근대한국외교문서 편찬위원회 편

近代韓國外交文書

조미수호통상조약

제4권

2013년도
대한민국학술원 선정
우수학술도서
이 도서는 교육부의 지원으로
대한민국학술원에서 선정한
"2013년도 우수학술도서"임

동북아역사재단

근대한국외교문서 편찬위원회 편

近代韓國外交文書

조미수호통상조약

제4권

동북아역사재단

간행사

저희 동북아역사재단에서는 2009년에 발행한 두 권의 외교문서(제1권: 『제너럴 셔먼호 사건 · 병인양요』, 제2권: 『오페르트 사건 · 신미양요』)에 이어 이번에 세 권의 외교문서(제3권: 『조일수호조규』, 제4권: 『조미수호통상조약』, 제5권: 『조영수호통상조약』)를 추가로 출간하게 되었습니다.

한국의 외교문서 편찬은 정조 때의 『同文彙考』에서 그 연원을 찾을 수 있습니다. 『동문휘고』는 사대교린의 예(禮)규범과 관련된 문서를 엮은 것으로, 정조의 명으로 1788년에 초편 60책이 발간되었고, 순조 · 헌종 · 철종을 거쳐 1881(고종 18)년까지 증보를 거듭하였습니다. 이 『동문휘고』는 중화질서 권역에 속했던 중국이나 일본에서도 그 유례가 없는 선구적인 외교문서집이었지만, 개항 이후 공식 외교문서집 편찬은 불행히도 단절되고 말았습니다. 그렇기에 본 『근대한국외교문서』 편찬 사업은 정조가 이룩한 『동문휘고』의 역사적 위업을 계승하는 민족사적 의의를 갖는 일이라 할 수 있겠습니다.

외교문서집을 간행하는 목적이 이곳저곳에 흩어져 있는 사료를 단순히 한 곳으로 모아 엮어놓는 데에만 있는 것이 아님은 주지의 사실입니다. 외교문서는 정부 간 상호작용과 외교행위*démarche*의 기록물인 동시에 국가 구성원의 대외인식의 정신구조를 담고 있는 과거의 역사적 자료입니다. 또한 그것이 한 국가의 현재와 미래의 외교 구상과 외교정책 수행능력을 보여주는 지표가 되는 이상, 외교문서집 간행의 목적은 상당히 다양해질 수밖에 없습니다.

그간 근대한국 외교문서집의 부재로 말미암아 역사 연구, 그중에서도 특히 관계사나 외교사 연구 등에서 외국의 외교문서집에 주로 의존함으로써 근대한국 대외관계의 객관적 사실이라든지 대외인식의 실체를 바르게 파악 · 포착하지 못하는 등 문제가 적지 않았습니다. 『근대한국외교문서』 편찬의 주된 목적은 근대한국이 행했던 외교행위에 대한 주체적 관점에서의 분석은 물론 주요 열강들의 대(對)한국 정책을 다각도로 분석할 수 있는 외교문서를 집록하는 것에 있습니다. 한국이 주체가 되어 주요 외교적 사건의 시말(始末)을 파악할 수 있도록 관련 외교문서를 기사본말체(紀事本末體) 형식에 의거하여 배열한 것도 그 목적의 일환입니다.

이번에 발간하는 세 권의 외교문서집은 근대한국이 동아시아의 전통적 외교질서체제였던 '조공·책봉체제'로부터 서구의 '조약체제'로 이행하는 시기를 다룬 것으로, 근대 한중일 3국이 신구(新舊)의 국제질서체제 속에서 각기 어떠한 위치에서 어떻게 대응했으며, 또 그 대응방식에 의해 3국의 명운이 어떻게 갈라져 나아갔는가를 파악할 수 있게 해준다는 점에서 상당히 중요한 외교자료·사료가 될 것으로 확신합니다.

『근대한국외교문서』는 앞으로도 계속 간행돼 총 30여 권으로 편찬, 끝마무리되는 것으로 알고 있습니다. 하지만 저희 동북아역사재단의 여러 사정 상 이번에 간행되는 외교문서집 3권을 포함해 총 5권의 발행으로 부득이 중간마무리를 하게 돼서, 그 애틋한 마음은 이루다 표현하지 못할 정도입니다. 그러나 다행히도 이『근대한국외교문서』편찬사업이 2010년 하반기부터 한국연구재단 토대기초연구사업으로 선정되어 그 편찬을 지속할 수 있게 되어 한편으로 크게 안도하고 있습니다.

그간 어려운 형편 속에서도『근대한국외교문서』편찬사업을 묵묵히 수행해 주신 근대한국외교문서편찬위원 여러분들과 김용구 편찬위원장께 심심한 감사의 말씀을 드립니다. 앞서 간행된 두 권과 함께 이번에 새로이 간행되는 세 권의『근대한국외교문서』역시, 외교사 연구자뿐만이 아니라 일반 독자들에게도 한국근대사에 대한 이해와 인식의 폭을 넓히는 데에 작은 도움이 되었으면 하는 바람입니다.

2012년 12월

동북아역사재단 이사장 김 학 준

서문

　수호조약의 체결로 사대질서를 규정하는 회전(會典, 1690~1882)과 교린질서를 뒷받침하는 약조(約條, 15세기~1875)의 시대는 종언을 고한다. 이제 한국외교사의 흐름은 조약의 시대로 접어들게 되었다. 편무적(片務的)인 영사재판제도, 비유럽세계의 불완전한 법 주체성, 5% 전후의 저율 관세 제도, 그리고 아시아·아프리카 지역을 유럽 세계에 예속시킨 차관제도를 특징으로 하는 19세기적인 세계화 과정이 시작된 것이다. 조선(1876~1910), 중국(1842~1949), 그리고 일본(1856~1911)의 조약 시대는 모두 이런 특징으로 점철되었으나 조선의 경우는 장정(章程, 1882~1895)의 시대와 겹쳐 형극(荊棘)의 길을 걷게 된다. 유길준이 말하는 양절체제(兩截體制)가 이것이다.

　용어 문제를 잠시 살펴보기로 한다. 본 편찬위원회에서는 이번에 출간되는 문서집 3책의 부제를 "개국조약"이 아닌 "수호조약"이라고 명명하였다. '개국(開國)'이란 낱말은 19세기 중엽 일본 정부가 자신들의 대외관계를 선전하려는 정치적 표어였다. 이를 서양 학자들이 한반도에 빗대어 'Opening of Korea'라고 즐겨 사용하였으며, 1950년대 이후 국내 학계 일각에서 무심코 이를 답습하여 "개국조약"이라고 불러왔던 것이다. 그러나 Opening은 야만단계의 지역이 서양 세계와 조약을 체결하면서 문화의 단계로 나아가게 되었다는 어감을 함축하고 있다는 데 유념해야 한다. 그리고 서양 공법에서 말하는 "조약"이란 용어는 병인·신미양요 시기 조선의 관찬사서(官撰史書)에 등장하기 시작해 1876년 이후로는 보편화되었다.

　조일조약은 메이지유신 일본 정부의 새로운 조선 정책으로부터 그 체결 문제가 대두되었다. 이는 "만국공법에 입각해 조선과의 관계를 다시 수립해야" 서양 열강이 납득할 수 있다는 명분에 근거한 것이었다. 이로 인해 교린과 공법의 두 질서가 8년 동안이나 충돌한다. 개념으로서는 자주(自主)와 독립(獨立)의 대립이었다. 강화도 조약

제1조의 '조선은 자주지방(自主之邦)'이라는 규정이 이를 상징적으로 말해 준다. 그런데 자주는 사대교린 질서의 개념이었던 바, 이것이 조선이 제1조의 구절을 아무런 반대 없이 수락한 배경이 되었다. 메이지 정부는 만국공법의 명분 이외에 "조선을 일등하(一等下)"의 국가로 간주한다는 정책을 명백히 하였다. 19세기에 들어오면서 나타나기 시작한 그들 특유의 조선관(朝鮮觀)이 현실 정책으로 구체화된 것이다.

조미조약은 1880년을 기점으로 획기적으로 변화한 중국의 조선 정책의 산물이었다. 『조선책략』, 「주지조선외교의(主持朝鮮外交議)」, 「삼책(三策)」, 그리고 조선의 양무(洋務)를 북양대신과 도쿄의 중국 공관이 관장하는 제도 개편이 뒤따랐다. 사대질서의 '조공국'을 공법질서의 '속국'으로 전환하려는 정책이 채택되었던 것이다. 중국은 이 정책을 수행하기 위해 미국을 이용하였다. 한편, 미국 정부는 한반도 문제에 무관심하였기 때문에 몇 명의 정치인과 해군제독의 정치적 입장을 손쉽게 수락하였다. 예컨대 10%의 관세율, 아편 금지, 자동 조정(調停)의 규정을 흔쾌히 삽입했던 것이다. 그러나 이윽고 미국 정부는 곧 서울 정부에 등을 돌리고 말았으며, 이러한 대(對) 조선 태도는 1905년까지 계속되었다.

조영조약은 어떤 열강도 한반도 문제에 개입하지 않는 한 영국과 러시아 두 세계 국가는 조선 문제에 간여하지 않는다는 침묵의 균형이 깨짐과 동시에 성립하였다. 강화도에서 일본의 운요 호 침략이 자행되자, 영국 정부 일각에서는 거문도 점령을 거론했다. 또 '아마추어'적인 미국 정부가 조선과 관대한 성격의 조약을 체결하자 영국 정부는 이러한 사태변화를 좌시할 수 없었다. 이러한 배경 속에서 외교 전문가가 아닌 해군 제독을 파견해 조미조약의 내용을 모방한 제1차 조영조약을 체결했으나, 영국 정부가 이를 비준할 리 없었다. 반면에 조선에서는 개화파 인사들을 중심으로 도교의 영국 공관을 통해 제1차 조영조약의 조속한 비준을 촉구했는데, 결국 영국 정부는 이를 빌미로 제2차 조영조약을 새로 체결함으로써 아편 및 관세 문제 등에 관한 그들 본래의 목적을 달성했던 것이다.

한 가지 애석한 점은 여러 행정적 이유로 말미암아 지난 수년간 작업해 온 조독(朝獨), 조불(朝佛), 조러(朝露)조약의 문서집이 이번에 함께 발간되지 못했다는 점이다. 이들 문서집은 추후에 별도로 발간할 예정이다.

우리의 『외교문서집』이 없다는 것은 세계 학계의 수준에서 보자면 실로 수치스러운 일이었다. 2007년 동북아역사재단 이사장 김용덕 교수의 지원은 이러한 난맥상을 바로잡는데 결정적 계기가 되었다. 동북아역사재단의 지속적 후원 하에서 본 편찬위원회에서는 지난 2009년에 『근대한국외교문서』 1, 2권(병인·신미양요)을 세상에 내어놓은 바 있으며, 금년에 다시 『근대한국외교문서』 3, 4, 5권(수호조약) 3책을 발간하게 되었다. 김용덕 이사장의 퇴임 이후에도 본 편찬사업에 대한 동북아역사재단의 지원은 계속되었다. 정재정 전 이사장, 그리고 김학준 현 이사장의 아낌없는 지원과 본 편찬사업에 대해 보여준 학문적 관심에 감사하는 바이다. 오랜 기간 번다한 실무를 맡아준 역사연구실 연구위원 김민규 박사의 노고 또한 잊을 수 없다. 끝으로 매 격주 토요일마다 한림대학교 국제대학원대학교와 서울대학교 규장각에 모여 토론과 연구를 계속해 온 20여 명의 교수 및 석·박사 연구원들의 열정에 더 없는 고마움을 전한다.

2012년 12월

『近代韓國外交文書』 편찬위원장 김 용 구

편집방침

1. 본 문서집은 한반도의 역사적 현주소를 밝히는 데 중요하다고 판단한 좁은 의미와 넓은 의미의 국내외 외교문서를 망라해 수록하였다. 좁은 의미의 외교문서는 정부의 토의 문서와 훈령, 외무 담당자들의 교섭과정 문서 documents préaratoires, 그들의 왕복 문서, 본국정부에 발송한 보고문, 그리고 국제조약을 가리킨다. 그리고 넓은 의미의 외교문서는 이 밖에 교섭 담당자들의 회고록이나 문집을 비롯한 개인 문서를 포함한다.

2. 본 문서집의 편집은 주요 열강의 외교문서집 편찬 방식에 따랐다. 주요 국가들은 외교문서를 보관하는 특별 기관을 보유하고 있어서 이 기관의 문서들 중 대외관계에 중요하다고 판단되는 문서들을 기사본말체로 편집하고 있다.

3. '중요하다고 판단'하는 편집자들의 '인식'이 외교문서집 발간의 국제정치적 성격을 나타내 주고 있다. 대외관계 문서집의 효시인 19세기 각국의 칼라 북스 *Color Books*, 미국의 *Foreign Relations of the United States*를 비롯하여 제1차 세계대전 이후 발간되기 시작한 독일의 *Grosse Politik der europäschen Kabinette 1871-1914*, 소련의 *Vneshnaya politika Rossii: XIX i nachala XX beka*, 그리고 *Dokumenty vneshnei politiki SSSR*, 영국의 *British Documents on the Origins of the War, 1898-1914*(G. P. Gooch & H. Temperley eds.), *Documents on British Foreign Policy, 1919-1939*(R. Butler & E. L. Woodward eds.), *British Documents on Foreign Affairs*(K. Bourne & D. C. Watt, eds.), 프랑스의 *Documents diplomatiques français 1871~1914*, 일본의 『日本外交文書』들이 모두 이런 방식을 취하고 있다.

4. 이들 외교문서집은 자국의 문서보관소의 문서들을 선별하여 편집하고 있다. 이들 선별된 문서들과 이를 채록한 원문서와의 관계를 검증하는 작업은 특수 분야를 연구하는 전문 연구자들이 담당하고 있다. 외교문서 편집과는 차원이 다른 연구 분야이다. 그러나 본 문서집은 '한국'의 '문서'집이기에 조선 문서의 경우, 채록 문서와의 관계를 가능한 한 규명토록 노력하였다.

범례

1. 조선에서 사대질서의 '外交' 개념과 전혀 다른 diplomacy의 번역어로 '외교'란 낱말이 사용되기 시작한 것은 1880년 이후의 일이다. 따라서 1866년 병인양요와 1871년 신미양요의 대외문서를 '외교문서'라고 지칭하는 데에는 비역사적인 측면이 있다. 그러나 본 문서집은 1910년까지의 문서를 편집하는 사업으로 1880년 이전의 자료를 편의상 외교문서로 분류하였다.

2. 조선은 1895년에, 중국은 1912년에, 그리고 일본은 1872년에 양력을 채택하였으나 본 문서집에서는 그 이전의 음력을 모두 양력으로 환산해 적었다. 1917년 소련 혁명 이전의 제정 러시아력(曆)도 양력으로 환산하였다. 19세기 제정 러시아력은 양력보다 12일이 앞서 있다. 이들 날짜를 모두 양력으로 환산시킨 것은 특히 아편전쟁 이후 한반도 문제를 포함한 세계의 모든 문제들이 세계외교사의 흐름과 연결되어 있기 때문이다. 다만 독자들이 동양 자료를 검색하는 데 도움을 주기 위해 중요한 날짜인 경우 음력을 병기하되 한자로 표기함으로써 양력 날짜와 구분하였다.

3. 중국과 일본의 인명, 지명은 모두 원음으로 표기하였다. 러시아어의 영문 알파벳 전자(轉字)는 *The Current Digest of Post-Soviet Press* 방법에 의거하였다. 한글 표기는 한국 교육인적자원부 편수자료를 따랐다.

4. 본 문서집은 연구자들에게 검색상의 편의를 제공하기 위해 문건 별로 문서의 내용에 관하여 간략한 정보를 표시하였다.

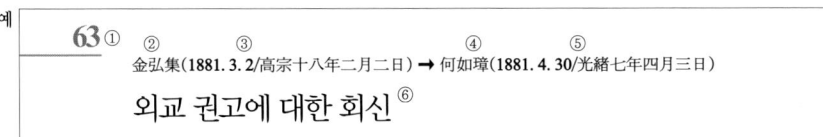

① 본 문서집이 부여한 고유의 문서번호이다.
② 문서의 발신인(기관)을 가리킨다. 문서의 수/발신인(기관)은 직함 등을 생략하고 인명만을 원어로 적는 것을 원칙으로 하였다. 인명을 특정하기 어려운 경우엔 문서에 나타나는 관직명만을 표기했다. 한편, 일본과 같이 일부 동일 인물의 성명 및 동일부서의 명칭이 시기별로 달라지는 경우에는 아래와 같은 원칙에 따라 표기하였다.
 • 대마번(對馬藩)의 경우 폐번치현(廢藩置縣)과 관련하여 공식적인 명칭이 수차례 변

경되었다. 관례적인 의미로 '對馬藩'으로 통일해 표기하였다.
- 宗義達과 같이 인명이 변경되었을 경우, 고친 이름[改名]을 기준으로 표기하되 기존의 이름을 괄호 내에 병기하였다.

    예) 宗重正(宗義達)

- 동일한 부서가 여러 가지 다른 이름으로 원문에 나타나는 경우 독자의 혼란을 피하기 위해서 단일한 명칭으로 통일하였다.

    예) 朝鮮事務辨理中, 朝鮮事務辨理御中, 朝鮮事務 → 朝鮮事務掛

③ 문서의 발신일을 가리킨다.
④ 문서의 수신인(기관)을 가리킨다.
⑤ 문서의 수신일을 가리킨다.
⑥ 본 문서집이 작성한 문서의 제목이다.

5. 문서의 수/발신일을 특정하기 어려운 교섭 담당자들의 회고록, 수기, 메모, 일기와 같은 사문서의 경우는 수/발신인 대신에 문서작성자의 이름을 표시했으며, 회담의 경우는 해당 회담의 기록자 이름을 표시하고, 제목에 회담 참석자를 나타냈다.

예
238
趙寅熙(1876. 8. 5/高宗十三年六月十八日)
趙寅熙 · 宮本小一 회담 (1)

6. 문건의 배열은 발신일을 기준으로 하였으나, 발신일을 확인할 수 없는 문건의 경우는 수신일에 의거하여 배열하였다. 어떤 문건의 발신일과 또 다른 문건의 수신일이 동일한 날짜에 겹치는 경우는 수신된 문서를 먼저 배열하였다. 문서에 발/수신일이 나타나지 않고 월(月)만이 표시된 경우는 그 내용을 분석한 후, 문맥상 다른 외교 문서와의 전후 관계를 고려하여 발송되었다고 추정되는 날짜에 의거하여 배열하였다. 내용으로 선후관계를 추정하기 어려운 문서는 해당 월의 말미에 배열하였다.

7. 중요한 외교문서의 경우, 각 국가의 외교관들이 이를 자국 언어로 번역해서 본국에 보고하는 것이 일반적인 관례이다. 이와 같이 특정한 문서에 대해 여러 언어로 작성된 번역문이 존재할 경우, 본서에서는 이를 [英譯文], [漢譯文], [日譯文], [佛譯文]이라고 표시하여 해당 문서 다음에 첨부하였다. 특정한 외교 교섭에 관해 참석

자들이 서로 다른 언어로 기록한 문건 역시 번역문의 범주에 포함된다. 번역은 단순히 문자 기호 사이의 등가적 교환이 아니고 번역자의 특정한 정치적 의도나 작위가 개재되는 실천적 행위이다. 특히 외교문서와 같이 정치적 성격을 띠는 문서에 있어서는 번역 과정에서의 특정한 언어의 선택, 미묘한 어감의 차이, 오역의 발생 여부 등을 더욱 면밀하게 살펴볼 필요가 있다. 본서에서는 원문서와 번역문을 병행 수록함으로써 연구자들로 하여금 사건의 시말을 보다 다각적으로 파악하는데 도움을 주고자 하였다.

8. 독립된 외교문서로 간주하기에는 형식적, 내용적 측면에서 부족한 면이 있으나 특정한 외교문서의 작성과정이나 사후처리 과정을 이해하는데 도움이 되는 문서는 [관련문서]라고 표기하여 해당 외교문서의 뒤에 첨부하였다. 또한 회고록이나 수기, 대화기록, 광범위한 보고서 등 근대한국 외교사에서 중요한 사료적 가치를 가지는 자료들은 [관계자료]로 분류하여 각 권의 말미에 별도로 수록하였다.

9. 동일한 외교문서인 경우에도 이를 기록하고, 전달하고, 재수록하는 과정에서 일부 자형이 변경되거나 오탈자가 발생하는 경우가 있다. 이 경우 본 문서집에서는 각 국가의 공식 외교문서집에 수록된 문서를 기준으로 수록하였으며, 오탈자가 있다고 의심되는 경우에는 (Sic.)라고 표시하였다. 원문의 오탈자가 문맥상 다른 글자로 추정되는 경우, [   ] 안에 별도로 표시하였다. 각 국가의 공식 외교문서집에 수록되지 않은 미간문서 가운데는 문서 자체의 훼손이 심하여 특정 글자나 단어를 판독하기 어려운 문서들이 존재한다. 이와 같은 미식별 문자의 경우 로마자는 [_____], 한자와 일본어는 ○의 기호로 표시하였다.

약어표

* 한글로 표기된 것은 한국 자료, 한자는 중국과 일본 자료, 로마자는 구미(歐美) 자료를 의미함.
* 자료의 나열은 한글 음 차례에 따름.

가오: 『嘉梧藁略』李裕元, 서울대학교 규장각한국학연구원 소장
고환당: 『古歡堂收艸』姜瑋, 서울대학교 규장각한국학연구원 소장
공거: 『公車文』편자 미상, 서울대학교 규장각한국학연구원 소장
구한국: 『舊韓國外交文書』고려대학교 아세아문제연구소 편, 22책(서울: 고려대학교 출판부, 1965~1973)
나암: 『羅巖隨錄』朴周大, 국사편찬위원회 편(서울: 국사편찬위원회, 1980)
대청: 『大淸欽使筆談錄』金宏集, 한국학중앙연구원 장서각 소장
동래계: 『東萊府啓錄』서울대학교 규장각한국학연구원, 한국학중앙연구원 장서각 소장
동문: 『同文彙考』국사편찬위원회 편, 4책(서울: 국사편찬위원회, 1970)
면암: 『勉菴集』崔益鉉(서울: 민족문화추진회, 1982)
미통: 『通商美國實記』서울대학교 규장각한국학연구원 소장
부록: 『修好條規附錄』서울대학교 규장각한국학연구원 소장
비변사: 『備邊司謄錄』국사편찬위원회 편, 251-265책(서울: 국사편찬위원회, 2010)
서계록: 『書契所報關錄』3책, 서울대학교 한국학연구원 소장
수신사: 『修信使記錄』국사편찬위원회 편(서울: 국사편찬위원회, 1958)
수호: 『修好條規』서울대학교 규장각한국학연구원 소장
실록: 『高宗實錄』3책(서울: 探究堂, 1970)
심행: 『沁行日記』申櫶, 2책, 고려대학교 한적자료실(상권)·국립중앙도서관(하권) 소장
영통: 『朝英通商條約』서울대학교 규장각한국학연구원 소장
왜사: 『倭使日記』서울대학교 규장각한국학연구원, 한국학중앙연구원 장서각 소장
용호: 『龍湖閒錄』宋近洙, 국사편찬위원회 편, 4책(서울: 국사편찬위원회, 1979)
운양: 『雲養集』金允植, 서울대학교 규장각한국학연구원 소장
윤치호: 『尹致昊日記』尹致昊, 국사편찬위원회 편, 6책(서울: 국사편찬위원회, 1973~76)
음청: 『陰晴史』金允植(『從政年表/陰晴史』, 국사편찬위원회 편, 서울: 국사편찬위원회, 1955)
일기: 『承政院日記(高宗朝)』국사편찬위원회 편, 15책(서울: 국사편찬위원회, 1967~1968)
일동: 『日東記游』金綺秀, 서울대학교 규장각한국학연구원 소장
일록: 『日省錄(高宗朝)』서울대학교 고전간행회 편(서울: 서울대학교 고전간행회, 1972)

자문: 『啓下咨文册』統理機務衙門, 서울대학교 규장각한국학연구원 소장
조미: 『朝美條約』서울대학교 규장각한국학연구원 소장
주연: 『珠淵集』한국학중앙연구원 장서각 소장
통상실기: 『美國通商實記』申櫶, 서울대학교 규장각한국학연구원 소장
환재: 『瓛齋集』朴珪壽, 서울대학교 중앙도서관 고문헌자료실 소장

東華: 『光緒朝東華錄』朱壽朋 編, 五册(『東華錄·東華續錄』王先謙·朱壽朋 編, 上海: 上海古籍出版社, 2008)
李文: 『李文忠公全集』吳汝綸 編, 七册(臺北: 文海出版社, 1962)
庸盦外: 『庸盦文外編』薛福成, 四卷四册(1893) 서울대학교 중앙도서관 고문헌자료실 소장
輶軒: 『輶軒抗議』余乾耀『近代中國史料叢刊續編』第百輯, 臺北: 文海出版社, 1983)
夷務始末: 『籌辦夷務始末』李書源 整理, 十册(北京: 中華書局, 2008-11) [지금까지 학계에서 일반적으로 이용한 판본은 國風出版社 影印本, 七册(臺北: 1963)으로, 본 문서집에서 인용한 판본은 영인본의 누락문서를 보완하고 문서 제목을 새로 추가한 것임.]
李鴻章: 『李鴻章全集』顧廷龍·戴逸 主編, 三十九册(合肥: 安徽教育出版社, 2007)
中日: 『清光緒中日交涉史料』故宮博物院文獻館 編, 二册(臺北: 文海出版社, 1963)
中日戰: 『中日戰爭』中國史學會 主編, 七册(新知識出版社, 1956) [『中日戰爭』戚其章 主編, 十二册(臺北: 中華書局, 1889~1996)은 1956년 본에서 누락된 문서를 보완한 것임.]
中日韓: 『清季中日韓關係史料』中央研究院近代史研究所 編, 十一册(臺北: 近代史研究所, 1972)
中朝續編: 『清代中朝關係檔案續編』中國第一歷史檔案館 編, 二册(中國檔案出版社, 1998)
中朝滙編: 『清代中朝關係檔案史料匯編』中國第一歷史檔案館 編, 二册(北京: 國際文化出判公司, 1996/1998)
清外: 『清季外交史料』王彦威·王亮 輯編, 九册(臺北: 文海出版社, 1964)
何如璋: 『何如璋集』吳振清·吳裕賢 編校(天津: 天津人民出版社, 2010)
黃遵憲: 『黃遵憲全集』陳錚 編, 二册(北京: 中華書局, 2005)

公文: 『公文錄』日本國立公文書館 所藏

陸奧文:『陸奧宗光関係文書』陸奧宗光, 日本國會圖書館憲政資料室 所藏
別錄:『公文別錄』日本國立公文書館 所藏
事務:『朝鮮事務書』日本外務省外交史料館 所藏
森:『森有禮文書』日本國會圖書館憲政資料室 所藏
三條家:『三條家文書』日本國會圖書館憲政資料室 所藏
續通信:『續通信全覽』通信全覽編集委員会 編, 五十四冊(東京: 雄松堂出版, 1983~ 1988)
雲揚記事:『明八孟春・雲揚朝鮮廻航記事』日本防衛省防衛研究所 所藏
伊藤:『伊藤博文文書』伊藤博文文書刊行會 編, 百二十七冊(ゆまに書房, 東京: 2007) [舊『秘書類纂』]
日外:『日本外交文書(明治年間)』外務省, 七十三冊(東京: 外務省, 1933~1963)
日韓資料:『日韓資料集成』金正明 編, 十冊(東京: 巖南堂書店, 1966)
雜纂:『對韓政策關係雜纂』日本外務省外交史料館 所藏
朝鮮御用控:『王政復古以來朝鮮御用筋相關ル候書付類控』국사편찬위원회 소장
條約類纂:『韓國條約類纂』朝鮮統監府(東京: 統監府, 1908)
黑田:『黑田淸隆關係文書』黑田淸隆, 日本國會圖書館憲政資料室 所藏

AADM: *Anglo-American Diplomatic Materials Relating to Korea, 1866~1886*, Park Il-Keun ed. (Seoul: Shinmundang, 1982)

ADPP: *American Diplomatic and Public Papers ; The United States and China*, Series II, *The United States, China, and Imperial Rivalries, 1861~1893*, Vol. 9~11, Davids, Jules, ed. 3 vols. (Wilmington, DE:Scholary Resources, 1979)

BDFA: *British Documents on Foreign Affairs*, K. Bourne & D. C. Watt, eds. Part I Series E Vol. 2; *Korea, Ryukyu Islands, and North-East Asia, 1875~1888* (Bethesda, MA: University Publication of America, 1989)

BFSA: *British and Foreign Papers*, Foreign Office/ Foreign and Commonwealth Office (London: H.M.S.O., 1814-1977)

FRUS: *Foreign Relations of the United States*, 1866~1882.

NARA I and II: National Archives and Records Administration Micro Films

RWS(국편): *Robert Wilson Shufeldt Papers*, 국사편찬위원회 소장

RWS: *Robert Wilson Shufeldt Papers*, Library of Congress, Washington DC

TNA: The National Archive(舊 Public Record Office)

편찬위원회 명단

편찬위원장 : 김용구 (한림대학교 한림과학원장)

편찬위원 :
김형종(서울대학교 동양사학과 교수)
김흥수(공군사관학교 인문철학부 교수)
신욱희(서울대학교 정치외교학부 교수)
우철구(영남대학교 정치외교학과 명예교수)
이근욱(서강대학교 정치외교학과 교수)
이상찬(서울대학교 국사학과 교수)
장인성(서울대학교 정치외교학부 교수)
최덕수(고려대학교 한국사학과 교수)
최희재(단국대학교 사학과 교수)

연구원 :

김종학(서울대학교 정치외교학부 박사과정 수료)
민회수(서울대학교 국사학과 박사과정 수료)
배민재(국사편찬위원회 사료연구위원)
이경미(서울대학교 정치외교학부 박사과정 수료)
이지영(서울대학교 동양사학과 박사과정 수료)
조병식(서울대학교 동양사학과 박사과정)
한보람(서울대학교 국사학과 박사과정 수료)
한승훈(고려대학교 한국사학과 박사과정 수료)
홍문기(서울대학교 국사학과 박사과정 수료)

연구조교 :

노진국(서강대학교 정치외교학과 석사과정)
송지예(서울대학교 정치외교학부 박사과정)
정민경(서강대학교 정치외교학부 석사)
정신혁(토론토대학교 역사학과 박사과정)
정연(서울대학교 정치외교학부 석사과정 수료)
조국(와세다대학교 대학원 문학연구과 박사과정)
조덕현(서울대학교 정치외교학부 석사과정 수료)
황수경(서울대학교 동양사학과 석사과정 수료)

차례

(1) 수신사(修信使) 金弘集 파견

1. 수신사 사폐(辭陛)시 전교 2
2. 서구 열강과의 수교 권고 4
3. 서구 열강과의 수교 권고 6
4. 부산 세관 설치 재검토 요청 7
5. 수신사 장계 8
6. 수신사 복명서(復命書) 9
7. 수신사 연설(筵說) 13

(2) 『朝鮮策略』의 전래와 신사(辛巳) 위정척사운동

8. 金弘集·黃遵憲 회담 (1) 20
9. 金弘集·何如璋 회담 (1) 22
10. 金弘集·何如璋 회담 (2) 23
11. 金弘集·何如璋 회담 (3) 25
12. 金弘集·黃遵憲 회담 (2) 28
13. 金弘集·何如璋 회담 (4) 31
14. 『朝鮮策略』에 관한 어전회의 33
15. 『朝鮮策略』어전 진상(進上) 통보 37
16. 『朝鮮策略』비판 상소 38
17. 李裕元-李鴻章 서한 (9) 40
18. 영남만인소(嶺南萬人疏) 41
19. 척사소(斥邪疏) 45
20. 척사소 49
21. 척사소 52
22. 척사소 62
23. 李鴻章 서한 변명소 64
24. 사직소(辭朝職疏) 65

(3) 조약체결 이전 미국의 조선 관련 보고

25. 대원군 실각 보고 68
26. 雲揚號 사건 보고 70
27. 雲揚號 사건 보고 71
28. 조선에 대한 일본과 청국의 입장 73
29. 조선-일본 관계에 대한 청국의 입장 75
30. 조일수호조규 체결 보고 77
31. 黑田淸隆로부터 입수한 조선 정보 보고 78
32. 수신사 金綺秀 도착 보고 80
33. 대조선 수호통상조약 체결 요청 결의안 83
34. 아프리카, 아시아 미개척 지역 탐사 지시 88
35. Shufeldt의 아시아, 아프리카 연안 항행 훈령에 관한 회신 ... 91
36. 조일 관세 문제에 관한 보고 95

(4) Shufeldt의 서한 전달 시도와 일본의 중재

37. 조선과의 협상 시기에 관한 조언 요청 98
38. 훈령 미도착 통보 99
39. Shufeldt를 소개하는 일본 측 서한 요청 101
40. 조선 개항과 관련한 협조 훈령 102
41. Shufeldt 소개 요청 거절 103
42. 부산 주재 영사에게 Shufeldt의 소개장 발송 105
43. 부산에서의 교섭 계획 보고 106
44. 협상 진전이 없을 경우 복귀 지시 108
45. 高宗에게 올린 Shufeldt 서한 109
46. 서한 전달 실패 보고 117
47. 近藤眞鋤를 통한 Shufeldt의 교섭 보고 120
48. Shufeldt 서한 재전달 협조 요청 121
49. Shufeldt의 서한 전달 요청에 관한 청훈 124
50. 서한 전달 협조 요청 수락 126

51. Shufeldt 서한의 접수 및 접수 지연 상황에 대한 대처 훈령 127
52. 서한 전달 협조에 대한 감사 129
53. 조선 교섭상황 보고 및 무력을 동원한 조약 체결 건의 130
54. Shufeldt 서한 접수 권고 133
55. Shufeldt 서한 접수 촉구 135
56. 일본의 협조에 대한 감사 137
57. Shufeldt의 서한 전달 시도 보고 138
58. Shufeldt의 서한 전달 실패 보고 139
59. Shufeldt 서한 관련 예조판서 답신 송부 140
60. Shufeldt 서한의 전달 경과 및 답신 통보 141
61. 조선의 서한 접수 거부 사유 통보 142
62. 조선의 서한 접수 여부에 따른 대처 계획 145
63. 조선의 서한 접수 거부 보고 147
64. 일본 외무당국의 서한 전달 상의 실책 비난 148
65. 일본공사를 통한 Shufeldt 서한의 전달 의뢰 151
66. Shufeldt 서한 전달 의뢰에 대한 회신 153
67. 주선 과정에서 일본의 불성실한 태도 보고 154

(5) 미국과 청국의 교섭

68. Shufeldt의 서한 전달 협조 요청 160
69. Shufeldt의 중국 해군 자문역 추천 161
70. 天津 회견 요청 163
71. 天津 회견 요청 승낙 164
72. 天津 초청 서신 166
73. 天津 초청에 대한 회신 167
74. 조선문제 협의를 위한 李鴻章 방문 계획 보고 168
75. Shufeldt의 天津 방문 일정 및 자문역 추천 170
76. Shufeldt와의 회견 기대 171
77. 李鴻章과의 회견 보고 172

78. 일본의 주선 및 李鴻章과의 회견 보고 174
79. Shufeldt의 중국 해군 개편 의견 찬성 175
80. Shufeldt · 李鴻章 회견 및 Prince of Genoa 조선 방문 보고 176
81. 李鴻章과의 회견 내용 전달 178
82. 何如璋의 적극적 협조 보고 181
83. 李鴻章과의 회견 내용 보고 183
84. 조선과의 조약 체결 전망 및 Shufeldt의 해군 고문 고빙 건 보고 186
85. 井上馨 · Bingham 회견 내용 전달 189
86. Shufeldt의 임무 통보 190
87. 조선 교섭 지침 192
88. 李鴻章의 조약 체결 권유에 대한 조선 회자(回咨) 보고 196
89. 조청(朝淸) 종속(宗屬)관계 보고 198
90. 조미조약 체결시 청국관료 파견 제안 보고 201
91. 李鴻章의 조미조약 초안 일부 전달 203
92. 조약 체결 관련 지침 205
93. 전권사절 임명 이후 조선과 청국의 정세 보고 207
94. 조약체결 전권대사 임명 사실 통보 210
95. 조선의 밀사 파견과 회견 방식 통보 211
96. 總署 회견 내용 보고 212
97. 保定府 회견을 원하는 李鴻章의 의사 전달 215
98. 保定府 회견 요청에 대한 회신 216
99. Shufeldt의 청국 해군 고빙 건에 관한 보고 218
100. 周馥 회견 결과 및 李鴻章 회견 계획 보고 220
101. 李鴻章 · Shufeldt 회견 223
102. Shufeldt 회견 보고 (1) 225
103. 李鴻章 회견 보고 226
104. 청국의 조청 종속(宗屬)관계 명문화 요구에 관한 훈령 228
105. 조미수호통상조약 초안 보고 229
106. Shufeldt 회견 보고 (2) 258
107. 조약체결 중재를 위한 馬建忠 파견 통보 260
108. 李鴻章 회견 보고 261

109. 조미수호통상조약 최종안 보고	263
110. Shufeldt의 조약체결 활동에 관한 보고	273

(6) 조선과 청국의 교섭

111. 조선에 조약체결을 권고할 것을 상주	278
112. 李裕元-李鴻章 서한 (10)	279
113. 李裕元-李鴻章 서한 (11)	281
114. 李裕元-李鴻章 서한 (12)	282
115. 李裕元과의 서한 왕복 보고 (1)	285
116. 李裕元과의 서한 왕복 보고 (2)	286
117. 주지조선외교의(主持朝鮮外交議)	287
118. 李裕元-李鴻章 서한 (13)	289
119. 조선에 대해 외교 및 자강책 권고 상주	290
120. 조선과 서양 각국의 통상 권유 상주	294
121. 卞元圭와의 회담 보고	295
122. 미국과 조약체결을 위해 밀사 李東仁 파견	298
123. 李裕元-李鴻章 서한 (14)	304
124. 高宗 밀명 전달	306
125. 李東仁・卓挺植의 밀보에 관한 보고	307
126. 조약체결시 조청 종속(宗屬)관계 명문화 건의	308
127. 李鴻章・李容肅 회담 (1)	310
128. 李鴻章・李容肅 회담 (2)	316
129. 李容肅 회담 보고	318
130. 李容肅 회담 상주	319
131. 외교 권고에 대한 회신	321
132. 영선사 사폐(辭陛)시 전교	322
133. 金允植・李鴻章 회담 (1)	324
134. 대미수교 주선을 청하는 서한	327
135. 金允植・李鴻章 회담 (2)	330

136. 조미조약 체결의 필요성 상주 333
137. 조미조약 체결 문제를 李鴻章에게 위임하는 상유(上諭) 335
138. 黎庶昌·魚允中 회담 336
139. 金允植·李鴻章 회담 (3) 339
140. 金允植·李鴻章 회담 (4) 342
141. 조청 종속(宗屬)관계 명문화에 관한 상소 345
142. 金允植·周馥 회담 (1) 347
143. 金允植·周馥 회담 (2) 349
144. 金允植·李鴻章 회담 (5) 351
145. 金允植·周馥 회담 (3) 354
146. 조미수호통상조약 초안에 관한 의견 356
147. 金允植·李鴻章 회담 (6) 358
148. 馬建忠·丁汝昌의 조선 파견 통보 364
149. 조미조약 교섭 전말 상주 365
150. 조약초안 관련 高宗에게 보내는 자문 367
151. 조미조약 체결 등에 관한 어전회의 368

(7) 조약 협상 과정

152. 반접관(伴接官) 임명 372
153. 馬建忠과의 회견 통보 373
154. 조선행 일정 통보 375
155. 조선 도착 및 조선의 조약 체결 태도 보고 377
156. 조선 입국 기록 378
157. 李應浚·馬建忠 회담 (1) 380
158. 조약 협상단 임명 381
159. 丁汝昌 파견 보고 382
160. 조선 입국 경과 보고 383
161. 조선 입국 통보 384
162. 李應浚·馬建忠 회담 (2) 385

163. 金弘集・馬建忠 회담 (1) 387
164. 金晚植・馬建忠 회담 392
165. 申櫶・金弘集 소개 394
166. 金弘集・馬建忠 회담 (2) 395
167. Shufeldt와 미곡수출 교섭결과 통보 401
168. 전권위임장, 조회문 도착 통보 402
169. 金弘集・馬建忠 회담 (3) 403
170. 金弘集・馬建忠 회담 (4) 406
171. 수호통상 요청 조회문 408
172. 조선 도착 이후 협상 경과 보고 410
173. 조인 일자 통보 416
174. 대통령의 신임장 제출 및 조인 일자 확정 417
175. 미 대통령 조회문에 대한 회답 조회 419
176. 조약 체결 축하연 초청장 421
177. 조미수호통상조약 조인식 기록 422
178. 金弘集・馬建忠 회담 (5) 423
179. 조약 체결 보고 424

(8) 사후처리 및 비준

180. 金弘集・馬建忠 회담 (6) 428
181. 高宗의 馬建忠・丁汝昌 인견(引見) 기록 431
182. 金弘集・馬建忠 회담 (7) 433
183. 조미조약 체결 통보 434
184. 조미조약 체결 통보 435
185. 조영, 조불 조약 체결시 조미조약 원용에 관한 의견 438
186. 조미수호통상조약 체결 전말 보고 439
187. 조미수호통상조약 체결 전말 상주 442
188. 조선 무역과 자원 현황 444
189. 조선의 비준 촉구를 본국 정부에 보고했음을 통보 448

190. 조청상민수륙무역장정에 관한 Holcombe의 견해 보고 449
191. 조약비준대표 영접 통보 464
192. 조약비준 전권 위임장 465
193. 조미수호통상조약 비준서 466
194. 비준 교환 일자 통보 467
195. 국왕 접견 및 미 대통령 국서 봉정 시각 통보 468
196. 高宗 알현시 Foote의 답사(答辭) 469
197. 조미조약 제6조의 개정에 관한 상주 471
198. 조약 비준 통보 472
199. 청국 연호 미기재(未記載)에 관한 문제 474
200. 조약문에 청국 연호 기재를 요구하는 자문 475
201. 청국 연호 기재 문제에 관한 자복(咨覆) 476
202. 보빙사(報聘使) 파견 통보 477

【關係資料】

1. 조미수호통상조약 480
2. 『조선책략(朝鮮策略)』 484
3. R.W. Shufeldt의 개인 서한 491
4. Duke of Genoa의 조선 방문 report 498
5. 『미국통상실기(美國通商實記)』 509

부록 문서 목록 513

(1) 수신사(修信使) 金弘集 파견

高宗(1880.5.1/高宗十七年五月二十八日)

수신사 사폐(辭陛)시 전교

庚辰五月二十八日 未時
上御重熙堂 修信使入侍時 右副承旨李乾夏 假註書朴壽昌 記事官鄭寅興閔
丙奭 修信使金弘集 以次進伏訖
上曰　　史官分左右
仍命修信使進前
上曰　　彼倭通好 已爲三百餘年 情狀自來狡黠 近日則雖云與前有異 而去益
　　　　難測 彼使頻來 不可無回謝之擧 以爾內明 且有學識 特此擇送 善爲
　　　　措處也
弘集曰 臣材質庸陋 識見淺短 恐無以堪承使命 秖切惶懼矣
上曰　　爾之內明 自在參下 予已知之 朝議亦然 似可堪當也
弘集曰 益切恐矣
上曰　　前修信使金綺秀去時 倭情叵測云矣 今則似更甚也
弘集曰 連年倭使來時 多有相持 今行必當更難於往年矣
上曰　　開港定稅等事 自政府必已授辭 而此外或有難處之事 須勿深慮 只圖
　　　　所以利國也
弘集曰 似多有意外之事 是庸憂悶矣
上曰　　出疆之後 無以稟定 不必過慮 隨事善處也
弘集曰 下教至此屢屢 然臣何敢擅斷 當以歸稟政府答之矣
上曰　　大事可歸稟 小事可自斷也
弘集曰 瑣細之事 謹當依下教奉行矣
上曰　　今日宿何地 何日抵萊府耶
弘集曰 今日當宿良才二十里 來月十五日當抵萊府矣
上曰　　留萊府 當爲幾何耶
弘集曰 乘船在廿五日 留萊府當爲十日矣
上曰　　乘船幾日 可抵達耶
弘集曰 年前信使 發船八日抵達矣
上曰　　今行亦當然也

弘集曰　前頭事何可預料 而以此爲準的矣

上曰　下屬輩 雖或出遊 至於雜亂偸竊之弊 必爲禁飭也

弘集曰　謹當操秉矣

上曰　中原使行 亦有此弊 而此處則異於中原 若有如是之弊 其爲貽羞 當如何哉

弘集曰　誠然矣

上曰　沿路支站 年前多有弊端 今番則當何如耶

弘集曰　今番則自廟堂另飭 特除出站 臣亦行關 除却浮文民弊矣

上曰　似得無苟艱之嘆乎

仍敎曰　今當遠離 仰瞻可也

又命仰瞻世子宮 弘集起立 仰瞻訖

上曰　萬里滄溟 冒炎作行 甚難也

弘集曰　王事何敢言勞乎

世子宮 敎曰　善爲往還也

弘集曰　謹當依睿敎矣

上命賜藥物節扇等 挾侍傳于乾夏 乾夏傳于弘集 弘集跪受訖

上曰　善爲往還也

仍命修信使先退 又命史官就座 又命退 承史以次退出

2

井上馨(1880.9.7) ➡ 尹滋承(1880.9.24/高宗十七年八月二十日)

서구 열강과의 수교 권고

관련문서 洪祐昌의 회신

庚辰外務卿告還遞米使書函 仍陳近日局勢書
敬啓 曩者 米國使船 欲通信於貴國 託我政府代遞文件 今准原封見却 卽據情節 還美使矣 因思方今海國大小交友 各立主權 强鄰有鬩 居身局外 以禦侵暴 所以獨鎖國門 絶交友者幾希 請觀淸有强鄰 耽彼東省 已非一日 頃者中俄繆轕 事勢日益迫切 殆將干戈相見於我兩國 所關甚鉅 坐不安席 如若一朝失和 則我兩國 終被餘害 而貴國自閉門戶 以爲守局外者 恐非易易 玆所望於貴國者 將來有外人至 彼能心存溫和 以禮求交 宜當無分畛域 輒相與之 以圖綢繆未雨 然則便益處多 國以咸寧 非啻我兩國幸甚也 臨金使行 爲之忠告 陳述詳盡 惟冀其歸國後 貴政府勉力開辦耳 耑此佈悃 順頌時祺 明治十三年九月七日 大日本國外務卿 井上馨 大朝鮮國禮曹判書 尹滋承 閣下

【관련문서】

禮曹判書答書
照回者往秋信輈還欣獲貴函已開歲矣尙爾披覽益覺輯睦枾深孰謂滄溟間之其所勉陳於信使者詳悉多感而稅則事與貴公使有所商確想當照諒是祈貴國泰平更頌時祺敬具
辛巳年二月日 禮曹判書洪祐昌

別錄
敬復我兩國維持如秤衡之相稱輻輳之相湊現事指機外侮指禦感誦盛意此所以永敦輯睦憂俄耽視貴我一般固當同謀協議隨機應備至若諸國之交通有不可以與貴國隣好比論也我朝廷嫺於待隣之禮修舊之誼且非不知宇內時事而虽虽野議泥古守規膠見莫回痼弊難醫實不可遽議於今者貴公使亦嘗稔揣習聆也必有

所詳陳貴政府益加照諒勿以我謂守局閉戶之爲焉更希燭悉不宣頌祉
辛巳年二月日 大朝鮮國禮曹判書洪祐昌 大日本國外務井上馨閤下

井上馨(1880.9.8) ➡ 金弘集

서구 열강과의 수교 권고

逕啓者 此次得貴使來京 日即溫雅 談及目今海外諸洲形勢 刻難疎防 況中俄之相軋 有如燃眉 斯憂固在洞燭之中 其關貴國安危 繁急若此 亦我邦之所不免也 至如花旗英法諸國 屢屢踵求交通於貴國 其意非由營彼貿遷之利 其為要旨 乃在扼俄遠圖之肆 故貴國亦莫若容其所求 藉為自衛之策 是我鄙衷 滿擬以忠告於貴政府也 適迓星臨 乃獲不顧忌諱 吐露肝膽 欣幸何似 此情 另繕一函 即煩趙便帶回 面尹判書前炤鑒 但筆楮未能罄 仰冀台旌此歸 詳達日來所與晤談情節 無所遺漏 俾得揮發另函所陳微悃爲囑 秋炎海涼 切惟珍重 敬具

明治十三年九月八日　　　　　　　　　　　　外務卿 井上馨(印)
修信使 金宏集 閣下

井上馨(1880. 9) ➡ 尹滋承(1880. 9. 24)

부산 세관 설치 재검토 요청

玆接庚辰年五月間來函 以我政府派遣禮曹參議金宏集 庸寓回謝之義 披閱之下 深感貴政府重申親睦之意 金使溫恭精覈 通曉事體 兼洽兩國之歡 良可敬也 至別錄收稅事 宜曾於明治十二年七月代理公使花房義質照會貴國沈判書文內備悉 兩國可以隨時會同訂立 今復以此意 面商於該使 其回旌後 想必有所陳述 庶可炳照 玆祈貴國康寧 竝頌台祉 敬具

明治十三年九月

金弘集 ➡ 議政府(1880.9.24/高宗十七年八月二十八日)

수신사 장계

修信使金宏集狀啓
本年六月二十五日自釜山浦發船之由已爲馳啓爲白有在果二十六日戌時止泊於山口縣赤馬關八百里下陸留館二十七日亥時發船二十九日巳時泊兵庫縣神戶港一千一百六十里船小不能馳大洋爲待大船之來留旅館五日七月初四日戌刻換乘大船初六日卯時止泊神奈川縣橫濱一千八百里下陸是白乎則自外務省委送權大書記官樓田親義屬官山之城祐長石幡貞等迎接同日乘火輪車前進九十五里到江戶城外本願寺仍爲駐接外務少輔芳川顯正辦理公使花房義質來見是白遣初八日巳時臣與正官等詣外務卿井上馨在外大輔上野景範少輔芳川顯正公使花房義質權大書記樓田親義等處所齎書一度傳致爲白乎旀同月二十七日太政大臣三條實美右大臣巖倉具視及外務卿以下設宴於遠遼館臣與譯官私禮單應給之處量宜分給是白乎旀八月初三日外務省回答書契一度別書契一度領付任譯使之齎去是白遣初四日自江戶離發十一日戌時還泊釜山鎭云云

金弘集(1880. 10. 2/高宗十七年八月二十八日)

수신사 복명서(復命書)

관련문서 수역(首譯) 李容肅의 문견사건(聞見事件)

庚辰修信使金弘集聞見事件
臣於本年五月二十八日辭陛 六月二十五日 自釜山浦賃乘協同商社船千歲丸 二十六日丑時離發 同日戌刻十個時 到赤馬關 二十七日亥刻行船 二十九日巳刻十九個時 泊神戶港 船小不能駛大洋 爲待大船之來 留旅館五日 七月初四日 戌刻 換乘和歌浦丸 初六日卯刻六十八個時 抵江戶 八月初四日還發發船後行船時刻計四十七時 酉時乘高砂丸 初七日卯時 泊神戶留一日 初八日酉時 換乘千歲丸 十一日戌刻 還泊釜山浦 計往回道里 水路七千三百二十里 陸路一百九十里 是白乎所 謹撤拾經歷聞見 庸備乙覽是白齊

釜山至赤關 羅針指巽巳 海路頗險 我人呼爲水宗 赤關神戶之間 爲內港 南北峽勢綿連 島嶼星羅 華人 以爲極似吳 越江行光景 由神戶東南行 出峽外至遠江州境 天水相接 四望無際 風定浪活之時 尙震盪靡定 卽所謂太平洋也 自此復折而東北抵橫濱 丙子以前信行 未嘗過此 彼言立春二百日後數十日間 風濤最怕 輪船亦難行云 而往還時 風日俱佳 無事利涉 此莫非王靈攸曁是白齊

始至之三日 往外務省 傳書契 卿井上馨在外 聞日間當還 大輔上野景範爲言 其國主當引見 又言各部長官 有往見之禮 故以我使所未行拒之 公使花房義質 又特來苦勸曰 淸使亦行之 若不見許 將於交情 大有妨礙 多日相持 不卽應之 下船宴 亦無動靜 因此疏節 來侮生衅 殊非得中 故於七月十六日 先拜孔廟 轉訪淸公使 其翌日 偕花房 歷見三大臣 參議及各部卿 皆卽來謝 幾處游覽 亦時勉行 至二十五日 其國主引見 二十六日外務省公幹 二十七日延遼館設宴 而後乃可還發 而輪船之行 自有定日 不得不遲待 致此淹延 極爲悚惶是白齊

定稅事 彼先問稅則擬定以來與否 故答以只得兩政府議協 可令地方官同領事官 商酌定之云爾 則彼曰 此事關係至重 兵端所由起 雖使臣 非委任專權 則不可云 故更以第依中東和約 擬一草案而歸 爲答 仍問出入貨時價於東萊通詞輩 用値百抽五例 抄成稅稿 私示公使 而未及面議 因淸公使 聞日人方議改約增稅 百抽三十 而各國姑未見許之由 仍秘錄其規例冊子以示 故見花房而言曰 前稿初非定本 待貴國改約事成 我亦當準此例 後於外務省公幹 亦如前

言 彼未敢顯拒 而以我未曉商務 而遽欲重稅 只滋爭端 不如姑先輕收 數年稍熟後 惟意改增未晚 米穀事 亦爲一切禁防 不如重稅而抑之云 似此重事 實難擅斷 以歸稟更議爲定 淸使亦曰 不須遽定 所收多少 亦不足計 惟有聲明條約 不失自主之權 爲第一要務云是白齊

開港駐京等事 初無公席發端 花房義質 只一次私問仁川事朝議如前與否而已 及至發行日 外務卿來別 仍言公使十餘日後出去 故答以使行九月初復命 備奏事機 朝廷爛確 又費一二個月 公使之行 量此少緩爲妥 彼曰 當更商 及至橫濱 見公使 爲誦前言 仍語 公使旣陞辨理 當帶國書否 丙子旣以不帶國書爲約 日後 亦只將外務書契以來爲妥云 則彼亦頗以爲然是白齊

俄羅斯 近日於圖們江海口 置軍艦十六艘 每艘有兵三千餘名 海軍卿領之 其意將欲由我國東南海 轉向中國山東省海岸 直入北京云 以是淸使及日人 僉以爲時日急切之憂 扼腕噓唏 近日上海公報與日本新聞紙 莫不以此講揣 以爲若果有事 則我國與日本 幷受其害 西洋各國 亦皆畏俄 如虎狼 欲與宇內合從以擯之 修好通商意 專在是云是白齊

日本公使 派往各國常住 亦有朝官 非公事而往游 以察其動靜者 故言宇內形勢如比隣事 江戶 近設語學 廣敎各國言語文字 已有朝鮮學校 蓋以不識事機 不通言語 則無以應變以自保云 日人 近又私開一社 名興亞會 淸公使及中國人士 多與焉 其意 欲與淸日本及我三國 同心同力 無爲歐羅巴所侮云 而外務省公幹之日 井上馨曰 見今宇內情形 日變一日 貴國速派公使來此 亦遣人學言語 此兩事 必歸稟政府 懇懇不已 淸公使 亦以不可不遣使久往爲言是白齊

沿海山勢環繞 類多古秀 無險峻雄拔之氣 過駿河境 遙望富士甚高 七月初 尙有雪痕 其終年不消可知 其南島 聞有火山 黑煙盤盤 夜視有光 相距不遠 截然殊觀云 江戶經線 與我嶺南蔚山機張等地相直 天氣多熱 回還時 正當白露節 而船中薰悶 不可堪 居人飮氷 多於茶酒 而冬不成氷 皆自北海島輸來售買云 頻雨卽晴 罕有多日成霖之時 地多震 數月輒一有之 間十數年 有大震 則屋舍人畜 大被損害云是白齊

人物 男女類多巧慧 質柔而性褊 罕見深沉雄偉者 村武則以薩摩長門等州稱奉國主廢關白者 此數處人爲多 今幷列高官 年前 武將薩摩人西鄕隆盛 議犯我國 而今右大臣巖倉具視 以爲不可 西鄕意不平 煽其徒作亂 與之相戰 久乃討平是白齊

其國主 古來徒擁虛器 關白 稱將家握重兵 予奪自專 殆爲三百年之久矣 邇者二十年來 强鄰交逼 大開互市 憂時之士 謂政令乖隔 無以自主而禦侮 乃倡尊

主攘夷之論 一二幹濟之村 乘時制變 强公室杜私門 擧積世流弊而更張之 易如反手 時事轉移 亦有自然之勢而然歟 往時儀節 多尚虛文 尊卑懸絶 上下否隔 近則務從質直 不飾邊幅 太政官各部卿以下百執事 逐日赴公辦事 如治家之勤 下午始散徇歸家 其出行也 官高者乘雙馬車而無騶從 惟在將相之列者 有騎兵四五名 露刃而衛之是白齊

其國內外官職 皆世襲 各州稱藩國 明治初 拜收其土 而居之都下 從其位 優給其祿 而不任之事 乃合六十六州 爲三十七縣 縣置令 如我國道伯 秩滿而遞 用人惟才 有華族士族平民之稱 華族 卽宗姓及舊藩臣之族云 昔時藩臣各君其民供賦 無藝農民 歲收七八于公 改制後 減稅至十分之三 近又蠲之 爲二分有奇 又通商惠工凡厚生之方 無不爲之 故民無一遊食 而日以繁庶云是白齊

陸軍之制 京外六鎭四十營 常額三萬餘名 演武時 坐作擊刺 動中師律 聞是新抄敎練 纔爲四朔 而已能如此 海軍有礮船二十四艘 蓋海軍用英國制 陸軍用法國制 而陸軍當又改從阿蘭陀法云 其外有警卒 俗稱巡查 分布里閭 遊徼緝捕 以故 使客過時 甚整肅無譁 或有爭鬨 輒執而送之法官 其刑法 凡鬪歐爭訟 必罰鍰 其罪重者 衣之赭衣 役作於公 隨其犯 而年限爲之久 近以故犯之者少 殆近古意是白齊

凡有敎習 皆有學校 如兵礮舟車測算開礦農商技藝等事 國中大學區七 餘中小之區 不可勝計 使婦孺就而學之 雖宗室及公卿子女 皆在焉 官以董之 師以敎之 作圖式與樣子 目存而手揣之 學成則送之諸局 每局或千餘人 或累百人 逐日執業 勤敏不懈 其製造之局 無不用機輪而爲之者 火輪之外 又有水激磁吸 而爲機輪者 至於舂米剉芻之微 亦皆有其機 用工省而收效速是白齊

舊俗 本皆精巧而好潔 民居多架木爲之 四面凉㯖 舖地以板 加莞席而坐 室雖小 必存隙地 裁花竹 養池魚 間以山石點綴之 時時掃滌 不留微塵 男女均寬衣博袖 而無褲褌 不能深掩其體 足躡木屐 只有底繫一絇 以鉤足指而已 近年國規 悉從洋制 屋則甎築鋳溜 琉璃其窓 服用氊裘革履 然自官府學校以外 多用板屋 舊式衣服亦然 雖朝士 在家時輒着服 其遺老逸民 不得嚮用於世者尙有 能談經學 硬硜然守舊俗不改者 頗爲可尙是白齊

其國計 一歲所收 約五千萬金 地租關稅爲鉅 鉄道電信各局製造及舟車牛馬 皆有收入 百方不遺 然官吏月俸 八百金 至十二金不等 加之養兵雇役 日增月加 外他宮府 經費甚博 所出多於所入 恒苦不繼 於是日造紙幣以當之 然實多虛額 浮於現在錢數 故物價日以昂貴 況西洋人去時 必投紙幣換金錢而歸 漏巵不塞 詎爲其福 大凡利必有害 盛則有衰 乃天道固然 人力無以善其後是白

齊 光緒六年八月二十八日

【관련문서】

修信行別遣首譯李容肅聞見事件
日本王 專意富强 少無怠倦 至於馳馬試劍 無不慣熟是白齊
日本王 五月初 巡至大和州 謁先陵 遊覽大坂城神戶等地 六月念後旋歸是白齊
宮室 乙亥回祿後 尙未重建 日本王居在赤坂離宮 而自明年經始 限二十年迄役爲計云云是白齊
日本王 接見信使於屋內 衣洋服 無所戴 佩劍而立 親王二人外務大輔一人民部小輔一人 左右排立 傳語官一人 檻外恭立是白齊
締盟諸國 若大淸英吉伊米利堅露西亞佛郞西伊太利和蘭白耳義澳地利獨逸秘露西班牙丁抹瑞西布哇葡萄瑞典 合十七國是白齊
日本人派往各國者 大淸獨逸米利佛郞英吉澳地露西伊太和蘭各國 曰專權公使 朝鮮有辦理 總領事各一人 又有領事七人 而朝鮮一人 大淸二人 米利三人 英吉一人 此外一等二等書記之出仕各國者 十五人是白齊
各國公使之來駐日本者 合十三國 而名稱不同 大淸米利露西伊太白耳義獨逸 曰專權 大淸又有副使 英吉佛朗西班丁抹 曰代理 和蘭澳地瑞典 曰辨理 而和蘭辨理 兼察丁抹代理是白齊
自草梁至江戶 各處市肆民戶 比丙子有加無減 京外各樣製造之局 增至幾分 猶爲不足 新建新備 不可枚擧是白齊
電線 丙子所見 多不過十四行 今則增至二十四行是白齊
彼地年成 雨暘均適 今已向熟 可期大登云云是白齊
光緒六年八月二十八日

金弘集(1880. 10. 2/高宗十七年八月二十八日)

수신사 연설(筵說)

庚辰八月二十八日 酉時

上御重熙堂 回還修信使入侍時 右副承旨洪承穆 假注書申容善 記注官吳致恒 別兼春秋李容稙 修信使金弘集 以次進伏訖

上曰　史官分左右

仍命修信使進前

上曰　萬里滄溟 无事往還乎

弘集曰　无事往還矣

上曰　彼使又爲出來云 當在何間耶

弘集曰　臣於臨發時 始聞於外務卿 而爲言事勢稍令緩其行期云矣

上曰　聞見別單已覽之 而此外更無可奏者乎

弘集曰　梗槩已備達於別單中 別無更奏者 而彼情似无惡意矣

上曰　旣无惡意 則其言果何如

弘集曰　彼人酬酌 專要親睦无間而已

上曰　親睦爲主 則果有厚待之耶

弘集曰　供饋贈給等節 雖不爲之 留館時賃屋及來往時滊車之費 皆自外務省措處矣

上曰　彼國孔廟制度何如

弘集曰　孔廟 奉安先聖及顔曾思孟塑像 後壁展掛周程朱子影幀 更无東西廡從享之規 翼室多貯經史書籍而已

上曰　訪見淸公使 果爲欣接耶

弘集曰　淸公使果甚欣款 其言以爲他鄕逢故人云矣

上曰　想爾心亦當懽欣也

弘集曰　臣心果慰洽矣

上曰　倭主見爾時節次何如

弘集曰　其君椅前立見 稍前有親王 將兵者 杖釖對立 臣之入見時 有外輔大輔式部頭二人 分左右同入矣

上曰　其君不草草云 果然否

弘集曰　其爲人 頗似英明矣

上曰　彼國官職 間有遞改云耶

弘集曰　它官遞改未詳 而外務卿遞改 井上馨爲之矣

上曰　何故改遞云耶

弘集曰　遞改未詳其由 而前外務卿寺島宗則 時爲政府參議官 而井上馨 亦以參議官兼帶外務卿矣

上曰　留住 以本願寺爲之 而何不住延遼館乎

弘集曰　聞延遼館有妨碍 故使之留住於本願寺云矣

上曰　定稅事 姑未歸正而來耶

弘集曰　別單已爲繫達 而聞其國方有改約事 故未可遽定矣

上曰　開港等事 更先言耶

弘集曰　花房義質 一次私問 故答以朝議與前无異 則更不發說矣

上曰　俄羅斯 自圖們江 直向山東云 若果有事 當在不久耶

弘集曰　彼人所言如此 而問諸淸使 則中國事 似可善了矣

上曰　然則當无事云耶

弘集曰　崇厚聞已放釋 而不之罪 則伊犁似終許之乃已云矣

上曰　崇厚 何爲不之罪乎

弘集曰　崇厚擅許土地 信有罪矣 中國旣委以專權 而其所許者 從而背之 是失信於隣國 所以不得罪之云矣

上曰　我國受害云者 或非誘嚇之端乎

弘集曰　彼言以爲 此非爲貴國代謀 實爲渠國而然矣

上曰　旣云自爲渠國 則其言似或然矣

弘集曰　彼言雖未足深信 然問諸淸使 亦以爲其實情然矣

上曰　淸公使 爲人何如

弘集曰　其人甚宏通 有幹局矣

上曰　日本廣設各國語學而敎之 其學規果何如

弘集曰　臣未嘗往見其處 而各國言語 皆設學敎之云矣

上曰　如我國譯學乎

弘集曰　然矣 其國朝士子弟 皆令就學矣

上曰　遣人學語 使之歸告朝廷耶

弘集曰　此事蓋爲我國而發也 施行與否 惟在朝廷處分 而不容不以歸告爲答矣

上曰　此事雖未遽行 而歸告則爲可也
又敎曰　富士山果何如 而七月雪尙不消耶
弘集曰　未及橫濱 遙望其山 甚高峻 尙見有雪痕矣
上曰　南島有黑烟云 然否
弘集曰　其地有火山 故地常多震云矣
上曰　地震果頻而大乎
弘集曰　數月輒有地震 間十許年大震 則屋舍人物 多被傷損云矣
上曰　雨事頗頻乎
弘集曰　頻雨而亦無久雨云矣
上曰　男女人物 果何如耶
弘集曰　其人物 類多巧慧 而勤幹矣
上曰　年前薩摩人 欲向我國 而其大臣巖倉具視抑之 使不得逞 此事眞然乎
弘集曰　此說誠確矣
上曰　問於淸使 可以詳知也
弘集曰　雖不及問諸淸使 而見巖倉具視 言及此事 則自謂實有是事云矣
上曰　彼人皆以勤幹不怠爲主 故其事爲能若是也
弘集曰　誠然矣
上曰　彼國之六十六州 今皆統合云耶
弘集曰　廢六十六州 分爲三十六縣 縣實合 如我國監司之制矣
上曰　各州世襲之人 今皆失位 得無怏怏之意乎
弘集曰　其心似不樂 然亦皆優其廩 而居之都下云矣
上曰　其賦稅多蠲減云耶
弘集曰　誠然矣 凡係利民之政 必擧而行云矣
上曰　陸軍操鍊 其法何如
弘集曰　坐作進退 頗中師律矣
上曰　彼國果甚畏俄羅斯乎
弘集曰　擧國莫不以是爲急切之憂矣
上曰　彼之兵械 今則可以敵西洋各國云耶
弘集曰　彼之所學者 西洋兵法 而自以爲不及西洋云矣
上曰　其兵法 當更從阿蘭陀云 是何許國耶
弘集曰　阿蘭 西洋中最小之國 幅圓不過爲我國四分之一云矣
上曰　國小如此 用何術而能如是乎

弘集曰　國無大小 兵械精利 亦在自強務實而已

上曰　　巡査警路 頗爲肅然云耶

弘集曰　然矣

上曰　　彼國敎人 各隨其才 雖婦孺 亦皆學習 然則無一人可棄也

弘集曰　以故 无一遊食之民矣

上曰　　屋舍之制 多有變改乎

弘集曰　屋宇或從洋制 而亦多仍旧制矣

上曰　　或有尙着旧服 不改其俗者 其中必有可觀矣

弘集曰　其中文士多然 頗爲可尙矣

上曰　　首譯別單 以爲倭主好馳馬試釰 至於躬入演武之場 與士卒相逐云 此乃夷狄之風也

弘集曰　誠然矣 而專尙武强之故矣

上曰　　彼之宮闕營建 將以二十年爲限云 一何宏侈 至此曠歲云耶

弘集曰　傳聞如此 未可深信矣

上曰　　彼之通商 爲十七國云乎

弘集曰　傳說云然矣

上曰　　全權公使領事官之出住它國者 其數不一云耶

弘集曰　未及詳聞 而或因該國事務大小而然矣

上曰　　朝鮮獨有辦理公使 而花房之陞爲辦理 何故耶

弘集曰　似是進階而然矣

上曰　　不與我國相議而爲之 其意欲帶國書而然耶

弘集曰　聞辦理公使 當帶國書 故臣問諸花房義質而語之曰 丙子旣以勿帶國書爲約 則今何可不與我國相議 而遽爾行之 第只帶外務書契以來爲好云矣

上曰　　其答何如

弘集曰　其答亦頗以爲然矣

上曰　　彼之沿路市肆民居 果何如

弘集曰　所見頗爲殷盛矣

上曰　　彼亦務農 而今秋大登云 果以何穀爲重耶

弘集曰　亦以稻米爲重矣

上曰　　俄羅斯欲向中國 當由何路云耶

弘集曰　彼中所聞 槩云由我國東南海路 轉入中國矣

上曰　察其動靜 彼國於我國 果无怨意耶
弘集曰　以今所見 姑无近慮 臣以此事 問於淸使 亦以爲實情則然矣
上曰　然則可以永保無他乎
弘集曰　此事臣未敢質對 向後惟在我應接之得其道而已 以故淸使 亦以自强相勉矣
上曰　自强是富强之謂乎
弘集曰　非但富强爲自强 修我政敎 保我民國 使外釁無從以生 此實自强之第一先務也
上曰　淸使亦以俄羅斯爲憂 而於我國事 多有相助之意乎
弘集曰　臣見淸使 幾次所言 皆此事 爲我國懇懇不已也
上曰　彼人雖欲與我國同心合力 而此何可深信乎 卽要我亦行富强之術而已
弘集曰　彼情誠不可深信 而惟以我國 不識外事 爲悶矣
上曰　彼言如此 似是向我國之意也 淸使則必知其裏許也
弘集曰　淸使之言亦然矣
上曰　近日俄羅斯 橫行天下 紛紛如黑雲漫天也
弘集曰　聞海外各國 莫不以俄羅斯爲憂 擾擾不已矣
上曰　倭主見爾 不爲勞問乎
弘集曰　无一語相問矣
上曰　倭主果洋服乎
弘集曰　然矣
上曰　彼國形勢 想應外强內虛也
弘集曰　聖敎誠然矣
上曰　彼使又爲出來 當在何間耶
弘集曰　臣於臨發時 始聞於外務卿 而爲言事勢稍令緩其行期矣
上曰　今番往還日子 計爲幾許日乎
弘集曰　恰爲九十日矣
上曰　海路殊險 送爾之時 極爲關念 今焉無事竣還 甚用喜幸
弘集曰　聖念逮下 一至於此 感惶无地
上曰　雖下隷輩 別無生弊 不知見侮於彼否
弘集曰　下隷輩 另操束 幸无大弊矣
上曰　到神戶 換乘輪船時 淂無洋人乎 年前使行 有洋人入船中云矣

弘集曰　自釜山至神戶 係是專船 故切禁外國人 而換船時 則附載商船 勢不
　　　　能一從我令 惟深處艙屋 不見其面而已 有此從權 萬萬悚悶矣
上曰　　此事深得其宜 不與之相關可矣 何可膠固不通乎 北京使行 亦多見洋
　　　　人於市肆街路云矣
仍敎曰　回路留萊府幾日乎
弘集曰　三宿卽發矣
上曰　　琉球國 問已復國云耶
弘集曰　此事存嫌 未嘗問人 而傳說已廢其國爲縣云矣
上曰　　彼人私禮單 皆受之乎
弘集曰　然矣
上曰　　旣以私禮贈之 不以公體 故彼亦不辭也
仍敎曰　萬里往返 仰瞻可也
弘集　　起立仰瞻 還爲俯伏訖
上曰　　大國使行 雖從陸 尙以爲難 此處涉險 不可與燕行同日語 而如此遄
　　　　返 誠可幸也
弘集曰　臣以萬萬无似之物 猥膺重寄 惟辱命是懼 今幸无事納節 此莫非王靈
　　　　攸曁也
上曰　　爾自綜核 兼有文識 如是竣還 固其宜也
弘集曰　不勝惶悚矣
上曰　　昨夜宿廣州山城 而入來耶
弘集曰　然矣
上曰　　遠役勞憊 夜又深矣 爾其先退
上命修信使先退 仍命史官就座 又命退 承史以次退出

(2) 『朝鮮策略』의 전래와 신사(辛巳) 위정척사운동

金弘集(1880. 8. 20/高宗十七年七月十五日)

金弘集·黃遵憲 회담 (1)

七月十五日 大淸欽使參贊官黃遵憲楊樞來
憲曰 海程遼遠 王事馳驅 賢勞可敬 得接閣下大名 於四月 由釜山遞來消息
　　旣如雷灌 久盼 旌麾早臨 淂以略論時事 佈一切悃忱 今日初見 春風藹
　　然 使人起敬 第不知滯留此間 爲日多少 欽使何公 亟欲圖晤 從容半日
　　暢彼此懷抱 不審何日 乃淂暇 使僕敬聽命
宏曰 今蒙兩先生辱臨 甚愜夙願 欽使何公 業擬卽謁請敎 連有冗擾 又値家忌
　　迄此遲滯 悚甚 定當晉候
憲曰 朝廷之於貴國 休戚相關 憂樂與共 近來時勢 泰西諸國 日見凌逼 我兩
　　國 尤宜益加親密 僕輩居東三年 日與異類相酬酢 今淂高軒之來 眞不啻
　　他鄕遇故人 快慰莫可言
宏曰 敝邦於中朝 蒙同內服 近日外事紛紜 蘄望更切 他鄕故人之喩 實獲我心
憲曰 以僕鄙意 若淂閣下常住東京 必於國事 大有裨益 方今宇內大勢 實爲
　　四千年來之所未有 堯舜禹湯之所未料 執古人之方 以醫今日之疾 未見
　　其可 以閣下聰明 聞見日拓 將來主持國是 必能爲亞細亞造福也
宏曰 此行 約於數旬間 竣事卽還 不可常駐 宇內大勢 高論誠然 敝國僻在一
　　隅 從古不與外國毗連 今則海舶迭來 應接戞戞 而國少力弱 未易使彼知
　　畏而退 甚切憂悶 所恃者 惟中朝庇護之之力
憲曰 讀此數語 足見忠愛之忱 溢於言表 朝廷之於貴國 恩義甚固 爲天下萬國
　　之所無 然思所以保此恩蒙 使萬世無疆者 今日之急務 在力圖自强而已
宏曰 自强二字 至矣盡矣 敢不敬服
憲曰 聞高論 使人豁然開朗 又使人肅然敬恭
又曰 使節之來 聞有大事三 不知旣與日本外務言之否 唐突敢問
宏曰 使事槩爲報聘 書契中 有定稅一事而已
憲曰 欽使何公 於商務 能悉其利弊 於日本事 能知其情僞 有所疑難 望一切
與商 我兩國如同一家 閣下必能鑒此
宏曰 僕此來 大小事 專仰欽使指導 而形迹亦不能不存嫌 所以稍遲遲 庶諒此
　　意

憲曰 貴國日本所締條約 僕未見漢文稿 能飭人惠鈔一分 感謝不已
宏曰 謹當如敎 僕向讀大著日本事詩 仰重大名久矣 又日本志未及見 敢問卷帙可爲幾何
憲曰 今日承雅敎 懽慰之極 僕著日本襍事詩 近遊戲之作 不知閣下何處見之 然旣承靑覽 他日過訪 再當敬呈數部 乞正 日本志 僕與何公同爲之 卷帙浩博 可爲三十卷 姑未淸草
宏曰 雜事詩見惠之敎 多感 日本志 異日入梓 亦乞波及
憲曰 明日何時枉顧 歸當稟告 必應掃逕拱候也 天晚敢告辭 筆談數紙 乞以見惠 感甚感甚
宏曰 明日拜聖廟 仍轉晋計 似稍晚也

金弘集(1880. 8. 21/高宗十七年七月十六日)

金弘集·何如璋 회담 (1)

七月十六日 往大淸公署

宏曰 旌節久駐海外 聲望遠播天下 引領東望 常切傾慕 今也萍緣幸湊 荊願獲遂 但叩謁此遲 是爲悚仄

璋曰 過譽媿不敢當 閣下冒暑遠役 此行良苦 明日敝署黃參贊上謁 荷延接周至 謝謝 今日又承枉顧 得親雅敎 快甚

宏曰 賜接款洽 極爲逾分 愧甚悚甚

璋曰 旌節已來 希在此多住幾日 得以從容過從 暢聆大敎 尤爲快事

宏曰 在此時 敢不源源拜誨

璋曰 我朝與貴國 誼同一家 今日海外相逢 尤爲親密 彼此均不拘形迹 容日僕當趁晤暢談也

宏曰 盛敎 更爲親切 視同一家 感刻何極 寵臨之命 猥不敢當

璋曰 此間天氣 較貴國何如 月來酷暑逼人 想閣下行裝南卸 酬應紛紛 亦苦勞頓否 閣下情神志氣 正是英發之時 雖天氣稍暑不勞也

宏曰 此間晩暑 與敝處一般 涉海之餘 不能無憊也

璋曰 此間官府諸事 均極整理 閣下有暇不妨 約宮本先生 到各處一覽

宏曰 指敎 可見相愛之至 才已偕宮本公 歷覽一處而來

璋曰 敝同事魯生先生 是我國最通時務之人 今年踰六旬 神明猶如四十許人 亦異稟也

宏曰 近讀萬國公法序文 魯先生蘊抱 早已仰悉 年高德邵 神明益旺 尤可敬也

璋曰 承高軒旺過 謝謝 改日走謁 暢聆大敎

金弘集(1880.8.23/高宗十七年七月十八日)

金弘集·何如璋 회담 (2)

七月十八日 大淸欽使何如璋·副使張斯桂來
璋曰 前日承惠顧 得領大敎 欣慰之至 今日特偕張君親來趨謝 竝暢談一切也
宏曰 卽蒙兩位大人光臨 感不可言
璋曰 此寺頗寬 道園金弘集別號先生及諸公 想俱安適 聞日間閣下 須謁見日皇 曾定期否 所商事如何
宏曰 日主引見 姑無定期 所商事 因日來始歷訪太政官各部卿 未暇更探
璋曰 從前貴國 與此間所換條規 及此次送商之件 有鈔稿否 如有所檢出 一分借覽爲荷
宏曰 條規及此次所商之件 本擬鑑正 方飭人繕寫 明當送納
璋曰 近日此間 方擬與泰西各國 議改條約 其議改之意 在管理寓商及通商 稅則各事 其稿極詳細 亦極公平 大約係西洋各國通行之章程 若各國通商均照此行 固無所損也
宏曰 昨日已送草案矣 若早拜誨 可無製碍 因存嫌 不克先事稟質 恨恨 或說米穀不得禁 則重其稅 其餘出口貨 幷不責稅 進口貨 亦於洋貨重稅 而日本零瑣産物 特免其稅爲佳云 此說未知何如
璋曰 此說弊端極大 切不可行 閣下第觀議改之稿 自知之 若答應添開口岸極好 俟其來議 將趁此與之議立妥善章程 彼自不能不答應也
宏曰 領悉 敝邦全不諳商務利害 極悶極悶
璋曰 此間 自通商以來 於各國交涉情形及辦理通商善法 均已知其曲折本末 俟取其此次議改約稿 細閱之 便悉中庸云 以人治人 亦一法也
宏曰 承示感深 其議改約稿 已入刻 可得一覽否 如可覓惠 尤幸
璋曰 先生所見極是 僕當爲先生圖之 第事須秘密爲要 又敝意 此間情形 總須貴國有人久駐此 徐徐審察之 自然容易辦理 卓見以爲然否
宏曰 秘密之敎 愚見亦然 此間情形 久駐審察 爲敝邦籌畫至矣 第本國 尙如中朝三十年以前風氣 士大夫未悉外國事情 辦此極不易易 是爲憂悶
璋曰 尊論 一切此事 眞無如何 第目前情事 較前時尤急 不特此間之爲難也 若固守舊習 恐非長策 且刻下有機 可乘圖之 尙易過此 則時會難逢 更

爲費手矣

宏曰 見敎鄭重 敢不服膺

璋曰 頃俄人 在貴國北界圖們江口一帶 經營布置 究竟情形如何 聞貴國民 往彼處者頗多 閣下詳悉其事 請以見告

宏曰 俄土 近雖接壤 從未相通 經營布置 無由聞知 北民之逃入彼地 時或入聞 亦末如之何 切悶 向後接應如何 方淂其宜 更乞詳敎

璋曰 近日西洋各國 有均勢之法 若一國與强國隣 懼有後患 則聯各國 以圖牽制 此亦目前不淂已應接之一法也

宏曰 均勢二字 近始從公法中見之 然本國 凜守舊規 視外國如洪水猛獸 自來斥異敎甚峻故也 大敎如此 弟當歸告朝廷

璋曰 僕與張公 擬治茗 邀閣下及諸先生 到舘一敍 閣下何日淂暇 請示知以便其具帖相邀也

宏曰 盛眷感謝 念後當如戒

金弘集(1880.8.26/高宗十七年七月二十一日)

金弘集·何如璋 회담(3)

七月二十一日 往大淸公署

璋曰 今日承道園金弘集先生及諸先生見過 溯慰下懷

宏曰 今蒙盛速 謹偕諸君上謁 穩奉大誨 爲榮實多 三生之幸

璋曰 進謁日皇之期 曾已定否 前呈之件 係此間由英文詳書者 其中所言 頗公平詳悉 尊覽以爲如何

宏曰 日主 當於二十五引見云 抄惠冊子乍閱 未及詳究 然其言殊爲公允

璋曰 西例 通商惟欲己國有益 故兩國往來稅則 無論出入口 均由本國自定 凡進口稅則 以値百抽三十爲率 更有所謂保護稅則 不欲此貨進口 更加重稅以沮之 出口之貨 則或輕或重 均由自己酌定 告知通商之國 照行 如何貨 欲其多出口 卽免稅 以便本國商民 亦無不可 總之 權由自主 則利益自歸本國 不致爲他國占盡便宜 故與萬國通商 亦有益無損之事 若秪論稅 而不分別出進之貨 或稅則自己不能定 而爲通商之把持 則有損無益矣 前日所譯之稿 彼便是言明 稅則之輕重 由本國主持一語

宏曰 開諭至此纖悉 雖甚魯愚 豈不曉淂

璋曰 條約施行一節 尙無定期 經東京各國公使 寄呈政府察核矣

宏曰 聞諸花房 改約可於明年妥定云 中國稅則 何尙未行此法乎 敢問

璋曰 尊問可謂留心之至 我亞洲各國 以前均未悉此種情形 故受損實多 此日因近日始知 故欲與西人議改 鄙見 欲貴國乘機會 先一步爲之 此難淂之事也

宏曰 敬悉

璋曰 閱昨日送來鈔件 貴國與此間所締之約 幷未言及稅則 趁此時 議開他港之時 與之定稅則 且卽以其向西人議改之法行之 彼自然不敢力駁 所謂第一好機會也 卓見以爲何如

宏曰 昨見花房 談及此事 欲待改約事定 我亦准此行之 彼頗持難 故我以爲貴國此法 必無十年議改之難 且非我爭利害 獨未准他國例 則有碍體面 彼亦不能更詰

璋曰 尊論極爲明暢 足以析之 請到席小酌後再談

宏曰 僕未曾遊燕 常以爲慊 今於海外 獲見中邦盃酌之盛 又飽以德 感幸莫名

璋曰 貴國負山瀕海 宇內所需之物産 類皆有之 今日時變如此 計不如開港通往來 與各國 幷馳大洋也

宏曰 我國家典章 以成周 士夫趨向 以趙宋 民俗儉嗇 有唐風遺意 今日時變雖如此 實無以與各國往來 勢則然耳

璋曰 有一語相詢 現西人競言功利 而俄尤橫暴 如戰國虎狼之秦 聞其近年 於圖們江口一帶 極意經營 且本年 又增設水師於東海 此事大爲可慮 遲則變生 我朝與貴國 誼同手足一家 殊難漠然也

宏曰 俄事最爲目下急切之憂 未知伊犁一事 如何究竟

璋曰 中土西邊之事 以近情揣之 與俄人不致搆隙 但觀其兵舶 絡繹東來 悉泊於圖們江口 恐其心懷叵測也 去歲李伯相鴻章寄書貴國 亦以近日情形迫切爲言 不知貴國公論何如 昨言均勢之法 亦爲不得已之事

宏曰 去歲李伯相寄書 備述近日情狀 爲小邦多費籌畫 擧國感誦 然朝野風氣如上所陳 只知守經之爲正 所以不能一朝開擴 奈何 往伯相書中 再擧閣下來信爲諭 述及東洋動靜 敝邦之荷閣下厪任久矣 感之次骨 敬謝敬謝

璋曰 聞俄人 近日有來元山津 議開口通商之說 果否 又美國兵船 前日赴釜山口通信 聞近日又再去釜山口 現貴國如何應付 先生知之否

宏曰 俄人春間到北地 欲與通好 邊臣直斥之 美船向抵釜山 欲納書不達而去 嗣又日本外務 代爲紹介 我國以其書勝國國號 且直呈至尊 爲違式而繳還 僕所知者 止此而已

璋曰 愚見 俄事頗急 現宇內各國 惟美係民主之國 又國勢富實 其與列國通好 尙講信義 不甚圖占便宜 此時彼來 善求通商 若能仿此間議改之約稿 與之締立條規 彼必欣願 如此 則他國欲來通商者 亦必照美國之約 不能獨賣 則一切通商之權利 均操自我 雖與萬國交涉 亦有益無損之事 此萬世一時之機會 不可失也 若必欲深閉固拒 致他日別生波瀾 事急時 所結條規 必須虧損無類 卓見以爲然否

宏曰 俄美情形 披示無隱如此 敝國事勢 雖未可遽議交涉 然盛念豈不知感 日昨伊藤博文亦言 與一國立善約 則他國皆遵之 交萬國 與一國無異云 又聞美國 不欲以西洋自居 其意欲附於東洋云 然否

璋曰 先生所述伊藤之言 自是實話 項日人議改之約 美國已許之 卽此一節 亦徵其厚於東方之意 僕頃所云云 正是此意 又不相往來之擧 今日屈指數之 宇內無幾國 此事有決難終拒之勢 固不如先一着爲之

宏曰 指敎懇懇不已 弟當歸告朝廷 稅則一事 日人改約未成 無以遽定 姑先歸
　　稟 再商處之如何

璋曰 尊論極是 此事自不能遽定 先生不妨 先歸 俟與其議開仁川口時 以此稿
　　大意 與之議 彼如有遲難之意 可專遣使來此議之 彼方與西人議改此條
　　必不敢顯拒貴國也 又此間人有欲占貴國之便宜耳 若稅則如此定議 則
　　彼無便宜可占矣 是彼不願者 其本心也 愚見 不如趁此機會 與美國人締
　　結如此條約 彼必允行美人已行 則列國一律照行矣 此萬世之計也

宏曰 日人情態 瞭如指掌 尤爲感服 彼言 中國現亦不禁米穀 未知果否

璋曰 日本米穀出口不禁 中國歲仰給安南之米數百萬石 雖不禁 亦無出口 但
　　禁出口 自是舊章 我國固未明言開禁

宏曰 此間新聞紙 有爲敝國論說者 以爲朝鮮 不欲日使之駐京 若令於開港處
　　常駐 遇有可議 以時赴京辦理爲妥 此說未知何如

璋曰 使臣駐京 無關緊要之事 近淂通商與交涉利害 全在約條稅則之善否而
　　已 善則內地通商亦無害 否則開一港 便是漏巵 爲患不淺矣

宏曰 所敎切當 閣下大著使東述略 敢乞多惠幾本 欲以歸布敝國也

璋曰 拙著已無存矣 無以副盛意 慚愧 他日再詣尊寓 暢談一切也 今日簡慢無
　　怔

金弘集・黃遵憲 회담 (2)

金弘集(1880.9.6/高宗十七年八月二日)

八月初二日 黃參贊遵憲來
憲曰 行旋之發有日 特來一話 能稍假從容幸甚
宏曰 行期此迫 悵甚 午後通有幹 伊前可以拜晤
憲曰 聞花房公使同行 信否 將附三菱商社輪船往耶 別乘何船耶
宏曰 花房行期 尙未聞 歸時當乘三菱社船爲計
憲曰 僕平素與何公使 商略貴國急務 非一朝夕 今輒以其意見 記之於策 凡數千言 知閣下行期逼促 恐一二見面 不能達其意 故邇來費數日之力草 就謹冒瀆尊嚴上呈 其中過激之言 千萬乞恕 鑑其愚而憐其誠 是禱
宏曰 見示冊子 萬萬感銘 勝似逢場筆話多矣 得暇奉閱 仍當携歸 俾我國人咸知上國諸公之眷念 如是其厚且摯矣
憲曰 乞於暇時 再熟覽而深思之 第其中所未及 有近日商量之禁輸出米定稅則二事 何公使尙有一二意見 容徐陳大槪 敢問此二事 旣議妥否
宏曰 防米定稅 向與外務公幹 兩言不相合 且非委任 實難擅行 姑俟歸後 再行議妥 彼謂我全昧商務 而遽爾重稅 必滋葛藤 非渠堅執云 本國從未識外國事情 此等處 極是難辦 悶甚悶甚
憲曰 何公使每見日人 常勸其事 事務持大體 且告之曰 旣欲兩國之交 以防俄 而多所要挾 益滋朝鮮疑懼 恐大局亦壞 彼亦必以爲然 故不甚堅執也 第輸米一事 査日本全國産米甚富 所仰給於朝鮮者 惟對馬島耳 輸出亦不足爲大患 且我有所輸出 彼亦有所輸入 若遇饑饉 亦有利益 若欲防其輸出太多 則惟有稅則由我之一法 加稅以防之 則操縱皆自我矣 前所送日本約稿 今縱不必仿其値百抽三十之重 但與之聲明 稅則由我自定之一語 則事之不掣肘也
宏曰 指敎明晰 感甚 輸米事 彼亦曰 重其稅而抑之 又限石數而節之 何害於國 我又詰其轉售他國 則曰 在公法 萬國穀價 常欲均平云 第俟定稅時 另立重稅却好 稅尙未定 而米稅之自我先言 恐無濟於事
憲曰 萬國公法 不禁輸米 若遇凶年 亦可以禁 英德之米麥 常仰於俄 而今年俄不熟 亦禁輸他國 亦不得有後言 故曰 不如聲明稅則由我自主之一語

之爲善也 僕料禁輸之事 彼不難應命 蓋此事於彼 無關大要也 特爲朝鮮本國計 與其一切禁輸 致碍他日凶年之輸入 不如加稅防之 由我自主也

宏曰 今觀日人動靜 只以我未識外事 代爲悶鬱 苟得交情益固 似不以從前得失掛心 此果出於眞情 而無可疑乎

憲曰 日本今日情勢 萬萬不能朝鮮 僕策中旣詳言之矣 其望朝鮮 强欲與朝鮮聯衡 實出於眞情 特其國人 好勝貪利 不甚闊達 故時時有所碍難耳 朝鮮急圖外交 於一切通弊 了然於胸 彼自不能多所要求也 稅則一事 以彼圖近事爲言 所謂以矛陷盾 極爲妙事

宏曰 往在丙丁 敝土奇荒 彼輸米到釜港出售 南民多得此粒食 未始不出於好意

憲曰 從前輸米一事 彼非有別心 極欲望朝鮮之締交 而爲是而市歡心也 其所以如此者 僕策中詳述之 而日本舊日收稅收米 不收金 是皆政府之所儲販之 又可以圖利耳

又曰 收稅之法 有一極妙策 但使我定一值百抽多少之主意 如欲值百抽十 則於貿物到關時 由稅吏佔量時價 貨值一百 則取其十 彼商人不願 則官吏受而購之 旣與時價等 轉賣之人 亦不之虧 彼商人無怨言 此日本稅則中所不將事事物物逐一臚列者 卽用此法也 此萬國通行之例 能知此無難事耳

宏曰 此策果絶妙 僕亦來此聞之 若爲此 則稅關得其人 且有財然後可行

憲曰 此事究可行 關吏能知物價人爲之足矣 受賣貨物 不必國有財 蓋明知値百之貨 估以九十 則不吃虧也 總之 此刻貴國講論稅事 尙無關大得失 惟切切記 與他人立約 必聲明稅則由我自主之一語 以待他日 不然 則如日本需十數年 乃能議改 而尙未定矣 日本新擬約稿 係法文 由法譯英文 由英譯漢文 故其文意 頗未明顯 其中用意甚深 措辭甚微 卽花房公使所謂 考求十數年而後有此者也 恨爲日無多 不及與閣下述其故 然閣下解人細觀之 必知其情 但能師其大意 爲益多矣

宏曰 節節情到 稅入多寡不足計 遲速不足論 惟自强不被人牽制 爲今日最急切之要務 敢不敬服

憲曰 稅之多寡 於國計 關係不足重 惟輸出之金銀 多於輸入 則民生窘而國計危矣 財爲生人養之源 拱手而致之他人 民貧而亂作矣 日本通商十數年 輸出金銀 至於十二千萬之多 朝野上下 幾不聊生 此稅則 由他人商定之害也 苟能重課進口貨 則外貨來源不多 卽金銀輸出不多 何至於此

故稅則自定之一語 乃全國安危之所係 不可以不謹也

宏曰 輸出價値 多於輸入 則通商有利 安見其害 見今敝處輸入 想亦不多 而輸出則國貧無産 尤當少少矣 輸入之物 非公然與人 不失我之錢耶 欲捄其弊 不得不師彼之所爲 務農興商 使我之出品 亦足以取人之金錢而後可耶 敝國朝野 只有凜遵成憲 安於儉嗇而已 萬不可議也

憲曰 去年一歲 朝鮮輸出之貨 多於輸入 値價七萬有餘 今日通商尙無害 惟他日 須設法防之 籌策救之耳 朝鮮苟能閉關 未始不樂國 特無如不能何也噫

宏曰 通商雖無顯害 日後應接極難 以是爲苦 閉關豈不是無上善策 我國讀書人 皆以通商爲不可 此論於時務何如 竊想 中朝亦多有至持正大之論矣

憲曰 今日尙欲閉關 可謂不達時務之甚 僕策中旣詳及之 請歸而與當局有力者 力主持之 扶危定傾 是在君子

又曰 歸國之後 他日欲通音信 當從何處寄 乃不付浮沉

宏曰 惠函 由釜山領事館 轉寄似好 或由北京托永平游太守 遞送如何

憲曰 由北京轉寄 殊稽時日 由釜山寄 又慮萬一爲人偸視 若得釜山商人住址 收到此間由商人歸去 交東萊府伯 乃妥善耳

宏曰 敝土 無商業可信者 釜山有辦交官常住 若此處商人 到釜交伊 可免浮沉

憲曰 僕意 所慮偸視 按日本郵便規則 本無慮 此特慮萬一有急報 不得不密耳 尋常書函 由釜領事官交府伯 必無阻碍否

宏曰 尋常書函 由領事交府伯無碍 密線若未易

憲曰 機事務密 萬萬如此 惟今日形勢 萬國皆無所諱 在有心人求之耳

宏曰 當更深思 明晤時再告

憲曰 明日再晤 僕有一團扇 在院西李祖淵手 乞賜書數字 明日見還 又有何公使之友人 代購朝鮮碑帖一紙 請歸國後 擇其都市通行者 每樣購二三分 其遠道難致者 則不必也 費神感甚

宏曰 僕筆甚劣 恐徒汚扇面 然吾輩相與 工拙亦不須計 當如戒 碑帖歸後廣求副敎 東人罕嗜金石 得之未易 多少不欲預告

憲曰 都市中有者 購之足矣 瑣事不足介意也 他日或有 由釜山寄來亦可

又曰 今日承麈敎 悵慰莫甚 天涯相聚 可謂奇緣 未知何日 再得良晤耳

宏曰 天涯相逢 又當相別 此恨何堪 未知欽使 何當復命 若得復見閣下於金臺之上 何幸何幸

憲曰 本係三年任滿 卽爲爪代之期 代者 未聞其人 恐在此再駐耳 若得相見於北京 幸甚幸甚

金弘集(1880. 9. 7/高宗十七年八月三日)

金弘集・何如璋 회담(4)

八月初三日 往大淸公署
宏曰 明當乘船 卒卒無暇 今才撥忙 特來告辭
璋曰 日來閣下 酬應紛紜 想不疲乏 聞明日卽掛歸帆 將來順途 至大阪各處
　　 仍有淹留否 又同來諸君 一同歸去 抑有人在後始歸耶
宏曰 到神戶 換船直去 不須迂入大阪 諸人一同携歸 無留在者 國規則然
璋曰 花房公使 同去否 稅則各節 日間仍有談及否 此事不妨從容商辦 又仁川
　　 開港一節 亦不關繁要 且此時各國通商情形 其口岸須近都會爲宜 以都
　　 會稍爲繁盛 一切可以全力維持也 若僻遠之區 則恐照料不周矣 昨日黃
　　 君所呈 係揣度今日情形如此 望閣下 恕其狂直 而辱敎之
宏曰 花房仍未聞其出去 稅事竟未定 俟再行議妥 昨日黃公見惠冊子 忙未一
　　 披 容淂暇細讀 而揣度籌畫 無所不用其極 萬萬感服 敢不存心
璋曰 現此間 知近日情形危迫 欲與貴邦 聯唇齒之交 以維持東洋大局 殆其實
　　 也 又議稅事 他日不必遽議加 第與言明 稅由本國自酌 則操縱之權在我
　　 自無流弊 又近日俄兵船來圖們江口者 已增至十餘號 又派一大員來 督
　　 辦已至 申情形頗急 不知其有何詭謀 愚見 如隨後有俄人來議通好 似不
　　 宜力拒 恐其猝然生事也
宏曰 才見井上馨爲言 俄兵船將由敝國東南海 轉向山東省海岸 莫爲關慮
璋曰 前有新聞云 俄兵船赴山東煙臺 此言不確 其在圖們江口者 陸續來長崎
　　 運煤至琿春海口 其擧動究未知如何 現中國與之商議伊犂事 此事有幾
　　 分可了 若此事已了 則其兵船在貴邦之北者 恐以請通商爲辭 藉生事端
宏曰 伊犂事果了 則敝邦亦蒙其禍 然藉通商而生事 固至之勢 未知如何應
　　 之 可爲保國之策否
璋曰 今日情形危迫 計不如先與美利加結約 藉以牽制之 亦急則治標之法也
　　 若此事一時能行 則萬一俄人 扣關請議通商 不如勉强許之 第俄人素橫
　　 與之結約 恐多周折也
宏曰 俄美事 所敎周至 豈不能理會此曲折耶 朝廷命意 雖未敢知 第當歸告也
璋曰 將來彼此通信 如何方所達 且有機密事 又當如何 請告我

宏曰 昨與黃公議此 夜來思之 苦無異算 此間有對馬人鹽田眞 向我國事不泛
　　　頗可托 其人主遷有商社 釜山有支店 由此交送辦察官 却不妨
璋曰 此間有郵便 寄至釜山自易 惟鹽田究係日人 有妨否 若有貴國商店在釜
　　　山者尤妥 閣下若寄使舘信 外封可書寄橫濱口永昌和華商店收坼 其內
　　　封令其轉送敝署 自無不達
宏曰 敝邦本無商店 如此間會社之規 所以苦無可托處奈何 僕欲先寄信 當如
　　　敎 轉交橫濱華商處
璋曰 鹽田眞釜山支店係何名 卽是遷有二字否 其在橫濱有支店否 交送辦察
　　　官 屬其轉呈閣下 仍須另封否
宏曰 釜山支店想亦號遷有 橫濱又有支店未及聞 當更問後 錄告 交送辦察官
　　　用另封 自不妨
璋曰 近日情形甚急 如閣下歸國 衆論稍通 請飛函告我 當相謀一善法也
宏曰 謹當留心
璋曰 明日何時乘汽車 當至鐵路關送別
宏曰 鐵路枉別 萬萬未安 且臨岐慁慁 筆談也不淂究 何益焉 請卽此告別

李最應, 閔致庠 等(1880. 10. 11/高宗十七年九月八日)

『朝鮮策略』에 관한 어전회의

관련문서 제대신헌의(諸大臣獻議)

庚辰九月初八日 未時
上御重熙堂 大臣政府堂上引見入侍時 同副承旨金晳根 假注書兪鎭奎 事變假注書韓必殷 記注官韓用皜 別兼春秋趙秉升 領議政李最應 行刑曹判書閔致庠 行戶曹判書洪祐吉 行禮曹判書李豊翼 吏曹判書李鎬俊 右參贊洪鍾雲 同知三軍府事申正熙趙羲復 行護軍閔泳翊 校理李範九 以次進伏訖

上曰　史官分左右
仍敎曰 大臣進前
最應進前
(中略)
上曰　修信使無事往還可幸矣
最應曰 果無事往還矣
上曰　萬里滄海 雖極危險 一船來往 比中原容易矣
最應曰 修信使氣質素弱 故始極爲慮 而克竣其事 誠萬幸矣
上曰　聞修信使之言 則日本人 極爲款曲云矣
最應曰 臣亦聞之 而丙子年金綺秀入去時 不知其情實矣 今番則見待頗異 信好意矣
上曰　日本人問答中 俄羅斯國事 不無爲慮矣
最應曰 俄羅斯國 近頗强盛 中原亦不能制之矣
上曰　中原猶如此 況我國乎
最應曰 年前宮本小一燕饗時 促坐 語及俄羅斯 此是眞情也 而我國人果疑之 今以信使行中 淸人所送冊子觀之 可驗其實情矣
上曰　俄羅斯則雖爲慮 日本人則果極盡之樣矣
最應曰 今番信使之供具行中 譯官從人之優待 異於丙子年 則此可見實情矣
上曰　我國人空然不信 而多浮言矣
最應曰 聖敎至當矣
上曰　信使行中所來冊子 淸使所傳 而厚意甚於日本矣 其冊子 大臣亦見之

	乎
最應曰	日本猶此款曲 況淸人乎 必有耳聞 故俾我國備之 而我國人心 本來多疑 將掩卷而不究矣
上曰	見其冊子 則果何如乎
最應曰	臣果見之 而彼人諸條論辨 將符我之心算 不可一見而束閣者也 大抵俄國 僻在深北 性又忌寒 每欲向南 而他國之事 則不過興利而已 俄人所欲 則在於土地人民 而我國白頭山北 卽俄境也 雖滄海之遠 一帆風猶可往來 況豆滿江隔在兩境乎 平時亦可以呼吸相通 而成氷則雖徒涉可也 方今俄人 聚兵船十六隻 而每船可容三千人云矣 若寒後 則其勢必將向南矣 其意固不可測 則豈非殆哉汲汲乎
上曰	見日本人之言 則似是渠之所畏在俄 而要朝鮮備之 其實非爲朝鮮 而爲渠國也
最應曰	其實似爲楚非爲趙 而朝鮮若不備 則渠國必危故也 雖然 我國則豈可諉以俄人之意在日本 而視若尋常哉 且以壬辰事觀之 稱以假道 空然出來 實非假道也 安知俄人無假道之意乎 今不聽人言 而急必難防 見今城郭器械軍卒兵粮 不及於古 而百無一恃 終難無事 目前之備 寧容少緩乎
上曰	防備之策何如乎
最應曰	防備之策 自我豈無所講磨 而淸人冊中論說 若是備盡 旣給於他國 則甚有所見而然也 其中可信者信之 而可以採用 然我國人必不信之 將爲休紙而已 六月 米利堅來東萊 此本非讎國矣 彼若以書契 呈萊府 則自萊府受之 未爲不可 呈禮曹 自禮曹受之亦可也 而謂之洋國 拒而不受 仍爲播傳於新聞紙 終爲羞恥見侮矣 若言讎國 則日本眞世讎之國也 米利堅有何聲聞之及 而謂以讎國乎 其在柔遠之義 恐不可生釁矣
上曰	米利堅 烏可謂讎國
最應曰	聖敎誠然矣 我國風習 本來如此 爲天下嘲笑 雖以西洋國言之 本無恩怨 而初由我國憸人輩之招引 以致江華平壤事之釁隙 此是我國之自反處也 年前洋人之入送 因中原咨文 好樣周處矣 大抵洋船入境 輒以邪學 爲籍口之說 則洋人之入住中原 未聞中原之人 皆爲邪學也 其所謂邪學 當斥之而已 至於生隙則不可矣 今日筵席 左相姑未出肅 臣獨承敎 宜與諸宰講究 而我國擧朝之人 只貪好仕 皆占自便之計 臣獨有

何策乎

上曰 諸宰則何如乎

致庠曰 大臣已爲備奏矣 無容更達

上曰 原任大臣 俱見其冊 而有何言乎

最應曰 姑未言之 而諸宰則曰 我國事本有廟堂 有何廟堂云爾 而雖十人同坐 無一言之可否矣 然而人孰無惻 爲父母保妻子 固是所欲 而無一講究 退爲高談 此非名節 非義理也 臣之計 則宜思宗社生靈之太平矣 若一朝俄人渡江而來 則想必曰 內修外攘 而修攘非一朝一夕之可爲也 顧今人氣國規器械財用 不如古矣 莫如以柔遠之義爲急務 而以爲安宗社之策也 於此於彼 聖衷牢確然後 可以無患矣 聖衷若不決於疑信之間 則釣名之人朋起 不待俄人 而必起中亂

上曰 廟堂似有可否之論矣

最應曰 未知何時 時原任入侍 而臣今登對 有未穩之語 然含糊不告於君父之前 則臣實有罪 惟冀聖衷之牢定矣

上曰 時原任終當有議 而今非臨渴之事也

最應曰 今日便是臨渴矣

上曰 俄人將往山東云 果然乎

最應曰 以若氣勢 何處不往乎

上曰 三使臣聞見錄 亦已見之 而寧古塔侵奪之說 未詳眞假矣

最應曰 未可知矣

上曰 天何生此類 橫行天下 誠可痛忿矣

最應曰 氣數然矣

上曰 中國若道光時 則此類似不如是矣

最應曰 雖道光之時 氣數所關 亦無奈矣

又曰 外道之器械申飭 何等切嚴 而不善修繕 無一可用 且火藥鳥銃 每下吏輩 乘間換出 誠可痛矣

上曰 然則國財不過虛費矣

最應曰 花房義質 不遠出來云 觀其動靜 又聞其議 庶有措處之方 然今日筵奏後 外論似騷擾 不勝悶然矣

(下略)

【관련문서】

諸大臣獻議 五大官會于左揆家 有下敎于領揆會議 而奉賀姜洰參席 亦因下敎

俄羅國處在北地 虎視耽耽 天下畏之如虎 厥惟久矣 近年以來 每因中國及外各國文字 常以是國爲憂 朝鮮壤界相接 安知不先受其弊乎 今玆修信使回啓 賫來中國人冊子 其所爲對策 自問自答 設疑設難 憂深慮遠者 比諸前日所見各國文字 益加詳密 雖未知其言 言皆是 亦安知非大加講究於安不忘危之義乎 其曰 親日者 二百年來我國事大誠 未嘗一分或懈 上國亦待之以內服 尙今曲加庇覆 更有何別般勸親者乎 此未可解也 其曰 結日本者 近年講信修睦 公使年年出來 聽許其難從之請者 在我國 可謂靡不用極 但我國習俗駭眼 其於留館之際 不能爲蓄憾之端 由是而疑我之不信渠國 此寔出於我之誠信未洽也 見今公使 非久出來 先從在我道理 務盡誠信 毋或如前輕忽 以示申好之意 其出來也 必有渠國受約者存 自謂京城住館也仁川開港也 彼發難從之請 豈可容易聽許乎 住京許之 仁川不許 京城至於仁川 京城尤不得安 雖或仁川許之 住京不許 彼又從渠所欲 强聒不已 若一是京城住館 仁川開港 聽我邈邈 挽回不得 將若之何 此則公使公幹時 隨其所請 以爲究竟之如何矣 其曰 聯美國者 今天下各國 無不合從 以沮俄國輕蔑之威 況我國處在海路要衝 孤立無據 其所聯好者 非不良策 而我國規模 非徒自來不通 相左數萬里 聲息不及之地 今何以自我先通 以爲聯交爲援乎 泊船投書 則見書而好言答之 泛海告難 則隨力而賙恤撫之 不妨爲柔遠之道 而如是然後 其國必曰善待 而亦豈無此際相通者乎 在因其時措處之如何矣 蓋此論 以我國之安危 有關於大淸日本 故如是纖悉爲言 雖在我國 不可尋常看過 而其語如是急迫 寧容玩歲愒日乎 領揆 李最應 左揆 金炳國 領府事 李裕元 領敎 洪淳穆 判府 韓啓源

金弘集(1880. 10. 19/高宗十七年九月十六) ➡ 何如璋(1880. 12. 30/光緖六年十一月二十九日)

『朝鮮策略』 어전 진상(進上) 통보

照錄朝鮮前修信使金宏集來函 六年十一月二十九日收到
子莪欽使大人閣下 自賦河梁 月已再圓 寤寐德音 心焉如痗 伏諗體祺淸旺 勛猷茂著 額手溯頌 不任蕘鋪 魯生夫子暨黃楊兩公諸度綏和 重爲之馳係 宏集前月旬一泊釜山 廿八復使命 家國一切托芘順平 差堪告慰耳 嚮也猥附還往 厚蒙閣下盛眷 體中朝字小之恩 不以宏集樗昧 引而敎之 將中外時事 剖示無蘊 又黃公所贈策略一通 代爲籌畫 靡不用極 謹已一一歸稟 敝廷莫不感誦大德 異聲同歡 現衆論雖未可曰通悟 殊不比往時矣 然敝邦規模 自來拙澁 況又憂虞頗洞 臨事茫然 計不知所出 玆敢飛函仰告 幸憐其愚 而鑒其誠 重賜之大誨焉 則敝廷奉如著蔡 用以稽款 獲受終始之惠矣 惟閣下裁之 言短意長 不能悉暴 統希勻照 不莊
庚辰九月十六日 朝鮮金宏集 再拜

16

劉元植(1880. 11. 3/高宗十七年十月一日)

『朝鮮策略』비판 상소

兵曹正郞劉元植疏曰 伏以臣跡出草野之微 名忝科籍之早 猥荷洪造 歷歇淸塗 奈以庸闇之質 蔑有絲毫之報 惶魔愚忱 食息靡懈 而臣亦化育中一物 粗具彝性 以忠君孝親 知爲天地之常經 以崇聖尊賢 知爲古今之大義也 夫忠孝本自一體 義理固無二致 臣子之於君父 寧諫而不可訑 後學之於前賢 可尊而不可訑 故晉欒子曰 人生於三 事之如一 孟子曰 能言拒楊墨者吾道也 挽近年來 凶役洋酋 枝尙奇巧 學主邪淫 輪行各國 煽惑蚩氓 其所謂敎者 卽無君父 蔑禮義 此鴻濛剖判以來所未有之穢種 粵在丙寅 臣家與沁府 只隔牛鳴 故詳有所聞知者矣 以坂貨色倡邪敎 看作能事 駕異舶張虛聲 誇爲神算 雖尺童愚婦 咸曰犬羊也 禽獸也 恨不一洗妖氛 廓淸區宇 而迄迄有染邪樂禍之徒 以甘利之說 餌誘蠢氓 一域靑邱 幾湮洪水 倚歟我殿下 以天縱之大聖人 秉執卓確 衛正闢異赫怒一師 爰識匪類 日月春秋 永有辭於天下後世矣 若曰洋夷 眞個有絡天網地之勢 挾泰超海之術 則迄今幾年 不敢東漁 轉借倭人之巧舌 藉播俄夷之騷訛 百歧恐動 期欲講和而止哉 惟我東邦 地則三千里 海岱俗尙二千年禮義 周孔程朱之淵源道學 家絃戶誦 逮我朝彬郁益彰 此隆三代 故以若倭若洋之人面獸心 言必稱爲禮義之邦者 良有以也 臣於伊間 得見今番修信使所持來之黃遵憲私議冊子 至於耶蘇天主之學 猶吾敎有朱陸之句 自不覺髮竪膽掉 心寒骨竦 朱夫子生丁盛宋 上接孔孟之遺統 親炙周程之正學 道炳千載 師表百世 雖蠻貊之邦 莫不遵奉爲大賢 況黃遵憲中國人 必無不知朱夫子之爲斯文尊師 今於遣辭之際 何患無證 乃以如彼耶蘇天主之穢 肆然憑據乎朱陸之異趣 若非染邪 焉敢侮賢 以修信使言之 奉使外國 係所公幹 則片辭隻字 雖不得私自閣之 若見此種凶慘之句 合有聲言面責 以示尊賢崇道之意 庸表衛正斥邪之原 不此之爲 安而受之 以館學言之 地是首善 義當崇賢 而此書此句 視若茶飯 寂乎緘口 漠然無聞 幾百年禮養培育之意 果安在哉 大抵此書 以臣愚見 我國邪孽 猶有餘種 潛結異類 做出此等文字 欲其騷擾人心 熾染邪道者也 以我聖上孔昭之天鑑 伏想洞燭無餘 而尙未有處分 或出乎天大包容之盛念也歟 愚憤所激 不能安住 玆敢冒瀆 伏乞聖明 廓揮乾斷 鋤得潛伏之凶徒 殄殄無遺 快雪輿憤焉 且伏念年前書院之毁撤 縱由於省弊之擧 其在乎右

文之化 實是盛代之欠典 胥均士林之抑欝 臣請特下復院之處分 使八域弁髦 益加講誦 明辨向背 則庶爲萬一之補於扶正熄邪之政矣 臣無任云云 省疏具 悉

17

李鴻章(1881. 2. 26/光緒七年一月二十八日) ➜ 李裕元

李裕元-李鴻章 서한(私函) (9)

照錄復朝鮮致仕太師李裕元函
橘山尊兄太師閣下 頃李君容肅到津 接展客冬十一月十一日惠書 遇承獎飾
祇增慚悢 嘉貺十二種 情文稠疊 籍尤潔〇精良 琳瑯滿目 拜登之餘 愧謝無已
比諗道履康愉 林泉養望 遠猷入告 宏濟時難 至爲企頌 貴國爲中土東方藩蔽
脣齒相依已數百年 邇者西洋各國航海東來 地球大勢爲之一變 吾輩不幸値此
時局 必創非常之原 然後可以禦非常之變 客歲貴國王深惟大計 以講戎敎械
爲兢兢 鄙人以爲當務之急 欣慰實深 因是不分畛域 亟思竭力襄助 甚願貴國
振興武備 風氣日開 庶有以禦外侮而固圉〇 前與卞君議定各條 原不拘定成
數 亦不限以歲月 在貴國量力行之 積久冀有成效 李君容肅攜來另冊 所詢八
事已遂條答覆 自必籍邀鑒詧 至論貴國目前形勢 雖不必近攻 而不可不遠交
我中國駐倭參贊黃遵憲所擬貴國策略一本 想已早達台覽 此策揆時度勢 實爲
貴國固圉之圖 亦卽異日富强之本 執事老成謀國 識略闊通 尙望蠲拘墟之成
見 擴久遠之宏規 貴國王及執政大臣 僕尙未通書 不便貿然相聒 惟執事千里
神交 相契已非一日 故不憚煩數之嫌 再三瀆告 諒高明當鑒其苦衷也 刻下中
俄和約雖成 而俄之重兵久駐東瀛 貴國東北海口多與毘連 靜念輔車 隱憂何
極 李君往返匆促 未及具不腆之物 一報雅貺 姑待來日 歉念無似 貴國王及執
政大臣 希爲代致擧 春寒惟千萬珍重 書不盡意
辛巳正月二十八日

李晩孫 等(1881. 3. 25/高宗十八年二月二十六日)

영남만인소(嶺南萬人疏)

慶尙道儒生李晩孫等上疏姜參判晉奎製
慶尙道儒生幼學臣李晩孫等 謹百拜上言于統天隆運肇極敦倫主上殿下 伏以 臣等 俱是嶺外疎迹之踪耳 韋布之賤名 未登於仕籍 管蒯之微才 不通於世務 而尙幸其生也 勛華聲明之時 其居也 鄒魯仁賢之鄕 而所誦說者 周公孔子之書也 所服習者 周公孔子之敎也 惟其疎逖微賤 未能有以萬分一裨補維新之治 庶幾講明執守 益篤尊衛之誠 征邁指引 益嚴扶斥之義 上不負菁莪作育之化 下不負降衷秉彝之性 以爲不報之報而已 卽伏見 修信使金弘集所賚來黃遵憲 私擬一冊而流傳者 不覺髮豎膽掉 繼之以痛哭流涕 於乎 天下之生久矣 堯舜周孔 開之於前 思孟程朱 明之於後 惓惓乎民彝物則之本 兢兢乎敍秩命討之實 一或有邪說詖行 擘芽其間 則必距闢之棄絶之 驅除之殄滅之 是以楊墨之學 仁義而斥之 甚於洪水 老佛之見 心性而討之 急於私讎 左道惑衆之誅 著於王法 黨與先治之訓 載在春秋 千五百年之間 由是而安 反是而危 由是而民生奠於袵席 反是而人類淪於鬼魅 由百等百 莫之或違 蓋以爲天地立心 爲國家立命者 舍是則無他道故也 洪惟我朝建極 列聖相承 崇儒重道 式至今休 諸百于六藝之科 詩書之敎者 罔敢售其胸臆 聘其頰舌 一道同俗之美 猗歟自三代以下 未有臻斯盛者也 而不幸有耶蘇邪敎 出於海外夷種 禮義廉恥 尙矣勿論 倫綱彝則 一切掃盡 其言也 宏闊勝大 而老佛之所不敢道 其術也 奸騙狙詐 而楊墨之所不忍爲 傳襲乎黃巾白蓮之妖 而狡獪過之 依托乎紫羅黑帽之科 而謊誕甚焉 直一禽獸耳 犬羊耳 闖我無人 思易天下 蝨蠧中土 浸淫東國 而周孔邈矣 程朱已矣 平陂之時運不常 好惡之民志靡定 則鋤耨汎掃之責 其不在吾君吾相乎 肆我先王正宗純祖 以及憲廟 先酉後申 增其式廓 干犯者必殺無赦 誆誤者雖小不貸 軒鏡高懸 禹鼎增重 妖腰亂領 咸就顯戮 逮我聖上踐阼 遹追先王之志事 率由先王之典憲 丙寅沁都之變 彼自送死 我乃致討 天怒斯赫 群醜遠遁 已膏之鐵鑽尙在 已明之日星未昧 而曾不十年 凶言醜說 狼藉旁午 前之潛相誑誘 潛相詿誤者 今乃肆然而筆之於書 前之渠自傳習渠自付受者 今乃顯然而投之於我 勝於周孔之說 猶吾朱陸之句 何等誣聖 何等侮賢 何等辱國 而有徵進而奏御之者 有登對而傳布之者 然猶上之人 恬然

不以爲怪 下之人 靡然不以爲恥 視若薄物細故 看作微眚小過 而無一人忠信
義士 明自張膽 沫血碎首 爲周孔爲程朱而伸其誣 爲先王爲殿下而盡其節 僅
有一卑微潛郞 劉元植 而旋以四凶之罪隨之 殿下試觀 自古以來 衣君之衣 食
君之食 冠儒之冠 服儒之服 膺專對之任 居具瞻之地 而賫奉辱國之書 達之天
陛 藏弄誣聖之說 播之朝著 張皇寇賊之勢 恐動君心 憑籍勻衡之威 箝制衆口
者 果皆何如人也 何況在先王 則斥之如此其嚴 而在殿下 則容而納之 在丙寅
則討之如此其正 而在今日 則優而接之 臣不敢知殿下 將何以仰報於先王 而
有辭於後世耶 廈氊肅穆 宮庭如水 永夜邃寂 丙枕無寐 以殿下之明 反以思之
必惕然有追舊之感 而喟然有鮮終之悔矣 孔子曰 自古皆有死 民無信不立 孟
子曰 死亦我所惡 所惡有甚於死 臣愚死罪 竊以爲寧以國斃 不可使先王典
憲 至於殿下之身 而破壞之 先王禮樂 至於殿下之身而弁髦之 先王疆土 至於
殿下之身而捐棄之 先王臣庶 至於殿下之身而淪陷之也 此則義理旣然 而惟
其利害之說 至巧且憯 粧出無形影之俄夷 嗾起不係關之美國 日本 強悍爲其
機關脈絡 則中間聽者疑懼於是 議者劻勷於是 爲建德報仇者 托重於是而逞
其怒 爲劉氏左袒者 顧忌於是而噤其口 恬憘玩愒 浸浸然載胥及溺 臣等請復
就其所論私議者 逐條辨之 其議曰 朝鮮今日之急務 莫先於防俄 而防俄之策
莫先於親中國結日本聯美國 夫中國者 我之所服事也 課歲玉帛 結轍遼薊 謹
守侯度 祇服藩職者 二百年于玆 而曰皇曰朕 優然二尊之稱 一朝安而受之 寵
其人而留其書 則烏在其親之也 萬一執此爲詰 致煩嘖舌 則殿下將何以解之
也 此其利害之較然者一也 日本者 我之所羈縻也 三浦之往事如昨 壬辰之宿
怨未平 而關阨險夷 渠已稔知 水陸要衝 渠已占居 非我族類 其心必異 乘時
陸梁 豈無其便 萬一暇我無備 恣其豕突 則殿下將何以制之也 此其利害之較
然者二也 美國者 我之所素昧也 空然被他慫恿 自我引惹 駕風濤涉重險 疲弊
我臣僚 尾閭我財賄 萬一觇我之虛 侮我之弱 強以難從之請 委以不繼之費 則
殿下將何以應之也 此其利害之較然者三也 俄夷者 我之本無嫌也 空然信人
間貳 損我威重 靠遠交挑近隣 擧措顚倒 虛聲先播 萬一藉此爲釁 來尋兵端
則殿下將何以救之也 此其利害之較然者四也 又況俄美日本 同一夷虜 難置
厚薄於其間 而豆滿一帶 疆界又相接 萬一循日本已行之例 援美國新設之約
請地而來居 請貨而交權 則殿下將何以拒之也 此其利害之較然者五也 又況
薄海內外 如日本 美國者 不可殫數 萬一各自效嚬 各自征利 請地請貨 一如
日本之爲 則殿下將何以遏之也 不許則前功盡棄 而衆怨叢集 爲仇爲敵者 不
但俄夷一國而已 許之則一隅靑邱 地不甚大 將無地之可容矣 此其利害之較

然者六也 又況夷虜之種 素性貪婪 今古一轍 南北同然 萬一蚯蚓相依 蚌鷸相持 裏應外合 坐圖漁利 則殿下將何以禁之也 此其利害之較然者七也 自有此事以來 無知者疾首怨詛 有識者撫心隱痛 民心已離 國勢已削 將使俄夷 一向岸視則已 眞如遵憲之言 力能幷呑而志在侵凌 則殿下將坐待萬里之來援 而抑將與彀下之羌戎禦之乎 此其利害之較然者八也 殿下何苦以爲此有百害無一利之擧 啓俄夷無心之心 生美國無事之事 以致寇而召戎 剜肉而醫瘡乎 其議又曰 從事於西學 盡力於致財 盡力於勸農 盡力於用工夫 財用農工 自有先王之良法美規 欲輕之於先王之道 貊也 欲重之於先王之道 桀也 勞來振德 不傷不害 則民恒安矣 節之制度 食寡用舒 則財恒足矣 不以無益害有益 不以異物賤財用 則工恒勸矣 唐虞之時 比屋皆封 成周之世 居積行裹 而漢之紅腐貫朽 由之有勇知方 何嘗舍先王之道 而從事於別樣妙術耶 政使奇拔淫巧 攫挐罔利 妖器幻術 鉤鉅引貨 天地之間 只有此數 決非可以神運而鬼輸 水湧而海溢也 何況先王之敎已熄 先王之法已壞 赤子化爲龍蛇 冠裳變爲甌脫 則雖有粟 殿下其得以食諸 雖有兵 殿下其得以用諸 臣等請復就其古事之載於史籍者 比類陳之 昔六國合從以擯秦 而皆壤地相接 風俗相隣 未聞越重溟之海 涉萬里之途 而結脣齒之援也 吳 蜀締交以距魏 而皆嚴其界限 愼其封守 未聞借我之地 循彼之敎 而重輔車之勢也 晉武徙氏羌於關右 維翰割幽燕於契丹 當時豈不自以爲受降不殺之仁 權時濟事之智 而終成尾大不掉之勢 遂致夷戎猾夏之變 此豈非前鑑之孔昭 覆轍之當戒者乎 尤可痛者 彼遵憲者 自稱以中國之産 而爲日本說客 爲耶蘇善神 甘作亂賊之嚆矢 自歸禽獸之同科 古今天下寧有是理 無乃向時渠魁漏網者 憤於沁都之敗 而知其不可以兵力取勝 譬於東俗之正 而知其不可以邪說見欺 要以甘言餂之 危辭脅之 逞其僬倖稍食之慾 售其輾轉熏染之奸乎 如其不然 則甘美之言 誘說之已極矣 危怖之辭 恐嚇之已盡矣 又何以傳敎無害之說 尾之於後也 其心所在 不難知也 由此觀之 其人之是眞是假 且不可知 而設使眞而非假 不過邪徒以是欺宰相 而宰相以是欺殿下耳 伏乞殿下 淵然深思 廓揮乾斷 深追旣往之失 痛念將來之禍 其人則盡爲發遣 其書則投之水火 明示好惡 布告中外 使一國蒼生 曉然知聖意所在 而益明周孔程朱之敎 人皆有親上死長之心 益修周孔程朱之法 民皆有安生居業之樂 則衆心成城 師直爲壯 不惟鴨江以東 馬島以北 醜類邪種之無所容奸 縱或有蟊螣之毒 不忍其螫 可使制挺 以撻其堅甲利兵矣 臣等忝在縫掖之列 均被培養之澤 不忍負先師 不忍負聖上 百舍重繭 來伏闕下 而顧今大小恘泄 未聞出一謀發一奇 以舒國家之憂 而徒慈慈然求比於侮聖猾夏之夷倭 以

苟逭目前之無事 一有違忤 又復飾刑以威之 臣等疏逖 臣等微賤 何啻洪水之尺葦 原燎之勺水 非不知嶺海金木 乃分之宜 而爲周公而死 爲孔子而死 爲朱子而死 爲先王而死 爲殿下而死 得與古之胡銓錢塘 遊於地下 榮亦極矣 雖我殿下 以包荒之度 推好生之德 不以狂妄爲罪而恕之 臣等寧蹈海而死耳 不忍與禽獸犬羊 雜處苟活也 人鬼判於今日 華夷決於此行 憂憤絪中 按住不得 大聲疾號 言不知裁 伏惟殿下 哀憐宥赦而採納之 則非獨一國之幸 實天下之幸 非獨一時之幸 實萬世之幸

洪時中(1881. 4. 21/高宗十八年三月二十三日)

척사소(斥邪疏)

武科及第洪時中疏曰 伏以臣 一赳赳武夫 何敢與聞於國家大計 然顧今三千里封疆 化爲異域 五百年宗社 將無地可安 此誠忠臣義士忘身殉國之日也 與其不善變而苟且寄生 寧伏出位妄言之誅 而不目見其敗也 噫 倭夷之爲患於東土 其來久矣 至若壬辰之變 尙忍言哉 夷陵之慘禍 義不可共戴一天之讐也 去鬴之恥辱 又不可一日忘于心者也 嗚呼 我皇明再造之洪恩 莫報 吾君臣百世之深仇 未滅 使有識者病焉 英雄者痛之 一部春秋 常存於其間 義理之昭著 不以氣數之不齊 有足相關而泯沒者 實由我列聖相承 崇正闢異 治敎隆盛 丕基我億萬年無疆之休 內有周召之輔 扶植世道 外得頗牧之材 嚴截奸宄 尙可昇平 思見德化 夫何挽近以來 美俗漸渝 良法生弊 文恬武嬉 駸駸然莫之收拾 於是乎貪戀寵祿之人 謂此時固然 袖手傍觀 行險儌倖之輩 謂此時可乘 接跡而起 援引已露之賊勢 挾持吾君父 張大未露之凶鋒 恐動我君父 邪說橫議 能移君父之志 潛賂奇貨 又導君父之慾 以至掃館厚饋 敬以大賓 備儀受書 把作典禮 割地許港 視若茶飯 冠裳淪於禽獸而不知爲羞 足跡交於犬羊而不知爲變 典常弁髦 廉恥刓鈍 至於人莫爲人 國不爲國之境 此輩之罪 可勝言哉 可勝誅哉 此輩見欺於彼倭 故欺殿下 殿下見欺於此輩 故又見欺於彼倭也 臣請以殿下見斯者 一一明辨之 此輩曰 我和倭 是舊制也 非今日剏行 此有大不然者 古之和 纔經大亂之餘 特存羈縻之策 東萊一隅 雖設館市 條規井井 防閑嚴肅 有若鐵梱金鍵 使不敢一步爛越 是倭受制於我也 今之和反是 任擇形便 控據要衝 直泊畿沿 海禁壞弛 爛入城圍 關譏莫施 小有不叶 渠意 則輒加咆喝 一或不允其請 則便動威脅 有若豪奴悍僕之蔑視其家主 是我受制於倭也 惟殿下猛省焉 此輩又曰 我和 是倭非洋 無傷也 此又有大不然者 古之倭 八十三洲 出沒蟹眼 盤據蛟窟 頑愚俗習 常滾其中 無暇外戀 變遷 今之倭反是 服洋制用洋器 乘洋船輸洋貨 其所與通商十四國 箇箇是大洋以西各種也 電線火輪 朝發夕至 或來有設產於神戶等地 或往有伴行於法美諸國 肺腑相輸 頭面換改 倭而洋 洋而倭 不待智者而可卞焉 惟殿下猛省焉 此輩又曰 開港設市 稅則立規 如鴉片烟及邪學書 互相譏捕 卽用一律 我無患矣 此又有大不然者 巧術之嚼利民口 如甘蜜 邪說之傾隱人心 如漬水 愚迷者第嘗其味

而悅焉 傑鶩者 姑閼其書而惑焉 末流之弊 人皆服鴉 人盡染邪 使已服者 察欲服者 是以蠻攻蠻也 使已學者 察欲學者 是以燕伐燕也 向所謂譏捕用律 適足爲空言虛套也 惟殿下猛省焉 此輩又曰 和倭諸國 即防俄之急先務也 且倭欲和我 亦畏俄也 此又有大不然者 今倭已與洋和 一變其俗 漸服其敎 爲其前導 而對我則曰 渠亦嚴禁邪學云者 深知我素習禮義之邦 如聞其爲邪學 則恐和事不成 故諱之也 今與倭和之日 即爲邪學之日也 爲邪學則國不亡 不爲邪學則國亡 抑將爲邪學而國不亡乎 且俄是洋之一大國 今學洋敎 即學俄敎也 蓋其學 同而異 異而同 大同小異 一再轉而同歸一轍 則安有同其學而貳其人之理乎 如使倭 眞若畏俄而和我 則倭之弱可知 今欲賴弱倭之餘力 以緩俄之來侵 不亦謬乎 又倭雖弱 我亦弱 同是弱 則合力拒賊 或冀萬一 若不合力 拒賊難矣云 則倭距我水路數千里 我猝有急 我何暇請援 彼何暇來救乎 以火輪駕海 若平陸大路 其來必速云爾 則俄亦以火輪 駕海如倭 必由此水路來時 倭由何水路速來乎 惟殿下猛省焉 此輩又大言曰 今天下地球上 莫强莫大之俄兵 一至 將束手無策 此又有大不然者 所謂俄羅斯 即歐羅巴也一名魯西亞 其國本在太平洋以外 西夷之一種 距我數萬餘里之層溟 風馬牛不相及之地 則假使俄 有深怨於我 其不動兵遠涉 恣行侵暴也 審矣 設有聽諸洋夷之甘誘 敢携無名之兵 輕涉數萬里之狂浪 或泊沿邊 我以堂堂千乘之國 以逸待勞 以主制客 何患不勝 年前沁都之役 浿江之擒 前鑑昭然 但俄夷今日之勢 稍强頑猾 爲諸洋夷之所畏憚 故彼常以俄 爲劫盟之一大欛 是猶胡奴之誇單于者 使衛霍諸將 聞之 不滿一笑之資矣 臣嘗遊北關 蓋聞之 自六鎭越百餘里 遼東界首白頭山北 黑龍江東 蒙古外壤 一面東濱太平洋 其間幾三四百里之地 即中原之極東邊廢棄者也 近古以來 中朝之徒流者處之 亡命者往焉 散盜餘黨淵藪焉 因漸着土 稍成部落 其耕鑿 初無徵歛之煩 故於是四方之困於苛政者 又引領歸之 北鎭愚民 冒越潛逃 所以有今 北伯臣金有淵 年前安撫而不能招還也 淸政亦失 不能奮武於此荒圍 以致猖大其勢 疑貳於中國 彊限於我東 自成一局 一局之中 所先着手者 不幸是邪學之巨魁 跋扈於各都 漏網於我東者 引黨化類 俛作酋長 遂擧土衆 遠附于渠之阿好 俄夷錫以西比利亞之名 許以俄東京之稱 爲俄夷計 是來者不拒之意 然甚不以心腹視 故必不爲些利動兵 搆怨於我 未判勝負之事也 明矣 以比利言之 初爲其學之同源 雖附庸於俄 亦不足爲手足使 故決不爲俄夷興兵 啓釁於我也 必矣 何以知其然 我近而俄遠 則近若有急 遠不暇之致也 而俄國亦洋也 比利亦洋也 大抵洋夷之計 專在乎廣布其學於天下 遠植徒黨 其宗旨 本無實脚 徒外馳末流 故欲使人人崇信其敎 敬

畏其虛位 推許其空名 至有民主之國 槪可知矣 意不在於拓土地得人民 則俄比利 俱無以兵血爭之理也 惟殿下釋慮焉 此輩又大言曰 俄夷東得樺泰洲地於日本 北拓黑龍江界於淸國 且以上國之大畏其強暴 賣銀二百萬之多 而平成 則其鋒莫敢嬰 此又有大不然者 日木之和洋爲學 臣已陳之矣 樺泰洲之種子 服其敎尤早熟 故效嚬于比利附俄事 而附比利 比利受之 日本不能禁也 黑龍江之鮮介 再變異類 而附比利 亦如比利之初 是猶大貊之小貊 蓋其學之所成就 一串貫來事也 今我之所大懼者 不在於比利之兼幷 乃在乎吾道之或不明 邪敎或乘虛入也 嗟呼 中州之無人已久 邪說之橫天下漸矣 俄近以犂耳事潛結中朝 中邪學者 紛爲恐動 輕裝火輪 直向威脅 索還動 兵浮費 要分犂耳地 在淸國計 寧爲棄銀 無捐土棄民之義 故有是事耳 其來也 初不欲戰得中原 其和也 亦不在畏強示弱也 惟殿下猛省焉 此輩又曰 今之兵器 愈出愈奇 彼有此無 勝負已判 不可不往各國學造 然後可以應變 此又有大不然者 自軒轅戰蚩尤以後 談兵之家 歷歷陳陳 不可殫記 而第其至精神妙不測一款 捲藏於人君之心一字上而已 人君以此一心任將 將以此一心御衆 衆以此一心向上 則三軍之制勝 不待接刃可決也 人君之心 一或反是 將帥之材 士卒之勇 城郭之固 器械之利 皆無足恃也 兵家器械 未嘗不欲精利 其與吾君之心精確 相距固霄壤懸殊矣 凶奴之鵰射 蠻酋之籐甲 何嘗不精利 而皆被擒獲哉 今我之長槍大釰 強弓勁弩 足可殲賊 大砲小銃 足可破陣 但患不得其人 繕其器 用其器也 今欲禦敵於外 而學兵於敵之耳目覩記處而能取勝 使愚者不許其算矣 惟殿下猛省焉 噫 此輩以此諸件 打成一片 壅遏天聽 鉗勒衆口 潛引外禍 暗弄權柄 馴致一國動搖 萬民離心 自滿朝諸臣 下至輿儓皂隷 及野外士女 孰不知殿下見欺 孤立於上而若將有不測之禍 迫在朝夕 用是憂懼 我殿下 深居九重 晝夜爲此輩之所困 外言無由得聞 故以此時 謂無事也 而莫之省悟 臣切痛之 傳曰 七年之病 求三年之艾 今日國勢之病 內虛莫補 外邪闖入 粒食已絶 元氣大脫 加以直下之別証 其泄莫救 又兼壅滯之重勢 藥餌不能下 使扁鵲當之不敢下手救起 豈不大可悶哉 何幸一條陽脉 或浮或沈 微微不絶如線 因連時刻 或不至七年之將至 則須不以三年之艾 爲一試之良劑乎 然則三年之艾 求畜之方 恐不可一日少緩也 是知今一日浪過了 便得他一日之效遲也 殿下以堯舜聖知之姿 先立精一之心法 去夫外誘之私 存吾天理之公 涵養省察之工無或間斷 則第於乙夜丙枕無寐之時 昧爽待朝未與物接之時 澹然虛明氣像自可見矣 乃以往日己行之事 何者爲正 何者爲邪 自語于心 自反于躬 則其是非得失 昭著于斯時也 殿下此心一開 然後今日之事可爲也 今日之事 臣請以

兵家之說解之 兵法曰 善戰者 因其勢而利導之 今不幸和倭 爲五六年之久 冠蓋相望於水陸之路 耳目已洩於虛實之機 今若一朝嚴斥 是使倭得構釁之資而來其兵 所謂削之反速之勢也 爲今之計 莫如別立條規 以十年一信使我往越明年彼使來 其九年之間 巨細事務 皆自萊伯 隨啓隨决 我使往彼留館 無過十日之限 又毋得出館外遊行 彼使來亦如之 雖利害議論 足可決於十日之內也 使行隨員 定以十人 彼此如數 所謂國書 非其主新立 勿施 使行船具 以彼船等待 責以港地之報代 港口三處不幸已許之事 雖難索還緊閉 然其一處將設之港 尤係我咽喉防賊之門也 此門已開 則末流之弊 必有納賊之患 其鎖鑰之方 不得不講定的確 然後或保其無憂 畫地設柵 嚴束防閑 半步踰柵 立斷一律 陸仁川爲水營 富平爲兵營 統重兵守禦 又設數鎮柵外 極擇有武略者居之 別設一烽於港口 彼船來泊 專管照燭 彼來商舶 多不得帶二三隻 設市以亥日爲定 一月兩次交易之物 凡經洋夷手者 幷嚴禁 潛商現發 依邪學律 即施梟警 非日本所産 不許買賣 買賣之法 非公文者 屬公 又米穀布木等物 三港皆不許貿 且以物易物 不許銅貨幣 本國商賈稅 以十之五 著爲定式 使我人 少利而罕見往 使彼倭稀販而頻不來 誠如是 不幾年 港市之弊 庶乎 其祛矣 今日所謂中西聞見 萬國公法 公史地球 瀛環申報 與亞會雜事 詩續今日 投我誘我 漸入邪學嘗試之計也 請一一搜出 都聚于鍾樓街上 付之以火 渙發德音 深陳旣往之悔 用布斥邪之義 俾萬姓明聽敬服 咸曰一哉王心 大哉王言 人莫不磨勵振刷 精白修德 以承休敎 大夫立朝 盡忠補闕 有堯舜吾君之志 士而居家習六藝之文 講明春秋大統之義 小民日遷善 納之仁壽之域 安其生樂其業 皆有親上事長之心 上下相濟 中外充積 遠近歸一 衆和消矣 衆心成城 可使制梃以撻堅甲利兵矣 夫何患乎倭 何患乎洋 何患乎俄之强哉 伏願殿下 勿以人賤其言 言可用采之 言不可用 治臣誣罔之罪 以謝國人焉 臣無任云云

黃載顯(1881. 4. 21/高宗十八年三月二十三日)

척사소

出身黃載顯疏曰 伏以臣 一箇出身 九重納書者 有違罪分之責 敢犯難赦之罪 然臣竊伏海濱 讀兵書十有餘年 其精微蘊奧 雖不足爲彷彿其皮膚糟粕 亦頗得其裏許也 然則臣所學者 兵也 所言者 兵也 所任者 亦兵也 今當此世道危懼之時 惜其一死之言 而棄其公忠之計哉 夫兵者 善用之而足可霸於天下 不善用之 而足爲致寇招禍也 是故其勝敗 不在於交兵接刃之後 而在於廟堂之上 其得失 不在於城郭甲兵 而全在於擇將鍊兵也 擇將鍊兵 豈在亂離之後而爲哉 古之春蒐秋獮 振旅治兵 皆用安不忌危 預立素具之道也 試論今日天下大勢 則上國不能令於天下 而邊徼反亂 齊楚古境 燕雲舊墟 或守或失 其餘洋海之間 如俄羅斯 法國 美國 英國等地 氣勢張大 恣其不道 時興干戈 與中國抗衡 此皆聖遠敎弛 駸駸然長夜乾坤之中 而盖由治入亂之時也 一或擧而擬之於我東方編小之上 則其爲患也 不啻若泰山壓卵之勢也 且疑似之信息 有遵憲之策 的歷之事機 有日本之使 此誠危急存亡之秋也 是故殿下之丙枕無寐 夙夜憂懼 三千里江山 至於朕之身而或有損失歟 五百年宗社 至於朕之身而或有傷敗歟 內無良將 外多敵國 而倉庫空虛 甲兵不利 則計無所施 勢無可爲 故乃出非常之計 又營不世之功 刱設機衙 齎煩使行 其意 不過是結連隣國 防禦外患 有無通商 彼此適用而已 則善爲之 似可富國强兵 不善爲之 反易招寇致禍也 其計之利不利 雖不能預籌 然使行之資裝疲於道路 異國之服色 駭於畿甸 上自搢紳 不至韋布 僕漱之類 莫不驚動於一國 此或古人之智者作法 愚者拘焉 賢者更禮 不肖子議之者乎 臣留連京師 酌宜京鄕人心 則輒不可以不知沒覺 歸之於蚩蚩之中而徒欲遽行之也 何則 人心之維持 爲國者 猶抒索之御六馬 古今有國家之切戒也 而古之人 雖或有厚生利民之道 不由舊制 刱出己意 庶可濟事者 未敢率爾變更者 爲是國係於民 而民一動擾離搔 則其爲利者 將不知其成功 而爲禍者 是存亡所關故也 今者 上不信度 下無法守 民散久矣 盖民情 常係字牧之如何 而自八道道伯 至三百六十州之守宰 都不知善治仁政之所在 惟以不奪不厭之苛政 徒欲交征於民人 則一國蒼生 盡入於水火之中 是日曷喪及予偕亡之語 猶在歇后 其困憔無告之情 不可忍言 而自數年以來 火賊黨起 嘯聚山谷 水盜群集 裝載兵器 白晝大道 禦人奪金 甚至

於稅錢軍木 往往見失 或至數十百人 或至七八百人 其餘市井閭巷間出沒餘黨 不可勝記 而都城之內 屢有盜驚火怪 此誠有深憂遠慮者 當緩彼急此也 若于斯之際 有一夫猖獗 張奉關動 則關西以北 嶺湖以南 非我有也 當此方蹶之時 惟泄泄然不知爲慮 臣徒吟夜上戍樓看太白之詩 而淚不可禁也 仰天而太息 長風颸颸 望洋而張目 怒瞻弸裂 臣第乃降心低徊 就諸實地 而商量 則方今國步日艱 民心日離 外倭請港 盜賊竝起 士氣沮喪 妄訕朝廷 文恬武嬉 奔競軒晃 上下扞隔 載胥溺焉 其前頭之禍 不啻若子胥之抉吾目掛東門 而此近禍起蕭墻 無用防胡者 不其然乎 今竊料之 兵政有五 擇將一也 習陣二也 儲食三也 兵卒四也 淸野五也 若將帥 苟得其人 則握萬機之權於掌上 運千里之目於心中 制勝妙用 決於未戰之前 而使外寇內盜 狼顧狐疑 莫敢生心於其間 則此所謂上兵伐謀也 如陳法熟鍊 則奇正有法 天地無方 雖當猝伏强弩 旗隊行伍 便成泰山之勢 撼動無計 鼓進 赴湯蹈火錚止 棄金遺玉 何師不濟 何寇不平乎 如士卒强壯 筋氣膂力 堅忍勁悍 則此所謂荊楚六郡 良家子弟 奇材釰客也 制之有道 養之有義 則可以爲子弟之衛父母 手足之捍頭目也 若軍糧充積 漕運無乏 則覘其形便 可戰可守 任其食飽 此所謂以逸待勞也 淸野者 無使野積民穀 藉寇之食也 賊若眞知吾境之淸 則恐其躔除戚施 畏首畏尾 不敢輕動 亦足爲次也 而其法井井方方 非但武備誌尹氏之堡約而已也 年前 今將臣申櫶 有所草記 布令各邑者 亦豈非知其急先務乎 盖自秦漢以來 至于宋明之末 屢試屢驗 百不一失 其爲法也審矣 然則五政之中 擇將之法 視今時原任諸將臣 未試一方 臣猥不敢輕議於其間也 戰陣鍊熟與否 亦未知其詳悉 然臣年前 行遊北關湖營 採聞於所謂兵校聽執事者 則我國之兵書淺近者 是指南一帙 而雖旁通曲暢 當於蒼黃行陣之間 失手違格者 猶爲十常八九 況其平時鍊習 一不介意 全不知束伍隊伍奇正鼓金 爲何件物事 而坐作進退 放丸箭檑木石 休番更代 視若夢中譫語 是可知八道郡縣營鎭 無一箇兵校之軍勢行陣得其糟粕者 若脫有不幸 將束手待死 如壬辰之席捲千里 直搖京城矣 使有識者 豈不寒心哉 盖各邑所謂兵校者 是亂時之將爲軍正者也 揣其蒼黃之日 或有忠義天性者 不棄印策馬 焦口乾脣 呼得數十名兵卒所能通者 任之以兵校之役 不能者不入 而任之者 授以渠廳中第一要窠 則其勢 不踰年 能精通者多矣 儲食之方 我邦不過是三南船漕 而近年之破船傷失 歲不下三四十隻 惣計爲五六萬石 而雖有徵民責出 終歸於糜費而止也 臣生長海邑 頗知其漕運之生弊 盖京江船主 與倉船篙師 貪其船價剩條之多餘 本自造船 巨創浩大 載卜 小不下二千餘石 且或有添卜之米 則欲於事半價倍之利 信其行險僥倖之

心 輒加添卜 其重斤 恰如泰山相齊 風帆波濤數十日程 有狂浪惡颷 則納之海濤之上 非但暴殄天物也 國步軍糧之受困 亦多矣 嚴關各道 稅運之船載卜 略不過千石許 則其傷敗必小矣 兵卒 今各邑軍惣 徒擁虛簿 束伍牙兵 舟師旗手 都是虛名也 薄籍之名號 盡是塚中枯骨 採鍊額數 太半懷中兒 只蒼黃有事之日 驅出此類 以之禦蓄銳之鋒 豈制勝之道乎 勢家墓村 鄉校校生 嚴立課條 入之兵籍 每月朔望 訓鍊以各邑兵校廳所學 則足可爲精兵 但嚴禁其奸鄉猾吏之受賂圖脫也 然則設有淸野之法 非士卒 不能保其勝也 雖有士卒 非儲糧不能保其勝也 雖有儲糧 非陣法 不能保其勝也 雖有陣法 非將帥則必不能保其勝也 是故人存政擧 人亡政廢 丞相之栢 水鶴來巢 忠武之墓 石麟凄凉 豈殿下之今日撫躬長吁者 其在此乎 然則今日之勢 不可不先守後戰 先守之道 莫如民堡 其法也 上可以爲國禦敵 下可以安民定産 簡易而天下之理 得矣 其餘兵之要領 事之機變 有不能以筆端可旣 臣不勝禹慮之至 獻此淺近之策 惟殿下 勿以人賤其言 言可用 采之 不可用 治臣以妄言之罪 以謝國人焉 臣無任云云

21

洪在鶴 等(1881. 8. 30/高宗十八年閏七月六日)

척사소

관련문서 洪在鶴이 閔台鎬에게 보낸 서한

伏以魯論有曰 不在其位 不謀其政 臣等固知此訓是守身之常法也 然難之大 則人人有救難之職 患之急 則人人有濟患之位 是以孟子曰 能言距楊墨者 聖人之徒 朱之註之曰 邪說害公 人人得以攻之 不必聖賢 如春秋之法 亂臣賊子 人人得以誅之 不必士師 又曰 謂賊當捉當誅是主邊人 謂賊可殺恕已可是 賊邊人 若曰邪說害正 必也聖賢然後可以攻之 亂臣賊子 必也士師 然後可以討之 云爾則洛閩世遠 士師貴賤 人人噤口 家家袖手 則少焉必將家家而邪詖 人人而亂賊矣 當是時也 果有能超然特免於禍者乎 所以古聖賢於此 則無論賢否 必盡力扶之 斷之以主邊之人 於依違傍觀 噤口袖手之徒 則無論賢否 必盡力抑之 斷之以賊邊之人 此豈非人人居濟患之位 人人有救難之職者乎 臣等草莽賤品 蒙被烈聖覆燾之恩 食息元氣開闢之間 皎皎而不知爲者矣 玆有莫大之患 切急之憂 不容泯然者 彛性所發 按住不得 謹從諸路儒生之後 伏叫天閽 籲此惶悶之至情 少垂察焉 臣等竊聞之 人之所以異於禽獸者 以其有五倫五常之典 華夷向背之性也 先王先聖之繼天 立極於萬世者 此也 後王後聖之講明傳授於後世者 此也 勸之以五常之服者 以其能此也 威之以五刑者 以其背之也 此窮天地 亘古今之大義 一或有違 冠裳淪於裔戎 人類化爲禽獸 而天地爲飜覆矣 洪惟授命聖神承繼 儒賢輩出 非文武周孔之訓不習 非顔孟程朱之敎不行 是以三綱明 九疇敍維持鞏固 累百餘齒 所謂磐石之宗也 詎意百年以來 洋胡妖氣浸潤 漸播於邦域之內 壘人心志 幻人臟腑 壞五品之典 亂羅之敎 而一種善幼厭常之輩 猶水就下 如獸走壙 窟穴盤據 涵淹卵育於名敎之下 其禍于人家 凶于人國 奚啻洪水橫流稽天 猛獸之狂奔 蹄蹢哉 惟我正祖純祖憲宗三大王 如是之憂 殄殄滅之 斷不饒貸 而擧兵犯闕之凶賊 同條共貫 垂關和之典 懸象魏之高 使民庶於是而知畏 萬代聖神於是而遵守 於是妖言凶敎 漸次屛去 人類免於禽獸 宗社免於危亡 大聖人之作爲 出於尋常萬萬矣 若於是時 少有寬假之意 則宗社不得有今日久矣 不幸於丙子辛未間 邪黨滿憂於內 洋賊突逼於外 浮言脅動 不可復制 而皇天眷顧 朝宗旣佑 朝廷決死社之議 謀臣致殉國之誠 成敗利鈍 置之度外 而邪黨魚駭 洋賊獸散 義理根于宇宙 而其於三聖之功 爲有光矣云 何近年以來 邪說肆行於廟堂之上 以致獸

蹄鳥迹 交橫於國中 凶敎異言 狼藉于都下 使先祖之宗廟社稷 危於綴旒 三聖
之盛德大業 入於剝蝕 竊不敢知 此何故也 此何事也 殿下其可恬然而已乎 臣
等伏讀聖批之答嶺南儒生者 有曰 衛正斥邪 何待爾等之言乎 臣等固如殿下
之本心在此而靡他也 雖然殿下果以爲孰邪而孰正乎 臣等請得以詳陳之 孟子
曰 服堯之服 誦堯之言 行堯之言 是堯而已 服桀之服 誦桀之言 行桀之行 是
桀而已 此萬世不易之大訓也 由此言之 我國之承薰家煥 我國之洋也 歐羅之
邪蘇三拔 歐羅之洋也 日本之花房義質 日本之洋也 何謂日本之洋 彼服洋之
服 言洋之言 行洋之行 有洋之技 能居洋之貨賄 洋之樣備矣 我國之承薰家
煥等 三聖則誅而鋤之 日本之花房義質等 殿下則容而接之 非特容而接之而
已 一言之偪逼于彼者 竄逐如不及 盡力而媚悅乎彼者 爵賞如不及 無乃三聖
之政敎 一南一北乎 夫楚王好高髻 四方高一尺 楚王好細腰 宮中多餓死 上有
好者 下必有甚焉者 殿下扶抑之如彼 國人皆知之矣 況從善如登 從惡如崩 臣
等竊恐 每瑟邪蘇之妖氛 日永月長 如烈火之燎原 而不可撲滅 孔孟程朱之大
道 日消月亡 如大廈之傾覆 而不可支吾 少焉將家家而亂倫敗常 人人蔑法棄
義 於此時也 殿下將誰與爲國乎 今日國勢之殆哉岌岌 擧國之所知也 一年二
年 因循推過 至今無事者 殿下寧不知其所由乎 良由列聖代作 正風化 立紀綱
禮義廉恥 以左支右梧 孝悌忠信 以前撑後亘 如大廈之棟梁傾倚 而欓槌楨幹
以撑柱之 墻壁土石 以維持之 何自撥藩籬 而莫之疑 自壞長城 而莫之恤使賊
人凶黨 心獨喜自負 忠臣義士 私憂竊歎也 臣等賦上天所降之彛性 被列聖培
養之厚澤 粗知彼此邪正之大分 雖然擧世而邪敎 則臣等之本心 亦難保其有
終 殿下根天之德 因不以質之神明 而至於左右諸大夫國人皆是邪敎 則未知
殿下之彛性 亦能保眞堅白無累也 所以臣等此擧非特爲殿下之宗社 亦要臣等
之不染於邪也 非特爲殿下之一身 實爲殿下之聖子神孫也 非特爲殿下之聖子
神孫 亦爲臣等之子孫兄弟親戚也 夫磨而不磷 涅而不淄 惟聖賢然後可以能
而不然 不能不因物而遷 是以聖賢之敎人也 必目不觀不正之書 耳不听非
禮之聲 必曰 寧可終齒不讀書 不可一日近小人 朱子之告君也 有曰 蓬生痲中
不扶而直 白沙在泥 不染而黑 習與正人居 不能不正 猶生長於齊 不能不齊言
也 習與不正人居 不能無不正 猶生長於楚 不能不楚言也 故參判臣李恒老之
言曰 當愼所居 所居者刑類之 當愼所近 所近者氣類之 當愼所執 所執者心類
之 所謂刑類 魚龍水居 其鱗波流 麋鹿山居 其角崢嶸 龜鼇石居 其甲巖險 何
謂氣類 藏鐵于石 亦能指南 沈木于水 亦能潤下 何謂心類 矢人猶恐不傷人
函人猶恐傷人 此至切之言也 擧國之所服者 洋織也 洋染也 擧國之所用者 洋

物也 所接者 洋人也 所以津津而流涎者 洋之奇技淫巧也 是所居所近所執者 俱是洋也 刑氣心神 安得不俱化爲洋乎 蓋洋之學 亂天理 滅人紀之甚者 無容更言 洋之物 太半長淫導欲戰倫敗常 亂人神逆天地 耳得之 而幻腸易牡 目寓之 而翻臟倒胃 鼻嗅脣接而易心失性 是則如影響之相應 癘疫之相染 不問其人好惡向背 亦不必立天柱之象 讀耶穌之書 而始得罪於聖人也 殿下臣民果有無耳無目無鼻無口乎 此則旣然矣 所謂中西聞見 泰西聞見 萬國公法 許多異類之邪書 光滿於國中 而所謂名士碩儒 好新尙氣之輩 論胥以入 樂而忘反 更相稱美 而各與位祿不同而滋 或有詰之者 從而爲之辭曰 此是彼國記事之書 未必是滅倫敗常之敎也 從事於此者 要以廣見聞 而開胷衿 未必是滅倫敗常之學也 噫只此一言 已是陷溺之甚也 昔我純祖大王 斥邪之敎 有曰 顧一世好新之風 卽近世蠱俗之習 動稱考證各物 競倣艶異博奇 一轉而作索隱行怪 再轉而爲異端佛經 大哉王言 其眞萬世之大訓也 彼所謂廣見聞 而開胷衿者 旣非六藝之科 孔子之術矣 此非好新蠱俗之謂乎 此非考證名物 艶異博奇之謂乎 此非索隱行恠 異端佛經之謂乎 從古異敎 例皆騁其似是之非 以惑亂人心 終至於率獸食人 而人不知察也 墨氏之無父 而託乎仁之近 楊氏之無君 而假乎義之疑 鄕愿之亂德 而借乎中庸之似也 況乎耶蘇利瑪竇心肝之所吐 態三拔萬濟國臟腑之所據 其似也分錢 而其禍也山嶽 其近也毫釐 而其遠也燕越也 以至廣見聞開胸衿之實 是何異於飮鴆毒 而要以解其渴 食餉吻 而要以饒其飢也哉 三聖之世 果有此等凶書之資行乎 殿下嗣服之初 果有從事於此而靦然無羞者乎 若欲無變今日之事 則承薰家煥之鬼 伸其冤枉可也 鐘三鳳周之子孫 訪問之 存恤顯榮之 可也 胡然廢罪禁錮 至於今日乎 彼不亦含冤呼慟於地下乎 若夫所謂黃遵憲之私擬冊 則臣等以爲未是人所爲 恐是殿下臣僚陷溺於彼者之所自爲也 假曰實是黃虜之所爲賫來 而進之天陛 揚之朝班 而其言曰 彼之諸條論辨 相符我之心算 曰 洋人人居中原 未聞中原之人 皆邪學也 是果截天履地者 所敎發諸口乎 是果不自爲者 有尺寸之間乎 夫水流濕 火就燥 正與正相求 邪與邪相應 不易之理也 如使殿下專對之臣 嚴乎扶正斥邪之義 凜然秋霜烈日 則彼安敢肆然而發此凶口乎 如使殿下之宰相執政 少持正議 嚴毅而不可犯 則彼所謂專對之臣 安敢肆然而進此悖書乎 由此觀之 使臣宰執 乃耶蘇之腹心 歐羅之內應 何意三千里箕聖古疆 至今日而陷溺於犬羊 五百年孔朱禮義 至今日而淪沒於糞壤哉 猶吾朱陸之說 傳敎無害云 延師習敎之奏 婦孺皆知凶悖 使臣之所以是說而進御者 殿下不能肆之市朝 宰執之勸殿下以牽確聖衷者 殿下不能以尙方之劍 而斫其頭 一二疎逖之臣 持正

議斥邪之敎者 放流罰殛 如恐不及 殿下扶抑 何若是差異也 若是不已 則臣等
竊恐承薰家煥之鬼將見其爲世宗師矣 孔孟程朱之書 明見其爲世大禁矣 誦法
孔朱之士 若存若已者 將見其爲凶黨矣 剃頭淨髮 裂冠毁冕之禍 將見其迫于
呼吸 而不可復制矣 蓋爲洋所制 無變不可事既到此 悔之何及 人之言曰 奚至
若見之甚乎 臣等以爲不思之甚也 始焉 木偶之殉葬 而終焉 七百之幷命 始焉
涓涓熖熖之端 而終焉 洪溟原火矣 是其次第件事 自住不得 況殿下今日扶抑
之差異 其木偶之小 涓熖之微哉 殿下何不反而思之 庶免無及於事之悔也 夫
國無不亡之國 道無不棄之日 豈可以國之存亡 破開先王疆土 養育日本之家
煥承薰 以種下種子于邦域乎 豈可以國之存亡 廢五倫五常之典 尊耶蘇之鬼
而行西洋之敎乎 豈可以國之存亡 顚覆先王金石之典 使先大王在天之靈 震
怒於冥冥乎 況古今天地未聞有守道亡國者乎 嗚呼神洲陸沈 四海腥羶 二百
年於此矣 皇壽一脈 特實吾東班 如天地肅殺之氣 碩果高懸生理於是即結梢
矣 此天地之所愛護 人物之所倚重 豈思幷此薄蝕 以爲純坤無陽之世乎 夫天
之生物之心 決不如是之昧然也 殿下誠能順天意 應人心 廓掃鬼魅之妖 高懸
日月之明 開聖路於旣湮 擎天柱於旣倒 則自然天助人順 不求利 而自無不利
其爲功於天下萬世 可與大禹之抑洪水 周公之驅猛獸 同其高大矣 豈不盛哉
古人有言曰 陷之死地 而後生 置之亡地 而後存 孟子曰 無敵國外患者 國恒
亡 田單之在即墨也 無可往矣 宗廟亡矣 有死之心 無生之樂 蹈劍戰 衝矢石
而不覺其悖劫 赴湯火 冒風雨 而未不覺其冷熱 所以即墨小城 破萬乘之燕 而
復臨之墟也 是知兵不徒以力而戰 在乎立心也 國不徒以地而强 在乎定計也
我國雖壤地數千里 山海之險 魚鹽之利 財粟之富 親上死長之民 足以自保 伏
願殿下奮發乾斷 能守死社之儀 決戰守之計 立志以師其氣 克己以御其心 刑
威以及乎遠 收境內西洋之物 聚境內西洋之書 焚之通衢 凡臣隣之倡爲橫議
以脅持上下 造爲飛語 以詿惑遠邇者 斷其頭 而懸之高街 凡侵淫邪敎 樂爲虎
前之長鬼者 誅鋤遏絶 無使易種于吾東三千里之境 凡東萊德原 設關逗留之
洋 城外城內出沒無常之洋 盡數驅除 無使汚染我禮義之俗 凡扶正斥邪 而得
罪於殿下者 隨其才德之高下 聲名之微著 進之朝 著寵之祿位 任以興復討賊
之職 咨以安民扶國之策 罷機勢之衙 復五營之制 移內營之費 厚軍卒之料 止
巫佛之禱 遠俳優之戱 革宴逸之舊 盡憂勤之德 選任將相 親近師友 收召賢
俊 放逐奸倖 裁省冗費 禁止奢華 廣開言路 沿受衆善 崇獎正學 屛遂淫巧 振
肅綱紀 變化風俗 愛養民力 修明軍政 上下遠近 精白一心 持久如金石 信實
如四時 則三軍之師 不戰而氣自陪 八路之民 不賞而心自固 風勢振動於六合

義氣洋溢於八紘 東倭西洋 有可制之策 北之俄羅 亦將慕我之義 憚我之威 而不敢加我以無禮矣 嗚呼死中求生 則一當百有餘 有生之樂 無死之心 則百當一而不足 非持患難之際爲然 雖袵席之上 憂勤者 生之道 而宴逸者 亡之術也 是故古人以燕安爲鴆毒 以酒色爲二斧 論兵則以有進無潰 將死鼓 御死轡 國君死社稷 爲萬世不易之常法 以衝矢石 赴湯火 爲禦賊之正經 以棄甲曳兵 和好苟全 爲謀國之大罪 此其聖經賢訓者 昭如日星 天下豈有二道哉 我國今日之形 雖凜凜若不保朝夕 而三千里 江山之大 三百州 民物之殷 其視莒卽墨之二邑 不啻相懸之萬萬 而胡爲從事於和之一字 斂四方之遠 貽萬古之羞 而使之禍亂隨興 而宗社顚覆也 臣等不忍見宗社之危亡於朝夕 不忍見殿下之貽羞於汗靑 不忍見千里父母之國湮沒於魑魅罔魎之窟 不忍見一脈陽氣 無處可尋於此天地之間 不忍生爲禽獸之身 而死爲禽獸之鬼也 玆敢踣繭而來 冒萬死哀呼於天地父母之前 斷斷衷赤 證在天日 伏願殿下哀衿財賜而採納 則非特臣等之幸 實宗社生民之幸 非特一時之幸 實天下萬世之幸也 臣等無任瞻天望聖 激切慟呼之至 謹昧死以聞

尾附
疏成未及進 伏而際次 伏見四道儒疏登徹後 傳敎下者 臣等讀之未竟 益不勝推胸之慟哭也 殿下何故牢拒一國士民 萬口一談之公論 而至於此極也 臣等聞之 從諫受善 聖王所以致興隆也 拒諫自聖 叔李之所致傾覆也 今考其見於經史者 有曰 稽乎衆 舍己從人 有曰 詢于四岳 開四門 明四目 達四聰 有曰 好問而好察邇言 隱惡而揚善 執其兩端 用其中 曰 設誹謗之木 建敢諫之鼓 曰 聞善言則拜 曰 從諫弗咈 改過不吝 曰 有言逆于汝心 必求諸道 有言遜于汝志 必求諸不道 曰 詢于芻蕘 狂夫之言 聖人擇之 此非二帝三王 所以日就興隆乎 子思謂衛侯曰 君之國事 將日非矣 君出言 自以爲是 而卿大夫莫敢矯其非 卿大夫出言 自以爲是 而士庶人莫敢矯其非 君臣旣自賢矣 而群羊下同聲賢之 賢之則順而有福 矯之則逆而有禍 如此則善安從生 宋孝宗時 主和之輩 進獨斷之說 朱子倡言排之曰 是將重誤吾君 使之傲然自聖 上不畏皇天之譴告 下不畏公論之是非 挾其雷霆之威 萬斤之重 以肆於民上 而莫之敢攖者 必此之由也 嗚呼其亦不仁甚於作俑者矣 此輩又恐公論之沸騰 而上心之或悟也 繼進國是之說 則朱子又極力卞斥曰 此安石章蔡之徒 所以馴致大禍者也 蓋其所是者 非天下之所同是 而強欲天下之是也 故懸賞以誘之 嚴刑以督之 然後僅足以創制士夫不齋之口 而天下之眞是罪 有終不可誣者矣 奈何

此尋亂亡之轍迹 而躬駕以隨之也 此非衛宋之君 所以日就於傾覆者乎 今以
殿下之明聖 負荷朝宗之世業 凡于政令施措 上法二帝三王 而致興隆之福可
乎 下法衛侯宋帝之致傾覆之禍可乎 此不待兩言而決也 今日之事 可否得失
原疏旣悉陳之無餘矣 抑不但臣等之疏爲然也 在丙子之初 崔益鉉 李學淵 張
浩根之徒 所爭者此也 近日文臣如許元軾 劉元植 武臣如洪時中 黃載顯 布衣
如李晩孫 金祖榮 金碩圭 韓洪烈 所爭之者此也 就其爲說詳略不同 而邪正利
害 安危存亡之大 則如出於一人之口 從其言 則邦域爲全衣裳之舊 宗社保磐
石之安 棄其言 則人數陷獸魅之域 赤子罹魚肉之慘矣 此其效害之必然 無智
愚皆能言之矣 殿下不惟不從願 乃刑之流之 不少顧措 此聖王從諫之事乎 叔
李拒諫之事乎 此謙然受善之事乎 傲然自聖之事乎 只此一事 旣非吉祥可願
之事 而向來嶺疏之批 近日傳敎之事 尤有甚焉 臣等請且條陳之乎 批旨旣曰
斥邪衛正 豈待邇言 而傳敎又曰 隨時隨捉 草薙而禽獼之 此敎一出 而四方之
人 莫不駭惑 殿下自親總萬機以後 何嘗一日而有斥邪衛正之政乎 邪學之黨
曾於何時 隨現隨捉 草薙禽獼之乎 如此批敎書之史册 天下後世 當以殿下爲
何如主乎 殿下試於閑燕之中 更加思量焉 如此而尙可以嚇人之口 服人之心
乎 何待爾等之指敎明示 訑訑自足 謂人莫已若之病哉 聖王心固當如是乎 聖
批有曰 他國文字 何必深究 夫他國之書 於我無利害 誠可放過也 而今見一墜
於此禍 將稽天而不可救 則安得不深究而痛卞乎 又以嶺疏誤看文字之少失
爲執言之端 要以伸彼而抑此者 必也是尙可謂斥邪衛正乎 至於李晩孫之被罪
駭聽尤大 夫看人文字 當領會其語意之所取 字句之小嫌 則略之可也 今夫爲
劉氏左袒之說 引類雖不親貼 而其無他心腹 則粗解文理者 皆可以知之矣 殿
下急於鉗制四方之口 扶摘以示威 則雷霆之下 雖不免摧折 而公議益激 安得
禁之乎 傳敎又以接倭通商 爲交隣修好之道 臣等又切惑焉 舊日和好之時 日
本果以皇帝僞稱 加我以無禮乎 果接數千戶於東萊乎 果豫德原之要地乎 果
許仁川之咽喉乎 果迎入於造紙署乎 果以我人學彼之奇術淫乃乎 果有惟其言
是從之事乎 古之交隣 所以畏天而保國 樂其天而保天下也 今之交隣 則割祖
宗之地 竭生靈之血 汚冠冕於獸魅 而墜赤子於塗炭者也 嗚呼異哉 古今之未
同也 傳敎又以不解道理 付疏儒 以退修學業勉之 臣等不和五典四維之外 有
可解之道也 孔孟程朱之外 別有可修之學乎 今如聖明之好惡豫奪 則修孔孟
程朱之學 解五典四維之道者 反恐如白晝罔魎 無所容於斯世也 臣等駭懼痛
隱 不知所以奉敎也 又以先敎後刑 斷以重律爲敎 則臣等冥頑不靈 今日之敎
不可奉承 伏見近日恩綸纔下者 固知聖意之謹嚴於斥邪於反經 然其曰雖不扶

摘破蔽以下云 尤切惑焉 夫薰猶同器 則薰變而爲猶 邪正 處則正變而爲邪 必然之理也 今東萊德原 都下之洋 依舊焉 好新尙奇 主和之徒 依舊焉 鍊習洋數 交易洋貨之事 依舊焉 若是而固可謂去莠而培苗 除惡而樹德乎 可使正道斯行 而善俗斯興乎 可使之不梁於邪 而能悛其習乎 殿下誠欲扶正道 而斥邪敎 則凡佞臣之主和賣國 而媚悅於彼者 斬其頭 而懸之高街 凡前日斥邪 而得罪於殿下者 赦其罪 而用其策 凡異類之接於邦域 而出沒無常者 一一迸逐 而火其書 燒其貨於市街之上 以快臣民之情可也 胡乃只設文具 以鉗萬口 以塗萬目 爲良策也 若一向如是 不實擧 則禍將稽天 而莫可下乎矣 臣等竊願速死 只得伏閣以竢陳東東市之刑而已 然爲殿下痛惜者 則有之 前批後敎 擧皆衛侯宋帝之所以傾覆 而殊非二帝三王之所以致興隆者 則臣等疏首若干人 殿下之力可以刑之於司寇矣 可以竄之於嶺海矣 可以肆之於市街矣 若夫八路萬姓家家而怨怒 人人忿恚 如烈炎急潮者 則殿下之力不得以制之矣 詩云 畀彼舟流 不知所屆 臣等之痛 實在於此 惟聖明小霽威怒 而徐觀事勢之是非 則宗社幸甚 又竊念 殿下所以作此無前之過擧 而漠然不悟者無他 由其平日不事學問 故知不足以燭理 心不足以勝私 甘於宴安之毒 悅於讒佞之誘 而惡夫瞺聒之藥 有以苦吾之口 以至此耳 殿下之所以不學者 又豈有他哉 由其頑鈍嗜利無恥之輩 深恐聖學開明 聖德將就 則必能進賢退姦 敍秩命討 較若畫一 吾輩不得接踵其間 而從其所欲也 自初至今 辮髦經筵 屛棄賢俊 以道學爲腐儒鄕暗 迂濶無用之物 以流俗爲忠實才智 緩急可使之人 抑揚予奪 一任腦臆 致誤聖明 至於此極 其罪可勝言哉 伏乞聖明竝賜省念 自今奮立聖志 勉進睿學 以爲淸化之源 革流弊之地焉 臣不勝懇迫之至云云

【관련문서】

洪在鶴抵閔判書台鎬書_{伏閣屢朔 登徹無期 故裁送此書於當路家 其翌疏徹}
嗚呼 孟子有言 天下之生久矣 一治一亂 朱夫子註之曰 氣化盛衰 人事得失 反復相尋 由此觀之 則其治其亂 不專在乎氣數也明矣 今日洋賊之橫恣邦域 壞亂先王之禮義 殄滅先賢之風化 禽獸一國之生靈 漁獵四方之少艾 戕伐五百年宗社 如綴旒而累卵 流毒三千里封壃 如魚爛而河決 果氣數之變者歟

人皆曰 氣數之變 而生等獨曰 人事之失而不關乎氣數也 何謂不關乎氣數 欲
爲而不能者 歸之氣數 固可也 可爲而不爲者 果何氣數乎 丙子之洋 卽丙寅辛
未之洋也 所乘者 丙寅辛未之舶也 所用者 丙寅辛未之砲也 丙寅辛未之甲兵
也 丙寅辛未之伎倆也 丙寅辛未之可逐者 丙子而不可逐者 生等不知爲何說
矣 自是五六年之間 禍日以熾 道日以熄 明公之噤其口愈深 於是風不縱而自
縱 燎由之以益肆 波不推而自推 瀾由是而愈漲 名士碩儒 服習乎妖書 大家世
族 茶飯乎異言 事已到此 何異湯湯洪水 蕩蕩而懷山 浩浩而滔天乎 嗚呼當
路者西人 而洋賊橫恣而莫之禁也 當路者明公 而異類熾盛而莫之制也 今日
罪謗之所萃者 非西人歟 罪責之所歸者 非明公歟 謗者所萃 責之所歸 既有
其人 又何氣數之論哉 嗚呼 西人縱不自愛 獨不念栗老 尤翁諸先生之捨死而
衛道 闢聖路而擎天柱乎 明公縱不自愛 獨不念驪陽 丹巖諸先生之捨死而衛
道 尊周室而攘醜虜乎 納洋者西人也 噤口者明公也 而萬代之惡名 則終歸於
聖躬 此不亦重可寒心而痛骨者乎 嗚呼 朝鮮 禮義之故邦也 今日則漫淫於腥
膻 西人 義理之宗主也 今日則汚染於糞壤 蒼天蒼天 此何事也 卽欲大聲而痛
號也 所謂機務衙門 未知裏許之果何如 而竊聽於一國之公論 既如是 決非衣
冠世族所可濡迹 而冒乎瓜田李下之嫌矣 亦當直言諫諍 牽裾折檻 而猶不可
止也 今也則不爲 巨家大族 入於此而恬然不愧焉 壯洞之金 而與於此 懷德之
宋 而又與於此 連山之金 而又與於此 輦轂之下 又有所謂固窮讀書者 而與於
此 巖峽之裏 又有離群長往者 而與於此 本心之難保 乃止於斯乎 所謂技藝之
鍊習者 不知鍊習乎此 而將何用也 所謂工徒 換其腸而反其胃 與寇賊而有骨
肉之憂 與親黨而成仇隙之怨 此輩非他日內應於洋賊而爲蕭墻者乎 所謂學術
之延師敎習者 未知四經五典之外 別有可學之術也 未知程朱尤栗之外 別有
可尊之師也 凡此兩端 皆機務所干涉 外議之峥嶸 如之何可免哉 生等以扶正
斥邪之義 進伏闕下 于今六十許日矣 天意向此漠然 挽回了無其期 得非群公
之壅蔽而然歟 若如今日之爲而無變焉 則三百六十之州 盡齲然於洋館 八路
萬姓之族 盡從事乎洋學 菽麥稻粱 無一非洋賊之資 馬牛鷄犬 無一非洋賊之
供 廢棄孔朱之學而盡崇奉於耶蘇 焚滅孔孟之編而盡傳神乎瑪竇矣 事如至此
何快於心歟 胡然乎佇見溢世之禍 越視燎原之炎 阻塘乎哀痛迫切之章 禁忌
乎救焚拯溺之擧 至此而極哉 人皆知噤口袖手之可以免謗乎彼此 而以愚所見
則計之主也 謀之窩也 如彼孔門諸子 當匡人之難 傍觀而無所左右 則是藉手
於傍人 以害聖師者也 其罪豈在於匡人之下哉 此義皎若 自不可誣 而安有畏
首畏尾 跋前疐後 既全七尺之軀 反逋乘陰之誅 以兩全而俱便哉 明公何不反

而思之 上告下諭 至誠而不已 以旋乾而轉坤 幹造化而贊陽春哉 今日禦戎 固
難其方 特延一國之賢 則不患無人 廣詢一國之言 則不患無策 堯舜是萬古首
出之聖 而亦曰嘉言罔攸伏 野無遺賢而已 今日諸君子之事不然 以爲朝廷之
外 則皆亂類也 以爲時論之外 則皆邪說也 杜絕四方之言路 勒定一國之是非
藉曰所執之或是 是天下至危之道也 況顚覆乎窮天極地之大道 從事乎洞宇亘
宙之大變 而乃莫敢矯其非 雖有孔孟之聖 管葛之才 遞在乎咫尺之地 又何救
乎宗社之危亡乎 議者之言問之 則我於彼 力不贍也 勢不敵也 力非不贍也 患
在乎無此心也 昔者 符堅以九十萬兵 渡江而南 謝玄後生孤軍以衂之 隋煬帝
以百萬之名 未攻高句麗 高句麗君臣 力戰而禦之 殄滅其十之八九 兀朮金虜
之良將 所向披靡 而劉錡以數千之名 挫十萬之兵於順昌之城 夫晉 宋 高句麗
之兵 未嘗有超天入地之才 其將未嘗有拔山蓋世之力 而能以小擊衆 以弱制
強 如建瓴然何哉 豈非有一定之計 於前有一定之規 於後有進無退 有死無潰
一衆心專衆志 氣勢風聲 自在於其中 自然勢如破竹 莫之敢攖也 況師之曲直
邪正 而壯老以之而分者乎 孟子之浩氣 塞乎天地 而養之之方 以直而無害 此
萬古不易之理也 若驚怵於一二海舶 無難以先王之壃土 持以與賊 資寇戎之
兵糧 決是無異三歲孩提之事耳 何足書之於史冊 貽羞於後世哉 人之言曰 聖
志已確然於此 而不可移易 朝臣縱能直言而無諱 何望其得力乎 是有不然者
明公若曰 不可 而捨死而力爭 則原任大臣之依違東西者 亦必曰不可 六卿三
司之依違東西者 亦必曰不可 於是乎風聲所曁 太學繼起進言矣 城裏士夫 方
外儒生 必群起血爭矣 聖上之意 豈不可以動得哉 況今日之事 非上意然耳 乃
朝臣之導而使然 以倭虜非洋之說而慰之 以防俄保國之說而動之 以富國強兵
之計而逢迎之 以傳教無害之說而惑亂之 以延師敎習之說而陳達之 一毛一髮
皆朝廷之罪也 敢曰天意之不敢移易乎 假使事不從心 有目前不測之禍端 大
義由之以明 邦國由之以光 可以有辭於天下後世 可以有辭於先祖先賢不昧
之靈矣 不亦善哉 淸陰被拘囚之辱 三學士罹殺戮之禍 趙忠翼金忠獻 敗家殄
宗 身陷大戮 而不之有後悔矣 明公獨不之聞知乎 獨不之敬服乎 況死生禍福
有命焉 不容人爲而可以安排矣 胡然未嘗主和 而爲和之魁 未嘗劃計 而爲計
之窩 來四方之笑 貽萬世之羞哉 嗚呼 擧世之所忌諱 生等言之不諱 到處挫折
隨事齟齬 又不知何樣禍端 隱伏於冥冥 而反以思之 無一毫之恨悔 豈曰樂禍
而然哉 所見亦非異於餘人而然耳 敢以此意仰告 或可密察而採納之 則非特
公家之幸 亦明公一身之私計然耳 所謂不求私而自無不利者也 如曰不然 治
亂之循環不窮 陰陽之消長無常 今日雖揚之以九卿之位 行呼唱於道路 而得

市童之憐 事變形移 水落石出 功罪自彰 榮辱始分 則于斯時也 明公之抱羞縮頭 其將無地可安矣 竊以爲明公代憫也 千人之諾諾 不若一士之諤諤 伏惟明公裁處焉 環顧一世 惟明公 爲可以此說進警 故若此仰告 伏惟鑑納

申櫶(1881. 8. 30/高宗十八年閏七月六日)

척사소

京畿儒生申櫶等疏略 天聰明 自我民聰明 天明畏 自我民明畏 自古人君 莫不以民心向背爲興喪焉 伏念 前月安置罪人李晩孫之疏徹也 聖上曲恕狂妄之罪 而旋施恩貸之仁 使之退去矣 都憲臣韓敬源 枉己循私 構虛露章 指姜晉奎爲製疏 而以李晩孫謂改疏語 至於請鞠島配 而竝無眞臟焉 彼徒知構陷斥和爲伎倆 而不知其自陷於罔上禦下之爲不敬矣 晩孫雖改疏語 在登徹之前 便同私稿也 私改私稿 有何罪過 而顧其血誠則舍生斥和矣 夫斥斥和之人 而靦然以爲得計者 卽是護倭也 朱夫子論距楊墨便是聖人之徒 而曰 如人逐賊 有人見之 若說道賊當捉當誅 這便是主人邊人也 若說道賊可恕 這便是賊邊人也 以此揆之 晩孫則如逐賊 而曰 當捉當誅者 主人邊人也 敬源則不但曰可恕 而現有護之之意 分明是賊邊人也 今也使主人邊人陷於不測之地 使賊邊人提揚呼唱於白日通衢 竊恐刑賞由此而失當言路由此而壅蔽 伏願殿下 痛施反坐之律 特著優儒之典 使八域含生 有以知殿下善善惡惡 出於尋常萬萬焉 且前修信使臣金弘集奉命出疆 何等重大 而不務不辱君命 誘惑於外人 所謂黃遵憲冊子 輕自受來 敢進於黼繡之下 而其主意 不過托彼北俄之鴟張 促我西美之通商 論說異敎之源流 至譬吾敎之朱陸 噫嘻 此何說也 俄雖日强 地雖接壤 限以水帶 便是風馬牛不相及 使節不通 恩怨初無可言 妄動干戈 侵擾疆域 豈有其理哉 此不過恐動以欲我和於西洋人也 夫美 耶蘇敎國也 與之通商 往來密接 則邪敎之漸染 必然之勢 此不待智者而可明也 此何異養虎於庭園納賊於門戶而望其護我棶我耶 弘集 以何心腸 出於此乎 被其鴆毒 失其本心 自陷於術中而不自覺也 先治其奉使無狀 嚴斥其冊子 無使聽聞駭惑焉 奉朝賀臣李裕元厚被鴻造 位極人臣 圖報之念 宜倍他人 而自犯人臣外交之罪 與李鴻章頻繁通書 未知有何關節 而籍託李書 謂通商可結於美國 租地可許於各港 謂遵憲之書 實爲我謀 至若邪敎之引譬 少不加斥 與弘集暗相綢繆之狀 不見是圖 而李書黃冊 分明是一串貫來 裕元弘集 分明是表裏相應 將以眩惑聽聞乖亂國是 是可忍也 孰不可忍也 由是論之 彼皆臣所謂賊邊人也 殿下何愛於此輩 而或縻以好爵 或禮遇加隆 而欲尊國威振國綱 不亦左乎 竊恐聖聰有欠於瀅澈 聖學未至於高明 不能無爲彼所擁蔽而然乎 傳曰人主一心 爲萬化之

原 殿下如欲卞淑慝察形影 莫如修明此心 如欲修明此心 莫如勉之學問 伏願
日開經筵 召接賢士大夫 講討經典 深究乎聖哲之傳授心法 鑑戒乎歷代之治
亂所由 久久化成 使天理流行 私意淨盡 如鑑空燭照 不爲邪說所動 早辨於微
逆 折其亂萌 則佇見太平萬世 實基於此 於不休哉 竊又伏聞前掌令郭基洛疏
語絶悖無倫 遽蒙寵擢 固仰聖朝包荒之美 而其曰有若大變急禍朝夕且至 且
指夫臣等之無中生事也 其意以爲方今國勢安如磐石 而臣等以爲危如累卵也
方今邪說朋起 異類橫行 內帑罄竭 火賊旁午 臺閣嘿默 忠臣憂歎 其將曰治耶
亂耶 其蔽人主視聽 反有甚於指鎭授兵也 其曰遵憲冊子不受之罪更大於受
之 此弘集之陰嗾也 所謂東寅(*Sic.*) 不知何自 而弘集謂以我人逋逃者 東還之
日 跟隨進之朝廷 髡髮纏長 官銜遽加 參謀別選 忽焉逃脫之計出於一夜 弘集
敢曰不知乎 東寅弘集腸肚相通 基洛弘集 便是一體人也 經曰 所令 反其所好
而民不從 今殿下 賞其宜罪 罰其宜賞 竊恐刑賞由是而顚倒 可以懼哉 臣草野
賤品 學識魯莽 固不敢妄論朝廷大事 然朱子曰 若國家危亡判斷之事 雖在韋
布 不可不言 見今强隣睢盱於四方 而國家積弊之餘 朝無犯顏强諫之士 世乏
伏節死義之人 委靡頹墮 苟安姑息 如魚遊釜中 燕巢堂上而莫之覺焉 臣憂憤
所激 出位妄言 嶺海鈇鉞 固所甘心 而苟臣言見探 有補於國家 雖死之日 猶
生之年 伏願殿下淵然澄省 廓揮乾斷 斥退姦佞 進用忠直 則可以回綴旒而奠
磐泰 宗社幸甚

23

李裕元(1881. 9. 1/高宗十八年閏七月八日)

李鴻章 서한 변명소

伏以臣伏蒙曠絶之異數 得遂三字之宿願 病伏窮鄕 尙阻叩謝之儀 晝宵惶慄 不禁戀結之忱 卽伏見京畿儒生申樔等疏語謄傳者 則臣攙入其中 張皇遣辭 擧臣之與李總督鴻章往復事也 臣常欲以此事 一番仰陳之計 非不熟矣 無階可暴 今幸因端以悉白之 臣於年前燕行時 適與此人往覆 乃中原首閣老也 或有相資之力 幾年通信 忽於己卯秋 自柵庭一械書來到 備言倭洋事 至有美國人借給於日本人開港之傍 同爲商販 臣病淹踰月 始入城闉 與諸大臣同議截嚴 答送曰 泰西之學 有異吾道 實乖民彝 據國法而拒之 後別咨官回自天津 言鴻章事 自歎未諧 又有書 臣竟不答 此等事從此迄無相關 至若黃遵憲冊子 金弘集之自倭出來者也 初不送於臣 且無來見於臣 而轉因京衚得見 則所道者乃美國事也 夫我國之於泰西諸國 聲氣原不相通 主敎本來邪穢 隔在滄溟萬里之外 維有咫尺强敵之患 其將倚以爲恃乎 富國之術 在我節用 未聞交外而富之 强兵之策 在我撫禦 未聞藉冠而强之 是何異於秦人失火 呼越以救之也 以臣愚見 已知李書黃冊 俱是挾雜 不足取信 而殊邦之人 難與分折 許久含默 一世皆知 今於此疏 何有呶呶卞白 以傷事面乎 鄕曲儒生 不知裏許 有此意外之說 以臣自視 不覺靦然 疏旣到院 露臣名字 則臣何敢晏然無故 不念廉方之重也哉 倩手草疏 從縣仰顧 伏乞聖上察臣前後事實 勘臣不愼之罪 以警具僚焉

金弘集(1881. 9. 24/高宗十八年八月二日)

사직소(辭職疏)

行右承旨金弘集疏曰 伏以臣 一自遭懼以來 辜戾彌天 嚴召屢降 而偃處鄉寓 臣之罪也 問啓連促 而不入禁扁 尤臣之大罪也 有臣如此 誅殛猶輕 而薄竄旋宥 敦飭隨下 霜雪雨露 曲費造化 臣雖頑如木石 豈無感激趨走之誠 顧乃一直 縮伏 迷不知變 是必有萬萬不獲已者耳 及至大僚論啓 姑先罷免 臣又一倍悚 慄 惟俟遄伏常刑 曾未幾何 新除特揀 恩旨相繼 載煩匪怒之敎 荐迫出膺之命 旣當律之未被 反異敎之遞紆 惶惑之極 悶隘轉甚 踢高蹐厚 此何人斯 噫 前 後儒疏之聲討臣構捏臣者 無非人臣之極惡 天下之大僇也 傳聞所及 骨顫膽 掉 其遣辭之罔測 用意之絶險 苟欲逐條較辨 適足以汚其口矣 第其執端 槩有 二說焉 其一曰黃遵憲文字事也 夫奉專對之命者 莫不以諮度採訪爲已責 假 令有人籌策 擬稿以贈 則只計字句之碍與無碍 罔念關係之繁與不繁 私自揮 却 終不受來 未知果合於奉使之道乎 況其人 乃上國之使 非他國之人乎 向伏 見儒疏批旨 若曰 爾等誤者而抉摘 天鑑攸燭 事理昭然 而猶且轉輾層激 必欲 甘心於臣 一何至此之甚也 其一曰李東仁事也 噫彼東仁 本以我國緇流 變服 犯越 按以國律 卽當擒斬之不暇 臣非病風喪性 豈或有招引潛隨之理乎 此則 聖明已所悉燭 同朝亦當見諒 今其捏合無據 一唱羣和者 抑又何故 藉曰疎遠 之蹤 動於浮訛之說 誣人以亂昧之科 不當於奏御之地 實不勝慨然也 至於郭 基洛一疏 不但臣 不識其爲何狀人 時則屛蟄於外 聞之且後於人 酒者畿儒 斥 臣以陰嗾之目 逞臆疑揣 不近事情 尤甚無謂也 向之論臣者一道 而今也諸道 迭攻 向之論臣者一事 而今也數事互擧 萬鏃叢湊 駭機衆發 臣心危怖 日甚一 日 從玆以往 惟有永謝簪組 退塡邱壑而後 衆怒有可息之期 餘生有可全之望 斷斷此心 自誓已久 臣情到此 無容他辭 則今我殿下 雖欲拂拭之督迫之 使之 復廁同行 而臣何敢蒙詬冒進 重喪其所守也 念臣身名俱敗 理合自廢 而由臣 無狀 貽累於淸朝 致煩於崇聽 此其臣罪 尤萬死而有餘勘矣 玆敢猥從縣道 冒 控哀籲 伏乞聖慈 下臣司敗 亟治臣前後罪犯 以昭國紀焉 千萬血祝 臣無任云 云 答曰 省疏具悉 擴遭之說 不足爲引 且有屢飭 卽爲上來行公

(3) 조약체결 이전 미국의 조선 관련 보고

S. W. Williams (1874. 3. 30) ➜ H. Fish (1874. 5. 26)

대원군 실각 보고

LEGATION OF THE UNITED STATES,

SIR: A Roman Catholic bishop, whose diocese comprises a part of Manchuria and the region contiguous to Corea, has lately reached Peking from Newchwang, and brings an account of an entire change in the government of Corea within the last three months, and the removal of the ruler who has usurped the chief authority during the past fifteen years. The principal facts, as he reports them, tally very well with some statements made years ago, and bear the appearance of authenticity, though many details yet remain to be supplied.

It is known that about fifteen years ago the succession of the reigning house of Ti to the throne of Corea became extinct, and the government came into the hands of the Queen Dowager. She sought out a remote scion of the house of Ti, and adopted a lad of eight years old as the heir-apparent, whose own father and grandfather were still living. This boy's father managed by force and fraud, to engross the entire authority; and his son and toe Queen Dowager became mere ciphers in his hands. It would seem that, stimulated by a feeling of insecurity in his seat, he began to oppress the people and remove his enemies. He took umbrage against everything foreign, especially foreign books and teaching, and the extension of foreign trade. In 1864 he exercised greater severity, and, as is well known, about that time began a deadly persecution against the Roman Catholics, putting to death hundreds and hundreds of native converts, and killing eleven foreign priests. The proceedings of Admiral Rose, in 1866, not being followed up by any ulterior measures on the part of the French, he took courage, having as he supposed, repelled both the Russian and French ships. It appears that a Russian man-of war had come on the eastern coast of Corea in 1864, which remained there a long time for the purpose of opening negotiations in respect to the new frontier between the two countries of Russia and Corea, near Port May and Possiet, but her mission was unsuccessful.

The result of the visits of American men-of-war, in consequence of the destruction of the "General Sherman." and especially of the United States expedition in 1871, were all regarded as a great triumph, by this usurper, who had, as he supposed, delivered the kingdom from subjugation by foreigners, and asserted the prowess of his army. But after the American flag had retired from his coasts, and there was time to review the whole affair, the more sensible part of the rulers began to see it in a different light. The members of the annual embassy had also had an opportunity to confer with the Chinese rulers at Peking, and learn from them all the real nature of Mr. Low's attempt to open amicable relations with their sovereign. At any rate we know that some of the Coreans in this city last year purchased many copies of all the books about foreign countries, including the monthly magazine published in this city, to carry back with them.

The conclusion now reported is, that the legitimate king and his adopted mother in conjunction with the ruling nobles of Corea, have compelled the usurper Ti to retire, and have assumed control. The change has been brought about without bloodshed, and the bishop (Monsignor R.) looks forward to a peaceable state of their missions, seeing that the new authorities are favorably disposed toward foreigners and Christianity.

He reports that the disastrous and bloody result to the Coreans of our attack on Fork McKee was used as a strong argument with Ti, of the uselessness of his resisting foreign nations, whose weapons and tactics were so superior to theirs, and their resources so great. On all these points there is much, no doubt, to be learned, but there seem to be full grounds for believing the report of an entire change of government in that kingdom.

I have, &c.,

S. WELLS WILLIAMS.

26

J. A. Bingham (1875. 10. 6) ➡ H. Fish (1875. 11. 9)

雲揚號 사건 보고

UNITED STATES LEGATION,
Tokei, Japan

SIR: It is with regret that I acquaint you that by public rumor in the press, and from private sources, I learn that war may be declared by Japan against Corea.

It appears from what has transpired to the public that a Japanese man-of-war was engaged in sounding off the coast of Corea and within its waters, and while so engaged was fired upon by a Corean fort and disabled. After retiring for repairs the Japanese vessel returned, attacked and took the Corean fort and captured its guns, some thirty in number, burned the village adjacent thereto, and returned to Nagasaki to await orders. Considering the relations of Corea and China, it seems to me, in the event of war between Japan and Corea, it would be proper to declare a strict neutrality touching both the powers as within the provision of the act of June 22, 1860, section 4090, Revised Statutes, treating both as powers with whom the United States are at Peace.

Should the fact reach you by telegram of a declaration of war or the commencement of actual hostilities between the two countries, I pray to be advised at once if the views herein expressed as to my duties in the premises meet the approval of the Department.

I have, &c.,

JNO. A. BINGHAM.

B. P. Avery (1875.10.26) ➜ H. Fish

雲揚號 사건 보고

No. 111

Legation of the United States
Peking
Oct 26th, 1875.

Benjamin P. Avery
To the Secretary of State, Hon Hamilton Fish

Subject
Corea versus Japan

Synopsis

   A collision has taken place between a Japanese gunboat and a Corea military force. The gunboat was first fired on from the shore, and subsequently landed a force and destroyed the Corean Batteries.

Sir,

   Calling your attention again to my No. 95 of sept 7th concerning the present attitude of Japanese government towards the King of Corea. I have the honor now to inform you that a few days since the Japanese chargé d'affaires at this court called at this legation and in the course of conversation stated that he had telegraphie advices from the foreign office in Yedo of a collision which had occurred upon the West Coast of Corea. Between a Japanese gunboat and a Corean military force occupying certain earth works. The details of the affair as receited by Mr. Lei are substantially as follow: The gunboat not expecting, and unprepared for hostile demonstrations of any sort, was engaged in taking soundings off the month of a river and near to the island Kokeva, where she was fired upon form certain forts upon the main land. The vessel proceeded until it became apparent that the firing was intentional and malicious, when she drew off out of range in order to put herself in a condition for defense, and to repair some slight damage which had been received. The next day, the gunboat drew in near the shore again, flying a flight of truce and dispatched a boat also burying a flight of truce with intention to land and enquire the reason for the hostile demonstrations of the day previous. Firing was once renewed on the part of the Coreans, no attention being paid to the peaceful signals displayed by the Japanese and the latter were obliged again to withdraw out of range. Upon the following day the Japanese war vessel again approached the shore and under a heavy but ill-directed fire from the Coreans batteries succeeded in landing a force which stormed the works capturing 17 cannon, and a large quantity of musket and small arms the Corean lost thirty killed and thirty prisoner, besides a number wounded, and inconsiderable damage done to their vessel. The offending fort and earth works were entirely demolished.

Mr. Lei remarked further that his information did not indicate what course his government intended to take in the matter as it was not yet decided. But the foreign minister stated that future course of the government would in due season the communicated to him and he assured me that he would at once inform me fully, so far as he could legitimately.

The fact herein recited are doubtless, not new to the department as they will have reached you from our minister in Japan in advance of this dispatch. I, however, deemed it best to report what I had heard upon a later day. The Japanese chargé inform me that he had communicated the facts of this collision to the Chinese foreign office, and that prince Kung in his reply merely acknowledged receipt of the information but made no comment of any sort whatever.

Whether, where China not embarrassed on account of the existing complications Great Britain, the Prince would have been quite so reticent in his answer to Mr. Lei, is a matter of doubt. But I am of opinion that in any event China would manifest no interest in this question of Corea vs. Japan, except in case of actual war it is doubtful whether even that she would interfere in any positive manner.

The location of these recent events is the same as that of the occurrences between the Coreans and the naval force of the United States under Rear Admiral Rogers in 1871.

I have the honor to be sir
Your obedient servant Avery

G. F. Seward (1875.12.28) ➙ J. L. Cadwalader

조선에 대한 일본과 청국의 입장

No. 1017

US Consulate General at Shanghai
Shanghai
December 28th, 1875

Mr. Seward
To the Department of State,
Honorable John L. Cadwalader
Assistant Secretary of State Washington

Subject
Japan and Corea

Abstract

States that the Japanese seem to just matters to the extreme, and that the Chinese will not interfere unless the Japanese attempt to a permanent occupation.

Sir

Mr. Bingham will doubtless have kept the Department informed of the disposition of Japan toward Corea. So far as can be seen here the insular empire is disposed to push matters to the extreme. The progress of the Japanese Minister to Peking overland from Chefoo at this inclement season is an indication that the situation has become urgent.

The relations between China and Corea are intimate but there is no interdependency of the respective governments. Corea will be at liberty to make a Treaty with Japan, or a war, as she prefers. China will not however permit Japan to make an extensive permanent occupation of Corean territory. It is her historical policy to keep peninsula independent and she will not hesitate if necessary to yield to it the force of arms.

I doubt much whether the ambitious Japanese look only to make a treaty of amity and commerce. They probably desire to occupy the peninsula. This task, if undertaken, will be a grave one, even if China holds aloof. It will be almost hopeless if the Chinese actively assist Corea.

I have the honor to be
Sir
Your obedient servant
(Sign) John F Seward consul General

G. F. Seward (1876.01.05) ➡ H. Fish

조선-일본 관계에 대한 청국의 입장

Copy
Doc No. 79

Shanghai
January 5th, 1876

Honorable John A Bingham
Tokio

My dear Mr. Bingham,

    The recent movements of Japanese ships and officials in Corea the mission of Mr. Mori to China, and the utterances of the native and foreign press in Japan indicate that the difficulties long known to exist between Japan and Corea have become very serious and may result in war.

    You remember that at one of the interviews which I had the pleasure to hold with you in Japan last summer we discuss the relations of the Chinese Government to Corea and the attitude she might be expected to assume in case of the outbreak of hostilities. In brief my opinion was that there is no essential interdependency between China and the Peninsular Government, that in case Japan goes no further than to seek redress at arms and an ordinary treaty of peace for any grievances which she may have sustained, China will not interfere but that this Empire will look with the greatest disfavor upon any permanent occupation of Corea by Japan, and will at last resort in such case make common case with the Coreans to expel the Japanese.

    This would seem to be traditional policy of China and I know now only two elements likely to disturb. One of there is the near approach of the Russian occupation north of Corea and east of the Manchurian provinces, the other the fact that a park at least of the army of japan is understood to be well drilled and well provided generally according to Western method of war fare.

    Upon the first point it may be remarked that whether rightfully or not the

Chinese can scarcely entertain a doubt as to the intention of the Russians to occupy ultimately the region in question and that she is likely together Japan to Russia as a neighbor in the Peninsula.

Upon the second it is to be said that the unwillingness of China to go to war with Japan at the time of the Formosa expedition when she believed undoubtedly that the course of Japan in occupying a part of the island was indefensible and an affront of a most serious sort which unwillingness led her to make a treaty that has been interpreted generally as a triumph for the latter Empire is very significant of the course which the Chinese rules will pursue in the contingency of which I am speaking.

It will interesting for me to know your view in regard to the general question. I think too that e to the advantages of our government to interchange information and opinion as fully and freely as possible.

Beyond mere matter of information and speculation it maybe well for us, further, to know what views are held by one another of the course which we should pursue toward our country people who in the event of hostilities may take part or be disposed to take part in them having reference in this respect specially to the instructions of Mr. Fish in the case of General Le Gendre

Believe me
My dear Sir
Yours very truly

J. A. Bingham (1876. 3. 9) ➡ H. Fish (1876. 4. 3)
조일수호조규 체결 보고

UNITED STATES LEGATION, JAPAN,
Tokei

SIR: It is gratifying to be able to say that a treaty of peace and commerce has been concluded between Japan and Corea without further conflict.

On the 2d instant His Imperial Japanese Majesty's vice-minister for foreign affairs, Mr. Sameshima, acquainted me of this by a private note, which he concludes by saying: "Mr. Kweoda reached Simonoseki yesterday, and telegraphed this news to us, at which I know you will rejoice as much as any of us in Japan."

On the 4th instant, in an interview with Mr. Terashima, I took occasion to say that I congratulated his government upon the result of the mission to Corea, and received from him assurance that, as soon as possible, I should be furnished the text of the treaty for transmission to the Department.

I understand that by the treaty three ports are to be opened to the commerce of Japan in Corea, and that Japan and Corea will hereafter be represented by diplomatic agents at their respective courts. Of the further details of the treaty I am not advised.

The peaceful solution of the difficulties between this government and Corea is especially satisfactory to me, in view of the opinions expressed by me to Mr. Terashima in reply to his inquiries touching the sending of a commission to Corea by this government, as communicated to you in my No. 306, of the 13th of December last.

I have, &c.,

JNO. A. BINGHAM.

31

J. A. Bingham (1876. 3. 21) ➜ H. Fish (1876. 4. 25)

黑田淸隆로부터 입수한 조선 정보 보고

UNITED STATES LEGATION, JAPAN,
Tokei

SIR: At an interview on yesterday his excellency Mr. Kweoda, late the Japanese ambassador to Corea, gave me some account of the people and resources of that country and of his reception. He informed me that the people are in great poverty, live chiefly on rice and fish, are poorly housed and poorly clad, and are intensely hostile to foreigners. He also informed me that there is no coal or iron or copper in the country, and doubts whether it is rich in gold, though they gather small quantities of gold-sand, it is said, about $130,000 of which in value they annually send to China. He further states that the whole population does not exceed 10,000,000, and that their forts and arms are indifferent. He says the tide rises in the bay approaching the town of Kakwa from 33 to 36 feet, and that at low water there are but from 2 to 3 fathoms in the harbor. On the evening of his approach to the shore with his vessel, at nightfall, there appeared on the hills near the coast many fires and many people. After some parley with the men whom he sent off in a small boat, the minister was received and taken to the capital, which is protected, as I understand him, by double parallel walls and gates.

As the treaty has not yet been published, Mr. Kweoda made no statement of its details, but seemed satisfied with the result.

I do not know that any effort will at present be made by the other powers to negotiate a treaty with Corea.

I have, &c.,

JNO. A. BINGHAM.

SIR: In pursuance of the treaty recently concluded between Japan and Corea, the latter has sent hither an embassy, which arrived in this capital on the 29th ultimo.

Supposing the account published in the Japan Daily Herald of that date descriptive of the embassy and of the reception thereof might be of interest, I inclose a copy thereof herewith in duplicate.

 I have, &c.,
JNO. A. BINGHAM.

J. A. Bingham (1876. 6. 1) ➡ H. Fish (1876. 7. 5)

수신사 金綺秀 도착 보고

[From the Japan Daily Herald, May 29, 1876]

THE COREAN EMBASSY.

The Mitsa Bishi Mail Steamship Company's steamer Korio Maru arrived this morning in port from Kobe, and at 8 a.m. the Corean embassy and suit, seventy-six persons in all, landed at the English hatoba, where a strong police force had collected. Preceded by their own hand of music, the Coreans went to the town-hall, whence they again started for the railway-station at 9:45, in order to proceed by train to Tokio. The ambassador is a man of very considerable stature and bulk: he wore a pair of very large spectacles, and was dressed in a violet crape robe. When he emerged from the town-hall and descended the steps, his followers, standing in the street set up a shout, and the band played on flutes, drums, and tom-toms. The prevailing sound, however, was a lugubrious one, something like the sound from a fog-horn and was emitted from some large wooden trumpets. The ambassador placed himself on a small seat covered with a tiger-skin, and fixed on an open litter, which was lifted on the shoulders of eight men; aloft, above his head, was carried a large white sunshade. The letter was preceded by the band of music which played the whole way to the station. Immediately before the litter walked two Corean girls, apparently about thirteen to fifteen years of age, in semi-Chinese costume, their hair in a long and thick plait hanging down their backs. After the ambassador's litter came four jinrikishas, each conveying a Corean; the rest of the suite made their way on foot. The men are tall and stoutly built, with rather a Malay cast of features. With the exception of the litter-carriers, who wore black felt hats, the rest wore small black hats of horse-hair adorned with peacock-feather; through the meshes of the hat the wearer's hair was visible, collected in a knot on the top of the head. The dress of the common men is of stout parti-colored cotton, not overclean. The five men composing the embassy are of the following rank: Shu-shinshi-reso-sangi, Bakan-do-sha, Kajan-tai-fu, Fahanji-jan-san-pan, Fuku-shiu, Bakandosha Kangi tai-fu. During the passage in the steamer they most scrupulously avoided partaking of anything of foreign origin, not touching wine or spirits. They would not even examine the vessel when they heard it was English-built.

From our special correspondent.

The Corean embassy arrived in Tokio this morning, by an ordinary train, at a quarter to twelve. Since 8 o'clock a large body of police had been collected in the neighborhood of shinbasi, as it was not then known by what train the strangers were to arrive. Soon after 11 a cordon of police was formed all the way from the railway-station to—gate, called Sukiya Bashi, and their appearance was the signal for the assemblage of an eager crowd. The wide, open space in front of the station was densely packed, and inside the station was a mixed crowd of Japanese and foreigners, among whom were most of the foreign ministers. When the train arrived, the embassy remained in their carriages till the ordinary passengers had passed out, occasioning to the spectators a momentary apprehension that they had had their trouble for nothing. At length the Coreans stepped out on the platform, and a very picturesque appearance they presented, looked at from a distance, reminding one of Italian brigands in a London theater. The costume appears to consist of kinickerbockers, with gaiters, tight from the knee to the foot, and a robe of either cotton or silk, fitting tight to the body, with flowing tails. The most striking part of the dress was the hat, which is shaped something like a cardinal's, with a small crown and large flat brim, but is made of a transparent black gauze, but perfectly stiff; through the hats one could see that the hair is worn twisted up in a tial on the top of the head.

The embassy came along the platform in state. First, fourteen bandmen, then flag-bearers and spearmen, then two women, with their black hair loosely plaited into tails like those of Chinamen, then a big umbrella, and then the great man himself. He was assisted, that is, literally supported, by two other richly dressed men, and followed by several others, who were evidently men of consideration. The cortege was closed by nine bearers carrying a chair, which was very much like a temple (kiyoku-roku) put on a large and fragile stand. The music was shrill, harsh, and discordant, at least to our ears. A friend with musical proclivities assured us that some of the sounds were sweeter than those of Japanese instruments. The men were tall and well set up—many of them old men, who wore a Tartar board and moustache. They stepped firmly as they walked, and seemed perfectly satisfied with themselves and indifferent to the laughter which the Japanese indulged in. They were conducted to the waitingrooms in the railway-station, and, after a few minutes' interval for rest, they set out for the residence which has been prepared for them in Kanda Nishiki Cho, in much the same order as they had marched up the platform. A detachment of the imperial mounted body-guard headed the procession, and the chief ambassador, a tall, stout, handsome old man, with huge spectacles, rode in his open chair, towering above the heads of the bearers. The superior members of his suite, several of whom had peacock-feathers in their hats, followed him in jinrikishas, and the interpreters, of whom there were a crowd, had enough to do to start them according to their precedence. One nice-looking young Corean was evidently much exercised in his mind at the misplaced zeal of his jinrikisha coolie, who would try and start before his turn. All, however, was finally happily arranged, and the cortege wound its slow way without mishap to the residence set apart for the embassy.

Sargent (1878. 4. 8)

대조선 수호통상조약 체결 요청 결의안

RELATIONS WITH COREA.

Mr. SARGENT asked, and by unanimous consent obtained, leave to introduce a joint resolution (S. R. No. 24) authorizing the President of the United States to appoint a commissioner to the King of Corea to arrange a treaty of amity and commerce between the United States and the King of Corea, and to appropriate the necessary expenses in making such treaty; which was read the first time at length, as follows:

Whereas the Kingdom of Corea is recognized as completely independent by the treaty of 1876, between Japan and Corea; and

Whereas the King of Corea has shown a disposition to enroll his great country among the family of nations, and to allow it to enjoy the reciprocal advantages of peace and commerce with other nation; and

Whereas the United States desires to remain in relations of peace with all peoples: Therefore,

Resolved by the senate and House of Representatives in Congress assembled, That the President of the United States be, and hereby is, authorized to appoint a commissioner to represent this country in an effort to arrange by peaceful means, and with the aid of the friendly offices of Japan, a treaty of peace and commerce between the United States and the Kingdom of Corea, and the sum of $50,000, or so much thereof as may be necessary, is hereby appropriated out of any money in the Treasury not otherwise appropriated to defray the expenses of said commission.

The joint resolution was read the second time by its title.

The VICE-PRESIDENT. The resolution will lie on the table, subject to the call of the Senator from California.

Mr. SARGENT. Yes, sir. I wish merely to remark that the population of that country is variously estimated at from twelve million to twenty million, and that, as this is a very important question, I want to present some considerations to the Senate before the joint resolution is referred.

RELATIONS WITH COREA.

Mr. SARGENT. I should like to call up for reference the joint resolution which I submitted the other day in reference to relations with Corea. I want it referred to the Committee on Foreign Relations, and I should like to occupy a few minutes of the time of the Senate in stating the reasons for the joint resolution.

The PRESIDENT pro tempore. Is there objection to the request of the Senator from California? The Chair hears none.

Mr. SARGENT. Mr President—

Mr. BURNSIDE. I ask the favor of the Senator from California to allow Senate bill No. 178 to be taken up for a moment in order to see if I can get a vote upon it.

Mr. SARGENT. How much time does the Senator ask?

Mr. BURNSIDE. I do not know of any one who has anything further to say on the subject, and it would only require a yea-and-nay vote on the passage of the bill. I ask the Senator simply to yield for that purpose.

Mr. SARGENT. That bill will lead to some debate.

Mr. BURNSIDE. I beg the Senator from California to yield.

Mr. SARGENT. If my friend will allow me to proceed, I shall conclude my remarks in fifteen minutes, and there will then be fifteen minutes left of the morning hour. I am informed by Senators around me that the bill will lead to discussion.

Mr. BURNSIDE. The understanding was very distinct yesterday that the bill should be taken up to-day, in the morning hour. The Chair asked if there was objection to that arrangement and there was none.

Mr. SARGENT. Does the Senator simply desire a call of the roll? Is that all?

Mr. EDMUNDS. It will have to be debated a little, Mr. President. There will be time enough. The Senator from California has just had unanimous consent, which we never refuse, to submit some observations to the Senate. I am sure we ought to allow him to proceed.

Mr. BURNSIDE. Very well.

The senate, as in committee of the Whole, proceeded to consider the joint resolution (S. R. No. 24) authorizing the President of the United States to appoint a commissioner to the King of Corea to arrange a treaty of amity and commerce between the United States and the King of Corea, and to appropriate the necessary expenses in making such treaty.

Mr. SARGENT. Mr. President, one of the most interesting events in the history of Pacific civilization was the opening of Japan to the five great western powers by the American treaty of March 31, 1854, the result of the United States expedition under Commodore Perry. On the 6th of January, 1869, the Mikado, or Emperor, emerged from his seclusion, and disregarding the tradition which forbade the "barbarian" to gaze on his face, received in state the foreign ministers residing at Yeddo, and exhibited a desire to maintain friendly relations. From 1858 to 1869 followed American, English, French, and Austrian treaties. As a result a great trade has sprung up, principally valuable to the United States, partly on account of our proximity and partly from the friendly feelings with which we are regarded by Japan. It is a fact that in those waters alone, of all the waters of the world, our tonnage exceeds that of all other nations. It is the only place where we have a fine American trade carried on in American bottoms.

But a still more striking result has been witnessed in this nation of thirty million people suddenly dropping a proud, isolation policy, opening relations with the civilized world, and rapidly adopting the appliances and modes of advanced civilization. Before that period all authorities concurred in depicting the Japanese as an effete, nonprogressive race, sunk in superstition, with strange customs and sanguinary laws, but with considerable excellence in the mechanical arts. By the wise action of our predecessors this great people have been brought into friendly relations, have developed into a civilized nation, and vindicated themselves as the possessors of a stalwart manhood and an enlightened, enterprising spirit. The apparent transformation has been wonderful; but the change has been one of development only, not of creation. All the elements of a great people must have been there; they had opportunity and expression when centuries of isolation terminated.

Neighboring to Japan on the mainland is another people, with most of their characteristics, perhaps all, treated of by the encyclopedists as they formerly treated the Japanese, now waiting for us to extend to them a friendly hand as we formerly did to Japan, and promising as noble reward for the service. I ask the attention of the Senate, and of the Committee of Foreigns, to whom I shall have this bill referred, to the promise held out to us by Corea if we know how to avail ourselves of our opportunity as our immediate predecessors did in the case of Japan.

Corea is described by Zell's Encyclopedia Dictionary as a maritime country of Northeastern Asia, consisting of a vast oblong peninsula with an adjoining portion of the continent and a great number of islands. Appleton's Cyclopedia states that it is bounded on the north by Manchooria, northeast by the Russian Amoor country, east by the Sea of Japan, south by the Strait of Corea, and west by the Yellow Sea and the Chinese province of Liaou-Tong, with an area of ninety thousand square miles. The population is estimated by various authorities from eight millions to twenty millions, and is probably about twelve millions. Its length is, from north to south, about six hundred and sixty miles, and the breadth is about one hundred and fifty miles. Its principal river is navigable for large ships twenty two miles, and for smaller vessels one hundred and twenty miles above its mouth. The climate in the north is severe, but temperate in the south. The mountains are covered with forests, and pine is common on the coasts. Most of our domestic animals are reared in Corea. The people are superior to the Japanese in strength and stature. Their dress is similar to that of the Chinese, but they do not cut their hair or wear a cue. They have a literature, a monosyllabic language; are generally educated; are fond of reading, music, dancing, and festivities. The government is jealous of intercourse with foreigners, and these are not allowed to land on their coasts, and the accounts of the treatment of shipwrecked persons are conflicting. In 1876 a treaty of amity of the people of any nation, friendly with Japan, they shall have kind treatment. And, I think, that illustrates the wisdom of our former action in opening intercourse with Japan. They have reached such a stage of intelligence and civilization, or development thereby, that they treat with a nation reputed barbarous, as they were at the time this intercourse was opened, for the purpose of protecting the lives and property of shipwrecked vessels of nations with which they are at amity. Of course that embraces the shipwrecked people of all nations, because Japan is in a state of peace with all the world.

The trade of Corea is with Japan almost wholly. No Chinese are allowed to settle in Corea, or any Coreans to leave their country. The northern frontier is abandoned for several miles to prevent any intercourse with the Tartars. The country is divided into eight provinces; the capital is on the Han or Kiang River, about the center of the Kingdom, and the government is despotic and the laws severe. Gold, silver, iron, and salt are said to abound, but mining is restricted by the government to its own requirements. The principal manufactures are silk, cotton, cotton-paper, grass-cloth, ricepaper, arms, and horse-hair caps. European manufactures to a limited extent reach Corea, and only through Japan. The Coreans live in a frugal manner, and articles of daily necessity to the Japanese and Chinese are still unknown among them.

In 1866 a French expedition sought redress for the execution of two Catholic missionaries, but were repelled with loss. These missionaries, contrary to the laws of the country, had penetrated into the interior of Corea, and it is said had succeeded in converting to the Catholic religion the queen mother. The king, fearing cabals in his home and that they might try to dethrone him, had them arrested. One account says they were all slain and another that two of them were slain the latter being the most probable fact.

Mr. CHAFFEE. What is their religion?

Mr. SARGENT. In religion they are Buddhists, I will say in reply to the question of the Senator from Colorado.

In that same year an American trading-ship, as it pretended to be the General Sherman, went into one of the rivers of Corea. The captain was an American, and she had a consul's trading register, a register given by a consul to trade. Perhaps she was American built. Of that I am not certain, but the presumption is that she was. She was manned by Chinese principally, and there were three other foreigners on board of her, one a Frenchman. A difficulty arose with the natives, and the vessel was burned, and they were all killed. Our commander in the Japanese waters went the United States ship Wachusett, under the command of their captain, now Commodore Shufeldt, to inquire into this affair. He penetrated into one of the rivers and addressed a communication to the king of the country, and I call attention to his correspondence and especially to the reply emanating from the King to show the sentiments which it contains—the sentiments of enlightened statesmanship and humanity which it contains, and that the people from whom such a document can emanate are worthy of our consideration, and that our recognition as a safeguard against the aggression of Russia or any other power, and also for the purpose of trade.

[Translated from Chinese document a copy of which is attached to this.—N.B. Chinese copy sent with original.]

34

R. W. Thompson (1878. 10. 29) ➜ R. W. Shufeldt

아프리카, 아시아 미개척 지역 탐사 지시

Navy Department
Washington, October 29th 1878
Commodore
R.W. Shufeldt
U.S. Flagship Ticonderoga
Special Services

Sir:

The Department having the fullest confidence in your capacity, discretion and [_____] fitness for the duty, directs that so soon as the Ticonderoga Commander Bartlett J. Cromwell, is prepared for sea you proceed with her to the unfrequented ports of Africa, Asia, the islands of the Indian Ocean, and the adjacent seas particularly where there are at present no American commercial representations with a view to the encouragement and extension of American commerce. While of course in the performance of this special service much must be left to your own discretion, both as regards the ports visited and your intercourse with the inhabitants, yet you will have no difficulty in ascertaining the main and important objects of the Department in fitting out this expedition. You will be expected-

First to report upon the articles of export and import, and the commercial facilities afforded by the laws of the respective countries and in the ports of entry.

Second to encourage and extend American influence by visiting countries where, like Liberia, we already have treaty relations; or like Muscat and Zanzibar, our treaties may need revision.

Third to come in contact with tribes or the coast of Africa not already under the control of European powers, for the purpose of familiarizing them with the advantages of trade with the United States.

Fourth to visit Madagascar and Burmah, at which latter place it is said an American citizen is now or has lately been maltreated.

Fifth to circumnavigate the island of Borneo and to have an interview with its Sultan. This immense island has but two foreign trading ports upon its two thousand miles of coast, Labuan and Sarawak. Both British and Americans have from time to time attempted the establishment of trading stations with the consent of the reigning Sultan, but have failed as it is alleged for want of protection. These fats will command your attention.

Sixth to visit some part of the Corea with the endeavor to re-open by peaceful measures, negotiation with that government. It is believed that the attack upon the Corean ports in 1871 is susceptible of satisfactory explanation and that a moderate and conciliatory course towards the government would result in opening the port of that country to American commerce. You will give special consideration to the subject.

Seventh to rectify errors when they are found to exert in latitude and longitude, to make sailing directions, to take tracings of unexplored coasts, and in every way possible to add to scientific knowledge, and give additional security to navigation in the seas visited.

You will also, if desired by the State Department, make reports in reference to the condition of all consulates in the ports of the world visited, or any such other information as that Department may desire.

The cruise thus designated will take the Ticonderoga along the line of the west and east coasts of Africa and by the adjacent islands, to Burmah, British East India and Borneo, thence through the Java seas to New Guinea and the surrounding islands, thence to the Corean and the China seas and thence home by way of the Pacific Islands and South America or by the Suez Canal and the Mediterranean as the Department may hereafter direct. It is supposed that it will occupy eighteen months or two years.

In April last, the British government through the Secretary of State expressed a desire that a naval officer of the United States should be dictated to act as arbitrator in a pending question between that Government and Liberia with regard to the northwest boundary between Liberia and the British possessions in conjunction with each officials as may be designed by her Majesty's Government. For this purpose the Department on April 5, 1878 designed Commander Robert F. Bradford commanding the U.S.S. Marion to act as such arbiter, and directed him to proceed to Gibraltar with the Marion and await further instructions. It has been indicated by the British authorities that this commissioner would meet in the first instance at Monrovia or Sierra Leone and although it was then contemplated that it should meet as soon as possible thereafter, the Department has since been notified, through the State Department, that it has been deferred until the month of January next. In the mean time, the Department has ordered Commander Bradford to return with the Marion to the United States and he either now is, or soon will be on his homeward cruise. It is, therefore, rendered necessary that some other officer shall be substituted for him, and the Department has decided to confide this duty to you. You will, consequently, upon reaching the coast of Africa put yourself in communication with the British authorities, and act in conjunction with the commissioner designated by them for this purpose.

In as much as the duties here assigned you are special in their nature you will consider yourself as having while executing them, a special command within the jurisdiction of the commanding officers of squadrons or foreign stations, which will exempt you from reporting to them except your arrival and departure from the limits of their command. And you will be expected to report directly to the Department from time to time during your cruise. All such matters connected with the expedition as you may deem of sufficient importance.

You may find it necessary to enter some of the rivers of Africa, in which event you will be permitted to remain on shore or go up these rivers without the restrictions usual to men of war upon that station. And you are authorized to employ natives for boatsmen and to pay their passage back to their homes, as is usual on the African coast.

The Department attaches great importance to this expedition in view of its probable bearing upon the future of American Commerce. An increase in the exchange of the productions of Africa, Borneo, and the islands of the Indian Ocean for those of the United States is eminently desirable; and there is no reason why our merchants should continue behind those of other nations in this respect. The present is perhaps a most favorable time for securing this increase and your selection for this special and important duty in view of your experience, ability and enlarged commercial views, give assurance to the Department that this expedition, under your charge will contribute very materially to this result.

Respectfully,
(Signed) R.W. Thomson
Secretary of the Navy

W. M. Evarts (1878. 11. 9) ➜ R. W. Thompson

Shufeldt의 아시아, 아프리카 연안 항행 훈령에 관한 회신

Department of State,
Washington, Nov 9, 1878
Hon. R.W. Thompson
Secretary of the Navy

Sir:

I have the honor to acknowledge the receipt of your letter of the 30th ultimo, accompanied by a copy of instructions which you have addressed to Commodore Shufeldt, who is about to proceed on a special cruise along the coasts of Africa and Asia and through the Indian Ocean.

In reply, I have the honor to inform you that those instructions have been read with much interest and are entirely approved. If carried out, as it is hoped, they may be from the high professional and personal character of the officer to whom they are addressed, they cannot fail to redound much to the public advantage. This Department has a special reason for forming a favorable opinion of the capacity and energy of Commodore Shufeldt, inasmuch as some years since, when his service in the Navy was of his own accord temporarily suspended, he was at a critical time Consul of the United States at Havana and discharged the duties of that onerous office with great diligence and sagacity.

Since the conclusion of the Treaty between the United States and the Sultan of Muscat of the 21st of September, 1833, there have been changes in that quarter which are not clearly understood here and which it is desirable should be explained. The Sovereign of the country now resides in Zanzibar, and is understood to acknowledge the treaty with Muscat adverted to. What were the political events which led to the change of the residence of the Sovereign and when did they take place? It has been represented to this Department that American vessels are not allowed to take cargo at places on the African continent belonging to the Sultan of Zanzibar but that at the productions of the Sultan's dominions on the mainland are carried to Zanzibar for exportation abroad. The cost of that merchandise to the foreign consumer must be considerable enhanced by the restrictions adverted to, which it is desirable should, if practicable, be removed. It is important to know whether, if the restriction exists it is general in its application. If there should be any discrimination in favor of the vessels of any other nation, we must claim the same privilege pursuant to the IV article of the Treaty.

The Consul of the United States at Tamatave, Madagascar, is of the opinion that the Treaty of 1867, between the United States and the Queen of that Island, is susceptible of improvement. A report from Commodore Shufeldt on this subject would be acceptable.

The British port of Aden, always important to commerce from its position at the entrance of the Red Sea, has in that respect much increased since the completion of the Suez Canal. At one time, Mr. William H. Nichols was the Consular Agent of this government there. He, however retired in 1869, and we have not since had any form of Consular representative at that place. The fees alone would not support one, but the Department has an application for appointment as Consular Agent there, from one Pieroslaw Buyorjee Sorabja of Aden, who says that Mr. Nichols on his departure, transferred to him the Consular effects. The application is supported by numerous testimonials of naval officers of the United States who have visited Aden. Commodore Shufeldt's views on the subject are desired. It is presumed from the manner of the application that he is either a Hindoo or an Arab, and an enquiry as to his nationality as well as his capacity is advisable.

In a dispatch to this Department of the 17th of September last, Mr. A.J. Studer, the intelligent Consul of the United States at Singapore, asks whether the treaty of 1850 between the United States and the Sultan of Borneo, is here regarded as in full force. As the instrument itself is unlimited in duration, the question can only be answered in the affirmative, in respect at least to all those parts of the Island, which that Sovereign may maintain within his own jurisdiction. If he should in due form have alienated to another Sovereign power any part of his dominions, the privileges promised to us by the treaty may be modified accordingly. It is understood however, that he has ceded or leased to individuals or companies pacts at least of the main Island and smaller islands adjacent thereto.

His competency to do this in disparagement of his stipulations in his treaty with the United States, cannot be acknowledged. This opinion is expressed despite the fact that one of the companies which obtained grants there was called the "American Tracking Company," the leading manager of which was M.J.A. Torrey, now Vice Consul of the United States at Bangkok, Siam.

It is understood that the lease of that company has been made voidable by a failure to comply with its conditions and especially the annual payment which it required to the Sultan. The extent of that Island and its resources, mineral and otherwise, are so great that it is important that the whole subject should be carefully enquired into. To this end Commodore Shufeldt may be advised freely to confer with Mr. Studer.

This Department is not aware that there is a material change in the prospect of opening commercial intercourse or entering into a Treaty with the Kingdom of Corea. Commodore Shufeldt may be referred to the accompanying reports on the Foreign Relations of the United States for 1870, 1871, and 1872 for the particulars of the abortive attempt for that purpose by Mr. Low, when Minister of the United States in China. In a dispatch to the department, however, of the 26th of March 1874, Mr. Williams, then Charge d'Affaires at Peking, represented that he had received credible information that there had been a change in the Government of Corea, and that the King during whose reign our overtures for diplomatic intercourse were rejected, had been dethroned, and that the dynasty by which he had been succeeded, might be regarded as more favorably disposed. If Commodore Shufeldt should find the same dynasty in power, he might cautiously sound it as to its inclination to enter into a treaty of Amity and Commerce with the United States similar in spirit and purport to those already in existence with other Oriental Countries, and it is desired that upon this subject he will report as early as may be practicable.

The volume containing the treaties of the United States with foreign nations is herewith transmitted for reference in this matter.

It will in any event be desirable for the Commodore to endeavor to ascertain the facts in regard to the American Schooner "General Sherman" and the persons on board of her. That vessel visited Corea in 1866, but never returned thence, and nothing authentic has since been learned of her officers or seamen. The accounts of their fate in the papers on file here, are so conflicting that a satisfactory opinion upon the subject cannot be formed. The failure of that vessel to return from Corea was the principal occasion for the mission of Mr. Low, above referred to.

This Department has information that Japan and Corea have recently entered into a treaty by one of the stipulations of which provision is made for relieving and returning shipwrecked mariners, not only of the parties but of other foreign countries. This is a proof of intimacy between those two governments, which may be taken advantage of in behalf of Commodore Shufeldt.

I have consequently addressed an instruction to the Minister of the United States in Japan, directing him to apply to the Japanese Minister for Foreign Affairs for such personal or official letters to the authorities of Corea in favor of Commodore Shufeldt as may tend to smooth his way and contribute to the success of his errand.

The opinions of the Commodore in regard to such Consulates as he may visit and as to the expediency of establishing others, would be appreciated, and any information that he may obtain in regard to opportunities for the development of American trade with the regions he is about to visit, would be gratifying to the Department as well as of public interest and importance.

I have the honor to be, Sir,
Your obedient servant,
Wm. M. Evarts
Accompaniments.
Volume of treaties and conventions between the United States and other Powers.
Foreign Relations of the United States for 1870-'71 and '72

S. Stevens (1879. 1. 24) ➜ W. M. Evarts (1879. 2. 24)

조일 관세 문제에 관한 보고

관련문서 보고에 대한 회신(1879. 3. 1)

UNITED STATES LEGATION.
Tokei, Japan

SIR: Referring my No. 13, of date of the 7th ultimo, on the subject of the recent complications between Japan and Corea, and the mission of Mr. Hanabusa to the letter country, I have the honor to inform you that Mr. Hanabusa has returned, and that, in an interview yesterday, Mr. Mori, vice-minister for foreign affairs, informed me that the difficulty between the two countries had been amicably and satisfactorily settled. But while the Corean Government has removed the duties upon exports and imports of which the Japanese Government complained, Mr. Mori said that the question of damages on account of the alleged illegal restriction upon trade resultant from the imposition of those duties still remained open. It is not probable, however, now that the main point in dispute has been conceded by the Corean authorities, that any serious complications will arise from the consideration of the losses which have been sustained by Japanese on account of the action of the Government of Corea.

* * * * * * * * *

I have, &c.,

D. W. STEVENS.

【관련문서】

DEPARTMENT OF STATE,
Washington

SIR: It has afforded me pleasure to receive your dispatch No. 35, of

January 24, reporting the peaceable adjustment of the main question in dispute between Japan and Corea. It is hoped that the recession of Corea from the position assumed may be indicative of a better disposition to cultivate relations of friendship and commerce with the rest of the world. That it should take a step in that direction with a neighboring people of the same race is a hopeful sign, and it may be that the influence of Japan may make itself felt in the interest of furthering the enlightened policy which should seek to open the hitherto inaccessible regions of the rich Pacific coast to the beneficial tendencies of trade and material development.

 I am, &c.,

WM. M. EVARTS.

(4) Shufeldt의 서한 전달 시도와 일본의 중재

R. W. Shufeldt (1880. 2. 13) ➜ J. A. Bingham

조선과의 협상 시기에 관한 조언 요청

If possible. If the occasion of the opening of the Korean ports to the Japanese government – which is said to occur in May – would not be as opportune time for me to make the effort of negotiating with the government of Korea.

I intend to be in Japan some time during May for the purpose of proceeding to the Korea, if by so doing I can forward the interests of our country.

I feel sure that such advice and assistance as you may feel justified in affording as reform our arrival in Japan, would be of very great service towards the successful execution of this mission.

I have the honor to be.
Very respectfully.
Your observant.

Commodore U.S.A.

J. A. Bingham (1880. 3. 12) ➜ R. W. Shufeldt

훈령 미도착 통보

U.S. Legations
Japan, Tokei March 12, 1880
Commodore R.W. Shufeldt
U.S. Flagship Ticonderoga
Special Service
Hong Kong

Sir:

I have the honor to acknowledge the receipt last evening of your communication of the 14th inst. in-relation to your telegram to me on the 13th inst.

I note your statement that your telegram was based on the "State Department instructions dated Nov. 9, 1878 addressed to the Hon. Secty of the Navy" and by him transmitted to you for your guidance "in a proposed effort to open negotiations with the Corean Government" and from which instructions, among other things you quote the following: -

"I (the Hon. The Secty of State) have consequently addressed an instruction to the Minister of the U.S. in Japan, directing him to apply to the Japanese Minister of Foreign Affairs, for such personal or official letters to the authorities of Corea in favor of Commodore Shufeldt as may tend to smooth his way, and contribute to the success of his errand."

This extract from the letter of the Hon. the Secty of State not only explains your telegram to me, but also discloses the entire propriety of it.

It is proper that I should acquaint you, that I have made examination of the records of this legation, but find no instruction to me, on to the legation, from the Department of State requesting me to make an application to the Japanese Minister of Foreign Affairs for such personal or official letters to the authorities of Corea in favor of yourself. I was absent on leave from the 25th of Oct. 1878 until the 21st May 1879, but am advised by Mr. Secty of this legation, who was left in charge during my absence, that no such instruction came from the Department.

I regret that I did not receive the instruction, and beg leave to thank you for bringing the same to my knowledge. I have today communicated with H. E. the Minister for Foreign Affairs, and hope to be able to obtain from him such letters BC- as may materially contribute to make your missions to Corea a success. Be assured that it will give me pleasure to see you in this capital at any time and especially in May next and to give you all advice or assistance possible in furtherance of your mission to Corea. May is a very good time in which to visit Japan.

I have received from H. I. J. M. Prime Minister Mr. Sanjo a proclaim action of date the 28th Jan. last, in which it is notified that the port of Geuzanshiro in Kan-Kodo. Corea, will under the 5th Article of the Treaty of Febry 1876 between Japan and Corea be opened for trade &c to Japan on the 1st May next.

Hoping to meet you as proposed and to be of service to you, I have the honor to be Sir
    Your obt svt,
    M.A. Bingham

J. A. Bingham (1880. 3. 12) ➡ 井上馨

Shufeldt를 소개하는 일본 측 서한 요청

第千百七十九號
以書翰致啓上候陳者今般我合衆國旗艦チコンデラゴ號暫時日本近海ヘ立寄可申筈ニ付貴政府於テ該艦ヲ致指揮候合衆國海軍水師提督アール・タブリユ・シユフエルトノ爲メ在朝鮮日本官吏并朝鮮官吏ヘコモドールシユフエルトヲ款待相成候樣依賴ノ書翰公書又ハ私書ニテモ拙者迄御贈付被下候得者我政府ニテ御懇情ノ事ト存シ可申候尤右水師提督ハ合衆國政府ヨリ朝鮮政府ヘ親睦ノ使命ヲ奉シ朝鮮國開港場ヘ入港可致心得ニ候就テハ日本國政府於テ我政府ノ爲メ拙者ヨリ申上候此請求御承諾被下候樣希望致シ候此段得御意度如斯候敬具

東京千八百八十年三月十二日合衆國公使館於テ
ジョン・エ・ビンハム
外務卿 井上馨 閣下

W. M. Evarts (1880. 4. 1) ➜ J. A. Bingham

조선 개항과 관련한 협조 훈령

No. 495
Department of State
Washington, April 1, 1880
John A. Bingham, Esquire.
&c &c &c

Sir:

A letter has been received from the Navy Department under date of the 31st ultimo, transmitting a copy of a dispatch from Commodore Shufeldt U.S.N., dated from Singapore the 15th of February 1880, containing an extract from a letter of this Department to the Secretary of the Navy, dated the 9th of November, 1878 which reads as follows:

"This Department has information that Japan and Corea have recently entered into a treaty, by one of the stipulations of which provision is made for relieving and returning shipwrecked mariners not only of the parties, but of other foreign countries. This is a proof of intimacy between those two governments, which may be taken advantage of in behalf of Commodore Shufeldt. I have consequently addressed an instruction to the Minister of the United States in Japan directing him to apply to the Japanese Minister of Foreign Affairs for such personal or official letters to the authorities of Corea in favor of Commodore Shufeldt as may tend to smooth his way and to contribute to the success of his errand."

Through some inadvertence the instruction intended for you was not sent.

You are, therefore, now instructed to lend your hearty cooperation to Commodore Shufeldt, in furtherance of his negotiations with the government of Corea on the occasion of the opening of her ports to the Japanese government, which event, it is understood, will probably occur in May next.

I am, Sir, &c.
Wm. M. Evarts

井上馨(1880. 4. 1) ➡ J. A. Bingham

Shufeldt 소개 요청 거절

His Excellency
John A Bingham
&c &c

Sir:

    I have the honor to acknowledge Y.E.'s dispatch dated the 12th March 1880, wherein Y.E. acquaints me that Commodore R.W. Shufeldt U.S.N. Commanding the U.S. Flagship, "Ticonderoga" is expected to shortly visit the open ports of Corea on a friendly mission from the United States Government to that of Corea, and requesting me to furnish Y.E. with letters to the Japanese Officials in Corea and also to the Corean Officials, commending the Commodore to their favorable consideration.

    I beg leave, in reply, to say that a very few years have elapsed since the conclusion of the treaty of friendship between Japan and Corea and that the time has not as yet arrived for putting into full execution the stipulations of the said treaty, furthermore that the Corean Government, not being familiar with foreign intercourse, appears still disinclined to open the country to foreigners. I beg therefore to say that if the introduction of Comdore Shufeldt to the Corean Officials should be granted according to Y.E.'s request, I fear that it might give rise to some complications whereby the execution of our treaty with that country might be somewhat prevented. I greatly regret, therefore, that I am at present unable to comply with Y.E.'s wishes.

    I may add that in my opinion, it would not be the best policy for the present to furnish any letters of introduction to the officials of Corea, but I am willing to advise the Japanese Officers in Corea to do the best in their power in facilitating the said mission.

    I avail myself &c
    (sgd.) Inouye Kaoru
    H.I.J.M. Minister for Foreign Affairs

【日譯文】

(朱書)「第十四號」「四月七日」
米國公使宛
　　　　　井上外務卿

以書簡致啓上候陳者千八百八十年三月十三日附貴簡ヲ以貴國軍艦チコンヂラゴ號ヲ致指揮候コモドール、アール・ダブリユ・シユフヱルト氏貴國政府ヨリ朝鮮國政府ヘ親睦之使命ヲ奉シ同國開港場ヘ入港ノ筈ニ付在朝鮮國我國官吏及ヒ同國官吏ヘ右コモドール、アール・ダブリユ・シユフヱルト氏ヲ款待候様依頼ノ書簡御所望ノ趣致承知候然ルニ我國朝鮮國ト修好條規取結テヨリ日尚浅クシテ未タ右條約中ノ條款ヲ充分履行スルノ秋ニ不至且同國政府ハ外交ニ不馴忌憚ノ情アルヲ以テ今御来意ニ應シ同國官吏ヘ右コモドールヲ紹介スル時ハ或ハ為夫我國ト同國間ノ條約履行上多少障碍ニ可相成哉モ難計其邊懸念不尠因テ同國官吏ヱ添書ノ義ハ方今ノ良策ニ無之ト存候間乍御氣ノ毒御来意ニ難應尤出来丈ノ事ハ御都合ニ相成候様同國在留我官吏ヘ委曲內諭可致置候右様御了承有之度此段囘答得貴意候敬具

三年三月廿三日

上野景範(1880. 4. 20) ➡ J. A. Bingham

부산 주재 영사에게 Shufeldt의 소개장 발송

(朱書)「十三年四月二十日達了」
特命全權公使ビンハム閣下
　　　　　上野大輔
昨日御出省にて御依賴有之候貴國軍艦指揮官コモドール、アール・ダブリュ・シユフエルト氏朝鮮國へ進航被致候に付在釜山我領事へ紹介狀差進方の義外務卿にも相談いたし候處異存無之候に付則別紙一通さし進申候右は日本文にて同氏一覽に不便なるへくと存候まゝ英文譯相添さし出候此序を以同氏へ拙者の敬意を表章いたし度候此段申入候也
敬具
　　追て外に釜山の測量圖壹枚さし進候也

四月二十日付　井上外務卿ヨリ釜脚在勤近藤領事宛米國提督紹介狀
丙號
　　　　　　朝鮮釜山在勤
　　　　　　　　　　　　井上外務郷
近藤領事殿
以手紙啓上候然ハ今度米國軍艦チコンデラゴ號ノ指揮官コモドール、アール・ダブリュ・シユフエルド氏同國政府ノ命ヲ受朝鮮國政府ヘ親睦ノ使命ヲ奉シ釜山ヘ入港スルノ積ニ有之依テ同氏ヲ貴下ヘ紹介ノ義同國特命全權公使ビンハム氏ヨリ依賴候ニ付此書ヲビンハム氏ヘ相渡置候就テハ右シユフエルド氏其港ヘ参着ノ末同氏使事上ノ事ニ付テハ貴下右ニ關係被致候ニハ不及候併シ米國ハ我國ト從來ノ友誼モ有之候間同艦滯泊中ハ可成ノ周旋ヲ盡サレ候樣致度依テ此段申達候也
明治十三年四月

43

R. W. Shufeldt (1880. 4. 26) ➜ R. W. Thompson

부산에서의 교섭 계획 보고

U.S. Flagship Ticonderoga
Special Service
Nagasaki, Japan
April 26, 1880
Hon. R. W. Thompson
Secty of the Navy
Washington, D.C.

Sir:

I have the honor to inform the Department of the arrival of the Ticonderoga at Nagasaki on the 15thinst. from Hong Kong.

It was my instruction to proceed direct Yokohama, but owing to the prevailing strong headwinds outside I decided to put in here.

I telegraphed Mr. Bingham, our Minister in Japan, of our arrival and, as much time could be saved by going direct to Corea, asked him in case it was not important that we should first come to Yokohama, if he would kindly send me here by first mail all communications that could be obtained which might be of service to us in our future movements.

He replied that he would answer by next mail.

That mail is just to hand and I am in receipt of a letter from Mr. Bingham informing me of his request in behalf of our mission to Corea, and enclosing copy of the reply thereto from His Imperial Japanese Majesty's Minister for Foreign Affairs, and also a letter to the Japanese Counsel at Fusan, Corea. Copies of both are herewith enclosed.

Fusan, has occurred to me as being the best point in Corea from which to communicate with the Capital, and we will accordingly leave here about the 1st proximo for that port.

After dispatching a letter to the Capital we will return here, or perhaps visit Yokohama, preceding again to Fusan about the end of May for the purpose of receiving a reply from our communication.

I have been informed here that prominent officials in China have recommended the Coreans to make treaties with foreign powers, owing perhaps to the dread of aggression by Russia and possibly Japan, but while I feel this to be an opportune time to attempt the opening of negotiations, I am not over sanguine of success.

The officers and men are all well.

I have the honor to be very respectfully your obedient servant,
R. W. Shufeldt
Commodore U.S. N.
On Special Service

44

R. W. Thompson (1880. 4. 26) ➡ R. W. Shufeldt

협상 진전이 없을 경우 복귀 지시

Navy Department
Washington

Sir,

I have today read your cable message answering that you would today leave Nagasaki on your 1st visit to Corea and would return to that port and asking if the Department has any advice. This Department has no further instruction to give and can only repeat its orders for you to proceed to San Francisco touching at the Sandwich Islands if advisable en route, unless something should be developed on your visit to Corea which would warrant for remaining longer in Japan and asking advice by Cable.

Respectfully
RW Thompson
Secty of the Navy

R. W. Shufeldt (1880. 5. 4) ➡ 沈東臣

高宗에게 올린 Shufeldt 서한

U.S. Flagship Ticonderoga
Special Service
Fusan, Corea

To His Majesty the King of Corea

Your Majesty,

I have the honor to inform Your Majesty of my arrival in Corean waters with the U.S. Ship Ticonderoga, Commissioned by the Government of the United States to visit your Majesty's dominions, with the intent by means of a friendly correspondence to bring about that amicable intercourse between the Government of the United States and Your Majesty's Government, which owing to a misunderstanding has been unfortunately interrupted for several years past.

I wish to inform Your Majesty that I am the Officer who, while in command of the United States Steamer Wachusett, lying near the mouth of the Ta-Tong River, addressed Your Majesty the following letter:

"The United States Steamer Wachusett

Off Ta-Tong River, District of Chang-Yuen, Corea

January 24th 1867

To His Majesty the King of Corea,

The Commander of the American armed vessel Wachusett begs to inform Your Majesty that he has come to the borders of Your Kingdom not to engage in war nor any unlawful business, but in obedience to the command of the officer commanding the armed vessels of America stationed in these seas, who has heard with great pleasure and thankfulness of the kindness of Your Majesty's Officers and people to the ship wrecked crew of an American vessel in the month of June last, on the west coast of Corea, how Your Majesty had them transported to the confines of China from whence they safely reached their friends.

The whole American people cannot but feel thankful and praise your nation for this act of kindness and brotherly love.

The Officer commanding the armed vessels of America has since heard with pain and surprise that the people of another American vessel wrecked in the Ping-Yang River in the province of Ping-Yang in the month of September last, were all put to death and the vessel burned, and has ordered me to ask of your Majesty what evil these people had done that they should be made to suffer such cruel treatment.

But if any or all of these people are living the Officer commanding the armed vessels of America has directed me to ask of Your Majesty that they may be delivered to me on board of the Wachusett now lying in the harbor of Ta-Tong off the district of Chang-Yuew, or at any more convenient part Your Majesty may select.

This is especially desired that the peace and friendship which has heretofore been uninterrupted for many years may still continue between America and Corea. A speedy answer is requested to this communication in order that he may depart in peace."

I have the honor to state to Your Majesty that the same kindly sentiments which guided me then activate me now while addressing to Your Majesty this Communication

The following is a Copy of Your Majesty's reply:

To Commander Shufeldt:

The intendant of circuit in the Hwong Hae district, Corea and ex-office inspector of the imperial board of directors, makes the following reply to the Commander of the Steamer Wachusetts, anchored on our coast off the district of Chang-Tuen, namely, that he has examined your letter of the 18th instant, forwarding a communication which you simply wish to be transmitted to my sovereign, and proposing to await the reply of the Minister of the Frontier. The local magistrate of the said place was in duty bound to inform you that the road going and returning would be quite long, and to have treated you with kindness and sincerity, so detaining your honored vessel for a replay. Now however, before the arrival of the reply, the guest from afar has already departed; so doing how grievously have we offended the rules of propriety and violated true friend by feeling.

Aside from the fact that this local magistrate has received a demerit mark, I have prepared a dispatch in reply, to be kept in readiness in case your honored vessel should return; and first, I beg to state in general as regards the circumstances of the affairs that the legal regulation of our country with reference to the merchant ships of a foreign country driven her by adverse winds are that, in case the vessel is sound, we are to furnish provisions and whatever is needed while waiting for a wind to depart. In case the vessel is not sound, and there is no means of proceeding by sea, then we are to follow their wish in sending an officer to escort them by land to Pekin, which thing has occurred heretofore, not merely once. Such a course we look upon as in accordance with true benevolence. He who is in [____] above regards the people of neighboring nations as he does his arm. Your worthy communication, which I have just received, is so exceeding by complimentary as to make me feel quite ashamed.

With reference to the affair which transpired last autumn in the Ping-Yang River, I would state that at that time there was a foreign vessel entered the lower waters of the Ping-Yang River, and the local magistrate of the place, supposing that its vessel was driven hither by distress of weather, and coming in to seek a vessel to transship to, proceeded to make inquiries into the matter, but the men on board the vessel became greatly enraged at the messenger and refused to make any reply, shutting their eyes and lying down at their ease, clearly intending to offer insult. Our people restrained their anger, and, by the most humble address and earnest entreaty, found out that they were not driven here by storm. There was one man on board the vessel named Tsuy, calling himself a Frenchman, and another said to be an Englishman. They said a large number of Men-of-War was about to come to this place, and if the local magistrate would suffer them to open trade with the people it would secure the dispersion of the soldiers of the two armies. The local magistrate replied that the opening of trade was not a thing that a local magistrate could assume to promise.

The man Tsuy however, refused to regard it, becoming more and more unreasonable and violent. The water in the Ping-Yang River is shallow and unfit for running large vessels; but he disregarded this, and every day, riding on the tide, went up a few miles further. Our people were especially anxious that affairs should not become serious and so presented them with nice meats, vegetables, fruit and fuel. The man Tsuy replied that they would leave the next day; but when the next day came, instead of leaving they advanced again, evidently intending to push their way to the provincial city. The Adjutant-General went out in a vessel every day and escorted them, in order to guard against a collision between their people and ours. One day he threw out grappling-wires and ropes and captured the vessel of the Adjutant-General, seizing him, with his official seal, and confining him on board their vessel. In some cases the trading vessels they passing to and fro they sent to pieces with their cannon, carrying off the goods and killing their crew. I do not know to the extent how many far and near; all were exceedingly alarmed and fled in continuous streams.

How extreme was the disgrace of the adjutant general thus to be seized before hostilities had begun! Nevertheless we still resorted only to mild words and earnest entreaty, requesting that the Adjutant-General should be given up; but the reply was, "Wait till we enter the City and we will restore him." This man Tsuy could speak Chinese and was without a match in fierceness and [_____] and seemed determined to force his way into the provincial city, though we did not know what his intentions were, the whole city, including several ten-thousands of soldiers and people, yielding to their indignant rage, came out in a mass to the river and commenced an attack with all their might, intending to rescue the Adjutant-General.

Several tens of good people were killed by the cannon balls, when all, becoming infuriated, rushed on in a mass, the force of which was irresistible. Fire was opened by both sides and fire-rafts were used. Finally the powder stored in said vessel exploded rending it to pieces and sending the black smoke up to heaven. The vessel was entirely burnt up and the men all killed. We still do not know whether this vessel belonged to your honorable country or not. This man Tsuy, without cause pushed his way into the interior of another country and provoked this affair, and examination had to this time failed to discover his object in acting thus.

It appears from your honorable communication that the vessel of our guest is a different nationality from that claimed by Tsuy. The beginning and the end of this affair amounts simply to this. That your honorable country's customs greatly tends and produce propriety in intercourse with others is well known to all the provinces as well as our illustrious neighbor China.

As to what it said in your honored communication about containing former relations of friendship without an occasion of mutual injury, I will simply say this affair is but a particle of autumn dust, not worthy to be entertained as a matter of doubt and solicitude. I now respectfully present this reply, asking you to make all necessary allowances, and for this purpose this reply is made.

A necessary reply addressed to the American Commander, fifth year of the Emperor Tung Chi, twelfth month [___] day."

Unfortunately Your Majesty's reply did not reach me until several years after it was written owing to my absence from the Coast of China as well as the Coast of the United States.

If I had received it in time I do not hesitate to say to Your Majesty that in my opinion, the subsequent events which occurred in 1871, in the Kang-Kiang River would probably not have been of such an unfortunate character because I believe that the statement of Your Majesty in the above letter in reference to the lost vessel was essentially true, and, knowing as I do, the peaceful policy of the Government of the United States with respect to all foreign powers, I think I could have convinced its authorities of the truth of the fact as contained therein, and, I feel authorized to add, from the tenor of my official instructions from my Government, that notwithstanding the attack upon the ports in our Majesty's dominion in 1871 the Government of the United States entertains most friendly feelings toward the Government and People of Corea.

I have now the honor to express to Your Majesty the hope that in view of the progress of events both in China and Japan, and in Your Majesty's dominions, you will have arrived at the conclusion that the present time is opportue for the commencement of a new era by offering to the United States, under treaty, such commercial privileges as are granted to it by the two nations just mentioned.

I need not remind Your Majesty that the Kingdom of Corea is of all nations the only remaining which excludes other nationalities from its territory nor is it necessary to inform Your Majesty that the Government and People of the United States have never sought by aggression to extend their sovereignty in these waters nor have they ever meddled or interfered with the religious or political institutions of independent nations.

The United States Government only asks, first for the protection of its citizens if stranded upon foreign shores, and second, for such commercial facilities as nations universally grant to each other in the present day.

I need nor ask Your Majesty's attention to the fact that Corea surrounded by nations some of which may be more or less anxious to extend their territory, would be materially strengthened and benefitted by making a friendly treaty with the United States, a strongly armed power which has no such desire or intention, and which is indeed your nearest neighbor among the so-called

Western Powers of the world—lying as it does directly between Corea and Europe.

In view of these facts thus briefly stated I respectfully submit to Your Majesty the propriety of consenting to receive a commissioner duly appointed by the Government of the United States for the purpose of negotiating such treaty, or Your Majesty might exhibit a praiseworthy feeling deserving of Your Character as indicated in your letter to me, by selecting an officer of sufficient dignity to confer with me personally on this subject either on shore or on board of this vessel while lying in the harbor of Fusan for which purpose, or at least for receiving a reply to this communication, I will return to the same anchorage in 42 days from this date.

I beg leave to assure Your Majesty that while in the waters of Corea no act of hostility against Your Majesty's subjects or their property, unless wantonly provoked, will be permitted by the officers and men under my command.

Trusting that a bond of peace, friendship, and good understanding may now be brought about which shall henceforth and forever continue to subsist between American and Your Majesty's Kingdom.

I have the honor to be,
Your Majesty's humble servant,
(Signed) R.W. Shufeldt, Commodore &C

【漢譯文】

照錄抄單

照鈔美國太匡低羅嘉轟船特命總兵官上高麗國王修好書大合衆國特命查辦各國通商事務 坐駕轟船太匡低羅嘉總兵官 上書於高麗國王殿下 爲敬陳修好事 竊因前數年兩國情意 尚有未協 是以大合衆國朝廷特命總兵官乘駕轟船名太匡低羅嘉前來貴境 欲修舊好 敬爲殿下陳之 今總兵官卽曩時一千八百六十七年正月二十四號 在貴國大同海口 乘坐敝國華休屑軍艦 曾經陳書於殿下者 其詞曰 合衆國華休屑坐駕官到來貴境 非欲有所戰爭及一切違理之事 但因奉合衆國統帶東方水師提督之命 以舊歲六月間有敝國船隻駛至貴境西邊 破船遭難 其在船人等幸得貴國官民照料 復蒙殿下派員將更生之難民 遞送中國

疆界 然後得以安抵親友 凡敝邦之人 莫不感戴貴國仁愛之心 雖兄弟無異 水師提督不勝感激稱謝 厥後是年九月 又有敝國船在於貴國平壤河地方 船隻被焚 人亦遭害 提督聞之 極爲驚駭 痛惜實深 特派坐駕官前來 敬求殿下查明該船之敝國人民有何不法 致被此害 倘或尚有生存者 望交還坐駕官船上 或由殿下另擇更爲合宜處所 知會坐駕官 得至該處領回 均隨方便 敝國與貴國數年以來 共敦和好 今望彼此親睦 仍復如前 此事若何 求早日賜覆 俾修好而歸 幸甚等語 總兵記憶前言 至今猶存此念 再爲殿下陳之 前數年得接賜書開稱 貴坐駕官蕭孚爾 高麗國黃海道台前監督部官爲照覆坐駕官華休屑事 前十八日來函 本道經已覽悉 另有轉遞敝國主上書一封 欲候邊疆大臣回復 當經地方官報違 以往返路遙 須要貴艦逗貿 遲日方回後 不料復函未到 而遠客揚帆 似此不周 有傷睦誼 抱歉之至 地方官亦有受責 玆竊有陳者 凡外國商船如有在敝境遭風者 敝國立有章程 若該船尚堪駕駛 俟其動身之日 須供給火食及各項需用物件 倘船不能駕駛 即派官員將其難民護送北京 歷經照辦在案 我國以爲此仁義之擧 上帝臨之 四海之內 無分畛域也 今接貴函 情詞備至 殊覺抱愨 至去歲平壤河一事 敢據實覆陳之 是時有洋船一艘 駛入內河 地方官以爲遭風漂至 覓雇船隻 委人到船查問 不意船上人等見有委員來查 不勝憤怒 問之不合 閉目安睡 任意欺凌 敝國之人忍聲呑氣 再三訪問 始知該船非因遭風而來 該船之人有名睢者 自稱法國人 又有英國人一名 二人皆云不日有許多兵船到此 若地方官能准我外國人在此往來貿易 可免干戈等語 地方官答以通商之事 本官實無此權 睢等聞言不顧 愈加兇怒 平壤河水甚淺 洋船不便往來 睢亦不理 每日乘潮駛入數里 我國人民但望不致生事 自備米柴魚肉蔬果各物遞送該船 睢答云明日卽去 乃至明日 不惟不去 且更駛進 顯欲到城 我國副將官恐土人與該船生事 每日駕船伴送 一日洋人睢抛擲鐵鉤繩索拘繫副將之船 將副將及其鈴印押送過船 或遇敝國商船往來 該洋船開炮向擊 奪其貨而戮其人 不知多寡 敝國人民驚慌奔走 兩非對敵 而副將如此受刑 可云辱甚 然我國之人仍以溫言求懇 請其放還副將 該船答云 俟我等抵城之後 自將副將交還 惟是能說華語之洋人睢 兇暴愈常 其意決要進城 我等不解其何因是以全城數萬兵民 氣怒已極 齊赴河旁 互相攻擊 欲救回副將 反被擊斃民人數名 人心更忿 蜂擁而來 不能阻止 兩岸施放槍抱 兼用火桴 迨後該船藥艙被火 煙焰冲天 全船被焚 無能生活 是時敝國之人亦不知其是否貴國之船也 忖思兇悍如睢者 闖進他國內地 激成事端 彼實因何至此 迄今無從稽查 今查來函 貴坐駕之船非與睢同國者 然其事顚末 實係如此 貴合衆國禮義之邦 不但

于我國知之 卽有道顯榮之大淸國 亦共聞之 貴函又稱重修舊好 無傷友誼 則此事亦何足介意 爲此照覆 諸祈鑒原 須至照覆者

右照會大合衆國坐駕官 同治五年十二月等因 寄遞前來 不料其時總兵官遠離中國海疆 亦未回至敝國 竟遲至數年方接殿下賜敎 若得早接貴函 在總兵官甚爲篤信 可以布告己國人民 共釋疑惑 敝國政治和平 素欲與各國和好 諒不至有一千八百七十一年在漢江河不幸之擧 今總兵官銜命而來 不復記念前時砲台攻擊 但欲與貴國修好 友誼盖敦 近觀中國日本及貴國進益情形 正宜倣照規條 與敝國立約通商 現今天下萬國無不往來貿易 惟貴國尙未允行 伏念敝國向無在此貪人疆土之意 凡有自主之邦 其敎俗禁令 斷無干涉 致有阻難 其欲通好於貴國者 一則爲己國船隻遇有遭風 藉資保護 二則欲照各國一律通商而已 至于貴國鄰封有思拓其土宇者 固不必言 我國素稱强大 毫無此心 若貴國與之修好 邦家益固 其利非淺 況此處離泰西之國與敝邦最爲密邇 敢以此敬陳殿下 希惟允准接待合衆國公使 共立條約 或簡派本等大臣到船西議 或另擇相宜之處 彼此往來晤商 均無不可 總兵官准於 空格待簽日期 日 再至釜山拱候鈞覆 此次奉命來此 未有敵視貴國人民之心 除非貴國人民先以非禮相加 始許員弁從事 伏願允准施行 俾我兩國立約 永遠和好 正函譯函止此 尙未簽名

R. W. Shufeldt (1880. 5. 10) ➜ J. A. Bingham

서한 전달 실패 보고

관련문서 近藤眞鋤가 조선 정부에 보낸 소개장의 영역문

Sir:

I have the honor to enclose herewith copy of translation of a letter from Mr. Kondo, H.I. Japanese Majesty's consul, Fusan, Corea giving an account of his attempt to forward a communication from me to the Capital of Corea and his want of success.

I beg to express my regretful acknowledgments to His Excellency, Mr. Inouye, for the kind efforts made by Mr. Kondo to assist us, as if we are assured that his services were rendered to the best of his ability.

But from what Mr. Kondo said, I have reason to believe if the letter had been enclosed by the Japanese Government, it would have been forwarded to its destination; and inasmuch as a similar service was once rendered by the Chinese Government, I trust that His Excellency Mr. Inouye will revise his decision and transmit the letter with such comments as His Excellency may deem advisable-without therefore, assuming any responsibility, or establishing it as a precedent for granting similar favors in the future.

I have the honor to be very respectfully,
your obedient servant,
R. W. Shufeldt

【관련문서】

Sir;

I have the honor to communicate with Your Excellency to the effect that the United States Envoy on board the United States Steamer "Ticonderoga" recently visited the port of Fusan with the object of presenting a letter to Your Government through the Governor of Torai Fu through the medium of our Consul, Kondo Masuki, wherein he expressed the desire of establishing friendship, but he left that port vainly as the Governor refused to receive it.

The U.S. Representative here has requested me that the sentiments of his friendly mission will be conveyed to Your Government, and that the said Envoy intends to proceed again to Fusan for that purpose. I fear that if U.S. Steamer would go again to Fusan, her appearance might cause an excitement among your people, consequently I suggested to him to defer his visit there. The friendly relations between Japan and Corea being especially intimate and that between Japan and the United States of America existing many years since, I feel myself obliged to communicate to Your Excellency the following.

The said U.S. Envoy. Commodore Shufeldt, is the same person who visited your country in 1867 and presented a letter to your Government expressing the gratitude of the U.S. Government for the kindness which your Government manifested in saving shipwrecked American citizens, and also requesting the negotiation of a treaty of friendship, to which letter your Government has given a favorable reply.

The object of the present mission is simply to repeat the former request, this you will perceive from Commodore Shufeldt's letter which I beg leave to forward herewith.

The general state of the would is now very different from that of older times, and we know from our own experience the impossibility of rejecting foreign intercourse, and China also has the same experience. The best plan which I recommend you for the interests of your country is to comply with the request of the U.S. Government in a friendly sentiment, treating them with the sincere benevolence and being guided in such intercourse by the principles of right and justice. This is the only means of guarding against contempt from abroad, and of securing the right of independence of your country; otherwise a great injurious result may be arrived at and may endanger the welfare of your country. My Government, of course has no intention of interfering with Your Government's policy. I however, have long experience in foreign intercourse, and in reflectiong on the past of China, I cannot hesitate to offer the above suggestion to Your Excellency.

The said Envoy will stay at the port of Nagasaki for sixty days from this date, awaiting a reply to his letter. Your Government's reputed for civilities toward others, and I have no doubt your Government will give the answer desired, so that I can transmit it to said Envoy.

I avail myself of this occasion to renew to your Excellency the assurance of my highest consideration.

47

沈東臣 ➡ 議政府(1880. 5. 13/高宗十七年四月五日)

近藤眞鋤를 통한 Shufeldt의 교섭 보고

東萊府使沈東臣狀啓
洋夷所騎異樣船一隻下碇黑岩前洋緣由已爲馳啓爲白有在果異船哨探尤當審愼乙仍于卽令臣府軍校等連加偵探另飭譯學詳探事情是白乎加尼本月二十七日巳時留館領事倭近藤眞鋤率從倭五名等來抵本府故問其事由則同領事倭言內黑岩前洋下碇異樣船一隻亞米利加國之船該國人欲爲通知於貴國裁書以來而弊邦與貴國交鄰厥惟久矣要我以先往萊府詳告事由呈納書契云故俺等不得已有此來告先自本府接見該國人捧納其所齎書契轉達于貴朝廷俾爲兩國通好亦云故答以爲我國之於亞米利加國聲氣不通風馬不及則渠所云通和修書以來者萬不近理況日本人亦知其洋夷之在我遇輒剿滅而今以該國通和等說如是來懇者有欠交鄰厚誼更勿煩聒亦云則同倭言內今來亞米利加國之船卽南方之人也與西洋所屬諸國自有別焉故專爲兩國好有此告達是如故更答以爲凡於外國人之來泊我境者不接面不捧書已有我朝廷命令同書契不當捧納矣卽自館中飭諭於該國人處卽速回棹亦云則同倭旣知事體之所在似無強聒底意故優備酒饌依前饋給後申時還入館所爲白乎旀二十八日辰時到付釜山僉使任衡準馳通內黑岩前洋下碇異樣船一隻無弊經夜云云

J. A. Bingham (1880. 5. 21) ➡ 井上馨

Shufeldt 서한 재전달 협조 요청

United States Legation
Tokei 21 May 1880
His Excellency
Inouye Kaoru
H.I.J.M. Minister for J.A.

Sir,

  Referring to the conversation had on yesterday between Your Excellency, Commodore Shufeldt, and myself in relation to the Commodore's request of a letter from you covering his letter to the Government of Corea I again beg leave to call Y.E. attention to the fact of which I had the honor to acquaint you in my No. 1179 that I am instructed by my government to ask the good officers of H. I. J. Majesty's Gov. by personal or official letters to the Gov. of Corea to aid Commodore Shufeldt in transmitting a friendly communication in writing to that governor. Y.E. already knows that Commodore Shufeldt is possessed of a letter addressed to him some years ago by order of the King of Corea in which the Corean Prime Minister among other things expressly says that the written communication which Com. Shufeldt had at that time addressed to the King was improperly delayed by the lead Corean Magistrate for which neglect of duty that official [_____] thereby showing that it was the wish of HM the King of Corea, as it was HM's duty to receive the friendly communication of Com. Shufeldt which was wrongfully delayed by the lead magistrate until the Corea was constrained by the severity of the weather and the demands of duty elsewhere to quit Corea. Now Commodore Shufeldt upon his return to Corea by order of Gov. simply requests that Y.E. will be pleased to address a letter to the official of Corea, at the Capital of that Kingdom and enclose therein his friendly communication to the Corean Gov. to the end that its transmission may not be delayed. By this kind act neither Y.E. nor H.I.J.M's Gov incurs any responsibility whatever either present or future and allow me to add will thereby give another assurance of good-will towards the U.S. which will be appreciated. My Gov. confidently expects Y.E. to comply with this request asking only what it would cheerfully and promptly do for Japan if such a request should be made of the U.S. by Y.E. government. I pray Y.E. to acquaint me at the earliest possible day of your decision in relation to this request as the Com. desires to avoid unnecessary delay. Again expressing a hope that this favor of a letter from Y.E. covering that of Com. Shufeldt's which will arise its immediate transmission to the Government of Corea and not doubting that Y.E. will be pleased to do this act of kindness for my government, I beg leave to renew to Y.E. the assurance of my highest consideration.

　　John A. Bingham
　　N.S.E.E.J.M.P.

【日譯文】

第一千二百二十一號

昨日「コモドール、シュフエルド」同道ニテ閣下ヘ御面晤之節右「コモドール」ヨリ朝鮮政府宛之書簡閣下御添書ヘ御封入相成度旨同官ヨリ御依賴之儀ハ兼テ第一千百七十九號拙簡ヲ以テ申進置候貴政府之御紹介ヲ以テ我政府ヨリ朝鮮政府ヘ和親書寄贈之儀ニ付「コモドール、シュフエルド」御援助相成候樣貴政府ヘ御依賴可申旨我政府ヨリ訓示有之候儀ニテ且閣下御承知之通先般朝鮮國皇帝陛下ヨリ「コモドール、シュフエルド」宛之書翰ハ同官所持罷在候其書翰中特ニ朝鮮大臣ハ當時「コモドール、シュフエルド」ヨリ該國皇帝陛下ヘ呈シタル書簡ハ朝鮮地方官ニ於テ進達方不當之遷延ニ及ヒ其失錯ニ依リ該官ハ處罰ヲ蒙リタル旨ノ明文有之候左候得ハ朝鮮國皇帝陛下ニ於テハ「コモドール、シュフエルド」ヨリ差出シタル和親信書ハ陛下ノ義務トシテ受領セラレ度思召ニ有之候處地方官ノ過失ニ依リ遲延ノ内ニ天氣惡シク旁他ニ公務モ有之候ニ付無餘儀右「コモドール」ハ出帆ニ立至候儀ト相見候扨今般同官我政府之命ニ依リ朝鮮ヘ再航ニ付テハ單ニ閣下ヘ御依賴ニ及ヒ朝鮮國首府ニ在ル該國官吏宛之御書翰中ヘ右「コモドール」ヨリ該政府宛之和親信書（昨日閣下ヘ讀上候）御封入相成無遲滯贈呈相成候樣致度儀ニ御坐候尤右御懇切之御取計有之候儀ニ付テハ現時將來共閣下又ハ貴政府ヘ決テ御迷惑相懸間敷且右ハ我政府ヘ對シ一際貴政府御厚意之證憑トモ相成候儀ニ有之候將又右御依賴之儀速ニ御承諾相成候上ハ他日貴政府ヨリ我政府ヘ御依賴之儀有之候節ハ我政府ニ於テモ亦同樣早速貴國之爲メニ盡力可致候「コモドール、シュフエルド」ニ於テハ無益之時日ヲ不費候樣致度儀ニ付可成丈速ニ右御依賴御許否之御決答有之度候呉々モ右「コモドール」之書簡御封入之御書翰御投與相成速ニ朝鮮政府ヘ相達候樣致度此段偏ニ御依賴申進候敬具

一千八白八十年五月廿一日 ジョン・エ・ビンハム
日本帝國外務卿 井上馨 閣下

井上馨(1880. 5. 24) ➜ 三條實美

Shufeldt의 서한 전달 요청에 관한 청훈

甲第百三十號

米國軍艦チコンヂラゴ號ヲ指揮スルコモドール、シユフエルト氏同國政府ヨリ朝鮮國政府ヘ親睦ノ使命ヲ奉シ同國ヘ渡航候ニ付同國官吏ヘノ紹介狀申受度旨同國公使ヨリ千八百八十年三月十二日附ヲ以テ別紙甲號ノ通申出候處同國官吏ヘ紹介ノ義ハ彼レノ求ニ應シ難キ旨別紙乙號ノ通斷リ及置近藤領事ヘ先別紙丙號ノ通リ申遣シ置申候然ルニ五月四日右コモドール、シユフエルト氏朝鮮國釜山港ヘ渡航シ該コモドールヨリ朝鮮政府ヘ宛タル書簡屆方在釜山我國領事近藤眞鋤ヘ依賴シ同領事ヲ經由シ東萊府伯ヘ轉達候得共之ヲ不受取其儘差戻シ候旨ニテ尚今般右コモドール朝鮮國ヘ再航致シ候ニ付テハ同官ヨリ朝鮮國政府ヘ寄贈スル書簡ニ拙官ヨリ同國政府ヘノ書簡ヲ付添シ彼ノ書簡ヲ封入致シ同國政府ヘ屆方依賴ノ儀ニ付米國公使ヨリ面談ノ上尚別紙丁號ノ通リ申越候ニ付勘考候處右コモドールヨリ朝鮮國政府宛ノ書簡ノ主義ハ米國政府ヨリ朝鮮政府ヘ對シ和親ノ意ヲ表候迄ノ事ニ止マリ候樣相見ヘ且同國公使ノ來簡中ニ該書屆方取計候ニ付テハ現時將來共我政府ヘ迷惑相掛ケ間敷ト有之右樣同國公使ヨリ再應請求申出候ヲ謝絶致シ候ハ同國政府ヘ對シ交際上穩當ナラサル所モ可有之哉ニ付同國公使ノ依賴ニ應シ朝鮮政府ヘ添書致シ候方ニ可有之ト存候得共一應相伺候間速カニ何分ノ御指令相成度此段上申候也

　　　十三年五月二十四日

　　　　　　　　　　　　　　　　　　　　　　外務卿　井上馨

　　　太政大臣　三條實美殿

(朱書)「伺ノ通
　　　　明治十三年五月二十五日」
(貼紙)

本文別紙甲號ハ最初ニアリ即チ米國公使ヨリノ來翰、乙號ハ第十四號四月七月附同公使ヘノ往翰、丙號ハ無號四月二十日付同ク往書附屬ノ別紙ニシテ丁號ハ千二百二十一號五月二十一日付同公使ヨリノ來書ヲ添タルモノニヨリ皆茲ニ略ス

50

井上馨(1880. 5. 24) ➜ J.A. Bingham

서한 전달 협조 요청 수락

千八百八十年五月二十一日附貴簡落手イタシ候陳ハ過日コモドール、シユフェルト氏御一同御面晤之節御陳述相成候趣旨ヲ以テ今般同官ヨリ朝鮮政府ヘ差出可相成書簡ニ拙者ヨリノ書翰相添同國政府ヘ通達方ノ義縷々御依賴ノ趣致領承候右ハ再應御依賴ノ次第モ有之且ツ貴政府ヘ對シ友誼ヲ重シ候處ヨリシテ御所望ニ應シ右「コムモドール」ノ書翰ハ拙官ヨリ朝鮮國政府ヘ宛タル書簡ニ封入シ來ル二十九日午後橫濱開帆ノ郵船便ニテ差立候積リニ付右書簡英文譯御心得迄ニ差進候此段囘答得貴意候敬具

　　　五月二十八日

井上馨(1880. 5. 24) ➡ 近藤眞鋤

Shufeldt 서한의 접수 및 접수 지연 상황에 대한 대처 훈령

明治十三年五月二十九日發遣
釜山領事近藤眞鋤へ別信案 第三號
米國軍艦「タイコンデロガ」釜山浦滯泊中の形勢并に右軍艦及東萊府伯と往復談判之模樣等委細報告書によりて承知致し候右軍艦橫濱へ歸來候後貴下周旋振に付ては滿足之段謝詞有之候然るに右「コムモドール」より朝鮮政府へ可差出書翰は必す平和之手立を以相達候樣致度由にて拙者より朝鮮政府へ勸告之添書を得て再航致度段懇談有之事勢難辭却場合に付承引致候得とも今我添書を得て釜山に再航候ては朝鮮國內人心爲に訝怪を致すを免かれ難く忽ち我貿易上に影響を及し交際上にも不可言之損害を來すへきに付談判之末「タイコンデロガ」は長崎に在て答書の來るを待つへきに約し置且同船は近日中橫濱を辭し長崎に在て本日より六十日間滯泊可致候就ては右期日迄に返書無之時は自然再航可致に付可成長崎にて返書爲受取候樣致し度就ては朝鮮政席より返書御落手の節足下直に開封之上シューフェルト氏當之分有之候はゝ足下より直に長崎縣令を經て同艦え御屆方可有之其寫は本省へ御送達可被成候且亦東萊府使へ書翰屆方御依賴之節米使之書翰封入有無等は御談話無之方可然只我公使花房より同政府え宛有之故彼より尋ね候とも秘密の用向故子細不致承知と應答有之度候尤禮曹判書え宛遣す文は別紙寫之通り足下御心得迄に差進置候尚東萊府伯え御談判之節此封書に付ては我政府に於て至急貴政府より返書を要する事件之由申來り候故飛脚を以其返辭を受取渡し呉候樣日限を約し置無怠御催促有之度尤返翰自然右期日に至るも尙送り來らす候はゝ其何故に遲引するか東萊府使へ催促し其趣長崎より電報にて被申越度候

明治十三年五月二十七日

外務卿

近藤領事殿

尚々本文「チコンデロガ」へ書翰送達方都合の義は長崎縣へも懸合遣し置候也

　　追啓
本文東莱府使へ書翰届方依頼之節米使之書翰封入有無等御談話無之方可然と認たるは其爲め府使にて取次を拒む事ありて到達之遲々せん事を恐るゝか爲めに有之就ては右書翰封入有之段明に告たる方運ひ方よろしかるへき義に候はゝ大意明告相成候も差支無之候

R. W. Shufeldt (1880. 5. 26) ➜ J. A. Bingham

서한 전달 협조에 대한 감사

Sir:

I have the honor to acknowledge the receipt of your communication of May 24th, informing me that you had addressed a note to H.I.J.M.'s Minister for Foreign Affairs. Mr. Inouye on the subject of the proposed letter to the Corean Government, covering my communication to the King of Corea, in accordance with the request made in a personal interview between His Excellency Mr. Inouye, yourself, and myself, and enclosing a copy of your note of 21st inst to H.I.J. Majesty's Minister, the earnest and comprehensive character of which I feel sure to have led to compliance on the part of H.I.J. Majesty's Council of State to the request therein contained.

From a personal interview with you this morning and subsequently with the interpreter at the Foreign Office in Tokio, it is now, I believe, understood both by the Foreign Office and by yourself that my communication to the King of Corea, which has been left in the hands of the Foreign Office, is to be covered by a letter from H.I.J. Majesty's Government, and forwarded by it at the earliest possible moment to the King of Corea, and that the Ticonderoga is transmittal to proceed to Nagasaki and there await a reply, which, as soon as received by the Japanese Authorities in Fusan, is to be forwarded to the Governor of Nagasaki for transmittal to me.

Believing that this course, which has been adopted on the advice of H.I.Majesty's Minister and with your full concurrence, will be best calculated to carry out the order conveyed to me by our Government.

I have the honor to tender my acknowledgments of your very kind and efficient cooperation in the mater. On the arrival of the reply at Nagasaki, I will telegraph you in reference to its character and submit to your judgment any future action which may be contemplated.

I have the honor to enclose a copy of a letter addressed by the Honorable Secretary of State to the Honorable Secretary of the Navy, April 5th ultimo, and received by the last mail.

I have the honor to be your servant.
R. W. Shufeldt

R. W. Shufeldt (1880. 5. 29) ➜ R. W. Thompson

조선 교섭상황 보고 및 무력을 동원한 조약 체결 건의

Sir.

Referring to my despatch to the Department No. 13. dated April 26th, I have now the honor to submit the following in continuation of and pertinent to the subject of Corea.

On the morning of May 4th the Ticonderoga anchored in the harbor of Fusan, (Chosan) Corea, I immediately communicated with Mr.Kondo, Japanese Consul at that port, and delivered to him the letter (copy enclosed in No. 13) addressed him by his Government.

I also handed him my communication to the King of Corea with the request that this might be forwarded to Seoul, the Capital of Corea.

It may be well to state here that the Japanese here had for many years a settlement at Fusan of an extraterritorial character and under the jurisdiction of Consul. Fusan however is a large and commodious bay and has several Corean towns upon its shores.

After the expiration of about 24 hours, Mr.Kondo informed me of the failure of his mission to the Corean Governor of the District at Torai-Fu, who refused to forward my communication from him on the ground that under the treaty between Japan and Corea, the Consul could not address any communication to the Central Government,—his authority being limited to correspondence with the District Governor,—and on the further ground that he, the Governor could (would) not hold intercourse with any foreigners except Japanese.

What transpired while the ships remained at Fusan is substantially told in the accompanying ship translated from a Japanese Newspaper, and evidently composed by same person cognizant of all the facts.

It is enclosed herewith as a part of this despatch. (marked C)

Governed by the peaceful tenor of my orders, and feeling that a collision at this time with the Coreans would render further negotiations impossible, and knowing also that the good offices of Japan … in giving a simple letters to its Consul at Fusan, had not been exhausted or indeed tendered to the extent due to our Government.... I determined to leave for Yokohama with a view to further consultation with our Minister at Tokio.

The Ticonderoga arrived at Yokohama on the 11th inst. after various interviews with our Minister, Mr. Bingham, an H.I.J. Majesty's Minister for Foreign Affairs, and Sunday Correspondence- the desirable result has been obtained of securing a communication from H.I. Japanese Minister to the Government of Corea at the Capital- which covers my letter to the King of Corea. Out of deference to the opinion of the Japanese Government, and with the concurrence of Judge Bingham-and to avoid for the present all pretext of hostility, I have consented to wait for a reply at Nagasaki for a period of sixty years, instead of proceeding again to Fusan or any other port in Corea.

I shall accordingly sail on the 31st inst., via Kobe for Nagasaki and there await the time specified, unless something should be developed in the mean while to suggest another course.

In this connection I have the honor to acknowledge receipt of Department communication of April 26 ultimo and have noted its contents.

The opening of Corea, although at present a matters of litter commercial importance. But it is the only country in the world from which, at the present time, foreigners are excluded.

I am satisfied that European Powers…more particularly Russia, are pretending to effect treaties with it, either by persuasion or by force; any complication especially between Russia and China, would almost compel the former to take possession of some of the Corean ports. China is aware of this and, as I have before written, is urging Corea to make treaties with Western Nations.

The Corean question therefore is one of great interest here in the East, and it would be seen that the prestige which we acquired by the treaty with Japan should be maintained by being also the first to make a treaty with Corea.

It therefore after the present overtures (which are of the most friendly character) are received, that Government should refuse to entertain any proposition. Especially for the protection of shipwrecked mariners and property stranded upon the Corean coast, it will be for the Government of the United States to decide upon the property of using other and perhaps more forcible means.

I think, but do not state it positively that a display of our navel forces in these sea upon the Corean coast would bring about intercourse at least, and perhaps a treaty at all events; the squadron is strong enough to attack and hold any desirable point on the coast.

I have the honor to enclose herewith copy of my letter to the King of Corea, marked "A" with copies of the correspondence in relation to its transmitted to Corean Capital, marked BDFFGHI

I have the honor to be………
R.W. Shufeldt

井上馨(1880. 5) ➡ 尹滋承(1880. 6. 23/高宗十七年五月十六日)

Shufeldt 서한 접수 권고

관련문서 尹滋承의 회신

以書翰致啓上候然レハ此度米國使船チコンデロガト號スルアリ曩ニ釜山浦ニ抵リ我領事近藤眞鋤ヲ經テ東萊府伯ニ由リ書ヲ貴政府ニ呈シ修好事ヲ陳ント欲ス而ルニ府伯接セス徒歸ヲ致セリ是以テ更ニ敝國ニ託シテ此意ヲ貴政府ニ通シ再ヒ釜山ニ航シテ使命ヲ達セント擬ス本大臣窃ニ恐ル米國使船再ヒ釜山ニ航セハ貴國人心爲ニ訝怪センコトヲ於是少クヲ之遲コトヲ勸メリ敝國ノ貴國ニ於ル隣誼特ニ敦シ米國ト通交スル亦既ニ年アルヲ以テ義一言セサルヲ得ス米國使官ハ總兵名ハシュフヘルト丙寅年既ニ貴國ニ航シ書ヲ貴政府ニ呈シ難民ヲ送還スルノ恩ヲ謝シ併テ修好ヲ約センコトヲ請タルニ貴國乃チ好音ヲ以テ之ニ報ラレタリ米國今日ノ求メハ卽チ前年ノ請ヲ申ル所以ニテ他心アルニ非ス另ニ米國使帶ル所ノ一函ヲ呈ス想フニ其情ヲ諒セラルヘシ抑宇內ノ大勢曩昔ト異ナリ鎖國ノ今日ニ行フヘカラサル敝國踏テ之ヲ知ル獨リ敝國ノミニアラス淸國モ亦然リ今貴國ノ爲ニ謀ルニ柔遠ノ心ヲ以テ彼ノ請ヲ聽サレ忠恕以テ之ヲ行ヒ公道以テ之ヲ要ムルニ如カス則チ外侮ヲ禦テ而自主ノ權ヲ固フスル所以ノ者是ニ在ラン若シ不然シテ邊釁ヲ啓クヲ爲サハ則チ其害言フニ勝ヘスシテ大ニ國家ノ福ニ非スト存候敝國固ヨリ貴國ノ政略ニ干涉スル者ニ無之但外交情事閱歷已久シク又近頃諸ヲ淸國徃事ニ徵シテ感ナキ能ハス故ニ敢テ腹心ヲ布ク幸ニ怪マルル勿レ米國使自今六十日長崎港ニ在テ鈞覆ヲ拱候ス貴國素ヨリ禮義ヲ重ンセラル想フニ必ス米國使ニ答ヘラルル所アラン切ニ望ム鈞覆期ニ及ヒ本大臣之ヲ轉致スヘキヲ專ラ泐シテ悃ヲ致シ併テ台祉ヲ頌シ候敬具

明治十三年五月　　　　　　　　　　大日本國外務卿 井上馨（印）

大朝鮮國禮曹判書 閣下

【漢譯文】

庚辰外務卿緩美國船再航釜山附呈該使書函書
逕啓者玆有米國使船號太匡低羅嘉曩抵釜山浦頭經我領事近藤眞鋤由東萊府伯呈書貴政府陳修好事而府伯不接致徒歸是以更托敝國通此意貴政府擬再航于釜山以達使命本大臣竊恐米國使船再航于釜山貴國人心爲訝怪於是乎勸少遲之敝國於貴國鄰誼特敦與米國通交亦旣有年義不得不一言米國使官總兵名蕭孚爾丙寅年旣航于貴國呈書貴政府謝送還難民之恩倂請約修好貴國乃以好音報之矣米國使今日之求卽所以申前年之請而非有他心也另附呈米國使所帶一函想合諒其情矣抑宇內大勢與曩昔異鎖國之不可行于今日敝國踏而知之不獨敝國而已淸國亦然今爲貴國謀不如以柔遠之心聽彼之請忠恕以行之公道以要之則所以禦外侮而固自主之權者於是乎在矣若不然○爲啓邊釁則其害有不勝言大非國家之福敝國固非干涉貴國政略者外交情事閱歷已久又近懲諸淸國往事不能無感故敢布腹心幸勿見怪米國使自今六十日在長崎港拱候鈞覆貴國素重禮義想必有所答於米國使切望鈞覆及期本大臣應轉致之也專泐致悃幷頌台祉敬具 明治十三年五月大日本國外務卿井上馨 大朝鮮國禮曹判書閣下
米國使所帶一函月日係送在釜山所署致有遲四十二日之言爲期旣太迫故勸改之六十日間在長崎港待之云是以本函更日候覆六十日又幸勿見怪

【관련문서】

答書
謹玆照覆者敝邦素以自守不與外國交接貴國所洞悉疇曩萊府伯之不受米國書函在守臣重邊圉文義不得不退却者也今焉貴函鼎至辭意勤摯敷示腹心實庸感篆第當稟報我政府圖所以受納幸以此意轉及米國使船恐好且米使之四十二日爲期者貴下特念敝邦事勢寬之以六十日亦出於鄰好之誼銘謝無已統希照亮不戩故具

花房義質(1880. 5. 29) ➡ 尹滋承(1880. 6. 23/高宗十七年五月十六日)

Shufeldt 서한 접수 촉구

관련문서 尹滋承의 회신

以書簡致啓上候然ハ米國使員玆ニ再航セント擬シタルヲ少ク遲シメ候ハ外務卿先ツ書ヲ貴政府ニ致シ滋端ニ涉ルナクシテ使命ヲ達セシメントスルヨリ他ナク候蓋前ニ旣ニ一タヒ徒ニ歸ルヲ致セリ之ヲ再スル將可ナラン乎一再遲回シテ已ム無ク敝國居間停調セント欲スト雖トモ亦得ヘカラサルニ至ラハ恐クハ我兩國ノ福ニ非ルナリ切ニ望ム外務卿及米國使員ニ致サルヘキノ鈞覆其迅速ナランコトヲ事迫リ親晤傾誠ニ由ナク膽企ノ至ニ任ルナシ併テ台祉萬福ヲ祈候敬具

明治十三年五月廿九日　　　　　　　大日本國辨理公使 花房義質（印）
大朝鮮國禮曹判書 閣下

【漢譯文】

辨理公使求不令美使再次徒歸書
逕啓者 米國使員玆擬再航 然今俾之少遲者無他 外務卿先致書於貴政府 圖無涉滋端 以達使命也 蓋前者旣一致徒歸 再之將可乎 一再遲回無已 至敝國雖欲居間停調 亦不可得 則恐非我兩國之福也 切望可見致我外務卿及米國使員之鈞覆其迅速 事迫無由親晤傾誠 不任膽企之至 倂祈台祉萬福 敬具 明治十三年五月廿九日 大日本國辨理公使花房義質 大朝鮮國禮曹判書閣下

【관련문서】

答書
照覆者米國使船書函今承頻示兼因外務卿書詳悉辭意而今方稟報我政府圖所以受納有此仰覆想應照管也第向日萊府之不受此係守臣重邊圉之政勿致疑訝
敬具

J. A. Bingham (1880.5.29) ➜ 井上馨

일본의 협조에 대한 감사

一千貳百貳十五號
昨日之御書面幷ニ封中朝鮮政府禮曹判書宛之御書翰寫シ共石橋殿ヨリ致落掌候然ハ合衆國海軍「コモドール、シフエルト」ヨリ朝鮮國王ヘ相呈候書翰本日閣下ヨリ御遞送可被下旨御通知被下致承知候貴國政府合衆國政府ニ對シテ御厚情之段拙者ニ於テ不堪感謝候我政府ニ於テモ深ク閣下ノ御周旋ヲ感佩致候儀必然ニ御座候隨テ閣下ノ御周旋ニ由リ拙者ノ致冀望候如ク合衆國ト朝鮮トノ間ニ修好通商約定ヲ取結フベキ好結果ヲ得ルニ立至候ハ、其約定ニ依リ大ニ日本朝鮮兩國ノ利益ト可相成儀有之候事ト存候敬具

一千八百八十年五月二十九日

　　　　　　　　　　　　　　　　合衆國公使館ニ於テ
　　　　　　　　　　　　　　　ジョン、エー、ビンハム

外務卿　井上馨殿閣下

何如璋 ➡ 總署(1880. 6. 7/光緒六年四月三十日)

Shufeldt의 서한 전달 시도 보고

四月三十日 日本大臣何如璋函稱 三月二十六日肅呈第八十三號緘 當邀垂鑒 本月初四日奉到堂憲三月十一日所發第四十一鈞諭 敬謹捧讀 祗悉一切 竹添進一旣於我三月二十九日回到東京 有與同舟者 據所自述稱 在京住了七八日 今讀來諭 知其並未進謁 諒彼知議論不合 故不敢來 抑或與宍戶公使尙有別商之語 亦未可知 竹添之言與外務卿所云 如出一口 而宍戶公使口氣又自不同 然宍戶所云云 類皆游移閃鑠 了無歸宿 來示謂目前惟有急脈緩受 旣行文詢其派員姓名 且看其如何答覆 再作道理 至此間派員一事 查無聞見 卽此案如何 亦無人議及 想當一味延宕矣 彼族近情如常 前函所述愛國社之片岡健吉 聯合九萬餘人之名 上書請開國會 初上之太政官 後上之元老院 後復上太政官 挨延幾一月 卒却而不受 民情甚爲不願 然亦未聞有他 又前前函所述美國兵船往朝鮮議約一事 昨據長崎理事余瓗鈔到其上朝鮮國王書 辭氣和平 當不至於激變 今謹鈔錄 呈請鈞鑒 此船聞於前數日由高麗來橫濱 聞旣上書 隨後再往商議也 日本所派花房公使未往 聞朝鮮特派使來 在此議一切 大意請日本政府謂通商宜緩辦 不宜驟進 致激生別釁云 俟其到來 再以續陳 俄約想須俟曾襲侯到後 方有端倪 新聞慮其拒絶不接 聞之西使 皆謂必無此事 又新聞紙稱俄國兵船在中國海者甚多 慮其乘我不備 倉卒開釁 似亦爲近來盟約之國所無 惟暫時曾襲侯方在啓程 新疆一帶兩軍相望 亟應嚴飭士卒毋許滋事 以貽口實 乃爲穩著耳 餘俟續陳 專此敬乞代回堂憲察核訓示 敬請勛安

何如璋 ➡ 總署(1880. 6. 11/光緒六年五月四日)

Shufeldt의 서한 전달 실패 보고

五月初四日 出使日本國大臣何如璋等函稱 敬啓者 本月初十日肅呈第八十四號緘 並附鈔美國兵船上朝鮮王書 當邀垂鑒 美國兵船現泊橫濱 聞將再往 此間見釜山來報云 五月十四日 我四月初六日 美國兵船入釜山港 託日本領事近藤眞鋤爲紹介 近藤訪東萊府伯 告之 府伯變色曰 美國船前於江華灣曾被我民焚燬 恐爲我仇 雖由日本關說 亦難從命 近藤告之總兵官 總兵官曰 事雖未成 得少知韓地情形 亦君之力 當回寓日本 請本國之命 逗留七日而去 如璋聞美總兵官私以告人 則謂日本不願朝鮮與他國通商 不肯爲周旋云 又傳聞俄國欲與朝鮮通商 在咸鏡道開口 經已派使前往 方在議論間 未知果否 朝鮮所派使係工曹參議名金廣集 將於西歷六月初三日 我四月二十六日 自釜山啓行前來日本 將俟其到來 詳詢一切 再以佈陳 查釜山一口 西歷去年之六月至十二月 半年中凡進口貨值三十一萬餘 出口貨値三十四萬餘 出口多於進口 値三萬餘 而進口貨中之日本只有三萬一千餘 洋貨乃値二十八萬二千餘 是日本與朝鮮通商未見有利也 琉球一案派員之事 此間並無所聞 肅此佈臆 敬乞代回堂憲察核 敬請勛安

專啓者 此間經費 去歲所撥之件現已告罄 曾承鈞諭 於本年三月間與各國出使經費一件撥給 現在尙未奉到 敬求飭催江海關道作速撥寄 以濟要需 是所至禱 乞代回堂憲 再請勛安

近藤眞鋤(1880.7.31) ➡ 井上馨

Shufeldt 서한 관련 예조판서 답신 송부

十三年機密信第十二號
本月二十一日付機密信第拾壹號ヲ以具狀仕置候通同日米國書契ノ義ニ對ス
ル禮曹判書ヨリノ返翰到達致候得共遞送ノ郵船無之候ニ付商船便ヲ以テ馬
關ヨリ電報ニテ御通知申上且ツ郵便ヨリ委細具狀仕置候付敏ク御承達相成
候儀ト遙察仕候則チ今便ヲ以右返翰送呈仕候條御領收相成度候且亦下官領
事被任候付花房辨理公使ヨリノ書契ニ對スル返翰亦去ル二十九日到達ニ付
併テ御送致仕候此段上申候也

　　　　明治十三年七月三十一日

　　　　　　　　　　　　　　　　　　　　在釜山港
　　　　　　　　　　　　　　　　　　　　領事 近藤真鋤 (印)

　　　外務卿 井上馨殿

　　目錄
　外務卿ニ宛ル禮曹書簡　　　　　一通
　辨理公使ニ宛ル同書簡　　　　　一通
　米國書簡　　　　　　　　　　　一封
　橫文　　　　　　　　　　　　　一通
　　　右爲一包

　代理公使ニ宛ル禮曹書簡　　　　一通
　別封
　　　右爲一包

追テ右書契ハ大ナル黑塗箱ニ入有之候得トモ嵩ニテ郵便ノ扱ニ相成兼候ニ
付箱ハ留置候間此段爲念申上置候也

上野景範(1880. 8. 4) ➜ J. A. Bingham

Shufeldt 서한의 전달 경과 및 답신 통보

外務卿代理
上野 外務大輔

　　米國公使宛

以書翰致啓上候陳ハ千八百八十年五月二十一日附貴簡ニ對シ同月二十八日付書翰ヲ以テ及御廻答置候通リコモドル、シユウフェルド氏ヨリ朝鮮政府宛ノ和親信書ヲ外務卿ヨリ同國首府ニ在ル彼國政府禮曹判書宛ノ書信中ニ封入五月二十九日發郵船ニ托シ逓送致置候處右ニ對スル返簡中ニ前述コモドルヨリノ信書其儘封入七月二十一日釜山港我國領事近藤眞鋤迄達來候此返簡ニ付テハ先ニ閣下ノ御依賴モ有之開封ノ儀兼テ下命致シ置候間則同人ニテ開封シ不取敢定規外ノ商船便ヲ以テ其寫送リ來候尤原書并ニ前述コモドールヨリノ書簡ハ次ノ公便ヲ以テ送リ越スベキ旨申越候間該返翰寫并ニ飜譯相添此段及御通知候右得貴意候敬具

61

J. A. Bingham (1880. 8. 6) ➜ R. W. Shufeldt

조선의 서한 접수 거부 사유 통보

관련문서 조선 예조판서 회신의 영역문

Sir:

Herewith I have the honor to enclose a copy of a letter from His Excellency Mr. Wooyeno, the Japanese Acting Minister of Foreigner Affairs, and also a copy of the official translation of the letter of the Corean Minister of Ceremony to Mr. Inouye in relation to your letter to the King of Corea.

It is to be regretted that the Corean Minister refused to receive and has returned your communication made on behalf of the United States. You will observe that among other reasons given by him for rejecting your letter is that it was addressed directly to the King of Corea, instead of being addressed to the Minister of Ceremony of "Great Chosen", you will also observe in this communication, the following words: "If he (you) should wish to send any communication, he (you) might better address it to a local officer or to the Minister of Ceremony".

The Minister of Ceremony requests that Mr. Inouye will "consider the state of affairs" and "do his utmost to arrange it". It is by no means clear that this very unsatisfactory letter to Mr. Inouye gives any assurance that a letter addressed to the Minister of Ceremony would be received and be favorably considered by the Corean Government. In this you can judge-.

Should you conclude to make any further communication to the Corean Government, I shall be pleased to render you further service.

Please advise me of the receipt of this and of any additional action in the premises in which you may desire my cooperation.

I have the honor to be, Sir
John A. Bingham

The 4th, the 8th month, The 13th year Meiji

Wooyeno Kagenori → John A. Bingham

Sir:

With reference to Y.E.'s despatch under date the 21st May addressed to the Minister for Foreign Affairs, to which he replied on the 28th May to the effect that measures had been taken to forward to a letter to the Minister of Ceremony of the Corean Government in the Capital of that country by the mail of the 29th May, enclosing therein a friendly communication from Commodore Shufeldt, U.S.N., to the Corean Government. I have now the honor to acquaint Your Excellency that an answer to the said letter returning Commodore Shufeldt's communication was received by Kondo Masumi, our Consul at the port of Fusan on the 21th July and opened by him in obedience to instructions given at Your Excellency's request.

Our Consul sent a copy of the said reply to me without delay by a merchant ship leaving before the regular mail, and he writes that the original and the letter of Commodore Shufeldt will be forwarded by the next opportunity.

I beg to enclose herewith a copy of the said reply accompanied by a translation of the same-

I avail myself……
Acting for the Minister for Foreign Affair

【관련문서】

I have the honor to reply to your Excellency and at the same time congratulate you for the enjoyment of good health.

In relation to the letter of the American Mission I am greatly obliged for your great kindness-. It is well known to the world that our foreign relations are only with Japan neighboring to us, which has been maintained for three hundred years, and that other foreign nations are not only situated far from us but there has never been any intercourse with them.

The letter of the American Mission bears the address of "Great Corai", this name of the country was used in the period of the late dynasty. Now the name has been altered. Even if the letter were addressed "Great Chosen", how can I receive and present to my August sovereign the letter which has been addressed directly to His Majesty? If he should wish to send any communication, he might better address it to a local officer or to the Minister of Ceremony.

Upon deliberation of the matter I cannot receive the American Minister's letter. I therefore return the same herewith requesting you to explain the reason to the American Mission.

I am greatly obliged to you for having prolonged the term of 42 days to todays, of which many days have already elapsed. I respectfully request you will consider the state of affairs and do your utmost to arrange it.

I avail myself of this occasion to renew to Y.E. the assurance of my highest consideration.

Signed In-Jisho (Seal)
Minister of Ceremony of Great Chosen

R. W. Shufeldt (1880. 8. 10) ➡ R. W. Thompson
조선의 서한 접수 여부에 따른 대처 계획

Sir:

Referring to my despatch to the Department No. 15. dated May 29 last, I have the honor to transmit the copy of a communication from the Hon. John A. Bingham, U.S. Minister to Japan, with the copy of a letter dated June 10th from Mr. Kondo, the Japanese Consul at Fusan, Corea, in relation to the transmission of my communication to the Corean Government.

By these enclosures it will be seen that my communication has been received by the first Corean Authority-the Governor of Torai-Fu who promised to transmit it to Seoul, the Capital—it will be seen also that Mr. Kondo confidently expects a reply will be received within the specified time. The letter reached Fusan on the 10th of June, and the 40days promised therein expire today, but the steamer by which the reply may be received has not yet arrived at Nagasaki.

In view of these circumstances and governed by the Department's cable despatch, the following considerations occur to me for my guidance in the future.

1st, the probability of receiving a favorable answer from the Government of Corea, in which case I should proceed to Fusan to arrange at least the preliminaries for further negotiations.

2nd, the probability of receiving an unfortunate communication, in which event I shall consider it my duty under my present instructions to return to the United States with the object unaccomplished.

3rd, the probability of receiving no answer to the communication addressed to the Government of Corea, from whatever cause; such a contingency involves in it the question how long it would be considered proper to wait beyond the time specified. As we are now in the middle of the "Typhoon Season", I consider that no great delay would occur by the sailing of the ship for San Francisco about the middle of September or the 1st of October. This would give to the Government of Corea as well as to the Government of Japan every reasonable opportunity for the former to reply to the Communication and for the letter to exhaust its friendly offices in that direction. Any order to the contrary received by cable from the Department will of course, be strictly observed.

It may be as well to state that since the visit of the Ticonderoga to Fusan, Vice Admiral Coote, Commanding the British Naval forces in China, has personally visited that port on His Majesty's ship "Vigilant" and has also despatched His Majesty's Corvette "Pegasus" for a cruise in Corean Waters. I have also reason to believe that the French gun boat "Lynx" has visited Fusan, and perhaps other ports in Corea, and at the present time the Italian Corvette "Vittor Pesani" under command of H.R.H. the Duke of Genoa is cruising in the Corean Waters.

I mention these facts to show that the "Ticonderoga in inaugurating this work" has excited much interest among the European Powers whose navies are stationed in the East.

The health of the officers and men of the ship remains good and the ship herself is in good condition for service. I have the honor……

R. W. Shufeldt (1880. 8. 17) ➜ R. W. Thompson

조선의 서한 접수 거부 보고

Sir:

I have the honor to enclose a copy of the communication from the Hon. John A. Bingham, U.S.Minister to Japan, with the copy of a letter from His Excellency Mr. Wooyeno, Acting Japanese Minister for Foreign Affairs; also a copy of the official translation of a letter from the Corean Minister of Ceremony and a copy of my reply to Mr. Bingham.

While I consider that the Corean that the Corean matter is not entirely concluded, I think that I am authorized to predict an unfavorable result—without some exhibition of force upon the Corean Coast it will be difficult to convince that Government of earnestness of purpose, secluded as it has been for so many countries from contact with the outside world.—

A movement, however, has been inaugurated by the Ticonderoga which in all probability will not stop until Corea is open to commerce and foreigners permitted to visit its shores under treaty protection.

The ship's movements after the full completion of this work and her return to the United States have been heretofore fully reported to the Department.

I have the honor to be very respectfully.

64

R. W. Shufeldt (1880. 8. 17) ➡ J. A. Bingham

일본 외무당국의 서한 전달 상의 실책 비난

관련문서 Bingham의 회신

Sir:

I have the honor to acknowledge the receipt of your communication of 6th inst, enclosing copy of a letter form His Excellency, Mr. Wooyeno, the Japanese Acting Minister for Foreign Affairs and also a copy of the official translation of the letter of Corean Minister of Ceremony to H.E. Mr. Inouye in relation to my letter to the King of Corea.

Considering these despatches I have the honor to submit to you that following points:

First—that the reply of the Minister of Ceremony to the Minister of Foreign Affairs for Japan is evasive, because my communication itself contains the evidence that on a previous occasion a letter addressed to the King of Corea was answered by the Minister for Foreign Affairs of that country.

Second—that it is proper to address the highest authority of a country particularly when the organization of its Government is, as in Corea, not thoroughly understood, while it would be equally proper to receive answer to such communication from the duly constituted Ministers.

Third—the change of name from "Great Corea" to "Great Chosen", if of importance, should have been mentioned to me by H.E. the Minister for Foreign Affairs at Tokio when the document in question was handed to him transmission.

If you consider these points well taken, I respectfully submit to your judgment; 1st that the Japanese officials in Corea should not have received back the communication to the King, and 2nd that it is due to the dignity and self-respect of the Japanese Government that said communication should be returned to the Government of Corea to be properly answered. This could be done in accordance with the request of the Minister of Ceremony to H.E. Mr. Inouye to "consider the state of affairs and do his utmost to arrange it".

But I have the honor to inform you that by a cable despatch received July 1st ult. I was directed by the Honorable Secretary of Navy to use only persuasive means with Coreans and avoid hostilities-. In consequence of this order I consider myself compelled to avoid visiting Corea again in the Ticonderoga from the apprehension that by some unforeseen event hostilities might ensue, at the same time I am freed from any obligation to remain any longer in Nagasaki.

I have also the honor to inform you that I have received an official invitation, but confidential, from His Excellency Li Hung-chang, Minister for Foreign Affairs in China, to visit him at Tientsin—.

I deem it for the best interests of our country to comply with this invitation and consequently shall leave for Chefoo on Thursday next 19th, inst, returning in a few weeks either to Kobe or Nagasaki on route to the United States, at either of which ports I will on arrival communicate with you by telegraph, trusting that in the meanwhile you will submit to the Government of Japan such portion of this despatch as you may consider conducive to the public interest.

My visit to China may, and I hope will, have the effect of inducing that Government to use its influence in the opening of Corea.

But under my orders, without any further development, I shall consider my mission ended and will return to the United States in obedience to the same.

Any future action in this matter on the part of Japan, after my departure for the United States, might be submitted directly to the Government at Washington.

Thanking you sincerely Sir for your very cordial and hearty cooperation, and for the interest manifested by you from the beginning in this matter.

I have the honor to be with the highest regard your obedient servant

---

【관련문서】

Sir:

I have the honor to acknowledge your telegram of this morning and have answered the same, that I will communicate by tomorrow's mail.

I have carefully considered the news expressed in your letter to me of the 17th ultimo, and beg leave to say that I am in perfect accord with the same. It is true, and "pity tie is true", that the Corean Minister of Ceremony has made an evasive reply to this Government as to the address of your letter to the King of Corea. Man had good precedent, as you say very truly, in that you had addressed His Majesty before on behalf of you Government, and your letter was received and answered, as it should have been in this instance. Do not infer that because I especially note only this answer made in your letter, that I mean to question your other replies to the evasive statements of the Minister of Ceremony. As I have said, your letter in its entirety commands my approval.

I shall fully acquaint this Government of its contents, and that it is my opinion, as it is yours, that the Japanese officials in Corea shall not have permitted the return hither of your unopened letter to the King of Corea; that this government should return it with a request for a fitting answer thereto, and that, as the Minister of Ceremony of the King of Corea has been pleased to ask His Excellency Mr. Inouye "to do his utmost to arrange it" viz; the blunder of the Minister of Ceremony. This Government should respect its request that the letter be transmitted to the King of Corea, with a regard that such answer be returned, through the Government, as it will be fitting for the King of Korea to make and for the Government of His Imperial Japanese Majesty to receive and to transmit to that of the United States.

I shall bring this matter to Mr.Inouye's attention, if possible by tomorrow. Of course, some time will be need for consultation and consideration by His Excellency. I regret to have you return home without first exhausting all proper means to bring the Corean Minister of Ceremony to a right understanding of his duty to his own Government and to ours.

Should you deem it your duty to leave under your orders, I shall follow my further action in the premises and results thereof to the State Department directly.

I shall regret if you go away without my having again the pleasure of meeting you. Now I am on an honorable and praiseworthy mission, you have taken the initiative for its accomplishment most wisely, and I cannot doubt that, sooner or later, your wishes and the wishes of our Government toward Corea will, without violence, be realized.

With sincere respect.

John A. Bingham

J. A. Bingham (1880. 9. 11) ➡ 井上馨

일본공사를 통한 Shufeldt 서한의 전달 의뢰

第千三百二十六號
拜啓陳者去月十三日附ヲ以テ上野閣下ヨリノ書簡ニ關シ今マ閣下ノ御注意ヲ煩シ候ハ先キニ合衆國海軍「コンモドル、シユフエルド」ヨリ朝鮮國王陛下宛ノ書翰ニ關シ上野君カ云々セシ來意ノ事ニ御坐候該書翰ハ曾テ閣下ノ御周旋ヲ以テ貴翰ト共ニ朝鮮國王陛下ノ禮曹判書迄御傳達被下候儀ニ候而シテ上野君ヨリノ來旨ハ右「コンモドル、シユフエルド」ノ書翰ハ朝鮮國禮曹判書ノ拒ム所ト爲リ朝鮮王陛下ニ之ヲ奏上セス封緘ノ儘返却相成リシトノ趣ニ有之且又閣下ヘ申上度儀ハ去月十三日ニ上野君ヨリ併緘御廻シ下サレタル六月附朝鮮禮曹判書ヨリ閣下ヘ回答ノ寫ヲ過日拙者ヨリ「シユフエルド」氏ヘ送リ遣シ候處今般受領ノ旨申越候事ニ御坐候「コンモドル、シユフエルド」ハ以爲ラク右朝鮮禮曹判書ヨリノ書翰ハ全ク通信ヲ拒避スル迄ノ意ニシテ第一閣下ノ御懇誼ヲ顧ミス且我政府ノ爲メ命令ヲ受ケテ朝鮮王陛下ヘ宛タル「コンモドル、シユフエルド」ノ修交尊敬ナル書翰ヲ斥ソケテ之ヲ朝鮮王陛下ニ奏上セス封緘ノ儘ニ返下スヘキ理由ヲ一モ記載セサルナリト確言致サレ候

拙者ニ於テモ固ヨリ「ヨンモドル、シユフエルド」ト同説ニ有之乃チ是レ我政府ヘ對シ至當ノ儀ト存候夫レ朝鮮禮曹判書ノ回答ヲ拙者ノ看テ之ヲ遁辭ナリト做ス所以ハ他ナシ則チ彼レ云ク此書翰ハ直チニ之ヲ國王陛下ノ名宛ニシテ送達スルヲ得スト而シテ獨リ知ラス千八百六十七年一月二十四日ヲ以テ該「コンモドル」ヨリ直ニ朝鮮王陛下ヘ右同樣ノ書翰ヲ差シ出シタルニ該書翰ハ同陛下ノ欣然領收スル所ト爲リ且其判書ヲ經テ尊敬ナル回答ヲ致セシ事ヲ

又苟モ合衆國ヨリ朝鮮ニ派出スル全權公使タル「コンモドル、シユフエルド」ヨリ朝鮮王陛下ニ贈ル所ノ修交書翰ニシテ且ツ日本皇帝陛下ノ外務卿タル性質ヲ以テ閣下ヨリ御傳達下サレタルモノナレハ彼レ必ス應ニ之ヲ朝鮮王陛下ニ奏上シ王ハ之レヲ領收シテ慇懃ノ回答ヲ我レニ報スヘキハ亦是レ日本皇帝陛下ニ對シ至當ノ禮ナランカト奉存候然ルニ「コンモドル、シ

ユフエルド」ノ書翰ヲ其王ニ奏上セス封ノ儘之ヲ返却スルハ是レ朝鮮禮曹判書カ合衆國及日本皇帝陛下ノ兩政府ニ對シテ耻辱ヲ與ヘタルモノニ有之候然リ在釜山ノ日本領事ニ於テモ若シ預シメ朝鮮禮曹判書ヨリノ回答ヲ充分ニ理解シタルナラハ則チ此ノ如キ貴我兩政府ニ對シテ不敬ナル回答ヲ決シテ受領傳達セサルヘキハ拙者毫モ疑ハサル所也

抑モ「コンモドル、シユフエルド」ノ尊敬ナル書翰ヲ朝鮮王陛下ニ奏上スルナク其封ノ儘返却セラルヽ事ハ該判書ニ於テモ其非ナルヲ悟リ即チ其日本外務卿并ニ米國政府ニ對シテ故ナク耻辱ヲ蒙ラシムル事ナルヲ識ルモノヽ如シ故ニ朝鮮禮曹判書ハ閣下ニ乞フテ曰ク曲ニ諒事勢另ニ爲周章焉云々アリ是レ果シテ何等ノ言ソ拙者ハ則チ以爲ラク彼ノ事勢云々ノ語ハ今日ノ場合ニ於テ別ニ用フル所ナク唯タ其整理スヘキ事件ハ乃チ是レ閣下及ヒ「コンモドル、シユフエルド」ノ依頼ヲ拒ミ朝鮮國ニ通信ヲ委任ヲ受ケ政府ノ使命ヲ帶ヒタル米國特派全權大臣ノ書翰ヲ朝鮮王陛下ニ奏呈セサルカ如キ彼ノ禮曹判書ノ粗暴ナル舉動コソ爭テカ之ヲ整理セスシテ放過ス可シヤ

就テハ朝鮮禮曹判書カ貴政府及我政府ノ依頼ヲ拒絶シテ大誤見ヲ犯シタル事ハ閣下モ拙者ト御同説ナルヘシト存候條何卒「コンモドル、シユフエルド」ノ書翰ヲ今一應其封緘ノ儘ニテ在朝鮮日本公使ヨリ朝鮮王陛下ヘ御差シ遣シ被下度且ツ適當ナル回答ヲ得テ閣下ヨリ合衆國政府ヘ御傳送被下度此段及御依頼候

今回ノ事件タルヤ特ニ現時ノ形勢ニ於テハ朝鮮國ノ爲メニ謀ルニ夫ノ米合衆國政府ノ如キ外國ト修交條約ヲ締結スルハ其義務ニシテ且利益アル事疑ヒナク候合衆國政府ハ未タ嘗テ他邦ニ對シ正義至當ナル要求ノ外更ニ乞フ所ナキモノニ有之候右得貴意度如此ニ候敬具

東京千八百八十年九月十一日

米國 公使館
ジョン、エ、ビンハム

外務卿 井上馨 閣下

井上馨(1880. 9. 18) ➡ J. A. Bingham

Shafeldt 서한 전달 의뢰에 대한 회신

千八百八十年九月十一日附貴簡致落手候陳者過日御所望に應し貴國海軍コモドール、シユフエルト氏より朝鮮國王陛下宛の書簡に拙者添簡いたし同國政府へ傳達候處右コモドールの書簡同國禮曹判書より同國王陛下へ奏上せす封緘の儘之れを返却相成候は貴國及ひ我政府へ對し不敬の所爲に有之候旨御縷述且つ右コモドールの書簡封緘の儘今一應我公使より同國政府へ差出方等御請求の趣致了承候最初右コモドール、シユフエルト氏の書翰同國政府まで送達方御賴談の際該書簡同國政府に於て受領の有無に不拘兎に角拙者より添書いたし同國政府へ屆呉候樣御申聞の次第も有之候に付則ち該書簡屆方取計候義にて右コモドールの書簡を受領すると否とは同國政府の撰ふ處なれは素より之れを强る譯にも至り兼候義は兼て閣下にも御同意の義と存候将又該書簡返却等の義は同國方今の時勢に就て推量候得は彼に於て貴國に對し强ち不敬の擧動に及ひ候事には無之却て至當の處分を施したる樣自認候義と被考候然るに御來示の如く今一應該書簡を同國政府へ傳達いたし候とも前同樣之れを斥そけて受領せさる時は其結果たるや特に貴政府の不快を增すに過さるのみならす夫か爲め將來我國との交誼上多少障碍に可相成義を釀成候哉も難計其邊深く苦慮いたし候前陳の次第に付右コモドールの書簡再ひ同國政府へ傳達し其に候はゝ在釜山我國領事を以て東萊府使へ傳送する迄の事にして之か返簡を得るの責任無之候はゞ今一應該書簡送達方可爲取計と存候此段囘答得貴意候敬白

井上外務卿

米公使宛

67

R. W. Shufeldt (1880. 10. 13) ▶ R. W. Thompson

주선 과정에서 일본의 불성실한 태도 보고

Sir:

I have the honor to transmit herewith a receipt from Paymaster Thonon on the commercial interests of Corea, with a report from Lieut. Niles, being a brief compilation of its geography and history as far as known- and at the same time to submit some views on Corea, and American interests in the East.

The acquisition of Alaska and the [_____] Islands, the treaties with Japan, the [_____] Islands and [_____] are only [_____] to the proposition that the Pacific Ocean is to become at no distant day the governmental domain of America.

The Atlantic either by force of circumstance or national indifference has been given over to foreign flags, backed by the immense weight of European Capital, but under natural law the flow of commerce—as if emigration—is from the East toward the West and geographical position of the United States in conformity with this law—points to the Pacific Ocean—as the main channel of trade and our country as the source from which the Oriental people must obtain whether they need in the way of commercial exchange-. In all probability within next half century the United States will find its largest market in Asia rather than in Europe.

Thus a treaty with Corea becomes but another link with the chain which binds the East to the West and would give to our country that naval precedence in Corea which is so universally conceded to it in Japan.

But the marauding expeditions of Europeans and Americans for the purpose of ill traffic or the still more contemplate object of robbing royal graves of supposititions golden coffins, added to the (so considered) unprovoked attack of the French Squadron in 1866, and the American Squadron in 1871 have naturally rendered the Government and the people of Corea averse to any foreign intercourse.

Yet in the very logic of events, Corea can no longer remain secluded. Japan has already forced a treaty upon her and Russia is silently preparing to appropriate the Northern Ports, and if any means can now be found to get beyond the "barred gates" and reach the Central Government, I am convinced that Corea would be made to understand not only the policy of a treaty with the United States,—but its absolute necessity as a matter of protection against the aggression of surrounding powers.

Corea would in fact be the battle field of any war between China and Russia or Japan in whichever may these nations might confront each other. But to accomplish this treaty need to same [_____] of purpose that characterized the course of the Commander Perry in Japan. The commissioner must have done outward and visited [_____] of the power of tis government [_____] with oriental and particularly the Coreans who have seen so little of the world, though assorted in the [_____] power. Full language, now fail to convince some those willing to believe, unless they saw indexers of the power of the nation which sought their friendship.

Besides in the intervention between the United States and Corea I am not satisfied that Japan has been acting in perfect faith, it is her policy indeed to monopolize the commerce of Corea.—She possesses in that country extraterritorial rights, and rules the Corean with an iron rod.—Stringing to free herself from the obnoxious away of foreigners upon her own soil,—she is unwilling to have these foreigners—she has imposed these same laws in an aggravated form—upon her defenceless neighbors.

But the [_____] has inaugurated a moment in Corea as the "Columbus" under commander [_____] did in Japan and it only remains for the United States if it really wished to extend its influence in the East to follow up the moment in the one Country with a legation in the command of a distant affair—as it did in the other—controlled and guided so successfully by the fairmness and wisdom of the Great commander Perry—Otherwise we shall bestow upon some other nation the prestige and some which of might belong to oneself. Moreover, it is a duty which we are to these people to become the pioneers of a more enlightened policy in the East. European Power is not employed to "civilize" Orientals, but to subordinate them and to keep them subordinate for the purpose of trade or Proselytism. A distinguished Chinese officer recently said to me "What has European treaties done for China had to fuse upon her opinion and missionaries? The H.S. should take higher grounds and which demanding protection for its citizens should ask for nothing more than he is willing to [_____]. Although as we'll be seen paymaster Thompson report—the foreign goods imported through Japanese lands into Corea as well as there suggested on it northern [_____] from Russian territory are of American main factor yet the consumer is at present unimportant.

The Coreans are a poor people, and the country for the most part rugged and unproductive, a failure of the rice crop invariably creates a famine, its mineral wealth, of which such fabulous stories have been told, is at best Apocryphal. The Corean, therefore have but little to sell and consequently but little to buy with. The account of the French missionaries which are the most authentic, indicate that the people are formed most despotically and that their aversion to [_____] [_____] as much from the fear of their Rulers as from any innate [_____] to have intercourse with them. Judging from the member of Christian [_____] there missionaries are said to have made, the Coreans must be willing to leave. The conclusion has recurred among all class from the coast to the handless pleasant. Indeed it is probably [_____] to the officers zeal of the priests that much of the [_____] of the Corean Government to foreign Government is due. It dreads and perhaps has reason to dread [_____] [_____] [_____] of authority though priestly intrigues with discontented or turbulent subjects. The population of Corea is probably very much exaggerated – the peninsula is not over 600 miles by 300 *** (Sic.) and judging from what I have seen myself and from the account of others, it cannot possibly contain an estimated 15,000,000 of people or even half of that number. Urged by that greed of fain or that desire of [_____] which characterized the career of foreigners in the East. Some pretext has been constantly advanced by (foreigner) them to induce their Governments "to open Corea" as the last remaining "forbidden land"—for the pursuit of trade or Christian propagandism.

The destruction of the American Schooner General Sherman and the massacre of its crew in 1866 was the pretext used by English, and American in China for the forcible entry into Corea, by a naval force of the United States. The attempt, however gallant, was fruitless-expect in embittering Coreans against citizens of the United States and deferring the prospect of a friendly treaty.

Previous, however, in this attack the United States ships Wachusett and Shenandoah had visited the neighborhood of the wreck, and a correspondence had ensured between their commanding officials—, in which the latter stated distinctly that the massacre was brought about by the imprudence and insolence of the people of Schooner-, who were made up of a several nationalities and while the Schooner was ascending the Ping Yang River in defiance of the

Authorities of Corea and was undoubtedly engaged in illegal traffic. The statement seemed to be corroborated by the fact, that during previous year the crew of another American vessel wrecked upon the Corean coast, had been hospitably received and with their effects conducted to the Chinese Boundary, whence they safely reached their own country.

But this explanation although forwarded to Washington, never received any attention, and the Naval Expedition in 1871 under Admiral Rodgers accompanying Mr. Low the American Minister in China-visited Corea, apparently in utter ignorance of its existence. On the other hand the French Naval expedition in 1866 went to that country to demand satisfaction for the murder of French Missionaries, who had clandestine by [_____] it said remained there inspired by the [_____] intention of connecting Corea to Christianity. They suffered the [_____] which they apparently had counted by entering and remaining in a forbidden land.

This Naval Expedition was still more unfortunate than our own in the loss of life without attaining its object. The people and the governors of Corea remember these things to the detriment of future friendly relations with Western Nations- as well as to exult over the fancied defeat of the two powerful naval forces upon their coast. The object of the Ticonderoga was to do away in the first place with this unfavorable reminiscence- and in the second, to endeavor to pave the way to such a treaty as would at least give to the United States the right to protect its citizens and this property if wrecked upon the Corean coast. At present we submit to the humiliation of such protection from the Japanese Government, the only one which thus far has such right under treaty.

The risk of the ship to Corea, however insignificant in its immediate results, has nevertheless attracted the attention of European Government and has been followed by the visits of men-of-war of every nationality represented in Eastern Seas. It may therefore be regarded as "the first step which is difficult" in the attainment of the purpose.

While acceding to the desire and even the right of Corea- to remain secluded from the family of nations- no one I presume will deny to other countries the prerogative as well as the duty of protecting their citizens wherever they may be found.

The Peninsula of Corea just out into the Ocean big array of the world-. Wrecks are likely and indeed often do occur her unknown others. Commerce insists upon the right to travel upon this trick and merchantile world is justified in demanding its protection.

I do not wish to see the United States use coercive measures in Corea or any where in the East. Yet as I have said before, America is the pioneer of the Pacific-a position which she shall not only recognize but claim for this reason-. If for no other, I hope she will not resign her places in Corea to other Powers both willing and anxious to retard her progress or cripple her prestige in the East.

I have the honor- ……
R. W. Shufeldt

(5) 미국과 청국의 교섭

余瓛(1880. 5. 4/光緖六年三月二十六日) ➡ 李鴻章

Shufeldt의 서한 전달 협조 요청

光緖六年三月廿六日稟 北洋大臣李 稟知日本窺伺朝鮮情形並鈔呈美廷遣使致該藩王國書請核籌妥辦由

敬稟者 竊中書自駐長崎開辦以來地方交涉百端 雖屬煩難 然布之以誠心持之以敬愼 近則稟承星使遠亦可仰仗國威 徇分至今視港內情形尚無他虞 惟長崎密邇高麗 自日本在釜山開港後一切布置爲患日深 去歲屢命公使兵船測海趲行直達麗京議增開元山仁津等港 一在咸鏡道一在京畿道 中書迭經備函由江南海關劉道瑞芬處請其迅速報聞諒有轉陳鈞覽 近查此處英美各國領事目擊情形無不妬忌日人爭思染指日人拒之甚堅 以爲中國多事之秋必不能保護高麗彼獨通商希冀爲所欲爲以圖兼併耳 玆於本月初六日忽有美國巡視各口商務之兵船名太匡低羅格 其坐駕者爲水師總兵官係奉美廷之命專赴高麗議約通商 其總兵於十二日偕美國領事官特來拜晤告知將往高麗修好並請借助派員同往之話 中書婉言辭之並飛報電信請欽使吩示遵行在案 今美國總兵業於本月二十五日己刻啓輪前赴高麗 有本港美領事同去並顧一華人能畧識漢洋語言者隨之偕行 中書先於二十三日偕梁繙譯殿勲同往 兵船答拜聞美總兵稱說此次得日本太政官一函札 其釜山領事官就近照應其事或可周全等語 伏查美國前派兵船赴高麗議約者自同治三年以來其濫觴不止一次皆係今總兵蕭孚爾一手經理 此行得成與否尚未可知 然就高麗而論與其專許日本往來墮敗冥昧之中不知兼許各國通商儻能辦理得人或可相維 而相繫應如何立約保護之處亟宜預圖之 祗得將現在美國總兵與中書對答情形另照日記鈔錄一卷 並將該總兵擬呈高麗王國書譯漢文一紙及日本在高麗設警部官又國內添募民兵情形二紙 除稟欽使外理合繕函密陳 伏維察核賜示俾有遵循 再現長崎各國領事官欲與高麗通商者不過日本與稅關相議欲通貨物往來耳 日本尚且不允 惟美國先派總兵作爲欽差大臣欲與之議立條約 英國雖未同謀而東京使館參贊官及駐神戶之英領事各皆留心學習高麗話以待相機而行似可見微知著 順以報聞 肅泐寸稟 處請崇安 伏祈垂鑒

余瓛(1880. 6. 14/光緒六年五月七日) ➡ 李鴻章

Shufeldt의 중국 해군 자문역 추천

光緒六年五月初七日上 北洋大臣夾單

敬再稟者 查美國太匡的羅嘉大兵船自三月二十五日由長崎開行後卽於二十六日抵朝鮮釜山浦 而日本已派一大軍艦名天城者由東京駛赴該埠巡視情形 美兵船旣定泊朝鮮官無往見者 聞總兵自將國書封固託日本領事官代遞東萊守 守卻而不納 美兵船駐候兩日 僅有高麗文士一名偕日本人登舟游玩該高麗人一言不敢自達 惟日本人口吻(sic.)是瞻 美總兵卽於二十八日下午展輪出釜山口徑往橫濱拜見日本外務省卿及美公使至五月初四日復返長崎 初五日美領事官卽來拜晤所言情形大略相同 中書問遲日是否仍要再往 美領事答云此次如何行止已請朝命俟廷寄到來乃定 中書問有何新聞 神戶橫濱各處兵船多否 美領事答曰在橫濱刻下無外國大兵船 惟神戶則有英法兩國水師提督皆前數日由長崎開往者 俄之提督兵船一艘今早與我總兵船同時入港均由橫濱神戶而來 此外尚有英國緊駁數隻而已 美領事又私語曰我近察俄國大添兵船十餘隻不日駛來東洋 其事非在中國卽在高麗雖是否尚難逆料 然海軍設備乃爲長策 我聞中國水師雖則兵船不少然未得一外洋熟識水師眞本領之員輔助貴國水師大臣妥立章程認眞訓練 一旦有事在中國海疆或可庶幾若出外洋遇敵勢必進退兩難是以外國皆藐視之屢屢生事 中國地大人衆財力有餘而竟受此患 今俄又如此人則幸災樂禍我與總兵均歎不平 我總兵蕭孚爾與前統領格蘭脫爲莫逆交自南北花旗之亂總兵歷事戎行以功晉升今職 前時勳業疊見於我國新聞天下共知其人中正和平能知進退 我國特命以出洋辦事之權不久卽擢任提督 今總兵曠觀中外情形深以爲恨且聞前統領格蘭脫言貴國爵相之賢慨然欲假尺寸之階爲中國助其威武如肯信任則楚材晉用 雖與俄國戮力而不辭卽未啓兵端或貴國因俄麗有事要派大員出洋查辦或專任或同任如總兵者眞堪首選 此我之私言也未知貴國領事可以轉稟上游查核否 中書答云用人乃國家大事非我所敢妄言也 然深感貴領事同澤同袍之義似不可以恝然容俟得間當徐圖之 中書伏思察言必先觀人 查美領事孟良在美國爲著名律師然爲人忠厚 前在上海爲副總領事後調任長崎領事迄今已有十三年內外均多推重 去

年美廷因謀保護華人傭工者其大臣特貽書交該領事酌議是否應與各外國工人一體優待保護之處抑或視各外國稍為分別 而該領事尚肯力陳公道極言保護中國工人與待各外國一體無異其用心足見一斑 然則無論如何今其所言亦必出自總兵之意且為我效力起見彼既披心腹向中書言之 中書亦不敢壅於上聞理合附稟瀝陳 伏惟中堂採擇 幸甚 再美總兵蕭孚爾亦來晤談 伊言在神戶與英提督會晤得悉英提督亦聞俄人將謀高麗 提督乘駕大兵船親至釜山省視又派警駁數隻往高麗之元山地方查看提督又披圖指畫 言此次俄人必謀取元山以便兵船往來等語所言亦在意料之中 昨俄提督來本港 雖言尚無欲與高麗通商之事然恐其言未必確真 該提督已經滿任 聞俄國新提督乘駛新式大鐵甲船名美甯者遲數日可以到崎 該提督即要交卸回國 隨後俄國續有兵船十四艘添注來東內仍有三艘亦係大鐵甲特未出歐洲海疆即未知實否 而英廷預備不虞已添派一大鐵甲船駐守香港敢為貴領事言之以觀其後云云 計總兵所言不為無心 至昨日下午俄之新任提督已乘美甯入長崎港 其鐵甲之雄邁尚不如英提督乘駕之挨溫刁克兵船其中如何新式匆猝尚未得見 中書忝駐長崎密邇高麗以上所聞似關於大局輒忘僭越據以報聞 另日高交涉各情載於東京新聞紙者謹抄錄數條一併呈覽 統祈垂鑒 不勝悚惶之至 乾耀再稟

李鴻章(1880. 7. 23) ➡ R. W. Shufeldt

天津 회견 요청

Sir:

I have heard your name for a long time, but I have not yet had the pleasure of seeing you. Mr.Ü,our Consul of Nagasaki, has written me about you. I respect you very much for being a clever and just man and having a good feeling toward China.

I may tell you that the friendly relation between China and the United States has been much strengthened since General Grant came to our country.

Now, I would ask you to come to Tientsin at once in order to let me have a personal meeting with you and talk over matters.

    Your truly
    Li Hung-chang (in Chinese word)

Shufeldt to secretary Navy (received Sept. 10th)
Ticonderoga homeward bound all well

                                        Shufeldt

71

R. W. Shufeldt (1880. 8. 8) ➡ 李鴻章

天津 회견 요청 승낙

Copy of reply to Li Hung Chang's letter.
U.S.Flagship Ticonderoga
Special Service
Nagasaki, Japan
August 8,1880
To His Excellency
Li Hung Chang,
Viceroy of Chin-li,

Dear Sir:

I have the honor to acknowledge the receipt of your friendly letter dated Tientsin, 23rd last, in which you kindly say that you have heard of me before and in which you also express the fact that the friendly relations between China and the United States have been much strengthened by the visit of our renowned Genl Grant, and in which also you kindly ask me to make you a friendly visit to Tientsin for the purpose of discussing matters o f interest both perhaps to ourselves and the countries to which we have the honor to belong.

In reply, while I am highly gratified at this exhibition of kindly feelings toward my country and myself, I can fully understand and appreciate that the visit of Genl Grant to China should have the effect of strengthening the friendship which ought to and does exist between China and the United States.

Referring to your kind invitation to visit Tientsin it gives me great pleasure to say that if my government will permit me, and I shall ask for such permission per telegraph, I will do myself the pleasure of soon calling upon Your Excellency at Tientsin.

If anything should prevent a personal visit I will have the honor to inform Mr. U. Tsing, His Imperial Chinese Majesty's Consul at this port.

Hoping to have the pleasure soon of a personal interview with you.

I am, Sir,

Faithfully and respectfully
Your obedient servant,
(Sgn) R.W. Shufeldt
Commodore U.S. Navy
On Special Service

72

余瓗(1880. 8. 9) ➜ R. W. Shufeldt

天津 초청 서신

Sir:

I have the honor to inform you that I have received a letter dated Tientsin, the 18th day of the 6th moon of the 4th year of Kwang shu (24th July 1880) from His Excellency, Li Hung-chang, Viceroy of Chih-li, and Minister for Foreign Affairs, stating that your honorable name is well known to him and he has always felt a great desire to see you, but he has had as yet no opportunity to gratify his wishes—. He has at present some matters of importance which he desires to discuss with you, and consequently he instruct me to call upon you personally and request that you would be good enough at your earliest convenience to pay him a visit at Tientsin where he will be most happy to meet you.

I hope this will receive your favorable consideration—I also yesterday handed in a letter addressed to you by His Excellency the Viceroy.-

While writing, I take this opportunity of wishing you the blessings of the season.

I have the honor to be sir your most obedient servant.

Ü Tsing, His Imperial Chinese Majesty's Consul.

R. W. Shufeldt (1880. 8. 9) ➡ 余瓛

天津 초청에 대한 회신

Sir:

I have the honor and pleasure to acknowledge the receipt of your letter of this date in which you inform me that you had received a communication from His Excellency, Li Hung-chang, Viceroy of Chih-li, and Minister for Foreign Affairs under date at Tientsin 24th July 1880, in which letter His Excellency has done me the honor to express a desire to have a personal conference with me on some matters of importance and for which purpose His Excellency has invited me, if possible, to a personal interview at Tientsin.

I feel gratified by the confidence which His Excellency has thus placed not only in me but in the country to which I have the honor to belong.

Be pleased to convey to His Excellency my earnest desire to meet him, and to state that as soon as I can, consistent with my duty to my own Government and by its permission, I will do myself the great pleasure of visiting him at Tientsin. At the present moment it would be difficult for me to say at what precise time I will be able to accomplish this purpose, but I trust and believe it will be very soon.

In the meanwhile, Mr. Consul, I desire to thank you for the communication forwarded to me and to express my appreciation to the full extent of the kind wishes, contained therein-

I have the honor……

74

R. W. Shufeldt (1880. 8. 13) ➜ R. W. Thompson

조선문제 협의를 위한 李鴻章 방문 계획 보고

Sir:

I have the honor to inform you that since my letter of 10th inst, the Steamer from Corea has reached this port, via Kobe where she landed the Corean Ambassador to Tokio, and has brought no information in reference to the Corean matter—But in view of the fact that she has returned to Fusan and will be back again in Nagasaki about the 20th inst., I have decided to remain here until her return, although the sixty day specified have expired.

If this coming steamer brings no communication from the Government of Corea, I shall feel myself at liberty to leave Nagasaki, while waiting the proper interval as indicated in my despatch to the Department of the 10th inst (No. 18). I should consider it proper to make a brief visit to the coast of China (Cheefu) believing that the interests of the cruise would be extended thereby—

In this connection I have the honor to enclose a copy of an official letter from the Chinese Consul at this port containing a request from His Excellency Li Hung-chang, Minister for Foreign Affairs, that I should make him a personal visit at Tientsin-. To this official letter is also appended herewith the copy of a private note from the same officer to me.

Both of these letters indicate a friendly feeling on the part of His Excellency-the Foreign Minister, by China toward the people and Government of the United States.

I should feel it somewhat discourteous to entirely neglect such an invitation and have consequently written to the Chinese Consul at Nagasaki a letter, a copy of which is enclosed.

When this letter was written, it was my intention to telegraph the Department, but upon considering not only the expense of such a telegram, but the difficulty of explaining its object without a violation of the confidence evidently implied in the letter of Li Hung-chang, I determined to take the responsibility of making him a visit and informing the Department of the fact by mail.

I feel sure that this visit will have no other than a pleasant effect upon the relations between the two countries, and will in no wise interfere or conflict with either the diplomatic or naval authorities in this part of the world-

I have the honor to be your servant.

余瓛(1880. 8. 16/光緒六年七月十一日) ➜ 李鴻章

Shufeldt의 天津 방문일정 및 자문역 추천

光緒六年七月十一日稟 北洋大臣李

敬稟者 竊照中書於本月初四日肅函稟覆附呈美總兵回書一函幷所著極言西國事端論譯文一本寄由外洋文報處轉遞不日計登鈞覽 去後於初六日美國新授天津領事孟艮來館拜晤言總兵料理一切公務約遲數日中歷七月十四五日可以啓行赴津孟艮亦與同船之任 查蕭總兵不特熟悉水師並嫻於外務美廷曾派充大呂宋總領事所至藉藉有聲此次奉美廷特命由南洋而東洋查辦通商大抵以其人中正和平堪與各國議立條約 前月與中書及高麗事謂固當忍耐俟之不欲急遽致傷兩國之和然中國亦亟宜留意以保護之而勿任人覬覦自棄東三省之屛蔽等語此論何等正大 卽與他國水師提督晤談之際每及朝鮮事宜輒高言宏議亦如項莊舞劍意在沛公此中書所親見者也 觀其胸羅智畧於各國水師情形無不周知而又深惡他國憑凌氣習不欲中國授人以權此金日磾勿使匈奴輕漢之意也 察其言論愛中國之心甚熱顧身荷美廷重任則進退之間頗費躊躇似非出於我朝廷特恩令彼樂效馳驅 告辭本職以竟其用亦未易舍舊而圖新 竊聞之勞於用人逸於任事 伏惟中堂加意垂察 如果堪資臂助應如何敷以心腹策以利權在中堂必能善處之立賢無方以光前業 天下幸甚 肅泐寸稟 處請崇安

李鴻章(1880. 8. 21/光緖六年七月十六日) ➜ 余瓗(1880. 9. 11/光緖六年八月七日)

Shufeldt와의 會見 期待

復駐扎長崎正理事官員外郎銜內閣擬補中書余瓗
光緖六年七月十六日

尊兄中翰閣下
頃接七月初四日惠函 並美國蕭總兵復書譯書院條陳一本 均已聆悉 俄艦續來
長崎一艘 不及米甯之大 西報言俄兵將援阿夫汗 不暇與我啓釁 似未可信 俄
人陰鷙好兵 舉事亦深沈不露 惟貴處恭値萬壽聖誕 設筵慶敍 俄船然炮升旗
該提督佩刀登堂 鞠躬致詞 較平昔敬禮有加 美總兵以此覘中俄大局尚無決裂
之象 或不誣也 閱蕭君答函 詞意殷勤 至其來華之擧 必先發電請示於美廷 足
征行動不苟 其議論指斥招工販煙各條 極爲痛切 可見公憤在天壤心理皆同
中國力能自強而推誠相與 不患無助我之人 美廷本有派蕭君署理東方水師提
督之命 如其接任 與中國重敦睦誼 自必緩急有裨 倘其惠然來晤 再商進止 望
先致鄙忱爲幸 俄兵艦續有見聞 並希隨時馳示 泐復 敬頌台祺 諸惟雅鑒 不具
鴻章頓首

R. W. Shufeldt (1880. 8. 30) ➡ R. W. Thompson

李鴻章과의 회견 보고

Sir:

This interview partook largely of a personal and intimate character and lasted for nearly three hours.—

His Excellency asked me first- if there was anything I desired- I told him in behalf of Government. I desired that China would use her influence to secure with the Corean Government; a treaty of amity between Corea and United States that this country (Corea) laid directly between American and Eastern Nations with which our commerce was in constant communication, and although Corea as I knew was a poor country and promised but little in itself of commercial importance, yet as it was in the live of ocean travel. It was of importance to secure from that Government protection by treaty of American lives and property that might be stranded upon its shores—.

After a prolonged discussion in which the strategic position of the Peninsula of Corea with reference to Russia, China, and Japan was pointed out. His Excellency told me that I might say to my Government that he would use his influence with the Government of Corea to accede to the friendly request made by me in behalf of the Government of the United States to open negotiations with a view to such a treaty as before mentioned.

For this friendly act I thanked him and assured him that it would meet with the appreciation deserved—.

Before closing this subject it was decided that the action of the Corean Government would be imparted to the American Minister at Peking, and for the purpose of acquainting him with this fact I have written our Minister a communication copy of which is herewith enclosed.

Second. His Excellency then said that he had invited me to Tientsin with the view of getting the opinion of a naval officer in whom he had confidence on the result of a war between China and Russia so far as naval operations on the sea coast of the former were concerned.

He begged me to reflect on my answers because he desired my opinion to have full force and effect not only with himself, but in the counsels of the nation.

I replied by saying substantially that in view of the formidable Russian naval force throughly drilled and equipped already upon the coast of China, and in view also of the incomplete and chaotic condition of the Chinese Navy, of which I was well aware the result could only be one of disaster to China.

After discussing the crisis in an international point of view, His Excellency seemed much impressed and assured me that war should not occur between these two countries if China could possibly avert it.

He said that the two Empress and Prince of Kung-Prime Minister were decidedly in favor of peace as well as himself, and that the thought of these counsels would prevail.

The result of this interview is necessarily given in brief, but I cannot refrain from expressing any admiration for the intelligence and judgement displayed by His Excellency Li Hung-chang, and my extreme pleasure in the treatment received from him and the evident respect he entertained for my opinions.

In conclusion he expressed the hope that when peace was assured that my Government would permit me to assist China in the organization of its Navy. This, of course, is a matter to some extent personal insists nature, but if consumated would add very much to American influence in China, and probably and in the construction of ships for the Government in American ship yards.

I have the honor ……
R. W. Shufeldt

78

R. W. Shufeldt (1880. 8. 30) ➡ J. B. Angell

일본의 주선 및 李鴻章과의 회견 보고

Sir:

I have the honor to inform you that in pursuance of instructions from the Navy Department. I have been endeavoring for the last few months to open, by peaceful measures, negotiations with the Government of Corea for the purpose of making a treaty of amity for the protection of shipwrecked mariners and property on the Corean Coast.

In view of the fact that Corea and Japan had recently entered into treaty relations it was thought by the Honorable Secretary of State that the intimacy of the two countries might be taken advantage of and accordingly has instructed our Minister in Japan, the Honorable John A. Bingham to apply to the Japanese Government for such personal or official letters to the Corean Authorities as might contribute to our success—.

The Japanese Government acceded to Mr.Bingham's request and agreed to cooperate but this for the result has been unsatisfactory.

· ·

In this interview His Excellency assured me that he would use his good offices in our behalf and urge the Corean Government to make a treaty with the United States and that, while he could not predict what the result of his endeavor would be, he would acquaint you with the reply he received. I write in order to advise you of the promised action of His Excellency in this matter-.

As it is my intention to sail from Japan for San Francisco about the 1st of October next, not feeling authorized under my orders to delay longer on this duty the result of such action as His Excellency, the Viceroy may take can be submitted directly to the Government at Washington.

Trusting that His Excellency's influence may prevail and the end sought for attained.

I have the honor……
R. W. Shufeldt

余瓛(1880. 9. 13/光緒六年八月九日) ➔ 李鴻章

Shufeldt의 중국 해군 개편 의견 찬성

光緒六年八月初九日稟 北洋大臣李

敬稟者 竊照中書連接七月十八日暨廿五日所發鈞函疊聆槼誨祗悉愛才善任 延攬彌殷既蒙吐握於元公定卜張皇乎禹跡私心冀幸昌任軒鼇 蕭總兵讜論宏 抒謂揣中國時勢今欲整頓海軍非盡在乎速購鐵甲而在乎 先立總帥選用善法 明定章程務使將佐船主各員部署井井有條人才得所造就然後鐵甲可用而海軍 可成 且輪船水師與內地武員不同其將佐等官時有交涉外務之責規模詞令所 繫匪輕尤當愼選 文官統領擇材授任重其祿而觀厥成省去浮文務求實效非如 此不能自強等語 中書材學疏淺未敢輕言軍國大計然卻深味乎其言憶昔時供 職都門周旋吳江師相之間深知外務之不易未嘗不撫髀興歎 及隨使抵東遇事 留心探訪見其海軍一部卓然可觀推原其故亦祗在專立總帥延請西人講求兵法 至今不過敎民七年凡將佐船主皆用本國人材海口燈臺莫不皆然 今年各口稅 關亦已辭去西人其戰船雖不多而水師兵頗精練外國皆信其可以即戎矣 豈彼 能之而我獨不能乎未必然也轉移之機是在朝廷耳 昨初二日稟內曾錄日本兵 船名數一摺並爲蕭君代呈答書一函其意似言造用水雷人員不宜兼當船主恐其 分務難以專精因此欲候吩示然後遵行等情 該函諒蒙賜覽 現查該船已離神戶 海疆想當展輪回國矣 俄之海部大臣昨日攜眷乘三菱郵船抵崎如何行止尙未 得知 在港兵船仍前二艘此外無甚新聞 惟初四日下午此間接有英倫總局電報 言中俄齟齬之事已經定著將簽條約於北京云未知確否 長崎自五月後兵船往 來旣多水手醉酒橫行最易生事 中書加意提防彼此尙無形跡 俄之鐵甲兵艦其 在港未有龍旗者自前月始定造六張 如此似有轉機 知關厪注 謹以附陳 肅泐 寸稟 處請崇安 伏祈鈞鑒

80

J. B. Angell (1880. 9. 27) ➡ W. M. Evarts

Shufeldt · 李鴻章 회견 및 Prince of Genoa 조선 방문 보고

Honorable William M. Evarts
Secretary of State

Sir: -

I have received from Commodore Shufeldt, who writes from Nagasaki, a letter stating that in an interview which he had with Li Hung Chang, Viceroy of this Province, the latter expressed a willingness to assist the Commodore in gaining access to Corea by sending a courier thither with some helpful message. The Commodore suggests that, in case any duties in connection with the attempt to open Corea are laid upon this Legation, the knowledge of this fact may be useful, and possibly the aid of the Viceroy may be secured. The Commodore writes that he is expecting to sail for American about the first of October. I presume his dispatches to our Government contain a fuller account of his interesting visit to the Viceroy.

Count de Luca, the Italian Minister, gives me some particulars of the recent visit of His Royal Highness, the Duke of Genoa, to Corea on the Italian man-of war, the "Vittor Pisani," which are I think, of importance. The Duke went first to Fusan, the port where the Japanese Consul is stationed. This Consul endeavored to dissuade him from landing, intimating that there would be danger of commotion and conflict. However the Duke remained awhile, but failed to get a letter delivered to the authorities. He subsequently went to another port where there is no Japanese Consul, and was very kindly received. The Magistrate of the place came off to the vessel, and remained some hours. The Italians were allowed to land, and shot birds and dig oysters, and the Duke obtained what he specially desired, some of the silk worms of the country to take away with him. The impression which he received, and which Count de Luca has, is that the Japanese Consul is endeavoring to throw obstacles in the way of all nations, except his own, who desire access to Corea, and consequently that it is better to approach Corea from some other point than

Fusan.

Count de Luca has kindly promised me a copy of the official report of the visit of the Duke. But as I cannot procure it in time for this mail, I send you this statement as I have it from the Minister. I shall hope to be able to forward you the official report by the next steamer.

I have the honor to be, Sir,
Your obedient servant.

C. L. Fisher (1881. 3. 3) → R. W. Shufeldt

李鴻章과의 회견 내용 전달

United States Consulate
Tients in March 3rd 1881

My dear Commodore,

Since my last of the 22nd ultimo I have occurrence one or two important events that has come to my knowledge which I would communicate to you by "wire" were it safe, as it is I hope this will meet you in season to take action.

On the 1st inst I had a long interview of over two hours with the Viceroy. He made many kind enquiries of you and Major and is wondering why he does not hear from you and also why Major does not telegraph at the Viceroy's expense when he will leave for China, as requested at the time of his ending the Major's contract, &c.

He says be sure and write to the Commodore at once, telling him that in compliance with his request he had entered into correspondence with the Corean Minister storing your wishes &c that this question had been in referred to the home government, and that a short time ago a favorable answer was received and that they were willing to negotiate with you. The Minister (this sub rosa) asked the Viceroy what would be demanded by you in making this treaty and he told the Minister about what would be just to ask and to give, and made up a sort of memo for their guidance. The Viceroys say be sure and tell the Commodore to come out in the Spring and accomplish the work so well inaugurated and after that is accomplished he wants you to come here and see and have long talks upon the many questions that are surrounding China, and he says he feels such that when he sees you again you can come to some final arrangement about staying with him, as he wants your advice continually. He wound up our interview with the request that I should come and see him professionally the following day at 3 p.m. in compliance with this request I could yesterday over examined him. He has inflammation of one eye &c. I gave him a very close examination and at 5 ½ p.m. he let me off. Today I have placed him under treatment which I hope will have a favorable [_____]. He yesterday asked all about my medical experience—if I have my diploma, my army commissions &c, what I thought of Japanese doctors, and ten thousand more questions on telling him that I had with me my diploma, commissions &c. he manifested great pleasure, but I took the old man's heart when I took out my pencil and made a sketch of the eye in its natural state and then showed the contents of his eye, it was wonderful to see the catalyst, he got up, came, and stood beside me, just his hands on my shoulders and said I know now you understand your profession, you must remain here at Tientsin, I assure you to be the Consul and my Physician, here's much good you can do me and others, I have known of you when you were in Japan and I know you are a true friend for China; progress, you must stay here and not go home.

Now Commodore for the first time I ever held conversation with him upon this branch, I must say it looks very favorable, the more so when he has had two "dime [_____]" attached to his yamen and he has not called them professionally to see him. If I could only remain here in charge for a few months, say six or eight more, I am sure of final success and not leave everything here to the English.

Late news from Peking and authentic states that the question of the introduction of railroads has been negated in the Consul unanimously. The reasons given are- 1st it will deprive the civic labors of traffic of work and injure the Hotel [_____] of the country by taking passengers so rapidly though the country, 2nd that the [_____] tax of each station would be done away with and only one tax instead, for any number as the case might be, could be collected thus emerging great loss to the government revenue. The telegraph from here to Peking and Shanghai is permitted. Tsu, the former general in the West is at Peking. He is storing favor and has been made member of the Foreign Office, and now Li Hung Chang stands at the head of the peace party and the railroad and telegraph interests. Time will soon tell which is the stronger. If this is news to the Department kindly advise and if &c if prudent.

We are still frozen up, and have had no mail either way for many days as the outland [_____] has been stopped for the river to open, and it closed. Thermometer last night 11° above. Ice at Tokei forts 14 inches, so the Lord only knows when we shall have communication with the outside world again.

I shall try to write to Mannix tomorrow but should I not have time to drop a line tell him he is not forgotten.

  With kind regards and remembrances
  I remain my dear Commodore,
  Yours very truly,
  CL Fisher

 Laisun has just come in from the Viceroys and says- Be sure you write to the Commodore today, as the V.R. is very anxious I inform him that the letter was already written. This Corean business and the late news I have not communicated to anybody, though Capt. Johnson of the [＿＿] is continuously sending me on the subject so that he can write to—addressed.

J. A. Bingham (1881. 6. 20) ➜ J. G. Blaine

何如璋의 적극적 협조 보고

No. 1318
United States Legation
Tokei Japan
Hon. James G. Blaine
Secretary of State

Sir,

　　Referring to my No. 1238 of date January 6th 1881 in relation to Mr. Angell's dispatch concerning Corea and also to my interviews with His Excellency Ho Ju-Chang, His Imperial Chinese Majesty's Chief Minister at this Court and his kind intervention with the Corean government to induce it to make a Treaty of Commerce and Friendship with the United States in accordance with the expressed wishes of the Chinese government. I now have the honor to enclose a copy of a communication from Mr. Ho in which he reports the result of his efforts in that behalf as communicated to him by His Excellency Chiu Hung-chi formerly the Corean Minister to this Court.

　　It is to be observed that this gentleman informs Mr. Ho that "the Corean government has been very desirous to hold intercourse with the United States of America but the people still have a little doubt about the advantages of foreign relations" and for that reason Mr. Ho's proposal for opening negotiations with our government has not been accepted. In my opinion Mr. Ho and his government were moved thus to urge Corea to make a Treaty of Commerce and Friendship with the United States because at the time of their voluntary action in the premises, the Russian government as threatening China, and it was doubtless feared that Corea would be first appropriated by Russia as a base of operations, to foremost which it was supposed by the Chinese government to be essential that Corea should by Treaty assure to the United States certain rights and privileges within its waters and territory which Russia would be bound to respect. Now that Russia and China have come to a good understanding it is no longer desired by China (as I suppose) to be important or needful, that any such relations between Corea and the United States should be established.

    I have the honor to be,
    Sir,
    Your obedient servant
    Mr. A Bingham

R. W. Shufeldt (1881. 7. 1) ➜ J. G. Blaine

李鴻章과의 회견 내용 보고

Sir:

In conformity with the Department's instructions of May 9th ult., I have the honor to report the result of an interview had with His Excellency Viceroy Li Hung-chang as follow:

First.- His Excellency stated that as he had promised me in the month of August last that he would use his friendly efforts to bring about a treaty between Corea and the United States, he had in accordance with this promise held a long conversation with a Corean officer visiting China who although not a Minister, or officially authorized to represent the Corean Government, was yet a man of influence-. As the result of this interview the Corean was favorably impressed with the advantage of making a treaty with the United States.

Subsequently His Excellency the Viceroy wrote to the Government of Corea, but to this letter no answer has yet been received.- The current of event in Corea in the interval between my last visit and the present time seems to have been this; During the pending difficulty between Russia and China the Corean Government, harassed by the fear that Russia would in the event of war take possession of some of her ports, was not only willing but anxious to enter into treaty relations with the Western Powers-more particularly perhaps with the United States-. But when the treaty of peace was signed between Russia and China this apprehension was dispelled and Corea partially reverts back to its desire for isolation.

In the meanwhile two parties seem to have arisen in that country owing primarily to the visit of the "Ticonderoga", one for and the other against opening the country to foreign commerce.

The Viceroy states that the King and Court officials belong to the first of these parties while many of the men occupying some of the minor offices of the Government are opposed to any foreign intercourse whatever.

The Viceroy also says that while he is satisfied that the influence of China would have great weight with the Government of Corea in effecting the treaty contemplated which he himself is anxious to secure yet, he apprehends that if any direct action is taken on the part of his Government in favor of the United States, the representatives of every Western Nation would demand the same on behalf of their respective governments. While therefore he does not see at present exactly what course to recommend in the matter, he advises me to have patience as he has the conviction that a treaty can eventually he made-.

The Viceroy seems to have been somewhat annoyed by an effort which he understood had been made by our Minister in Japan through the Chinese Embassy at Tokio to persuade the Corean Government to send an Envoy to Japan to confer with him on the subject of a treaty between the United States and Corea.

I informed the Viceroy that I know nothing of this matter nor had judge Bingham mentioned it to me during my late visit to Tokio-.

The jealousy existing between China and Japan, at present enhanced by the delicate relations between the two countries, will account for the feelings exhibited by His Excellency on this occasion—.

After a conversation as to the importance of a treaty with Corea, not only to that country but to China, I told His Excellency that I was prepared to let the subject rest until I could see our Minister at Peking, as I had no authority at present other than to ascertain the present condition of things.

In this connection I would state that I ascertained when in Japan that while on the one hand the French Missionaries had again been deported from Corea, that on the other hand the Corean Government had sent forty young men to Tokio for the purpose of reporting to their Government and the country the advantages of Western Civilization as exhibited in Japan.

Thus, it will be seen that the visit of the "Ticonderoga" has created a party and aroused a feeling which will undoubtedly lead to the opening up of that country to foreign commerce-.

As peace, however, has ensued between China and Russia, and thus the apprehension that Russia would take possession of Corean ports has been removed, it will be readily understood that neither the Viceroy nor the Chinese Government feels so earnestly the necessity of securing the integrity of Corea by means of treaties with Western Powers-. Nevertheless I am inclined to the opinion that in the course of a few months the friendly offices of China might be obtained and a Commissioner of the United States might succeed in making a treaty on Corean soil; this of course, would require the assistance of a ship of war.-

Second, His Excellency in reference to the appointment of a U.S. Minister to Peking warranted, me expressly to say that he would regard the selection of Judge Denny, the present Consul General at Shanghai, as best both for the interests of China and the United States, and for the perpetuation of the present amicable relations between the two countries-.

To use his own language he said he would "guarantee" from his long personal acquaintance with Judge Denny that he would give perfect satisfaction in the post of American Minister to Peking-. His Excellency requested me to state this in my communication to the Honorable Secretary of State.

During the interview the new Chinese Minister to Washington, His Excellency Chen Tsou Jü was present and the Viceroy desired me to commend him to the friendly offices of the Honorable Secretary of state, Mr.Blaine, and to the Government of the United States generally, saying that he hoped he would prove acceptable and aid in maintaining our present friendly relations-.

The interview concluded with the satisfaction which His Excellency the Viceroy expressed in the selection of Lieutenant Marris of the U.S. Marine Corps as instructor in Naval Torpedoes and coast defence-. His Excellency stated his opinion that this officer would render valuable service to China-.

. . . .

I shall proceed in a day or two to Peking and have already informed our Minister of my presence here.

> I have the honor to be you obedient Servant.
> R. W. Shufeldt

84

J. B. Angell (1881. 7. 16) ➡ J. G. Blaine

조선과의 조약 체결 전망 및 Shufeldt의 해군고문 고빙 건 보고

No. 183 187
Corrected in record.
Once with Mr. Angell's
request.
See his No. 191 of July 30
Legation of the United States
Peking
James B Angell
the Secretary of State
Subject
Commodore Shufeldt's visit
Synopsis

The immediate prospect of securing a treaty with Corea has passed away. Reviews the situation of affairs in this connection. Commodore Shufeldt's services if sought, are likely to be sought by Li Hung Chang.

No. 183 187
Legation of the United States
Peking, July 16th, 1884
Honorable James G Blaine
Secretary of State,
Sir:-

  In your No. 94 (confidential) you informed me that Commodore Shufeldt U.S.N. was instructed to report to this Legation for special duty described in that dispatch.

  The Commodore arrived here on the 7th instant and remained as my guest till the 13th instant when he set out for Tientsin. I had the pleasure of presenting him to the Diplomatic Representatives here and also to Prince Kung and the Ministers of the Foreign Office. He and I concur in the opinion that for the present at least he can best perform his duties by remaining chiefly at Tientsin and visiting the capital as occasion required.

I have through the winter watched as carefully as I could from here the course of events in Corea. I think that the situation is correctly described in Commodore Shufeldt's dispatch of July 1st to you. If we had been ready to act say in November last, before the fear of a war between Russia and China was fully dispelled, it is very probable that we might have negotiated a treaty with Corea. I know that Li Hung Chang urged one of the Foreign Ministers here to go at that time to Corea, assuring him that a treaty could then be made. While the King and several of the high officers of the realm are disposed to establish relations with foreign powers, a strong and violent party is acting in opposition.

I do not learn here any tidings of a purpose of the Duke of Genoa to revisit Corea this season. Nothing that I see in the delegations here indicates the intention on the part of any of the Western Powers to press Corea for a treaty just now. They all seem to think that we are bent upon that work and for the present at least appear willing that we should do it, knowing well that they would soon share in the advantages to be secured.

The resources of the country are not great. The inhabitants now consume some of our cotton goods, and would consume more, if we had regular access to them. The peninsula lies near the pathways of Eastern commerce and it is very desirable that some treaty provisions for the relief of shipwrecked mariners be secured. As it is the only country upon the Asiatic seacoast to which access is denied, the whole world would rejoice to see it peacefully opened, and the United States may not improperly covet a glory kindred to that which she won by opening Japan.

Should our Government decide to make a persistent effort to secure a treaty with Corea, it may well heed one lesson which the experience of the past winter has suggested. It is this. The Commissioner or Minister charged with the negotiation should have authority to seize on any auspicious moment which presents itself. Had any one been authorized to act in November last, it seems probable that he could have accomplished something. But in the lapse of time required to write home and receive a reply, the opportunity must have been lost.

What the present temper of the Chinese Government is on the Corea question is not known. After conference, Commodore Shufeldt and I agreed that it was not yet time to approach them on the subject.

I note carefully your instructions concerning the conditions under which

Commodore Shufeldt can be permitted to enter the Chinese navy.

I may say that it is extremely improbable that the Imperial Government will ask for his services, since that Government practically has nothing to do with the navy. The Viceroys and especially the Viceroy of Chihli and the Viceroy of Nanking, who are the Northern and Southern Superintendants of Trade, control the naval forces. If the Commodore's services are sought, they will in all probability be sought by Li-Hung-Chang.

I think it would be well for us as it would certainly be fortunate for the Chinese, if as experienced and accomplished an American Officer as Commodore Shufeldt should for a time occupy a commanding position in the Chinese navy.

I have the honor to be,
Sir,
Your obedient servant,
James B Angell

R. W. Shufeldt (1881. 9. 14) ➜ J. B. Angell

井上馨 · Bingham 회견 내용 전달

Peking
My dear Commodore,

 I have just now [_____] Washn a copy of a dispatch of M. Bingham, dated June 20th, covering a communication [_____] the Chinese Minister to Japan on the subject of opening Corea. The gist of it is that the Minister (in M.B's opinion) wanted Corea to have a treaty with us to prevent in some (way) the use of Corea as a base (near) Russia against China, but that as soon as the danger of war was over China can do no more about it.

 If you have not seen the dispatch and would like to see it, I will send it down to you.

 Do you think I had better send the [_____] the matter upon 2 go? Absolutely no news here except the probable retirement of Tso from the [_____] or accruement of increasing infirmities.

 In the steamers pretty soon to leave for Shanghai Saturday or Sunday?

 I hope you and your daughter are enjoying this fine weather. Count on it for a few months.

Yours very truly,
J.B. Bryce

Commodore Shufeldt
Tientsin

J. G. Blaine (1881. 11. 14) ➙ C. Holcombe

Shufeldt의 임무 통보

No. 132

Department of State
Washington
Nov 14, 1881

Chester Holcombe Esquire Peking

Sir,

You are aware that Commodore Shufeldt was detailed for special duty at the legation in Peking, with a view first to a renewal of the negotiation in Corea, should that be deemed judicious and second to afford him the opportunity to make certain arrangements with the Chinese authorities for his temporary employment in their naval service.

Instructions in relation to the first subject have been sent him by this mail, with copies of which you will be furnished.

As to the second, while this government took no active part in the contemplated arrangement, it was willing in a spirit of friendship to the Chinese Government, to permit one of its distinguished and experienced officers to render such assistance as in terms of peace, he could properly offer in the organization of the Chinese Navy.

Mr. Angell was informed that if the Chinese Government made or desired to make an application to this effect, he was authorized to say that this government would reserve it favorably. But that if the appointment was simply one in the service of the Viceroy of Chih-Li, it would be a matter of arrangement between Commodore Shufeldt and the Navy Department not one in which this department would deem it proper to interfere but that even in that case [_____] would be granted by the secretary of the Navy to the Commodore, to undertake the service.

As we are now informed the service will be rendered to the Viceroy and in virtue of a personal agreement between him and Commodore Shufeldt. But we are, also, informed that some of the Foreign Legation at Peking especially the French have manifested great unwillingness that such an arrangement should be made and have earned their influence with the Yamen to prevent its accomplishment.

As the request is not from the Chinese Government to the Government of the U. S. you cannot with propriety intervene, officially, in the matter. But if upon investigation you should come to the conclusion that there has been diplomatic intervention at Peking, you are authorized and desired unofficially to counteract any misrepresentations as to the position and purposes of this government, which may have been made and to let it be understood that any arrangement between the Viceroy and Commodore Shufeldt would be acceptable to this government and that any diplomatic interference to prevent it, will, it is to be hoped, meet with proper rebuke from the Chinese Government which is entirely capable of judging of its own interests and duties and can rely with confidence upon any act of friendly service or advice on the past of the United States, which may be desired, either by the Government itself or any of its departments.

I am sir
James G. Blaine

87

J. G. Blaine (1881. 11. 14) ➔ R. W. Shufeldt (1882. 1. 19)*

조선 교섭 지침

Doc. No. 98
Department of State
Washington
Commodore R.W. Shufeldt, U.S.N.
&c.　　&c.　　&c.
On Special Service at Peking

Sir:

　　Your communication in reference to the service upon which you were specially detailed, indicate your believe that a successful effort can now be made to open commercial relations with the Kingdom of Chosan. You are therefore furnished in this dispatch with the necessary instructions and such credentials as will attest your character and authority.

　　As the propriety of this renewed effort must to a very large degree be determined by your own discretion, governed by the condition of things, existing at the time of the receipt of this dispatch, it is proper that I should impress upon you that the government of the U.S. is not willing to subject itself to another refusal at the hands of His Majesty the King of Chosan. It is therefore only upon the assumption that you are in possession of evidence sufficient to furnish reasonable grounds for very confidant hope that you are authorized to put into execution the instructions now sent you. The government would be seriously dissatisfied if your anxiety to accomplish a work, in which I recognize, that you feel a natural and honorable interest, should so far mislead you as to subject the friendly advances of the U.S. to another repulse.

　　It is of course desirable, should you determine to prosecute the mission, that the letter from the President should be presented to His Majesty in person but as we have no reason to believe that access to the Capital will be allowed you, it is to be presumed that your negotiations will have to be conducted at Fusan with some representative of the government. You will take care that such

---

*이 훈령은 같은 날 J.B. Angell에게도 발송됨.

representative is not an official of merely local or provincial consideration and you must be assured that any negotiator who may be appointed to assist you has full and direct authority from H.M. to discuss and sign a Treaty, and you will also require that the communication from the President be properly and honorably transmitted to the King, with a guarantee that it will be received and answered.

It may perhaps be judicious to put forward as the prominent purpose of your visit, a Treaty for the relief and protection of American vessels and crews who may be shipwrecked on the Corean coast, as the rare communications which we have already had with the Corean government have arisen from such recurrences and in any such negotiation you will take as your instruction the Treaty of May 17, 1880 with Japan, a copy of which accompanies this.

Should the temper and disposition of the Corean government be such as you anticipate, you will secure the right of trade at such port of ports as may be open. If I am rightly informed, the port of Fusan is at present the only port which is so open to foreign trade and even that trade is limited to subjects of the Emperor of Japan. I have no information as to what may be the limitations or conditions imposed upon this trade, but such a privilege would scarcely be satisfactory if it was anything less than the privilege of trade secured by Treaty to the citizens of the U.S. in the open ports of Japan and China.

Our experience with these Empires induces me to believe that a Tariff regulated by Treaty is not advisable and that you need only stipulate for an equality of duties, the rates being the same as those imposed upon native merchants or the most favored nations. But you will take special care to secure a provision that duties of import and export shall be paid only once for all at the ports of entry or shipment and that no further dues or internal taxes shall be levied or such merchandise in transition.

You will also endeavor to obtain the right of free travel into the interior for the purposes of trade under such regulations as you may deem fitting for the maintenance of a proper respect to the native laws and authorities and a sufficient and liberal protection of our own citizens.

In all cases of difference, or in the cases of commission of offences or crimes, you must insist upon the same exterritorial jurisdiction for Consuls and other officers, as is granted by the Government of Japan and China.

And in the Article which shall provide for the right of establishing Consulates, it is desirable that you should secure for the Consul the right of direct communication with the authorities at the Capital, until Diplomatic representation has been regulated, for you of course understand that Diplomatic representation is the necessary consequence of such a Treaty. The old and now happily terminated controversy with Japan and China over the right of Diplomatic residence at the Capital proves that no government can safely trust the persons and property of its citizens where it has not the right of equal and direct communication with the government which deals with them.

With these instructions, the Treaties with China, Japan, and Siam which are sent you, will be sufficient guide in your negotiations.

In your own experience and recognized ability, the Department has great confidence. While no political or commercial interest renders such a Treaty urgent, it is desirable that ports of a country so near to Japan and China should be open to our trade and to the convenience of such vessels of our Navy as may be in the waters, and it is hoped that the advantages resulting from the growing and friendly relations between those great Empires and the U.S. will have attracted the attention and awakened the interest of the Corean government. I look forward, therefore with confident expectations to the success which you anticipate, but in the negotiations upon which you may enter, the government desires that you shall avoid a complicated Treaty containing minute and multifarious provisions and that you shall distinctly refuse a prolonged and controversial discussion. If the government of Corea (or Chosan) is willing to open its ports to our commerce as China and Japan have done, we will with pleasure establish friendly relations, but we do not propose to force or to entreat such action.

Instructions will be sent from the Navy Department by the mail, to the Admiral commanding the Asiatic squadron, to place at your disposal such vessels as he can spare from the fleet. As it is to be presumed that he will cheerfully and cordially cooperate with you, your movements will to a reasonable extent, conform with such arrangement as he shall deem most judicious. You will be accredited to H.M. the King of Chosan, with your rank in the Navy and as Special Envoy from the United States.

While I do not feel disposed to put an absolute limit upon the time during which you may wait the result of your negotiations, the Government would not consider it compatible with a proper sense of its own dignity that you should remain in the Corean waters longer than two months unless the certainty of a successful termination of negotiations commenced in a friendly spirit and conducted with reasonable promptitude should require a moderate extension of time.

You will be allowed compensation at the rate of twenty dollars per diem and your actual travelling expenses from the day on which you shall leave your residence after the receipt of these dispatches until the return of the vessel to such point as the Admiral may designate upon the completion of your mission, and you will then consider the special service for which you have been detailed as completed. For while the government would learn with pleasure of the accomplishment of the other object referred to in your original instructions, it would not feel justified in prolonging indefinitely your details for special service at the Legation. It is presumed that such an arrangement as you contemplated at the time of your departure will at your return from Corea either have been effected or abandoned.

I am, Sir, &c
James G. Blaine

88

R. W. Shufeldt (1881. 12. 16) ➡ C. Holcombe

李鴻章의 조약 체결 권유에 대한 조선 회자(回咨) 보고

Dear Sir;

Referring back to the history of Corean matter since the month of June last, you will remember that His Excellency Li Hung-chang told me that he had sent a messenger or a message to Corea advising the Government to make a treaty of amity and commerce with the Government of the United States.

The Viceroy stated that he expected an answer within ninety days, and that he thought a treaty might be perfected with His Excellency's assistance, which he was willing to afford under certain circumstances.

When Mr.Angell, our late Minister passed through Tientsin en route to the United States, the Viceroy informed him that he had as yet received no communication from the Corea, although more than four months had elapsed since the message was supposed to have been sent, and he added that he did not know positively when a reply might be expected.

Yesterday (15th instant) Mr. Lo-Fong-loh the Viceroy Naval Secretary, called me, authorized by H.E. to say that a Corean offices had reached here and "that Corea was now willing to make a treaty with the United States".

I sent word back to the Viceroy that I did not know whether our Government wished to negotiate now with Corea or not, but if it should be so disposed, I thought it possible that I might receive the Commission or our Minister at Peking might be conferred upon the authority. At all events I did not think anything would be undertaken before the coming spring.

Although this matter was supposed to be confidential between the Viceroy and myself and was brought about during my visit to him in August of last year, yet Mr.Angell informed me at Peking that Sir.Thomas Wade had been asked by the Viceroy to inaugurate a negotiation between England and that country.

I am therefore inclined to think that the Viceroy has again mentioned the subject to Sir.Thomas Wade, during some of the conferences which have passed between them within the past ten days.

The Viceroy sent me a civil message of regret that he could not see me, — owing to his constant occupation, before leaving for Pao Ting Fu on the day after tomorrow.

If you consider the foregoing message of sufficient importance to telegraph to Washington, supposing you to be in possession of a cypher I can send if from here direct as the Shanghai line is now rowing order.

The value of a treaty with Corea would be more in the prestige than any immediate substantial results, if we are to make one, we should be the first.

89

C. Holcombe (1881. 12. 19) ➡ J. G. Blaine

조청(朝淸) 종속(宗屬)관계 보고

No. 30
One Enclosure
Legation of the United States
Peking, December 19th 1881
Honorable James G. Blaine
Secretary of State

Sir:-

I have just sent to the Department the following telegram in cipher: —
" Peking, 19/12.81
Secretary of State
    Washington, D.C.
Viceroy Li informs Shufeldt
Corea willing to make treaty
with us. Word has come
from Corea.' Holcombe, Chargé"

This telegram is based upon a letter which I received yesterday from Commodore Shufeldt, a copy of which is enclosed.

It is unnecessary for me to detail here the history of Viceroy Li's intention in this matter, and which has resulted in the message sent by him on the 15th instant to Commodore Shufeldt, as the Department is already possessed of all necessary information upon that point. You will not fail to notice the intimation in the letter enclosed that the Viceroy has broached this subject to Sir Thomas Wade.

It is generally understood that the anxiety of that high Chinese official to see Corea enter into treaty relations with Western Powers has been the outgrowth of a fear lest Russia should seize the Corean peninsula and so threaten the integrity of China in a far more serious manner than ever before. And he has doubtless correctly reasoned that, by bringing Corea to the front and causing her to take a place, and to enter into treaties, with the family of nations, he would materially lessen the danger of the occupancy of her territory, and the extinction of her autonomy by any foreign Power.

It is also whispered that the "certain circumstances" or conditions which Viceroy Li is ready to render us his assistance in this business, are substantially, that any treaty so made shall distinctly recognize the suzerainty of China over the Kingdom of Corea. I am unable to say whether this rumor has any foundation in truth. Nor is it for me to say whether such condition, if proposed, should be accepted. The Department is doubtless well aware that in the two treaties made between Japan and Corea in 1876, no such recognition is to be found.

It should, however, be understood that the word "suzerainty" does not properly express the relation that exists between China and Corea, the latter being to all intents and purposes an independent Kingdom. Once in each year the King sends an embassy with presents to the Emperor who makes certain presents to the King in return. In the train of this Embassador is found a number of Corean merchants who are permitted to bring their wares into China and to take away their purchase free of all duties and taxes of every sort. Upon the accession of any person to the Throne of Corea a high dignitary is deputed by the Emperor of China to proceed thither and recognize the new Sovereign. A similar formality is observed on the part of the Corean King when a change occurs in the ruler of China. And thus is described the entire relationship which constitutes the miscalled suzerainty of China over Corea. There is absolutely no interference on the part of this empire in either the domestic or foreign concerns or policy of her neighbor. The relation between the two Powers is that of a powerful to a weaker ally, and not that of a suzerain to a vassal.

It may be added here that the above will also serve as an accurate description of the relationship which existed for centuries between Japan and Lewchen, and between the latter Kingdom and China.

As to the practical value of any treaty which the United States may be able to conclude with Corea, I am at present able to say but little. That peninsula is, to all purposes an unknown land, and the very meager accounts which have been published of its population, wealth, products, etc. etc. are derived so entirely from unreliable sources as to be nearly worthless. A good deal has been written, comparatively speaking, of the mineral resources of Corea, but this has been based, not upon the reports of accurate surveys nor even upon the personal observation of trustworthy travelers, but purely on hearsay. It is at least safe to assume that, if that country possesses great mineral resources, they are as yet quite underdeveloped.

I may add in conclusion that I am now seeking such information as is available upon all these points and may serve to guide the Department in its consideration of the question whether to attempt to conclude a treaty with Corea. Whatever information I may obtain will be laid before you at the earliest possible moment.

I have the honor to be,
Sir,
Your obedient servant
Chester Holcombe

Enclosure
Commodore Shufeldt to Mr. Holcombe December 16th 1881

C. Holcombe (1881. 12. 29) ➜ J. G. Blaine

조미조약 체결시 청국관료 파견 제안 보고

Sir,

Since closing my despatch number 30. in regard to the negotiation of a treaty with Corea, I have become possessed of one or two further items of interesting and, it may be important information bearing upon the subject.

The Viceroy Li Hung-chang is evidently anxious to have treaty relations established between the United States and Corea, and has intimated that he would send a Chinese official in company with the Commissioner whom the United States may appoint to conduct negotiation.

Professedly, his object in taking such a step is to see that our Envoy is properly treated and enabled to bring his mission to a successful termination. That such may be his minor object is very likely. But there is strong reason to believe that his more important object or motive in sending an official with the Commissioner of the United States is to enable the Viceroy by this means to control and direct to a large degree the course of negotiations and nature of the treaty made.

In support of this view, I may say that I have been privately informed that the Viceroy has prepared a scheme of a treaty such as in his opinion Corea should conclude with the United States, and that this document is now in the hands of the Corean Government.

I have not been able to secure a copy of this very interesting paper, not to get more than a vague idea of its general features. It is said, however, to reflect with great accuracy the views of the Viceroy as to what would be a proper treaty between China and Foreign Power. Thus, it embodies Article II of the Commercial Treaty negotiated here in November, 1880, which prohibits traffic in opium; it stipulated that exterritorial jurisdiction by the United States over the people in Corea shall be temporary; makes several modifications in the articles on tonnage dues and duties as found in our treaties with this Empire, besides important changes in other directions.

It will thus be seen that should our Government undertake negotiations with Corea, and should Viceroy Li carry out his purpose to despatch a Chinese official to "assist" our Commissioner, the presence of such an individual might prove to be for more of a hindrance than a help in the transaction of the business. He would unquestionably have great influence with Corean Authorities and might indeed render the attempted negotiation an entire failure unless we consented to keep within the lines marked out in advance by the Viceroy.

There can be little doubt that the view taken by the Duke of Genoa, and Commodore Shufeldt, and communicated to the Department last year that the Japanese Government does not favor commercial intercourse between Corea and other Foreign Powers is substantially correct. If it be so, then our Commissioner would have both Chinese obstructiveness and Japanese intrigue to contend with in the transaction of his business. At the same time it is true that these two influences would counteract each other to a great degree. For the Chinese Government is constantly receiving bitter complaints from Corea of the overbearing and abusive conduct of Japanese officials and people towards Corean subjects, and is anxious on this account to bring some other Power besides Japan into relations with her neighbor.

On the whole I am of opinion that in case negotiations can be entered upon at all, they can, with patience, and persistence be brought to a successful termination, and secure to us a treaty which shall be reasonably satisfactory in itself and furnish a stepping stone to something better in the future.

I have the honor to be your obedient servant.
Chester Holcombe

C. Holcombe (1882. 1. 3) ➜ R. W. Shufeldt
李鴻章의 조미조약 초안 일부 전달

Legation of the United States
Peking

Confidential
My dear Commodore: ──

    Thanks for your note of the 1st instant with Irescots/Prescots letter which I return herewith. I am anxious to see you and talk over the Corean matter before long. I am convinced that Li's main idea in sending an officer of his over to Corea with our Commissioner is to thereby control to a large extent the course of negotiation and practically to dictate the nature of the treaty to be made. I have private information that he has drafted and sent to Corea a scheme for such a treaty as he thinks Corea should make with us and that this document is already in the hands of the Government at Seoul. I even know in a general way what source of its provisions are.

    I am afraid that if our Govt. gives any very definite instructions to its commissioner they may hinder quite as much as keep him, partly from the peculiar situation of affairs in Corea, and partly because of the fact their source of the most natural things to ask are just the last things which Corea would grant. For example, the right to travel under passport in the interior; and the so called "religious toleration article" will, so I am informed, not be conceded by Corea, and there is even danger of difficulty on the exterritorial question. Yet these are all points which our Government would naturally expect to be conceded, and the concession of the last she must of course insist upon. On the whole business I am strongly of opinion that the best course for the department to take would be to give only very general instructions to its Envoy in advance reserving naturally the right to accept or reject the treaty made upon a close examination of its details accompanied and explained by the reports of its Agent. But I want to talk over all this with you, and if you are agreeable perhaps you had better come up as soon as Levitts and his party go back. I will write you officially to this effect at a later moment.

Thanks for the information about Sir Thomas Wades' talks with Li on opium. It is safe to assume that neither England nor China will accept such a scheme.

You know of course that Frelinghuysen is Secretary of State.
With best regards to Miss Shufeldt and yourself in which Mrs. Holcombe joins,
Yours Sincerely,
Chester Holcombe

F. T. Frelinghuysen (1882. 1. 6) ➡ R. W. Shufeldt

조약 체결 관련 지침

Department of State
Washington
Commodore R.W. Shufeldt, U.S.N.
&c &c &c
On special service at Peking

Sir:

I was much gratified to receive on the 21st ultimo a telegram from Mr. Holcombe reacquainting me with the information received from His Excellency the Viceroy Li Hung Chang that word has come from Corea that the government of that island is willing to make a treaty with the U.S.

In view of the length of time required for communication with you while on this mission to so isolated a country, you are necessarily left largely to your own discretion in carrying out invitations furnished to you by the Department on the 14th of November last. It does not appear from Mr. Holcombe's telegram whether the Corean government has expressed willingness to negotiate both of the treaties contemplated, or, if only one of these, which one. A shipwreck conversation is, naturally, of the first necessity, and should you accomplish no more than this, your mission will still have yielded admiral results.

With regard to a commercial treaty, your own good judgment will doubtless have counseled the primary importance of not seeking to gain too many or too great advantages in a negotiation which, in the nature of things, is merely a first step in the discretion of opening a hitherto closely sealed country to our trade. The provisions of such a treaty should be so simple and few as not to excite any distrust on the part of a government and people whose jealous dread of foreign association and influence has been conspicuously manifested hitherto. That a moderate degree of friendly and mutually profitable intercourse at first will bring about its natural and necessary enlargement in time cannot reasonably be donated. Bearing this in mind, and regarding any concession however small, as an absolute gain, you may safeguard future interests by a judiciously worded clause giving to the United States whatever commercial privileges may be hereafter granted by the Coreans to other countries by treaty.

Congratulating you on the auspicious beginning of your mission, as reported in Mr. Holcombe's dispatch and expressing every appreciation of the friendly aid you have received from the Viceroy Li in your delicate task.

I am, Sir,
Your obedient servant
Fredk. T. Frelinghuysen

R. W. Shufeldt (1882. 1. 23) ➜ F. T. Frelinghuysen
전권사절 임명 이후 조선과 청국의 정세 보고

Sir,

I desire to express my sincere recognition of the great confidence placed in me by the President and the Secretary of State in the appointment forwarded to me by the last American mail as Special Envoy to Corea, with power to make a treaty with that country, and I also wish to thank the Honorable Secretary himself for the encouraging telegram forwarded to me by the U.S. Charge at Peking and received on the 19th inst.—

The instructions accompanying the Commission contain, very properly, a warning against the danger of permitting my zeal to outrun my discretion in the effort to be the first to enter this "forbidden land"-. I hope the Hon. Secretary of State will believe me when I say that I consider the dignity of the Government paramount always to my own advantage.—

A long experience in the East has taught me that nothing gives a Western Nation greater ascendancy than a successful manifestation of its power-, while a failure is never forgotten, and one great obstacle just now in Corea is the memory of the unfortunate issue of our efforts there in 1871.

But the Department will understand that success depends now not so much upon ourselves as upon the critical condition of the relation existing between China and Japan—between which countries Corea is a strategical point— A treaty made by the United States through the influence of China would tend to check the encroachments of Japan, against which China, while possessing the will, lacks the nerve to protest-.

His Excellency Li Hung-chang lends his assistance (without which I doubt if a treaty can be made) for this purpose and not from any desire to advance the interests of the United States in the East. Besides, he fears that some other nation less scrupulous might force these "barred gates".

Indeed it was his dread of Russia when I visited him in August, 1881, which urged him to offer his cooperation in making a treaty with Corea.— Following this period came the peace with Russia and when I saw him again June 1881, he told me that a treaty was no longer advisable- that the crisis had passed! But very soon afterwards complaints reached the Viceroy of the Japanese aggression in Corea and of the ill-treatment of its people, and then His Excellency again sent for me and said that he had dispatched a messenger to Corea advising a treaty with the United States.

The time he had specified for an answer elapsed while rumors of grievances multiplied.—

During this interval I was consulted about the "Chinese Navy" and my suggestions were adopted to such an extent that it was generally believed the Viceroy intended to place the Squadron belonging to his Province under my charge, and he quite understood from our Minister at Peking that our Government would not be unwilling to have one of its Naval Officers accept such a position—.

However serious the Viceroy may have been in this intention, it became evident in a few months that it would end in frustration-either by the intrigues of foreigners already in and about the Naval Service, or by the pressure of Foreign Representatives from their own countrymen— Under these influences His Excellency, the Viceroy began to grow less communicative on Naval Matters and finally placed me in such a position that I was obliged to decline any further connection with the Navy, or sacrifice the dignity due to my country and myself.

When I chose this alternative I heard no more from His Excellency until just before his departure for Pao-Ting-Fu (the Winter Capital), in December, when he sent me the message by his Naval Secretary which Mr. Holcombe transmitted to you viz:—"that the Corean Government was now willing to make a treaty with the United States and that the Viceroy would send an official with the American Envoy to that country"—This message is the result I have no doubt of a visit from a Corean Envoy who came here and went to Peking some time in the month of October last and I think that in sending it to me the Viceroy had the sanction of Yamên at Peking.

If the condition of things as I have stated them should remain unchanged in Corea until Spring about May 1st proxi—, I think the prospects of a treaty quite favorable-. But as the Department will by that time be in possession of this communication I can readily be advised as to the propriety of prosecuting the mission.

I do not take into account any wish of the Corean Government itself on this question because I believe it will be governed by the advice of Li Hung-chang. I have every reason to believe that the Japanese treaty was made under his sanction.

I speak of the Viceroy in these matters because he is virtually in all foreign affairs the ruler of China. I quite recognize the fact that there is no "urgency" in a treaty with Corea.

It is a poor country and its commerce is of small promise both at present and in future, but it lies in the Ocean highway of nations and must be opened sooner or later; it is a only question whether our Government will take the initiative as it did in Japan or leave to European Powers the prestige which such action will confer upon them. Our ships have almost disappeared from the surface of the sea- Our Navy is fast becoming a tradition, but if our diplomacy can by its <u>moral</u> force gain a point here upon the Pacific, I shall take great satisfaction in my share of the work.

Although the propositions for a Corean treaty were made to me confidentially, yet, I have reason to believe that the same project was submitted to H.B.M's Minister by H.E.Li Hung-chang.

The Viceroy however prefers the United States because he hopes to see "the opium clause" inserted which England would not agree to and the "religious toleration" question left out which either France or Italy would probably insist upon.

I am inclined to think that an "opium clause" would be very satisfactory to China. His Excellency Li Hung-chang has been informed of my appointment through the Chinese official in charge of foreign affairs at Tientsin.

Rear Admiral Clitz has placed the U.S.S. "Swatara" at my disposal and I have written asking for a meeting to discuss the question of cooperation which I have no doubt will be cordial and effective. I have proposed Chefoo about May 1st prox. or any other point in China during the month of April.

In a letter to the Assistant Secretary of State by the earliest mail acknowledging receipt of the despatches of the Department, I mentioned two or three minor points in the instructions which I respectfully request may meet with your favorable consideration.

I have the honor to be with great respect your obedient service.

R. W. Shufeldt
Commodore U. S. Navy

R. W. Shufeld ➡ 李鴻章(1882. 1. 23/光緒七年十二月四日)

조약체결 전권대사 임명 사실 통보

譯美國出使朝鮮大臣水師總兵辥斐爾上中堂書西曆一千八百八十二年正月廿三日 中曆光緒七年十二月初四日

太子太傅文華殿太學士李中堂爵前 敬啓者 本大臣近奉大美國伯理璽諭 派本大臣作爲出使朝鮮國 大臣 頒有全權字樣 以便與朝鮮 議訂和約 前承中堂於未啓節晉省之先 派令營務處羅牧豐祿轉爵諭 朝鮮願與美國訂約等因 已由本大臣電報本國華盛頓都城政府大臣 項得回信內稱貴大臣 此行諒可成議 可喜可賀等語 本大臣現擬於西曆本年五月初一日 由燕臺乘坐本國所派兵船 前赴朝鮮國 因本國國家不欲再將此事 未有可成之機 亦不願遽行開辦也 素蒙中堂許以提絜 俾朝鮮議約之可成 不但有利美國 且可兼益中華 玆因新承簡命 敢致書爵前 唯求雠奪施行 本大臣或應趨赴保定崇轅 面聆爵諭 或應仍駐天津 恭候節旋 諸唯示悉 以便恪遵 肅此奉瀆 敬頌崇祺

大美國出使朝鮮大臣水師總兵辥斐爾謹上

李鴻章(1882. 2. 2) ➜ R. W. Shufeldt

조선의 밀사 파견과 회견 방식 통보

Government House, Pao-ting-fu
2nd February 1882
To Commodore Shufeldt
Envoy Extraordinary and Minister Plenipotentiary of the United States to Corea

Sir,

    I have the honor of being informed by your letter, of the 23rd ultimo, of your appointment as a special Envoy to negotiate a treaty with Corea to the interests both of the United States and China. You requested by the same letter an interview with me either immediately in Pao-ting-fu or until I have now, first, to congratulate you on the sure success of your mission due to your tact and cordiality exclusive of the verbal message which I sent to you through Mr. Cheow Tinh the Haikwan Taotai and Mr. Lo Honghoh, my naval secretary. I have now to acquaint you that the Corean Government is contemplating to send a confidential envoy to me for the affair in question. Corea as you are well aware has been from time immemorial a dependant country on the Chinese Empire, its Government will consequently act under the instruction of China as the sincere friendship exists between ourselves in no less a degree than the most amicable relation between the two Governments it shall be my duty to render your mission successful in the most impartial manner. But as the success depends mostly upon keeping secrecy which, if once, be broken many obstacles would be thrown in the way by the parties who are jealous of your Governments' initiating Corea, so I have to request you, if you see fit, to come to Pao-ting-fu incognito as a private traveler in the interior I will then consult with you in the principal points of the question.

    I have the honor to be Sir
    Your humble servant,
    (a separate card)

96

C. Holcombe (1882. 2. 4) ➡ F. T. Frelinghuysen

總署 회견 내용 보고

Sir:

Two days since, at an interview with the Ministers of the Foreign Office, I brought up the Corean question with a view to learn what the attitude of this Government would be and what assistance might be expected from it, in our proposed negotiations for a treaty with Corea.

I conceived that it was of importance to secure some information upon these fruits, since all the assistance and encouragement which has hitherto been given to-Commodore Shufeldt has come from the Viceroy Li Hung-chang who, though a person of great influence and power, is only a Provincial Officer and not a number of the Central Government. It was desirable to learn how far his assurances of support and assistance would be borne out by the Imperial Authorities.

The Ministers answered with more freedom and readiness than I had anticipated, and furnished some information which has an important bearing upon the proposed attempt to negotiate a treaty by our Government.

The Department is doubtless aware that hitherto all business between China and Corea has been transacted through the "Board of Rites"- here in Peking. This is the highest, and most conservative, of the six bureaus or departments of the Government, and in past years has played the part of a most effective- obstruction to any intercourse, by means of the Government of China, between Powers and Corea. This was notably main fact in the attempts made here by Minister Low to pave the way for his mission to Corea in 1871.

The Ministers informed me that their Government had recently become convinced of the desirability of the establishment of commercial relations between Corea and Foreign Powers. About a year ago Prince Kung-effected the transfer of the charge of Corean matter from the Board of Rites to the Foreign Office. Immediately thereafter a letter was addressed by the Emperor of China to the King of Corea strongly urging him to enter into treaty relations with Western Powers and advising him to first conclude a treaty with the United States.

The Ministers frankly said to me that the action of their Government was mainly influenced by the belief that sooner or later the autonomy of Corea would be threatened by the aggressions of Russia and Japan, and that this serious danger could be best met by bringing the Peninsular Kingdom into the family of nations. And they were desirous that the United States should be the first to enter-into treaty relations with Corea because, in general, they counted much upon the conciliatory and moderate disposition and policy of our government, and because in particular, they were anxious that Corea, like Japan and unlike China should be spared the opium curse. They doubted not that our Government would willingly consent to the introduction of anti-opium article in a treaty made with Corea, which action on our part, would determine that question in any treaties made later.

Hence the Emperor's letter was prepared as indicated, and it was put into the hands of Viceroy Li to be forwarded.

The Ministers said-further that a reply had been received from the King of Corea, who expressed himself as willing and even anxious to conclude a treaty with us. They added that the King and a large portion of the people of Corea understand the situation and are ready for foreign intercourse, but that in Corea, as in China, there is an anti-foreign faction.

The Ministers concluded by expressing the readiness of their Government to aid the United States in any proper way to open friendly and commercial relations with Corea.

In absence of Commodore Shufeldt, to whom the proposed negotiations are entrusted, I did not think it wise to pursue the conversation further at the moment. After thanking the Ministers warmly for this information, and for their expressions of confidence in, and good will towards our government, I allowed the subject to drop.

It is perhaps unnecessary to warn the Department that, while there is much ground for satisfaction and encouragement in the attitude assured by China, Oriental Governments are not noted either for their frankness or consistency, and it is always possible that in the future, for reasons which cannot be discovered by us, the Imperial Government may see fit to assume an entirely different attitude and policy in this business.

I am expecting the arrival of Commodore Shufeldt in this city shortly, when we shall consult together in regard to these matters to the end that all possible cooperation and assistance may be afforded him by this Legation.

I have the honor to be Sir. Your obedient servant.

Chester Holcombe

周馥(1882. 2. 6) ➡ R. W. Shufeldt

保定府 회견을 원하는 李鴻章의 의사 전달

Tientsin

To Commodore Shufeldt,
Envoy Extraordinary and Minister Plenipotentiary of the United States to Corea
Sir

    I regret that I have not been successful to detain you from your departure for Peking through Mr. Lo. I beg now to enclose to you an answer (with a translation) from H. E. the Viceroy to your letter, inviting you to go to Pao-ting-fu.

    I hope you will change your course at once, if you [_____] Pao-ting-fu or you will return to Tientsin first, I will at the same time request Mr. Lo Honghoh to start for Pao-ting-fu at once to wait there for your arrival.

    I solicit an immediate answer from you to enable me to acquaint His Excellency the Viceroy of the course which you are now taking.

    I have the honor to be sir,
    Your humble servant

98

R. W. Shufeldt(1882. 2. 8) ➡ 李鴻章(1882. 2. 13/光緒七年十二月二十五日)

保定府 회견 요청에 대한 회신

Peking

His Ex. Li-Hung-Chang

Viceroy of Chihli; Senior Guardian to the Heir-Apparent; Grand

Secretary, &c &c

Your Excellency:

Your Excellency's communication of the 2nd inst. from Pao-ting-fu, reached me this morning at Peking.

Although the Hai-Kwan Taotai seems to regret my departure from Tientsin, apprehending that Your Excellency's letter would have induced me to visit you at Pao-ting-fu yet I think your Excellency will concur with me, that, under the conditions of secrecy which you think proper I should observe at present in Corean affairs, a visit to Pao-ting-fu would be inadvisable; as my journey there could not be made without attracting public attention.

But nevertheless, should Your Excellency still consider a personal interview at Tientsin during the early part of the coming month, as too late for any object you may have in view connected with the Corea, I will be pleased to join you from here at any time you may indicate. In the meanwhile I beg to assure your Excellency that I realize the importance of the caution necessary in initiating this negotiation, in order to avoid the obstacles which would be sure to intervene through international jealousies.

The trust placed in me by my own government, added to the confidence implied on the part of China, through your Excellency, will make me very careful of the obligations connected with this duty. Your Excellency need therefore feel no apprehension of any disclosures from me.

A treaty between the United States and Corea, would be a surprise to the world, to accomplish it, would be a matter of just pride not only to me, but to your Excellency, as one of the Rulers of the nation most interested.

I am with great respect

Your Excellency's most obt. servt.
(signed) R.W. Shufeldt
Commodore U.S.N.

【漢譯文】

太子太傅文華殿太學士直隷制府李中堂爵前 敬啓者 十二月十四日保定所發鈞旨 頃在都門奉到 據周道台之意 以本大臣急於晉京 不能在津 守待鈞函之至爲歉 然朝鮮議約一事 以秘密爲先 本大臣如遽赴保 不旣動人聽聞 由都赴保 尤爲未便 想貴爵中堂 必以鄙意爲然也 如貴爵中堂 適有朝鮮議約 要務相示 不能待至回津面談 尙乞卽日示知 以便登程赴保 本大臣敬禮鈞函之意 朝鮮議約一事 自當秘而不宣 以杜他國妬之計 美國國家旣付本大臣以重任 貴爵中堂 復示本大臣以盛情 本大臣斷不敢稍有孟浪 貽覆餗之譏 日後和約有成 實爲貴爵中堂謀國之宏謨 本大臣不過添附末光而已 肅此奉覆 虔頌爵祺 辥斐爾頓首
西曆二月初八日中曆十二月二十日 十二月二十五日到

99

C. Holcombe (1882. 2. 28) ➜ F. T. Frelinghuysen

Shufeldt의 청국 해군 고빙 건에 관한 보고

Sir,

In reference to the temporary employment of Commodore Shufeldt in the naval service of China, I was informed by Department instruction number 132 that it had come to your knowledge that some of the Legation of Peking, and notably the French, were unwilling that such an arrangement should be made and had used their influence with the Foreign Office to prevent it. The same instruction authorized and requested me, in case I found that these had been diplomatic intervention here, to counteract, unofficially, any misrepresentations as to the position and purposes of our Government which may have been made etc, etc.

In response to this instruction I have the honor to inform the Department that after cautious and yet thorough inquiry I am satisfied that no action upon this subject has been taken by any of Legations here with the Foreign Office. There has beyond a question been much intriguing and plotting hostile to the employment of Commodore Shufeldt in the Chinese naval service, but the issue of this had been before the Viceroy Li at Tientsin and not here.

Under the existing—system the Central Government of China has little or nothing to do with its naval marine. There is an annual appropriation for "Coast Defense" as it is called. This is decided by the Government between the Viceroy at Tientsin and Nanking who expend it, according to their own discretion on the construction, repair, and armament of land fortifications, in building or purchasing vessels of war, the purchase of cannon, small arms, or ammunition, in recruiting of sailors and soldiers, or in the employment of foreign naval or military officers. Contracts for the services of foreigners are invariably made between the parties concerned and these Viceroys. Only the vaguest and most general report is made upon the expenditure of the "Coast Defense" allowance to the Throne, and it is exceedingly doubtful whether any Minister of Foreign Office could tell today over the number of vessels of war which fly the Chinese flag. it is as though, in the United States, all naval matters were relegated by the General Government, to say, the Governors of New York and California, who contented themselves with reporting annually the most general facts connected with the expenditure by them of our naval appropriations.

The Department will readily see that, under such a system, any business connected with the engagement of Commodore Shufeldt in the Chinese naval service would be conducted with the Viceroy at Tientsin, and that all efforts to prevent such engagement would also center there. The Foreign Office has, in the past, invariably disclaimed all connection with or responsibility for contacts of the kind in question, and would doubtless decline to go further than to report what I might say to Viceroy Li.

It is true that, were the business to be entered upon officially, this disclaimer of responsibility on the part of the Central Government might justly be refused acceptance. But there are, in my opinion, important reasons affecting public interests for deferring any action upon this business for the present.

As the Department was informed in my despatch number 60 of the 4th instant, the Chinese Government has expressed its readiness to afford assistance to the United States in an effort to establish treaty relations with Corea.

On the part of our Government this business has been confided to Commodore Shufeldt, and Whatever aid China may see fit to render will be through Viceroy Li as its agent. It is therefore enumerately desirable that nothing be done which may in any way risk the loss to us of the treaty-cooperation of that influential and sensitive official.

In view of the grave interests at stake, while believing that the Viceroy has been influenced by outside parties to a gross breach of good faith toward Commodore Shufeldt, and that this Government should at a fitting moment be made to understand that the United States resorts the treatment which a distinguished officer of our naval services has received at the hands of the Viceroy as a reflection upon its own dignity, I have still decided in the exercise of that discretion which no doubt the Department intended to repose in me, to defer any action upon the matter at issue for the moment.

It is proper that I should say that the decision has been reached after full consideration with Commodore Shufeldt, who is now in Peking, to whom this despatch has been submitted, and who agrees in its conclusions.

I beg the approval of the Department

I have the honor to be, Sir, your obedient servant.
Chester Holcombe
With three inclosures
Tientsin, China

R. W. Shufeldt (1882. 3. 11) ➡ F. T. Frelinghuysen

周馥 회견 결과 및 李鴻章 회견 계획 보고

Sir:

I have the honor to acknowledge the receipt of the Department's despatch of January 5th, 1882.

While this communication gives me more direction in the pending negotiation for a treaty with Corea, than my original instructions, a discretion which is indeed essential to success, I yet fear that the Hon. Secretary, misled by the telegram of Mr. Holcombe stating "that Corea is now willing to make a treaty with the United States," places more reliance upon the active of the Chinese Government, and is consequently more sanguine of a formable result, than may be justified by events.

A rather close study of affairs in China for the past year, has convinced me that the present policy of its Government is reactionary, and marked by a feeling rather hostile than friendly to foreigners in general. Whatever may be done therefore in this matter by H. Ex. Li Hung-chang, or the Foreign Office at Peking, will be with a view rather to weaken, than to advance foreign influence in the East.

I am led to express, from an interview on the 9th inst. with the Hai Kwan Taotai, who is the representative of the Viceroy during the absence of the latter from Tientsin: that His Excellency will endeavor to have inserted in the Corean treaty (1) the dependence of Corea upon China. (2) prohibition of all religious books. (3) the right of Corea to establish her own tariff, and to tax foreign imports both a the ports and in the interior. (4) the right of Corean officials to arrest Corean criminals in the house of foreign merchants ext.

The first requisition of H. Ex. Viceroy, the acknowledgement of the dependence of Corea upon China, will be made because he wishes to obtain the official support of the United States for a proposition which China has not the usage authoritatively to assert to the world. As I consider such a proposition inadmissible and not even justified by the facts, it will, if insisted upon, of course terminate the negotiations so far as His Excellency is concerned.

The other clauses may be either omitted, or satisfactory shaped in accordance with our other certain treaties, particularly as my instructions indicate the propriety of expressing myself to the protection of shipwrecked seamen and property on the Corean coast.

This statement is made in anticipation of events; in order that the Hon. Secretary may feel no more disappointment than I shall myself, if after waiting nearly year upon the active of this Government, the negotiations should terminate in a failure.

Since my dispatch (No. 1) of Jan. 20 to the Department, I have informed H. Ex. the Viceroy of any appointment as Envoy to Corea, by a letter addressed to him at Pao-Ting-Fu under last June 23rd, 1882. (copy herewith inclosed)

In that communication I asked for an interview, either at his present capital or after his return to Tientsin. To this H.Ex.replied-under date of Feb. 12, -that he would be glad to see me at Pao-Ting-Fu provided I could come incognito (copy enclose).

In the interval between my letter, and the receipt of H. Ex's reply, I went to Peking and then I respectfully declined H. Ex's invitation to visit him incognito. (copy enclosed)

I did not desire, nor did I think it proper to give this negotiation the character of a personal intrigue between the Viceroy and myself, and I went to Peking for the purpose of ascertaining whether H. Ex. the Viceroy was acting in this matter with the sanction of the Chinese Government; and thus place the affair upon its proper basis as a friendly act on the part of this Government toward our own.

Mr. Holcombe entered cordially into my view; and in an interview with the "Tsung-li-Yamen" I ascertained that the Viceroy had been authorized and directed to act as its agent in the matter, and that the Yamen itself was quite as willing, and I thought more sincere than the Viceroy himself in its offer of cooperation.

He is now understand therefore; that whatever may be done in China in the matter of the Corea- by the Viceroy-has the authority of the Chinese Government.

His Excellency returned to Tientsin in a few day, and I have invited Mr.Holcombe to be present at the coming interview, in order to have the benefit not only of his counsels, but also of his knowledge of the Chinese language.

I have written thus frankly to the Department because I wish it to understand that I have no personal desire to remain one moment longer upon this duty than is necessary either to make it a success, or to ascertain its failure.

I do not consider it advisable to go to Corea without the assistance of the Government of China, and if this is refused, or so qualified by obstructions as to render it unavailable, I will telegraph the fact to the Honorable Secretary.

I am with great respect,
R. W. Shufeldt
Commodore U.S.N.

李鴻章(1882. 3. 25/光緒八年二月七日)

李鴻章・Shufeldt 회견

問　在京幾日 住在何處
薛云　在京一個月 住美國公使何天爵署中
問　貴總兵奉使朝鮮 勿聽何公使代出主意
薛云　此事本國專派本總兵辦理 惟國家給予本總兵之訓條 曾經外部抄示何公使 但朝鮮議約一事 惟總兵一人作主 何公使不過與聞而已 何公使不日來津 不知其另有何事 本總兵意欲何公使作繙譯也
問　本大臣在保定府時曾有朝鮮官來見 經本大臣飭令回國 屬朝鮮君臣預擬一約稿 此稿已於日前寄到 至貴大臣所擬之約稿 已由周道呈閱本大臣 將兩稿比較所差甚遠 現擬將朝鮮寄來約稿酌爲刪改 以期易於議成 遲幾日 當令周道將稿本轉交閱看
薛云　如此辦法甚善 周道於朝鮮議約之事甚爲明白 中堂稿本發下 本總兵與周道商妥 再將底稿呈請貴中堂削政
答云　甚好 朝鮮從古以來爲中國屬邦 其內政外交事宜向來得以自主 從前尙不願與日本立約 何況泰西 彼時曾經本大臣函勸 方肯與日本立約 惟朝鮮雖奉中國意指 未經來華請敎 只在本國倉猝議成 議成之後始知會中國 朝鮮今日乃大悔 從前日本立約受虧 現在萬不能以朝日原約爲依據也 本大臣在保定時已函屬朝鮮於二月間密派大員來津 與貴總兵先行面商 俟有端緖 再赴朝鮮定議 則事易成 現在尙未得有回信 大約四五個禮拜內回信可到 屆時再行知照
薛云　此事極承中堂關照 不特本總兵一人私心感激 美國國家尤領盛情 前奉有本國公文 令本總兵代爲道謝 已托周道代達 此次議約之事 本不應來催促 無如朝鮮辦事向多迂緩 本國所派兵船定於西曆五月初一日駛抵煙台 其時如朝使未來 本總兵必卽前往 可否懇請中堂派一大員同往 或給文書帶往亦好
答云　大槪派員同往爲妥 惟須俟朝鮮回信再定 聞朝鮮國王與二三大臣尙願與美國聯約 而以外臣工不願者甚多 如公然派員到津議約 或嫌先自來求 致招國人謗議 故其派員旣恐爲難 而貴總兵冒然獨往 亦恐彼此之情不

通 現在京各國公使果聞貴總兵奉使朝鮮否

薛云 已盡知之

問云 是誰告知 豈何公使轉告耶

薛云 不是何公使漏言 本國來文已久 難保無傳說者

問　各國公使曾知貴總兵在此與本大臣商議否

薛云 不知

問　各國有俟美約定後派員踵赴朝鮮議約之語否

薛云 此次尚未之聞 惟前年各國公使談及 似皆盼美國約成 則各國相續而來

問　此次議約必須格外公允 庶後來者可奉為程式 美國素講情理 貴總兵又最明達大局 朝鮮風氣固陋 中國休戚相關 不得不為之熟計

薛云 我亦甚願如此 朝鮮有釜山 仁川兩口 仁川近王京 釜山距其王京可十日程 此次船到朝鮮 擬泊釜山 不泊仁川 何如

因命取朝鮮海圖 密告薛曰日本已訂今年八月開仁川港 朝鮮意欲美國先往仁川 不欲日人先往

薛云 如此當知會本國 多派兵船二三隻前往仁川

答云 歸國不必多派兵船 屆時本大臣或派中國兵船同往

薛云 甚善

問　仁川港潮漲潮落 其淺深相較差多少尺

薛云 三十尺

問　貴兵船吃水若干尺

薛云 十七尺半

問　港內應於何處泊船

薛　於圖上畫有鐵錨之處 指云此處可泊

問　此處距王京若干里

薛云 僅六十里 坐小輪船可到 本日中堂接見指示 感荷之至 擬將所談各情節轉達本國

答云 務望秘密 勿使他人知之

薛云 謹遵命

李鴻章(1882. 3. 27/光緖八年二月九日) ➡ 總署(1882. 3. 28/光緖八年二月十日)

Shufeldt 회견 보고(1)

致總署 籌議朝鮮與美定約
光緖八年二月初九日

敬密陳者 美國與朝鮮議約一事 去臘初四日曾經具奏抄摺咨呈在案 歲杪聞美國復派定水師總兵薛斐爾即蕭孚爾爲朝鮮議約全權大臣 催令該總兵今春乘兵船東駛 其時適朝鮮陪臣金允植二次赴保定謁見 謂續奉該國王密諭 求敝處代爲主持速與美使商議 並寄呈該國機務大臣擬具約稿 屬爲鑒定 當卽密飭津海關周道設法婉留薛總兵 俟鴻章到津籌商 一面令金允植密稟朝鮮國王遴派大員 於二月間來津 借與薛總兵面議大略 再赴朝鮮 庶易成事 昨鴻章抵津 薛總兵訂期會晤 先將伊所擬約稿由周道譯呈 該使之意 欲以日本條約爲藍本 鴻章將兩稿比較 所差甚遠 且於中國屬邦一節均未提及 則敝處礙難與聞其事 將來各國效尤 久之將不知朝鮮爲我屬土 後患甚長 而萬國公法凡附庸小國不得自主者 又未便與各大邦立約 是左右均有爲難 鴻章先屬周道將此意諷示薛斐爾 謂約內必須提明中國屬邦 政治仍得自主字樣 意在不黏不脫 鴻章亦與金允植等議及 該陪臣翕服無異詞 玆爲酌量刪增約稿 並將各項應防之流弊應獲之權利一一包括在內 卽令周道與馬道建忠等密交薛總兵閱訂 該總兵素悉交涉機宜 難保不加改竄 然大致似不可出此範圍 謹將二月初七日問答節略及代擬約稿錄呈鑒核 俟後若何商辦情形 隨時奉聞 專肅密布 ○頌中堂王爺大人鈞祺 李鴻章謹上 直字二百九十六號 計抄摺並約稿各一件

103

R. W. Shufeldt (1882. 3. 31) ➡ F. T. Frelinghuysen

李鴻章 회견 보고

Referring to my despatch No. 2. March 11th, I have the honor to inform you that the promised interview on the subject of Corea between H. Ex. Li Hung-chang and myself occurred at this place on the 25th, inst.

His Excellency authorized the following statement, which I told him intended forwarding to Washington.

The King of Corea and his Prime Minister are in favor of opinion, the country to prepare treaty, and are not only willing but anxious to treat with the United States. But there is a faction at the Court and among the people intensively hostile to the Government. A Corean Envoy has recently visited H. Ex. at Pao-Ting-Fu and it was their determination to ask the Corean King to send an Ambassador to China for the purpose of making a treaty with the United States under the supervisions of H. Ex. the Viceroy to return to Corea show Sept. 5 for to that country the ratification.

To facilitate this arrangement I have submitted a draft of a treaty to the Viceroy, such as I thought would agree with my instructions, and H. Ex. in return has presented me with one which, while stipulating for the Quasi-political dependence of Corea upon China, and containing other features more or less objectionable, is yet not by any means incapable of being reconciled with our demands.

On Saturday next I am to present my objections to this draft to the Hai Kwan Tao Tai, who is empowered to discuss the question with me.

Both Corea and China are anxiously looking for protection against the pending oppression of Japan on the Peninsula. In this connection the Viceroy informed me in entire confidence that the King of Corea would now be glad to see an American man-of-war in the Seoul and H.Ex.advised me by all means to go to that point, and to get as near to the Capital as possible.

If the Corean Ambassador does not reach Tientsin within Thirty days proxi. the 25th inst, then H. Ex. promises either to send me an escort from a Chinese army or to give me such a letter as will insure a friendly reception by the Corean Government and in this annuciation he told me confidentially that he intented to send a Chinese gun boat accompanying me.

I informed H. Ex. that the United States had now been waiting more than a year for the action of the Chinese authorities in the matter of Corea; that the proposition to intricate came from His Excellency; that the United States had accepted it in the a friendly spirit and that I hoped there would be no delay in the actions for shadowed and I further told him that if there was no promise of success by May 1st proximo, I should telegraph the State Department at Washington and advise the abandonment of the proposal. His Excellency said that he had promised me his assistance in this matter, and he intended to fulfil it to the extent of his power.

If my confidence in the promises of the Viceroy has been somewhat shattered, it is from a freed conviction of this uncertainty for my work to Peking, which he is much dipricated has had the effect of impressing him with the fact, that I am no longer to be deceived by the Prefecture that his action is personal to me, or even the evidence of a friendly feeling for the United States.

He is presumed in the fact by the orders of the Imperial Government, and with the part and His Excellency are moved by a Peking which holds between their interest to their fears, not which permits to foreign treaties in the part of Corea, and that country from absorption by Russia and Japan to my fresh damage of the prestige of China.

If a treaty is to be made between the United States and Corea, it will require just care and circumspection. For it will be the basis for all further negotiations on the part of the other Foreign Powers. As the proposal hightens thinkful a render of the responsibility connected with this work, and to appreciate the cooperation of Mr.Holcombe who has twice invited Tientsin with the object of assisting me.

. . . .

I have the honor to be-
R. W. Shufeldt

104

C. Holcombe (1882. 4. 5) ➡ R. W. Shufeldt

청국의 조청 종속(宗屬)관계 명문화 요구에 관한 훈령

Legation of the United States
Peking

My dear Commodore: ──

    If Li insists on putting in something in reference to China's connection with Corea, could you not insert the following of which I enclose also the Chinese text: — "Chosen, in accordance with the advice of the Emperor of China, being desirous to establish permanent relations of amity and good will with the U.S." etc. etc. I don't see any objection on our part to such a phrase.
    How do you get on. I have had nothing from you since I reached home.

    Yours hurriedly,
    Chester Holcombe

R. W. Shufeldt (1882. 4. 10) ➔ F. T. Frelinghuysen
조미수호통상조약 초안 보고

Tientsin, China

Hon. Frederick T. Frelinghuysen
Secretary of State
Washington, D.C.

Sir:

Referring to my dispatch No. 4 March 30, 1882, I now have the honor to enclose

Copy of Draft of Treaty between the United States and Corea compiled by Mr. Holcombe and myself at Peking (Marked No 1);

Copy of Draft of Treaty between the United States and Corea; purporting to come from the Gov't of Corea, and modified by His Ex. Li-Hung-Chang, (Marked No 2);

Copy of Draft of Treaty between the United States and Corea; being a combination of Drafts No. 1 + 2, compiled by myself and presented to His Ex. Li-Hung-Chang for his consideration April 2nd 1882 (Marked No 3);

Also letter to His Ex. Li-Hung-Chang upon the subject of the First Article of the Treaty between the United States and Corea as proposed by Corea and exhibited in Draft No 3 (Marked A);

Also a memorandum of an interview between Li-Hung-Chang and myself in reference to this Article and the matters (Marked B).

These different Drafts have been the subject of discussion since the date of my last dispatch, which is still continued. At the present moment His Ex. has presented some modifications of Draft No. 3 and I have promised to consider them.

The First Article however, reference to, has been waived subject to a proposition on the part of His Ex. that I would make a request in writing for a messenger to accompany me to Corea, on the part of the Chinese Government, in which request I was to state, that owing to the fact that Chosen was in a certain sense dependant of China, I had asked the intervention of the Chinese authorities to the accomplishment of the purpose in view. On reflection I saw no objection to making this request, but deferred action until the Treaty itself could be perfected and approved by the Viceroy.

The other modifications of Draft No. 3 more particularly referred to the commercial articles, and to a desire expressed on the part of the Viceroy to substitute the favored nation clause recently introduced by China into the now Brazilian and German Treaties in place of that article used in the Treaty between China and the United States. To this I have hitherto objected.

The Chinese Authorities, both here and at Peking are manifesting an earnest purpose to have this Treaty accomplished; and I have every reason to believe, that there is at this moment in Tientsin, a Corean official of rank, who is being consulted at every ship and who when the discussion is closed, will be sent to Corea in a Chinese man-of-war, in order that the Government of that country may be prepared to conduct the negotiations to a favorable issue.

The main point which the Viceroy and the authorities at Peking seem to have in view is, the connection of China to Corea in this Treaty, realizing the fact, that by such connection the encroachments of other nations upon Corea may be checked. With this idea in view you will observe in the memorandum inclosed and marked B, that the Viceroy has submitted a proposition that when the Treaty is concluded, the King of Corea, shall write to the President of the United States, stating that he had made this treaty with the United States, by, and with the consultant of the Emperor of China. I simply promised on my own part, that if such letter were written, I would see it sent to its proper destination and thought I could promise a reply thereto.

Referring to the letter part of the same memorandum, which is personal to myself, while I do not desire to embarrass the Department, I still consider that the subject may at some future time be worth of consideration. For certainly for some reason or other, I have not only suffered in my own dignity, but this in some measure has been reflected upon my Government.

It is true, that before I came to China under orders as Naval Attaché of the Legation, I endeavored to impress upon the late Secretary of State, that I desired mainly to negotiate a Treaty with Corea, and that the Chinese Navy was only an incident of my coming. After my arrival here, and after an interview with the Viceroy I repeated the same desire to our Minister at Peking, but from May 1881, to January 1882, I received no intimation of any action of the Department in that matter. While I realize the embarrassment of the Department under the sad circumstances of the late President's illness, I can also understand why, among the intrigues of foreigners, the pressure of foreign representatives and the jealousies of the Mandarins, I should come to be considered by the Viceroy rather as adventurer seeking office, than as an officer, whose main desire was, by organizing the Navy of China to enhance the reputation of his own country. I remained in Tientsin for four months subjected to these influences, because I was determined to see whether an American officer could be thus treated with impunity.

I have but little faith in the friendship of China for any nation, and believe that friendship to be measured by the pressure brought to bear upon it; and I desire to repeat my conviction, that if a Treaty is made with Corea, it will be owing to circumstances surrounding that country which are as threatening to China as to Corea itself, and not from any particular friendship for the United States.

I am with great respect,
Your obedient servant,
R.W. Shufeldt
Commodore, U.S.N.

No 1.
Draft of Treaty between
The United States and Corea
Compiled by
Mr. Holcombe and myself at Peking

The United States of America and the Kingdom of Chosen, desiring to establish firm, lasting and sincere friendship between the two nations, have resolved to fix in a manner clear and positive, by means of a Treaty, or general convention of peace, amity, and commerce, the rules which shall in future be mutually observed in the intercourse of their respective countries for which most desirable object, the President of the United States has conferred full powers upon their Commissioner.

And the August Sovereign of the Kingdom of Chosen on his

And the said commissioners, after having exchanged their said full powers, and duly considered the premises, have agreed to the following articles:-

Art. I. There shall be a perfect, permanent and universal peace, and a sincere and cordial amity, between the United States of America on the one part, and the Kingdom of Chosen on the other part, and between their people respectively, without exception of persons or places.

Art. II. The United States shall have the right to appoint a Diplomatic Representative to reside at the Capital of Chosen, and Consular officers at such ports as one, or hereafter may be open to foreign trade. The King of Chosen shall also have the right to appoint a Diplomatic Representative to reside at the capital of the United States, and consuls at such ports and places within the territory of the United States as he may see fit. Official intercourse shall be carried on in terms of equality and courtesy, and all rules and precedents calculated to obstruct friendly intercourse shall be totally abrogated , and in their stead rules liberal and fit to secure a firm and perpetual peace shall be established.

Art. III. The citizens of the United States are permitted to frequent the ports and cities of

And any other port or place hereafter by treaty with other powers, or with the United States opened to commerce; and to reside with their families and trade there, and to proceed at pleasure with their vessels and merchandise from any of these ports, to any other of them. But said vessels shall not carry on a clandestine and fraudulent trade at other ports of Chosen not declared to be legal, or along the coasts thereof; and any vessel under the American flag violating this provision shall, with her cargo, be subject to confiscation to the Government of Chosen; and the United States will take measures to prevent their flag from being abused by the subjects of other nations as a cover for the violation of the laws of the Kingdom.

Art. IV. All citizens of the United States of American in Chosen, peaceably attending to their affairs, being placed on a commerce footing of amity and good will with subjects of Chosen, shall receive and supply for themselves and everything appertaining to them, the protection of the local authorities of Government, who shall defend them from all insult and injury of any sort. If their dwellings or property be threatened or attacked by riots, incendiaries, or other violent or lawless persons, the local officers on requisition of the Consul, shall immediately dispatch a military force to dispose the rioters, apprehend the guilty individuals, and punish them with the utmost sign of the law. Subjects of Chosen guilty of any criminal act toward citizens of the United States shall be punished by the Authorities of Chosen according to the laws of Chosen; and citizens of the United States, either on shore or in any merchant vessel, who may insult, trouble, or wound the persons or injure the property of the people of Chosen, shall be punished only by the Consul or other public functionary threats authorized, according to the laws of the United States. Arrests in order to trial may be made by either the Chosen or the United States authorities.

When controversies arise in the Kingdom of Chosen between citizens of the United States and subjects of His Majesty, which need to be examined and decided by the public officers of the two nations, it is agreed between the Governments of the United States and Chosen that such cases shall be tried by the proper official of the nationality of the defendant. The properly authorized official of the plaintiff's nationality, shall be freely permitted to attend the trial, and shall be treated with the courtesy due to his position. He shall be granted all proper facilities for watching the proceedings in the interest of justice. If he so desires he shall have the right to present, to examine, and to cross-examine witnesses. If he is dissatisfied with the proceedings, he shall be permitted to protest against them in detail. The law administered will be the law of the nationality of the officer trying the case.

Art. V. Whenever United States vessels either by stress of weather or by want of fuel and provisions cannot reach one or the open ports in Chosen, they may enter any port or harbor either to take refuge therein or to get supplies of wood, coal, and other necessities, or to make repairs, the expenses incurred hereby are to be defrayed by the ship's master. In such events both the officers and the people of the locality shall display their sympathy by rendering full assistance, and their liberality in supplying the necessities required.

If a United States be wrecked on the coast of Chosen, the nearest

Chosen authority, on being informed of the occurrence, shall immediately send assistance to the crew, provide for their present necessities, and take the measures necessary for the salvage of the ship and the preservation of the cargo. The whole shall then be brought to the knowledge of the nearest Consul or Consular Agent, in order that the latter, in concert with the competent authority, may take ships for sending the crew home, and for saving the debris of the ship and cargo.

Art. VI. The Coasts of Chosen, having hitherto been left unsurveyed, are very dangerous for vessels approaching them, and in order to prepare charts showing the positions of islands, rocks, and reefs, as well as the depth of water, whereby all navigators may be enabled safely to pass between the two countries, any United States mariner may freely survey said coasts.

Art. VII. His Majesty the King of Chosen hereby promises and agrees that no other kind or higher rate of tonnage dues or duties for imports or exports or [_____] trade shall be imposed or levied in the open ports of Chosen upon vessels wholly belonging to citizens of the United States, or upon the Produce, Manufactures, or Merchandise imported in the same from the United States; or from any foreign country; or upon the Produce, Manufacture, or Merchandise exported in the same to the United states or to any foreign country, or transported in the same from one open port of Chosen to another, than are imposed or levied on vessels of any other nation, or on those of subjects of Chosen.

　　The United States hereby promise and agree that no other kind or higher rate of tonnage dues or duties for imports shall be imposed or levied in the ports of the United States upon vessels wholly belonging to the subjects of His Majesty and coming either directly or by way of any foreign port from any other ports of Chosen which are open to foreign trade, to the ports of the United States, or returning there from either directly or by way of any foreign port to any of the open ports of Chosen; or upon the Produce, Manufactures, or Merchandise imported in the same from Chosen or from any foreign country, than are imposed or levied on vessels of other nations which make no discrimination against the United States in tonnage dues, or duties on imports, exports, or [_____] trade; or than are imposed or levied on vessels and cargoes of citizens of the United States.

His Majesty the King of Chosen hereby further agrees that the duties leviable on merchandise imported to; and exported from the open ports of Chosen shall in no case exceed the maximum rate of 10 percent ad valorem; and that such duties of import and export shall be paid only once for all at the ports of entry or shipment, and that no further dues or internal taxes shall be levied in such merchandise in transitive.

Art. VIII. The Governments of Chosen and of the United States mutually agree and undertake that subjects of Chosen shall not be permitted to import opium into any of the ports of the United States, and citizens of the United States shall not be permitted to import opium into any of the open ports of Chosen. This absolute prohibition which extends to vessels owned by the citizens or subjects; of either Power, to foreign vessels employed by them, or to vessels owned by citizens or Subjects of either Power and employed by other persons for transportation of opium, shall be enforced by appropriate legislation on the part of chosen and the United States, and the benefit of the famed nation clause in existing treaties shall not be claimed by the citizens or subjects of either Power as against the provisions of this Article.

Art. IX. Friendly relations having been established between the two contracting parties, it is necessary to prescribe trade regulations for the benefit of the merchants of the respective countries.

Such trade regulations, together with detailed provisions, to be added to the Articles of the present Treaty to develop its meaning, and facilitate its observance, shall be agreed upon at the Capital of Chosen, or at in the country, within eighteen months from the present date by special commissioners appointed by the two countries.

Act X. The two contracting parties hereby agree that should at any time the King of Chosen grant to any nation, or to the merchants or citizens of any nation, any right, privilege or favor connected either with navigation, commerce, political, or other intercourse, which is not confined by this Treaty, such right, privilege, and favor, shall at once freely [____] to the benefit of the United States, its public officers, merchants, and citizens.

In faith whereof the Respective Plenipotentiaries have signed and sealed the foregoing at in English and Chinese, being three originals of each text of even tenor and date, the ratifications of which shall be exchanged at within one year from the date of its execution.

No. 2
Draft of Treaty
between
The United States and Corea:

Purporting to have come from the Government of Corea, and modified by H. Ex. Li-Hung-Chang

The Kingdom of Chosen and the United States of America being sincerely desirous of establishing abiding relations of amity and friendship between these respective peoples, have therefore appointed that is today the King of Chosen

As his commissioner Plenipotentiary, and the President of the United States

As his commissioner Plenipotentiary, who having reciprocally examined their free respective full powers, have agreed upon the several articles as under,

Article I. Chosen, being a dependent state of the Chinese Empire, has nevertheless hitherto exercised her own sovereignty in all matters of internal administrative and foreign relations. After the conclusion of this Treaty, the King of Chosen and the President of the United States shall treat with each other upon terms of perfect equality, and the subjects and citizens of the two nations shall maintain perpetual relations of friendship. If other Powers deal unjustly or oppressively with either Government, the other shall render assistance and protection, or shall act as mediator in order to the preservation of perfect peace.

Article II. After the conclusion of this Treaty of commerce and amity, the High Contracting Powers, may each appoint Diplomatic Representatives at the Court of the other, and may each appoint Consular Authorities at the open ports of the other, at their own convenience. These officials shall have relations with the corresponding local authorities of equal rank upon a basis of mutual equality. The Diplomatic and Consular Authorities of the two ports shall receive mutually all the privileges, rights and consideration without discrimination which are accorded to the same class of representatives from the most favored nation. Consuls shall exercise their functions only after receipt of an exequatur from the Govt to which they are accredited. The consular authorities shall be bona-fide officials, and no merchants shall be permitted to exercise the duties of the office, nor shall Consular Officers be allowed to engage in trade. At ports to which no Consular Representatives have been appointed, the Consuls of other Powers may be invited to act, provided that no merchant shall be allowed to assume the duties; or the provisions of this Treaty may in such cases be enforced by the local authorities. In the relations between the people of the two nations if matters shall arise which are offensive to the local authorities and people, the Consular Authorities shall not arbitrarily interfere. If Consular Representatives conduct their business in an improper manner, their exequaturs may be revoked in conformity with the rules of international procedure.

Article III. If the vessels of either nation meet with stress of weather or one cast ashore upon the coasts of the other the local authorities upon being informed of the fact shall devise measures for their reserve and protection. All reasonable possibilities shall be afforded by the local authorities of either country to vessels of war or the other to make necessary repairs and to purchase supplies at the ports open to trade. But merchant vessels, except when forced by stress of weather shall not be allowed to enter ports not open to foreign trade, and shall be liable to penalties for violation of this provision.

Article IV. The subjects of Chosen who desire to proceed to the various ports of the United States for purpose of commerce shall conform to the laws and regulations of the United States. And the United States agrees to grant to them all the rights, privileges, and immunities which are accorded to the subjects or citizens of the most favored nations.

According to the international laws recognized by the European and American Governments, citizens of the United States who may frequent Corean ports open to foreign trade should be subject to the jurisdiction of the native authorities. But as Chosen has not yet arranged with the United States to modify the laws and procedure of the former in conformity with the laws of Western Nations, Chosen agrees temporarily that citizens of the United States in Chosen shall be subject to the jurisdiction of their Consular Authorities. If persons from vessels of the United States create disturbance on shore, the local authorities shall conduct measures with the Consul for suppressing it.

Article V. Merchants and merchant vessels of Chosen visiting the United States for purposes of traffic shall pay tonnage dues and duties and all fees according to the Customs Regulations of the United States.

Merchants and merchant vessels of the United States visiting Chosen for the purposes of trade, shall pay duties upon all imports and exports. But as the particular rate of duty to be lied upon each class of merchandise, has not yet been fixed, it is for the present agreed that upon such imports as are necessities of life an ad valorem duty of 10% shall be levied, and that upon such as are luxuries, as foreign wine, tobacco, clocks and watches an ad valorem duty of 30% shall be levied. Native produce exported shall pay an ad valorem duty of 3%.

American merchant vessels entering the ports of Chosen shall pay tonnage dues at the rate of five mace per ton, payable once in three months according to the Chosen calendar.

Article VI. Subjects of Chosen who may visit the United States for purposes of commerce shall be permitted to reside and to rent, purchase, construct residences or warehouses in all parts of the country. They shall be permitted to traffic in all merchandise, raw and manufactured, that is not declared contraband by law.

Citizens of the United States visiting to the open ports of Chosen, are permitted to reside at such ports to rent houses or land and to erect buildings, but no coercion or intimidation may be exercised. The land thus leased remains an integral part of the Kingdom of Chosen and the administrative functions of the local communities shall not be interfered with.

Native produce and foreign imports, not contraband, may be brought and sold at the ports open to trade. But American merchants are not permitted either to transport foreign imports to the interior for sale, or to proceed to the interior to purchase native produce. Nor are they permitted to transport nature produce from one open port to another open port. Violations of this rule will subject vessel and cargo to confiscation and the merchant offending will be handed over to his Consul to be dealt with.

The importation of opium is strictly forbidden. Persons who bring it into the open ports shall be punished by the Authorities of Chosen.

Article VII. All crimes and suits at law which may arise in Chosen in which the subjects and citizens of the two Powers are concerned shall be tried in the Court and by the law of the defendant's nationality. In the case of thefts and debts the proper officers of the two Governments will make effort to arrest and punish the guilty parties and to secure restitution or payment, but will not be held personally responsible for any losses incurred.

Should the plaintiff in any action be dissatisfied with the judgment, he may appeal through his official to the official of the defendant for a new trial.

Article VIII. The officers and people of either nation residing in the other shall have the right to employ natives for all lawful work. Should subjects of Chosen guilty of violation of the laws of the Kingdom, or against whom any action had been brought, conceal themselves in the residences of American officials or citizens, or in warehouses or on board American merchant vessels, the local authorities shall, on the one hand, notify the Consul, and, on the other dispatch constables to make the arrests.

American officials or citizens shall not be permitted to harbor such persons.

Students of either nationality who may proceed to the country of the other in order to study the language, literature, laws, or arts shall be given all possible protection and assistance in endurance of good will.

Article IX. This being the first Treaty negotiated by the Govt of Chosen, is necessarily incomplete and imperfect in provisions. It shall, however, in its stipulations be first carried into operation. As to stipulations not embodied herein, after a period of five years, when the officers and people of the two Powers shall have become more familiar with each other's language a further negotiation of commercial provisions and regulations in detail in conformity with international law and without unequal discrimination on either part shall be had.

Article X. This treaty and future official correspondence between the two contracting Powers shall be made, on the part of Chosen in the Chinese language. The United States shall either use the Chinese language, or if English is used, it shall be accompanied with a Chinese version in order to avoid misunderstanding.

The foregoing Articles having been agreed upon the Representatives of the High Contracting Powers are herewith, in the first instance signed and sealed by them in witness where of the whereof the King of Corea shall forward forward a copy to the Board of Rites of the Chinese Emperor and shall ratify as above.

The President of the United States, by and with the advice and consent of the Senate shall ratify this instrument and the certificates of ratification shall be exchanged at a place to be named, and thereafter they shall be proclaimed in both countries in order that they may be known and obeyed.

Chosen　　　　　　　　　　　　　　　　　　　　　　　　A.D. 1882

【漢譯文】

代擬朝鮮與美國修好通商條約
　　光緒八年二月

大朝鮮國與大美國切欲敦崇和好 惠顧商民 是以大朝鮮國君主特派全權大臣 大美國伯理璽天德特派全權大臣 各將所奉全權字據互相校閱 訂立條款 臚列於左

　　第一款
朝鮮爲中國屬邦 而內政外交事宜向來均得自主 今玆立約後 大朝鮮國君主大美國伯理璽天德俱平行相待 兩國人民永敦和好 若他國偶有不公及輕侮之事 必彼此援護 或從中善爲調調處 俾獲永保安全

　　第二款
此次立約通好後 兩國可按照通例 彼此各派秉權大員 往來駐紮 並於通商口岸設立總領事領事副領事署領事等官 均聽其便 此等官員官員與本地官交涉往來 均應用品級相當之禮 兩國秉權大員與領事等官 享獲種種恩施 與彼此所待最優之國官員無異 惟領事官必須奉到駐紮之國批准文憑 方可視事 所派領事等官必須眞正官員 不得以商人兼充 亦不得兼作貿易 倘各口未設領事官 或請別國領事兼代 亦不得以商人兼充 或卽由地方官照現定條約代辦 至商民交涉事件有與本地官民齟齬者 領事官不得任意爭執 如領事官辦事不合 彼此均可按照公例 將批准文憑追回

　　第三款
兩國船隻在彼此沿海地方 若遇遭風擱淺等事 地方官聞知 卽應設法救護 至兩國兵船往來 在彼此已開口岸 如遇買取食物煤炭甜水 修理船隻 地方官應妥爲照料 惟商船於未開口岸 除遭風外 不得駛往 違者罰辦

　　第四款
朝鮮國商民欲往美國各口各邑貿易 應遵守美國律例章程 美國亦准照待最優

國之商人一體看待 至美國商民前往朝鮮國 准開口岸貿易 若照歐美各國通例 原應歸地方官管轄 惟朝鮮國與美國政制攸殊 現尙未訂改東西交涉公律 是以 朝鮮國政府暫許美國商民歸領事官管轄 至美國船主諸色人等 如有上岸滋事 應由地方官會同領事官妥爲彈壓

第五款

朝鮮國商民並其商船前往美國貿易 凡納稅船鈔等事 應遵照美國海關章程辦 理 至美國商民並其商船前往朝鮮貿易 進出貨物均應納稅 惟各色貨物銷滯 不得預知 稅則暫難詳定 玆擬先訂大略 各色進口貨有關民生日用者 照估價 值百抽十 其奢靡玩要等物 如洋酒呂宋煙鐘表之類 照估價值百抽三十 至出 口土貨 槪值百抽五 美國商船進朝鮮口岸 須納船鈔 每噸銀五錢 按中歷一季 抽收一次

第六款

朝鮮國商民前往美國各處貿易 准其在該處居住 賃房買屋 起蓋棧房 所有土 産 以及製造之物 與不違例之例之貨 均許買賣 美國商民前往朝鮮已開口岸 准其在該處居住賃房 租地建屋 惟不得稍有勒遇 其出租之地 仍歸朝鮮版圖 不得有碍地方官治理之權 所有本國土産以及外洋運來不違禁例之貨 均可就 已開口岸收買發賣 但美國商民不得以洋貨運入內地售賣 亦不得自入內地採 買土貨 併不得以土貨由此口販運彼口 違者將船隻貨物入官 並將該商交領事 官懲辦 至鴉片煙素所嚴禁 如有運販進口者 由朝鮮官罰辦

第七款

凡美國商民在朝鮮已開口岸 遇有與朝鮮民人交涉財産及各罪案 俱由被告所 屬之官員審斷 各照本國律例定案 惟竊盜逋欠等事 兩國官員只能分別拏辦追 究 不能代償 倘案內原告有未甘服者 應聽其所屬官員照會被告所屬官員覆訊

第八款

凡兩國官員商民在彼此通商地方居住 均可雇請各色人等勤執分內工藝 惟朝 鮮人遇犯本國例禁或牽涉被控 凡在美國官民公館寓所行棧及商船隱匿者 由 地方官一面知照領事官 一面派差拘拏 美國官民不得庇縱捎留 至兩國生徒往 來學習語言文字律例藝業等事 彼此均宜勤助 以敦睦誼

第九款
玆朝鮮國初次立約 所訂條款姑從簡略 應遵條約已載者先行辦理 其未載者俟五年後 兩國官民彼此言語稍通 再行議定 至通商詳細章程 須酌照歐美各國通例 公平商訂 無有輕重大小之別

　　第十款
此次兩國訂立條約 與夫日後往來公牘 朝鮮專用華文 美國亦用華文 或用洋文必須以華文註明 以免歧誤

以上各款現由兩國所派全權大臣議定 先行畫押蓋印 用昭憑信 俟大朝鮮國君主一面移咨中國禮部 一面批准 大美國伯理璽天德由國會紳耆大臣議允批准後 彼此知照 指定一處互換 然後刊刻通行 使兩國官民咸知遵守

大朝鮮國 開國某年　月　日
大美國 一千八百某年　月　日

No. 3
Draft of Treaty
between
The United States and Corea
being a combination of Drafts Nos. 1 and 2
Compiled by myself and presented to His Ex. Li-Hung-Chang, for his consideration. April 2, 1882

The Kingdom of Chosen and the United States of America being sincerely desirous of establishing abiding relations of amity and friendship between their respective peoples have therefore appointed that is to say the King of Chosen and his Commissioner Plenipotentiary, and the President of the United States and his Commissioner Plenipotentiary, who having reciprocally examined their respective full powers, which have been found to be in due form, have agreed upon the several articles as under

Article I. The King of Chosen and the President of the United States shall treat with each other upon terms of perfect equality, and the subjects and citizens of the two nations shall maintain perpetual relations of friendship.
　　If other Powers deal unjustly or oppressively with either Government, the other shall under such assistance as friendly governments having treaty relations may afford to each other under the laws of nations, or shall act as mediators in order to the preservation of perfect peace.

Article II. After the conclusion of this treaty of commerce and amity, the High Contracting Powers may each appoint Diplomatic Representatives at the Court of the other and may each appoint Consular Authorities at the open ports of the other at their own convenience. These officials shall have relations with the corresponding local authorities of equal rank upon a basis of mutual equality.
　　The Diplomatic and Consular Representatives of the two Governments shall receive mutually all the privileges, rights and consideration, without discrimination which are accorded to the same class of representatives from the most favored nation. Consuls shall exercise their functions only after receipt of an exequatur from the Government to which they are accredited. The Consular Authorities shall be bona-fide officials, and no merchants shall be permitted to exercise the duties of the officer, nor shall consular officers be allowed to

engage in trade.

At ports to which no Consular Representatives have been appointed the Consuls of other Powers may be invited to act provided that no merchant shall be allowed to assume the duties; or the provisions of this treaty may for such case be enforced by the local authorities.

If Consular Representatives conduct their business in an improper manner, their exequaturs may be revoked subject to the approval previously obtained of the Diplomatic Representative of the Government by whom they are appointed.

Article III. Whenever United States vessels either by stress of weather or by want of fuel and provisions cannot reach one or other of the open ports in Chosen, they may enter any port or harbor, either to take refuge therein or to get supplies of wood, coal, and other necessities, or to make repairs. The expenses incurred thereby are to be defrayed by the ship's master. In such events both the officers and the people of the locality shall display their sympathy by rendering full assistance, and their liberality in supplying the necessities required.

If a United States vessel be wrecked on the coast of Chosen, the nearest Chosen authority, on being informed of the occurrence, shall immediately send assistance to the crew, provide for their present necessities, and take the measures necessary for the sabotage of the ship and the preservation of the cargo.

The whole shall then be brought to the knowledge of the nearest Consular Agent, in order that the latter in concert with the competent authority may take slips for sending the crew home, and for saving the debris of the ship and cargo.

Article IV. All citizens of the United States of America in Chosen, peaceably attending to their affairs, being placed on a common footing of amity and good will with subjects of Chosen, shall receive and enjoy for themselves and everything appertaining to them, the protection of the local authorities of the Government, who shall defend them from all insult and injury of any sort. If their dwellings or property be threatened or attacked by riots, incendiaries, or other violent or lawless persons, the local officers on requisition of the Consul, shall immediately dispatch a military force to disperse the rioters, apprehend the guilty individuals, and punish them with the utmost sign of the law. Subjects of Chosen guilty of any criminal act towards citizens of the United States shall be punished by the Authorities of Chosen according to the laws of Chosen; and citizens of the United States either on shore, or in any merchant vessel, who may insult, trouble, or wound the persons or injure the property of the people of Chosen, shall be punished only by the Consul or other public functionary thereto authorized, according to the laws of the United States. Arrests in order to trial may be made by either the Chosen or the United States Authorities.

When controversies arise in the Kingdom of Chosen between citizens of the United States and subjects of His Majesty, which need to be examined and decided by the public officers of the two nations, it is agreed between the Governments of the United States and Chosen that such cases shall be tried by the proper official of the nationality of the defendant. The properly authorized official of the plaintiff's nationality shall be freely permitted to attend the trial and shall be treated with the courtesy due his position. He shall be granted all proper facilities for watching the proceedings in the interests of justice. If he so desires he shall have the right to present, to examine, and to cross-examine witnesses. If the is dissatisfied with the proceedings, he shall be permitted to protest against them in detail. The law administered will be the law of the nationality of the officer trying the case.

It is however mutually agreed and understood between the High Contracting Powers that whenever the King of Chosen has so far modified and reformed the statues and judicial procedure in his Kingdom that in the judgment of the United States they conform to the laws and codes of justice in the United States, the right of exterritorial jurisdiction over U.S. citizens in Chosen shall be abandoned, and U.S. citizens shall when within the limits of the Kingdom of Chosen be subject to the jurisdiction of the native authorities.

Article V. Merchants and merchant vessels of Chosen visiting the United States for purposes of traffic shall pay tonnage dues and duties and all fees according to the Customs Regulations of the United States.

Merchants and merchant vessels of the United States visiting Chosen for purpose of trade shall pay duties upon all imports and exports. But as the particular rate of duty to be levied upon each class of merchandise has not yet been fixed, it is in the present agreed that upon such imports are necessities of life an ad valorem duty not to exceed 10% shall be levied, and that upon such as are luxuries, as foreign wines, tobacco, clocks and watches, an ad valorem duty not to exceed 30% shall be levied. Native produce exported shall pay an ad valorem duty not to exceed 3%. And it is agreed that these duties shall be paid once for all at the port of import or export, and that, no other dues, duties, or fees or taxes of any sort whatsoever shall be levied upon the goods in the interior of Chosen or at the port.

American merchant vessels entering the ports of Chosen shall pay tonnage dues at the rate of five mace per ton; payable not more than once in three months according to the Chosen calendar. The tonnage dues shall be applied exclusively to the proper and necessary envoy of the coasts of Chosen, and the construction and maintenance of lighthouses, beams, buoys, &c.-

Article VI. Subjects of Chosen who may visit the United States for purposes of commerce, shall be permitted to reside and to rent, purchase or construct residences or warehouses in all parts of the country. They shall be permitted to traffic in all merchandise, raw and manufactured that is not declared contraband by law.

Citizens of the United States visiting to the open ports of Chosen, are permitted to reside at such ports, to rent houses or land, and to erect buildings, but no coercion or intimidation may be exercised.

The land thus leased remains an integral part of the Kingdom of Chosen, and the administrative functions of the local authorities shall not be interfered with.

Native produce and foreign imports not contraband, may be bought and sold at the ports open to trade. But American merchants are not permitted either to transport foreign imports to the interior for sale, or to proceed to the interior to purchase native produce. Nor are they permitted to transport native produce from one open port to another open port. Violations of this rule will subject such cargo to confiscation, and the merchant will be handed over to his Consul to be dealt with.

The Governments of Chosen and of the United States mutually agree and indicate that subjects of Chosen shall not be permitted to import opium into any of the ports of the United States, and citizens of the United States shall not be permitted to import opium into any of the open ports of Chosen. This absolute prohibition, which extends to vessels owned by the citizens or subjects of either Power, to foreign vessels employed by them, or to vessels owned by the citizens or subjects of either Power and employed by other persons for the transportation of opium, shall be enforced by appropriate legislation on the part of Chosen and the United States, and the benefits of the favored nation clause in existing treaties shall not be claimed by the citizens or subjects of either Power as against the provisions of this opium clause.

Article VII. The officers and people of either nation residing in the other, shall have the right to employ natives for all kinds of lawful work. Should subject of Chosen guilty of violation of the laws of the Kingdom, or against whom any action had been brought conceal themselves in the residences of American citizens, or in warehouses, or on board American merchant vessels, the local authorities shall, on the one hand, notify the Consul, and, on the other, dispatch constables to make the arrests. But the warrants for such arrests shall have the Consular endorsement before it can be executed in premises occupied by American citizens.

It is to be understood, however that American citizens are not permitted to harbor such persons.

Article VIII. Students of either nationality who may proceed to the country of the other in order to study the language, literature, laws, or arts shall be given all possible protection and assistance in evidence of cordial good will.

Article IX. This being the first treaty negotiated by the Government of Chosen, is incomplete and imperfect in its provisions. It shall, however, in its stipulations be first carried into operation. As to stipulations not embodied herein, after a period of five years, when the officers and people of the two Powers shall have become more familiar with each other's language, a further negotiation of commercial provisions and regulations in detail, in conformity with international law and without unequal discrimination on either part shall be had.

Article X. This treaty and future official correspondence between the two contracting Powers shall be made on the part of Chosen in the Chinese language. The United States shall either use the Chinese language or if English used it shall be accompanied with a Chinese version in order to avoid misunderstanding.

Article XI. The contracting parties hereby agree that should at any time the

King of Chosen grant to any nation, or the merchants or citizens of any nation, any right, privilege or favor connected either with navigation, commerce, political or other intercourse, which is not conferred by this Treaty, such right, privilege, and favor shall at once freely [_____] to the benefit of the United States, its public officers, merchants, and citizens.

In faith whereof the respective Plenipotentiaries have signed and sealed the forgoing at [_____] in English and Chinese, being true originals of each text of even tenor and date, the ratifications of which shall be exchanged at within one year from the date of its execution.

【漢譯文】

美總兵薜擬子朝鮮約稿
大朝鮮國與大亞美理加合衆國切欲敦崇和惠顧商民(正本惠顧彼此人民)是以
大朝鮮國君主特派全權大次正本全權大官經理統理機務衙門事申櫶全權副官
經理統理機務衙門事金宏集大美國伯理璽天德特派全權大次水帥總兵薜斐爾
各將所奉全權字據互相較閱俱屬妥善訂立條款臚列於左

　　第一款(正本第一款不用另有照曾)
朝鮮爲中國所屬之邦而內治外交向來歸其自主今大朝鮮美國彼此明允定議大
朝鮮國主允此條約內外款按自主公例必要認眞照辦大美國國王允定認朝鮮國
爲中國屬邦嗣後永遠不相干預

　　第二款(正本此爲第一款)
嗣後大朝鮮國君主大美國伯理璽天德幷其商民各皆永遠和平友好若他國有何
不公輕藐之事一經照知必須相助從中善爲調處以示友誼關切

　　第三款(正本此爲第二款)
此次立約通商和好後兩國各交派秉權大臣駐紮彼此都城竝於彼此通商口岸設
立總(正本無總字)領事等官均聽其便此等友(官)員與本地方友(官)交涉往來
均應用品級相當之禮兩國秉權大臣與領事等官享獲種種恩施與彼此相待(正
本相待作所待)最優之國官員無異惟領事官必須奉到駐紮之國批準文憑方可
視事所派領事等官必須眞正官員不得以商人兼充亦不得兼作貿易倘各口未設
領事官或請別國領事兼代亦不得以商人兼充或卽由地方官照視定條約代辦若
駐紮朝鮮之美國領事等官辦事不合須知照美國公使彼此意見相同可將批準文
憑追回

　　第四款(正本此爲第三款)
美國船隻在朝鮮左近海面如遇颶風或缺糧食煤水距通商口岸太遠應許其隨處
收泊以避颶風購買糧食修理船隻所有經費係由船主自備地方官民應加憐恤援
助(正本援助之下添供其所需四字)如該船在不邇商之口潛往貿易拏獲船貨入

官如美國船隻在朝鮮海岸破壞朝鮮地方官一經聞知卽應飭令將水手先行救護
供其糧食等項一面設法保護船隻貨物幷行知照領事官俾將水手送回本國幷將
船貨撈起一切費用或由船主或由美國認還

　　第五款(正本此爲第四款)
美(國)人民在朝鮮居住安分守法其性命財産朝鮮地方官應當代爲保護勿許
稍有欺凌損毀如有不法之徒欲將美國房屋業産搶劫燒毀者地方官一經領事告
知卽應派兵彈壓幷查拏罪犯按律重辦朝鮮民人如有欺凌美國民人應歸朝鮮官
接(按)朝鮮律例懲辦美國民人無論在商船在岸上如有欺凌騷擾損毀朝鮮民人
性命財産等事應歸美國領事官或美國所派官員按照美國律例查拏懲辦其在朝
鮮國內朝鮮美國民人有如涉訟應由被告所屬之官員以本國律例審斷原告所屬
之國可以派員聽審審官當以禮相待聽審官如欲傳訊查訊分訊證見亦聽其便如
以審官所斷爲不公亦許其詳細駁辯大美國與大朝鮮國彼此明定如朝鮮日後改
定律例及審案辦法在美國視與本國律例辦法相符卽將美國官員在朝鮮審案之
權收以後朝鮮境內美國民人卽歸地方官管轄

　　第六款(正本此爲第五款)
朝鮮國商船前往美國貿易凡納稅船鈔幷一切各費應遵照美國海關章程辦理與
征收本國人民及相待最優之國稅鈔不得額外加增美國商船前往朝鮮貿易進出
口貨物均應納稅其收稅之權應由朝鮮自主所由進出口稅項及海關禁防偸漏
諸弊悉聽朝鮮政府設立規則先期知會(正本先期知會之下添美國官布示商民
遵行現擬十一字)先訂細稅則大略各色進口貨有關民生(正本民生下有日用二
字)者照估價値百抽稅不得過一十其奢靡玩要等物洋酒呂宋煙鍾表之類照估
價售百抽稅(稅不得過三十至出口土貨槪照値百抽)不得過五凡進口洋貨除在
口岸完納正稅外該項貨物或入內地或在口岸永遠不納別項稅費美國商船進朝
鮮口岸須納船鈔每噸銀五錢每船按中曆一季抽一次

　　第七款(正本此爲第六款)
朝鮮國商民前往美國各處准其在該處居住賃房買屋(正本買屋作買也)起蓋棧
房任其自便其貿易工作一切所有土産以及製造之物與不違禁之貨均許買賣美
國商民前往朝鮮已開口岸准其在該處所定界內居住賃房租地建屋任其自便其
貿易工作一切所有土産以及製造之物與不違禁之貨均許買賣惟租地時不得稍
有勒逼該地租價悉照朝鮮所定等則完納其出租之地仍歸朝鮮版圖除按此約內

所指明歸美國官員應管商民外(正本商民下添錢産二字)皆仍歸朝鮮地方官管轄美國商民不得以洋貨運入內地售買亦不得自入內地採買土貨幷不得以土貨由此口販運彼口違者將貨物入官幷將該商交領事官懲辦

第八款(正本此爲第七款)
朝鮮(正本朝鮮之下添國字美國彼此商定八字)商民不准販運洋藥入美國通商口岸美國商民亦不准販運洋藥入朝鮮通商口岸(正本通商口岸之下添幷由此口運往彼口亦不准作一切買賣洋藥之貿易所有二十三字)兩國商民無論雇用本國船別國船及本國船爲別國商民雇用販運洋藥者均由各本國自行永遠禁止查出從重懲罰

第九款(正本此爲第八款)
如有朝鮮國內有事故恐致境內缺食大朝鮮國君主暫禁米糧出口經地方官照知後由美國官員轉飭在各口美國商民一體遵辦(正本遵辦之下添惟於已開仁川一港各色米糧皆行禁止運出)紅蔘一項朝鮮舊禁出口美國人如有潛買出洋者均查拏入官仍分別懲罰

第十款(正本此爲第九款)
凡砲位鎗刀火藥鉛丸一切軍器應行由朝鮮官自行采辦或美國人奉朝鮮官准買明文方准進口有私販查貨入官仍分別懲罰

第十一款(正本此爲第十款)
凡兩國官員商民在彼此通商地方居住均可雇請各色人等勤執分內工藝若朝鮮人遇犯本國例禁或牽涉被控丸在美國商民寓所行棧及商船隱匿者由地方官照知領事館有或准差役自行往拏或由領事派人拿交朝鮮差役美國官民不得稍有庇縱指留

第十二款(正本此爲第十一款)
兩國生徒往來學習語言文字律例藝業等事彼此均宜勸助以敦睦誼

第十三款(正本此爲第十二款)
玆朝鮮國初次立約姑從簡略應遵條約已載者先行辦理其未載者俟五年後兩國

官民彼此言語稍通再行議定至通商(正本通商下有詳細二字)章程須酌照萬國公法通例公平商訂無有輕重大小之別

　　第十四款(正本此爲第十三款)
此次兩國訂立條約與夫日後往來公牘朝鮮專用華文美國亦用華文或有英文必須以華文註明以免岐誤

　　第十五款(正本此爲第十四款)
現經兩國議定嗣後朝鮮(正本嗣後下擡書大朝鮮國君主有何惠政云云)有何惠政恩典利益施及他國或其商民無論關涉海面行船通商貿易交往等事爲該國幷其商民從來未沾抑爲此條約所無者亦准美國官民一體均霑(正本一體均霑之下改以惟此種優待他國之利益若立有專條一體遵守方准同霑優待之利益)惟於優待他國利益係出於甘讓立有專條互相酬報

以上各款現經大朝鮮美國大臣同在朝鮮(正本朝鮮下添仁川府三字)議定繕寫華洋文各三分句法相同先行畫押蓋印以昭憑信仍俟兩國御筆批準總以一年爲期在朝鮮(正本朝鮮下添仁川府三字)互換然後將此約各款彼此通喩本國官員商民俾得咸知遵守

大朝鮮國開國四百九十一年 中國光緖八年四月初六日
大美國一千八百年月日

A.

Letter to His Ex. Li-Hung-Chang: on the subject of the First Article of the Treaty between the United States and Corea, as proposed by Corea

Tientsin, China

April 4th, 1882

His Excellency,

Li-Hung-Chang,

Grand Secretary, Senior Guardian to the Emperor, Viceroy of Chihli, &c. &c. &c.

Your Excellency,

By an understanding with your Ex. I had the honor to meet in conference on Saturday last, with H. Ex. The Haikwan Taotai, Ma Taotai, and Mr. Lo-Fung-loh on the subject of a treaty between the United States and the Kingdom of Corea.

I submitted to these officials, acting on the part of your Ex. a draft of each a treaty combining the projects of the two Parties which had previously been interchanged, in such form as I thought would meet with your approbation and thus secure your assistance in the accomplishment of the object in view.

This draft seemed to me liberal in terms, and eminently just towards Corea, which country is unaccustomed to foreign intercourse, and one by which it might shape its future policy with reference to all foreign nations.

I was met by these officials however with the propositions contained in the first article of the Corean project to wit: "Chosen, being a dependent state of the Chinese Empire, has nevertheless hitherto exercised her own sovereignty in all matters of internal administrative and foreign relations. After the conclusion of this Treaty, the King of Chosen and the President of the United States shall treat with each other upon terms of perfect equality, and the subjects and citizens of the two nations shall maintain perpetual relations of friendship.

If other Powers deal unjustly or oppressively with either Government, the other shall render assistance and protection, or shall act as mediator in order to the preservation of perfect peace."

My assent to this article was made the "sine-qua-non" of any further discussion.

I do not deny the right of a semi-dependant state to make independent treaties, on the contrary if (as the article referred to asserts) the Kingdom of

Corea is a dependent state in possession of sovereign powers as to its foreign and domestic relations; then I respectfully submit, that the United States has the right to treat with it irrespective of the suzerainty of China. It is eminently proper that the King of Corea should take the advice and be governed by the counsel of his suzerain the Emperor of China, and the United States has no cause whatever of complaint, but the privilege remains unimpaired for the two countries to negotiate upon terms of perfect equality and without any reference to, or acknowledgement of any other power that contained in themselves.

Any reference therefore to China in this treaty would not be pertinent to it, and might be the cause of complications which the United States always desires to avoid in its foreign relations. Moreover the article in question more or less directly connects China and the United States, in such a way as to make these two great powers, the joint protectors of Corea. However willing I might be personally to see Corea enter the family of nations under such powerful escort, your Ex. will understand, that I am only authorized to make a treaty of amity and commerce, and not to enter into any political alliance.

Under these circumstances I submit to your Ex. that you should not ask me to insert in this treaty, an extraneous article which might before reaching in its effects, but which has no bearing upon the object, and which at the same time has no precedent.

I have the honor to submit these views, with the hope, that your decision as indicated by your advisers may not be final.

I have the honor to be,
Your Excellency's obedient servant
(signed) R.W. Shufeldt
Commodore, U.S.N.
Envoy to Corea

D.
Memorandum of an Interview between His Ex. Li-Hung-Chang and myself, on the subject of the Corean Treaty and other matters. Tientsin, China.
Thursday, April 6th, 1882
Had an interview yesterday, April 5th, with His Ex. the Viceroy at his Yamen, upon the subject of the Treaty with Corea.
At this interview were present His Ex., the Haikwan Taotai, Ma Taotai, and Mr.

Lo-Fung-loh interpreter.

His Ex. began the interview by saying that the draft of a treaty which I had previously exhibited to him, met with his approval, with the exception of some small emendations, which he would send to me for consideration. (This draft is a combination of the perfect purporting to come from Corea, and one previously arranged by Mr. Holcombe and myself at Peking.)

His Ex. however said, that the insertion of the first article of the Corean treaty (which will be found in [_____] in the foregoing letter to His Ex. dated April 4th and inclosed: marked A) was indispensable; otherwise he could not send either a messenger or a gun-boat to accompany me to Corea; that the instructions of his own Govt made this imperative. I then sent to him the letter of April 4th as an agreement why this article was regarded as inadmissible on the part of the United States in any treaty with Corea. Subsequently to his own request, the letter was handed to him and His Ex. after considerable discussion, asked for four days further consideration, when a final interview might take place but intimated that in any event, this article would be sent to Corea, to be inserted there; as he insisted that it was written at the desire of the King of Corea himself. I told him that in that event I could not take the to Corea under the auspices of China, because the article was entirely inadmissible. A discussion then ensued as to the propriety of the Corean Govt addressing a communication to the Govt of the United States, after the signature of the treaty, stating that such treaty had been made, by and with the consent of the Govt of China. In reference to this, I would only commit myself so far, as to promise to see that such communication reached its destination; but again insisted distinctly upon the fact, that the United States had nothing whatever to do in its treaty with Corea, with the Govt of China, except so far as its friendly offices were concerned.

His Ex. then to my surprise, stated to me, that a friend of his in America had telegraphed him, that in a published letter of mine to my Govt I had said that "force was the only argument to use in Corea." He asked me if I had written any such letters to the Govt. I told him I had not. He then repeated the question with regard to Eastern Nations generally. I then replied that I did not propose to hold myself responsible to him for any correspondence of mine whether official or personal. I then said to His Ex. that since he had broached a subject outside of the matter under discussion, I wished him to understand that I appreciated the studied indignity with which I had been treated by him for four months. That I had on two or three occasions sought an interview, and it had been denied me. That his manner had been more or less reflected by the mandarins surrounding him, until the foreign residents in Tientsin had come to consider me as an adventure seeking officer in China, although he himself will know that I had come here by his own invitation and with the approval of my own Govt. His Ex. could not suppose that I would submit to such treatment without intimating it to my own Govt or resenting it in any other meaner that I might think proper. I had never, to my knowledge, given His Ex. any reason for this palpable disregard both of my age and position, and yet it had been so marked, that my own Minister had on two occasions advised me to leave Tientsin rather than submit to it. (I had remained however, quietly bearing it, in order that I might see whether an American officer could be compelled to leave China under a condition of ignoring, when his conduct had been irreproachable. I then said to His Ex. that I did not wish any further discussion of this subject, and that I respectfully desired him to understand, that our intercourse hereafter must be of an official character.

The subject was then changed by His Ex. asking me if he might recommend Mr. Patrick as interpreter, in case I went to Corea. I told him I had applied to my Govt two months since for an interpreter; that I desired one who would be responsible to my own Govt for his work, and that I should prefer Mr. Holcombe, if he could be spared from Peking, to any other person the Govt might select.

The interview ended with the understanding before mentioned, that a final arrangement might be made at the end of four days.

R.W. Shufeldt
Commodore U.S.N. and Envoy to Corea
N.B. The impression may have been conveyed to His Ex. that I denied positively having so written to my Govt in reference to the use of force towards Eastern Nations generally, but if so it was owing to the existing nature of the conversation and its passing through an interpreter.

李鴻章(1882. 4. 11/光緒八年二月二十四日) ➜ 總署(1882. 4. 12/光緒八年二月二十五日)

106

Shufeldt 회견 보고 (2)

二月二十五日 北洋大臣李鴻章函稱 再奉二月十八二十一日六百六十二六十五號兩次密諭 以美國與朝鮮立約一事 重費盡籌 曷任感佩 薛總兵接閱鴻章前擬約稿後 於各款略有增改 大致尙無甚出入 惟於第一款聲明朝鮮爲中國屬邦 堅不允從 先經周馬二道與之力持 十七日該總兵復來署謁商 鴻章謂此款若不允行 中國卽未便與聞其事 將來亦未便派員同往 該總兵意甚決絶 留下所擬洋文照會稿 譯出呈鑒 今幸何署使在鈞署議添認明屬邦一節 應俟該署使到津會晤 再堅持原議 與相駁辨 未知果就範圍否 惟據薛總兵面稱此事責在全權 何署使位望旣卑 祇可贊襄繙譯之事 未能攬越立約之事 除俟議定若何再行詳達外 附鈔譯薛斐爾照會草底 奉呈鈞鑒 再敬台祺

　　照錄淸摺
　　照譯美總兵薛斐爾照會中堂稿
照得本大臣前承貴大臣鈞允 於本月十四日會同津海關周道 營務處馬道 羅牧商議朝鮮合衆兩國擬訂約稿 當將本大臣所改約稿相示 該約稿係將兩國原擬者融會爲一 鄙意貴大臣必以爲然 許以勷助議約一事 必易成功 查明朝鮮國與外國交際來往 尙未爛熟 現在本大臣所擬約稿相待朝鮮殊極公允 可爲朝鮮後來與各國通好之程式 惟據周道等稱 朝鮮原擬第一款內所載朝鮮係中國屬邦 而內政外交向來得以自主 立約後大朝鮮國君主大美國伯理璽天德平行相待 兩國人民永敦和好 若他國有不公輕蔑之事 彼此必須援護 或從中善爲調處 以期永保安全等因 此條如美國不允 和約卽勿庸議 本大臣査半主之國 於訂約一事原可自主 今按朝鮮原擬第一款 朝鮮係中國屬邦 而內政外交向來得以自主 是在美國固可與朝鮮訂約 不必認朝鮮爲中國屬邦 在朝鮮於議約一事須奉中國大皇帝旨意 美國亦不必過問 是朝鮮合衆兩國平行議約 於兩國之外並不必徵引他國也 如引用中國字樣 與本旨旣不相涉 而復易滋疑義 殊非美國愼重邦交之意 且循繹其義 有援護字樣 是立約後中美兩國公保朝鮮一國矣 本大臣深願朝鮮能得强大之國如中華合衆者爲之保護 自存於列國之中 惟本大臣此次欽奉本國訓條 專立通商條約 殊無議立援護條約之權 是第一款旣與

通商和約無涉 復於美國諸多未便 歷溯美國訂約 並未有辦遇此等成案 惟乞貴大臣俯察情由 許將原議第一款刪改 再行妥議 俾朝鮮合衆議約一事 不至中輟 實深盼望之至

李鴻章(1882. 4. 23) ➜ R. W. Shufeldt

조약 체결 중재를 위한 馬建忠 파견 통보

To His Excellency
Commodore Shufeldt U.S.N.
Envoy Extraordinary and Minister Plenipotentiary to Corea
Sir,

    I have the honour to inform you that His Majesty the Emperor of China has been Gracious to approve of my memorial whereby I have prayed the Throne to appoint Ma-Rietchong an expectant Taotai of the Honorary Title of the Second Rank to proceed to Corea in a man-of-war of the Chinese Imperial Navy to act as an intermediary for facilitating the final arrangement of the forthcoming treaty between the United States of America and Corea.

    The recommendation to appoint a high official for this purpose was especially made at the request both from your part and from the part of the Corean Government.

    As Ma Taotai has followed the whole course of the negotiations of the said treaty from beginning to end he will unquestionably be able to render valuable services towards the initiating of the perpetual friendship and amicable relation between the two countries. I therefore trust you will place your whole confidence in him so that my hope for the accomplishment of an affair in which I have taken so deep an interest may not be frustrated and the status quo of the great East may be maintained.

    I avail myself of this opportunity to assure you my highest consideration and esteem.

Grand Secretary of the Chinese Empire and Viceroy of Chili

Li Hung Chang
Tientsin Apr 23, '82
Letter informing of the appointment of Ma-Rietchong as intermediary.
Answered
May 6, 1882

C. Holcombe (1882. 4. 24) ➜ F. T. Frelinghuysen

李鴻章 회견 보고

Sir:

 I have the honor to report to the Department that in compliance with the request of Commodore Shufeldt, and in accordance, as I have judged, with the wishes of our government, I have made three visits to Tientsin in order to render assistance in the negotiation of a treaty between the United States and Corea.

 In the opinion of both Commodore Shufeldt and myself my presence and assistance were imperatively necessary. The entire business has been conducted in the Chinese language, and mainly with the Viceroy Li Hung-chang. Our representative had no interpreter, and Mr. Waclay, who is I believe, acting interpreter to the Consulate at Tientsin, having been absent from his post-almost continuously since last September. His services could not be secured, and it was found decidedly unsafe to trust to the interpreter who were in the pay of the Viceroy. There were moreover, many important points in the negotiation of a treaty with Corea in which Commodore Shufeldt was good enough to ask for my advice and council, which could only be given effectively by being on the spot where negotiation were conducted.

 On my first visit I was absent from Peking six days, on the second, nine, and on the third, twelve. I was in daily communication with Peking, and could have reached here in a few hours had my presence been necessary.

 In my opinion, the public interests here have suffered no detriment by these visits to Tientsin, and I trust the negotiations with Corea have been substantially advanced.

 I beg the approval of the Department for my action as described herein.

 And as these journeys were made safely upon public business, and not with any view to private interests, I enclose a statement of my expenses for the three trips, and request most respectfully to be authorized to draw upon the Department for the amount.

I have the honor to be, Sir your obedient servant.
March 12-17. 23-31. April 11-16 all expenses $ 191.75cent
Peking April 24th, 1882

R. W. Shufeldt (1882. 4. 28) ➡ F. T. Frelinghuysen

조미수호통상조약 최종안 보고

No. 7
Shanghai, China
Hon. Frederick T. Frelinghuysen
Secretary of State
Washington, D.C.

Sir:

I have the honor to enclose herewith a copy of Draft No. 4 – and the final one, of the Treaty between the United States and Corea. Duplicate originals in the Chinese language of this Draft were certified to as correct, by H.Exc. the Viceroy and myself. One of these, I have reason to believe, has been sent to Corea; with a recommendation on the part of the Viceroy that it be adopted.

The First Article in the Corean Project of the Treaty referred to in my dispatch No. 5, you will observe has been entirely omitted, in the enclosed Draft. I had insisted upon this, as being outside of the object of the Treaty, and beyond my authority. The final understanding was, that I should ask the Viceroy to send the Treaty to Corea with an Envoy or messenger, as an act of friendship on the part of the Government of China towards that of the United States.

This proposition would have been agreed to if, during an interview between Mr. Holcombe and the Foreign Office at Peking, that Office had not proposed to him whether in some way less positive, the suzerainty of China over Corea might not be mentioned in the Treaty. To this proposition Mr. Holcombe did not see the objections which had occurred to me; consequently the Foreign Office addressed a letter to the Viceroy on the subject, and out of deference to the wishes, both of the Foreign Office, and of H. Exc. The Viceroy, although contrary to my own judgment, I sent to the Department on the 12th inst. the following telegram:

Tientsin, April 12th, 1882.

"May I insert in Treaty with Corea an Article admitting dependence of Corea upon China. China conceding sovereign powers to Corea. They desire it. I have

objected. Answer.
Shufeldt."
which at this date remains unanswered.

After the completion of the Draft at Tientsin, I also telegraphed on the 19th inst. the following effect.

"Business arranged except subject of [_____] telegram ready start for Corea, must have interpreter suggest Holcombe his assistance very necessary thirty-day probably sufficient can you send him putting Taylor in charge of anchors at Peking.
Shufeldt."

By reference to any dispatch to the Secretary acknowledging the receipt of my instructions, you will observe that I asked for the appointment of an interpreter to accompany me to Corea. I know no one is competent as Mr. Holcombe, or so responsible to his own Government. The evident desire of the Chinese Government to make this Treaty as advantageous as possible to China, renders it absolutely necessary that a competent Chinese scholar should accompany me if I go to Corea.

I have made arrangements to be at Chefoo on, or about the 1st prox., in order to meet there the 'Swatara,' detailed to convey me to Corea; as well as a messenger appointed by the Viceroy to accompany me, either in that vessel, or in a Chinese gun boat; and for that purpose shall leave Shanghai within a few days.

But the death of the mother of the Viceroy, which, under the customs of China necessitate his immediate retirement from public life at least for the time being, may derange, or delay action on the part of the Chinese Government. If however, I find the messenger at Chefoo, and that this Treaty has been sent to Corea with the unconditional approval of the Viceroy, I shall, with absence of further instructions from the Department, proceed at once to that country, either to Fusan, as the Viceroy now desires, or to the mouth of the Seóul River.

I have no reason to change my opinion hitherto expressed as to the object of China and only in making, but in hastening this Treaty, but if the one here proposed can be made independent of political considerations, then I see no objection under favorable circumstances to making the effort.

If however the Treaty has not been forwarded unconditionally, I shall remain at Chefoo until the time will have elapsed necessary to hear from the Department by mail in answer to the telegram of the 12th inst, before referred to; when, not hearing, and no further action being taken on the part of the Chinese Government, I shall apply by telegram to be relieved from the duty assigned me.

I have our doubt however, that the preliminary efforts of our Government in this matter, will bring the attention of the world to Corea, and lead to the opening of that country.

Judging from the newspapers, the antagonism between China and Japan is growing daily in importance. Two parties representing these Governments respectively, are said to have been formed in China; and it is safe to predict, that at no distant day, it will become the battlefield of the two nations. From this same sources I learn, that the French Admiral has secretly dispatched a vessel to the coast of Corea, which will probably be followed by vessels of war of other nations, as it seems to be a fixed idea here in the East, that Corea is about to be opened.

I am,
With great respect,
Your obedient servant
RW Shufeldt
Commodore U.S.N.

No. 4

The United States of America and the Kingdom of Chosen, being sincerely desirous of establishing permanent relations of amity and friendship between their respective peoples have to this end appointed, that is to say, the President of the United States, as his Commissioner Plenipotentiary, and his Majesty, the King of Chosen, as his Commissioner Plenipotentiary, who, having reciprocally examined their respective Powers, which have been found to be in due form, have agreed upon the several following Articles.

Article I.
There shall be perpetual peace and friendship between the President of the United States and the King of Chosen and the citizens and subjects of their respective governments. If other Powers deal unjustly or oppressively with

either Government, the other will exert their good offices, on being informed of the case, to bring about an amicable arrangement, thus showing their friendly feelings.

Article II.

After the conclusion of the Treaty of amity and commerce, the High Contracting Powers may each appoint Diplomatic Representatives to reside at the Court of the other, and may each appoint Consular Representatives at the ports of the other which are open to foreign commerce, at their own convenience.

These officials shall have relations with the local authorities of equal rank, upon a basis of mutual equality.

The Diplomatic and Consular Representatives of the two Governments shall mutually all the privileges, rights, and immunities, without discrimination, which are accorded to the same classes of Representatives from the most favored nation.

Consuls shall exercise their functions only on receipt of an exequatur from the Government to which they are accredited. Consular authorities shall be bona-fide officials. No merchants shall be permitted to exercise the duties of the office, nor shall Consular officers be allowed to engage in trade. At ports to which no Consular Representatives have been appointed, the Consuls of other Powers may be invited to act, provided that no merchant shall be allowed to assume Consular functions, or the provisions of the Treaty may in such cases, be enforced by the local authorities.

If Consular Representatives of the United States in Chosen conduct their business in an improper manner, their exequaturs may be revoked subject to the approval previously obtained of the Diplomatic Representative of the United States.

Article III.

Whenever United States vessels either because of stress of weather, or by want of fuel or provisions cannot reach the nearest open port in Chosen, they may enter any port or harbor, either to take refuge therein, or to get supplies of wood, coal and other necessities, or to make repairs, the expenses incurred thereby being defrayed by the ships master. In such event the officers and people of the locality shall display their sympathy by rendering full assistance, and their liberality by furnishing the necessities required.

If a vessel of the United States carries on a clandestine trade at a port not open to foreign commerce such vessel with her cargo shall be seized and confiscated.

If a United States vessel be wrecked on the coast of Chosen, the local authorities on being informed of the occurrence, shall immediately render assistance to the crew, provide for their present necessities, and take the measures necessary for the salvage of the ship and the preservation of her cargo. They shall also bring the matter to the knowledge of the nearest Consular Representative of the United States in order that steps may be taken to send the crew home and to save the ship and cargo. The necessary expenses shall be defrayed either by the ship's master or by the United States.

Article IV.
All citizens of the United States of American in Chosen, peaceably attending to their own affairs, shall receive and enjoy for themselves and everything appertaining to them the protection of the local authorities of the Government of Chosen who shall defend them from all insult and injury of any sort. If their dwellings or property be threatened or attacked by riots, incendiaries, or other violent or lawless persons, the local officers on requisition of the Consul, shall immediately dispatch a military force to disperse the rioters, apprehend the guilty individuals, and punish them with the utmost sign of the law.

Subjects of Chosen guilty of any criminal act towards citizens of the United States, shall be punished by the authorities of Chosen according to the laws of Chosen; and citizens of the United States, either on shore or in any merchant vessel, who may insult, trouble, or wound the persons or injure the property of the people of Chosen, shall be arrested and punished only by the law of Consul or other public functionary of the United States thereto authorized, according to the laws of the United States.

When controversies arise in the Kingdom of Chosen between citizens of the United States and subjects of His Majesty which need to be examined and decided by the public officers of the two nations; it is agreed between the two Governments of the United States and Chosen, that such cases shall be tried by the proper official of the nationality of the defendant according to the laws of that nation. The properly authorized official shall be freely permitted to attend the trial, and shall be treated with the courtesy due to his position. He shall be granted all the proper facilities for watching the proceedings in the interest of justice. If he so desires, he shall have the right to present, to examine, and to cross-examine witnesses. If he is dissatisfied with the proceedings, he shall be permitted to protest against them in detail.

It is however mutually agreed and understood between the High Contracting Powers, that whenever the King of Chosen shall have so far modified and reformed the statutes and judicial procedure of his Kingdom that, in the judgment of the United States, they conform to the laws and course of justice in the United States, the right of exterritorial jurisdiction over United States citizens in chosen shall be abandoned, and thereafter United States citizens, where within the bounds of the Kingdom of Chosen, shall be subject to the jurisdiction of the native authorities.

Article V.
Merchants and merchant vessels of Chosen visiting the United States for purposes of traffic, shall pay duties and tonnage dues and all fees according to the Customs Regulations of the United States, but no higher or other rates of duties and tonnage dues shall be exacted of them, than are levied upon citizens of the United States or upon citizens or subjects of the most favored nation.

Merchants and merchant vessels of the United States visiting Chosen for purposes of traffic shall pay duties upon all merchandise imported and exported. The authority to levy duties is of right vested in the Government of Chosen. The tariff of duties upon exports and imports, together with the Customs Regulations for the prevention of smuggling and other irregularities will be fixed by the authorities of Chosen and communicated to the proper officials of the United States, to be by the latter notified to their citizens and duly observed.

It is however agreed in the first instance as a general measure, that the tariff upon such imports as are articles of daily use shall not exceed an ad valorem duty of ten per centum; that the tariff upon such imports as are luxuries, as for instance foreign wines, foreign tobacco, clocks and watches, shall not exceed an ad valorem duty of thirty per centum; and that native produce exported shall pay a duty not to exceed five per centum ad valorem. And it is further agreed that the duty upon foreign imports shall be paid once for all at the port of entry, and that no other dues, duties, fees, taxes, or charges of any sort, shall be levied upon such imports either in the interior of Chosen or at the ports.

United States merchant vessels entering the ports of Chosen shall pay tonnage dues at the rate of five mace per ton, payable once in three months on each vessel, according to the Chinese calendar.

Article VI.

Subjects of Chosen who may visit the United States shall be permitted to reside and to rent premises, purchase land, or to construct residences or warehouses in all parts of the country. They shall be freely permitted to pursue their various callings and avocations, and to traffic in all merchandise, raw and manufactured that is not declared contraband by law.

Citizens of the United States who may resort to the ports of Chosen which are open to foreign commerce shall be permitted to reside at such open ports within the limits of the concessions and to lease buildings or land, or to construct residences or warehouses therein. They shall be freely permitted to pursue their various callings and avocations within the limits of the port, and to traffic in all merchandise, raw and manufactured that is not declared contraband by law.

No coercion or intimidation in the acquisition of land or buildings shall be permitted, and the land sent as fixed by authorities of Chosen shall be paid. And it is expressly agreed that land as acquired in the open ports of Chosen still remains an integral part of the Kingdom, and that all rights of jurisdiction over persons and property within such areas remain vested in the authorities of Chosen, except in so far as such rights have been expressly relinquished by this Treaty.

American citizens are not permitted either to transport foreign imports to the interior for sale, or to proceed therein to purchase nature produce.

Nor are they permitted to transport nature produce from one open port to another open port.

Violations of this rule will subject such merchandise to confiscation and the merchant offending will be handed over to the Consular Authorities to be dealt with.

Article VII.

The Governments of the United States and of Chosen mutually agree and undertake that subjects of Chosen shall be permitted to import opium into any of the ports of the United States, and citizens of the United States shall not be permitted to import opium into any of the open ports of Chosen, to transport it from one open port to another open port, or to traffic in it Chosen. This absolute prohibition which extends to the vessels owned by the citizens or subjects of either Power, to foreign vessels employed by them, and to vessels owned by the citizens of either Power and employed by other persons for the transportation of opium, shall be enforced by proper legislation on the part of the United States and of Chosen, and offenders against it shall be severely punished.

Article VIII.

Whenever the Government of Chosen shall have reason to apprehend a scarcity of food within the limits of the Kingdom, His Majesty may by decree, temporarily prohibit the export of all breadstuffs, and such Decree shall be binding on all citizens of the United States in Chosen upon due notice having been given them by the Authorities of Chosen through the proper officers of the United States.

Chosen having of old prohibited the exportation of red ginseng if citizens of the United States clandestinely purchase it for export, it shall be confiscated and the offenders punished.

Article IX.

The purchase of cannon, small arms, swords, gunpowder, shot, and all munitions of war is permitted only to officials of the Government of Chosen, and they may be imported by citizens of the United States only under a written permit from the authorities of Chosen. If these articles are clandestinely imported they shall be confiscated, and the offending parties shall be punished.

Article X.

The officers and people of either nation residing in the other, shall have the right to employ natives for all kinds of lawful work.

Should, however, subjects of Chosen, guilty of violations of the laws of the Kingdom, or against whom any action has been brought, conceal themselves in the residences or warehouses of United States citizens, or on board United States merchant vessels, the Consular Authorities of the United States, on being notified of the fact by the local authorities will either permit the latter to dispatch constables to make the arrests, or the persons will be arrested by the Consular Authorities and handed over to the local constables.

Officials or citizens of the United States shall not harbor such persons.

Article XI.
Students of either nationality who may proceed to the country of the other in order to study the language, literature, land or arts, shall be given all possible protection and assistance in evidence of cordial good will.

Article XII.
This, being the first Treaty negotiated by Chosen, and hence being general and incomplete, in its provisions, shall in the first instance be put into operation in all things stipulated herein. As to stipulations not contained herein, after an interval of five years, when the officers and people of the two Powers shall have become more familiar with each other's language, a further negotiation of commercial provisions and regulations in detail, in conformity with international law and without unequal discrimination on either part shall be had.

Article XIII.
This Treaty and future official correspondence between the two contracting Governments shall be made, on the part of Chosen, in the Chinese language.
　　The United States shall either use the Chinese Language, or, if English be used it shall be accompanied with a Chinese version, in order to avoid misunderstanding.

Article XIV.
The High Contracting Powers hereby agree that, should at any time the King of Chosen grant to any nation or to the merchants or citizen of any nation any right, privilege, or favor, connected either with navigation, commerce, political or other intercourse, which is not conferred by this treaty, such right, privilege and favor shall freely insure to the benefit of the United States, its public officers, merchants, and citizens; provided always that whenever such right, privilege or favor is accompanied by any condition, or equivalent concession granted by the other nation interested, the United States, its officers, and people shall only be entitled to the benefit of each right, privilege or favor, upon complying with the conditions or concessions connected therewith.
　　In faith whereof the respective Commissioners Plenipotentiary have signed and sealed the forgoing at in English and Chinese, being three originals of each text of even tenor and date, the ratifications of which shall be exchanged

at within one year from the date of its execution, and immediately thereafter this Treaty shall be in all its provisions publicly proclaimed and made known by both Governments in their respective countries in order that it may be obeyed by their citizens and subjects respectively.

 Chosen
 A.D.   1882

 Draft No. 4 and Final of Treaty between The United States and The Kingdom of Chosen.
 Tientsin.
 April 11th 1882

G. Young (1882. 5. 1) ➜ F. T. Frelinghuysen

Shufeldt의 조약체결 활동에 관한 보고

Sir:-

In obedience to your several instructions given to me when in Washington, I have the honor to submit this memorandum, in reference to the duties of Commodore Shufeldt as naval attaché to the Legation in Peking.

On May 9, 1881, Commodore Shufeldt was directed by Mr. Blaine to report to the American Minister, Mr. Angell.

He was instructed to stop at Tientsin and inquired "as to the readiness of the Corean Government to resume the negotiations for a treaty of a amity and commerce", which he had been instructed to conclude on a "visit to the Kingdom,"

He was instructed to report fully- "on the military and naval organization of the Chinese Empire, and the present condition and probable extension of our commerce there."

In a despatch of the same date, Mr. Blaine writes to Minister Angell at length in reference to the mission of Commodore Shufeldt. The special point in this despatch is, "a desire for more precise knowledge, not only of the direct interest to the United States of a treaty with Corea, but of the general conditions of the political relations of the East."

Mr. Blaine alludes to the possibility of the Chinese Government desiring to engage American naval officers in its service. He expresses the President's willingness that Commodore Shufeldt should accept any offer of that nature from the Chinese Government.

On November 1st, 1881, Mr.Blaine writes to Commodore Shufeldt as to the stipulations in a proposed treaty with Corea. Seamen were to be protected. One or more ports were to be opened for trade.- The principle of extraterritorial jurisdiction as it now exists in China and Japan was accepted. Corea was to be at liberty to determine her own tariffs with the understanding that the United States would always stand with the most favored nations.

On the same day a despatch was addressed by Mr.Blaine to J.W. Holcombe, Charge d'Affairs, which contemplated an objection from the diplomatic Representatives of the other Power to the appointment of Commodore Shufeldt to a high command in the Chinese Navy. J.W. Holcombe was instructed to insist that the Chinese Government shall be allowed to act as an independent power.

On February 4, 1882, Mr. Holcombe wrote an important despatch detailing a conversation at the Foreign Office, Pekin. The Foreign Office was anxious that the King of Corea, should enter into treaty relations with the outside powers, and more particularly with the United States.- This Mr.Holcombe, believes, arose from the fear on the part of China, "that sooner or later the autonomy of Corea would be threatened by the aggressions of Russia and Japan, and that this serious danger could be best met by bringing the Peninsular Kingdom into the family of nations."

In other words the geographical position of Corea was such that whoever annexed or governed the Kingdom would be in a position to menace the independence and integrity of China. If therefore the United States could be induced to recognize the independence of Corea, -Russia or Japan would hesitate before carrying not the policy attributed to them, the policy of annexation- Corea on treaty isolations with the United States would in some way place its independence under the moral protection of the United States. This would be another's guarantee to the Chinese of the freedom from invasion.

In April 19, 1882, Commodore Shufeldt telegraphed from Tientsin that Treaty negotiation with Corea were in progress,—that the Chinese wished an article admitting the dependence of Corea upon China, as a tributary power,— which China concealed sovereign rights to Corea.—

This telegraphic message read in the light of the confidential despatch of Mr. Holcombe, a summary of which I have just presented, would seem to incite the question as to whether the proposed treaty was for the benefit of China or Corea.

How far should be commit ourselves to a convention which China would regard as protecting her frontiers from some dreaded ultimate danger on the part of Russia, or Japan and which Russia and Japan might deem an unwarranted interference in Asiatic politics.- It is difficult for any Western Power to determine the delicate and lazy conditions pertaining to the "Independence" of Asiatic Powers.- Thus Siam claims independence,- and its King has long ceased to pay tribute to China.- China has never relinquished sovereign rights, and may at any time service them.- The Loo Choo Islands have long been tributary to China. Japan not long since assented sovereign rights, dethroned the King,- annexed his dominions to the Empire as one of the Departments, and carried him as a prisoner to Tokio.- The same thing may be seen in Corea at any time.

If Corea is an independent Kingdom, then we can treat with its sovereign without regard to China.- If Corea is a province of the Chinese Empire, then we should treat directly with the Pekin Foreign Office.- If the question is in doubt, as is most probably the cast,- then we should consider the wisdom of the United States endeavoring to settle it by the indirect method of a commercial treaty.

I am not insensible to the value of a commercial treaty with Corea. I should also be disposed to think that as far as our good offices could be gracefully and efficiently given they should be used to protect Corea either in the "Independence" which China will recognize- or in the tributary position which the Peking Government is indisposed to surrender.—

I am Sir, with great respect, your obedient servant.
John Russel Young.

(6) 조선과 청국의 교섭

總署(1879. 8. 21/光緒五年七月四日)

조선에 조약체결을 권고할 것을 상주

總理各國事務衙門奏擬勸朝鮮交聘各國片
再東洋三國曰日本曰琉球曰朝鮮琉球朝鮮久隷中國藩屬琉球接壤日本而朝鮮
尤爲中國東三省屛蔽實有脣齒相依之勢咸豊年間中原多故英法等國恃其船砲
之利乘隙要挾通商傳敎各事悉立條約自是西洋大小各國先後皆以議約接踵而
來且皆往與日本國立約雖以蕞爾琉球亦間有一二國與立約者惟朝鮮未與西洋
各國通各國以其爲中國屬屢向臣衙門請爲介紹臣等惟以政敎禁令聽其自爲等
語却之英法美國昔嘗自行法辦朝鮮拒之皆未來得志而返而其心未嘗釋然朝鮮
也近年以來朝鮮屢有囚禁法國敎士之案法國使臣婉請轉求釋放臣等恐其藉端
尋釁勉照所請奏明辦理實爲朝鮮息事起見日本朝鮮兩國積不相能自日本用西
人主謀改藩封爲郡縣事事崇尙西洋遂來中國訂立條規名爲通好實圖窺伺旋以
兵威脅制朝鮮强令通商非朝鮮心所願也日本恃其詐力雄視東隅前歲臺灣之役
未受懲創今年琉球之廢益張氣燄臣等以事勢測之將來必有逞志朝鮮之一日卽
西洋各國亦必有羣起而謀朝鮮之一日中國將往助而力有未逮將坐視而勢有不
能臣等爲朝鮮計有不能不爲中國慮查本年五月據丁日昌條陳海防事宜摺內聲
稱朝鮮不得已而與日本立約不如統與泰西各國立約日本有呑噬朝鮮之心泰西
無滅絶人國之例將來兩國啓釁有約之國皆得起而議其非日本不致無所忌憚若
泰西仍求與朝鮮通商似可密勸勉從所請並勸朝鮮派員分往有約之國聘問不絶
等語丁日昌所稱自是按時立論辦法近日威妥瑪等來臣衙門亦以爲朝鮮若不與
各國交通必爲琉球之續是其意仍欲與朝鮮通商可知朝鮮爲中國屬政敎禁令雖
聽自爲未便强以所不欲惟大局所繫亦未可知而不言光緒二年十二月據北洋大
臣李鴻章函稱朝鮮使臣李裕元係該國執政之列曾致書該大臣道其仰慕該大臣
復書略及外交之意該大臣與其執政前有信函往來此時若以此意藉爲開導尙非
無因而至可否飭下該大臣查明丁日昌所陳各節設法轉致朝鮮俾知理貴因時治
期可久知彼知已利害宜權庶該國可免杌隉之虞而中國亦藉資屛蔽之力臣等因
事關大局理合縷晰附片密陳謹奏請旨

李鴻章(1879.8.26/光緒五年七月九日) ➔ 李裕元

李裕元-李鴻章 서한(10)

答肅毅伯書 附 原書
橘山尊兄太師閣下 正月抄裁復寸函 旋於二月間 接到客臘望日惠書 反覆於
交邦一事 推究得失 剖晰情勢 忠謨碩畫 傾佩無涯 比諗頤養脩齡 平章大政
保釐禦侮 措注咸宜 至爲企頌 承示日本與貴國交涉各節 倭人性情 桀驁貪狡
爲得步進步之計 貴國隨時應付 正自不易 客歲駐倭公使何侍讀來書 屢稱倭
人倩爲介紹 願與貴國誠心和好 兩無虞詐 鄙人思自古交隣之道 因應得其宜
則仇敵可爲外援 因應未得其宜 則外援可爲仇敵 倭人之言 雖未必由中 尙冀
迎機善導 杜彼爭端 永相輯睦 是以曾寓書奉勸 勿先示以猜嫌 致令藉爲口實
也 近察日本行事乖謬 居心叵測 亟宜早爲之防 有不能不密陳梗槪者 日本比
年以來 宗尙西法 營造百端 自謂已得富强之術 然因此致庫藏空虛 國債纍纍
不得不有事四方 冀拓雄圖 以償所費 其疆宇相望之處 北則貴國 南則中國之
臺灣 尤所注意 琉球係數百年舊國 並未開罪於日本 今春忽發兵船 劫廢其王
呑其疆土 其於中國與貴國 難保將來不伺隙以逞 中國兵力餉力 十倍日本 自
忖尙可勉支 惟嘗代貴國審度躊躇 似宜及此時 密脩武備 籌餉練兵 愼固封守
仍當不動聲色 善爲牢籠 凡交涉事宜 恪守條約 勿予以可乘之端 一旦有事 則
彼曲我直 勝負攸分 第思貴國向稱右文之邦 財力非甚充裕 卽今迅圖整頓 非
朝夕所能見功 現聞日本派鳳翔日 進兩戰艦 久駐釜山浦外 操演巨礮 不知何
意 設有反覆 中國卽竭力相助 而道里遼遠 終恐緩不及事 尤可慮者 日本廣聘
西人 敎練水陸兵法 其船礮之堅利 雖萬不逮西人 恐貴國尙難與相敵 況日本
諂事泰西各國 未嘗不思藉其勢力 侵侮鄰邦 往歲 西人欲往貴國通商 雖見拒
而去 其意終未釋然 萬一日本陰結英法美諸邦 誘以開埠之利 抑或北與俄羅
斯勾合 導以拓土之謀 則貴國勢成孤注 隱憂方大 中國識時務者 僉議以爲與
其援救於事後 不如代籌於事前 夫論息事寧人之道 果能始終閉關自守 豈不
甚善 無如西人恃其慓銳 地球諸國 無不往來 實開關以來 未有之局面 自然
之氣運 非人力所能禁遏 貴國旣不得已而與日本立約 通商之事 已開其端 各
國必將從而生心 日本轉若視爲奇貨 爲今之計 似宜用以毒攻毒 以敵制敵之
策 乘機次第 亦與泰西各國立約 籍以牽制日本 彼日本恃其詐力 以鯨呑蠶食

爲謀 廢滅琉球一事 顯露端倪 貴國固不可無以備之 然日本之所畏服者泰西也 以朝鮮之力制日本 或虞其不足 以統與泰西通商制日本 則綽乎有餘 泰西通例 向不得無故奪滅人國 蓋各國互相通商 而公法行乎其間 去歲土耳其爲俄所伐 勢幾岌岌 英奧諸國 出而爭論 俄始斂兵而退 向使上國孤立無援 俄人已獨享其利 又歐洲之比利時丹馬 皆極小之國 自與各國立約 遂無敢妄肆侵陵者 此皆强弱相維之明證也 且越國鄙遠 古人所難 西洋英德法美諸邦 距貴國數萬里 本無他求 其志不過欲通商耳 保護過境船隻耳 至俄國所踞之庫葉島·綏芬河·圖們江一帶 皆與貴國接壤 形勢相逼 若貴國先與英德法美交通 不但牽制日本 並可杜俄人之窺伺 而俄亦必隨卽講和通好矣 誠及此時 幡然改圖 量爲變通 不必別開口岸 但就日本通商之處 多來數國商人 其所分者日本之貿易於貴國 無甚出入 若定其關稅 則餉項不無少裨 熟其商情 則軍火不難購辦 更隨時派員 分往有約之國 通聘問聯情誼 平時旣休戚相關 倘遇一國有侵佔無禮之事 儘可邀集有約各國公議其非 鳴鼓而攻 庶日本不致悍然無忌 貴國亦宜於交接遠人之道 逐事講求 務使剛柔得中 操縱悉協 則所以鈐制日本之術 莫善於此 卽所以備禦俄人之策 亦莫善於此矣 近日各國公使 在我總理衙門 屢以貴國商務爲言 因思貴國政敎禁令 悉由自主 此等大事 豈我輩所可干預 惟是中國與貴國 誼同一家 又爲我東之省屛蔽 奚啻脣齒相依 貴國之憂 卽中國之憂 所以不憚越俎代謀 直抒衷曲 望卽轉呈貴國王察核 廣集廷臣 深思遠慮 密議可否 如以鄙言爲不謬 希先示覆大畧 我總理衙門 亦久欲以此意相達 俟各使議及之時 或可相機措詞 徐示以轉圜之意 從前泰西各國 乘中國多故 併力要挾立約之時 不以玉帛而以兵戎 所以行之旣久 掣肘頗多 想亦遠近所稔知 貴國若於無事時 許以立約 彼喜出望外 自不致格外要求 如販賣鴉片烟 傳敎內地諸大弊 懸爲厲禁 彼必無詞 敝處如有所見 亦當隨時參酌一二 以盡忠告之義 總期於大局無所虧損 夫政貴因時 治期可久 知己知彼 利害宜權 用間用謀 兵家所尙 惟執事實圖利之 法國敎士崔鎭勝經貴國挐禁 該國使臣在京 婉求我禮部行文 轉請釋放 實爲調停息事起見 想已查照施行 緣迭奉來函 諄諄於交隣之道 用敢不彈覼縷 密布腹心 復候起居書復盡意

李裕元(1879. 10. 7/高宗十六年八月二十二日) ➡ 李鴻章

李裕元-李鴻章 서한(11)

照錄朝鮮原任太師李裕元函稿
肅毅伯爵前 猥以海外微踪 過蒙錯愛 尺素不遐 已積歲月 下情慰感 何日忘諸 徂夏屆秋 凉煥不調 鈞體候對時萬康 寅亮鎭綏 軍民樂生 德望遠曁 不勝攢頌 小邦間有倭使之來留 雖屬過境 尙未出場 極可悶然 此去憲書咨官李容肅有所兼管 特送者也 此人曾與游太守有雅分 故使之齎[札]入見 且將其所幹細細面白爲喩美 游太守必以李容肅之言 轉達於爵前 幸忘卑賤 特垂[威]眷 隨事周便 到底指敎 俾完玆事 千萬至仰 小生優游鄕山 調病便宜 莫非國恩所庇耳 不備白 小生李裕元再拜 己卯八月二十二日

114

李裕元(1879.12.24/高宗十六年十一月十二日) ➔ 李鴻章(1880. 3. 15/光緒六年二月五日)

李裕元-李鴻章 서한 (12)

관련문서 『용호한록(龍湖閒錄)』 수록본

答肅毅伯書
李中堂文華殿太學士肅毅伯相爵前 中秋間 因憲書咨官李容肅 謹裁上函 屬
游太守轉呈 卽於十月念間 獲見李容肅手本 縱知書函似經勻鑒 猶未得其詳
下懷結轎 不勝憧憧 今於年貢使祗 冒白衷曲 伏望垂憐焉 本年七月九日下書
自瀋陽專到 乃八月垂暮之時也 其時身滯鄕山 久不入城闉 所以得聞天下事
而未卽上答 自阻我爵前殷注之誼 亦負我爵前疵恤之念 顧此不敏 懯悚交切
大抵異舶之遍滿海上 爲中外所憂 果如勻敎中開闢以來未有之局面 自然之氣
運 非人力所能禁遏者也 彼專仗火礮以威 礮是兵器 而武備志等書 素不載者
居多 彼之精攷 豈勝於古名將方畧而然哉 當今爵前恩威德望 布於海內 謨畫
籌策 運之掌上 以及東土一隅 其所論議者 無非稱衡平施 其所指敎者 無非塞
茅頓開 雖千里之外 怳如合席之間 而小邦大小 孰不感鏤肝肺 仰之若泰山北
斗 重之若九鼎大呂乎 日本則公使連年懇請釜山浦外 別開新港於南北 而德
源乃關防之地 不無難愼 然終未可一切牢拒 不得已許之矣 何爲又顧仁川 期
欲占得 充其無厭也 上國之臺灣 何等重地 而妄自窺覦 已是可駭 小邦之仁川
距都城未滿百里 來頭爲弊 有不可勝言 許久頡之 塞於國論 竟乃辭屈而退 爲
其王臣者 誰無敵愾之心 泰西則通商一欵 莫可議到 盖小邦僻在海陬 遠隔數
萬里 聲旣不及 道亦不同 自來不與此國人相接 章條至嚴 民皆畏犯 卽與日本
之三百年交隣有異 此上國之所洞悉 而近獲法國人 雖已奉咨 節次解送 國法
則不然爾 強弱之相維 關稅之少裨 有以仰勻敎眷眷之至意 而但小邦事勢 萬
不及於上國廣大規模 且年前日本立劵也 以他國人不得容接於港口 已著金石
之科條 今何可着影於其間也 第念日本與泰西之尙不能肆其意者 實賴爵前鎭
壓之澤 而向後事端 設或爲虞 此皆專倚于默運而裁處 隨事而通報 聲氣應求
與共維持也 伏惟上國之於小邦 視同內服 字小之恩 河海莫量 仰望之忱 曷任
尋常 伏請勻體度對時萬康 小生寄身山野 餘生無多 又無堦趍拜於榮戟之前
罄陳情悃 冲悵何極 不備 勻下察

【관련문서】

李中堂文華殿大學士肅毅伯爺爵前 間因憲書吝官李容肅 謹裁上函 屬遊太守 轉呈 卽於十月念間 獲見李容肅手本 縱知書械 似經勻鑒 未得其詳 下情結轖 今於年貢使行 冒白衷曲 庸冀付達焉 本年七月九日所賜下書 伏奉於八月晦間 捧手盥讀 伊後便使蹉違 至今謝忱未伸 雖尋常箋儀 不宜逋慢如是 矧承諄複辭旨 崙爲鄙邦機密事布囑 而朦然若罔聞知 其不敏之咎 內訟曷已 猥玆追籲 所以愈急切於餘辰 庶蒙聆察否 邇來弊邦之與日本交好 立約通商 固出於萬不得已 而其接應之宜 寔遵前後勻敎 勿示猜嫌之意 一以含容巽順 挫其桀騖性氣 而維彼言動 不無警急 干請多在科外 指開別港 無非重地 相持多時而後 以元山津施許 仁川係是畿甸 竟不副其求 則其去也 頗惟怏怏 而其諸際幸不至相失 若其貪狡之志 專在鯨呑蠶食 今春廢滅琉球 近日探演礮船等事 苟非此密喩開示 顧玆聾瞽 那由得知 我爵前之仁之德 庇復我小邦 厥惟久矣 酒玆郵患于未危未亂 爲之代籌 何圖至此之極 今日西人之局面 寔由自然之氣運 旣是至訓 而防患之要 又有以毒攻毒 以敵制敵之策 縷縷示下在焉 維以款啓昧晦 細細溫繹 詎無灑然而有省者乎 泰西各國 先與交通 則日本自可牽制 日本旣已牽制 則俄國窺伺 亦無可憂 斯爲勻敎綱領 而以至定關稅也 熟商情也 諸弊之廣禁也 又何其處分詳察也 誠惶誠感 敢不聞命 而第自念弊邦 僻在一隅 謹守規度 恬居文約 自治邦內 不暇外交 而況泰西之學 有異吾道 實乖民彝 則嘗畏之如烈火 避之如毒矢 敬而遠之如鬼神 近如干法國人潛踪者 非奉旨解送 而鄙邦人染敎 罔或肆赦 推此庶有以洞諒 而敗炯行敎 卽其贏家之孚 恐非貙牙之攸制 庶亦可以燭照矣 古昔謀國者有曰 遠交而近攻 有曰以蠻攻蠻 斯乃以敵制敵之術也 目下局面 與古昔頓異 雖武强自力者 朝幣夕戈 待於二境 將疲於奔命 我先取敗而已 豈文弱如鄙邦 而可以效古昔者乎 寔不能也 非不爲也 神皇之嘗百草 遇毒而死 死而復起 非神皇而效爲 則一遇毒而能起者鮮矣 今學制敵而我先受敵 學攻敵而我先中毒 竊恐一遇毒而不能起也 奚暇以制敵乎 惟我爵前 盛望振於陬滋 謨劃愷於中外 以彼俄國之强梁 泰西之尨雜 日人之反覆 靡不折心焉屈膝焉 則日人之耽視臺灣 無足爲憂 而弊邦久沐覆露 亦尙恃而不恐 且泰西公法 旣不許無故奪滅人國 以俄之强 而斂兵於土國 則弊邦無辜 或遇呑噬之毒 亦庶幾諸國之所共禁乎 惟獨有憪憪懷疑而不釋然者 日人之廢琉王呑其疆 卽桀宋之得欽洲列卯 似宜有齊桓興師遷邢

封衛之擧 或以義喩日人 俾復置許君 如鄭莊所爲 而側耳無聞何也 救土國於 垂亡 公法可伏 而興琉邦於已滅 則公法有難行歟 抑日人之桀黠 輕視各國 雖 縱恣專利 而公法莫能行歟 利時丹馬 以痣小國 介於諸大邦 賴以强弱相維 而 琉王以累百年舊國 不得相維者 以其所處孤弱 與各國隔絶 而公法有不及行 而然歟 弊邦則崎嶇者乎 地雖盡處 其視土琉利丹等國 尤貧儉凿窳 距泰西 又 踔遠莫攀 兵戎頡頏 尙矣勿論 玉帛周旋 亦難自振 夫以日人之慣於通商 巧於 營造 盡得富强之術焉 尙致枵其藏累其債之歎 則設令弊邦改圖 廣置港埠 畢 通遐邇 悉學其巧 必於藉茅承匡應酬之際 立見稛橐蕭然 奚翅藏枵債累 蹈日 本之轍也 且況偏邦地産之薎裂 貨物之沽惡 四方所稔聞耳 各國之遠來交貿 恐如三家之市 難容千金之商 不亦主客俱無得乎 其難於自振 實際然也 曁痿 而思行遠 毋寧奧突之坐守爲得歟 盖上國規模 譬如天地之大也 巨細咸宥 橐 鑰嫩惡 畢就釵規 獜鳳蛇龍 無適無莫 時或掣肘 施措磐泰 固萬方所歸極 而 小邦遽欲 則反不猶醯鷄之學鵬鳥乎 我爵前心腹敷喩 務欲趨吉避害之愈惻怛 肫摯 雖父兄之於子弟 曷以過此 而形格勢禁 末由奉承 大愚之終身不靈 無乃 謂是歟 然而私自依怙者 泰西與日本 旣無敢憑肆於爵前盛饋之下 則小邦永 賴大德 機事輒荷提命 是所日夜祈祝之至 情窮辭迫 不知攸裁 但惟哀其愚而 宥其罪焉 伏惟勻軆度 對時萬康 小生 寄寓山野 餘生無多 又無階趨拜於棨戟 之前 罄陳情悃 冲悵何極 不備 勻下察

李鴻章(1879. 12. 25/光緖五年十一月十三日) ➡ 總署

李裕元과의 서한 왕복 보고 (1)

致總署 籌朝鮮
光緖五年十一月十三日敬肅者
七月間欽奉寄諭並五百三十八號鈞函 令查照雨生所陳各節轉致朝鮮 勸與泰西各國立約通商 以杜日本之詭謀 當卽遵旨寓書朝鮮致仕太師李裕元 密爲勸導 已繕疏復奏幷泐函略陳梗槪在案 旋于十月初七日由永平游守智開遞到李裕元來信 絶不提及前事 似有未便明言之隱 据游守密稟稱 李裕元另函謂 該國本意不欲與他國往來 日本開港實出於不得已 若西人通商 則莫敢開口 渠前于七月晦間奉到敝處書緘 曲爲小邦多方指導 旣勤且摯 當經言之於朝 而以解官歸鄕不敢力爭 務求鑒原 此番如蒙賜復並求勿露七月間書函事 屬代爲密陳等語 其賷咨官李容肅復與游守籌商 欲來謁晤 將制器練軍等事面陳一切 鴻章以旣有要務 未便阻其前來 卽函告游守專派妥人伴送 茲接游守稟稱 專人由京折回 携到該賷咨官復信 謂身充使者 出入不得自由 躊躇中止 幷云李裕元信中有要務細細面白者 盖因該國興論擬仿古外國入學之例 咨請禮部揀選明幹人員在天津等處學習軍器武備 特屬游守轉達請示 鴻章竊思裕元之不能獨主謀議 與該賷咨官之不敢淹留內地 均系實情 而該國講求武備實難再緩 因緘復游守 告以所請似屬可行 將來該國咨文到部 應由禮部奏明 轉咨鈞署 酌度辦理 如以后朝鮮有員到津 敝處于練兵製器之法不難罄其秘要 隨宜指授 俾獲有成 借作自强之基 增我藩籬之固 屬俟該賷咨官李容肅道出永平詳爲道達 幷宣示朝廷微旨 務使該國規模日新 邊備日嚴 庶勿爲强隣所窺伺 另復李裕元一函 則但作通候寒暄之語 不提七月間所商各節 令其順便携交 謹將李裕元來函及敝處復函抄呈鈞鑒 朝鮮旣堅不欲與西人通商 中國自難强勸 敝處似不必再行瀆奏 可否請於召對之頃敷陳及之 伏候卓裁 轉肅密布 敬叩中堂 王爺 大人鈞祺 李鴻章謹上 直字二百二十四號 附抄函

李鴻章(1880. 3. 17/光緒六年二月七日) ➡ 總署(1880. 3. 19/光緒六年二月九日)

李裕元과의 서한 왕복 보고 (2)

致總署 籌朝鮮
光緒六年二月初七日
敬肅者 客秋欽奉寄諭 查照雨生所陳各節 寓書朝鮮致仕太師李裕元 勸與泰西各國立約通商 以杜日本之詭謀 已於七月十一月兩次泐函 略陳梗槪在案 去冬李裕元來信 絶不提及前事 據永平游守智開密稟 李裕元另給伊函 謂該國本意不欲與他國往來 雖經言之於朝 而以解官歸鄉 不敢力爭等語 昨游守復遞到李裕元十一月十二日來書 反復千言 大致謂泰西之學素所深惡 不欲有所沾染 又以該國向稱貧瘠 不能多容商船爲詞 謹將原函抄呈鈞鑒 朝鮮僻處東隅 風氣較晚 雖中國爲謀至周且密 然非洞達時務 橫覽全局者不能見到 今通國人情囿於見聞 勢難家喩戶曉 李裕元牽牽於衆議 玩其辭旨 亦似未以此事爲然 因勢轉移 相机利導 殆非一朝夕之功也 專肅密布 敬叩中堂 王爺, 大人鈞祺 李鴻章謹上 直字二百叄十二號 附抄函

何如璋 ➡ 總署(1880. 11. 18/光緒六年十月十六日)
주지조선외교의(主持朝鮮外交議)

主持朝鮮外交議
朝鮮一國 居亞細亞要衝 其西北境與吉奉毗連 爲中國左臂 朝鮮存 則外捍大洋 內擁黃海 成山 釜山之間 聲援聯絡 津港數千里海道直達 斯神京門戶益固 而北洋一帶無單寒梗阻之憂 朝鮮若亡 則我之左臂遂斷 藩籬盡撤 後患不可復言 故泰西論者皆謂朝鮮之在亞細亞 猶歐羅巴之土耳機 爲形勝之所必爭 自我大淸興東土 先定朝鮮 而後伐明 當康熙乾隆朝 無事不以上聞 幾無異內地郡縣 其餘越南之疏遠 緬甸之褊僻 相去萬萬 而二百餘年字小以德 事大以禮 朝鮮託庇宇下 得以安全 恩深誼固 相安無事 可謂幸矣 乃至於今日 北有至强之俄羅斯與之爲隣 蓋俄自得樺太洲全島 又經營黑龍江之東 屯戍圖門江口 高麗建瓴 久有實逼處此之勢 朝鮮危 則中國之勢日亟 故論中國今日之勢 能於朝鮮設駐箚辦事大臣 蒙古西藏之例 凡內國之政治 及外國之條約 皆由中國爲之主持 庶外人不敢覬覦 斯爲上策 顧時方多事 鞭長不及 此策固未能遽行 不得已而思其次 莫取俄國一人欲佔之勢 與天下萬民互均而維持之 令朝鮮與美德英法國通商之爲善也 頻年以來 我總署及南北洋大臣 合力同心共圖此擧 徒以朝鮮僻處東隅 風氣所囿 聽我藐藐 幾無如何 逮 乎今日形勢危逼 彼乃幡然改圖 此豈非天牖其衷 爲該國危急存亡之一轉機乎 雖然如璋嘗考泰西屬國 皆主其政治 每謂亞細亞貢獻之國 不得以屬土論 又考泰西通例 屬國與半主之國與人結約 多由其統轄之國主政 又考泰西通例 兩國爭戰局外之國 中立其間 不得偏助 惟屬國乃不在此例 今欲救朝鮮我吞滅之急 不得不藉他國之力 以相維持 然聽令朝鮮自行與人結約 則他國皆認其自主 而中國之屬國 忽去其名 救急在一時 貽患在他日 亦不可不預爲之計也 如璋因又偏[sic]查萬國公法 德意志聯邦向各有立約之權 今中國許令朝鮮與人立約 原無不可 惟應請朝廷會議速遣一幹練明白能悉外交利害之員 前往朝鮮 代爲主持結約 庶屬國之分 因之益明 他日或有外隙 而操縱由我 足以固北洋鎖鑰此至計也 卽或不然 應請由總署 奏請諭旨 飭令朝鮮國王與他國結約 並飭其於條約開端聲明 玆朝鮮國奉中國政府命願與某某國結約云云 則大義旣明 屛藩自固 如璋竊念朝鮮之於中國 戴高履厚 素稱恭順 宗田法國敎士一案 我一

言而卽釋拘囚 而朝鮮告於日本者 每曰上國 曰天朝 彼近日本國 是稍破舊習 觀彼君臣上下私相告誡之辭曰 淸人之厚意 甚於日本 則由朝廷勅諭 彼自當唯命是聽 而泰西諸國正當求成請盟未可必得之時 由我主持 彼自欣感 況又有德意志聯邦之例可援 則奉中國命云云 外國亦無辭可拒也 若朝鮮旣經開港之後 應飭令彼國襲用中國龍旗 或圍繞以雲 微示區別 以崇體制 應飭令朝鮮商人來中國貿易 亦令華商前王釜山元山津等處通商 以通聲息 又飭令彼國學生來京師同文館習泰西語言 來福州船政局上海製造局習造船簡器 來直隷江蘇等處練軍 習洋鎗以修武備 總之 今日時移事變 中國待朝鮮 總須稍變舊章 方能補救 如璋又念現今俄海軍卿理疏富斯基率兵船十數艘 屯泊琿春 天寒冰凍 必將南下 若不幸而鯨吞蠶食 肆其毒惡 則朝鮮必將割地以求自存 臥榻鼾睡 後患滋深 卽幸無此事 而俄之西北利亞 欲藉朝鮮之民以開拓 藉朝鮮之未以轉輸 蓄志旣非一日 苟盡率兵船以劫盟約 朝鮮亦何敢不從 朝鮮一土 今日鎖港 明日必開 明日鎖港 後日必開 萬不能閉關也必矣 顧與其爲他人威逼勢劫 以成不公不平所損實多之條約 則何如自中國急圖之 以攬大權 以收後效 夫亞細亞諸小國喪微久矣 越南旣割地與法 緬甸復受制於英 徼天之幸 朝鮮僅能瓦全 而固守舊習 執迷不悟 屢勸不悛 至於今日懷于厥心 旣有措手不及之嘆 而當此形迫勢切間不容髮之際 幸有一線之生機 時會不可再來 則安得不圖所以補救 如璋實不勝憂悶屛營之至 而發此議軍國大事 深恐無裨於萬一 伏望迅賜裁奪 天下幸甚

李裕元(1880.8.14/高宗十七年七月九日) → 李鴻章

李裕元-李鴻章 서한(13)

文华殿大学士肃毅伯爷爵前
本年季春贡使回 得承永平游太守书 盛传爵前仁政布于寰内 威名施诸海外 莫非尊主庇民 有辞千秋 小邦黎庶咸思沾溉之恩 非不欲种种恭探钧节 山海 漠漠 界疆有限 末由展诚景仰 结轖曷有其极 秋凉骤至 钧体度对万康 警铎不动 卫戟凝瑞 瞻望津云 若拜床下 小邦 日本之人稍似讲好 德源开港 商舶來往江户 送使书契修谢 姑无圭角 实赖爵前左右之力 实遵爵前指教之方 而忽于春夏间 佛国及米国书本自莱馆 要其送纳 小邦以非约条中事 措辞退却 盖他国书之自日本借送 不得施行 曾有交铃而然也 若有意外层节 则不得不仰告于爵前 更蒙乙亥冬斥退森有礼之泽 此举国之所仰望也 小邦国王此际忧虞宵旰靡弛 文而崇儒重道 武而讲戎渶械 先选六条之士 广开百技之门 惟我上国是则 亦惟我爵前是倚 派定别咨官卞元圭前往京都 赍文陈白于礼部 未知回施之如何 而上年因游太守言 已知爵前之微意 故敢将咨草先从永平以为转达 伏维慈惠之念 必有周全 若或准可 则下次事无巨无细 专仰爵前禀定 而不以卑鄙随外戒饬 俾有实效 奚特一邦之幸 亦获藩屏之固矣 小生依旧在林泉逍遥之间 老聩转甚 无足相问 而今于兹 事不敢辞 为张皇诉衷 兼奉礼单 庶或亮收不备 谨呈直隶总督伯爷爵前 庚辰七月初九日

礼单

倭缯匹纽十端, 曲生绡十端, 土绸二十端, 上黄细絺布十端, 上白细絺布十端, 加重生绸五十端, 细绵布五十端, 大漆箄二百把, 芭蕉圆扇一百柄, 大圆扇十柄, 细帘子五双, 满花席子十立, 色纸二十轴, 大搗厚纸叁十轴, 白楮二百束, 上上制山稺清心元一百丸, 红仁参五十斤, 白仁参三十斤, 大鳆鱼二百个, 江瑶珠一百贴, 柚子清一缸, 姜果一缸, 计二十二种

119

李鴻章(1880. 10. 7/光緖六年九月四日)

조선에 대해 외교 및 자강책 권고 상주

관련문서 근대식 기기 학습을 청원하는 조선 자문

妥籌朝鮮武備折
光緖六年九月初四日
奏爲朝鮮講求武備 遵旨妥籌 恭折密陳 仰祈聖鑒事 竊臣承准軍机大臣字寄 八月二十九日奉上諭 禮部奏据朝鮮國王咨稱 該國講究武備 懇爲轉奏請旨 俾該國匠工學造器械于天津廠等語 著李鴻章妥籌具奏 其咨內所請簡選解事 人員或于邊外習敎一層 幷着李鴻章詳審其意 一幷妥籌迅奏 該國使臣經該部 安置居住 俟該督復奏到日再降諭旨 原咨着鈔給閱看等因 欽此 仰見聖謨广 運 眷顧東藩至意 欽佩莫名 伏查朝鮮僻處海隅 向于外交之道 御侮之方漠不 介意 日本窺其孤弱脅以兵威 先與立約通商 實則隱圖侵逼 去年七月臣密奉 諭旨 查照前福建撫臣丁日昌所陳各節 致書朝鮮原任太師李裕元 勸以密修武 備 愼固封守 與英法德美諸邦逐漸立約 借以牽制日本 卽可備御俄羅斯 幷告 以熟悉西國商情 軍火利器不難購辦等語 已將原稿鈔呈御覽 是年十月 朝鮮 貢使入都 道出永平 据前永平府知縣游智開密稟 李裕元給伊另函 謂該國本 意不欲與他國來往 牽于衆議 不敢主持 惟該國輿論擬倣古外國入學之例 咨 請禮部揀選明干人員赴津學習練兵制器之法 臣謂果有成議 未始非該國自强 之基 曾密屬游智開詳告該使 本年二月復由游智開遞李裕元去冬復函 大致 謂泰西之學素所深惡 不欲有所沾染 又以該國貧瘠不能多容商船爲詞 已將 原函鈔寄總理衙門存案 竊思地球諸國惟朝鮮開風氣最晩 該國士大夫囿于見 聞 昧于時勢 墨守成法 閉拒忠謀 雖曰卽于危弱而不顧 此殆有氣運主之 非人 力所能爲者 今該國卽以講武爲請 正可因其一線之明 迎机善導 增彼軍實 固 我藩籬 惟是該國練習此事 卽使始終勤奮 其收效亦在數年之后 就目前事勢 而論 則有迫不及待者 自去冬以來 中俄和約未定 積有違言 俄之鐵甲快船兵 船二十餘隻陸續東駛 幷厚集陸軍分布吉林海濱之海參崴 摩闊崴一帶 豫儲煤 粮軍火甚富 六月間 有美國水師總兵薛佛尔赴朝鮮議約被拒 旋來津與臣會晤 据稱美國尙无用兵逼勒之意 但俄人已費巨餉遣將調兵 勢必不肯中止 若不圖 中華 恐遂呑幷朝鮮 八月間 法國水師提督瞿貝賽過談 謂探聞俄海部尙書里 沙士几之意 欲赴琿春攻奪朝鮮海口 陸則斷奉吉之右臂 水則扼北洋之襟喉

規劃甚爲雄遠 又謂朝鮮東界海口 形勝爲東方之最 俄人故欲取之 以與琿春
海參崴等處掎角 其餘各處探報及新聞紙所論 大致相同 盖俄人所据之海參崴
綏芬河 圖們江各境 皆與朝鮮東北接壤 彼旣占東海口岸爲巢穴 自必漸圖開
拓 若呑幷朝鮮 卽拊我東叁省之背 使中國岌岌不能自安 是朝鮮與我國實有
脣齒相依之勢 不能无休戚相關之情 當此兵餉兩絀 中國沿海各口尚未能處處
周防 斷无餘力兼顧藩服 似只能就其力所逮者而利導之 万一俄事稍紓 俾朝
鮮得于數年內力擴新机 整軍經武 保衛東隅 未始非中國之幸也 惟該國匠工
來津學習机器 此中亦有繁難之處 查天津初設机器局 不過仿造洋火藥 銅帽
等項 厥后迭次擴充 添購机器 火藥多出數倍 自造士乃得林明登后膛槍子 克
鹿卜格林后門炮子 蚊船大炮子之屬 光緒元 二年間 亦曾自制后門槍 因工費
甚巨 較購自外洋者价几逾倍 卽經停止 各軍所用槍炮 專向西洋定購 但源源
供給子葯零件 今朝鮮匠工來學 卽使盡嫻各法 聞該國所用土槍僅與中國綠營
之抬鳥槍相等 其制造机器及新式槍炮仍須購自外洋 是无其器而不能用也 西
洋槍炮其准線 口令 步伍 非操演數年難以純熟 是无其人而不能用也 臣愚以
爲旣准該國來學机器 將來必須代爲購器 代籌練兵 皆事之連類而及 缺一不
可者 又 該國匠工言語不通 來局之后應如何設法敎導 俾獲漸窺門徑 擬請敕
下禮部揀派通事人員 伴送該國使臣卞元圭到津 由臣督同局員與之熟商辦法
再行奏明請旨施行 至該國王原咨內所稱 簡選解事人員或于邊外習敎及來學
往敎等語 文義似未甚明晰 臣就事理度之 今如中國派員往敎 該國旣无机器
匠工 又无現成槍炮 斷難獲益 自應先由該國挑選匠工來廠學習 幷選聰穎子
弟來津分入水雷 電報各學堂 俾研西法 本末兼營較有實際 至練兵一事 將來
或選派熟悉員弁往敎 或由該國派隊來從我兵操演 購器一事 或乘中國訂購之
便寬爲籌備劃付 均應隨時酌度情形 妥商辦理 臣比接李裕元來書 頗知戒備
不虞 以講戎敎械爲兢兢 幷致送禮物甚厚 想因所圖之事關係頗重 意在豫聯
情誼 從前李裕元以該國邊事與臣通問 每附土議數種 臣援古人贈帶獻衣之義
兼仿盛世薄來厚往之經 必爲加倍酬答 此次禮物較多 未敢擅便 謹將原函及
禮單鈔呈御覽 應否收受 由臣加倍酬答之處 伏候聖裁 至朝鮮與西人通商一
節 實系謀國要圖 與練兵制器相輔而行 其李裕元來函 俟奉諭旨后卽當裁復
臣仍擬不憚苦口 善爲開導 冀其或有轉机 庶免爲他國所兼幷 所有朝鮮講求
武備遵旨妥籌緣由 恭折由驛密陳 是否有當 伏乞皇太后 皇上聖鑒訓示 謹奏
光緒六年九月初六日 軍机大臣奉旨 欽此

附 光緖六年八月二十九日寄諭 軍机大臣字寄大學士直隸總督一等肅毅伯李鴻章 光緖六年八月二十九日奉上諭 禮部奏据朝鮮國王咨稱 該國講究武備 懇爲轉奏請旨 俾該國匠工學造器械于天津廠等語 著李鴻章妥籌具奏 其咨內所請簡選解事人員或于邊外習敎一層 幷著李鴻章詳審其意 一幷妥籌迅奏 該國使臣業經該部安置居住 俟該督復奏到日再降諭旨 原咨著抄給閱看 將此諭令知之 欽此 遵旨寄信前來 九月初一日奉到

附 光緖六年九月初六日寄諭 軍机大臣字寄大學士直隸總督一等肅毅伯李鴻章 光緖六年九月初六日奉上諭 李鴻章奏遵籌朝鮮請派匠工學造器械一摺 朝鮮爲東北藩服 脣齒相依 該國現擬講求武備 請派匠工前來天津學造器械 自宜俯如所請 善爲指引 本日已諭令禮部揀派通事 伴送該國賚奏官卞元圭赴津 俟該員到后 著李鴻章詢問一切情形 再行奏明辦理 李裕元致李鴻章書函幷禮物卽可收受 從厚酬答 以聯情誼 幷著酌度情形作書答復 俾知領會 將此諭令知之 欽此 遵旨寄信前來 九月初七日奉到

【관련문서】

竊以小邦久沐聖化 遍荷洪私柔遠之德 每矜其不能字小之恩 多崫其不及 无幽不燭 有願必施 當職恆與一國臣庶北向攢祝隕越于下 圖報万一之念 不忘跬步之頃矣 今有區區切至之願 而徒懷嚴畏 不思轉聞 則是皇慈視均內服 而小邦還自疏外也 惡乎可 蓋聞兵可百年而不用 不可一日而无備 奚謂之備 卽兵戎之具是已 良兵良器以待大用 見于周制 除戎器戒不虞 着于易象 良有以焉 惟小邦屛翰上國 竭力御侮 何翅如子弟之衛父兄 手臂之捍頭目 而其捍衛之要 不亦在乎兵備歟 矧又邇年 強隣窺覘 憂殷伏莽 正須戒不虞待大用之時也 著禮部有咨 使小邦悉習籌畫 計出万全 不得稍涉疏虞可也 云云 職由是耳蒙此警示 非止一再對證砭葯 銘肌難忘 而第念小邦以朴拙 其俗荒嬉成極 武備講究 徒凭古書而无异談 寵器械善修只依圖式而便 聞刻鵠五兵飭材一任鈍工 其句則彈 其刺則蜎 其鍛則不摯 每思器械不利 以其卒予敵之古語 不覺寒心 于是一國興論 咸以爲上國軍器精利以威天下者 欽仰久矣 而天津廠等處

實四方巧工之所會 各國神技之攸萃也 亟宜選送明干人員 情願學造器械之意 聞于皇上 恭候誕綸 爲今急務 當職仍伏念我皇上聲敎訖海 欝郁鑄世 威不憚達于四極 郵旣溥于万區 至若小邦 常欽醇和 最被覆露 苟此輿情之得徹 庶幾寵施之不靳 而惟畏越是懼 不敢直具奏本 先玆悉陳情事于部堂大人 仰冀曲加怨察 卽爲導達 特降隆旨 俾小邦匠工學造于津廠 且簡選能事人員 或于邊外極徽獲來學之願 亦紆往敎之道 隨處方便 竟能有成 則內而竭屛翰之職 外而盡御侮之方 環東土數千里幾萬生靈永賴以妥 頌戴帝力 豈特與窮壤而无究也 不任誠懇訴祝之至 專差行副司直卞元圭賫咨前去 爲此合行移咨 請照驗轉奏施行

120

李鴻章(1880. 10. 24/光緒六年九月二十七日)

조선과 서양 각국의 통상 권유 상주

朝鮮通商西國片
光緒六年九月二十七日

再 朝鮮與西人通商一事 係其今日謀國要圖 臣前奏明 俟復李裕元函仍擬善為開導 冀有轉機 惟李裕元致仕家居 雖尚得與聞朝政 而一切謀議設施 究由該國君相主持 此次賞叅官卞元圭來津謁見 臣與筆談良久 觸類引伸 俾徐悟保邦之大計 即臣上年七月致李裕元一函 彼亦知為忠告 因與開誠佈公 迎機善導 剴切而詳示之 聞朝鮮與日本通商數年 尚未收稅 彼並不知稅額重輕 臣告以西洋各國通例 令勿為日本所蒙 且知重稅之有裨國計 朝鮮與法美有怨 慮其見侵 臣告以法美志在通商 並無用兵強逼之意 而俄人則窺伺甚急 朝鮮東北海口與俄接界 防禦太疏 臣告以德源永興口既准日本開埠 倘俄人以兵船闖入 或先禮後兵 應派員相機接應 酌允通商議約 免致動兵後格外吃虧 朝鮮欲在德源埠筑臺置炮 恐為日本借口 臣告以東西各國通商口未有不筑炮臺以自防護者 乃係自主之權 凡此皆所以破其惑 而使之自強 開其意 而使之自悟 該使臣似聞所未聞 中心悅服 一切俟歸報國王妥為酌度 當不至如從前之扞格 查朝鮮三面環海 其形勢實當東北洋之衝 而為盛京吉林直隸山東數省之屏蔽 其民人能耐勞苦 物產亦非甚絀 五金煤鉄之礦未經開採 倘為俄人佔踞 與吉林黑龍江俄境視若連雞 形若拊背 則我東三省及京畿重地皆岌岌不能自安 關係甚重 日本近與開埠 陽為各國先容 而陰嗾朝鮮堅拒 其意亦甚叵測 玆欲杜俄日之隱謀 惟有與泰西各國一律通商 尚可互相牽制 孑然常存 然聞見以閱歷而始廣 風氣由倡導而漸開 該國於製器練兵既知加意講求 商務一端或終有擴充之望 謹照錄臣與卞元圭筆談問答節略 恭呈御覽 除密咨總理各國事務衙門知照外 謹附片密陳 伏乞聖鑒 謹奏

李鴻章 ➡ 總署(1880. 10. 31/光緒六年九月二十八日)

卞元圭와의 회담 보고

謹將九月二十二日接見朝鮮賚咨官卞元圭筆談問答照鈔 恭呈御覽
問　該國相臣何名
卞答　領議政李最應六十六歲 今王叔父 宗親封君 初爲興寅君
問　議政亦猶中朝之軍機大臣否 其人中外政務兵事均洞悉否
卞答　議政卽古之丞相中書今平章事也 中外諸務均得與聞
問　與日本通商兩口曾設關否 歲增稅項若干
卞答　東萊口已有關 德源口方設關未完 稅額尙未一定
問東萊開口已數年 何以稅額尙未定 聞日本輪船常至 豈能有貨無征
卞答　兩口俱完工程 行將一倂定稅
問　中國初設洋關 未知西國通例 接貨値百抽五 貴國定額擬値百抽幾
卞答　此在兩國論定 廟堂必有成算 而陪臣位下 無由預知 敢問抽幾庶可得中
告以泰西各國大率入口稅重 出口稅輕（土貨出口稅輕 所以恤吾民生利吾物
產也）又分別貨之貴賤 銷之暢滯 酌定等差 有每百抽二三十者 有每百抽十數
者 故歲入較多 中國初不知此例 爲西人所蒙 進出口槪定爲値百抽五 條約旣
定 至今一成不可易 雖販運內地 加半稅二五 然喫虧實多 貴國甫問通商 稅額
必須加重 可以自主 否則各國援例而來 必有後悔
卞答　出入口稅參酌輕重 實維石畫指敎 敬當據以歸告 思所以恤吾民利吾產
　　　仰副德意之萬一
問　吾去年七月致李太師密函 勸與西國通商 蓋稔知各國見日本開埠 必有
　　繼往求索者 貴國主意須早自定 若不得已而與各國通商 重加稅則 利可
　　在我 妥定條約 害亦有限 不圖貴國衆議不以爲然 而各國覬覦 終無已時
　　兵力又恐不能自守 爲害甚大
卞答　此國之大事 陪臣雖位下人微 亦有所聞矣 非不知前秋密函下示 備極忠
　　　告 而特因與彼有怨 未便遽和 謹將尊敎一一歸告
問　所謂與彼有怨 想指法美兩國前事而言 聞法美尙不欲遽加兵 但求通商
　　而已 俄界逼近 實欲在東海開拓口岸土地 目下兵船麕集海參葳土們江
　　一帶 與貴國擊柝相聞 貴國何以備之 又聞貴國民人在俄界貿易工作者

甚多 彼得藉以偵察虛實 貴國官府向與有文書往來否
卞答　俄之爲虞 浮於法美 小邦之北陲 卽慶興慶源等地 雖蠢逐末之類 種種越
　　　去爲其雇傭 則偵探虛實 想亦必然之勢也 但犯越者爲本國所獲 法不容
　　　貸 故輒一往不返 邊民有爭桑之漸 邊民或有文書開解云 非有按例往來
問　　德源永興海口 聞各國艷稱 形勢險固 爲東海之最 俄人有意圖之 貴國於
　　　該口有礮台兵船否 吾於此甚爲焦系 請以實告
卞答　海口要害雖有船礮 然船是木板 礮皆舊製 庸是憧憧 從前小邦之事 全仗
　　　中堂維持 今當艱危之秋 伏願加倍留念 仰紓宸東顧之憂 俯慰褊陬北
　　　拱之誠 無任祈懇願祝之至
問　　俄人詭詐異常 吾曾詢有此意否
答云　無之 然各國從旁窺探 謂其實有是謀 但尙未發動 明春必須謹防 若屆時
　　　彼之大隊兵船竟回 貴國須早留意
卞答　武經云知彼知己 百戰不殆 所以寡君憂深慮遠 另加偵刺 來咨有強鄙窺
　　　覘之語 卽謂此事也 苟非中堂視均一室 誰肯明教而代籌其將來耶 伏乞
　　　連加詢探 而亦或有鎭壓排解之道 更願隨機方便 保無他患 千萬至祝 固
　　　知早蒙關垂 無待陪臣縷白 然情窮勢迫 安得不屑瀆乎 庶可原其心而有
　　　其罪矣
問　　鄙意永興口旣准日本通商 倘俄人遞以兵船間入 或先禮後兵 貴國須派
　　　委員與之接應 相機酌允通商 議約如何議法 權仍在己 此卽排鮮之道 若
　　　待動兵後議約 喫虧甚矣
卞答　敬當一一歸告 而鎭壓之要在乎中堂 伏願特垂終始之惠焉 小邦咸鏡道
　　　卽國祖康獻王肇基之地也 四世仙寢於是乎安 且五金之類於是乎産 其
　　　民勇而無謀 習於騎射 堪稱北方之剛 惟是德源元山爲陸海咽喉 所以小
　　　邦多年靳持 究竟萬不獲已 而許其開埠矣 倘或有事於此地 則咸鏡一道
　　　非我之有 何則 扼其喉則呼吸豈能通乎 握管焦心 不知所裁
告以中國陸軍尙可自立 水師仿造兵輪船多隻 僅能自護口岸 勤辦土寇 或與
他小邦角勝 若俄水軍強威 目下吾力尙未足與馳逐大洋 其勢實未便遠顧東海
卽未敢云鎭壓貴土永興一帶也 俟數年後鐵甲快船稍備 鄙意今其出巡 偶泊貴
國海東各口 聊作聲援 蓋本大臣北洋轄境與貴邦海岸毗連 誼若一家 本無畛
域 現今力量萬難兼營 若俄意不測 貴國委蛇待之 羈縻勿絶 亟圖練兵製器自
強之策 猶可爲善國也 泰西通例 公法無無故稱兵奪人土地者 若堅拒固閉 彼
得有詞 不可不熟慮之

卞答　先禮後兵　先兵後禮　固當商敵爲資　未可預料　而德源埠頭之役已自春間
　　　經始矣　今忽添築礮台　多排大砲　則日本之人必將藉爲口實　若束手坐待
　　　尤非禦侮之策　伏乞明賜指敎　俾有準從　千萬祈懇
告以東西各國通商口　未有不堅築砲台以自防護者　日本似不能藉口　果相詰問
答以此係我國自主　万國通例　但須約束弁兵　不得滋事耳
卞答　謹承明敎　辭旨鄭重　披露無隱　忝在下風　曷任感激　數年之後　轄境巡泊
　　　威聲所被　想足震憴　而目下憂虞　靡所止屆　寡君智勇仁明　諒有以善後
　　　而陪臣漆室之見　自不免憧憧　竊有隣邦滋惑之事　琉國爲日本侵奪　卽公
　　　法所不許也　天下各國其將公議而興亡繼絶乎
告以日本之於琉球　自謂前明中葉卽爲藩屬　倂球後　以新聞紙徧告各國　各亦
輕信之　公法乃泰西所訂　東土未必照行　但各國通商公共之口　一國不能獨佔
佔之　則必羣起而爭　故去秋蜜商貴國　酌允各大國通商　亦慮俄日之將有事於
朝鮮也
卞答　無論鉅細　歸候寡君掛酌
問　　貴國所求派人學習製器練兵各事　業令諸位道台與之妥議數日　昨呈略摺
　　　大端　已甚詳晰　貴官能遵允否
卞答　此事係前古所未行　素意所不畜　乃敢容請者　仰恃大朝之於小邦　有籲必
　　　從　無願不遂之德意　亦維我中堂眷茈之惠澤　如有所敎　敢不奉遵
告以玆有節略草藁一本　望携回細閱　條議具復　或有疑難　再與諸道酌商轉稟
卞答　各條周密精核　無庸更議　若有事時　乞從海道往來　前布告於諸位道員　諒
　　　蒙鑑燭
告以朝貢信使來往　必須恪遵成憲　此係破例之擧　若徑從海道　自更便捷　仍今
諸道會商妥議章程凴票等事　呈候具奏請旨定奪
卞答　陪臣前日仰請　本自如此　而不必今日明日　隨便裁處　惟圖濟事

何如璋 ➡ 總署(1880. 12. 3/光緒六年十一月二日)

미국과 조약체결을 위해 밀사 李東仁 파견

관련문서 (1) 조미 조약 체결을 위한 淸의 관여 요청
        (2) 이동인이 밀교한 조선 내부 의론
        (3) 이동인이 밀교한 조선정부회의절략

附 駐日本何使由長崎來電
光緒六年十一月初二日到

玆有朝鮮委員李東仁 身帶國王密詔 據稱現朝議一變 由國命金使致書與璋 書意欲璋勸美來結約 此事可否代爲周全 現請總署電示 以便收到金信後遵行 又 現探實俄海軍卿仍在琿春 尙無來東日期 餘俟後詳 十月十九日

【관련문서 1】

十月十六日 出使大臣何如璋等函稱 本月十四日肅呈第一百五號緘 當邀垂鑒 前聞俄海軍卿將來橫濱 續於十六探確 日本駐劄琿春領事小林新有電報告外務稱 理疏富斯基尙無來濱準期 又聞理君年旣七十餘 二十年前卽曾乘船來日本 凡次俟其到來 日本擬待以賓禮云 中俄萬一有事 日本自然中立 惟萬國公法中立有二 一曰嚴正中立 則一切泊船買煤買米之事 盡行拒絶是也 一曰友誼中立 則泊船買煤購米亦准接濟是也 此二中立 隨其國形勝時勢利益而擇用之 今日本自爲計 自應守嚴正中立 故新聞主筆多勸政府爲此 然必須自行設備 方能杜絶俄人之請 不知日本力量做得到否耳 惟近日傅聞伊犁之事旣經妥結 前奉堂憲來諭 謂俄國限議一月 卽我九月底 今旣過期 不聞有決之信 妥結云云 或是確音 至以爲念 日本近情如常 肅此敬乞代回堂憲察核爲禱 卽請勛安

專啓者 本月十七日下干 有朝鮮人李東仁 來館見參贊黃遵憲 其人通日本語

言 亦解筆談 坐定寒暄數語畢 卽解衣襟取出紅綾包裹之一紙 見有巨印三顆 內云今爲嚴密探偵事 特委李東仁前往航海云云 又取出圓式如盒之木具一 上有火印 彼云此印朝鮮國王密詔 其圓木 乃符驗也 又云朝鮮朝議現今一變 伊於九月初三日受命由漢城啓程 在道六日 至元山津 駐十餘日 得友人信稱 國主現命前修信使金宏集 致書何公使 勸令美國前來結好 惟金使此函由驛遞寄來 未知何日可到 十八日早晨復來 先出書函數件 云係友人寄彼之書 字畫各別 內有一云 自上命金信使致書何如璋 而致書之意都在使何公勸美速送之_{原文如此 妥謂勸其來也} 從此我國庶幾開荒耳 又有一云 近日諸大臣會議 與主上世家幾處公論 與年前迥異 欲隨花房公使_{按卽日本公使} 所請看勢諒處 且美國公使到日 隨其所請隨勢答之云云 又出筆記一紙 謂係國主與首相密商當筵筆記 又出其政府公議一紙 檢其文意在防俄 有待日本務盡誠信 待美國臨時操處之語 朝鮮國是果將一變矣 先是朝鮮金使之將來 如璋欲勸外交 荷承總署指示 又素知北洋李爵相屢經致書勸論 而近來南洋峴莊制府亦主此議 因於其來也 危詞異語面爲開導 渠頗覺悟 復慮言語未通 不能盡意 中亦有如璋礙難盡言者 因命參贊黃遵憲作一朝鮮策略 設爲問答論難之辭 先告以防俄 而防俄在親中國 結日本 聯美國 以圖自强 卽今筆記中所謂冊子是也 瀕行 如璋復執其手告之曰 今俄海軍卿率兵船十五艘屯泊琿春 若天寒南下來劫盟約 未便抗拒 慮遭翦滅 又告之曰 美國差爲公平 若於無事時預與結好 他國依樣爲之 利益無窮 閣下歸國 廷議若變 幸惠緘告知 可代爲周旋 彼唯唯而去 今觀李東仁所遞諸文件 則朝鮮欲與美國結好 自屬可信 如璋於十九日申刻寄電請示遵行 寄電之後 於二十日下午英署使堅尼迪來見稱 現聞朝鮮旣願外交 日來德意法諸使派船偕往之言 恐英國亦不能不往 如璋謂朝鮮卽願外交 若諸國偕往 操之太蹙 吾決其事必不成 英使無他言 如璋伏思泰西諸國之欲通朝鮮久矣 而俄人虎視耽耽 包藏禍心 更不可測 今俄師方屯琿春 若率而南下 雖朝鮮願與行成 幸可不至滅國 不至割地 而成逼勢劫 乞盟城下 恐屬國之名 中國不能復保 正謂防俄之呑噬 憚泰西諸國之要挾 不得不擇一較爲公平之美國 早與結約 以圖結援 以圖舒禍 今天氣日寒 俄船難於久泊 其旌麾所指未知何逼如璋不揣冒昧 謹爲主持朝鮮外交議 別繕上呈 若以爲可採 切望迅速由禮部行文以期補救至如璋此間一面俟總署電示 一面俟金使來函 然後相機妥籌 務期著著穩實 著著有益 雖彼國噬臍之悔 事旣過遲 有無裨益皆敢知 惟求盡一分心力 圖一分補救而已 玆事重大 如璋日夕惴惴 然慮失事機 敬求代回堂憲 迅逮察核訓示遵行 並求秘密 是所之禱 再請勛安

外呈主持朝鮮外交議一件 又附呈李東仁來二件 查此係李東仁自行密交之件
若由禮部行文 又或由總署致函與朝鮮國 其中云云 皆未便提明 謹附藏於此
本月十九日酉刻發電 錄呈查核 玆有朝鮮委員李東仁身帶國王密詔 據稱現朝
議一變 由國主命金使致書與璋 書意欲璋勸美來結約 此事可否代爲周全 應
請電示 以便收到金信後遵行 又現探實俄海軍卿仍在琿春 尙無來濱日期 餘
詳後械

【관련문서 2】

朝鮮偵探委員李東仁密交朝鮮國王與大臣密議當筵筆記

上曰　修信使無事往還可幸

領相曰 果無事往還矣

上曰　萬里滄海雖極危險 一船往來 比中原容易矣

領相曰 修信使氣質素弱 故始則爲慮 而克竣其事 誠萬幸矣

上曰　聞修信使之言 則日本人極爲款曲矣

領相曰 臣亦聞之 而丙子年金綺秀入去時 不能知其情實 今番則見待類異信
　　　好意矣

上曰　日本人問答中 俄羅斯國事不無可慮

領相曰 俄羅斯國近頗强盛 中原亦不能制之 誠爲可慮

上曰　中原猶如此 況我國乎

領相曰 年前宮本小一燕飡時促坐語 乃俄羅斯國 此是眞情也 而我國人果疑
　　　之 今以信使行中 淸人所送冊子觀之 可驗其情寔

上曰　俄羅斯雖爲慮 日本人則畢極盡之探矣

領相曰 今番修信使之供具行中譯官從人之優待 異於丙子 則此可見實情矣

上曰　我國人空然不信而多浮言

領相曰 敎至當

上曰　修信使行中所來冊子 淸使所傳 而厚意甚於日本 其冊子大臣亦見之
　　　乎

領相曰 日本猶此款曲 況清人乎 必有耳聞 故俾我國備之 而我國人心本來多疑 將掩卷而不究矣

上曰 見其冊則畢何如乎

領相曰 臣畢見之 而彼人之諸條論辯 相符我之心算 不可一見而束閣者也 大抵俄國僻在深北 惟不耐寒 每欲向南 而他國之事則不過奧利而已 俄人所欲則在於土地人民 而我國白頭山北 即俄境也 雖滄海之遠 一帆風猶可往來 況豆滿江之隔在兩境乎 平時亦可以呼吸相通 而成冰則雖徒涉可也 方今俄人滿兵船十六隻 而每船可容三千人 若寒後則其勢必將向南矣 其意固不可測 則豈非殆哉汲汲乎

上曰 見日本人之言 則似是渠之所畏在俄 而要朝鮮備之 其實非為朝鮮 而實為渠國也

領相曰 其實似為楚非為趙 而朝鮮若不備 則渠國必危故也 雖然 我國則豈可諉以俄人之意在日本 而視若尋常哉 且以壬辰事觀之 稱以假道 空然而來 實非假道也 安知俄人無假道之意乎 今不聽人言 而急必難防 現今城郭器械軍卒兵糧不及乎古 而百無一恃 終雖無事 目前之備 寧容少緩乎

上曰 防備之策何如乎

領相曰 防備之策 自我豈無所講磨 而清人冊中論說若是備盡 既拾於他國 則深有所見然也 其中可信者 則信之 而可以採用 然我國必不信之 將為休紙而已 六月米利堅來東萊 此本非仇國 彼若以書契呈萊府 則自萊府受之未為不可 呈禮曹則自禮曹受之亦可也 而謂之洋國 拒以不受 仍為播傳於新聞紙 終為羞恥見侮 若言仇國 則日本真世仇之國也 米利堅有何聲聞之及而謂之仇國乎 其在柔遠之意 恐不可生釁也

上曰 米利堅烏可謂仇國乎

領相曰 聖教誠然 我國風習本來如此 為天下嘲笑 雖以西洋國言之 本無恩怨 而初由我國愚人輩之招引 以致江華平壤事釁隙 此是我國之自及處也 年前洋人之入 近因中原咨文將探內處矣 大抵洋船入境 輒以邪學為藉口之說 則洋人之入住中原 未聞中原之人皆為邪學也 其所謂邪學 當斥之而已 於隙則不可矣 今日筵席 左相未出 肅臣獨承教 宜與諸宰講究 而我國擧朝之人 只貪好仕 皆與自便之計 臣獨有何策乎

上曰 諸宰則何如意

領相曰 大臣已為備奏 無容更達

上曰　原任大臣俱見其冊 而有何言乎

領相曰　姑未言之 而諸宰則我國事本有廟堂 有何別廟堂云爾 而雖十人同座 無一言之可否矣 然而人孰無慚 為父母保妻子固是所欲 而無一講究 退為高談 此非名節 非義理也 臣之計宜思宗社生靈之太平 若一朝俄人渡江而來 則想必曰內修外攘 而修攘非一朝一夕可得也 顧今人氣國規器械材用不如古矣 莫如以柔遠之義為急務 而以安宗社之策也 于此于彼 聖衷不決於疑信之間 則釣名之人朋起 不待俄人而必起內亂

上曰　廟堂似有可否之論

領相曰　未知何時原任入侍 而臣今登對 每有未穩之語 然含糊不告於君父之前 則臣實有罪 惟冀聖衷之牢定矣

上曰　時原任終當有議 而今非臨訐之時也

領相曰　今日便是臨訐矣

上曰　俄人將往山東云果然乎

領相曰　以若氣勢 何處不住乎

上曰　三使臣聞見錄亦已見之 而寧古塔侵奪之說 未詳真假

領相曰　未可知也

上曰　天何生此類橫行於天下乎 誠可痛忿矣

領相曰　氣數然矣

上曰　中國若道光之時 則此類似不如是

領相曰　雖道光之時 至於氣數所關 則亦無奈矣 又曰 外道之器械 申飭何等切嚴 而不善修繕 無一可用 且火藥鳥銃 每下吏輩乘間櫻出城 可痛矣

上曰　然則國財不過虛費

領相曰　聞花房義質不遠出來云 觀其動靜 又聞其議 庶有操處之方 然今日筵奏後 外論似騷擾 不勝悶然

上曰　大臣就座

按 據李東仁稱 領相曰 相即朝鮮首輔 名李最應 觀其所論 國主首相 皆願外交 其所未願者 惟原任大臣耳 領相之言頗有譏諷之意 又東仁謂原任大臣即李裕元 曾寄書與李爵相者 又嘗聞之日本外務官宮本小一曰 李裕元即今王之父 朝鮮人 為大院君 未知確否 詢李東仁則云未悉也 如璋附識 又按 內有壬辰事云云 即指平秀吉攻朝鮮事

【관련문서 3】

又李東仁密交朝鮮政府會議節略

俄羅斯國處在北 虎視眈眈 天下畏之如虎 厥惟久矣 近年以來 每因中國及外各國文字 常以是國為憂 朝鮮壤界相接 安知不受其弊乎
今前修信使回還 賚來中國人黃君冊子 其所謂朝鮮策略 自問自答 設疑設難 憂深慮遠者 比前日所見各國文字 益加詳密 雖未知其言言皆當 亦安知非大加講究於安不忘危之義乎
其曰親中國者 二百年來我國事大之誠 未嘗一分或懈 上國亦待之以內服 至今曲庇復更有何別般效親者乎
其曰結日本者 邇來講信修睦 公使年年出來 聽許其難行之請者 在我國可謂靡不庸極 而但我國習俗駭眼 其於留館之際 彼使不能無蓄憾之端 由是而疑我之不信渠國 此實出於我之誠信未洽也 現今公使匪久出來 先從在我道理務盡誠信 毋或如前輕忽 以示申好之義 其出來也 必有渠國受約者存 自謂京城駐館也 仁川開港也 彼發難從之請 豈可容易聽許乎 駐京許之 仁川不許 京城之於仁川 京城尤不得安 雖或仁川許之 駐京不許 彼又從渠所欲 強聒不已 若一邊京城駐館 一邊仁川開港 聽我邈邈 挽回不得 若將之何 此則公使公幹時隨其所謂以為究竟之如何矣
其曰聯美國者 方今天下各國無不合縱 以阻俄國輕蔑之威 而況我國處在海路要衝 孤立無援 其所聯好者非不良策 而我國規模 非徒自來不通外國 相去數萬里 聲息不及之地 今何以自我先通 以為聯交為援乎 泊船投書 則見書而好言答之 泛海告眠 則隨力而以周恤接之 不妨為柔遠之道 而如是 然後其國必曰善待 而亦豈無此際相通者乎 此在臨時操處之如何矣
蓋此論以我國之安危 有關於大清日本如是 纖悉為言 在我國亦不可尋常看過 而言語如是切直 詎容玩歲愒日乎

按 以上二款 李東仁行囊中所攜來者 持出閱看 彼初不肯留抄 強之乃可 切望秘之

李裕元(1880.12.12/高宗十七年十一月十一月日) ➡ 李鴻章

李裕元-李鴻章 서한(14)

照錄朝鮮原任太師李裕元來函
文華殿大學士 直隷總督 肅毅伯爺爵前 本年冬至月初伏奉下答書 乃九月二十八日出卞元圭齎來者也 伏維爵前威惠日隆 天下仰望 而小邦偏蒙厚春 有擧必顧 有呼必應 雖難從難副之事 上達天陛 下收廷議 有若家人之愛護 尊師之敎導 軍情至愼也 而一質而開牖 局勢其測也 而屢運而代籌 孰不慕德廣河海 量恢山藪 而小邦之大小倚靠 非比尋常 不爲遠交 而爵前之彈壓愈重 不爲近攻 而爵前之維持斯在 然則何待乎層溟以外之國 何憂乎隔江至逼之敵也哉 料以爵前曲念 則如鰕生之賤 久不遐棄 如齋官之微 猶賜容接 推以知爵前之於小邦視同骨肉 費其心膂 實由小生託契下風 貽憂彌大 罪悚之至 無望厚贖 但所欽誦者 國王深感德意 命小生恭作復函 下寄禮物二十四種 亦爲收納 興榮之忱 曷有其極 至於入學事 不圖若是之順成 固當不留晷刻 而辦備之間 自致月日非漫也 實事勢然也 容俟更白 惟冀惠念之終始統垂也 伏請鈞體度對時萬康 小生蒙恩休致 永歸鄕里 從此棲息有暇 感鏤腑肺 無以形達 玆因貢使修緘 敢呈肅毅伯爵前
嘉梧退生李裕元再拜
庚辰十一月十一日

禮單

論語一帙
孟子一帙
中庸一帙
大學一帙
詩傳一帙
書傳一帙
周易一帙

春秋一帙
頂上山蔘四本
鹿茸二對
上上製山䅉淸心元一百丸
苔紙二十卷
計十二種

卓挺埴 ➡ 何如璋(1880.12.22/光緒六年十一月二十一日)

高宗 밀명 전달

上國之屢屢開示於敝邦者 皆出於親切愛護之隆眷 而敝邦之不能奉敎者 果爲習見之所結 有難於一朝頓釋也 今於信使之歸 復蒙懇懇指敎 方覺時事之急務有所先後 而況上國之所親經歷鑑照無遺者乎 然敝邦臣民素無海外眼目 誠難勇敢發起也 若彼美國復來求和 而所約公平 則斷當眞情相接 必無冷却之理 然事之大者 豈可謀於衆而後方欲成之乎 是所以小生之密奉君命而轉達也 又如昨日所囑結連美國 實爲保國良策 則伏望急速商議 毋違積年庇護之宏圖焉 欽差大臣閣下 卓挺埴再拜

何如璋 → 總署(1881. 2. 1/光緒七年正月三日)

李東仁·卓挺植의 밀보에 관한 보고

正月初三日 出使日本大臣何如璋函稱 上月二十七日肅陳第一百十一號函 當邀垂鑒 二十九日奉到堂憲本字第四十八號賜諭 敬謹讀悉 琉球一案 此間傳聞謂未經畫押盖印 猶未定議 玆承縷示 一一祗悉 俄海軍卿仍在長崎療養 尙無動靜 送經函飭駐崎理事余瓗 俄船若有往中國往朝鮮各信 由電告知 現在並無他信也 西歷正値新年 此數日中亦無甚新聞 如璋等自去歲十一月起 至本年十月止 又屆第三次報銷之期 謹備公續呈達氷案 開除以外所存一萬七千餘兩 計到七年正月約署告罄 各員續支薪水 及歸國應領辦裝銀兩 求飭江海關道 滙寄以資應用 聞許竹篔侍御開凍以後方能東駛 所有署中一切公文函件 及各國交涉文件 業隨時料理鈔存檔案 其各處来往函件有關公事者 亦旣陸續摘抄 屆時自當滙入交代也 肅此 敬乞代回堂憲察核是禱 順請勛安

十二月初二日午後九點鐘四十五分奉到來電 鈔呈查核來緘竝鈔單 所議極正 朝鮮能連絡外交 誠於大局有益 但由中國代爲主持 恐生疑慮 且多關礙 閣下答金信 仍望迎機以導 立約一層 聽其自主 中國不爲干預 只可密爲維持調護 北洋所見亦同 先行電聞

專再啓者 朝鮮外交一事 本初三日晩戌刻奉到電示 譯讀祗悉 查此事以金使函遲久未到 礙難發端 續因朝密探委員卓挺植來東 有密奉君命之稟 曾與美使一商 均作從旁聯絡之詞 未著痕跡 至如何結約 因李東仁卓挺植詳細探問 曾將利害各節告知 俾其轉達該國有所依據 經詳前函 諒邀洞鑒 前函所云卓挺植歸國因誤船期 一時未及啓程 旋接到金使來函 其中不過云朝鮮現在衆論雖未通悟 殊不比往時 仍望賜教等語 於聯美一事 未經提及 仍未能將書意達美使勸之前往也 卓挺植於本初二日附英國公司船往長崎回國 如璋仍告以俟朝鮮有願交美國之函 美使方能前往 惟卓挺植屢稱 國主與領相二三大臣決意外交 以憚李裕元之故 未能遽發 若得中國勸諭之力 事必有成云云 觀金使函亦有此意 可否請仍由總署寄書朝鮮勸令外交 庶可以決其疑 而堅其信 仍望鈞裁 現在朝鮮情形未敢必其能成 若有回信 謹當遵照電示 密爲維持調護 此事理應秘密 如璋在此均係不露聲色 格外嚴密 並再三叮囑李卓諸人 不得少有疏漏矣 專此 再乞代回堂憲察核訓示 再請勛安

何如璋 ➡ 總署(1881. 2. 21/光緖七年正月二十三日)

조약체결시 조청 종속(宗屬)관계 명문화 건의

正月二十三日 出使日本大臣何如璋等函稱 本月十五日肅呈第一百十三號緘 當邀垂鑒 伊犁一案 自前次英倫來電稱 中俄事旣了結 以後未有續電 俄海軍卿理疏富斯基仍在長崎 據長崎理事余瓗函稱 曾往見一面 尙坐而握手 步履猶未便也 現泊橫濱之阿非利加船提督某 曾來東京見外務卿井上馨 井上答拜 次日復坐其船偕往熱海(在伊豆之近海地方 去東京約二百里 有溫泉 日本高官巨室時時往遊之所也) 昨有外務書記官來坐 談及此 彼謂井上偕其夫人及女答拜提督 言及溫泉之遊 提督强邀之同往云(到後 船卽歸泊橫濱) 惟有無他項詭謀 須再密探 又此月中先後往熱海有參議大隈重信 伊藤博文 黑田淸隆 現皆未歸 或云帶有太政書記官 及大藏省飜譯之書記官 恐係會商借債事 則井上之往 仍爲此事 亦未可知也 肅此 敬乞伏回堂憲察核爲禱 卽請勛安

專再啓者 如璋等現屆三年期滿 所有隨帶之參贊理事繙譯隨員等員不無微勞 現旣援案籲請恩奬 此摺仍由輪船寄到上海文報局 轉遞到日 求鈞署代爲遞進 如璋等從前摺件係求代遞 曾奉賜諭 謂以後可照此辦理 此次仍備奏事處咨文 又謹鈔原摺片繕文呈達鈞案 統求察核辭理 附片中之丁憂任敬和等五員 除任敬和一員留差旣滿三年外 神戶理事官劉壽鏗雖到差未久 而神戶大阪之華商閩廣三江分幇不睦 該員創辦之初 盤根錯節 苦心調護 甚爲出力 至隨員吳廣霈 何定求等 草創之始 事屬繁難 而該員當差 旣過二年 毫無貽誤 其時旣有奏定丁憂人員章程 本可留差 皆以堅請守制 未便强留 其立心制行 似可嘉尙 又念該員離鄕井 別父母 而遠役海外 念以中道丁艱 上未霑朝廷之隆恩 下不免家庭之隱痛 其情亦未免向隅 如璋等本欲分別酌量開奬 繼以未滿三年 保奬未有章程 恐經部駁 再四籌思 所以叩請恩旨交鈞署核議 是否有當 伏候鈞裁 再乞代回堂憲察核訓示爲禱 再請勛安

再如璋等到東以後 所有公事摺件 均係會銜具奏 與出使美英各國單銜陳奏者微有不同 此次保奬人員 因摺內之隨員張鴻淇係斯桂之子 斯桂年過六旬 遠涉重洋 飭令隨侍來東 經如璋商派充作隨員 現屆差滿 張鴻淇自應一律保奬 是以斯桂未便會銜 謹此附陳 務希於摺到之日 卽回堂憲察核 均不勝翹禱之至 再請勛安

再正在等待輪船 未及發函間 接奉大文並堂憲本字第四十九號賜諭 敬謹捧讀 祈悉一切 朝鮮外交一事 如璋前呈主持朝鮮外交議 院旣經繕呈之後 再四籌思 所議派員前往代爲主持 及奏請諭旨飭令立約 一時皆未便行 惟念朝鮮前與日本立約 約中有朝鮮爲自主之邦一語 嗣以朝鮮禮曹行文日本外務中 有上國指揮等字 擡頭繕寫 而日本公使花房義質竟無理取鬧 行文駁詰 如璋私心竊冀除立約仍由朝鮮外 但使其能於約中 不觸不背 順便露出中國屬國影子 則外人不認爲自主之邦 庶幾將來無事時 可互相聯絡 以壯聲援 有事時 可互相策應 無須中立 而朝鮮外交 一切仍係由彼自行辦理也 但不知能辦得到否 又堂諭命如璋措詞之間 作爲如璋意 尤覺泯然無迹 如璋前晤美使 卽係作爲如璋意 與之妥商 與鈞旨正同 所陳一百十號十一號函 旣經詳陳 又李伯相謂仿照華約 不利朝鮮 如璋所亟亟然欲先與美國結約者 正爲此事 伯相又謂他國相率偕往朝鮮 反恐中阻 前英署使堅尼迪言及此事 如璋亦經以婉言辭之 所有辦法均幸不至乖謬 現在俄師仍泊長崎 新聞傳說 亦時有遣船前往之言 究難保其無事 朝鮮前次之委員李東仁 早旣抵國 後次之委員卓挺植 近亦當到釜山 苟使朝鮮自此開悟 決意外交 誠於亞洲大局大有裨益 事機至逼 間不容髮 如璋日夕傍皇 惟禱祝朝鮮破除舊見 妥速辦理而已 肅此 敬再乞代回堂憲察核訓示是禱 再請勛安

李鴻章(1881. 2. 26/光緖七年正月二十八日)

李鴻章・李容肅 회담(1)

酌覆朝鮮詢問各條正月二十八日
小邦今與日本開港通商 然小邦素昧商規 恐被欺壓 上下胥願倘邀上國商人來會開港諸互相交易情志旣乎 依賴必大云 而又有黃參贊策略 卽奏請推廣鳳皇廳貿易 令華商乘船來開港各口通商 以防日人壟斷之句語 此論恐未知如何 伏候亮敎 具呑仰請 而措詞主何妥當乎 並望訓示
朝鮮向無海道貿易之例 現旣擬與外國通商 則華商前往貿易亦所不禁 至於黃參贊策略防日人壟斷 將來如願華商前往貿易 應由國王將寔在情形咨請核奏辦理
敢問小邦他日有不得已與各國相交之際 自主自强 利權在我 不爲他要挾 且不失先後早晚之策 此條已於上年九月二十二日曾與賫奏官卞元圭詳晰言之 當必於回國時面陳 總宜先事豫防 自主之權操之在我 玆有馬道台所擬與外洋通商約章節略一冊 交付帶回 以資採擇
小邦釜山元山兩港定稅 旣蒙大人訓示 敢不卽速議定 第伊言非全權委任 不可擧擬 若値全權之來議値百抽幾 當恪遵指津 隨機圖之 各國修好立約 通商章程 稅則額條款 稅關設官凡例 伏想已有印行文字 願蒙賜下各一件 謹當帶回 援釜山元山兩港定稅 宜由國委員予以議稅全權字樣據 俾與彼國使臣互換觀看 以資取信 此乃各國遣使議事之通例也 至稅則値百抽幾 不必援中國所定通商稅則爲例 緣前者中國於外國情形尙未深知 僅爲體恤商民而設 進出口各貨皆係値百抽五 若洋貨運入內地 再抽二五子口稅 其實未可執一而論 上年亦面告賫奏官卞元圭矣 若外洋抽稅 皆視貨物之暢滯 以定稅則之多寡 竟有値百抽三十以至値百抽百者 若以各物統扯論之 大約不在値百抽十五以下 今朝鮮國擬與外洋通商 倘各貨暢滯未能預知 則値抽幾亦難預定 不若定一試辦統例 進口貨估價値百抽十 出口貨估價値百抽五 至食用等物數滿十件者亦照則抽稅 如此試行三五年 貨物之暢滯可知 卽則例之多寡可定 然後與外洋各國重定稅則 洋人決無不從之理 盖和約與商約有異 在我不背和約 決無開釁之端 在我欲修商約 斷無興戎之擧 不然甌洲瑞士比利時藎爾彈丸 介於諸大國之間 將商約不修 稅則不 加國不足爲國矣 至中國各口稅關 或設監督

專管 或飭巡道兼管 從前初開通商口岸 華人罕諳洋文洋語 收稅事件僱用洋人司理 仍歸監督巡道節制 今朝鮮擬與各國通商 日本窺知朝鮮未諳西洋語言文字及稅務事宜 難保不以管稅一職自荐充當 但日本朝鮮僅隔一水 往來商貨必多 且聞通商五年尙未收稅 喫虧已甚 倘僱日人司理稅務 尤恐滋弊 祇有暫僱西人之明白稅務兼通漢文者 令其隨同朝鮮所派管關官員料理收稅 較爲妥當 並一面速選聰穎子弟 從所僱西人學習語言文字稅務事宜 學成之後 自無容再用西人矣 日本初與各國通商 於暫僱西人料理稅務兼司敎習一節辦理甚妥 是以該國現在稅務辭退西人 已能自行管理 茲將中國所有通商章程稅則稅額條款飭津海關道檢交該員帶回 以資考證

北洋咨式似依禮部咨式書呈 而內書北洋督署大臣 外書一體繕寫 恐未知如何

北洋咨式應咨禮部相同 外銜稱應書欽差北洋通商大臣衙門字樣

伏見禮部咨示中有委員弁兵學徒通事人等 由北洋大臣衙門給發空白憑票交該國按名塡給之語 空白憑票許令此次帶回 以爲隨用之地 伏望

據關道等面詢稱係先派學藝人來 業由該道等詳請給發憑票十張 交該員具領帶回呈收 如學藝人分起前來 應按每起塡用一張交管領之員執持 以憑查驗

學習人徒往旣蒙徑從海道自便捷之敎 恐是賃乘汽船吉利涉海 當自何處賃船 可以無碍 亦蒙公文不致盤詰

據關道等面詢稱 由朝鮮進鳳凰廳邊門計程一千一百餘里 再到牛莊營口約三百餘里 卽從營口或附輪船或附帆船來津較爲便捷 應於進邊門時將憑票呈東邊道衙門查驗 於到營口時將憑票呈奉錦山海關道衙門查驗 均候加戳放行 若遇有交涉事件 仍由地方官約束訊斷

小邦船舶本無旗標 令將議造 而黃參贊有奏請襲用中國龍旗之論 敢問中國船上旗身畫樣而小邦則用某色某畫是否有當乎

凡西國商船旗式皆係國主之旗 因海上往來俾知爲某國船隻 今貴國王自用之旗 據稱是畫龍方旗 亦與中國龍旗相仿 自可以畫龍旗爲國旗 卽作爲船舶旗標 應於定用之先將龍旗尺寸顏色繪具圖式咨明本大臣衙門 以憑核奏咨行

卑職未渡鴨綠 聞日本使花房義質賫其國書而來 敝朝以爲條約中曾有我禮曹與伊外務省書契往來而已 無國書往來之規 今何遽變條約乎 以此難之 彼云見陛辦理公使 不可恃外務書契 且各國皆有國書然後益加親睦 力懇不已 國王特念隣誼 親臨便殿 召接彼使而受之 書辭敬白等句 頗恭非慢 至若皇帝字 朕字 極涉礙眼 上下俱爲不安 且書中所註箚 最難應從 彼言仁川開港 亦

不可輕許 廷議仁川開港强許以遷就幾年 駐箚則欲因仁川事彌縫 然彼之從否
姑未可知 國書不可不答 而稱他日帝 實所不願 至於自稱又無援照 往復之際
如何撰措 庶不失國體而免笑於各國乎 彼之意望又在專价修答 非徒事力不敷
隨請隨行 豈不損弱乎 大人旣垂厚念 視均一室 故玆敢謄上彼之國書與口奏
伏乞俯鑑指賜良策 使我東藩得以固圉全安焉

使臣駐京 西洋各國皆同 蓋旣通商 必有交涉事件 公使之駐京猶之領事之駐
口岸 非此不能遇事互酌 以聯兩國之誼 以平兩國之爭 實有益而無損也 特東
西風氣相殊 猝議駐京 鮮不意存顧慮 中國從前初與西國通商開口時 情形亦
然 揣度事勢 旣經立約通商 斷難始終拒絶 與其勉從於後日 似不如慨允於目
前 況日本使臣駐京一節 查光緒二年貴國與日本立約 業於第二款載明 現彼
據約而求 倘不允許 卽爲背約 其曲在己 未免授人以隙 至仁川一港係由海道
達王京必由之路 如已允開 卽踐守前諾 似亦無碍 至所云自稱又無援照 往復
之際 如何撰措 庶不失國體而免笑於各國等語 玆日本遣使賫奉國書 將來貴
國答以國書 乃兩國禮尙往來之義 答書如何措詞 想貴國自有討論而潤色之者
至於國書內所稱名號 歷查西洋各國書籍內所載 聘問國書譯其稱謂 本非一律
如德意志俄羅斯奧斯馬加等國主 皆自稱爲帝 意大利日斯巴尼亞瑞典等國主
皆自稱爲王 間有譯漢文爲君主及君主者 英吉利國主男則稱王 女則稱后 迨
前六年始加印度皇后之號 如稱王之國 致書於外洋稱帝之國 彼此亦各從其本
稱 未嘗以稱帝爲尊稱王爲小也 貴國久受中朝冊封 如有報答日本之書 理應
仍用封號 將來傳聞各國 衡以西洋通例 當無笑貴國爲失體者

　　照錄清單
謹將酌覆朝鮮詢問各條照繕清單 恭呈御覽

　　第一條
小邦今與日本開港通商 然小邦素昧商規 恐被欺壓 上下胥願但邀上國商人來
會開港諸處 互相交易 情志旣孚 依賴必大云 而又有黃參贊策略 卽奏請推廣
鳳凰廳貿易 令華商乘船來開港各口通商 以防日人壟斷之句語 此論恐未知如
何 伏候亮敎 具咨仰請 而措詞主何妥當乎 並望訓示 朝鮮向無海道貿易之例
現旣擬與外國通商 則華商前往貿易亦所不禁 至於黃參贊策略防日人壟斷之
語 果能與各國通商 日人自無從壟斷 將來如願華商前往貿易 應由國王將實
在情形咨請核奏辦理

第二條
敢問小邦他日有不得已與各國相交之際 自主自强 利權在我 不爲他要挾 且不失先後早晚之策
此條已於上年九月二十二日曾與齎奏官卞元圭詳晰言之 當必於回國時面陳總宜先事豫防 自主之權 操之在我 玆有馬道台所擬與外洋通商約章節略一冊 交付帶回 以資採擇

第三條
小邦釜山元山兩港定稅 旣蒙大人訓示 敢不卽速議定 第伊言非全權委任不可擧擬 若値全權之來議値百抽幾 當恪遵指津 隨機圖之 各國修好立約通商章程 稅則稅額條款 稅關設官凡例 伏想已有印行文字 願蒙賜下各一件 謹當帶回援照
釜山元山兩港定稅 宜由國王委任妥員予以議稅全權字據 俾與彼國使臣互換觀看 以資取信 此乃各國遣使議事之通例也 至稅則値百抽幾 不必援中國所定通商稅則爲例 緣前者中國於外國情形尙未深知 僅爲體恤商民而設 進出口各貨皆係値百抽五 若洋貨運入內地再抽二五子口稅 其實未可執一而論 上年亦面告齎奏官卞元圭矣 若外洋抽稅 皆視貨物之滯暢 以定稅則之多寡 竟有値百抽三十以至値百抽百者 若以各物統扯論之 大約不在値百抽十五以下 今朝鮮國擬與外洋通商 但各貨暢滯未能預知 則値百抽幾亦難預定 不若定一試辦統例 進口貨估價値百抽十 出口貨估價値百抽五 至食用等物數滿十件者亦照則抽稅 如此試行三五年 貨物之暢滯可知 卽則例之多寡可定 然後與外洋各國重定稅則 洋人絶無不從之理 盖和約與商約有異 在我不背和約 決無開釁之端 在我欲修商約 斷無興戎之擧 不然歐洲瑞士比利時蕞爾彈丸介於諸大國之間 將商約不修 稅則不加 而國不足爲國矣 至中國各口稅關 或設監督專管 或飭巡道兼管 從前初開通商口岸 華人罕諳洋文洋語 收稅事件雇用洋人司理 仍歸監督巡道節制 今朝鮮擬與各國通商 日本窺知朝鮮未諳西洋語言文字及稅務事宜 難保不以管稅一職自薦充當 但日本朝鮮僅隔一水 往來商貨必多 且聞通商五年尙未收稅 喫虧已甚 倘雇日人司理稅務 尤恐滋弊 祗有暫雇西人之明白稅務兼通漢文者 令其隨同朝鮮所派管關官員料理收稅 較爲妥當 並一面速選聰穎子弟 從所雇西人學習語言文字稅務事宜 學成之後自無容再用西人矣 日本初與各國通商 於暫雇西人料理稅務兼司敎習一節 辦理甚妥

是以該國現在稅務 辭退西人 已能自行管理 玆將中國所有通商章程稅則稅額
條款 飭津海關道檢交該員帶回 以資考證

第四條
北洋咨式似依禮部咨式書呈 而內書北洋督署大臣 外書一體繕寫 恐未知如何
北洋咨式應與咨禮部相同 內外銜稱應書欽差北洋通商大臣衙門字樣

第五條
伏見禮部咨示中有委員弁兵學徒通事人等 由北洋大臣衙門給發空白憑票 交
該國按名塡給之語 空白憑票許令此次帶回 以爲隨用之地 伏望
據關道等面詢稱 係先派學藝人來 業由該道等詳請給發憑票十張 交該員具領
帶回呈收 如學藝人分起前來 應按每起塡用一張 交管領之員執持 以憑查驗

第六條
學習人徒來往 旣蒙逕從海道自更便捷之敎 恐是賃乘汽船吉利涉海 當自何處
賃船可以無礙 亦蒙公文 不致盤詰
據關道等面詢稱 由朝鮮進鳳凰廳邊門 計程一千一百餘里 再到牛莊營口約
三百餘里 卽從營口或附輪船或附帆船來津 較爲便捷 應於進邊門時 將憑票
呈東邊道衙門查驗 於到營口時 將憑票呈奉錦山海關道衙門查驗 均候加戳放
行 若遇有交涉事件 仍由地方官約束訊斷

第七條
小邦船舶本無旗標 令將議造 而黃參贊有奏請襲用中國龍旗之論 敢問中國船
上旗身畫樣 而小邦則用某色某畫 是否有當乎 凡西國商船旗式皆係國主之旗
因海上往來俾知爲某國船隻 今貴國王自用之旗 據稱是畫龍方旗 亦與中國龍
旗相仿 自可以畫龍旗爲國旗 卽作爲船舶旗標 應於定用之先將龍旗尺寸顏色
繪具圖式咨明本大臣衙門 以憑核奏咨行

第八條
卑職未渡鴨綠 聞日本使花房義質齎其國書而來 敝朝已爲條約中曾有我禮曹
與伊外務省書契往來而已 無國書往來之規 今何遽變條約乎 以此難之 彼云
見陛辦理公使 不可持外務書契 且各國皆有國書 然後益加親睦 力懇不已 國

王特念鄰誼 親臨便殿 召接彼使而受之 書辭敬白等句 頗恭非慢 至若皇帝字
朕字 極涉礙眼 上下俱爲不安 且書中所請駐箚 最難應從 彼言仁川開港 亦不
可輕許 廷議仁川開港強許以遷就幾年 駐箚則欲因仁川事彌縫 然彼之從否
姑未可知 國書不可不答 而稱他曰帝 實所不願 至於自稱又無援照 往復之際
如何撰措 庶不失國體而免笑於各國乎 彼之意望又在專价修答 非徒事力不敷
隨請隨行 豈不損弱乎 大人旣垂厚念 視均一室 故玆敢謄上彼之國書與口奏
伏乞俯鑑指賜良策 使我東藩得以固圉全安焉

使臣駐京 西洋各國皆同 盖旣通商 必有交涉事件 公使之駐京猶之領事之駐
口岸 非此不能遇事互酌 以聯兩國之誼 以平兩國之爭 實有益而無損也 特東
西風氣相殊 猝議駐京 鮮不意存顧慮 中國從前初與西國通商開口時 情形亦
然 揣度事勢 旣經立約通商 斷難始終拒絶 與其勉從於後日 似不如慨允於目
前 況日本使臣駐京一節 查光緒二年貴國與日本立約 業於第二款載明 現彼
據約而求 倘不允許 即爲背約 其曲在已 未免授人以隙 至仁川一港 係由海道
達王京必由之路 如已允開 即踐守前諾 似亦無礙 至所云自稱又無援照 往復
之際如何撰措 庶不失國體而免笑於各國等語 玆日本遣使齎奉國書 將來貴國
答以國書 乃兩國禮尙往來之義 答書如何措詞 想貴國自有討論而潤色之者
至於國書內所稱名號 歷查西洋各國書籍內所載 聘問國書譯其稱謂 本非一律
如德意志俄羅斯奧斯馬加等國主皆自稱爲帝 意大利日斯巴尼亞瑞典等國主
皆自稱爲王 間有譯漢文爲君主及君主者 英吉利國主男則稱王女則稱后 迨前
六年始加印度皇后之號 如稱王之國致書於外洋稱帝之國 彼此亦各從其本稱
未嘗以稱帝爲尊稱王爲小也 貴國久受中朝册封 如有報答日本之書 理應仍用
封號 將來傳聞各國 衡以西洋通例 當無笑貴國爲失體者

光緒七年二月初四日軍機大臣奉旨 覽 欽此

李鴻章(1881. 2. 26/光緒七年正月二十八日)

李鴻章・李容肅 회담 (2)

與朝鮮委員李容肅問對節略
朝鮮委員李容肅對 鴻臚寺出身 陞任郎中 曾經中樞府知事 見無所帶職名
問 由科甲出身否
　李對 中漢文科
問 貴國科名亦有擧人進士翰林否
　李對 有進士科文科
問 足下此來專爲赴津請示 抑兼辦貢差 另有貢使何人
　李對 卑職此來專爲奉辦武備學習事 而順差於貢使行中 正使任應準 副使鄭
　　稷朝 書狀官洪鐘永
問 從前屢次來京係爲何事 往日本又爲何事
　李對 或差貢行 或賫咨之行 兩次赴日本 隨修信之行
問 金宏集自日本回後 又派何人赴倭 晤中國何公使究爲何事
　李對 去年金宏集回後 無派送人 金宏集去時 因國命同往拜何公使
問 我接何公使去年十月來書 云貴國派有人去 賫閱廷議節略
　李對 呈鑑黃遵憲策略 卽去年金宏集帶來
問 黃參贊策略係交金宏集帶回 嗣後又有人往日本 將貴國廷議漸有回悟大略
　告知 閣下知其人否
　李對 金宏集回還後 有送何公使書 略言敝廷議而已 嗣後更無送人送書之處
　　然卑職起身以後事 未得聞知 不敢仰對其有無
問 你看以後若有西洋各國 派使往朝鮮商議結約 當無拒絶否 我斷不肯爲西洋
　作說客 但慮貴國再三堅拒或釀衅端
　李對 寡君之意已屬於此 廷臣亦有回悟者 若有美意來請 恐不當如前堅拒
問 日本花房義質見在王京 貴國如何款待 亦適館授餐否
　李對 今此款待之節 雖未獲聞 前此已爲優待 今亦如前優待
問 如何優待之處 詳細告之
　李對 住館務要干淨華麗 伺候人等亦加操飭 委派二品官住偏近處 隨事周察
　　寡君種種遣官問其安否 時或餽饌 而小邦貧乏自如 不敢以恰滿其心仰
　　對

問 聞金使等在東京 日人款待至周 花房之莅王京 自應有以酬之 嗣後若常住京 或西國有公使至各口岸 向例皆只派員應接 似無須代備公館伏食 以免煩費

李對 謹當一一歸告敝廷 以爲恪遵訓敎

問 貴國弁兵派人來津學操否 卞元圭帶去洋槍已試驗否 較舊用鳥槍若何

李對 弁兵派送學操 係是遵旨擧行之事 而小邦仰籍累百年皇靈 無外侮 自致恬嬉 軍額多虛 事力亦多不敷 故今方以此逡巡 若蒙終始輪念 稍俟紓力 更請來操 伏未知如何 卞元圭帶去洋槍 當抵達於卑職離發後 未聞已試與否

問 紈知琉球平日無兵無器 故日本唾乎得之 貴國軍額旣虛 器械不利 日本現與通商 必多輕視 若再與他國結約 易啓窺伺 是擴充源 脩整武備 最爲要政

李對 訓下詞旨 亦當詳細歸告于敝廷

問 國用每歲約若干 稅入若干

李對 國稅每歲所入 以銅錢計之僅爲五百萬吊 所用之外 別無羨餘

每萬僅合中國制錢一千文

問 稅入太少 無怪如此艱難 若與各國開口通商 重立稅則 歲入必可倍加 無政事則財用不足 無財不足以養人 歸告執政 須亟變計

李對 謹遵命

問 日本來朝鮮貿易用銀錢否

李對 每以物換易 而小邦人或給銅錢 亦受之 以爲他日貿資

問 用銀及買賣銀兩之禁 須設法速開 庶便於流通

李對 謹又歸告

問 帶來冊子係朝廷意旨 抑執政大臣之意

李對 寡君之意 執政亦已知悉

問 我已將所詢事件逐條酌覆 並給空白憑票十紙 又派員代擬朝鮮與各國通商章程 屆時自行參酌妥辦 然取益防損之大要 固不出此

李對 蒙賜酌覆及憑票十張 謹幷帶歸呈告國王 代擬通商章程 一時詳告呈納

問 橘山予告後尙預聞朝廷否 現年幾何 精力健否

李對 橘山休退後不預國事 而有詢咨 不敢不遵 今年六十七 精力尙好

問 玆有復書 望帶交 何日由津起程 回國後 國王及執政大臣 均代道意

李對 下覆書函 謹當帶回面呈 起程伏計來月初二日發向北京 一同貢使歸國 下敎道意 亦謹奉遵

光緖七年正月二十八日

129

李鴻章(1881. 3. 1/光緒七年二月二日) → 總署(1881. 3. 2/光緒七年二月三日)

李容肅 회담 보고

復總署 論朝鮮外交
光緒七年二月初二日

敬密復者 正月二十九日奉二十八日公函並抄奏一件 以朝鮮外交遇有關係繁要之件 由敝處及出使日本大臣通遞文函等因 仰見籌度機宜 權衡至當 欽佩曷勝 適有朝鮮國王委員李容肅隨本屆貢使來京 於正月二十日赴津稟謁 據稱專為奉辦武備學習事 並賷呈該國請示節略書冊一本及原任太師李裕元函 鴻章查閱節略所開各條 內有領議政李最應啓本 頗悔去年六月堅拒美利堅來使為非計 末則歸重于及今之務莫如懷遠人而安社稷等語 另條又問他日不得已與各國相交先後早晚之策 又索中國與各國修好立約通商章程稅則 帶回援照 是子峨函述該國廷議漸有回悟 願與美國立約 已有明證 惟李裕元函仍隱寓不欲外交之意 鴻章因其節略諮商事件繁瑣 先令津海關道鄭藻如等會同傳詢一切 擬議大概 旋於二十八日傳見李容肅 與之筆談良久 詢及各國若派使議約 當無拒絕 該員答以寡君之意已屬於此 廷臣亦有回悟者 若有美意來請 不當如前堅拒等語 該國於外交情事生疏 節略內既有披露腹心 願一一開誨碩畫之語 自須乘機切實指示 導引迷途 因屬前在西洋學習交涉事宜之道員馬建忠與鄭藻如等代擬朝鮮與各國通商章程草底 參酌目今時勢及東西各國交涉通例 豫為取益防損之計 俾該國有所據依 不至多受洋人蒙蔽 仍緘復李裕元 婉切開導 冀其勿再從中作梗 至其所詢日本國書稱謂一節 在我頗難措詞 亦難保彼非意存嘗試 因查西洋各國稱帝稱王本非一律 要皆平等相交 略無軒輊 該國王久受冊封 實有報答日本及他國之書 自應仍用封號 國政雖由其作主 仍不失中國屬邦之名 庶為兩得 謹將李容肅帶呈節略一本 敝處酌復朝鮮詢問各條 代擬朝鮮與各國通商約章 與李容肅問對節略 李裕元來往函稿照抄六摺 奉呈電核 除撮要敍摺具奏外 專肅密復 祇叩中堂王爺大人鈞祺 李鴻章謹上
直字二百七十五號 計鈔摺六件

李鴻章(1881. 3. 1/光緖七年二月二日)

李容肅 회담 상주

答復朝鮮所問事宜摺
光緖七年二月初二日

奏爲朝鮮委員來津請示 斟酌答復 相機開導 恭摺仰祈聖鑒事 竊上年九月間 朝鮮賫奏官卞元圭來津 奉旨令臣妥籌該國學習製造練兵各事 業經詳晣復陳 在案 嗣接出使日本大臣何如璋函稱 朝鮮外交一事 近日廷議 漸知變計 又准 總理衙門函商 隨時設法維持調護 並奏請嗣後遇有關係洋務緊要之件 由臣與 該國通遞文函 相機開導等因 奉旨 依議 欽此 欽遵密行知照前來 適有朝鮮國 王委員李容肅 隨今屆貢使來京 於正月二十日赴津稟謁 據稱專爲奉辦武備學 習事 並賫呈該國請示節略一本 內載有領議政李最應奏章 頗悔去年六月堅拒 美國來使爲非計 末則歸重於及今之務 莫如懷遠人而安社稷等語 又問他日 不得已與各國相交先後早晚之策 又索中國與各國修好立約通商章程稅則帶 回援照 是何如璋所稱 朝鮮國王與執政大臣決意外交而未敢遽發 固已確有明 證 臣因其節略咨商事件繁瑣 先令津海關道鄭藻如等傳詢一切 擬議大槪 旋 准李容肅進見 與之筆談良久 該國軍額極虛 餉力極絀 誠慮無以自立 而所據 形勢實爲我東三省屛蔽 關係甚重 現其君相雖幡然變計 有聯絡外邦之意 國 人議論紛歧 尙難遽決 自應乘機開誠曉諭 冀可破其成見 固我藩籬 惟該國於 外交情事生疏 卽如與日本通商五年 尙未設關收稅 並不知稅額重輕 設再與 西國結約 勢必被其欺蒙 無益有損 臣因其來牘有披露腹心 願一一開誨碩畫 之語 出於至誠 遂令前在西洋學習交涉事宜之道員馬建忠與鄭藻如等 參酌目 今時勢及東西洋通例 代擬朝鮮與各國通商章程底稿 預爲取益防損之計 交李 容肅賫回 俾該國遇事有所據依 不至多受蒙蔽 又聞該國君相已漸回悟 惟原 任太師李裕元等不無異議 臣於光緖五年七月間曾遵密諭 轉致李裕元 詳切開 導 嗣接復書 尙未敢遽爾信從 此次李裕元來書 似仍有不欲遠交之意 臣復函 又加敦勸 使不至從中作梗 此後無論何國再派人往朝鮮議約 當無堅拒之理 但未便由中國强爲驅迫耳 至其節略所詢各條內 惟答復日本國書稱謂一節 倘 稍涉含混 卽於屬邦體例有礙 臣查西洋各國稱帝稱王本非一律 要皆平等相交

該國王久受我朝冊封 其有報答日本及他國之書 應令仍用封號 國政雖由其作主 應不失中國屬邦之名 除將朝鮮寄呈節略及代擬通商約章 李裕元來往函稿鈔送總理衙門查核外 謹將酌復朝鮮詢問各條照繕清單 恭呈御覽 是否有當 理合恭摺由驛密陳 伏乞皇太后皇上聖鑒訓示 謹奏

光緒七年二月初四日 軍機大臣奉旨 該衙門知道 單並發 欽此

金弘集(1881. 3. 2/高宗十八年二月二日) ➡ 何如璋(1881. 4. 30/光緖七年四月三日)

외교 권고에 대한 회신

照錄鈔單
鈔錄朝鮮前使日本金宏集來函
　　光緖七年四月初三日到

子峩欽使大人閣下 卓姓人自東還 獲拜下函 夢因不到 若從天降 且驚且喜 曷可名狀 信後歲籥載新 伏諗體覆萬禧 引領東望 不任勞禱 玆奉大敎 洋洋千言 指示機事 靡有底蘊 兼以條約冊頁 多方周旋 尤出望外 卽將右件轉達敝廷 具細眷庇 逈出尋常 萬萬感服 銘肌鏤髓 誠不知何以塞報也 第以來敎參究敝邦事勢 則朝論雖或差殊 民志尙屬難回 恐無以卽地裁斷 用是爲悶 非敢有負於盛念也 惟閣下鑒原千萬幸甚 爲此敬謝恩 不莊

　辛巳二月三日 朝鮮金宏集再拜啓

132

高宗(1881. 11. 17/高宗十八年九月二十六日)

영선사 사폐(辭陛)시 전교

辛巳九月二十六日申時
上御興福軒 領選使從事官官弁入侍時 行左承旨金聲根 記事官俞鎭奎尹相翊 金天洙 領選使金允植 從事官尹泰駿 官弁白樂倫 以次進伏訖

上曰 史官分左右
仍命領選使從事官官弁等進前訖
上曰　今天下大勢 不可操守矣 領選使文學知識 可以專對 故特差送之 善爲
　　　往返 而廣詢博采 期有實效可也
允植曰 臣百無一肯 厚蒙聖恩 至承專對之命 感激洪造 豈敢言驅馳之勞 而此
　　　與年例貢使 有異 不得無以事相關 以臣庸愚 不知何以對揚 深恐債誤
　　　晝宵憧憧矣
上曰　豈其然乎
仍敎曰 毋論某事 量宜措處 而大事之不可自斷者則伏聞 又有不得已難處之
　　　事 與李鴻章 相議爲之似好矣
允植曰 事之小者 或可相機措處 而如有大段難者 豈敢專斷乎 若李鴻章 則深
　　　知我國事勢 有事相議 庶獲其力矣
上曰　從事官與官弁 亦皆聰明有知識 故特爲擇送 悉心對揚可也
泰駿曰 臣以常調末蔭 知識蒙昧 猥膺從事之命 入彼之後 固當隨事傍贊 而未
　　　知將何以圖報聖眷之萬一 不勝憧憧矣
上曰　入彼境後 東局南局 皆可請究 而若才有不合於用者 卽爲回送可也
允植曰 試其才 而僅可成就 則可幸 而若不可解悟者 則卽當還送矣
上曰　今番則寒候已屆 不由海路 而若明年春夏 則可由海路來往 庶可容易
　　　矣
允植曰 聖敎誠然矣
上曰　今將遠離 須起立仰瞻 而東宮在座 亦仰瞻也
允植等起立仰瞻 還卽俯伏訖
上曰　天津 距皇城幾許乎

允植曰 二百八十里云矣

上曰 大事則狀啓 若狀啓有不可盡者 或以書啓 而大抵隨便爲之 且行中 若有秘密語 從事官譯官 先送可也

允植曰 謹當依此奉行矣

上曰 大國之於我國 極爲歎曲 以感謝之意 言于禮部 而亦以予意 言于李鴻章 以表慇懃之意好矣

允植曰 謹當以聖意備言矣

上曰 程途絶遠 且將屢朔留住 須善爲往返也

允植曰 聖敎至此 不勝惶感矣

上曰 今日宿於何處乎

允植曰 出宿於南大門外矣

上命賜貂帽扇子藥物等屬 聲根跪傳于允植等跪受訖

上曰 領選使從事官官弁先退

仍命史官就座 又命退承史 以次退出

金允植(1882.1.17/高宗十八年十一月二十八日)

金允植・李鴻章 회담(1)

二十八日 晴 督府將於未刻請見 午刻隨游藏園 詣督署門外 兵衛甚盛 至一空堂 亦有交椅床卓 鋪設整齊 各官請見時來待之所 若我東公廨之歇所廳也 候之至未正 請入中堂交椅上 余捧咨文 而入中堂下椅而立 傳咨文於藏園 藏園受獻中堂 置卓上 余行一跪三叩頭 主人三揖 從事官弁別遣 以次行禮畢 分交椅而西坐 中堂問 國王安寧 及行中安否 各人出身年紀 令從事官弁先出 從事官 尹泰駿 官弁白樂倫 別遣堂上卞元圭同入 留余及卞吉雲筆談

問 工匠學徒年紀
對 以自十六七至四十餘不等
問 年紀何如是過多
對 年幼昧方 不如素所執業
問 李應俊逢於何處
對 逢於義州 想已達王京矣
問 魚允中逢於何處
對 夏間往游日本 姑未復命
問 聞已由津回國 何以不逢
對 在途雖聞風傳 一路曾未相遇
問 魚允中官居幾品何職
對 弘文應敎曾經三品
問 魚允中論外交事明白 頗有聲望否
對 有志氣有識見人 外交情形 素能諳究 居官到處有聲
問 此來學習之外 更有何幹
對 中堂以聯美事 屢有指敎 我寡君 深感謀忠之德意 奈國俗創見 議論不一 迄未歸正 寡君屢致意焉
問 機務府 創於何時
對 自明今春始設
問 統理者爲誰

對 大臣二員 一領府事 李最應 今王之叔父 一左議政 金炳國

問 旣管機務 何無書於余 余與橘山相往復 國王亦有咨文 大臣有何嫌疑乎 吾於貴國視如肺腑昆弟 推心置腹 尙未喩余意乎

對 中堂屢度勤函 苦心代籌 我寡君感謝不已 但機府新設 凡百艸創 兩大臣年老多病 未及上書 且未承尊命 何敢遽先往復乎

曰 孔子云所求乎朋友 先施之未能也

對 謹聞命矣

問 花房義質 尙在否

對 花房義質 因事還國 姑未再來 隨員副田節 領衆留館

問 學徒等何許人

對 一半少年書生 一半素習工匠

問 書生何爲

對 以其年少聰明 或有可學之道耳

問 居住之限

對 隨其成就早晚 姑無定限

問 兵丁之數

對 都下各營軍簿雖云三萬 除羸老外不過什之三四問 一年餉銀

對 通計地部一年所入錢 計之不過數百萬

問 行中人員資斧

對 每人日銀子或二兩一兩不等

問 帶來耶換給耶

對 帶來換給 隨便措置

問 將留京赴津

對 自此 直向天津 學徒等步二十七日 自京離發計 今明間可達津門卞曰元圭同向天津 觀學徒奠接 留數日 由京還國 趁來春正月旬間 王世子加元服 爲參慶會耳

中堂曰 卞君與天津諸局員熟迷 偕往照料甚好

且曰 國王厚遺 不可無回禮 而此間難以備辦 送天津備送 臘中起程可否

對謹遵尊命擧燭後半箇時辰 罷還寓舍 俄者呈咨 繼呈自內所送禮單曲生絹二十疋山紬十疋盆紬二十疋熙紬十疋白細苧布二十疋白紬綿布二十疋奎章全韻十卷古碑拓本十六種紅蔘四十斤白蔘四十斤極廣頂細簾子十掛楹聯次各色扇子紙二百幅十束苔紙二百幅十束上品山樝淸心丸一百箇蝴蝶別繡香囊四雙別

繡香匣四雙 永定河道游智開十六種 節藻如許其光王德均劉含芳四人 各十二種 通州轉漕部繼格十種
夜闌還寓 見有駕車馬二疋 高大骨聳 異於生馬 驚怪問之 店裏有客死者其家治喪運柩而出 乃造馬也 簷下列果餌紙錢 堂中延僧徒誦經 追薦僧徒皆袍 終夜喧舌

金允植(1882.1.17/高宗十八年十一月二十八日) ➜ 李鴻章(1882.1.18/光緒七年十一月二十九日)

대미수교 주선을 청하는 서한

上北洋大臣李鴻章書辛巳冬在保定府時
伏以小邦情形 惟中堂燭照纖悉 勝於小邦之自知 是以前後代籌時宜 提撕警覺 無所不用其極 非知明仁深 何以至此 我寡君深感中堂之德 欽誦靡已 此次專差陪臣 率領學徒 前赴天津 恭聽指敎 允植辭朝時 承寡君面諭 諄復鄭重 使之代達景仰之忱 且曰罄陳衷私 無有所隱 允植受命以來 不敢遑安 曉夜趨程 旣到京城 卽聞駐節保定 逶迤前進 敬致國書 仰蒙中堂慰藉備至 誨誘拳拳 藹其如春 頓忘覊旅之苦 然初筵賜接 嚴畏在心 敬勝於情 辭不能達 卽將轉向天津廠局 僻處一隅 趨陪稀闊 恐負寡君面命之意 玆敢書陳所懷 仰塵崇覽 伏願垂察焉 小邦山川險陿 聞見局滯 往在羅麗時 疆場不靖 頗尙武備 自小邦開國以來 境內乂安 民至老死 不聞金鼓 或數百年而一見兵革 旋復忘廢 現今武庫所存 皆數百年前無用之器仗 而國人猶恃而自壯曰何苦費財勞衆 遠學新製 夫器仗猶不欲學 遑欲交遠人乎 往者法國陰遣敎士 煽布邪學 其爲敎大抵瀆倫廢祭 惟利是趨 自恭宣王以來 立法痛禁 誅夷相繼 猶不滅息 國中士夫及良民莫不痛心疾首 誓不與此夷共戴一天 伊後西勢日旺 氣運大變 治兵護商 旁洋天下 察其意趣 不專在於行敎一事 設爲約條 網羅四海 入者相與 出者孤立 互相連合 如七國之時 此與往日局面 又大不同矣 夫有國有土者 惟以保存宗社 奠安生民爲務 春秋二百四十年之間 通聘會盟 殆無虛日 不第諸夏衣裳之會 卽蠻越鱗介之國 玉帛相續 此豈不知義理而然哉 惟小邦則不然 不問時勢可否 惟以守經爲正理 斥和爲淸議 與其通洋而存 不如絶洋而亡 言及交際 輒以邪學目之 爲世所棄 自丁卯以後 日本投書求好 朝議以爲近日日本變用洋制 通倭卽通洋之漸 却而不受 及乙亥秋 日本兵船入江華 衆論沸騰 幾致生事 故相臣朴珪壽倡議調停 復修舊好 國受平和之福 而論者猶至今咻咻 上自朝廷縉紳 下至巖穴草茅 以及市井屠販之流 所見皆同 以爲不必交鄰 恐納侮也 不必講武 恐滋事也 閉境自守 無如我何 惟我寡君超然遠覽 卓然不惑 念孤弱之不可久支也 知凡愚之難與慮始也 又慮衆論之殆難力勝也 撫循含容 默運獨斷 交隣鍊兵等許多急務 次第籌度 將欲擧而措之 昨年秋令中外廣薦人才 量加擢用 今年春設統理衙門 分治機務 秋又令擇文武子弟年少者 使習語

學兵技 今又選徒遠赴 學習製造 我寡君之有猷有爲 宵旰憂念 欲保民社之苦
心 斷可知矣 奈獨勞於上而無將順之人 雖有一二臣同 姑無鎭物之望 是以寤
寐英賢 託情遠交 相臣李裕元往者入京 得達姓名於榮戟之下 中堂爲陳保邦
固圉之道 賜以手書 歸獻寡君 寡君一見契悟 傾慕不已 自後連年書幣 皆出寡
君之意 緣李相昏耗 將中堂密函示人 遂至傳播於日本 今年夏有悖儒投進斥
和之疏 其中並論李相不當與中堂往復 我寡君怒其不密 即日竄逐李相於嶺南
之巨濟府 且念中堂爲我謀忠 以德取怨 並致日人之憾 不勝慨惋 分送朝士 遊
歷於日本 語及書函事 必今到底分疏 無使貽累於中堂 朝士等承命東往 詳晰
辨明 回奏日廷 恍然覺誤 幾釋初憾 寡君猶爲之憧憧不安 臨朝屢歎 今年八月
又有逆臣安驥泳等 聚不逞怨國之徒 托言伐倭 將欲犯闕 事發鞠治 渠魁雖已
就戮 餘黨迄未盡瘳 以致領選之行久已派定 而國內多故 不能即程 遂至奄迫
深冬者也 竊伏念小邦處環海之中 尙孑然特立於萬國之外 久爲衆手所指 觀
其成敗 而北俄東日 形勢相逼 燕雀之處堂 猶未足以喩其急也 從前每有緩急
悉仰上國 若今日則駭機一發 水陸電迅 四面受敵 所謂雖鞭之長 不及馬腹 所
以中堂屢示警告 丁寧反覆 使之先事周旋 冀或紓東顧之憂者也 雖然小邦積
弱之餘 急難自振 縱云通商鍊兵 非可時月見效 爲今之道 惟有擇邦善交 講信
修睦 從以彌縫疏失 以備陰雨 庶幾爲目下之急務 而泰西諸國中久聞美邦國
富兵强 心公性和 國富則少貪 兵强則可恃 心公則處事平 性和則執禮恭 且聞
近日頗豔慕華風 購買經籍 周孔之道 未必無西被之理 先通美國 公平立約 俾
嗣後來欵者 一遵成式 無害我自主之權 此又急務最當先者也 凡此數畫 皆不
出於中堂之成算 辛勤胹迷 若恫在己 使小邦君臣幸得一二開悟者 寔中堂之
賜也 雖然邦人之最惡者洋人也 我寡君重違民情 姑未嘗顯言通洋 若美船一
朝來泊 則美亦洋也 國內橫議 必將歸咎於寡君 迎接之際 事事掣礙 反有起釁
之慮 觀於安驥泳之事可知矣 欲藉中堂之重 以鎭服羣情 則中堂威著四裔 誰
不敬慕 獨小邦愚俗 不知畏憚 觀於李相之事 亦可知矣 今此小邦聯美之計 環
瀛各國不應不心許 而惟東北隣比及本國人 所不欲樂聞者也 東北隣比若知此
機 則必忮害沮撓 事未可知 國人若知此機 則必譁然蠢動 功難順就 此事宜速
不宜遲 宜密不宜疎 事體重大 彈壓國人之心 宜名正言順 以消狡隣之謀 惟有
我皇上明降詔旨 先期曉諭於明春年貢使之回 踵遣派員 協美議約 則我寡君
得以憑仗皇靈 隨宜酌辦 保合東洋 永固藩屛 庶其在此 惟願中堂默運玄機 與
神爲謀 俾事成之後 渾然無形迹之可尋 如泰山喬嶽 不見運動 而功利及人 使
小邦愚民 獲福而不自知 豈非盛德之事乎 嗣後凡干事務 更煩指敎 克圖有終

亦惟中堂之惠 我寡君深有望焉 允植受命專來 不敢不盡其所蘊 言所難言 張
皇冒瀆 死罪死罪 拙手自書 辭冗筆荒 伏望領其意而恕其僭 尤增惶恐 謹白
敬稟者 竊下官前在津沽 仰聆訓誨 叩辭東下 瞬抵藩疆 遙望旌麾 依依左右
伏惟爵中堂 衣上公服 爲帝者師 一代偉人 萬方式仰 鄙邦武備久弛 當經吳筱
帥派員訓鍊 已于上月今月 先後有成 凡此士民 莫不額手喜有磐石之固 惟下
官所守江華東境 有南北兩海口 爲一國門戶 其南口水深 乘潮可駛輪船 其北
口水淺沙浮 乘潮則小舟可入 均係出入漢江必經要路 舊設屯兵三千 以爲防
守之備 然承平日久 武事漸忘 老弱廢殘 無能爲用 自下官涖任後 簡閱部伍
汰弱留強 僅得千五百人 兵貴精不貴多 果能有勇知方 卽足折衝禦侮 功歸實
用 餉不虛糜 綢繆宜亟 因于十月十四日 奉國王命 約同慶軍營務處袁丞世凱
馳赴江華 詳勘沿口礮台 並閱所有原兵 以及軍械地勢 袁丞亦亟稱此地若失
漢江難守 較天津之大沽 尤爲險要 一朝有事 敵人必全力先攻此地 以爲退步
且四面受敵 孤立無援 非有精兵守之 則劒門適足資敵 所擇之兵 尙稱精壯 加
以訓鍊 可以轉弱爲強 至所存鎗械大礮 均邅古制 重而不能及遠 鈍而不能利
用 非急購洋鎗洋礮 不能得力 然目下亟欲鍊兵 一時又難猝致 只好姑以原存
之土鎗土礮 操習泰西口令陣法 俟有洋器 再行換給 至舊有之礮台 雖不合用
然沿岸多山 因山成台 尙易爲力 歸以此仰告筱帥 擬于明正望後 酌派妥員 仍
赴江華 敎鍊沁兵三營 惟國儲支絀 購器甚難 可否俯賜 暫假藉資操鍊 容俟國
力稍裕購得時 敬當奉趙 伏思爵中堂軫念藩服 中外所瞻 仰體皇上字小之仁
俯察屬邦時務之急 用敢冒威上告 縷晰詳陳 不勝悚惶待命之至 肅此具稟 恭
請勛安 伏惟慈鑒壬午冬

135

金允植(1882. 1. 19/高宗十八年十一月三十日)

金允植・李鴻章 회담(2)

三十日 晴 督署送名帖 約明日十一點鍾午初 赴署喫飯 且於今日三點申初鍾 請余及吉雲入見 未正與藏園吉雲 同入外茶房候之 良久請入拜 長揖各就椅坐 如昨日 中堂先使通詞 傳言國王禮物使臣所送 不必番番有之 彼此貽弊 不如省事 此後置之爲好 仍始筆談

中堂問 前年 我與李裕元察書 何以傳播日本 刻出新聞 察 我爲貴國代謀 名正言順 何畏乎日本 但自洩情實 於貴國不利耳
答　　我寡君 爲是憧憧 今夏游歷朝士之往日本也 諭令到底發明 日人頗釋初憾云
問　　如何登答 詳晰見告無隱
答　　日人亦憑傳說 未嘗見原本 朝士之去 日人 有問書函事 答以中堂書中聯美事有之 至於事涉貴國 初未曾有此 奸細之徒 欲間兩國之好 做播謊說 此采苓之所以作也 日人稍解前惑 不如初頭氣色云
問　　八月間 安驥泳輩如何作辭 聚衆若干
答　　同謀者送四十人 方欲募兵起事 爲徒中人所告 次第就捕得情
問　　派往日本之趙秉鎬李祖淵是何官職 李祖淵係國王同族否
答　　趙秉鎬官禮曹參判 李祖淵現任機務主事 俱係國王親信之臣 非同族也
問　　修約議稅則 底稟曾見過否
答　　曾見過 而稅則姑未敦定 信使此行 爲議定稅則
問　　趙秉鎬等 已於十月廿六日 由日本起程回國 擬於明年三四月 奉使來津 稟商外交事宜 確否
答　　領選之行 距信使發行 不過一月之間 伊後信息 更未聞知
問　　六月問[間] 鄭大人藻如交李應浚 帶程察議辦法 甚妥 貴國果允行否
答　　鄭大人察議 實稟中堂旨意 代籌詳察 寡君感佩無已
中堂曰 魚允中在津 接晤兩次 論外交等事 甚詳據云 歸告國王矣使臣等問 魚允中 何時抵津候謁 歸時由旱路水路 中堂所答如此

問使臣問 趙秉鎬等回國之信 何以入聞否
答中堂答 頃何星使函稱趙秉鎬等與日本議稅則 不成 擬明春奉使來津 再商與 美總兵 議定條約稅則 日本自不能獨異 甚合機宜
問使臣問 蕭孚爾與書斐路爲兩人否 現在何處 明春來津否
答中堂答 卽是一人 自去夏來津 見示該國察旨 與朝鮮結約之事 因貴國 尙未 定見 款留至今 若明春 貴國仍無確信 彼決意回國矣 余月初由津啓 程時 屬美總兵住至 來春余回津時再議 該總兵 唯唯
問中堂問 去秋 帶回毛瑟鎗後 問別遣答 槍弁兵知其用法否
答別遣答 頗解使用矣
問別遣答[問] 何大人書中云 俄事不如去歲之急 何謂耶
[答]中堂答 俄約已定 言歸于好 何星使謂其事稍緩 然俄使十月初 自其國過津 晤談 亦求與朝鮮結約 余答以緩議 不獨俄也 英使亦向余屢言之 皆 以婉詞拒阻 竊見美總兵蕭孚爾 人極和平 美國又無貪求要挾之意 是 以欲成此擧也
卓子上展示我國地圖 詳問通商各口要害 以紅墨點開港處
問　　各國人皆言 通商港口 永興最好云 永興距德源幾里
答　　隣境而永興有先富[當]所重 故不許開港
問　　釜山開港亦係新設否
答　　釜山自壬辰以後 仍爲許和通商 但規模盡變耳
問　　所變者何事
答　　前日日本留館人 自嶺南輸米餽之名下納米 今皆革罷 一直賣買而已
問　　自貴國向日本 惟有東萊一條否
答　　湖南沿海固城等處 皆可直向一歧·薩摩等島
問　　對馬島 今屬何國
答　　屬日本
問　　元時再攻日本 見敗而還 知之否
答　　知之
問　　仁川距王城水陸幾許里
答　　水路迤由江華近二百里 陸路一由旬有餘
指幸洲項而問曰 此距王城幾里
答　　十里遠近
問　　江水深廣如何

答　　廣可一里 最深處數三丈 海潮出入

驚問曰 然則輪船無慮往來 天津港口甚涉不過一丈水 各國兵船無難出入 況三丈之水乎

大有憂歎之色曰 輪船曾無來碇之時乎

答　　丙寅年 法國船一隻 幾到此處 船樣不大 若大船則不可入矣

問　　伊時貴國 曾無騷動否 問國內沿海地面 曾經行歷否

答　　未嘗行歷

微笑曰 讀書不曾出門

別遣曰 沿海往嘗一遭遊覽

問　　俄人所在土們 卽是豆滿江 距何地最近

答　　 六鎭諸邑 皆距不遠

指會寧而問曰 此是與中國互市處乎

答曰　 然

問　　中國何處人赴市 答吉林凡剌渾[琿]春等人 或皇城商賈亦出來

問　　中國商賈出去貴國 供給朝夕 其費皆歛於民間 果然否

答　　果有是事

問　　此是弊風 可以革罷

答　　商賈出來者 本非多人 且自前已行之例 別無爲弊

問　　罷則罷之 何難之有 其費官亦分當耶 民間全當耶

答　　官民分當 行之已久 不必革罷

問　　貴國多山 必産石煤

答　　間間有之 姑未采用

問　　何不採取 一爲民間柴薪之用 一則賣於各國來船 必獲大利 日本船石炭 何以繼用

答　　彼國 隨乏載來而用

問　　貴國曾向日本 講究採煤之法否

[答] 日本人未嘗不自請 而弊邦 每事專仰上國 擬從近送人上國 學得採鑛之法 故姑未許也

李鴻章(1882. 1. 21/光緒七年十二月二日)
조미조약 체결의 필요성 상주

密議朝鮮外交摺
光緒七年十二月初二日

奏爲朝鮮陪臣金允植密陳該國王議商外交情形 相機開導 恭摺密奏 仰祈聖鑒 事 竊査光緒五年七月初四日奉上諭 總理各國事務衙門奏泰西各國欲與朝鮮 通商 著李鴻章査照丁日昌所陳各節 作爲該督之意轉致朝鮮等因 欽此 當經 臣欽遵函致朝鮮前任太師李裕元 密勸其與泰西各國立約通商 以牽制俄日各 情 並鈔函具奏在案 本年正月二十五日 總理衙門因屢接出使日本大臣何如璋 函述朝鮮近日漸知變計 商與美國立約 請由中國代爲主持 擬變通舊制 嗣後 遇有朝鮮關係洋務繁要之件 由北洋大臣及出使日本大臣與該國通遞文函 相 機開導等因 奏奉旨 依議 欽此 專函知照前來 五月間適有美國水師總兵薛斐 爾來津面稱 該總兵上年乘兵船赴朝鮮投遞國書 欲與結約通好 朝鮮堅決不納 今奉該國密諭求臣爲之轉達 並出示該外部原函 臣知朝鮮廷議尚未甚洽 密屬 薛斐爾留津緩待機會 六月間朝鮮委員副司直李應濬賷文來津 臣卽令津海關 道鄭藻如繕具節略 力勸朝鮮派員赴津 就便與美總兵商議 俟有頭緖 再奏派 大員同往 面訂條約各等情 交李應濬帶回 已由鄭藻如於七月間在京密致總理 衙門王大臣矣 玆朝鮮國王派領選使金允植帶領學徒來直 又別遣去冬使員卞 元圭同赴保定謁見 據稱李應濬帶到密函 該國王深相契合 奈國中論議不一 有難調停 總求大皇帝作主 先期宣諭 則諸般難便之端自歸妥貼 旋據金允植 呈遞密書一件 詳布原委 並以聯美之計 日俄及本國人所不樂聞 擬請明降詔 旨 於明春貢使之回踵 遣派員協美議約 該國得以憑仗皇靈隨宜酌辦等語 情 詞雖甚恭順 究於事體非宜 臣與筆談 開誠曉譬 以向來中國於外交各事 必先 由大臣等與各國商定 然後請旨遵行 若事未辦而先奉旨 轉予外人以挾持之 柄 汝國王此論似未深知馭外情勢 鄭藻如前議該國借學生赴津爲名 派員協同 前來與美總兵商辦 尤無痕跡 況昨接何如璋十月杪由日本函稱 朝鮮近遣使 臣趙秉鎬李祖淵赴日 修改通商章程 議立稅則 日本不允 業經辭歸 欲於明年 三四月奉使來津 與美總兵薛斐爾晤商 如能與美國結一善約 日本亦可仿照定

議 與臣所見相同 幸蕭孚爾經臣留住 或者其事易成 該陪臣等聞知 均尚領會 謂此行不專在學造一事 面承國王密諭 深以此事為重 專望臣設法方便 隨機指教 卞元圭擬即由津回國 稟商該國王酌辦 金允植亦赴津照科[料]學徒 靜候本國消息 臣維朝鮮久隷外藩 實為東三省屏蔽 與琉球孤懸海外者形勢迥殊 今日本既侵滅琉球 法國又割據越南 沿海六省中國已有鞭長莫及之勢 我藩屬之最親切者莫如朝鮮 日本脅令通商 復不允訂稅則 抑勒把持 計甚陰狡 非先與美國訂一妥善之約 則朝鮮勢難孤立 各國要求終無已時 東方安危 大局所係 中朝即不必顯為主張 而休戚相關 亦不可不隨事維持 多方調護 保兹屬土 即以固我藩籬 除俟卞元圭回國後 該國如何籌派 明春臣到津後 美總兵如何進止 再行察辦具奏外 所有朝鮮陪臣金允植密書謹照抄恭呈御覽 並臣與相機開導各緣由 理合繕摺由驛密陳 是否有當 伏乞皇太后皇上聖鑒訓示 謹奏

光緒帝(1882. 1. 23/光緒七年十二月四日) ➡ 李鴻章

조미조약 체결 문제를 李鴻章에게 위임하는 상유(上諭)

附 光緒七年十二月上奉上諭旨

李鴻章奏朝鮮陪臣密陳該國王議商外交情形一摺 據稱美國欲與朝鮮結約通好 該大臣勸令朝鮮派員赴津與美總兵薛孚爾商議 現在該陪臣回國酌辦等語 朝鮮久隸藩屬 自應隨時維持調護 卽以固我邊陲 該國必與美國訂約 則他國不至肆意要求 於大局實有關係 着李鴻章隨時相機開導 妥爲籌辦 該國聯美之計 爲日俄各國所不願 該大臣亟應加意愼密 毋貽口實 將此諭令知之

魚允中(1882. 1. 27/光緒七年十二月八日)

黎庶昌·魚允中 회담

照錄筆談

辛巳十月二十八日 高麗翰林院魚允中來公所謁見 與之筆談

魚云　久仰大名 今始獲見

答　　前日聞機器局李大人說及閣下 甚顧一見

魚云　允中曾往遊日本 與何 欽憲大人黃參贊陪晤多度 顧今東洋時事 與前不同 可相與綢繆 今此來謁大人 非欲紓私心仰慕 抑公也 望於日後事事認眞見敎 大人在外洋多年 已著威望 如允中愚蒙 從此可蒙厚庇

答　　東洋改效西法 閣下意思以爲何如 貴國人意中又以爲何如

魚云　爲彼計則可謂善變 其間或有失當者 可論大體而略其小失 隣國之强 非我之福 從可力求富强乃已

答　　尊見頗是 日本變法稍嫌太驟 且有不必變者而亦變之 然其大段總是振作有爲 貴國與彼爲隣 亦以力求富强爲第一義 富强何在 此不能不稍稍參用西法 而目前急務又似以與各國通商爲要著

魚云　謹受敎矣 通萬國而後富强可論 不然徒虛言而已

答　　富强二字 須圖之一二十年 始可見效 通商各國 先使戢其戎心 然後在已 乃可施圖富圖强之術

魚云　大敎亦然 但辦法隨時而異 乘外人搆釁之際 不可不先使戢其戎心 講求武備 不然則可力求內政 以定根基 兼治戎備 可免耗費之害 軍火槍砲之具 皆耗財之源也 徒務於此 不求內政 亦如今之土耳機矣 故范蠡用計然之策 先富其國 而後用以○吳

答　　所論亦然 通商所以應外 講求武備所以治內 以今日時勢而論 二者皆當兼之 不可偏廢 西洋何嘗不是兵商幷營 兵商之本卽是內政 未有內政不修而外能自立者

魚云　時人皆知武備之可以制外 不知商務之可以制外 善營商務可不勞而制之 彼以通商來 我以商務對 彼無所售 我可專制 大人有此言 深可欽仰 現本邦信使在日欲與定稅約 而嘗托之何大人 未知果已出抄也 如或未竣 望勞大算

答 善營商務可不勞而制外 累年以來 中國所望貴國與日本及別國通商者正
　　是此意 惟稅約似應由貴國酌定 不知所託何大人者采係何仲
魚云 采略有所定 以未諳外務之故多不稱 或彼不願准者 可設法妥定故耳
答 貴國與日本通商已有數年 曾有定約否
魚云 未有定約 曾與日人通商 自皇明萬曆間 行之前 反給餼料而無稅矣 在丙
　　子改定條約以後 當如法徵稅 彼以港務未完 乞於三年後議稅 故亦許之
　　尙未徵稅 而前次不知外國事狀 欲只從彼國現行抽五之稅 更爲察看 則
　　抽五乃極不平不公之稅 所以欲抽十抽二十 恐彼必斬待
答 兩國旣經通商 必須早爲議定 稅約方有依據 值百抽五最不平允 貴國初
　　次通商 正好因勢利導 與之另議 縱不能抽十抽二十 然一槪値百抽五則
　　不可行也
魚云 誠然 欲以抽十爲通常之額 酒類則三十五 鐘表等物二十五 洋織類則
　　二十 金珠寶玉珍玩之類抽五十 汽機類抽五也
答 此事亦如買賣貨物 先高其價 與之商議 因貨價定等級 斯爲平允
魚云 然而物價失定 故始先如此 待稅務稍就緖 而後再商量計耳 英美各國稅
　　款之漢譯者願見之
答 所見甚是 英美各國稅則 容覓一部奉贈 然中國初定條約之時 亦因未能
　　深知外國情事 所定稅則 頗有吃虧之處 異日尙須議改
魚云 中國現行約款已見之 願見考 英美所行之約款也
答 英美稅則漢譯者尙未見專書
魚云 本邦與日本交涉 多用彼之舌人及商賈之徒 深有不便 故允中嘗率往
　　二三人士族子弟 方在彼學他文字語言 而本邦無使臣之駐彼者 大人可
　　視爲一國人 而時賜顧念指敎
答 敝國與貴國誼屬一家 理宜照應
魚云 感激 感激
答 閣下此次來游敝國 到過幾處 現欲可往 曾見過李中堂否
魚云 只到滬及津 而嘗上謁李中堂數度 方欲歸航
答 何時再到日本
魚云 今欲付東洋船到長崎 直向本國 而更到日本 未可質對 日本各港理事諸
　　大人皆歸華云 未知何公分駐于彼乎
答 日本各港理事 余到後應有更換 然繼任者與前任無異
魚云 琉球之衆從何以妥帖

答　　琉球之衆 中國所以未肯遽結者 正爲防後患耳

魚云 彼之有此事極無理 大失着

答　　原是如此 問貴寓在何處

魚云 金利源帳房樓上

答　　容再謝步

魚云 明晚可付輪船東走 恐不必勞光臨 更拜當有其日 謹此造退 乞保重

答　　將來到東洋一定可以叨敎

　　　　羅星垣鈔

金允植(1882. 2. 7/高宗十八年十二月十九日)

金允植·李鴻章 회담 (3)

十九日 已初入督署 候外茶房 良久請入 長揖就坐 李中堂以筆談
問曰 游道游智開也 示貴國王書意竝閔公書稿均閱悉 何以公等出境時 未先商
　　定 不久又有此信
允曰 允植辭朝時大略旣承命意 以國勢民情 仰禀酌議 故向有所仰陳者矣 此
　　次專信想美使之尙留 今始入聞 又以俄人致書邊臣 雖姑未受 多應是求
　　好之意 却之亦難 受之亦不無商量 故欲先妥美事者 今番亦無公文 然李
　　應俊所齎書 以待領選使面剖 卽公文也
李曰 前已告知俄使 十月初過津面稱 欲與朝鮮通好 頃又聞俄人 擬於明年夏
　　間 派兵船前往 屆時恐有他國隨之而去 可惜 李應俊齎書到時 貴國未能
　　遽定立意 立遣員來津 與美使商議 已失 機會 昨聞美使薛孚爾 奉到國
　　書 已赴北京 諒駐京各國使臣 必共聞知 將來議約 恐不易就範耳
允曰 俄人事 頃於席間陪話時 旣已聞命 敝邦不及聞知矣 若於夏間來到 則伊
　　前先與美使議約 恐 不爲晚 但美使之遽奉其國書 赴京聲張起來 實有將
　　來議約 不能如意之慮 機會易失 可惜之甚
李曰 向來各國議約 必有全權大臣 憑據朝命 互相看閱 始允商辦 閣下旣未奉
　　公文 是無此憑據 美使未必與商
允曰 敝邦事勢雖不得不聯美 事成之前 不欲露出於公文 顯示國人以邀來之
　　意 寡君之意 則鄭玉軒書中所言玉軒卽鄭藻如 自此酌議 派員出送 則寡君
　　預爲密飭於沿海守臣 勿大驚小怪 船近港委員會議 一邊彈壓 一邊修睦
　　無所不可 允植旣未奉 全權之命 雖美使請與會商議所不敢
李曰 玉軒書 原請朝鮮派官來華 與薛面商 則本大臣可居間調停 較易操縱 若
　　朝鮮無人 與美使議論 竟是中國一面之事 美使旣不見信 亦有難於指詞
　　之處 尊示顯示國人以邀來之意 實未明萬國公法 凡不顯通商 則壹意堅
　　拒 旣可議約 則必派全權大臣 若議不成 雖一兩年 再三往復 自無妨也
允曰 若依各國之規 必派全權 可以議約 則須今急發一函 奏達於寡君 但恐國
　　中事勢 不能如意 是可悶也
李曰 昨接薛斐爾卽薛孚爾 本月初四日來書 役擬西曆五月初一日 乘兵船赴朝

鮮中曆三月 貴國 如尙遲疑 不早派全權來華 本大臣實亦無法阻美使之行
允曰 若兵船一到 雖云匪寇昏媾 不既事多阻礙 允 今將歸津 卽發急使 願明
示方便 海關道卽周馥也 或游藏園卽游智開 以此意 致書敝邦政府 錄送美使
書一通 囑令派員來商 帶有全權字樣事 乃可成云云 則允亦將備達此意
以俟寡君處矣
李曰 薛書 請卽照鈔 密速寄去 津海關道台 於貴國政府 尙未通問 恐未便多
瀆 藏園則未知何如
允曰 謹當如敎 而敝邦 自來不諳外交情形 最以目前橫議爲難 若美國兵舶出
去云 則一邊議論 必有坐而待之 兵到後 議和未晚云 則全失機會 爲之
奈何 卽欲以此意 專報敝邦 而若派全權 則事涉張大 以敝人心之囂囂
恐難趁期來議 反貽他邦之羞 允雖承全權之命 先於此處 與美使一面 以
示傾○之意 開春後 任其東出 卽當議約 便是邀來之意 未如可否
李曰 昨已緘復薛使 請其來保定一商 據關道報稱 辥使業於十七日起程進京
未知其果由京赴保定否 如來此 可就與閣下會面道達 貴國目下人心囂
囂之情勢 及傾慕友邦之誠 本大臣再相機開導 勸其少留津門 以待貴國
後命 但聞辥使與關道密談 欲照日本條規成式 則事殊不妥 且若聯合俄
英諸國偕往 更慮激成事變 倘辥使回來執事 式遵貴國王密札 變通權宜
另擬全權密旨一道 給與閱看 以堅其信 在此將約稿 議有頭緒 較在津各
國交訌已僻靜多矣
允曰 權宜另擬 在他國 或有是例否 敝邦則行不得 此何等事 而允植 敢擬全
權密旨乎 若與美使 在此一會 道達情意 以緩其東出之事 則儘好 一邊
飛奏本國 須奉有全權之旨然後 事面正大耳 美使之欲照日本條規者 指
稅則而言耶 稅則尙未歸正 未知所照何事否
李曰 彼所謂日本條規 想係初訂之約 稅則尙未定議 何從援照 辥使人尙公平
吾勸其增訂稅則
允曰 以若公平之見 欲照日本條規者 豈緣敝邦 以此事延擱 故少變其好意耶
李曰 嚮在津會晤時 未曾談及和約如何議辦 只說要公平耳 今彼旣奉全權之
命 未有不欲見好本國者 其云照日本國條約之言 不得爾 吾嘗設法權導
之 但慮貴邦 旣多延擱 各國互相交通停留 長智事 未可知 此事須趁機
會 估先著也
允曰 今欲急發一函 期於來正月晦內或二月旬前 得奉回旨 尙未過晚否 美使
或當來此 允植姑留俟 一面爲可耶 竝乞明敎

李曰 卽可照辦 若貴國另派全權來津 仍作爲照料學生 臨時相機 辦理較妥 外間不至張揚
允曰 謹遵尊命 以此意專達于寡君矣 談草乞暫借 欲歸寓謄出 以爲遠外信蹟
李曰 謄就 望卽將原稿封還 此來帶有幾人 能分派回國 開寫名條卽繕給護票
允曰 此來所帶者 通詞外奴子二人伴倘一人伴倘奴子一人而已 自此急發一便 則卞君想離京不遠 可以追及
李曰 請轉達貴國王曁政府 如卽派全權於二月初旬到津 使吾必從旁爲力 俟議約稍有眉目 奏明派員 同美使前往近港 再行畵押定議 若遲逾期限 只好聽美使自去矣
允曰 請便告退還寓 裁函速發 專足以及卞君之行 自此至山海關以內 雖無憑票 庶可無礙 但恐不能速馳耳
李曰 明春開河較早計 正月二十外營口卽通輪船 來使就赴營口 搭船到津 僅二三日 尙可以速補遲
允曰 但速派使 不患不及 謹當力奏 無失此期 因揖辭而出

金允植(1882. 2. 14/高宗十八年十二月二十六日)

金允植・李鴻章 회담(4)

二十六日朝 省署巡捕來言 中堂於十點鍾請見 遂於巳刻 乘車詣省署 二品官
入見還出者 爲三人 少頃請入 始筆談

○中堂問 卞元圭何時由京起程
　對 擬於今月十九或二十日起程云矣 姑未聞到京信息 未知果能如期登程否
○問貴國 派有生徒 往日本學習何事
　對 未有派送學生於日本之事 日人留住王京 故使兵弁往學技藝
○送去兵弁若干已否 前往何項技藝
　對 春間選送八十名 八月 又聞有加選之命 所學者先習於法 次習鎗砲 敎師
　　姓掘本 而所學不甚精微云
○余知日本步兵 倣法國操法 聞尙整齊 貴國派人往學甚好
　對 彼旣屢懇 難拒好意 中堂傍書曰是好意 且彼方留飯無事 故就遣學習 然友誼
　　數則斯疏 寡君 常欲邀上國敎師數人 授兵弁技藝 勝似請學於日人
○中堂曰 似無不可
　對 請學於上國 面勢也好寡君期欲圖之
○問 派往日本學習之兵弁 交何人管帶 用何器械
　對 所選兵弁 原屬武衛營 現今武衛都統使 閔尙書台鎬 帶往學習者韓聖根
　　尹雄烈 器械則允未嘗目擊 似是日人所用鎗砲矣
○問 貴國舊器械全屬無用 旣學西洋兵法 卽新式鎗砲 於易多得自國中 雖有
　　倣造 試可而已 恐不中用 稍稍振作然後 乃可言儲備耳
○問 昨接美使辪斐爾 自京城復函云如 遽赴保 不旣動人聽聞 種種不便 約俟
　　回津面談 是閣下可先回津 專候來春貴國朝命如何
　對 美使做事縝密 可喜 第欲一面者 爲彼此通犀而已 今已略相照領 奚遽相
　　接 允卽當還津 以俟敝邦回音
○允曰 此事無論差早差晚 想究竟乃已納條 宜豫爲講究停當 謹齎議稿三本一
　　李中堂所送 一黃參贊遵憲所送 一機務府參謀官李東仁擬呈本 及日本條規謄本 或可慶
　　覽否

中堂曰 望見示允曰 玆有在寓荒膽之本 敢呈
○中堂曰 李東仁所擬稿本 語意頗爲簡括 但美使未必盡允 第七款派駐官員 通商章程 俟五年再議尤恐難行 約內以頂須添一條大意云 朝鮮久爲中國屬邦 而外交內政事宜 均得自主 他國未便過問 方覺不觸不背 尊意以爲何如

對 雖有擬稿 敝邦原無閱歷 未諳便否 故 以此仰稟商酌 無致異日深悔 此寡君之意也 派駐及通商事 彼若堅執 亦非例外之事 恐難終拒 但與日本修好時 係是創行創聞 不免事事相持 今則稍異於前 然日本 公使駐京一款 至今在未許中 彼自托事來留耳 未知開春 敝邦派送何員 來時承朝廷命意如何 具未敢質對 惟敝邦在中國爲屬國 在各國爲自主 名正言順 事理兩便 條約中 此一款 添入似爲極好

○問 余所以預料 美使必不允 五年後再派駐通商者 緣辭使在關道處已言 須仿日本約稿 將來縱不能事事仿照 但日本久經派駐通商 美人豈甘獨後 且貽各大國笑柄也 卽第十款之不立敎堂十一款悉照萬國通例 亦有難行 美國耶蘇敎 尙不滋事 中日訂約皆未能照萬國通例 豈獨讓於朝鮮耶 至另款聲明中國屬邦 前已與魚允中商定 彼必回奏耳 英使前詢及朝鮮議約 亦與泛論及此 渠亦謂應如是

對 擬稿雖如此 派駐通商之限 以五者彼未必允 敝邦亦有日本前例 惟當仿行而已 惟不立敎堂一款 不容不力言 他日聞見漸廣胸次稍豁 則未可知也 惟今則實難許立 且敝邦之望於美國者 以其和平無乖僻之性 欲保始終友誼 而若以敎堂 先失民心 實爲可惜 雖云耶蘇敎 本不滋事 愚民 安知天主耶蘇之分耶悉照萬國通例者 欲得公平之分耳 若未得公平之分 則又安有衣裳議和之本意乎 末段事外面與裏許 均爲極妥 竊想寡君入聞 稱善感謝也

○問 不立敎堂一節 言極有理 竊就貴國時事揆之 實多不便 余必與美使力言之前說 係默揣其意耳 但能堅拒 或不因此節誤約事萬國通例 通商口岸及內地 無論何國人民 寄居 皆歸本國地方官管理 東西刑律 風俗禮敎未可强同 是以地方官 未能兼管他國人民 日本現欲與各國議變通舊約無成者 戢是故耳 此一節 各國必不能行

對 黃參贊遵憲 已以此有所論 著於擬稿中 竊念西國通例 他國寄居人民 歸本國地方官管理 惟中東不然 西人謂之不公 然 抑其事勢然也 况敝邦素昧外情 雖使兼管他民 實多難便之端 若日本改約 中國亦改前規 則敝

邦邦 固當隨而改之 約條中先依黃參贊所擬立言 似宜 教堂事 伏望另設
　　方便 務回彼意 實爲敝邦之萬幸
○中堂曰 黃參贊原擬第四款 暫許美國領事館管轄 較虛活 又書其傍曰 此二
　　款甚合情理 立言亦得體第十款查照歐米公例 定立關章較着實 將來議
　　約 可卽用此兩條 改擬之 第一款 太覺渾融 美使恐難允許 教堂一節 貴
　　國使臣 必應詳切辨阻 余亦當從旁道達國人疑畏之意
　　對 謹以領會
○問 閣下還津 照料學生 餘於正抄 想可抵津 屆時看美使動靜若何 再行奉告
　　對 旣在此無幹 卽今已天晚 明曉卽程歸津 恭俟節旋進謁

金允植(1882. 2. 15/高宗十八年十二月二十七日)

조청 종속(宗屬)관계 명문화에 관한 상소

臣竊伏念 美使旣以全權出使 奉其國命 早晚議約 勢所難已 約條不可不豫爲
構定 而有難懸空說去 故 下送議稿三件 合膽一冊 指示某某所擬 幷日本修
好條規謄本 出示李中堂 請商酌可否 中堂一番披覽後 不診自己所擬 但於黃
李二稿 先說李東仁所擬 頗爲管括 而第七款派駐官員及通商章程 五年後議
定 尤恐難行 此在問答中 而臣伏念 派駐官員一事 往在與日本議約時 我國以
此相持 然此是各國之例 議約後 最先務也 若不派官互駐 情意一向不熟 與不
和同 我雖不往 寧能禁彼之來駐乎 曾於日本 雖堅執不許 而日本則來駐自如
今於約美之後 恐難更申前說 徒傷事體 通商章程一事 各國議約 專爲通商一
款 若待五年議定 其間憑何法例 我國於日本議約之時 不知裏許 不定稅則 六
年之間所失不勘 已爲各國之所竊笑 豈可再蹈前轍乎 此事非徒彼所不肯 在
我自謀 恐不當如是 不如初頭議立公平章程 如有未盡 更則照他國例 限年追
改 未爲不可 此二款李中堂所云難行者 似非謬見 又曰第十款 不立敎堂之難
便 臣旣以書以談 力言不可 中堂亦以爲然 當從旁力勸云 具在談草中 又曰第
十一款 悉照萬國通例 亦有難行 中東訂約 皆未能照萬國通例 豈獨讓朝鮮耶
臣之所答 具在談草中 而中國 日本用兵後議約 故事未洽 今番以好意修約 何
獨不得萬國之例乎 不過爲弱小 不能優占地分耳 然 在我不無可言之端 縱未
能件件滿意 恐不宜與用兵後議約同例也 但我國所得見者 惟中國 與各國相
通之條規而已 不知萬國通例之如何 只以稅則一事言之 泰西諸國 則似用値
百抽十 或二三十之法 而中國日本 則至今用値百抽五之制 此其用兵後議約
之害也 今次不必照其例也 又論黃遵憲所擬第四款 暫許美國領事管轄 較虛
活 第十款查照歐美公例 定立關章 較着實 已上亦在談草中 而虛活者 外樣甚
好 而裏許則從其事勢之便也 着實者 緊着而有實利也 於此二款 大加稱歎 連
稱好好 加圈於傍 蓋美其深中機宜也 以此觀之 查照歐美公例 定立關章云者
卽與實照萬國通例者 何以異焉 中堂所以斥彼而扶此者 以汎稱萬國通例 驟
看甚大 而汗漫無實 不如黃議之較緊也 故云將來議約 可卽用此 兩條改議之
改者 改李東仁所擬稿之謂也 又曰第一款 大覺渾融 美使恐難允行 此指黃稿
第一款朝鮮奉中國政府命云云 若如是 則美國 亦渾入於中國命令之中 故彼

必難允者也 臣謂此條立言 非徒美使難允 在我亦旣自主之權 恐難仍用 又曰
約內似須添一條大意云 朝鮮久爲中國屬邦 而外交內政事宜 均得自主 他國
未便過問 方覺不觸不背 臣之所答 亦具在談草中 此亦黃氏所擬奉中國命之
意 然特其立言 不倖耳 我國之爲中國屬邦 天下之所共知也 常患中國無着實
擔當之意 以若我國孤弱之勢 若無大邦之作保 則實難特立 今李中堂 卽中國
掌兵大臣也 幸而擔去我國之重 毅然自任 旣已聲明於各國 大書於約條 異日
我國有事 若不竭力救之 必貽天下人之笑 天下人 見中國之擔任我國 則各國
輕我之心 亦從而小阻 且於其下 以均得自主繼之 是則與各國相交無害 用平
等之權矣 不觸失權之忌 不背事大之義 可謂兩得 中堂此論 大有益於吾邦 故
屢屢稱謝 伏未知何如 右所論諸條 皆係約條之大者 其餘 均屬例言 別無可論
玆敢附錄 以備乙覽 恭候聖裁 明春或有派使之擧 須奉有成命 庶幾臨事無礙
竊伏念議約大節 不可隨意專斷 又遠外取 稟 臣不任豫切憧憧

金允植(1882. 2. 27/高宗十九年一月十日)

金允植·周馥 회담(1)

初十日 陰寒有雪意 午刻與李應俊 往海關道 訪周玉山筆談 未末還今日復始服歸
茸君子湯飯後啜天門冬茯苓茶
海關道談草與首堂李應俊同入

周問 李君年幾何 何號 現定何職 幾時由至此 卞君幾時啓程回國
李答 卑職今年五十 號相庵 官居鴻臚寺四品 去年臘月二十八日到北京 今初
　　八日到此 卞君昨臘二十五日 在小凌河相逢
周問 閣下去年與大家 分先後行耶 抑到北京 復回本國而來耶 在津能常駐否
李答 早分先後而行也 今月底回本國 再來津常住耳
周問 去歲十二月二十三日 聞有人回國 今正李瓚等又去 大約二月底 當有的
　　信來
金答 想二月 必有回信 今次李君之來 又奉到寡君手札辭旨 如前無異 大略敝
　　邦物情 斷不可先派員來 由美船自去爲好 另有錄呈可賜覽否
周曰 謹將此意及來冊 寄保定 俄國有書來 不宜屢拒 以好辭答復而已 日本性
　　狡 此時但其力不足耳 然貴國與中國一氣 彼自不敢輕動
金曰 俄書之四次退却 亦已過矣 此後來書 飭令受上 但恐俄人託以旣通書札
　　不時來泊 遽欲議修好通商等情事 或窘迫未能妥善之慮耳 日人之性如
　　婦女 難遠難近 此次數條語 甚覺憤惋
周曰 昨 保省有書來 言中堂 正月尾到津 但未定準何日 請李公 不必往保定
　　候中堂到此 見過兩面 略得端倪 再回國不進 貴國若許美船 到仁川港口
　　甚善 惟慮議約一節 彼此意見相去太違 而中國又無人 在仁川幇忙約成
　　或亦吃虧約不成 更多後慮 愚見就金公在此 或一二月有貴國人 來在此
　　密議大約派全權大臣到此一節 想貴國難行 槪使美使胸中 有幾分可成打算 再聽
　　其乘船 而往仁川也 似於事機更順 不見日本乎 日本與各國所定之約 並
　　不甚好 卽貴國去年 與日議修 而未成之約稿 亦覺不甚周到 惟此事宜
　　机察遲則恐漏 毋論貴國 二月 有無全權大臣來天津 察商此事 至多不得
　　過一月工夫

金曰 李君行止 固當依敎爲定 冊子所錄 幸望因使速達 亦望大人傾助 若遂寡君之意 則甚幸甚幸 總之敝邦不便 先派議約之使 卽敝邦物情 實難强拂故耳 自天津還寓 聞慈橋伯從兄主 已於客臘初三日下世 由玉河舘 得本國邸報 知之 痛哭痛哭 昨秋拜辭時 但以脚步不仁爲慮 不知有何深祟 至於此境 天涯訣別 容音永阻 亦從兄弟惟餘兩人 門戶零替 不堪傷痛 且念慈橋事勢 想無措手之道 喪人兄弟 何以支過 喪具何以經紀 事事茫然 不勝痛哭

金允植(1882. 3. 7/高宗十九年一月十八日)

金允植·周馥 회담(2)

十八日 周玉山談草

周曰 美使乘船到仁川 勢所必然耳 所慮不妥 中國昔年用兵所訂之約 大爲吃虧 現觀日人與各國 貴國與日人 貴國欲改議約稿 皆不妥當 前年本國與巴西換約 從前日人與本國換約 卽非用兵時所議 大槪可知也 現美使意中 所必求者幾件 貴國所必不能允者幾件 須見面問過 方可代籌否 則不必空言也 貴國與中國一氣 將來邦基鞏固 外人自不敢輕視 且貴國與他邦議約 本朝應得與聞 苦援昔與日議約 竝未與聞爲例 他國 將欲繼日人接踵而至 一槪按日人已成之約 後患何可勝言 此時本朝以主少 一切未敢輕動 然日日講求 安知十年二十年之間 氣像不逈異耶 倘聽日人之謀 是認賊爲子 本朝何所利於貴國 而有壞心待之耶 中堂何曾勸美使不往 何曾要彼此定在天津議 亦因邦交情誼故耳 竊見前日說帖 有獨立半主之語 故放言及請察

允曰 大人 於敝邦事情 終有所未盡諒察矣 敝邦 自古慕華慕義 仰庇上國 如帲幪覆幬 況今委弱已甚 諸國窺覦之時 敢以自尊特立 如計有理乎 是不爲也 亦不能也 往者與日人議和時 船泊港口 事急無暇仰聞 故 伊時事過之後 卽發飛咨 據實轉奏 今次美國事 卽敝邦通洋之創例也 爲國論攜貳 縱不能止彼之行 實難派使迎來 旣經許好之後 議約通商諸般事務 一聽中朝處分 奚止望與聞而已乎 向者獨立半主等語 卽日人構間之計 敝邦原不以此動心 豈不見諒耶 若美船自出 則議約之誠 恐未妥 此所以縷縷仰祈 方更設法 俾無受屈者也

周曰 本無不見諒 竊細繹前說帖 似以議約難辦之爲輕 而爲乘船通好 易行之事爲急 若此間 故留美使者 語意未暢 是以傾吐 勿以爲實話

又曰 議約在用兵後與未用兵前 本逈然不同 然 東西之勢 頗不易說

又曰 魚允中幾時回國 想李應俊來時 當見過矣

允曰 魚允中 自天津 由上海還走長崎島 與信使同爲復命 在應俊已發之後 故不得見過耳

周曰 魚允中 前在此 請本朝開海禁與貴國通商 本是因是制宜辦法 然必貴國
　　先奏 或咨請總署及北洋大臣代奏 方可議准 能先奏否 有所聞否 當今之
　　時 外來生客日多 防維不易 與舊相識之人 更要親切 方於事體有益也
　　此言譬得中理否 日人在貴國恣肆 聞者無不切齒 因只有兩家 若有他人
　　幇說 不至如此 如人入市中 不能說大無禮話 以人多故也
允曰 開海禁事 謹當隨使奏達 諒敝朝廷必無異議 此豈爲中國商民之地耶 古
　　人云 數見顔面情重 昔時大小邦相孚之義 日以益親 此敝邦之所願聞也
　　市中不敢恣話之敎 譬喩切當 本諺云 無虎洞中狸作虎 政類於此
周曰 先開海禁 有中國官商 在貴國暗中幇忙 庶免外人許多猜嫌耳
又曰 此間諸人 有送貴國王禮物 一月後可到 望趁便雇車 與信使同路發 特此
　　先聞

金允植(1882.4.4/高宗十九年二月十七日)

金允植·李鴻章 회담(5)

十七日 風寒 早朝王筱雲來訪 少頃李君應俊及通事 鄭麟興自東局來 雇四人 轎 共向中堂衙門 俟於外茶房 馬眉叔羅稷臣在焉 九點鍾入見中堂 是歲後初 見 與首堂李應俊同入 行一拜三叩頭 禮畢分坐敍話

當日談略 談草未收而來 隨想記而錄之
中堂問 李應俊幾時離王城
○應俊曰 去年至月二十七 離京
○中堂問 間以何事入京
○俊曰　爲見年貢使臣
○中堂曰 年貢使官幾品
○俊曰　判府事正一品大臣 猶中國之中堂也
○中堂曰 然則出疆踰年 相府事務盡爲廢曠否
○允植曰 議政府 備三事 雖一人出疆 無曠務之理 自古奉使中國 必遣一品大臣 例也
○中堂問李應俊曰 年貢使臣 應知美約事
○俊曰　不知
○中堂曰 他不曾問過否
○應俊曰 不曾問 亦未敢說
○中堂曰 你國事何其秘密也 你是小官也 國家大事 豈有小官知之 而大官不知之理乎
○觀其辭色 似是認年貢使 方在政府 而不知國家邊務 深爲疑惑
　余對曰 年貢使臣 不曾過三事之任 每年進貢時 相臣無幾人 故就列卿中 加銜奉使 亦自古有例
○中堂曰 然則今之年貢使 現居何官
○允曰　前任工曹判書
○中堂曰 今已解任否
○允曰　今已解任 特奉使命而來

○中堂曰 何不早言如是 使我疑惑不定
○中堂問 向日專人送函 有回信否
○允曰 姑沒有
○中堂變色曰 是何說也

以上口談通詞傳言

○去年臘月十八日往保定府筆談時中堂屢囑傳達此意 期於今年二月旬前 有回音 今過旬已久 而未承回音 此次說話 如終出於大不平 又時時回顧周馥等 刺刺歎咄 不知爲何語 臣於還寓後 問諸通詞 則以爲皆歎我國之言云

○以下筆談

○中堂問李應俊曰 汝奉國王面諭 是何事
○俊曰　寡君以國論未定 諭俊仰稟中堂 善圖方便也
○中堂曰 此次亦有貴國王手札否 可呈閱 因使李應俊移椅 來就允植之傍 漸看其辭氣峻厲
○允曰　此次亦有宸札 而在東局 未曾奉來
○中堂曰 國王手札 不曾來示面商 可見執事之將命不誠也
○允曰　不敏甚悚 然君臣間私札 不便呈覽 所以不敢奉到也
○中堂曰 書中若有他言 不必過問 若只爲聯美事 則何不便之有乎
○允曰　下書中 別無他事 但寡君函諭中 未承呈覽於中堂之敎 允 私自呈獻 分所不敢 旣承旬命 此與私意擅呈有異 謹當送人奉到呈覽矣
○中堂曰 貴國王書函旣不來示 則但憑一介行人之三寸舌可乎
○允曰　但念自下難便之義 見識原不到此 惟望敎其不逮 以示益國便民之道
○中堂曰 貴國事 常如欲吐不吐 如是而事可做乎 派員之來不來 非吾所知 而吾歷年忠告 貴國 尙不知利害乎
○允曰　中堂之爲敝邦 悉心代籌 寡君深感無已 前已仰達 允 在此承敎 不止一二 豈敢曰 專昧利害之分乎 但敝邦國論 尙未寧縣 寡君之意 寧小失時於交際 不欲大拂吾民之情 使臣在外 惟有奉承君命而已 雖有粗知利害 豈敢擅便乎
○中堂曰 美使雖欲勿去 不可得也 貴國有解洋語洋文者乎 若無則難以辦事
○允曰　敝邦素無外交 安有解洋文洋語者乎 通情之際 須藉華人 庶不致齟齬之弊 不知美使何日發船 李應俊急宜先送 以達美使之奇
○中堂曰 此次中國 亦不必派員 由他自去
○允曰　李應俊來時 奉到宸札 是在專函奏達之前 早晚苦奉專函回信 又未

知如何 派員之必不來 亦出臆料 縱或不來 美船自應依期東出 東出
後無幫辦之人 敝邦初接素眛之遠人 當如何應接 願加三思 矜其不
能 而無至僨誤 允不敏之罪 恭俟譴何

○中堂曰 李應俊似宜候至二十五日 乃發何如

○允曰 美使若不待敝邦回音而出去 則李應俊 急宜先還 不可稽留 若待敝
邦回音 而爲進退 則李應俊之少留幾日 似爲無妨

○中堂曰 自津乘輪船至營口回國 二十日內外 可達王京否

○允曰 假量二十二三日可達

○中堂屈指 顧左右云云 似問洋曆日子也 乃曰 美使三月望前乘船 七八日可
抵仁川 李應俊留至二十五 如有不及之慮 自此專給官火輪船一隻
自能速達 未知可否

○允曰 專撥輪船 極爲感悚 然爲敝邦事 眷念周至 期欲速達 在美使之前
唯命是依 不敢飾讓臨別 以歲時賞給學徒等銀子及近日加造東國朝
鮮館宇事 致謝

中堂又口囑曰 貴國王手札 須於今天封寄 如有專函回信 立刻示知爲可

對 謹如命

與周玉山王筱雲馬眉叔羅稷臣 同至海關署喫飮 周玉山 錄示馬眉叔 觀察 印
建忠 江南丹徒人 精法國文學 兼通各國交際事宜 游學西方 西人奉爲師友 志
氣超然 非庸庸仕路者所可比擬 羅稷山自云候補知州刺史 福建閩縣人 印豐祿年
三十三 精英美各國文字 尤善今古文詞 游學西方 練習兵船之藝甚精 操履謹
篤 爲我輩珮服 二公可諦交 於公家之事身心之學 皆有益也 玉山所示止此 二人
外貌俱淸秀精明 羅稷山襟懷沖澹 動止端凝 與余坐

近問 東國科制 且言顧亭林胡朏明 皆有用之學

余曰 亭林先生日知錄 僕嘗得見過 胡先生所著 僕固陋未之得見

稷山曰 僕 游歷英法德三國 見西國良法 多合於顧胡二先生之言 以是知二先
生之學 非徒資考據而已也

余曰 西人之善處 必不出於先聖之範圍 二先生之言 無怪見施於西國也 亦
可曰暗合古人 問游歷環瀛幾年 何時東還

羅曰 尊論甚是 僕前游英法德三國 計三年有餘

余曰 壯觀非徒山川之助 博察天下郡國利病之源 足以繼亭林之志 甚盛甚盛

羅曰 豈敢豈敢 遂辭別諸人

以起還東局寓所 卽封御札及幷來文蹟 送鄭麟興 奉交中堂衙門

金允植, 周馥(1882.4.8/高宗十九年二月二十一日)

金允植·周馥 회담(3)

二十一日 海關署談草

余曰 向日蒙中堂示諭 使李應俊 乘火輪官船 先歸奏達 極知感悚 然昨夜與從事尹君相議 敝邦之尙無回信 却不知何故 李應俊若從水路而行 與陸路回信相違 則更多難便 愚意候至二十五日 自此乘輪船至營口 二日可到 自營口到柵門 三日可抵 自柵門至義州爲一日程 義州至王京有飛遞 二三日可達 總不過一旬之工 中路若遇回信 還與俱來 若不遇 則直達京城 預講接應之道 亦不爲晚 未知盛意如何 向日所云旱路二十二三可達 以常時之程計之耳 倍道晝夜趲行 必不蹟十日

○周曰 議約大事 貴國王必願趁早入聞 必不願晚後得聞 李應俊之行 雖先美使十日抵京 講究停當 尙云太迫 況由旱路 更費多少日子 得無誤了事機乎 中堂 特念貴國王懸企之情 專撥輪船 俾便歸奏 今更違中堂之命 倘誤事機 竊爲不取

○余曰 美使當於何日發船

○周曰 西曆五月初二日 卽中曆三月十四日

○余曰 十四日發船 則何日可抵仁川

○周曰 念內可抵

○余曰 然則李應俊 雖於今晦間由旱路發程 可先美使十日之前 輪船一動 爲弊甚大 由陸似好耳

○周曰 中堂方與美使 爲貴國議約 稍有眉目 奏聞皇上 李應俊出去時 奉約條底稿及中堂公文 乘船前去 此不可暫緩

○余與從事尹友 相視而議曰 似此則從旱從陸 更非吾輩可擅當 奈何 遂書曰 旣有公文所重 中堂所送 允何敢干預 請勿復敢言

○周曰 貴國有洋語者乎 議約緊要之務 惟在傳譯

○余曰 敝邦 素無解洋語之人 已於日前 稟知中堂矣 願一通曉洋語及交際事務之人 偕往幫辦 深爲萬幸

○周曰 日間閣下進院時 面請於中堂可也 此次又必奏派大員 乘兵船前去 此非幫美國也 專幫貴國也

○余曰 通曉洋語之人 久欲仰請 而近日緣敝邦之無回信 滿心惶蹙 不敢更煩他事 日間如得進院陪話 當依戒仰請矣
○周曰 中堂方議和約底稿 日本之所不允者 皆欲允之 又有貴國所未想到者 亦爲補入 此實爲貴國也 爲閣下也
○余曰 允 庸昧蔑裂 將命不善 中堂不以使臣之不敏 移咎於國 悉心代籌 俾和約無虧 敝邦君臣暨一國之民 同受其賜 豈獨使臣乎 但愧不能奉副其至意耳
○余又曰 與美使議約時 彼倘無不肯順從處否
○周曰 豈得無之 多有缺裂處耳
○余曰 何者爲肯從 何者爲不肯從乎
○周曰 議約數日可定 伊時必有邀議 今未大定耳

146

李鴻章 ➡ 總署(1882. 4. 21/光緒八年三月四日)

조미수호통상조약 초안에 관한 의견

관련문서 협상 대리를 청하는 李最應 서한

三月初四日 北洋大臣李鴻章函稱 密肅者 美國與朝鮮議約一事 何署使於二月十四日到津 次日來謁 果謂薛總兵堅執原議 該署使在京所擬改第一款未能增入 經鴻章再三駁辨 謂汝旣在鈞署議定 豈可復行翻悔 該署使力稱此事本國專派薛總兵主政 伊僅可商辦 薛之不允載明中國屬邦者 慮於兩國立約平行體統有礙 他日國會紳員亦必議駁 不得不格外愼重耳 鴻章因商令汝兩人旣未敢擅允 可先電請本國核示 該署使遂與薛總兵於廿五午後發電請示 滿擬三四日內必得覆音 乃至今八日 尙無回報 疑竟爲該國所不許也 二十七日 三月初一日薛總兵與何署使偕來商訂此外各款 有敝處續增而該使酌改者 有該使續增而敝處酌改者 大致較原本似更周密 然何署使狡獪頗甚 未免多費唇舌 現議暫空第一款 俟該國回信 再議去留 稿本旣定 鴻章於紙尾鈐一圖章 並屬薛總兵簽字爲據 擬交朝鮮陪臣 迅齎回國 以爲屆時該國另派大員與薛使商辦之依據 謹照鈔一本 奉呈鑒核 薛總兵卽日赴煙臺 與該國水師提督會商 約於三月二十日開駛東行 諄請敝處派員偕往 而去冬以後 朝鮮屢次來員 亦懇派員同美使前去 鴻章反覆籌維 該兩國約稿旣憑敝處議有頭緒 誠如二月十八日來示 在我隱然主盟 若不派員同往 恐主客之間形迹隔○ 易生疑衅 或再有他人從旁唆聳 約事無成 而日俄强隣轉得遂其離間侵陵之詭計 亦東方大局之憂也 昨已面許薛何二使 擬派馬道建忠與統領北洋水師丁提督汝昌 於三月望後會於煙臺 酌帶兵船偕同薛總兵東駛 馬道精明幹練 於交涉公法研究素深 當密屬其相機妥辦 屆期再具奏請旨 合先奉聞 頃又接朝鮮丞相總理機務李最應該國王之叔父 二月初三日來書 照鈔呈覽 書內渾言美使東來 惟敝處是仰是依亦隱求主盟之意 派員一節 似屬義無可辭 其所派考選官魚允中李祖淵二員 魚允中於去歲十月來謁 頗能洞達時務 李祖淵則去秋赴日本議稅則未成者 據金允植報稱 該二員現至營口 搭船未到 先專人投書也 容俟魚李二員到後 再傳同馬道晤商一切 隨時布陳 何署使日內回京 當赴尊處 提及該署使未來津之先 鴻章已與薛總兵議及 如中國屬邦未能於約內載明 或俟畫押後 由朝鮮另備照會美國外部 聲明朝鮮久爲中國藩屬 內政外交向來歸其自主云云 將來卽連約本奏報中國朝廷 庶爲不觸不背 薛總兵已可允行 今則專候該國回信 前議不

便再訂 亦未與何署使說破 姑於約後提明光緖八年字樣 稍顯出奉中朝正朔而已 仍密屬馬道屆時商辦 鴻章因母病請假歸省 心緖瞀亂 此事關係屬邦外交要政 不敢置爲緩圖 惟智慮未周之處 尙祈匡導所不逮 幸甚 專肅縷布 祗敂鈞福

【관련문서】

朝鮮丞相總理機務李最應來書
李中堂肅毅伯閣下 頃李橘山裕元有幾遭書械 深荷曲軫之念 臨事綢繆 隨機靜鎭 俾小邦永有依賴 受賜無涯 翹首斗南 朝野咸頌 洒玆小生冒據廊廟 兼總機務 責任綦重 瘝隳是懼 而竊有所蘊 不容泯默 敢此槩陳 伏乞垂鑒焉 蓋年前美國人之來泊釜山港口也 不受書契 實因本國素無外交 輿論所在 止竟不許 該國人旋卽回船而去考 寔由中堂維持之攸曁也 近見領選使金允植書報 則美國使臣又將東來云矣 第念小邦 惟中堂是仰是依 則安得不以前日之所庇者 復望於來許乎 機務主事魚允中 李祖淵 爲董飭學徒 現派考選官 前赴津門 聽候指導 謹玆付上一函 伏冀到底涵燭 克垂終始之惠 以副褊隅跂祝之誠 千萬祈懇 滿腔衷情 有非寸楮可罄 瀆擾爲悚 不盡縷白
中堂肅毅伯閣下
　　總理機務事李最應再拜

　　壬午二月初三日發
　　　　二月十九日到

147

金允植(1882. 4. 21/高宗十九年三月四日)

金允植·李鴻章 회담(6)

관련문서 (1) 李鴻章의 기록
　　　　　(2) 조약 초안 조관별 논의

北洋大臣衙門談草 尹石汀及周玉山 馬眉叔觀察建忠 同在座

李中堂問 魚李兩人 尙無來信否
余曰 姑未來到
李曰 想至營口候船 故此耽延
余曰 候船不遇 則必由旱路
李曰 李相之官職姓名別字年紀可書示
以上口談
余書對 現官領敦寧府事 興寅君 原任議政 李最應 號山響 年六十六
李曰 興寅君是否 封爵有信與卿等否
余曰 興寅君 係是宗親府封爵 書函想付魚 李之行
李曰 現與美使 已有成議 美使已赴煙臺取齎 剋期東駛 而魚李等不知何日可到 將若之何
余曰 誠極悶鬱 雖有旱路 從令似不過三四天可到 亦未可確知
李曰 魚李到遲 於此事 却無甚關係 愚意 可遣李應俊乘輪船先回 我卽復山響一函 將本大臣與美使議定約稿 賚去報知貴國王 以免遲誤何如
余曰 帶約稿 均屬妥愜於敝邦之望 雖先去 亦似無妨於事 惟在中堂裁處
李曰 約稿副本 可先奉覽 本大臣與周道馬道等 會商美使 辦論二十餘日 始能辦到 如此地步 諒能愜貴國之望 將來美使到後 另派大員 與之議辦 或可小有更易 大致必無甚出入 否則美使決不從命也
余曰 第一款第五款 已於昨冬 在保省承敎 亦已轉達於寡君 其餘各款 均洽素望 惟禁米穀一事 最礙通商 而奈敝邦民情 以滲穀爲大患 與日人相持多年未許開 今若於平年開禁 明裁約條 未知敝邦朝議當如何耳
李曰 朝鮮與日本初次約本第六則 載明糧米雜穀 得出入 出者出口之謂也 殊欠分明 故日人力持 不得嚴禁 此次 亦與美使 辦駁數日後 使謂永禁斷不能行 只可聲聲明 因有事故 暫禁出口 在我 尙可有酌辦之權 將來到

貴國議約時 不妨再與爭論 若爭之不可 似未便 因一事而敗和局也

余曰 日人議約時 米穀出入云者 卽萊館居留日人之糧米也 遣辭欠明 以致日人之藉口 然 此事本非可禁 但有礙國人之情 通商稍久 庶可自知 昨年趙李二人 在日本 與何太史商論此事 似應歸奏於寡君 方苦企魚李之來 正爲此事憧憧故耳

李曰 魚李來與敝處議此 亦屬無益 只有俟美使入境 再與斟酌

余曰 李應俊之去 謹當以此先奏寡君 此稿 寔出代籌密妥 想敝朝廷 不輕刪增也 又曰 美船方在煙臺 將由彼使獨往否 敝邦不諳交際事務 又無解洋文洋語之人 若不自中國派員同去 則竊恐事多窒礙 然允植不敢煩請

李曰 卿等如必欲余派員前往 襄助成人之美 所不敢辭 擬卽派馬道台 坐中國兵船 同美使前去 幷有水師提督丁大人偕行 使中國與貴國 聲勢一振 馬道台名建忠 號眉叔 曾游學西洋各國 精通英法語言文字 熟諳萬國交際公法 介紹其間 必能通達兩國情好 我將奏明大皇帝派往

余曰 爲敝邦事 到底眷庇至勞 馬公 遠涉滄溟 不勝感謝

李曰 李應俊 擬於何日起程 我前已告知鎭海船主預備 但魚李二君來遲 再由陸路回國 恐趕不及美使入境議約之期 此間別無輪船可送矣

余曰 美船當於何日起碇否 李應俊之行 恐不得緩 伏望指日見教

李曰 美使辟斐爾 訂於三月二十日 由煙臺開駛 一日夜可至仁川港 李應俊似應三日內啓行 至貴國後 籌備一切方妥

余曰 不謂若是迅速 李應俊之行 恐不宜過三日以外 擬於初六發程 望前抵王京 可無後時之患矣

李曰 本大臣向來用兵謀國 皆是謀定伏動 今日特召兩君來商 卽欲立地定議也

余曰 敝邦於此事 惟仰成於中堂 若謀之臧 卽敝邦之福 中堂之惠也

李曰 約稿正本 末由鄙人鈐印美使畫押爲憑擬 封寄興仁君 副本卽交兩君持去 將來第一款 美國家 若不肯添入 貴國須照此款大意 於定約後 另備照會美國外部 存案爲要

余曰 謹當一遵句命 此次議稿 事事妥協 以敝邦之弱小 何以得此 一副妥約於外國之交耶 寡君聞之 必深喜且感

李曰 請問美使兵船一隻中國兵船二隻 逕入仁川港 抑泊釜山 再轉仁川耶

余曰 若自煙臺 一日夜可達仁川 必無迤從釜山之理 敝邦學徒有故當還者爲八九人 而道遠難致 此次付送船便 未知可否

李曰 鎭海船已議泊鴨綠江口 李君就便登岸 隨行若干人 開名草送周道知照

【관련문서 1】

照錄與朝鮮陪臣金允植筆談節略
壬午三月初四日 與金允植筆談節略
問　　李山響官職姓名別字年紀
允植對 現官領敦寧府事興寅君 原任領議政 李最應 號山響 年六十六
問　　興寅君是否封爵 有信與卿等否
允植曰 興寅君係是宗親封爵 書函想付魚李之行
問　　現與美使已有成議 美使已赴烟台取齊 剋期東駛 而魚李等不知何日
　　　可到 將若之何
允植曰 誠極悶鬱 雖由旱路 從今似不過三四天可到 亦未可確知
問　　魚李等到 遲於此事 却無甚關係 愚意可遣李應浚乘輪船先回 我即復
　　　山響一函 將本大臣與美使議定約稿賷去 報知貴國王 以免遲誤 何如
允植曰 帶約稿急先報知 極爲便好 而未知魚李之來奉有旨意何如 若所議約
　　　稿 均屬妥愜於敝邦之望 雖先去亦似無妨於事 惟在中堂裁處
問　　約稿副本可先奉覽 本大臣與周道馬道等會商美使辦論卄餘日 始能辦
　　　到如此地步 諒能愜貴國之望 將來美使到後 另派大員與之議辦 或可
　　　小有更易 大致必無甚出入 否則美使決不從命也
允植曰 第一款第五款已於昨冬在保省承敎 亦已轉達於寡君 其餘各款均洽素
　　　望 惟禁米穀一事 最礙通商 而奈敝邦民情 以滲穀爲大患 與日人相持
　　　多年 尙未許開 今若於平年開禁 明載約條 未知敝邦朝議當如何耳
問　　朝鮮與日本初次約本第六則載明糧米雜穀得出入 出者出口之謂也 殊
　　　欠分明 故日人力持不得嚴禁 此次亦與美使辦駁數日 該使謂永禁斷
　　　不能行 只可聲明因有事故 暫禁出口 在我尙可有酌辦之權 將來到貴
　　　國議約時 不妨再與爭論 若爭之不可 似未便因一事而敗和局也
允植曰 日人議約時 米穀出入云者 卽萊館居留日人之糧米也 遣辭欠明 以致
　　　日人之藉口 然此事本非可禁 但有礙國人之情 通商稍久 庶可自知 昨
　　　年趙李二人在日本與何太史商論此事 似應歸奏於寡君 方苦企魚李之
　　　來 正爲此事憧憧故耳

問　　　魚李來與敝處議此 亦屬無益 只有俟美使入境 再與斟酌
允植曰　李應浚之去 謹當以此先奏寡君 伏想此稿寔出代籌密妥 敝朝廷不輕
　　　　刪增也
允植又曰　美船方在烟台 將由彼使獨往否 敝邦不諳交際事務 又無解洋文洋
　　　　語之人 若不自中國派員同去 則竊恐事多窒礙 然允植不敢煩請
問　　　卿等如必欲余派員前往襄助 成人之美 所不敢辭 擬卽派馬道台坐中
　　　　國兵船同美使前去 並有水師提督丁大人偕行 使中國與貴國聲勢一振
　　　　馬道名建忠號眉叔 曾遊學西洋各國 精通英法語言文字 熟諳萬國交
　　　　際公法 介紹其間 必能通達兩國情好 我將奏明大皇帝派往
允植曰　爲敝邦事到底眷庇 至勞馬公遠涉滄溟 不勝感謝
問　　　李應浚擬於何日起程 我前已告知鎭海船主預備 但魚李二君來遲 再
　　　　由陸路回國 恐趕不及美使入境議約之期 此間別無輪船可送矣
允植曰　美船當於何日起碇否 李應浚之行恐不得緩 伏望指日爲敎
問　　　美使薛斐爾訂於三月二十日由煙台開駛 一日夜可至仁川港 李應浚似
　　　　應三日內啓行 至貴國後籌備一切方妥
允植曰　不謂若是神速 李應浚之行恐不宜過三日以外 擬於初六發程 望前抵
　　　　王京 可無時之患矣
問　　　本大臣向來用兵謀國 皆是謀定後動 今日特召兩君來商 卽欲立地定
　　　　議也
允植曰　敝邦於此事惟仰成於中堂 若謀之臧 卽敝邦之福 中堂之惠也
問　　　約稿正本末有鄙人鈐印美使畫押爲憑 據封寄興寅君 副本卽交兩君持
　　　　去 將來第一款美國家若不肯添入 貴國須照此款大意 於定約後另備
　　　　照會美國外部
允植曰　謹當一遵鈞命 此次議稿事事妥協 以敝邦之弱小 何得此一副妥約於
　　　　外國之交耶 寡君聞之 必深喜且感
問　　　請問美使兵船一隻中國兵船二隻逕入仁川港 抑泊釜山再轉仁川耶
允植曰　若自煙台一日夜可達仁川 則必無迤從釜山之理 敝邦學徒有故當還者
　　　　爲八九人 而道遠難致 此付送船使 未知可否
答　　　鎭海兵船已議泊鴨綠口 李君就使登岸 隨行若干人 開名單送周道知照

【관련문서 2】

北洋大臣衙門筆談事情及海關談略 此亦錄於談草之下

本月初四日 海關道周馥 以李中堂之意相邀 當日申時量 與首望(堂)李應俊 卽往海關署 同周馥馬建忠 詣北洋大臣衙門筆談 定李應俊行期 中堂辭色平和 不似曩時峻勵爲言 與美使議定約稿之事 蓋知我國 雖有派員 亦未有全權之使 美使議定行期漸迫 不容遲延 故先議約稿 齎送李應俊還奏也 仍出示約稿 凡十五款 詳細奉閱

第一款 特書中國屬邦 末係中國年號 似礙自主之權 日本人見之 必爲藉口 而李中堂之意自初確定 以此一款 爲我國大關鍵 嗣後各國 若侵侮我國 卽是侵侮中國 同聲相應 一氣相貫 使各國不敢侮視 卽中堂之主意也 我國 方服事中國 若以有礙自主爲言 則便疑我國 有自尊各立之心 故不敢發口 議約時美使 以第一款 須稟問于彼國然後 乃可妥定 電報已久 當無回信 想矣美國 亦以此條 議論未定 電報回後 彼若不從 中堂使我國 另備照會于美國 外部存案云 可見以此一款 預爲聲明於天下 他日我國 或彼各國侵凌中國 理宜幫助各國 不得以交涉他國例 言之也

第三款 互派秉權大臣駐京此一款 曾所不許於日人者 今乃許之 亦有異同之嫌 然此是萬國通例也 若日本 則猶得以前日相交之例 爭之 其他各國 無辭可拒 誠爲難處

第九款 米穀事通商之禁 米穀本是拙法 中堂特爲我國物情 屢與美使相持 終不順從 不得已以如有事故 暫禁米糧出口爲言 使他日或開或禁 其權尙我國 若猶不合於國論 則在港口議約時 更爲爭論無妨云云 紅蔘亦爲我國物情 以禁出口載物約 而此間議論 皆云紅蔘不必禁 多種廣售 厚收其稅 其利斯博 近年潛蔘 多於官蔘 日人賣於廣東福建上海等地 北京蔘價爲之頓低 以此觀之 非徒中國地方爲然 必滲布於各國 許多漏稅之弊 實爲可惜 敎堂一款 初不擧論於約條中 他日若有言 當以條約之所不載 爭之矣 敎堂 彼國之所重 中堂似必難於措辭 辭恐傷和局 故置之耳 此外稅則之値百抽十 章程之酌照通例 諸般條約 比中日向時立約受屈於西人者 反爲大勝 此中人所謂 爲貴國可慶 正指此等 酉時量辭出 共至海關署 主人設飯待之 馬眉叔建忠號曰 仁川 有城市否 余曰 小去處無城市 馬曰 我到仁川後 豫於岸山 定一居住之所 以便與美國相會商議 余曰 自當有接待之節 不勞過慮 馬曰 我等食費 自有銀子 辦買

給用 不煩貴國用慮 余曰 敝邦爲主之道 豈容疏慢 馬與周屢屢稱不必費心 余曰 此次寡君 如或邀見兩位大人 則美使亦難異同 日本使臣到敝邦 以臣禮見君 美使亦應用日本之例 而同時行禮 大人於以客禮見 美使以臣禮見 得無礙乎 馬曰 此次美使爲通好而來 不應面君 他日公使奉國書而來 則時有延見之禮耳 此次幷不宜入城 余曰 若大人 見寡君時 其禮當何如 周曰 雖兩位 似不必入至京城 如或貴國王邀見 不必見於公堂 見於便殿 只用一揖爲好 雖失禮亦無大妨 此次雖奏明派員體例 與詔使有異 若過爲隆崇 與美使迥殊 則美使必懷猜恨之心 惟在貴國深諒處之 竊念李中堂之特派文武大員 乘兵船二隻提幾百水師 同美使出去 不惜許多浮費 爲此張大之舉者 蓋欲爲我國 大振形勢 聲明於各國也 丁馬兩人 便是一二品大官 因中堂奏明派送 事體不爲不重在我國 待之宜極優厚 而周馬兩人之言 不必與美使 過有厚薄 亦深慮之言 似宜外面一體優待 裏面則另致慇懃於二人 以示尊親中國之意 至於當施於美使者 亦詢於馬建忠 務歸停妥 至於派全權議約之事 各國之例皆用當朝頭等大臣 中國與日本議約時 李中堂爲全權大臣 不如是 不能見重於各國 況有中國大員 其迎接之道 恐不可疏薄

148

李鴻章(1882. 4. 22/光緒八年三月五日) → 李最應

馬建忠·丁汝昌의 조선 파견 통보

山響尊兄興寅君閣下 頃奉二月初三日惠書 情文兼摯 津沽浿水 延企爲勞 往歲橘山太師垂詢邦交 殷殷商榷 郵筒往返 略竭紆籌 想貴國王與在廷諸臣均所深悉 矧執事以親賢之碩望 膺軍國之重寄 平章大政 悉協機宜 東方柱石卽中朝屛蔽 此鄙人所昕夕引領 願與識時俊傑爲輔車之依也 貴國君臣權時審勢 幡然遠交 洵能破除成見 美國直接大東洋 向無侵人土地之心 今先與彼立一平善條約 旣可杜東隣覬覦 卽他國續議通商 亦得有所依據 間執要求之口 鴻章竊不自揆 輒思居間主持 冀爲二國講信修睦 深恐載書所述偶一失當 流弊滋多 入春已來 督同津海關道周馥 二品銜候選道馬建忠 與美使薛斐爾往復辯論二十餘日 易稿至十數次乃稍就緒 較之中美原約及貴國與日本約款 取益防損之處似更周密 惟第一款聲明貴國爲中朝屬邦而政治向歸自主云云 美使未敢遽定 已電商本國 將來若于正約中刪去 必須另行聲明 俾貴國數百年事大之誠昭示天壤 想貴國王執禮素恭 定不河漢斯言耳 其餘各款俟美使入境 另派大員與之復議 卽使小有更易 而大致不出範圍 比經面同美使于約稿末 分別鈐印畫押爲憑 玆將原定草本奉呈臺覽 來員魚允中李祖淵尙在途次 而美使未肯久留 已赴煙臺取齊 克期東駛 只得先派李應浚賫約稿由兵船駛回報知 以便籌備一切 美使與領選使金允植等皆力懇敝處派大員前往襄助 擬卽奏明大皇帝 遣派馬觀察與北洋水師提督丁汝昌乘兵船偕往 二君周歷瀛海 熟悉洋情 馬君尤精通西國語言文字 熟諳交際公法 介紹其間 必能爲兩國通達情好 到時希與美使一體款待 貴國遠在東陲 鴻章仰體大皇帝綏靖藩服至意 但視力所能爲 不分畛域 竭誠代謀 惟冀宏此遠謨 匡濟時艱 講求馭外之道 以爲固圉之圖 途遙意邈 不罄欲言乎 此布復 敬頌時祉 文華殿大學士直隷總督北洋通商大臣李鴻章再拜

李鴻章(1882. 4. 23/光緒八年三月六日)

조미조약 교섭 전말 상주

奏爲遵旨籌辦朝鮮與美國議約事宜 現經商定約稿 並擬請旨派員前往會辦 恭摺馳陳 仰祈聖鑒事 竊查美國欲與朝鮮結約通好 經臣勸令朝鮮派員赴津與美總兵薛孚爾商議 適朝鮮國王派陪臣金允植爲領選使 帶學生來津 就便籌議外交 臣於光緒七年十二月初二日奏奉上諭 朝鮮久隷藩屬 自應隨事維持調護 卽以固我邊陲 該國如與美國訂約 則他國不至肆意要求 於大局實有關係 仍著李鴻章隨時相機開導 妥爲籌辦等因 欽此 仰見聖謨廣運 綏撫屬邦 莫名欽服 臣於歲抄卽聞美國派定水師總兵薛斐爾卽薛孚爾爲朝鮮議約全權大臣 催令今春乘兵船東駛 朝鮮陪臣金允植亦來保定謁見 謂續奉該國王密諭 求臣代爲主持 速與美使商議 並寄呈該國機務大臣擬具約稿 屬爲鑒定 當卽密飭津海關道周馥設法婉留薛使 俟臣會商 臣二月初抵津 薛使訂期謁晤 先將伊所擬約稿由周馥譯呈 其意欲以日本條約爲藍本 臣將兩稿比較 所差甚遠 且於中國屬邦一節 均未提及 將來各國效尤 久之將不知朝鮮爲我屬土 而萬國公法 凡附庸小國不得自主者 又未便與各大邦立約 是彼此均有爲難之處 臣囑周馥諷示薛使謂約內須提明中國屬邦 政治仍得自主字樣 臣亦與金允植等議及 該陪臣翕服無異詞 因與酌量刪增約稿 將各項應防之流弊 應獲之權利 一一包括在內 令周馥及道員馬建忠密交薛使閱訂 該使於各款頗有增改 大致尙無甚出入 惟於第一款聲明朝鮮爲中國屬邦 堅不允從 意甚決絶 適美國署使何天爵在京與總理衙門議添認明屬邦一節 經總署王大臣將何天爵擬改第一款照錄專函知會前來 何天爵旋於二月二十五日來謁 乃謂薛斐爾堅執原議 慮於兩國平行體統有碍 且他日國會紳員亦必議駁 是以該署使在京擬改第一款未能增入 臣謂旣經議定 豈可復行翻悔 該署使力稱此事本國專派薛斐爾主政 伊僅可商辦 臣以該兩人旣未敢擅允 令先電請本國核示 該署使允爲發電請示 至今尙無回報 二十七日三月初一日 薛斐爾復偕何天爵來署商訂 此外各款有臣處續增而該使酌改者 有該使續增而臣處酌改者 較原本似更周密 於一切取益防損之道 再三斟酌 總期於朝鮮政有裨 將來不致爲他國肆意要求 以冀仰副朝廷軫念屬藩 維持調護之至意 此事與薛斐爾何天爵四五次辨論 二十餘日始有成議 所訂約稿擬暫空第一款 俟美國回信 再議去留 臣於稿本

紙尾鈐一圖章 並邀薛斐爾簽字畫押爲據 先交朝鮮陪臣李應浚迅賫回國 以爲該國另派大員與薛使商辦之依據 並傳見金允植 諭知現辦情形 告以美國若不肯將第一款添入 須於定約後另行設法聲明 以符初議 此送次與薛斐爾等議辦朝鮮立約之實在情形也 朝鮮今春續派陪臣魚允中等 尙未到津 薛斐爾已赴烟台與該國水師提督會商 約於三月二十日間駛東行 諮請臣處派員偕往 而朝鮮屢次來員 亦懇派員同美使前去 頃又接朝鮮國王之叔父總理機務李最應來書 內言美使東來 惟臣處是仰是依等語 臣反覆籌維 該兩國約稿旣經議有頭緖 若不派員同往 恐主客之間形跡隔閡 易生疑衅 或再有他人從旁唆聳 約事無成 而日俄強隣轉得遂其離間侵陵之詭計 亦東方大局之憂 關繫實非淺鮮 查有二品銜候選道馬建忠 精明幹練 於交涉公法 硏究素深 此次臣與薛斐爾議約 該員皆在座 詳悉顚末 堪以派往 會同朝鮮國王所派議約大員相機妥辦 應卽請旨特派前往勷助 由臣咨明朝鮮國王知照 再薛斐爾乘坐該國兵船前赴朝鮮 臣處北洋水師兵輪船 本擬於春夏之交 飭赴東洋等處游歷 藉以測量沙線 練習風濤 拟卽派統領北洋水師記名提督丁汝昌 於三月望後與馬建忠會於烟台 酌帶兵船偕同薛斐爾東駛 以壯聲勢 而杜要挾 除將議定約稿曁臣與朝鮮總理機務丞相李最應來往函件 及與金允植筆談底稿 照鈔淸摺 恭呈御覽外 所有臣遵旨籌辦朝鮮與美國議約事宜 並請旨派員前往會同商辦各緣由 理合恭摺由驛五百里密陳 伏乞皇太后皇上聖鑒訓示遵行 謹奏

李鴻章 ➡ 總署(1882. 4. 28/光緒八年三月十一日)

조약초안 관련 高宗에게 보내는 자문

爲密咨事 竊照美國欲與貴國結約通好 派水師總兵薛斐爾爲議約全權大臣 薛總兵前已來津 商請本閣爵大臣代爲先容 貴國王亦派陪臣金允植爲領選使 帶學生來津肄習機器 就便籌議外交 該領選使等屢求本閣爵大臣代爲主持 速與美使商議 並寄呈機務大臣擬具約底 面懇鑒定 而美使初擬約稿 欲以日本條約爲藍本 比較兩稿 所差甚遠 本閣爵大臣仰體大皇帝綏靖藩服至意 冀爲兩國講信修睦 督同二品銜津海關道周馥 二品銜候選道馬建忠與美使薛斐爾往復辨論二十餘日 易稿至十數次 乃稍就緒 較之貴國與日本約款 取益防損之處 似更周密 比經商同美使 於約稿末暫行分別鈐用圖章簽字畫押爲憑 仍俟行抵貴國後 再行妥議辦理 貴國來員魚允中 李祖淵尙在途次 而美使未肯久留 訂於三月之杪乘兵船東駛 只得先派貴國委員李應浚賫約稿由輪船駛回報知 以便籌備一切 美使與金允植等皆力懇本閣爵大臣奏派大員前往襄助 貴國總理機務李最應來書 亦言美使東行 惟敝處是仰是依等語 玆已奏請大皇帝特派二品銜候選道馬建忠 與北洋水師提督丁汝昌 酌帶兵船偕往 欽奉諭旨允准 馬道丁提督周歷瀛海 熟悉洋情 馬道尤精通西國語言文字 熟諳交際公法 詳知此事顚末 介紹其間 必能爲兩國通達情好 三月望後卽於煙台偕美使東行 望貴國王遴派大員 商同馬道等與美使籌議妥定 仍俟和約辦竣 由貴國王鈔錄約本照會各稿 備文咨呈中國禮部及北洋大臣衙門轉奏備案 除將詳細情形函復李最應並告知金允植等轉達外 相應審咨貴國王 煩請查照辦理

151

洪淳穆, 金炳國 等(1882. 5. 5/高宗十九年三月十八日)

조미조약 체결 등에 관한 어전회의

大臣箚對三月十八日

上御熙政堂 時原任大臣次對入侍時 領相洪淳穆辭免事云云 領相捕廳戢盜事云云

上曰　諸大臣俱見李鴻章書乎
領相[曰] 其爲敦定約條也 甚爲備詳矣
上曰　自我接待之節 何以則可以得當耶
領相曰 旣爲同行出來 而淸人非是勅使 則在我接待之節 宜無差等 而至如供饋凡百 務從精略 一體善待 無乾糇之歎似好矣
上曰　無咨文 是皇帝不知而然耶
領相曰 鴻章雖主其事 皇帝必無不知之理 皇帝旣知之 則在庭之臣 自當皆知 而此非可特咨之事 故只有鴻章書也
上曰　此必是各國之請得於中原而有此擧也
領相曰 西宮太后及恭親王在矣 必有外請內圖之計也
上曰　日本修好 亦中國咨文也
領相曰 各國交和相濟 皆因鴻章而受命于皇帝矣
上曰　大皇帝之大字 甚近自尊矣
金判府炳國曰 然矣 皇帝無上 旣曰皇帝 則又安知大字乎
上曰　今此大國之欽送使朝鮮 取信無疑矣
判府曰 然矣
上曰　以一品官出送云 反高於勅使之品何耶
領相曰 勅使則擇官自有定品 而此使則擇人故 不拘品之高下矣
上曰　西使均接之際 淸使無介意之慮乎
領相曰 似無是理矣
上曰　迎接之地 多送譯官 必有弊端 擇其謹愼解事幾人 簡率以送好矣
領相曰 謹當如敎矣
上曰　美國人 不可處之城內 淸人亦不可無同處 而倭人則在於城內矣 美國

	與淸人 恐各有言 且在我待淸人待倭人 體貌不無失當者乎
領相曰	雖是上國人 自非特勅之使 而同來同處 待之無間之理 宜無介意之慮 而淸人旣在城外 則美國亦何嘗言之乎
上曰	彼在烟臺云 仁川相去八百餘里也 順風張帆 不過一日程 而非久當來到矣 迎接之節 所居之處 退而爛商 告稟預備 無至窘迫之歎 先使畿營 關飭沿海諸邑 以爲無滯應接之弊可也
判府曰	謹當如敎 而二十一二日間 來抵云耳
上曰	迎接官 何以稱之可也
領相曰	伴接官爲稱 而機務堂上中差定好矣 而接應之節 專爲戶曹擔着 而戶曹方在筵中 當在準備擧行矣
上曰	美國人容貌 異於他人 我國人必有驚邊侵撓之弊 道路觀者 別般操飭 然後 可無見侮之慮矣
領相曰	然矣 深目高準 白面黃瞳 髮如羊毛 殆同獸形 但心與人同矣
上曰	曾見在內屛風所畵 則亦有紅毛國 此果何國人乎
領相曰	此亦中原幅員中所在 而未知其何國人也 盖是東洋之人 多白晳 西洋之人 多蒼黑矣
上曰	接應之節 必到善處好矣
判府曰	戶曹事 極爲可悶耳
上曰	當百錢淸錢革罷後 戶曹尤爲蕩竭 而事急矣 退以爛議 以爲善接之道好矣
領相曰	謹當如敎矣
承旨曰	諸宰奏事云云

(7) 조약 협상 과정

152

統理機務衙門(1882. 5. 2/高宗十九年三月十五日)

반접관(伴接官) 임명

金晩植以統理機務衙門言啓曰 卽見領選使金允植書報則 淸國使臣與美國使臣並爲騎船 將匪久到泊云矣 經理趙準永伴接官差下解事 譯官自舌院泒送 所住舘宇 令度支擇定於京江近處 斯速修理 供饋接待之節 亦令戶禮曹 參酌磨鍊 而上來時延接官 還歸時護送官 以沿路地方官差下 何如 傳曰 允

R. W. Shufeldt (1882. 5. 6) ➡ 李鴻章

馬建忠과의 회견 통보

#2
Chefoo, China
His Excellency Li Hung Chang,
Grand Secretary, Senior Guardian to His Heir Apparent, Viceroy of Chihli, &c &c &c

Your Excellency:

I have the honor to acknowledge the receipt of your communication, dated at Tientsin, April 23th, 1882, in which your Excellency informs me that in consequence of your application, His Majesty, the Emperor of China, has been pleased to direct that Ma-Hietchong, an expectant Taotai of the honorary title of the second rank has been appointed to proceed to Corea, in a man-of-war of the Chinese Imperial Navy to act as an intermediary for facilitating the final arrangement of a treaty between the United States and Corea.

This appointment was signified to me by your Excellency during a personal interview at Tientsin and at that time met with my approbation. The appointment of such an officer will, I have no doubt, be regarded by the Government of the United States as an evidence on the part of the Government of China of its desire not only to facilitate, but to perfect a treaty of lasting friendship between the Government and people of Corea and the country which I have the honor, on this occasion to represent.

I take this occasion to inform your Excellency that in an interview with Ma Taotai and Admiral Ting, held yesterday, it was arranged that such of the vessels of the Chinese Imperial Navy as were destined to proceed to Corea, should leave Chefoo on the morning of the 7th inst., while I promised them that we would follow these vessels to a pre-determined anchorage on the Corean coast on the morning of the 8th inst.

Your Excellency will, I am sure, concur with me in the opinion that if this treaty is to be made it is advisable to proceed at once, in order that no further obstacle may intervene to prevent.

I avail myself of this opportunity to express to your Excellency my appreciation of your Excellency's earnest endeavor by means of this treaty to create another alliance between my own country and one in the great east, which hitherto has not entered into the family of nations.

I have the honor to subscribe myself, with great respect, Your Excellency's most obedient servant.

 (sg'd) R.W. Shufeldt
 Commodore U.S.N.
 and Special Envoy to Corea

R. W. Shufeldt (1882. 5. 6) ➡ C. Holcombe

조선행 일정 통보

Chefoo, China
Hon. Chester Holcombe
U.S. Charge d'Affairs
U.S. Legation, Peking

Sir:

I have the honor to inform you that upon my arrival at Chefoo, on the 4th inst., I found the U.S. Ship Swatara, Commander Cooper, at this port, and the following morning Comd'r. Cooper reported his ship in readiness to convey me to Corea, under instructions from Rear Admiral Clitz, commanding the U.S. Squadron on this station. I also found the Chinese gunboats under command of Admiral Tuig, of the Imperial Chinese Navy, in the port, ready to proceed to Corea.

Ma Taotai, a messenger from His Excellency the Viceroy at Tientsin, forwarded to me a letter from the Viceroy accrediting him to me as a messenger on the part of the Chinese Government to proceed to Corea. In a subsequent interview with this gentleman I ascertained that the draft of treaty (No. 4) which has previously been presented by you and myself, had been forwarded to the Government of Corea without any conditions of a political character being imposed upon it by His Excellency the Viceroy, and he announced himself ready to proceed on the morning of the 7th inst. in a Chinese vessel-of-war.

While at Shanghai I wrote to the State Department under date of April 28th, that if on arriving at Chefoo, I found the state of affairs as above indicated I should proceed to Corea, in the absence of any further instructions from Washington. I have therefore determined if the Chinese officials leave here on the morning of the 7th, to follow them on the next morning, to the coast of Corea, to the pre-determined anchorage. I confess myself somewhat surprised at the evident desire of the Chinese Government to act upon this treaty, without imposing any conditions whatever and under these circumstances and in the absence of answers to the telegrams, I feel it my duty to carry out my original instructions.

I regret exceedingly that the State Department has not authorized you to accompany me to Corea, and shall no doubt feel the need of your experience and knowledge, but I take this occasion to express to you my sincere obligations for the services you have already rendered. If the treaty is perfected and ratified it will be due very much to the interest you have taken in the matter. It is of course, difficult to say when I shall return or to what port, but by the earliest opportunity I shall inform you of the results. I am very respectfully

Your obedient servant
(sgd) R.W. Shufeldt
Commodore U.S.N.

馬建忠(1882. 5. 7/光緒八年三月二十四日) ➡ 李鴻章

조선 도착 및 조선의 조약 체결 태도 보고

照錄馬道建忠來稟
宮太傅中堂爵前 敬稟者 竊忠於前月十八日在烟台肅上一稟 諒早蒙鈞鑒
二十日起椗後 行一晝夜 至次日四點鐘駛抵漢江口虎島旁 依山停泊 日本公
使花房義質已乘兵船先半時許至 亦於此地下椗 李應浚偕同彼國三品以下官
數員 先在海口伺候 望見旗幟 卽駕小舟來謁 云其國王已令於仁川府預備行
館 所派伴接官二品參判趙準永次晨卽到 忠因將憲台咨朝鮮國王文交李應浚
令速派妥員賫去 二十二日晨 伴接官趙準永率李應浚數人來舟 諄請登岸 意
不可却 遂徇其請 暫至行館 丁提督留舟靜候美使 是日午後 花房義質來見 忠
已登岸 與丁提督寒喧而去 忠至行館後 與李應浚等筆談消遣 將微覘其朝議
應浚等狡甚 凡所問有稍近此事者 答語皆諉爲不知 二十三日凌晨 李應浚辭
赴王京 催派議約大員 趙準永等相繼來 忠復與筆談 秘密如故 固告以我中堂
奏請大皇帝派員來此 專爲調護屬邦起見 分宜推誠相待 安用是模棱爲 準允
等雖引咎不遑 仍無一字吐實 午間丁提督以美使未至 亦遂登岸 晚膳後 有機
務衙門二品參事金景遂進謁 云自王京奉命而來 議約大員已派定經理總理機
務衙門事申櫶 越宿當至 景遂年六十餘 其國王於派定議約大員後 命之來 知
其胸中當有成議 爰略以筆談相詆 辭意之間頗涉桀黠 狡展心機 似已流露於
語言之表 忠因責以應對失體 拂衣欲去 景遂等再四挽留 忠皆堅不允從 意將
小試操縱 使知中國來員不可玩狎 冀稍折其恣雎之氣 或將來辦理略可應手
遂於次晨偕丁提督毅然歸舟 方欲出館 忽花房義質來見 忠以英語與談 其意
頗涉窺探 而二十一二等日 李趙諸人來謁後 亦皆至日本兵舶晤談良久 其間
有無情弊 均未可知 花房義質去後 忠亦旋卽歸舟 伏念此事關係朝廷體制與
憲台威望 忠以駑鈍 謬膺斯任 自當竭盡心力 相機辦理 於懷柔之中寓窾竅之
意 務期於事機有濟 以仰副憲台委任之意 若彼國始終頑梗 自外生成 則忠亦
不敢遇事遷就 致辱使命 惟薛斐爾約定於二十一日東渡 至今未至 不知因霧
阻滯 抑別有他項情事 故與丁提督商令鎭海兵船回至烟台 沿途探覘 並附便
將抵朝鮮後一切情形專肅具稟 恭叩爵綏 伏惟崇鑒 職道馬建忠謹稟
二月二十四日

R. W. Shufeld (1882. 5. 8~1882. 5. 12)

조선 입국 기록

#5, 6 + 7
May 8th, 1882

The U.S.S. Swatara got underway for the coast of Corea at 7 o clock in the morning with Commodore R.W. Shufeldt, U.S.N., on board as Special Envoy to that country. Took on board as interpreter, Ah Ling and with him a Chinese teacher.

May 12th

Anchored at 2:15 am today at the mouth of the Salie River, Corea a little below Rose or Albei Island, and found there the Chinese corvette Wei Yuen, bearing the flag of Admiral Ting, I.C.N., the steel ram Yang-wei and the dispatch boat Chen-hai; also the Japanese gunboat Banjö.

The commanding officer of the Banjö delivered a letter from the Hon. J.A. Bingham, U.S. Minister to Japan, of which the following is a copy:-

Legation of the United States
Tokei, Japan
April 26th, 1882

My dear Commodore:

It gives me pleasure to introduce and command to your most favorable consideration the bearer of this note, Mr. Hanabusa, H.I.J. Majesty Minister accredited to the Court of Corea. Should your business or pleasure call you to Corea, I have no doubt that you will find it to your advantage to cultivate intimate and, if need be, confidential relations with Mr. Hanabusa.

I remain my dear Commodore,
Very sincerely yours
(sgd) J.A. Bingham

Commodore R.W. Shufeldt, U.S.N.
&c &c &c

To which the following reply was sent through the commanding officer of the Japanese Gunboat Banjö:-

U.S.S. Swatara
At Anchor in the Salie River
May 12th, 1882

157

馬建忠(1882. 5. 8/光緖八年三月二十一日)

李應浚·馬建忠 회담(1)

三月二十一日 威遠舟次與李應浚筆談
忠曰 約事諸多未定 如日本人問 決不可稍有漏洩 亟宜知會貴國官員 愼重其事
李曰 當如戒矣
忠曰 貴國現派來二品官趙準永住在何處
李曰 今在仁川府 明早當來此相迓
忠曰 閣下此來 曾見貴國相臣與興寅君李山響否 有何屬付
李曰 卑職曾見李相國 則多有感謝之意
忠曰 貴朝見我中堂議訂約稿 有何意見
李曰 感謝周便 僉意洶同
忠曰 此次約事經我中堂籌議 十分妥善 亟宜速定 不可遲悞 僕自烟台臨行時 聞英法德等國將各調集兵艦前來 果爾 則約事必多掣肘
李曰 如此事機 當轉達朝廷矣
忠曰 貴國若與美國訂一妥善之約 他國踵至者 卽可奉美國約稿爲依據 將來 強隣斷難肆其要挾 亦貴國之福也
李曰 朝議亦然
忠曰 約內第一款貴朝有何議論
李曰 姑無詳聞者 未知美國電報聞回音否
忠曰 烟台曾晤美使 詢及尙無回電 大約第一款之意 必當設法聲明
李曰 此亦轉達朝廷矣
忠曰 現貴國王所派一品大員 其姓氏乞示知 幷何日可至
李曰 聞大人到境後派出 故卑職姑未詳聞
忠曰 執事已將第一款之意轉達貴朝 貴朝之意究竟若何
李曰 卑職轉達之日 聞知槪有感意 未詳其裏許矣 早晚秉權大臣相接時 當有 確論 又曰 皇上特派大人之諭旨賫來否
忠曰 業由我中堂轉咨貴國王矣 此事非係成例 故未由禮部轉行

統理機務衙門(1882. 5. 11/高宗十九年三月二十四日)

조약 협상단 임명

又以統理機務衙門言啓曰 卽見仁川出去伴接官與淸使問答說話則 我國一品大員速爲派送云矣 經理事申櫶下送于彼使留住處 凡諸事務 使之商辦句當 而經理事金弘集副官差下 副主事徐相雨從事官差下 竝令除下直同爲出往何如 傳曰 允

李鴻章 ➡ 總署(1882. 5. 11/光緒八年三月二十四日)

丁汝昌 파견 보고

三月二十四日 北洋大臣李鴻章文稱 據統領北洋水師記名提督丁汝昌呈稱 竊照提督現奉憲台札派 酌帶兵船會同水師營務處馬道前往朝鮮 照料該國與美國結約通好事宜 已經提督商明馬道 帶同威遠揚威鎮海三兵船 約同美國總兵薛斐爾 先後由烟台起程 所有留駐旅順快砲等船 應派管帶超勇快船林泰將泰曾暫行督率 照章認眞操練 酌量出洋巡閱 幷將旗書燈語照現定各類編成 晝夜相通號令 卽將未盡事宜詳細添載 俾得呼應便捷外 令各船管帶大副等輪流先繪行陣變圖 將各船於港口內外操試嫻熟 再領各船於附近海面演試各陣 倘須領用煤頓及遇有礙難事件 幷令該參將隨時稟明前敵營務處黃道瑞蘭核示遵辦 劉遊擊步蟾起程赴德國後 大沽口駐操各船如來旅順 均歸一律辦理 除札飭林參將參曾 幷移明前敵營務處黃道外 理合申報查核等情到本大臣 據此相應呑明 爲此合咨貴衙門 謹請查核

李鴻章 ➡ 總署(1882. 5. 11/光緒八年三月二十四日)

조선 입국 경과 보고

三月二十四日 北洋大臣李鴻章文稱 據二品銜候選道馬建忠 統領北洋水師記名提督丁汝昌詳稱 竊職道等於十六日午後在大沽會齊 乘鎭海兵船出口 十七日午正駛至烟台 美使臣薛孚爾施未至 候至十八日早間 薛孚爾歸自申江 職道等當卽往晤 議定職道等於二十日自烟台啓程 薛孚爾於二十一日自烟台啓程 彼此至朝鮮漢江口虎島旁會齊 除以後至彼議約情形 當俟隨時陸續稟報外 所有職道等自烟台啓程日期 理合詳報憲台鑒核施行等情到本大臣 據此 相應咨明 爲此合咨貴衙門 謹請査核

161

R. W. Shufeldt (1882. 5. 12) ➡ 花房義質

조선 입국 통보

To His Excellency
Yosimato Hanabusa
H.I.J. Majesty's Minister resident in Corea

Sir:

It has given me pleasure to receive through the hands of the Commanding Officer of the I.J. Gunboat Banjö, a letter of introduction to you from the Hon. J.A. Bingham, Minister of the United States at Tokei.

I have no desire to conceal from you the fact that I have arrived in Corea with the purpose of negotiating a treaty of amity and commerce between this country and the United States.

Any attention you may think proper to give to this subject, towards its accomplishment will I have no doubt, be duly appreciated by my own government.

I shall remain at this anchorage until some settlement can be made either favorable or otherwise, while delay will be considered by the government of the United States as undesirable.

I have the honor to be
Your obedient servant
(sgd) R.W. Shufeldt,
Special Envoy to Corea

馬建忠(1882. 5. 12/光緖八年三月二十五日)

李應浚·馬建忠 회담(2)

二十五日威遠舟次與李應浚審談
李曰 立約之時 大人應說是不是全權大臣 否則不能立約 各國通商之法都是
　　　全權方可定約 蓋我朝建公論不一之故也
忠曰 我對別位貴國官員當如此說 是否
忠曰 現派來議約大員申金二公 有正副之別否
李曰 申大官 金副官
忠曰 我當說申金二位當是全權 方能議約否
李曰 是也
忠曰 到底我問你貴國王已予全權否
李曰 我國王欲予 興寅君無通商意而阻矣
忠曰 何以知興寅君無通商意
李曰 興寅君說 我的沒有請通商之事 何以書我曁金允植商請之說乎
忠曰 我中堂接興寅君之書內有立約一事惟中堂是仰是依之語 此說何來
李曰 興寅君說 我書則防美國人東出之意 而無通商之說云
忠曰 我中堂與興寅君函 渠可呈於貴國王否
李曰 興寅君尙未見之 而卑職已看之也 是大人書械一般之言
忠曰 你由津回來 不是帶有中堂與彼之書麽
李曰 有是有 而卿函上沒有這樣話
忠曰 金景遂可是興寅君私人否
李曰 金景遂與韓文奎都是
忠曰 申金正副使可見中堂與興寅君之函 並吞貴國王之文否
李曰 申年老 金似可見之
忠曰 金君爲人何如
李曰 甚是明白
忠曰 貴國王親信
李曰 果然親信
忠曰 金君見中堂兩次書函 有何話說

李曰 尙未逢晤 未知得見兩次書函否 而鄙意思之 則似可見之耳

忠曰 你說此事可速成否

李曰 與金君說約則好

忠曰 但是申公爲正使 難以○開

李曰 正副使同往訂約 則大人問事 金君必答之也

忠曰 吾想申公年老 難以登舟 而美使與本道不能先施 迄至仁川議事 法莫若
　　 金君一人來舟議事 然後轉達申公 但是如此解法 必須申金二位同一事
　　 權方可

李曰 他二位今日斷當赶來也 一切明日再商

忠曰 金君甚麽官

李曰 二品官禮部參判

金弘集(1882. 5. 14/高宗十九年三月二十七日)

金弘集·馬建忠 회담(1)

관련문서 馬建忠 기록

我曰 仁川府館宇湫隘 殊爲未安 敢祈下陸一就 俾正事面

馬曰 均期兩便 不必下陸

我曰 禮欠敬客 但切歉愧

馬曰 條約議定日子 乞卽訂示

我曰 歸後酌商 訂日再告

馬曰 全權字據 現卽帶來否

我曰 今次未曾奉到 嗣當留心也

馬曰 後次帶來 以便交閱

我曰 敬聞命矣

馬曰 立約之處 就海岸近地爲定 明日當令舟人上岸 搭盖帳屋

我曰 搭盖一事 祈早止之 此當主人爲之 不至過費注念 且要在訂期後也

馬曰 此次傳相爲察貴國商務 命招商社五人 現在舟中 要往正城 一番觀看 可命人護往否

我曰 此事未敢遽對 容緩稟知朝廷 待回敎更告

馬曰 切須速稟回示 愈速愈好

我曰 當圖迅告

馬曰 前美使在津 與爵相商議 謂貴國久爲中國屬邦 不若在津與中國定一美好約條 而爵相 答以貴國雖爲屬邦 內治外交均得自主 美使終不釋然於心 謂難與貴國平行相待 此美使至此 亦屢屢以此爲信 彼謂 法莫若由貴國王給一照會 與彼國國主 內稱貴國雖爲中國屬邦 而立約一事自主云云 則何如 美使之意 欲將傳相所議第一款之言 在約外聲名[明?] 若列入約內 則有碍兩國平行之禮 僕自津面辭中堂時 中堂亦諄諄以此爲囑 若由貴國王先備一照會 與彼國國主 不必訂奉 送與美使看明 彼卽可先爲坧看 立約以平行相待 而立約後 彼亦可將照會與條約一並携回美國 呈明國主也

我曰 指敎周悉 兼示方便 極用感紉 第此事係寡君處分 不得不傳達 奉有裁允 然後可以走告

馬曰 此事旣係貴國王出面 應由公等轉奏定奪 惟此事決不可少之一着 爲貴國立定地步 歐美各國 方不渺視 且此次傅相奏派鄙人 隨帶兵輪 來此相助 亦曾定明貴國事大素恭 今日各國通商 時局大變 宜允貴國立約必須平行 方不受他人欺挾

我曰 敝邦服事中朝 垂三百年 偏荷庇覆之恩 此次又蒙爵相勻慈 審度時局 代爲畵籌 期欲立定地步 不受別人欺挾 萬萬感服 況兩大人親馭兵輪遠臨 爲敝邦主持 尤切悚無已

馬曰 傅相爲貴國某事 視如家事 誠以貴國逼邇強隣 事變難測 故屢次郵函以與美國開口爲請者 職是故也 僕等馳輪貴國 從中代達結好 分所應爲 何須言謝 惟此照會之文 須斟酌周至 四面圓到方可 更文 何日當訂期

我曰 謹領敎意 訂期一事 不得不俟照會文字稟裁 然後乃可指告

馬曰 誠是 但僕爲此事 難以此辭 不揣冒昧 謹代擬一稿 執事可能一看否 仍出示照會擬稿一紙

我曰 此稿至荷代擬 不勝感通 事關重大 僕不敢擅對 唯當轉達朝廷耳

我曰 米穀則與日本締約 初不許交易 只許港口糧米 去年改議通商新約 而爲禁米另立一款 與日使辯論屢次 只許港口糧米 去年改議通商新約 而爲禁米另入一款 與日使辨論屢次 我則堅持不變矣 此次條約 只云恐致境內缺食 暫禁米穀出口 則便是開禁 大違所料 幸燭蔽國事勢 妥議釐改

馬曰 此二句 揷入約內 權操貴國 與不開禁無異 若直禁米穀出口 美使定難照議 且傅相在津 已與之屢辨矣 矧美商來至貴國 販運洋貨 必無暇運及米糧也

我曰 蔽處朝野之論 僉以米穀一事 爲民命收關 期欲堅守不變 願得閣下主持

馬曰 中國貴國日本皆産米穀 不過有此貴彼賤之別 各國自開禁通商之後 沿海決不因通商之故 致呼庚癸也

我曰 蔽處民貧 唯以穀不出洋爲樂土 而若至外人輸米 以致價値日昻 則貧者坐困 豈非大憂 若得與中東章程初定時 特立違禁一項 俟幾年硝熟商務後 再議恐妥

馬曰 此意僕當傳告

我曰 仁川口禁米 日人已有另議之言 合於本款下註明 美使若以爲難 姑先限年嚴防 則稍可合邦人之望

馬曰 僕俟議約時再行轉告美使 註明此條如何

我曰 甚好

【관련문서】

與副使金宏集筆談
忠曰 客歲執事奉使日本所議通商章程 在津捧讀 周密之至 不勝欽佩
金曰 愧不敢當 何星使黃參贊兩大人近節何如 間已須代復命否
忠曰 何太史現已回國 黃太守調往美國舊金山接任總領事 朝廷現派黎觀察庶
　　 昌持節日本云 前日花房義質入京 道過仁川 曾與深談 微覘其意 於稅則
　　 一事 恐費唇舌
金曰 盛教誠然 花房來敝邦議稅有年 兩言終不相合 極屬憂悶 未知何如可以
　　 妥協
忠曰 中堂在津接閱執事去歲與日本所議稅則 其外務府未能定允 故中堂乘此
　　 次美國來議條約 將稅則概列於內 貴國若及早與美國定約 以示日本 日
　　 本雖狡 斷難始終强項
金曰 伯相大人爲敝邦籌畫周至 萬萬感頌 不可形告
忠曰 美使先至港口 二位後至 按照公法 後至者應先往拜 午後二位前少帶僕
　　 從爲佳 酌隨官員四五位卽可 至有願往彼舶觀看者 他次再往未爲晚也
金曰 謹領敎

二十七日午後兩點半鐘偕同申金二使往美舶晤
薛使與金宏集筆談
忠曰 薛使云 今日初見 非辦事之時 但諸公擇定一日在岸沿帳內 互將全權諭
　　 旨較閱 以便商議
金曰 薛使盛指謹悉 而貴使一行不以敝邦爲嫌 下陸就館 以安主人之心 切望
　　 商辦一事 容當訂日更告
忠曰 薛使云 上岸諸多未便 且打擾君等 心實不安 莫若在岸就近商議 旣免二
　　 公登舟之勞 且於約事有濟也
金曰 薛使執意如此 不敢更欲强請 在主人之心 夫益歉悚不自安也

忠曰 辦事總期兩便 各無所歉 明日本道卽命舟上人上岸搭盖帳房可也
金曰 搭盖帳房本不必煩大人過念 況訂期後再商未晚 明日分付 幸亟止之
忠曰 此事俟本道回舟 再與執事細商
金曰 領敎

四點二刻回威遠船與金宏集筆談.

忠曰　明日搭盖帳房 由僕等自備 並不費事 緣船上帳帆甚多 且水手等習於此事 俟搭成後 再行訂日商酌

金曰　盛敎雖極感悚 毋論由某處搭盖 容俟確訂日期 然後搭成甚妥 不須預期指揮

忠曰　誠是 但執事約於何日方能辦事 美使催促 望速示焉

金曰　美使催促 庶可仰揣 而不得不下船與大官酌商訂定 恐無以在此遽對 幸乞涵宥

忠曰　俟執事回舘與大官商定日期 卽乞示知

金曰　敢不如敎

忠曰　去歲魚允中在津與傅相面談 曾有商請華商前來貴國貿易 以奪倭商之利 現由傅相飭派招商局五人在舟 欲往王京察看商務 不識執事能派人護送前往否 並無卽刻貿之事 惟先行察看商務耳

金曰　承示貴商五人欲往王京之由 未敢遽對 容偕大官面詳轉告政府 待有回音 卽行仰報

忠曰　愈速愈妙 至禱至感

忠又曰 前美使在津與我中堂商議 謂貴國久爲中國屬邦 不若在津與中國定一美朝條約 而當時中堂答以貴國雖爲屬邦 內治外交均得自主 美使終不釋然於心 謂難與貴國平行相待 比美使至此 亦屢屢以此爲言 彼謂法莫若由貴國王寫一照會與彼國國主 內稱貴國雖爲中國屬邦 但立約一事 本可自主云云何如

忠又曰 美使之意 卽將中堂所議第一款之言在約外聲明 若列入約內 則有碍兩國平行之禮 僕自津面辭中堂時 亦諄諄以此爲訓 若由貴國王先備一照會與彼國國主 不必訂封 送與薛使看明 彼立地可立約 平行相待 俟約成畫押後 彼可將照會與條約一幷携回美國呈明國主也

金曰　指教周悉 兼示方便 極用感紉 第此事係寡君處分 不得不偕大臣酌商
　　　即行轉達 奉有裁允 然後可以走告
忠曰　此事旣係貴國王處分 應由公等轉奏定奪 惟此實係決不可少之一着
　　　爲貴國立定地步 歐美各國方不藐○ 且中堂奏派鄙人隨帶兵輪 來此
　　　襄助 曾言明貴國事大素恭 今日各國通商 時局大變 宜允貴國立約通
　　　商 以杜他人之欺挾
金曰　敝邦服事中朝垂三百年 偏荷芘覆之思 此次又蒙爵相勻慈 審度時局
　　　代爲籌畫 期欲立定地步 不受別人欺挾 萬萬感服 僕雖愚昧 豈不仰揣
　　　此至意耶 況兩大人親駛兵輪遠臨 爲敝邦主持 尤切感悚無已
忠曰　傅相爲貴國謀事 視如家事 誠以貴國逼邇強隣 日俄包藏禍心 事變難
　　　測 故屢次郵函以與美國開口爲請者 職是故也 僕等馳輪貴國 從中代
　　　達情好 分所應爲 須言謝 惟此照會之文 須斟酌周至 四面圓到方可
金曰　謹領敎意 訂期一事 不得不俟照會文字稟裁 然後乃可指告
忠曰　試是 但僕爲此事難以措詞 不揣○昧 代擬一稿 請執事一閱
金曰　此稿至荷代擬 不勝感誦 事關重大 僕不敢擅對 惟當共大官面商轉奏
　　　耳

金晚植·馬建忠 회담

金晚植(1882. 5. 16/高宗十九年三月二十九日)

관련문서 馬建忠의 기록

馬曰 僕等駛舶至此 祗緣公事尙未就緒 不克分身馳赴王京 玆承貴國王不棄 遣執事恭賫御帖問好 惶悚曷已 煩執事敬稟貴國王 僕等擬於蕆事後 躬赴貴朝請安

答曰 寡君此訊 只緣虛竚大人之就留江館 致此晼晚矣 鄙人來時 屢有歉仄之敎

馬曰 貴國王御帖 實不敢當 謹具銜束 祈執事賫回奉璧

答曰 謹領敎意

仍曰 此禮之不當行於美使 事體爲然 而美使若或致訝 幸明信其屬邦與友邦之自有等級甚好 不致訝 則不必提說

馬曰 美使深識屬邦友邦之分 必不饒舌 且僕等必不令美使知也

又曰 前承申金二公登舟光顧 幷屢承諸君辱臨 明日擬與丁軍門赴仁川答拜 兼以閒談公事 卽煩回時轉知地方官 爲僕等 明日午初 在浦岸備轎二乘馬八騎

答曰 當趁期等候 俄見大副官 盛說兩大人德意 且言有些病恙 不能踐昨日之約 甚用歎嘆 若聞明日回謝之敎 當欣感無比也

馬曰 全權諭旨 果已下來 而照會文字 那當來到乎 唯祈迅速蕆事 歸帆無 幸甚幸甚

答曰 全權諭旨 似已不來 而照會文字 明再明間可來到耳

【관련문서】

二十九日午後五點鐘威遠舟次與承政院副承旨金晚植筆談

忠曰 僕等駛輪至此 祗緣公事尙未就緒 不克分身馳赴王京 心正歉然 乃承貴國王謙抑先施 遣執事恭賫束帖問訊 愧汗無已 煩執事回奏貴國王 僕等

擬待約事畢後 躬赴王京請安

金曰 謹領敎 回朝轉奏明

忠曰 諸費淸神 先明謝悃

金曰 寡君此訊 祗緣虛竚大人之暫留江舘 致此晼晩矣 鄙人來時屢有歉愧之敎

忠曰 貴國王束帖實不敢當 謹具銜柬 祈執事賫回奉璧

金曰 謹領敎意

忠曰 前承申金二使登舟先顧 幷屢承諸君惠臨 明日擬與丁軍門赴仁川答拜 兼以閒談公事 卽煩回時轉知爲禱 幷代請地方官爲僕等明晨在浦岸備轎二乘馬八騎

金曰 當趁期等候 又曰 俄見大副官盛說兩大人德意 且言有病 想不能踐此日之約 甚用愧歉云 若聞明日回謝之敎 想當欣感無比也

忠曰 僕想約內諸款除集米糧出口一節外 無甚更張 美使屢屢催促 不識貴國王全權諭旨何時可頒 照會之文何時可至 本道亦因我中堂四月初旬回藉奔○百日 欲乘中堂未行之先思得一面 先慰中堂眷念貴國之心 故甚欲約事速成也

金曰 大人之歸期甚迴 安得不然 全權諭旨俄已下來 照會之文 明再間當來到矣 不須深念焉 又曰 鄙人允植從弟 厚蒙傅相眷庇之德意 每見書信 輒言傅相忠政 闔門感激 何可形告

忠曰 傅相度待人接物 無分畛域 矧令弟領選使謙恭和協 在僕等亦所心折

金曰 日前專便致書 出於大人勤念 從弟書中專遵此意 故知之而感謝僕僕 又曰 寡君束帖一節 此禮之不當行於美使 軆爲然 而美使若或致訝 大人幸明言其屬邦與友邦之分 有等級 甚好 不致訝 則不必提說

忠曰 美使素知屬邦友邦之分際 必不致訝 且僕等亦詎必令美使知也

165

花房義質(1882. 5. 17) ➡ R. W. Shufeldt

申櫶 · 金弘集 소개

My dear Commodore R.W.S. Shufeldt,

    I have received with the greatest pleasure your note of the 12th inst., and thank you very much for your kind information, and the same time I congratulate you upon your safe arrival in Corea.

    I understand in your letter that you have come to this country with the purpose of negotiating a treaty of amity and commerce between this country and the U.S. Now I beg leave to say that it is only a year since the Corean government has began her improvement and there seem much troubles prevailing among themselves, but in spite of it, the government sent the commissioners to meet you with a full power to negotiate a treaty between the two nations. The chief officer, so empowered is the man who had negotiated and concluded the treaty with Japan and the second officer or the assistant was once an envoy to Japan; so they understand something about the world. I therefore believe that your object of this mission will, no doubt be successful. I was waiting for your arrival there wishing to speak something about our relations with Corea &c, but I had been obliged to enter Saoul without any delay for some urgent business, but I think I can visit you within four or five days.

    I have the honor to be,
    Your obedient servant
    (sgd) Yasimoto Hanabusa

金弘集(1882. 5. 17/高宗十九年四月一日)

金弘集‧馬建忠 회담(2)

관련문서 (1) 馬建忠의 기록
　　　　　(2) 조약문 개정 사항 초록

馬曰 美使屢屢催促 謂全權諭旨一下 卽加記議 今晨特遣其船主來舟 待明日
　　會議 諸公意見何若 且謂照會之文 若貴國王已允 賫呈其國主 後至無妨
我曰 本欲指定日字 專訊趁告 因委員往京城未還 所以遲待至此 可得回音 當
　　卽走報
馬曰 諸公約於何日起義 緣美使今晩專俟准信也
我曰 專等委員之回 大略不出數日
馬曰 會議原是虛文 總是私自商議妥當 一經會面 卽可定議 昨日舟中無事 曾
　　向美使 抄出洋文 細細與漢文校閱 無甚不符之處 間有一二句 微覺參差
　　已由僕將漢洋文更呈 今特携來呈閱
我曰 紹介周至 萬萬感
馬曰 唯約稿第八款 美使堅持 不願去 不識諸君有何卓見 原議稿內 有因有事
　　故之句 嗣後任有何故 卽可由貴國禁止出口 此乃寓禁於不禁之中也
我曰 米穀出洋 蔽土事勢 萬不可議 前已備陳 專望善爲紹介 就原稿內註明
　　今承敎示 殊違所望 此時民命收係 不可不嚴立防禁而後已 所以期欲與
　　中東章程初定時例耳 況仁川一口 日人已有另議之言 更乞補入言明若
　　何
馬曰 美使於米粮一節 似已決然不願刪去 而諸公又堅持遏糴之議 僕居間 甚
　　難調停 且所議約稿 甚屬妥善 爲貴國通籌日後取益防損之道 若因米粮
　　一節 以致和議不成 甚爲可惜 我傳相在津 屢以此意告知金允植 其問答
　　筆談 亦已轉寄貴朝矣 諸公亦已詳閱矣
我曰 領選使談艸 姑未及見 但任有何故 由敝國禁止出口之意 可爲防損之道
　　耶 民情事勢誠爲悶瀜
馬曰 若決意照約稿辨理 諸公之意何若 祈以實告
我曰 傳相寄敝大臣函中 有卽使少有更易 而大致不出範圍之敎 窃謂此款補
　　明 不過是少有更易處 且國論民心咸以爲大憂 此僕等所以堅持不撓者
　　也

馬曰 諸公於第八款擬改之處 可示知否

我曰 第八款一禮遵辦下 惟仁川口不許出米一句補明 則稍可答朝野之望 馬使卽於約稿本款添書云 仁川一口 米糧一槪不准運出

我曰 如此補明 萬萬感幸

馬曰 僕回舟後 當與美使言明 或可允議

我曰 荷此周全 只得誦

馬曰 設或美使仍有執拗之處 僕想 第八款可改爲朝鮮米糧向禁出口 今玆立約 美國商民於叫運米糧一節 當遵已開口岸章程辦理 如此 若貴國與日人約仁川不准運出米糧 則美商自宜照辦矣

我曰 所教切當

馬曰 前由李應浚 奉到通商章程 包括在內 不必於約外重言申明

我曰 誠是 所欲補明者 特細章耳 此則少俟通商後再定 無妨否

馬曰 詳細章程 須俟兩國將約批准開口時另行妥議 故十二款尾 有至通商細章程云云

我曰 理會得

馬曰 約稿別款 有何斟酌 尙乞指示

我曰 前呈通商章程中 西教冊子嚴禁懲罰一節 與洋葯幷論 而今此約稿 只擧洋葯一款 西教禁防 不少槪見 何也

馬曰 西教一事 若於約內提明 歐美各邦必致缺裂 古傳相再四籌維 莫若不必言明 而於第十二款內 加應遵條約已載者先行辦理 如立約後 遇有教事 卽可由貴國嚴行止絶 此約內亦不載明准洋人遊入內地 若立約後 遇有外洋教士在內地遊歷 卽可照約懲辦

我曰 指教或然

馬曰 此外尙有何增刪 卽乞指示

我曰 約稿各款 均屬妥善 僕等不識外務 更無可以仰質子 嗣後如有所見 再於立約後徐議恐妥

馬曰 約事一立 無可再議 當趁未立之先 與僕商約 以便與美使辦議也

我曰 一依原稿協定無妨

馬曰 第八款 僕當與之力辨 以冀其成 所有原稿改易較對處 卽乞貴處改訂

我曰 當於敝處所存原稿 逐款改正 第八款釐改 旣承明教 當奉若金石矣

馬曰 承教謂約稿均屬妥善 則改日一經會商 諒可指定畫押之日矣

我曰 俟委員會 卽當躬指承誨 仍須面定畫押之日

馬曰 畫押之日 總須與美使會商後 方可訂期 委員明日果能回來否
我曰 委員俟於數日回來
馬曰 昨承貴國王遣副承旨官齎帖來舟 僕等汗顏曷已 應俟事蕆 躬詣貴朝請安 乞先容焉
我曰 昨於承旨回 業聞大敎 承旨復命 自當轉奏
馬曰 招商局委員五人 欲往王京 察看商務 不日內 想有確示
我曰 此事李應浚回 始可指告
馬曰 諸公等宜於約前官銜商量妥當 以便塡寫 又漢洋文各三分 三分畫押 各攜其一 其未畫押批 俟兩國批准盖印 頃與美使商定 彼繕洋文三分 諸公飭繕華文三分
我曰 官銜謹當妥定更告 華文三分亦當依敎飭繕 而第洋文一分 須令以華文註明 以爲憑據 甚幸
馬曰 洋文卽係注明 華文 其較對之役 僕當庖也
我曰 甚感甚悚
又曰 我國從來不通西洋 而今此英國人隨伴兩大人而來 雖不得牢拒 殊涉未安
馬曰 此是葛雷森 現住北洋水師總敎習天津副稅司 是中國所雇 旣爲中國所用 亦華人而已

【관련문서 1】

四月初一日午初赴仁川答拜申金二使與金宏集筆談
忠曰 與諸君別三日 渴念之至 想皆佳勝
金曰 冒淋无顧 不勝悚皇 僕等托芘無恙 荷詢感甚
忠曰 古人冒雪訪戴 今僕等冒雨造訪 藉得暢談 快何如之 美使屢屢催促 謂全權諭旨一下 卽可議事 今晨特遣其船主來舟約明日會議 諸公意見何若 且謂照會之文 若貴國王已允 齎呈其國主 卽後至亦屬無妨
金曰 使催促 謹聞命矣 本欲指定日子 專誠趨告 因委員往京城未還 所以遲約至此 如得回音 當卽進拜報知 萬乞寬暇勿罪是幸 至照會文字 委員回當

帶到也
忠曰　諸公約於何日起議　緣美使今晚專俟準信也
金曰　專等委員之回　大約不出數日耳
忠曰　會議原是虛文　總是私自商議妥當　一經會面　即可定議　昨日舟中無事　曾
　　向美使抄出洋文　細細與漢文較閱　無甚不符之處　間有一二句微覺參差
　　已由僕將漢洋文更正　今特攜來呈閱
金曰　紹介周至　萬萬感紉
忠曰　約稿第八款美使堅持不願刪去　不識諸君有何卓見　原議稿內有因有事故
　　之句　嗣後任有何故　即可由貴國禁止出口　此乃寓禁於不禁之中也
金曰　米穀一事　敝土事勢萬不可議出洋　前已備陳　冀幸善爲紹介　雖原稿內注
　　明　今承敎示　殊違所望　敝邦全昧商務權操自我之理　目下雖立嚴防　尙慮
　　有潛輸之弊　所以期欲如中東堂章程初定時例耳　況仁川一口　日人已有
　　另議之言　更乞補注言明若何
忠曰　美使於米糧一節　似已決然不願刪去　而諸公又堅持遲耀之議　僕居聞甚
　　難調停　且所議約稿甚屬妥善　爲貴國通籌日後取益防損之道　若因米糧
　　一節　以致和議不成　甚爲可惜　我傅相在津　屢以此意告知　金允植其問答
　　筆談　業已轉寄貴朝　想諸君亦已詳閱之矣
金曰　提敎懇至　還切悚恧　領選使談草　僕等姑未及見　但任有何故　由敝國禁止
　　出口之意　可爲防損之道耶　民情事勢　則裁爲門隘
忠曰　美使若決意照約稿辦理　諸公之意何若　祈以實告
金曰　傅相寄敝大臣函中有雖少有更易　大致不出此範圍之敎　竊謂此款注明不
　　過是少有更易　敢爾屢煩以敝處事言之　國論民心　咸以此爲憂　僕等辦事
　　安得不辨論如此
忠曰　諸公於第八款擬改之處　可示知否
金曰　所敎至此　誠爲幸甚　第八款一體遵辦下　惟仁川口不許出未一句注明　則
　　稍可答朝野之望　如此補明於正約內　萬歲幸不知爲謝
忠曰　僕回舟後　當與美使言明　或可允議
金曰　荷此周全　只得攢誦閣下德意而已
忠曰　設或美使仍有執拗之處　僕想第八款可改爲朝鮮米糧向禁出口　今玆立約
　　美國商民於販運米糧一節　當遵已開口岸章程辦理　如此若貴國與日人約
　　仁川不准運出米糧　則美商自宜照辦矣
金曰　所敎切當　四面圓到

忠曰 約稿於第八款外尙有何增刪 卽乞詳示
金曰 俟進菲膳後再告

午飯畢與金宏集續談
忠曰 前由李應浚奉到通商章程二本 在津時業捧讀一過 約稿業將章程包括在內 不必於約外重言申明
金曰 誠是 誠是 所欲補明者特細章耳 此則少俟彼此商民來往時再定 可無妨否 惟大敎是仰
忠曰 詳細章程須俟兩國將約批准開口時另行妥議 故十二款尾有至通商詳細章程云云
金曰 理會得
忠曰 約稿別款有何斟酌 尙乞指敎
金曰 前呈通商章程中 西敎冊子嚴禁懲罰一節與洋藥並論 而今此約稿只擧洋藥一款 西敎禁防不少槪見 何故 敢乞確敎
忠曰 西敎一事 若於約內提明 歐美各邦必致決裂 故傅相再四籌維 莫若不必言明 而於第十二款內加應遵條約已載者先行辦理 如立約後遇有敎事 卽可由貴國嚴行止絶 且約內亦不載明准洋人遊入內地 若立約後遇有外洋敎士在內地遊歷 卽可照約懲辦
金曰 指敎明暢 欽服 欽服
又曰 約稿各款均屬妥善 僕等不諳外務 更無可以仰質者 嗣後如有所見 再於立約後徐議恐妥
忠曰 約事一立 無可再議 當於未立之先與僕商酌 以便與美使辯議也
金曰 實無更商 惟一依原稿協定 伏企 伏企
忠曰 第八款僕當與之力辯 以冀其成 所有原稿改易數處 卽乞貴處改訂
金曰 謹當依敎 將敝處所存原稿逐款改正 第八款厘改旣承明敎 當奉若金石矣
忠曰 承敎謂約稿均屬妥善 則改日一經會商 諒可指定畫押之日矣
金曰 謹聞命矣 俟委員回 卽當躬詣承誨 仍須面定畫押之日耳
忠曰 畫押之日 總須與美使會商後方可訂期 委員明日可能回來否
金曰 委員似於數日回來 姑難指的仰告 更乞少寬
忠曰 昨承貴國王遣副承旨官賚東帖來舟 僕等汗顔曷已 應俟事歲 躬詣王京請安 乞先容焉

金曰 昨於承旨回 業承大敎 想伊復命 自當轉奏耳
忠曰 招商局員五人欲往王京察看商務 不日內想有確示
金曰 此事李應浚回 始可指告
又曰 葛君英人 然英國從來未曾相通 今因兩大人隨伴 不得不合席 而終於無外交之義 實爲欠處
忠曰 葛敎習旣爲中國所同 亦華人而已

【관련문서 2】

條約改正草
惠顧下常民 改以彼此人民 此行則頭辭
第一款刪去 第二款陞爲第一款 餘倣此
第一款 並其下商民 改以人民
第二款 總領事 改以領事
第四款 折毀 改以搶劫燒毀 渠魁 改以罪犯
第六款 買屋 改以買地 應官商民下 錢産二字添入
第八款 遵辨下 惟仁川一口米粮一槪不準運出十三字添入
　　　　頭部筆話此一款 惠指美商在貴國而言 較原文稍覺體面
第十四款 朝鮮二字 改以大朝鮮國主五字 惟於優待地國利益 係出於甘讓 立有惠條 改以惟此種優待地國利益 若立有惠條 彼此須照酬報瓦訂之惠條 改以美國官民必將五訂酬報之惠條 方準同霑下 惠條二字抹去 跋尾 同在朝鮮下 仁川府三字添入 一年而期在朝鮮下 付樣指定何處四字

丁汝昌(1882. 5. 17/高宗十九年四月一日) ➡ 申櫶, 金弘集

Shufeldt와 미곡수출 교섭결과 통보

敬啓者 日間暢聆塵敎 兼擾鯖廚 醉酒飽德 感謝曷已 米粮出口一事 承囑於薛
使處代爲轉圜 歸途順至美舶 與之轉輾商略 雖未峻絶 亦未明允 揣其意 似以
貴國全權諭旨與自主照會均尙未至 故不肯遽定可否 顧薛使迫欲歸國 亟思約
事早蕆 便可鼓輪而去 倘能於一二日內 將諭旨照會一倂賷至 再由鄙人從中
關說 彼內迫於速成之心 外屈於媚商之誼 或可勉如所議 希執事亟派妥員 歸
告貴國王及政府諸公 毋以濡滯坐失事機也 專泐奉佈 敬頌勛祺

　　　　　四月朔日燈下　　　　名正肅

申櫶·金弘集(1882. 5. 18/高宗十九年四月二日) ➜ 馬建忠

전권위임장, 조회문 도착 통보

관련문서 전권위임장(1882. 5. 15)

敬覆者 昨蒙賜貢 暢聆大誨 經宿充然 愈挹度芬 匪意專价奉到尊函 敬諗體氣佳裕 慰玆不忱 承詢全權字據照會備文等件 今早委員李應峻賫來 刻當馳詣面告 諒必關聽也 率泐不莊 統祺勻鑒

　　　　四月三日午刻　　申金 同頓啓
　　　　　附請丁大人長安

【관련문서】

全權諭旨

光緖八年三月三十八日 統理機務衙門奉諭 着申櫶爲全權大官 金宏集爲全權副官 前往仁川 與美國全權大臣 妥議和好通商條約 欽哉

金弘集(1882. 5. 19/高宗十九年四月三日)

金弘集·馬建忠 회담(3)

관련문서 馬建忠의 기록

馬曰 前晚薛使 將米粮一節 與之力爭再四 彼縱未嘗明允 若今晚見諭旨照會 二文 諒可允准

我曰 深感閣下至意

馬曰 今晨美使復遣其船主來晤 欲請明日會面時 美使尚有國書一通呈遞 未經拆封繙譯漢文 貴國王接其國書 亦宜預爲商覆 議約書出自美國 故以國書先施 美使至今遲遲未呈者 專爲諭旨照會之事耳

我曰 訂期一事 多荷提示 美國國書 未曾慮到 漢文譯本 旣未及見 且呈遞之際 儀節極爲難便 不可不奏達朝廷

馬曰 明日會面 不過略商 至畫押日期 可緩數日 明日僕可約美使於午後二點鍾 至仁川一晤 國書不過通示聘問之意 幷不提及公事 呈遞儀節 毫無不過[可]由美使親手遞與執事 托專弁送至王京賫呈 而執事手受 不必行禮

我曰 領敎 約事一定 繕寫冊子 從此事已藏矣

馬曰 繕寫冊子 不過一二日 卽可藏事 初六初七皆可 明日與美使會面 須將全權諭旨互相較閱外 錄一紙互換存案 故全權諭旨 君等先攜回館 照錄一紙 以便明日交與美使收存 彼已備文 明日亦面交 至照會之文 僕將攜往 以示美使 然後暫存僕處 俟押約日 再行送交 以昭愼重

我曰 謹遵命也

【관련문서】

初三日未刻金宏集來威遠舟次筆談

忠曰 和約上執事官銜如何塡寫

金曰 經理總理機務衙門事全權大官某 全權副官某 金又曰 敢問和約上寫君

主乎 抑寫國主

忠曰 君主國主意義相同 惟英國條約稱君主 依大利國亦稱君主 美國文書來往則稱國主

金曰 鈐用印章 則不必畫押耶

忠曰 押在本名之下 印在年號之上

金曰 若用畫押 寫姓不寫名乎

忠曰 官銜姓名都要寫明 又曰 前晚見薛使 當將米糧一節 與之力爭再四 彼縱未曾明允 若今晚見諭旨照會二件 諒可允准 惟原文仁川一口米粮一概不准運出 語氣含糊 僕謬加已問與各色等字 較爲穩妥

金曰 深感閣下至意

忠曰 今晨美使時遣其船主來晤 謂昨接花房公使來函 內稱不日回舟細談一切事務 美使懼有擾越 欲請明日會面 面訂畫押日期 乘日使未來之先 及早定計 且明日會面時 美使尚有國書一通呈遞 未行拆封繙譯漢文 貴國王接其國書 亦宜預爲商復 議約出自美國 故以國書先施 美使至今遲遲未呈者 專爲諭旨照會之事耳

金曰 訂期一事 多荷提示 感服 感服 但明日甚促 不可不歸與大官商酌 酌更告美國國書未曾慮到漢文譯本 旣未及見 且呈遞之際 儀節極爲難處 此是剏有不諳各國之例故耳 不可不走達朝廷也

忠曰 明日會面不過略商 至畫押日期可緩數日 明僕可約美使於午後二點鐘至仁川一晤 國書不過通好聘問之意 並不提及公事 呈遞儀節毫無 不過由美使親乎遞與執事 託專舟送至王京賫呈 而執事手受 不必行禮

金曰 多謝 多謝 更乞祕之 祕之

又曰 約事一定 繕寫冊頁 從此事已藏矣 設於畫押 花使突至 想不至多生枝節

忠曰 若乘日使未至之先畫押 則更妙矣 好在繕寫約冊不過二日即可藏事 初六初七皆可

金曰 指敎切當 切當 今日此話萬乞勿漏

忠曰 遵敎 約款卽於畫押後亦不可今日使知之 須俟換約後方可宣示

金曰 謹當銘心 但日使住京 耳目甚多 又極點 甚是關慮

忠曰 若公等同僚中無人漏洩 日使絕無他處可以通消息也 因日使若知 或由彼國政府函知其駐美公使從中挑唆 致美國不能批准來換 甚無謂也

金曰 此事極未易 甚悶 甚悶 僕等何敢漏洩 然只是未敢明言終秘 因國人不諳此等關係故耳

忠曰 此事僕言之鄭重者 亦未兩綢繆之意耳
金曰 領敎
忠曰 明日與美使會面 須將全權諭旨互相較閱外 錄一紙 互換存案 故全權諭旨君等先携回館照錄一紙 以便明日交與美使收存 彼已備文 明日亦面交也 至照會之文 僕將携往 以示美使 然後暫存僕處 俟押約日再行送交 以昭愼重
金曰 謹遵命也

金弘集, 馬建忠(1882. 5. 20/高宗十九年四月四日)

金弘集・馬建忠 회담(4)

관련문서 馬建忠의 기록

馬曰 僕昨持照會文往美舶 與薛使商酌 美使始釋然無疑 而米粮一節 力辯再三 始能照議 今彼來館 一以答二公之拜 一以示全權字據 不識諸公可將全權諭旨 另錄一分否

我曰 美使商酌 多蒙閣下周旋 米粮一節 亦已照議 不勝感幸 全權諭旨 已錄存一分矣 條約冊子 亦已連夜飾繕三分 特來將就 未識閣下一鑑 轉示美使 仍行鈐印畫押若何

馬曰 美使此來 不過初次商議 如尊處條約冊子已就 卽約初六日十點鍾 在浦涯畫押甚妙 冊子不必裝訂 惟日後換約冊子出自貴國王批訂 當稍爲裝潢耳

我曰 領敎

馬曰 美使全權字據 想臻妥善 卽乞諸公收下 以爲左證

仍曰 此國書封訂 幷無附譯漢文 僕意此書由公等先行開坼 僕可代譯 收下代坼 今晚差專弁呈王京 可卽擬答 必趁畫押日 交與美使持去 甚好甚好

我曰 謹當遵敎 答書 惟在敝朝廷處分

馬曰 答書不過申明通好之意 無須斟酌

我曰 美國書純用洋文 此係約前 故不得不受 此後必用華文乃可

馬曰 此係國書 非平等文牘可比

我曰 敝國無解洋文者故也

馬曰 日後通商 自宜附以漢文

仍曰 傳相咨文 尙有請貴國王將條約照會等稿咨行禮部與北洋大臣之語 玆請作速繕就 專人偕僕等 一幷賫回爲幸

我曰 謹當轉奏也

【관련문서】

初四日午後偕薛使往晤申金二使於仁川舘署
忠曰 昨金君登陸後 僕持照會文往美舶與薛使商酌 美使始釋然無疑 而米糧
　　一節 力辯再三 始能照議 今彼來館 一以答二公之拜 一以示全權字據
　　不識諸君可將全權諭旨另錄一分否
金曰 美使商酌 多蒙閣下周旋 米糧一節亦已照議 不勝感幸 全權諭旨已錄存
　　一分矣 條約冊子亦於僕歸後連夜飭繕三分 特未裝潢 未識閣下肯賜一
　　鑒 俟美使至 今席仍行鈐印畫押若何
忠曰 美使此來不過初次商議 如尊處條約冊子已就 卽約初六日晨十點鐘在浦
　　岸畫押甚妙 冊子不必裝訂 惟日後換約冊子 出自貴國王批訂 當稍裝潢
　　耳
金曰 領敎
美使至 各出全權字據互閱
忠曰 美使全權字據悉臻妥善 卽乞諸公收下 以爲左劵
金曰 多謝 日使明日可至 恐生枝節
忠曰 頃已明定初六晨畫押 明日日使縱來 諒無虞也
金曰 領敎
美使呈其國書 忠曰 此國書封訂 並無附譯漢文 僕意此書由公等先行開折 僕
可代譯 然後賫呈貴國王 卽可答復 金宏集因將國書遞忠
忠曰 現留君處 待僕行時携回代譯 尋復細閱洋文
又曰 國書之意與全權字據大約相似

171

R. W. Shufeldt(1882. 5. 20/高宗十九年四月四日) ➡ 申櫶, 金弘集

수호통상 요청 조회문

관련문서 (1) 전권위임장
          (2) 미 대통령 국서

大美國欽命總統水師全權大臣薛 爲照會事 窃照本大臣奉命前來貴國 進呈國書 盖欲永敦友睦 信好通商等情 並奉有國君御筆憑據一通 今飜譯漢文 貴大臣代呈御覽 本大臣在舶恭俟示覆 貴大臣公忠體國 澤專治民 亦必從速爲襄成也 至國書 候畫押後 再行進呈外 爲此照會貴大臣 請煩查照施行 須至照會者
   計移送飜譯漢文諭一道
   右照會
大朝鮮國執政大臣
       中華光緖八年四月初四日　　移

       皮封
大美國欽命總統水師全權大臣　薛 公文移至
大朝鮮國執政大臣衙門　　　　　　　當臺開披
       皮封後面
    內二件
       中華光緖八年陰四月初四日　　　移

【관련문서 1】

   美國全權字據
大亞美理駕合衆國大伯理璽天德阿爾惑 特派水師總統薛斐爾 念爾眞誠信實智慧能幹 命爲全權大臣 卽往朝鮮進呈國書慶賀 並與大朝鮮國主或執政大臣 商立和約 永敦友誼 永遠通商 所定條約賫回本國 紳耆大臣議允 卽批准畫押

此諭

於一千八百八十一年 自主一百六年十一月十五日 在華盛頓都城用寶 著爾執
爲的確憑據

【관련문서 2】

美國主國書 譯漢文

大美國伯理璽天德 致書於大朝鮮國君主 窃惟美國與中華日本和好通商 歷有
年所 今願偕美國與貴君主子民一體和好通商 且祈貴君主永享昇平 茲特遣水
師總兵薛斐爾 前赴貴國 議立一妥善和好通商條約 以冀吾民國人兩[兩國人
民] 益敦友誼 專此特佈 敬頌遐祺

美國國主 阿爾惑 押
時西曆一千八百八十一年十一月十五日 京都華盛頓 發
大朝鮮君主 開坼

172

馬建忠(1882. 5. 20/光緖八年四月四日) ➡ 張樹聲

조선 도착 이후 협상 경과 보고

관련문서 東行日錄

敬稟者 竊忠於去月二十四日因薛使失期不至 恐有事故 擬遣鎭海輪船回至 烟台 沿途探視 並特抵朝鮮後一切情形 縷悉具稟 今就便賫呈 稟甫繕就 而美 舶已至 故未卽發 玆特附呈鈞鑒 仍將二十四日以後情形撮擧大槪 爲憲台陳 之 薛斐爾二十四日入口 次日抵港 二十六日彼此往拜 談及約內第一條 彼終 謂有碍平行體 且電復未至 斷難擅允 詢以何天爵在京所譯第一條洋文 則謂 未經携來 亦並不知所譯是何言語 詞意之間 甚爲決絶 若必欲以此條列入約 中 將至以堅持廢事 不得已議令朝鮮國王另備照會一通 聲明爲中國屬邦 則 於我旣存藩服之名 於彼亦無碍平行之體 薛使謂曩在烟台答中堂書時 曾允聽 朝鮮設法聲明 今旣不列入約中 則亦無所不可 忠因思此項照會須令寫明係於 未經五約之前先行聲明 則美國於此條雖不允列於條約之內 而已許申明於立 約之先 似卽與認明朝鮮爲我屬邦無異 惟朝鮮自受日人蠱惑 雖未敢箕踞向 漢 而亦不無狡展之心 自二十二日回舟 小示決裂 始知中朝人士不容狎玩 由 是景遂諸人及後之來自王京者 皆益形恭謹 而國王遂遣承旨官賫名東來拜 桀 黠之氣固已非復前日 玆若臨以大義 令其將中國屬邦一節遵照聲明 以理勢揆 之 似不敢或有違悖 然萬一中於簧鼓 稍涉支吾 則日美二舶 瞻視非遙 深恐於 國體有碍 爰欲稍參權變之術 以駕駛之 於二十七日其所派議約大官申櫶副官 金宏集登舟來謁時 先令站隊聲砲 以張吾威 復傳諭陪臣某某代國王行三跪九 叩禮 恭請皇太后皇上聖安 以折其氣 然後以筆談所載諸言 從容誘掖 使之樂 就大範圍 已乃爲代擬照會一稿 寬假以自主之名 實申明其屬邦之義 金宏集 等閱之 乃皆欣然願從 卽於次日命李應浚賫回王京 請國王照稿繕用 繼復議 及他款 大都無甚出入 惟米糧出口一條 申櫶金宏集等謂於其國朝議民情有碍 堅欲議禁 而薛使則堅不允禁 相持屢日 金宏集乃議改註惟仁川口不准出米一 句 忠與美使重加商略 擬更改爲惟於仁川已開一口 各色米糧槪行禁止運出 較爲周密 美使迫欲歸國 亟思約事早蕆 復經忠反復開陳 彼內迫於速成之心 外屈於婉商之誼 亦遂勉强允行 初二日李應浚歸自王京 初三日將照會送來 照稿繕寫 一字未易 擬暫存忠處 俟定約時交薛使 與國書條約一並賫回 頃偕 薛孚爾同至仁川 已與申櫶金宏集將全權字據互相交換 卽訂於初六日會集畫

押 忠於蔵事後赴王京一行 答其國王賞帖之拜 初十內外當可起椗回津矣 玆
恐仰縈憲慮 特遣鎭海先歸 謹將二十四日以來辦理情形 專肅具稟 恭叩爵綏
伏維崇鑒 職道馬建忠謹稟

四月初四日
附呈日記筆談各一冊

【관련문서】

東行日錄
光緒八年壬午春三月 我東方屬土朝鮮國始與阿美利加合衆國立約通商 其國
之政府亦不諳外交條例 願得中國大員主持壇坫 於是合肥傅相請朝廷以建
忠行 北洋水師統領丁禹亭因巡洋之役 率兵船三艘 曰威遠、曰揚威、曰鎭
海、以偕 將先至烟台 會同美國議約全權大臣薛孚爾駛赴朝鮮 襄助議約事宜
十四日自析津起程 十六日乘潮致輪出口 是日潮漲丈有三尺 嚮夕風平
十七日晨微霧 緩輪行 十二點舟抵烟台 美國兵船名汕島者 在口內望望見水
師提督旗幟 站舷申敬 入口後渡至威遠兵舶 俄而汕島船主哥貝來謁 云薛使
滬游未返 卽夕當可至 又云英國水師提督頃赴析津 間亦將迎威妥瑪往朝鮮議
約 而水師總敎習葛雷森來 亦述新報內載有英法德三國調集兵艦 將赴朝鮮議
約 而日人亦以兵船直指漢江之語 無何哥貝辭去 復有四人來見 詢知爲招商
局及附舶東渡者 告以行期旣定 令鎭海管駕官知會登舟
十八日凌長報薛孚爾已至 卽專弁賫傅相書函去 附以洋文一緘 訂相見期 隨
偕丁軍門登岸拜東海開道方佑民觀察 歸途遇寄船主謂薛使候於寓 與禹亭改
道往訪 促談良久 薛使謂在烟台宜捐棄往拜升砲繁文 以免譁屬 且頃聞英法
德日四國威將調集兵艦□至朝鮮 果爾則定議遂難 宜乘問先期駛往 遂訂中國
兵舶於二十日辰刻起椗 美國兵舶於二十一日辰刻起椗 陸續進發 順約貝船主
午後在汕島船會議入漢江口停泊處所 俾先後來集 於是三點鐘偕丁軍門往晤
哥貝於具船 與披國指定於漢江口虎島旁下椗 盖遇此則水淺溜急 輪舟不能停
泊矣 虎島屬朝鮮京畿道仁川府治 去王京五十餘里 回舟繕稟上傅相 報起程

日期

十九日五點二刻起椗東渡 首威遠 次揚威 次鎭海 各舟相距八百碼 魚貫而進 速率每小時行八邁半 前舟晝於橫檣懸速率表 夜綴燈以屬後舟耳目 諸習流軍將往觀東瀛風景 令下之後 理索試器 莫不躍躍從事云

二十日晨五點二刻起椗東駛 風平浪淨如拭 九點二刻遇劉公島 一點鐘薄成山岬 自此迤東偏南太半度行 直指漢江口仙俠島外之小島 距水程一百七十邁 先是海道往朝鮮無入漢江口者 隋書開皇十八年伐高麗 以一軍自東萊泛海趨平壤城 唐書貞觀十七年 上親征高麗 以張亮爲平壤道行軍大總管 帥戰艦自萊州泛海趨平壤 平壤箕子故都 漢書稱王險城 今屬平安道 據大同江上流 其皆進大同江無疑 宋徐明叔宣和奉使圖經云 由定海乘南風北行五日程 可歷大靑島 入急水門 則亦由大同江進 又唐書永徽五年 命蘇定方爲神丘道行軍大總管 帥師伐百濟 定方引軍自成山濟海 百濟據熊津江口以拒定方 進擊破之 熊津在今忠淸道公州下流 由成川入海 則自成川口進 而以一帆東渡 直指漢江 記載以來都所未有 蓋其口外島嶼碁布 水淺湍急 沙線無常處 巨艑至此 率以觸礁擱淺爲懼 故往時泛海者至大靑島成山岬二處 皆分迤南北而去 同治中有法國水師提督某駛往測驗繪圖極審 爲海舶指南 於是始稍稍有知漢江口者 國朝魏默深聖武記謂熊津江卽漢江 係屬舛午 熊津與漢江相距遠甚 良以從前地圖簡略 經緯不明 故雖通材 亦不能無誤歟

二十一日晨四點鐘舟指仙俠島 微霧 島靄沒不可辨 緩輪繞行 有輪舟自南來 望其旗幟 如爲日本兵舶 有頃 霧歛微而 五點二刻 遇仙俠島外小島 八點鐘過仙俠島 島四合 如行江中 水淡靑色 溜急 溯流而上 日本兵舶以道熟先駛 相距十邁 十二點三刻 過立岐島傍小貓島 折而北 右掠小阜島 左□燕興島 已復迤東兼北行 鐘報三點 望見日本兵舶已於虎島旁下椗 四點鐘我舟相繼至 下椗與日舶隣 其副管駕剌艉板來 與我舟管駕官相慰勞 兼詢東來故 亦遣大副剌艉板答言 日舶名磐城 自內海口下開 載駐紮朝鮮公使花房義質來 逢中行十日程 道泊釜山巨文島各數日 其舶大與鎭海埒 俄而小艇二隻自山隙出 張蒲帆駛赴鎭海 以逮鏡窺之 見有烏帽藍袍僑舫而立者 則朝鮮四品鴻臚李應浚也 應浚曾以議約事至沂津 本月初先以鎭海送至鴨綠江口歸國者 故識之 鎭海管駕官旋以舢板送之來 則與偕者 又言三品鴻臚韓文奎 五品鴻臚高永周登舟寒喧畢 筆談數則固以登岸爲請 云其國王已令於仁川埽除行館 並派二品參判趙準永爲伴接官 明晨當來晉謁 薄暮應浚等辭去 丁軍門傳令三舶 仍蒸汽以待

二十二日十點鐘 李應浚諸人與趙準永先後至 準永以登岸請 余以美使未來 而朝鮮議約大員亦未派至 適館 無所事事 則固辭 準永等固請 乃允於午後二點鐘登岸 留準永等同飯舟中 飯畢 準永謂往者遊日本 識日使花房義質 請往訪於其舟次 卽命以舢板送之去 約令二點鐘回威遠同行 李應浚別偕諸人往揚威觀看機器 鐘報二點二刻 應浚等歸自揚威 準永猶未返 余與李應浚等別乘舢板先行 中流見準永自日本兵舶下 花房義質亦刺舢板至威遠來見丁軍門與余云 三點鐘抵埠 仁川府使武二品鄭志鎔迎謁道左 並以肩輿來迓 輿如車箱狀 跌坐其中 四人昇之行 導以靑旗皁蓋 輿隸呵殿 漫聲長謳 前後互答 迤邐循山麓行 景色明秀 如在江南道中 村人扶老携幼來觀者以數百計 越嶺者三約十五里許 見兩山廻抱中嵌茅屋數十家 如一村落 問之 卽仁川府也 仁川無城郭 官廨在東山之麓 正對文岳 今卽以爲賓館 入館 則屋宇傾圮 堂皇側有小室三四間 備余輩棲息之所 室簇比如蜂房 地薦蒲蓆 壁障紙屛 無几案牀榻 給事者先於門外解履乃入 其俗略似日本 而簡陋特甚

二十三日 侵曉 陸倫華回舟 李應浚辭回王京 催派議約大員 趙準永等相繼束問訊 因與之筆談 將乘間覘其朝議 準永等獪甚 凡所問有稍涉政府者 答語皆諉爲不知 因告以傅相奏請大皇帝派員來此 實爲調護屬邦起見 分宜推誠相待 安用是模棱爲 準永等咸悚慴謝過 午後與高永周筆談 諮其政治風土 與夫古蹟之沿革 遂留之晩膳 膳畢 而朝鮮國王遣二品參事堂備官金景遂來 云已派定經理機務事申櫶爲議約大員 越日當馳至 景遂年六十餘 外若恭謹 而與之筆談 詞令間頗涉諷刺 知其不免有輕量之心 遂欲以操縱之術制之 因責其應對失禮 立傳伴接官 飭質明備輿馬回舟 漏三下而準永等獪來固留

二十四日 晨起 金趙諸人復來固留 峻詞謝之 丁軍門先行 余方將登輿 而日使花房義質策馬往王京 道仁川 適館請見 與語良久 別詳問答 語畢出館 各分道行 至舟而美舶仍未至 雖達晨霧塞 而後期至三日 恐別有事故 爰與丁軍門商定 明晨遣鎭海返棹烟台 沿途探視 因以一稟上傅相 令就便賫回 稟甫繕就 報見美國兵舶入口 時已晩七點鐘矣 登舵樓以達鏡窺之 則於口門下碇 相距猶三十里

二十五日 霧 美舶未起碇 十點鐘丁軍門邀赴揚威閱操 午後二點鐘美舶駛至傍威遠旁下碇 金景遂李應浚等亦來威遠 遂歸自揚威 而我舟管駕官呂翰適自美船回 詢知美舶在口外阻霧 停四十八點鐘 故失期 薛使致聲謂 明日十點鐘來答烟台之拜 景遂等尋入見 稱申櫶今夕乃至 詞氣謙抑 非復前日 數語後 李應浚攝衣請問 遂引入別室 應浚謂昨歸王京 聞政府議論歧出 興寅君李最應

頗非外交 金景遂卽附之阻撓新政者也 因與筆談數則而出 應浚等請往款接薛使 適美船船主來答呂翰之問 稱薛使兩日內不理公務 乃轉語景遂諸人 五點鐘辭去

二十六日九點鐘 美舶船主哥貝來拜 十點鐘薛使來拜 寒喧畢 薛使謂其全權字據已譯出 並繕就公文一通 擬咨行朝鮮機務總理衙門 顧以匆促就道 未携繙譯 僅帶有烟台領事所雇之華人文案 不審華洋文果相符否 擬乞代爲一閱 余允以午後四點鐘報謁時順爲勘對 薛使辭去 余與丁軍門議 翌夕七點鐘邀薛使暨美日二船主晚膳 旋膳發洋文請單 薛使辭以疾 謂弗克夜出赴宴 二船主答書如約 三點鐘趙準永率李應浚諸人 持其大官經理機務事申櫶 副官經理機務事金宏集 與從事官機務副主事徐相雨三刺來問訊 訂明日十點鐘登舟晉謁大官意卽大臣之謂 下國陪臣不敢稱大臣 降而稱官 禮也 未幾鐘報四點 遂往美船答薛使拜 渠永等留待舟中 薛使出國書與全權字據華洋文各一通 較閱無誤 薛使商於余謂 條約未定 不便遽遞國書 擬先以公文咨朝鮮政府 國書俟約定後再呈 何如 余謂國書呈遞先後 無關輕重 第先將全權字據咨行朝鮮政府 便可會議 薛使因問朝鮮正副二使是否全權 余謂其國王旣特派議約 諒無不予全權 且我中堂所議約稿內寫明全權字據 彼政府恪遵所議 非有窒碍 亦不敢擅行增損焉 旋辭回舟 復與準永等筆談 論及全權事 李應浚復請往別室 求代擬全權諭旨一稿攜去

二十七日九點鐘 丁軍門邀同點名 九點二刻薛使來商請議約時在近岸支立帳房 不必往仁川行館 並問朝鮮正副二使登舟 升炮與否 余謂近岸議約 免涉跋省供億 計誠兩得 少頃當與申金二使言之 升炮則按中國禮用三響焉 十點鐘趙李諸人先至 十一點二刻申金二使率徐相雨 及申櫶之子奭熙孫德均登舟 命舟師站隊以迎 升炮三響後 令通詞傳語陪臣某某入艙 先行三跪九叩禮 代國王恭請皇太后皇上聖安 然後行賓主相見之禮 於是余偕丁軍門在艙屛立兩旁 俟櫶宏集行跪叩禮畢 乃與相見 送茶後 余偕丁軍門立問其國王安 櫶宏集立問中堂安 周旋之間 頗極整肅 蓋自二十三日回舟小示決裂 彼始知中朝士大夫不可狎玩 嗣是景遂諸人及凡來自王京者 罔敢稍有䙝越 而兩使臣則入倔僂益恭云 就坐寒暄數語 遂留飯舟中 飲間與金宏集筆談甚長 申櫶卽光緒初與日本議約者 年七旬餘 雖步履甚蹇 而風度仍復端凝 金宏集年邁四十 望之似三旬許人 與之談 通達識時務 往與日本議加稅則 章程周密 是其所定 蓋國中矯矯者 飯畢偕赴美舶拜薛使 薛使待之禮有加焉 已而周視炮位 駭嘆無已 四點鐘回舟 申櫶請先歸 余復與金宏集筆談良久 六點鐘始以小輪船送之去 七

點二刻美日二船主來赴宴 盡懽而散

二十八日午後四點鐘 仁川府使鄭志鎔以牛一頭豕二肩曁雞魚等物 致饋美舶 遣通詞登舟請示 且言李應浚復往王京面陳機務 中國派員至此主持壇坫 凡有交際 罔弗來告 亦恭順之一端也 初志鎔亦數以禮來饋 余與丁軍門皆斐辭却之 一無所受 以體國家優岫藩服之意

二十九日晚五點鐘 國王遣承政院右副承旨金晩植賫名東來勞問 東貯匣內 襲以紅綾 跪而進獻 余長揖受之 啓視 則於右側下方書朝鮮國王李㷩六字 細若蠅頭 起坐筆談數則 囑其歸告國王 謂於蔵事後躬詣王京晉謁 希先容焉 與丁軍門各附銜帖 璧束 曉植復跪而受之 因順令轉囑仁川府使 明日備輿馬至浦岸伺候 將與丁軍門往行館答拜申金諸君

四月初一日 雨 美舶船主哥貝將薛使命來催訂議約日期 十點鐘促具膳 膳後偕丁軍門登岸至仁川 入館與申金諸君相見畢 就坐 筆談良久 二點鐘進食 食時接談 胥金宏集主筆 率以米穀出口於朝議民情有碍 須設法議禁爲請 余答以見薛使時當相機爭之 四點二刻辭歸 復往美舶 以米穀出口一條與薛使往復辯論 七點鐘回舟作書 以所議告申金兩君

初二日曉晴 專弁往仁川致書 一點二刻李應浚持申金二君復函來云 歸自王京所需文件摒擋完好 明日金宏集當來舟商略壹是 招商局五人已言於朝 卽飭人護送至王京 察看商務 訂後日起行 且爲其國王致願見之忱 請余與丁軍門蔵事後赴王京一遊 云已令館人除室以待 三點鐘後應浚辭去 薛使在汕島船望見朝鮮人來 隨遣隨員至我舟詢議約日期 答以俟明日金宏集來舟議定再告

初三日二點鐘 金宏集率徐相雨李應浚來舟 坐定 金宏集出交王京文件 復以約事與余往復商略 語載筆談 四點鐘辭去 是夕余以約事粗定 至朝鮮且十餘日 尙無一字抵津 恐傅相垂注 因與丁軍門議令鎭海兵船於初五日賫稟先歸

初四日 晨起 申金二使令李應浚來 以國王命璧還銜束 幷致我兵舶各牛一頭豕十蹄 雞子二百枚 白粢五石 以犒勞軍士 故受之 十二點鐘薛使赴仁川行館答申金二使之拜 卽互換全權字據 邀與同行 遂登岸偕至仁川行館 相見畢 申金二使出全權字據 與薛使互相較閱 遂訂於初六日支立帳房在近岸 會集畫押 四點鐘美使先歸 余獨留與金宏集筆談 乃返回舟繕稟上傅相 並附以筆談日記二冊 交鎮海管駕官陸倫華 令遲明五點鐘起椗 賫至烟台後 沿途探投

173

R. W. Shufeldt (1882. 5. 20) ➡ C. Holcombe

조인 일자 통보

#12
U.S.S. Swatara
At Anchor Salie River
Off Yin Chuen, Corea

Hon. Chester Holcombe,
Charge d'Affairs, U.S. Legation
Peking, China

Sir,

By reference to my letter of the 6th instant you will be aware of my intended departure for Corea, and now have the honor to inform you that the ship anchored in the Salie river on the 11th inst., and that on the morning of the 14th I received a visit from the commissioners appointed by the King of Corea to negotiate the treaty we have had so long in contemplation.

Today I visited these commissioners at a town five miles in the interior and exchanged credentials with them. On Monday next, the 22nd inst., a final meeting is appointed for the purpose of signing the treaty; in which I do not apprehend any difficulty as both the government and people of Corea have been perfectly friendly.

The Swatara will probably sail on the 24th, but her destination is at present, undetermined. I give you this information, because, as we are so entirely cut off from communication, some apprehensions might be felt about the ship in the event of any lengthened absence.

I am very respectfully
Your obedient servant
(sg'd) R.W. Shufeldt
Commodore U.S.N.

R. W. Shufeldt(?) (1882. 5. 20)

대통령의 신임장 제출 및 조인 일자 확정

#13
May 20th

By invitation of the Royal commissioners appointed by the King of Corea to make a treaty with the United States, Commodore Shufeldt visited their official residence at Yin Chuen, accompanied by Commander Cooper, Lieut. Comdr. Perry and Lieut. Stanton and Paymaster Harris of the Swatara. After the ceremonies incident to the arrival, they royal commissioner presented their power to negotiate, a copy of which in English will be forwarded on a subsequent page.

Commodore Shufeldt then presented the following documents as the evidence of his authority on the part of the President of the United States (in Chinese) to conduct the negotiation. These were accepted by the commissioners who then received from the hands of Commodore Shufeldt a letter from the President of the United States to the King of Corea. It was understood that this letter would be delivered and answered in terms of equality as existing between two sovereign rulers of friendly nations.

Upon the conclusion of this ceremony it was settled that at a joint meeting of the commissioners to be held on shore in view of the ship, on Monday the 22nd instant, the treaty which had previously been perfected was to be sealed, signed and delivered follow:

Great America, United States

Great President Arthur I now send Commodore Shufeldt of the United States Navy with this letter. Greeting: to meet and confer with your honorable nation and your government, and to consult as to signing a treaty of friendship and commerce. Reposing confidence in Commodore Shufeldt's integrity and ability I give him full power of the United States to sign a treaty. This treaty to be transmitted to the United States and the senate to be satisfied. In proof of this I seal it and sign it in Washington, November 15th, 1881, and the one hundred and sixth year of the independence of the United States.

Great America, Imperial Decree of Commodore Shufeldt U.S.N. Special

Envoy with full power.

I enclose a copy in Chinese of a letter to me from the President of the United States authorizing to make a treaty of friendship and commerce and will also send a letter from the President of the United States to his Majesty the King of Chosan, after the treaty is signed.

I will be obliged if you will give them your consideration. I am awaiting your reply on board my ship and hope that you will act justly for your nation in order to accomplish this treaty.

To the Full Power Board of Civil Office of Chosan
With Complements &c.
(sgd) R.W. Shufeldt
Commodore, U.S.N.

申櫶, 金弘集(1882. 5. 22/高宗十九年四月五日) ➜ R. W. Shufeldt

미 대통령 조회문에 대한 회답 조회

관련문서 (1) 申櫶, 金弘集 신임장
　　　　　(2) 속방조회문(屬邦照會文) 초안

朝鮮國總理大臣答照會

大朝鮮國特命總理統機務衙門大臣金爲照覆事 准貴大臣照會稱 本大臣奉命前來貴國 進呈國書等語 本大臣幷奉准貴大臣照會 謹已進徹御覽 奉有回照國書 恭祈貴大臣 代呈貴國君主 竊惟貴大臣殫誠體國 講信修好 立約通商 悉臻妥協 俾我兩國永徵休祥 本大臣不勝忻慰 爲此照覆 須至照會者
　　　　右照會
大美國欽命總統水師全權大臣　　薛
　　　　大朝鮮開國四百九十一年卽中國光緒八年四月初五日

　　外封式
大朝鮮國特命總理總理機務衙門大臣　　金　　　　　公文移至
大美國欽命總統水師全權大臣　　　　　　薛　　　　當臺開坼
　　後面
大朝鮮開國四百九十一年卽光緒八年四月初五日

【관련문서 1】

答國書擬草

大朝鮮國君主 致書於大美國伯理璽天德 竊聞貴國政治公平正直 久欲通好無綠爲歉 今承貴國主先遣大員 來此議約 不穀已派申金與之計議 不日卽可畫押 仍由薛總兵賷回面呈 卽乞速爲批行 派員前來互換 以使吾兩國人民從

此益敦和好 有厚望焉 專此泐覆 敬惟邇祺

大朝鮮國開國四百九十一年卽中國光緖八年四月　日
大美國伯理璽天德　開坼　　　　　　　外封如照會式爲妥 各行各體故也

【관련문서 2】

照會擬稿　爲朝鮮國王代擬照會美國伯理璽天德照會稿

大朝鮮國國主 爲照會事 窃照朝鮮素爲中國屬邦 而內治外交 向來均由大朝
鮮國國主自主 今大朝鮮國大美國 彼此立約 理屬平行相待 大朝鮮國國主明允
將約內各疑 必按自主公例 認眞照辦 至大朝鮮國爲中國屬邦 其分一切應行
各節 均與大美國毫無干涉 除派員議立條約外 相應備文照會 須至照會者
　　右照會
大美國伯理璽天德
大朝鮮國開國[四百九十一]年卽中國光緖八年四　月　日

　　封皮式前面
大朝鮮國國主　|盖寶|　　　　　公文移至　　|盖寶|
大美國伯理璽天德　　當臺開坼
　　後面

大朝鮮|國開國| [四百九十一]年卽光緖八年四　月　日　　　　　　移
　　　|盖寶|

丁汝昌, 馬建忠(1882. 5. 21/光緒八年四月五日) ➜ 申櫶, 金弘集

조약 체결 축하연 초청장

관련문서 축하연 초청에 대한 회신

再書初五日
威堂道園兩位尊兄台右 明日貴國與美國定約通商 從玆彼此邦交固於膠柒 因以是爲權興矣 僕等薄治菲具 於明日畵押後 屈執事等曁美使 至敝艦一敍 聯兩家賓主之懽 薛君已惠然肯來 執事等不我遐棄 當亦勿吝玉趾焉 威翁憚於登陟 原不能强以所難 然坐無車[申]公 終覺不樂 倘其時水軟風平 扁舟安隱務祈俯賜辱臨爲幸 李桐菴可携而同來 俾爲通達壹是 此外諸君 以舟中地仄弗克遍請 殊歉然也 專泐奉佈 卽頌均祺
　　　　初五日 申刻　　　　　愚弟 丁汝昌 馬建忠 頓

　初六日午刻 潔樽候敎
申大人　威堂
金大人　道園
趙大人　松澗
徐大人　相雨
　　　　　　　　　　　　丁汝昌 馬建忠 同拜訂　席設威遠兵舶

【관련문서】

答書
禹延眉叔兩大人閣下 此次敝邦與美國 締定約好 多蒙兩大人紹介主持 克恢永遠之圖 感紉五中 不知攸云 玆奉勻諭 於明日畵押後 速僕等至尊艦 一時陪歡 薛使又肯惠然 俾全槃敦之會 敢不唯命 某脚痺添苦 登陟維艱 用是爲悶容俟明席面佈 另單已轉及兩友 李君亦當拉之偕送也 肅此奉覆 順頌辰祺
　　　　四月初五日戌刻　　　　申金仝頓啓

馬建忠(1882. 5. 22/光緒八年四月六日)

조미수호통상조약 조인식 기록

初六日風定 午前九點鐘 偕丁軍門減從登岸 美舶四艇偕行 花旗颭風 銜尾而進 至濟物浦 有朝鮮官備肩輿來迓 詢知帳房在山陽 因辭輿步行 越嶺見篷揭崖麓 環繩爲衛 守之以兵 美使率水師官弁十餘人 火器兵二十人踵至 偕行 甫及帳 申金二使趨出 肅迓入帳 送茶畢 卽爲指授儀節 請兩國使臣中坐行事 余偕丁軍門退居他室以待 約本漢洋文各三冊 悉當場鈐印簽押 冊尾年月均以漢文塡寫朝鮮開國若干年 卽中國光緖某年月日字樣 事畢 申金二使復起立 以其國王致美國伯理璽天德約外照會一通 捧交薛使 託賚歸轉呈 於時哥船主於帳房燃火箭一枝 俄而美舶升礟二十一響 致敬朝鮮國王 諸臣各肅立以聽 已復升礟十五響 致敬丁軍門及余 威遠亦升十五礟答之 礟聲止 余偕丁軍門出室稱賀 因邀薛申金三使曁趙準永徐相雨李應俊等至我舟宴集 爲敦槃之會 申櫶辭以疾 趙準永因事不赴 餘人悉至 登舟已十一點二刻 小憩入座 與宏集筆談甚長 薛使卽席邀余與丁軍門曁金徐諸人翌午會飮 金徐以復命辭 席散薛使辭去 金宏集復留筆談 四點鐘 宏集辭登岸 且謂 項聞薛辭云 於初八日起椗 請順至美舶送行 因遣我舟管駕官偕之往 美舶升礟十五響 敬之 六點鍾 申金二使復遣李應俊以其國王命持答美國伯理璽天德書二冊來 請余擇用書中一列名 一不列名 余謂 照會旣無國王名 則答書亦不必列名 以歸畫一 應俊卽以一冊留舟中 託代致美舶

馬建忠(1882. 5. 22/光緒八年四月六日)

金弘集・馬建忠 회담(5)

初六日席工有薛斐爾與金宏集筆談
忠曰 薛使云今夏美國兵舶前往釜山元山 現請貴國政府先行知會
金曰 當將此意告知政府也
忠曰 明日國王答書可至否
金曰 似不出明日
忠曰 薛使急於回國 初八卽行起椗
金曰 領敎 明日交付國書 初八行期可無悞也
忠曰 薛使○請諸位明日至該舟午時便飯
金曰 明交付國書 僕與大官仍當復命 不敢再留 且今日應召 卽爲與薛使叙賓
　　 主之好也 不須更煩厚泣 僕今日歸時 當送薛使至該艦以爲謝 兼行拜別
　　 恐妥

179

R. W. Shufeldt (1882. 5. 29) → F. T. Frelinghuysen

조약 체결 보고

Sir;

I had the honor on May 7th the telegraph you that I had gone to Corea and on the 27th instant I telegraphed you that I had returned from that country with "the treaty made and intercourse established"

I now have the honor to forward herewith in the despatch bag of U.S. Consulate General,
one original in English and
one original in Chinese
if the treaty made on the 22nd instant at Yin-Cheun, Chosen by myself and the two Commissioners, duly appointed on the part of the Government of Chosen.

This treaty is the same in its essential features, as the Draft 5#; forward to you on my communication of April 28th, and was agreed to without any political consideration whatever, and only upon the promise which I had previously made and repeated, that I would forward to the President of the United States, a letter from the King of Chosen, stating the political relations existing between Chosen and China. This letter with a translation accompanied has despatch and will, I trust, meet with such a response from the President as I may deserve. I also forward herewith another communication from the King of Chosen with a translation, which is an answer to one that I had the honor of learning from the President of the United States to Chosen.

I also forward with his despatch the original in Chinese, together with a translation in English of document presented to me but the Corean Commissioners as an evidence of their power to make the treaty.

Owing to the early departure of the mail, I have only time to say in this brief despatch that the whole translation was of the most friendly character not only on the part of the officials but also of the people of the country. The treaty was signed in view of the Ship in a tent erected on the shore by the Corean Commissioners. We were appreciated by a large number of the officers of the U.S.S. Swatara and by a filt of marines bearing the American flag. On it completion in the Swatara fired a salute of twenty-one gun, having the first salute ever given by any Western Nation to the King of Chosen.

This friendly treaty was signed very near the spot where the collision occurred between our naval forces and the Corean in 1871, and thus obliterates at least from the minds of the Coreans the memory of the event. I hope that it may be considered of sufficient importance to American interests in the East to secure to ratification.

At my request the Government of Chosen has issued instructions to the authorities of the three open ports to receive in friendly manner the visits of any American vessels of war that may be directed to go there. You will, no doubt, see the importance of such visit, pending the ratification of the treaty.

A detailed report of the whole translation and correspondence connected herewith will follow by the near mail, thus ending my intercourse the special duty to which I had been assigned by the Honorable Secretary of the Navy for permission to remain abroad on naval duty, and that I have this day written to the same effect to the Navy Department. If this is granted I will send home the remaining two copies of the treaty, either by mail or in such way as the Honorable Secretary of State may direct.

I have the honor to be with great respect your obedient Servant.

R. W. Shufeldt
Commodore U.S.N.

(8) 사후처리 및 비준

金弘集(1882.5.22/高宗十九年四月六日)

金弘集·馬建忠 회담(6)

관련문서 馬建忠 기록

馬曰 諸事告畢 賀賀
我曰 約事縱成 專由閣下周旋之力 甚感
馬曰 此皆皇上威德 傳相聲望所致 僕何力之有
我曰 皇上綏靖 傳相經畫 不知何以爲報 乞於回津之日 先爲敝邦 代達謝悃於傳相切盼
馬曰 美使云 今夏美國兵船前往釜山元山 現請貴國先爲知會
我曰 當將此意告知政府也
馬曰 答國書今明可至否
我曰 似不出今明
馬曰 薛使急於回國 初八卽行起碇
我曰 領敎
馬曰 傳相已奔喪回籍 不若由貴國王送一祭幛或輓對 亦可床巾之類
我曰 小邦僻陋 不諳中國禮節 愚意則不若只由總理大臣具書奉慰 兼呈奠銀 用表區區之誠 甚好 未知若何
馬曰 亦好 奠銀可不必 情到卽可 若送銀兩 甚不稱也
我曰 傳相丁憂回籍 仍當報復視事否
馬曰 傳相百日後 卽當回任視事 刻雖在籍 大事亦皆傳相主裁
我曰 爲中外事務甚幸
馬曰 另於咨文內 將約事順成之意 申明卽可矣 我曰 所敎良是 謹圖轉達敝朝廷也
馬曰 現有一事奉告 貴國不可無國旗 以示遠人 昨李應浚袖至旗式 似與日本相混 貴國旗式 究竟何若 前黃參贊謂貴國宜用中國龍旗 以僕觀之 似亦未安
我曰 此論良是 更乞明敎
馬曰 國旗以昭示各國 甚難定式 僕當歸府乃可
仍問 貴國王服用紅色蟒袍否
我曰 雲文紅袍 兩肩及胸背 金繡升降龍

馬曰 貴國色尙白否

我曰 朝野服着多尙靑 然庶民喜白衣 此乃殷太師遺風云

馬曰 吾想貴國國旗可用白底靑雲紅龍 惟龍用四爪 暗示區劃 何以區別 只在
　　　四爪五爪耳 靑雲者 亦取雲從龍之義 君臣以民爲本 故質用白色

我曰 旨意甚妙 當告知朝廷 從可以表屬邦之倣用中國儀章耳

馬曰 旗式商定 可一倂咨行北洋大臣爲妥

我曰 尙須熟商妥定 緩行咨請爲好

馬曰 貴國剏始通商 當思所以設立關卡之法

我曰 關卡之法 俟隙賜敎是幸

馬曰 中國初開口岸 亦未深諳通商條例 大爲吃虧 今則遣人至外洋 察看考究
　　　方知底蘊 貴國須雇一熟諳此事者 以總司之

我曰 敝邦幸蒙中朝指導 可望將來不至吃虧否 願終始庇護

馬曰 無已 則可由貴國王咨商北洋大臣 轉奏朝廷 或派人前來襄理 或由貴國
　　　派人至中國海關學習 否則 由貴國王自行奏請亦可

我曰 領敎

馬曰 僕等擬于初八日赴王京 初十日回舟 十一日起碇 所有貴國王咨文各件
　　　或可派李應浚 乘敝舟賷去何如

我曰 啓駕來京 不勝忻幸 回舟一事 敢乞再遲五六個日 以副寡君之望 回咨附
　　　舟一節 已經轉達 而姑未承朝廷旨意

馬曰 此次赴京 專爲拜謝貴國王遣帖之禮 不敢久留 津門尙有事 更乞轉達

我曰 到京再作商量極好 此言亦當轉達 而歸帆勿邅幾日 至禱

馬曰 在京住宇何處 尙宜奉拜

我曰 敝寓在城內 如聞駕至 謹當造候 徐從事亦當偕進

馬曰 不敢當

【관련문서】

四月初六日畫押後金宏集來舟筆談

忠曰 諸事告畢 賀賀

金曰 約事順成 專由閣下周旋之力 萬萬感激

忠曰 此皆大皇帝威德 傅相規畫所致 僕何力之有

金曰 皇上天恩 傅相大德 誠不知何以爲謝 只是西望攢頌 乞於回津之日於傅相前爲僕等代達謝悃 切盻 切盻 傅相丁憂回里 仍當起復視事否

忠曰 傅相百日後卽當回仕 現雖在籍 大事亦皆傅相裁決

金曰 爲中外事務 幸甚 幸甚

忠曰 僕等擬於初八日赴王京 初十回舟 十一起椗 所有貴國王咨文各件 或可派李應浚乘敝船賫回何如

金曰 初八起駕前來敝京 不勝欣幸 回舟一事 敢乞再遲五六日 以副寡君之望 行咨附舟一節 已經轉達 而姑未聞朝廷旨意

忠曰 此次赴京專爲答貴國王遣帖之拜 不敢久留 津門尙有事事 尙乞轉達

金曰 遵駕到京 再作商量 極好 此敎亦當轉達 而歸勿遽 少緩數日 千萬至禱

高宗, 馬建忠, 丁汝昌(1882. 5. 26/高宗十九年四月十日)

高宗의 馬建忠·丁汝昌 인견(引見) 기록

壬午四月初十日申時
上御便殿 中國使臣接見入侍時 行都承旨李載完 行左承旨趙東鎬 假註書朴
歧勳 別兼春秋鄭寅興 指教閔泳韶 以次侍立訖
上命統理大臣經理事入侍 賤臣承命 傳諭統理大臣李最應金炳國經理事金弘
集入侍 清使納上名帖 上覽訖 命史官還傳 賤臣承命 往傳于清使 上出楹外
清使陞殿 立于楹外 上請行揖禮 清使作揖 上答揖訖 請坐椅子
清使曰 請先坐
上命傳語曰 皇上諸節何如
清使曰 平康
上命傳語曰 皇太后諸節何如
清使曰 平康
上命傳語曰 天氣不好 海路悠遠 兩位大人跋涉之餘 體上何如
清使曰 往來輪船 始爲無恙矣
上命傳語曰 兩位大人光臨 實在難得 而路上伺候不恭 敬聽回往船上云 主人
　　　云心不安極矣
清使曰 路上伺候 都是懷意 而至此勞問 還爲不安矣
上命傳語曰 公館狼窄 各樣辦理 不能盡禮 而兩位大人 雖然不恠 還是面爲
清使曰 舘宇乾淨 好爲影息
上命傳語曰 傅相大人 仰體皇上柔遠之恩 護庇小邦 奉旨派官 和美國通好立
　　　約 彼此妥當 實在感心 而咨報於傳相大人及禮部矣
清使曰 中堂奏達大皇帝 使我們送到 便是一家事 何必道謝
上命傳語曰 兩位大人回朝後 道此感謝之意於傳相大人面前
清使曰 我們回去 自然告稟中堂
上命傳語曰 兩位大人尊庚幾何
丁使曰 今年四十七
馬使曰 今年三十八矣
上命傳語曰 賓主初會 天氣不早 請進茶

清使曰 准准

上命傳語曰 兩位大人遠來 皇不榮耀 畧備筵席 聊表東道之禮

清使曰 不敢當

上命傳語曰 膳雖微薄 意則懇摯 幸賜下著

清使曰 膳爲珍異 敢不飽德

上命傳語曰 隨員們場外賜菜何如

清使曰 隨員不復沾恩 感謝感謝

上命傳語曰 兩位大人 遠路辛苦不少 天氣傍晚 不敢請久坐 早回公館 累日平安歇息 少慰主人之心

清史曰 盛意感謝 而前路有限 當於明日發程矣

上命傳語曰 甚是悵缺 明日當送近臣 探請起居 兼修餞別之禮矣

清史曰 眞是不敢當 不必如是勤伺矣

上命傳語曰 欲使東宮 獲憩感儀 或可肯議否

清史曰 我們初意亦然 從此卽往東宮矣

仍出檻外 上出檻外 請行揖禮 清使作揖 上答揖 仍命傳語曰 隨員們亦爲好去影息 又命退諸臣 以次退出

金弘集(1882. 5. 27/高宗十九年四月十一日)

金弘集・馬建忠 회담(7)

馬曰 國旗之事 乞君留意 我曰 向論紅龍靑雲 製造須費工 李應浚鑒正本 謂與日本相混 若用紅質中靑白合成圈子 則可免相混否 馬曰 國旗之事 關係究非輕 歸當與政府細商 日前議此事後 曾思仍用白底中用太極圖 外週用八卦 則恰合八道之數 八卦純用黑色爲顯 太極用半紅半黑 旗外又綠以紅色何若 但此係鄙人所見 歸當語我政府也 我曰 領敎 僕亦當告知敝朝廷也

高宗(1882. 5. 27/高宗十九年四月十一日) ➜ 禮部

조미조약 체결 통보

朝鮮國王爲會咨事 竊照小邦 僻在東隅 惟皇靈是仗 藩職是修 邇來時局漸變 交涉轉滋 顧小邦用是憂慮 思所以維持彌綸 幸蒙我皇上隆恩天大 洪猷遠彰 深軫小邦 曾無他國之往來 未免應接之齟齬 曲費造化 綏靖藩服 至有北洋大臣密咨 審時度勢 開論諄摯 將小邦與美國 通好事宜 前後指敎 纖悉周至 又轉奏此等情形 奉旨派遣觀察馬建忠提督丁汝昌 同美國總兵薛斐爾 乘兵船來泊于仁川港口 以襄助兩國通好 當職用是感結衷腸 卽以陪臣經理統理機務衙門事申櫶金宏集 充差全權大副官 出迎仁川港 迺於本年四月六日 面同美國公使 薛斐爾 講定修好通商條規十四款 鈐印畫押 互相憑據 以爲永遠金石之信 此莫非中朝視屛藩如手足 特垂鴻渥 俾禦外侮 且由馬觀察丁提督兩大人 克體聖旨 殫力周章 剋日竣事 順成和約 小邦臣民 莫不北望攢頌 隕越于下 擬俟前頭使行 恭修表謝之擧 而先將條約冊子照會文字 及美國國書小邦答國書 兩國全權字據等備文各稿 另行鈔錄 庸備轉奏載案 玆憑揚威艦西駛 專差副司直李應浚 齎咨前往 泧詳條報 煩乞轉奏天陞 以達事情 嗣後或有他國交涉事端 亦卽請旨暫留馬道丁提督 在此商辦 俾小邦終始徹惠 區區幸甚 爲此合行移咨 請照驗轉奏施行 須至咨者
右 咨
咨報事
光緖八年四月十一日 啓
藝文提學 臣 鄭範朝 製進 禮部 光緖八年四月十一日 撥送 光緖八年四月初十日

高宗(1882. 5. 27/高宗十九年四月十一日) ➡ 張樹聲(1882. 6. 5/光緒八年四月二十日)

조미조약 체결 통보

朝鮮國王爲會咨事 竊惟弊邦 介在東陲 惟憑仗皇靈 恪守候度 邇來宇內時局 歲變月異 港口事務 疊生層出 幸蒙中堂大人 特推皇上字小之恩 深諒弊邦交際之勢 前後開導之庇佑之 不翅若同舟竝力 今於美使之東駛也 亦爲之先事而謀量時之宜 指敎詳密 十分妥當 又念弊邦 曾無外交 未嫺時務 禀旨差遣馬觀察丁提督兩大人賫密咨 同美使專來襄助 遂令弊邦 得以左右藉力 訂立條約 當職用是感結衷腸 寤寐衞戢 卽以經理統理機務衙門事 申櫶 金宏集 充派全權大副官 出迎于仁川港 迺於本年四月六日 面同美國總兵 薛斐爾 講定修好通商條規十四款 鈐印畫押 互相憑據 以爲永遠金石之信 而惟第一款 不得於正約中存留 將小邦之爲中國屬邦等語 另行照會聲明 恪遵中堂大人提示之微義 此莫非中堂大人仰體聖念 綏靖藩服 經劃遠圖 俾有取益防損之道 亦惟兩大人居間主持 殫力周章 乃底剋日竣事 立約平善 由此弊邦臣民 莫不翹首攢頌 隕越于下擬 俟前頭使行 恭修表謝之擧 而先將條約冊子照會文字及美國國書小邦答國書兩國全權字據等備文各稿 悉行鈔錄 庸備轉奏載案 玆憑揚威艦駛西 專差副司直 李應浚 賫咨前往 涓詳條報 煩乞轉奏天陛 以達事情 嗣後或有他國交涉事端 亦卽請旨暫留馬道丁提督 在此商辦 俾小邦終始徼惠 區區幸甚 爲此合行移咨 請照驗轉奏施行 須至咨者
右咨
咨覆事
光緖八年四月十一日 啓
藝文提學 臣 鄭範朝 製進 欽差北洋通商大臣衙門 光緖八年四月十一日 撥送
光緖八年四月初十日

美國國書
大美伯理璽天德致書於大朝鮮君主 竊惟美國與中華日本和好通商 歷有年所 今切願偕貴國與貴君主子民一體和好通商 且祈貴君主永高昇平 玆特遣水師

總兵薛斐爾前赴貴國議立一妥善和好通商條約 以冀吾兩國人民益敦友誼 專此特佈 敬頌遐祺 美國國主阿爾惑押 時西曆千八百八十一年十一月十五日京都華盛頓發

────────

朝鮮國答國書
大朝鮮國君主致書於大美國伯理璽天德 竊聞貴國政治公平正直 久欲通好 無緣爲歉 今承貴國主先遣大員來此議約 玆特派全權大官經理統理機務衙門事申櫶 全權副官經理統理機務衙門事金宏集與之計議 不日卽可畫押 仍由薛總兵賷回面呈 卽乞速爲批行 派員前來互換 以使吾兩國人民從此益敦和好 有厚望焉 專此泐復 敬候遐祺 大朝鮮國開國四百九十一年 卽中國光緖八年四月 日

────────

朝鮮國照會
大朝鮮國君主爲照會事 竊照朝鮮素爲中國屬邦 而內治外交向來均由大朝鮮國君主自主 今大朝鮮大美國彼此立約 俱屬平行相待 大朝鮮國君主明允將約內各款 必按自主公例認眞照辦 至大朝鮮國爲中國屬邦 其分內一切應行各節 均與大美國毫無干涉 除派員議立條約外 相應備文照會 須至照會者
右 照 會
大美國伯理璽天德
大朝鮮國開國四百九十一年 卽光緖八年三月二十八日

────────

美使照會
大美國欽命總統水師全權大臣薛爲照會事 竊照本大臣奉命前來貴國 進呈國書 蓋欲永敦友睦信好通商等情 並奉有國君御筆憑據一道 今繙譯漢文 祈貴大臣代呈御覽 本大臣在船恭候示覆 想貴大臣公忠體國 澤惠治民 亦必欲速爲襄成也 至國書俟畫押後再行進呈外 爲此照會貴大臣 請煩查照施行 須至

照會者 計移送繙譯漢文上諭一道
右 照 會
大朝鮮國執政大臣
中華光緒八年四月初四日移

朝鮮國總理大臣答照會
大朝鮮國特命總理統理機務衙門大臣金爲照覆事 准貴大臣照會稱 本大臣奉命前來貴國進呈國書等語 本大臣並奉准貴大臣照會 謹已進徹御覽 奉有回照國書 恭祈貴大臣代呈貴國君主 竊惟貴大臣殫誠體國 講信修好 立約通商 悉臻妥協 俾我兩國永徵休祥 本大臣不勝忻慰 爲此照復 須至照會者
右 照 會
大美國欽命總統水師 全權大臣薛
大朝鮮國開國四百九十一年 卽中國光緒八年四月初五日

朝鮮國全權字據
光緒八年三月二十八日 統理機務衙門奉諭 著申櫶爲全權大臣 金宏集爲全權副官 前往仁川 與美國全權大臣妥議和好通商條約 欽哉

美國全權字據
大亞美理駕合衆國大伯理璽天德阿爾惑 特派水師總統薛斐爾 念爾眞誠信實智慧能幹 命爲全權大臣 卽往朝鮮進呈國書慶賀 並與大朝鮮國主或執政大臣商立和約 永敦友誼 永遠通商 所定條約賫回本國 紳耆大臣議允 卽批准畫押此諭 於一千八百八十一年 自主一百六年十一月十五日 在華盛頓都城用寶 著爾執爲的確憑據

張樹聲 ➡ 總署(1882. 6. 5/光緒八年四月二十日)

조영, 조불 조약 체결시 조미조약 원용에 관한 의견

四月二十日 署北洋大臣張樹聲函稱 朝美議約已定訂期會集畫押各節 業於十七日專函馳達鈞覽 本日接馬道建忠稟少荃中堂函 據稱 初六日美高兩國使臣在近岸濟物浦支立帳房 會集畫押 當將朝鮮國王照會與國書條約並交美使 美卽於初八日起椗歸國 英國使臣韋力士已乘兵舶駛至 大約一切可照美約定擬等因 惟現定條約尙未據該道寄到 除俟專摺詳晰奏報並將馬道節次日記筆談錄呈鈞署外 謹先將馬道原稟照錄馳布 仰慰藎廑 專肅 恭敬崇安 樹聲謹肅 敬再肅者 昨日奉直字二十七號鈞函抄件 祇悉一一 法國與朝鮮議約一事 亦明知必難與他國兩歧 因少荃中堂極言法人專重傳敎 而朝人深皮洋敎 恐致扞格 且寶使旣未親到津門面議 亦未作函相託 不得不小作節次 以昭詳愼 玆蒙垂示機宜 慮周見遠 業經卽日鈔錄鈞函 轉致馬道 寄至煙臺 覓便船遞去 屬其遵照指示 妥爲辦理 並屬其暫行留駐 勿遽西返矣 肅復 再敬鈞棋 敬附肅者 再誦另示 並抄寄粵字二百九十九號信函 謹聆種切 鈞署致澤生中丞公丈一角 亦已卽日交招商局船速遞矣 再請崇安

R. W. Shufeldt (1882. 6. 8) → F. T. Frelinghuysen

조미수호통상조약 체결 전말 보고

Nagasaki, Japan
Hon. Frederick T. Frelinghuysen,
Secretary of State
State Department
Washington, D.C.

Sir,

I have the honor to request that this dispatch may be considered a continuation of my dispatch No. 7 dated Shanghai May 29th.

The causes which brought about a treaty between the United States and Corea, and the events which lead up to it, have been narrated in my several communications to the Department.

The antagonism between China and Japan, extending even to parties among the Coreans themselves, has been the underlying reason for the action of China, which made me from my long communication with the subject, the medium for securing the American treaty with Corea.

Two years ago the same effort on my part through the intervention of Japan failed, I yet have reason to know, that if from any cause China had declined to assist at the present time; Japan would have seized the opportunity of retrieving the mistake which she made, and which she now realizes that she made on the former occasion.

Nonetheless it is due to the Government of China to acknowledge its friendly offices, and the very efficient and practical manner in which they were rendered. It is also proper to add, that the Commissioners of Corea were manifestly in favor of concluding the treaty rather through the intervention of China, than of Japan. Ma Taotai, the agent of the Chinese Government sent over to Corea to act as the intermediary, managed the negotiation with great skill; inspired perhaps by the knowledge that Mr. Hanabusa the Japanese Minister resident in Corea, was watching every movement, and was only prevented from offering his services by the sudden, and to him unexpected conclusion of the treaty. The Department must have been made aware of the reasons for the action of China by my dispatch of Jan 23th (No. 1) in time to recall my commission if it so desired. My telegram also of April 12th, indicating that I was ready to go to Corea, could have been answered in the interval between the date and May 1st the day fixed for my departure, in time to countermand the movement if anything had occurred to render such action advisable. Not receiving however any further instructions either by mail or telegraph, I felt myself obliged under those already in my possession to proceed to Corea. Accordingly after a correspondence between his Excellency Li-Hung-Chang and myself at Chefoo (enclosures Nos. 1 +2) it was arranged that Ma Taotai should proceed me by one day to the anchorage in the Salie River at Yin-Chuen or [____] the seaport of Séoul the capital of Corea.

This was done, and on my arrival at that port I found anchored there, two Chinese man-of-war with an Admiral on board, and also a Japanese corvette.

May 14th occurred, as stated in enclosures Nos. 8+9, the first visit of the Corean commissioners to the 'Swatara' the first visit of an official character ever made by Corean official on board of a man-of-war of any Western nation.

On the 17th of May, I was informed by the commanding officer of the Japanese corvette 'Banjo,' of the presence in Séoul of Mr. Y. Hanabusa H.I.J.M. Minister resident in Corea. At the same time was handed me a letter of introduction to that gentleman, from the Hon. John A. Bingham, U.S. Minister at Tokei. The correspondence resulting from this letter will be found in enclosures Nos. 7&9.

In inclosure No 13 will be found the details of the first visit made by myself, accompanied by a staff of officers to the Corean Commissioners at Hen-Shaw, six miles in the interior; where credentials were exchanged, the letter of the president of the United States to the King of Corea delivered for transmission, and a day fixed for the signing of the treaty.

May 22nd I proceeded, as agreed upon, to the place appointed for signing the treaty; accompanied by fifteen officers of the ship, and proceeded by a file of marines bearing the American flag. Full details of the ceremony will be found in inclosure No. 14.

After the conclusion of the ceremony, salutes were exchanged between the Chinese Admiral and myself, Mr. Hanabusa was also saluted, as well as one of the Corean Commissioners who came on board to make a farewell visit.

On the morning of the 24th of May, I left Corea for Shanghai, arriving on the evening of the 26th.

I visited that port, because, in the absence of any authorized interpreter with me in Corea, it became necessary to secure the services of the Government interpreter attached to the U.S. Consulate General. All the documents forwarded with the treaty were translated by that officer, and may therefore be regarded as entirely trustworthy.

After this work was accomplished and forwarded to the Hon. Secretary of State by mail, I came to Nagasaki in the 'Swatara' on the 4th inst., and notified Comdr Cooper commanding, that my mission was accomplished by letters to him, and to Admiral Clitz, as per inclosures Nos. 15 & 16.

The Department on the receipt of this dispatch, will be in possession of as complete a [_____] as in my power to give, of an event which may become an important era in modern history.

England and Germany are following in the footsteps of the United States. In all probability they will make treaties based upon our own, and will no doubt be the first to reap the fruits of the new commercial field.

    I have the honor to be,
    with great respect,
    your obedient servant,
    R.W. Shufeldt
    Commodore, U.S.N.

張樹聲(1882. 6. 9/光緖八年四月二十四日)

조미수호통상조약 체결 전말 상주

直隷總督兼理通商事務大臣張樹聲奏朝鮮與美國議約事竣摺
光緖八年四月二十四日
署直隷總督兼理通商事務大臣兩廣總督臣張樹聲跪奏爲朝鮮與美國議立和好通商條約現已事竣恭摺仰祈聖鑒事竊前北洋大臣李鴻章籌辦朝鮮與美國議約事宜務將商定約稿請派二品銜候選道馬建忠前往朝鮮會辦並派統領北洋水師記名提督丁汝昌酌帶兵船偕美總兵薛斐爾束駛以壯聲勢各緣由於本年三月初六日奏奉俞允欽遵在案馬建忠等於前月二十日自烟臺起有次日駛抵朝鮮漢江口停泊時有日本公使花房義質已乘兵船先在該處下椗馬建忠登岸至仁川府行館連日接見朝鮮伴接官趙準永及金景遂李應浚等每與言及約事答語支吾意頗閃爍花房義質來見語氣亦涉窺探馬建忠以日使意存蠱惑朝人情近猶豫不得不稍權變因爲指存大義斥其不知推誠相待深負大皇帝調護屬邦至意徑出行館回舟金景遂諸人惶恐挽留自是王京來人皆益恭謹二十四日薛斐爾抵港馬建忠議原據約內第一條彼堅執有礙平行體制且本國電復未到斷難擅允詞意甚爲決絶乃議由朝鮮國王另備照會於未經立約之前先行聲明再四熟商始行首肯在彼則謂不列約中尙不礙其體面在我則先聲明而後立約是彼已認明朝鮮爲我屬邦較初議於立約後設法聲明尤有根據二十七日朝鮮國王所派全權大副官經理統理機務衙門事申櫶金宏集登舟謁議於此節皆無異詞次及原擬第九款米粮出口一條申櫶金宏集謂於朝議民情有礙堅欲議禁薛斐爾堅不肯允相持累日金宏集乃議添注惟仁川口不准出米一句馬建忠復與美使重加商酌改爲惟於仁川已開一口各色米粮槪行禁止運出較爲周帀美使急欲定約勉強允行其餘各款間有一二處改易數字於大指均無出入計議定條約十四款卽於四月初六日在仁川港由申櫶金宏集會同薛斐爾鈐印畫押據馬建忠節次稟報本月二十日並准朝鮮國王將約本及照會底稿兩國書全權字樣抄錄咨送專差副司直李應浚齎呈請奏前來伏查中西互市之初中國罕通西例各國來立條約大都因利以乘便損我以益彼沿至今日挽救爲難朝鮮僻在東北近偪於日俄兩國日人以議稅未定惟事挾制俄人以拓地爲志尤所覬覦其國中士大夫又多拘守常經自安積弱因應失當勢難圖存朝廷深惟藩衛之誼疊諭李鴻章妥籌指引該國王與一二臣工始知幡然變計李鴻章

爲該國密擇邦交先聯美國乘薛斐爾東來之機令馬建忠往莅其事謀畫經年次第就緒如第二款領事必須奉到批准文憑視事及辦事不合追回一節則於領事予奪之權不致動與地方官齟齬碍難鈐制第五第六第七第十二等皆商務緊要關健自操利權預防流弊悉已包括無遺第四款審案之事雖不能如西國案件俱由地方訊斷亦由朝美律法不同之故但西人通商之處被告多屬本地之人玆定爲由被告所屬官員以本國律例審斷則可持平辦理朝人不致喫虧其日後改定律例一節尤有關係雖一時未必辦到特存是說可待將來第十款拏犯之事各口本地民人多恃洋人爲護符犯案則領事必爲庇匿玆定有或准差役自行往拏之條可免戢法縱奸肆無顧忌其第十四款提明互相酬報專條以救一體均霑之弊卽遇強國亦不能以勢力相偪至洋人入內地傳敎朝鮮尤所深惡近年因有敎士私往屢滋事端但朝人有必不能容之情而公法又無於條約內明有禁止之例現在約內不提傳敎一節而於第十二款內議明應遵條約已載者先行辦理其未載者俟五年後再行議定則立約後如有洋人前往傳敎朝鮮卽可照約相拒不至以民敎起釁多生枝蔓以上各節均照西國通例斟酌後辦理取益防損之道實已籌慮周密此皆憑藉皇靈故美使迅就範圍辦理尙屬順手朝鮮守而弗失他國續議通商持此約爲依據可以杜窺伺而絕要求從此講求馭外之道以立自強之基庶可世守東藩仰承聖主以大字小之德除照鈔朝鮮國王咨文曁約本照會及兩國國書全權字據恭呈御覽並將馬建忠節次來禀及日記筆談各件一幷抄送總理各國事務衙門查核外所有朝鮮與美國議約事竣緣由理合恭摺由驛馳奏伏乞皇太后皇上聖鑒訓示謹奏光緒八年四月二十六日軍機大臣奉旨該衙門知道單三件片一件幷發欽此

J. A. Bingham (1882. 8. 28) ➡ F. T. Frelinghuysen (1882. 9. 26)

조선 무역과 자원 현황

[Extract.]

UNITED STATES LEGATION,

Tokei, Japan

SIR: In the Japan Daily Herald of the 23rd instant I find an article entitled "Corea, its trade and mineral resources," which it seems to me is worth recording, and a copy of which I have the honor to inclose.

*　　*　　*　　*　　*　　*　　*　　*　　*　　*

I have, &c.,

JNO. A. BINGHAM.

[Inclosure in No. 1555.—Extract from the Japan Daily Herald, August 23, 1882.]

COREA: ITS TRADE AND MINERAL RESOURCES.

The interest that is at present taken in Corea makes any reliable information with respect to the trade and mineral resources of this hitherto forbidden land of great importance; and the following extract from Mr. Walter Lay's (commissioner of customs) report to Sir. Robert Hart, inspector-general of customs, on the trade relations between Newchwang and Corea during the year 1881, will be read with interest. Mr. Lay says:

"The exchange of commodities between Newchwang and Corea has not been on such an extensive scale lately as it was at one time, owing, it is said, to the footing which the Japanese have secured for themselves on the eastern side of the Corean peninsula. By virtue of a treaty which they have concluded with Coreans, two places on the seaboard, called Bushan, in the south, and Yüanshan, In the east, have been opened to them, and through these new ports they have been supplying the country with many things which were formerly admitted into it on its western side through this port. Many influential Corean merchants, who at one time carried on their business at the Corean Gate, have transferred their operations to the new ports, leaving behind them a class of traders who are simply peddlers.

"The old conservative ideas of exclusiveness are fast disappearing from the Corean people, and the Corean Government, unable to stop the march of events, is now allowing its subjects both to leave and to return to their country. Formerly, commercial transactions between Chinese and Coreans were carried on at the Corean Gate, the Coreans having to obtain a pass to go thus far, and being forbidden on pain of death to go farther. Now, it appears that a Corean has simply to pay duty on his goods to enable him, if he cannot dispose of them at the Gate, to carry them where he likes. He can bring them down here, if he thinks the market will suit him better, but he cannot take them beyond Shanhaikwan, unless he holds a proper pass, which is a wooden ticket, and he can only obtain this if he is attached to the suite of an embassador.

"An embassy is sent from Corea to Pekin at periodical intervals, the number of individuals composing it being about two hundred. To each of these a passport is given so that he may have something to show should his official right to travel be called in question. The holders of passports either bring with them Corean productions for sale, or, for a consideration, they transfer their passports to other for that purpose. Without a passport a Corean can come as far as this port, but he cannot travel in the direction of Pekin.

"The restrictions against the exit of Coreans from their country having been relaxed, there is no longer any necessity to confine operations to the Gate, and the fairs, therefore, which have been held there three times a year, are now losing all their former importance. The Chinese are beginning to feel dissatisfied at the influx of Coreans into their country, arguing very rationally that privileges to trade should be reciprocal. Whilst Coreans can come in this direction with freedom, Chinese who venture across the border do so at the peril of their lives. Far north, in the wilds of Manchnria, the Coreans have been induced to settle on Chinese territory, and in one of the Peking Gazettes issued a few months ago there appeared a memorial from the Tartar general of Kirin, requesting the imperial sanction to allow taxes to be paid in cattle to suit the convenience of settlers, who were not allowed to bring away money from their own country.

"The chief item which the Coreans bring across the border is ginseng, and this is the most valuable. Wild ginseng is found among the hills, and takes more than thirty years to arrive at perfection. The root can be used when it has been in the ground about twelve years, but it is not so valuable as that of mature age. The other kinds of ginseng, known as first and second quality Corean, are a special branch of culture. Only well-to-do people can afford to set apart the ground for its cultivation, and to devote to it the time which it requires. The usual period allowed for the root to attain its full growth is from five to six years; it is then dug up, washed, and dried in a pan over a fire, and after the skin has been scraped away it is ready for the market. Once every year a small flower is put forth, the seed from which is carefully preserved and sown the following year. The root thrives best in a sandy soil.

"Among other things that Corea produces are gold dust, tiger skins, sable skins, and human hair. An experimental shipment of the last-named to England was made last year, but with what result has not yet been ascertained. Tigers and leopards abound in Corea: but few skins from that country pass through this port.

"In his work on Corea, Perè Dallet affirms that the mountains conceal a wealth of gold, silver, and copper. Gold, he says, may be met with in the north by merely turning over the soil, but that excavations for this hidden treasure are not allowed under the severest penalties, the people not even venturing to pick it up on account of the impossibility of disposing of it. Some assert that the government discourage mining enterprise, because they are afraid of exciting the cupidity of powerful neighbors; others attribute it to the fear of a revolt, which they are afraid would infallibly break out if a large number of workmen were concentrated on ground far away from the Capital and where there is little or no official authority. Iron, Perè Dallet says, is so plentiful in some places that after heavy rain it may be freely obtained—people picking up as much as they like of it.

"A country with such mineral resources as Corea is said to possess can scarcely remain closed much longer to the outer world. The Japanese have secured a footing there, and it now remains for England, with her large commercial interests, to obtain one also. I am given to understand that Coreans generally are in favor of opening the country to trade and simply await the advent of foreigners to receive them with open arms. This may mean that the mercantile portion of the people would like to see foreigners appear; it does not necessarily indicate a desire on the part of the official class to welcome a change.

"In exchange for the various articles which Coreans bring down here, they obtain foreign piece goods, native cloth, silk piece goods, and treasure. They also like foreign dyes, and are not proof against the seductive charms of opium. As the trade of this port has been almost entirely in the hands of the Chinese since it was first opened, it is more than likely that it has been the Chinaman, and not the foreigner, who has introduced this well-known narcotic into this new and unexplored country."—Shanghai Courier.

189

J. R. Young(1882. 9. 29/高宗十九年八月十八日) ➡ 趙寧夏, 金弘集

조선의 비준 촉구를 본국 정부에 보고했음을 통보

大亞美理賀合衆國欽命駐箚中華便宜行事全權大臣楊爲照覆事 前准貴大臣 於八月初七日由津來文內開 本國六月初九日之事 係屬內難 玆幸壹是敉平 所有前經簽押條約 自應按照公法 悉遵原議辨理 如貴國批准派員前來 卽請 馳往仁川互換 以便兩國人民一體遵守 共亨利益 本大官等 因公來津 誠恐外 間訛傳 致生疑議 備文照會 查照等因前來 查本國與貴國 首立通商和約 係開 貴國與各國以聯絡之階 並爲貴國與各國商民彼此均得通商之益 是以於貴國 君民之休戚 本國甚有相關 玆閱前因 知貴國亂事粗[敉]平 並聞與日本國重 訂和好之款 實深欣慰 除譯錄來文轉報本國外 相應照覆 貴大臣查照可也 須 至照會者
　　右照會
大朝鮮國欽差全權大副官趙金
　　一千八百八十二年九月二十九日卽壬午年八月十八日

J. R. Young (1882. 12. 26) ➜ F. T. Frelinghuysen (1883. 2. 23)

조청상민수륙무역장정에 관한 Holcombe의 견해 보고

LEGATION OF THE UNITED STATES,
Peking

SIR: I have the honor to inclose a translation of a treaty made between the Chinese grand secretary of state, Li Hung Chang, and the Corean envoys to China.

This convention has excited much attention among the representatives of the powers which have signed conventions with the King of Corea.

I inclose also a memorandum written by Mr. Holcombe, pointing out the salient points in this convention, wherein it diverges from the existing treaties, and the objections the western powers must advance to its enforcement.

Mr. Holcombe's familiarity with the negotiations which culminated in the treaty signed by Commodore Shufeldt will give value to his analysis as a thorough presentation of the whole subject, and I therefore commend his memorandum to your attention.

* * * * * * * * *

Taking everything into consideration, the legation will hear with pleasure that the Shufeldt convention has been ratified. I think it very important that the United States should have a footing in Corea, and that, having opened the door, we should not close it nor give any other power precedence.

I look upon all our conventions with these Asiatic powers as tentative. We have very little to lose whether Corea becomes a province of China or is annexed to Japan or remains independent. The only power whose presence in Corea would effect our trade would be Russia, as the policy of Russia would be to open trade channels overland and limit the seaboard commerce.

Our convention with Corea is, commercially, a step in the path of progress, and made, as was our first convention with Japan, with the view of extending into Asia the advantages of our civilization. With the other powers it is political, and is bound up with the aims and schemes of western nations for aggrandizement in Asia. As we have no interest in these enterprises, as we have at heart the independence of these Asiatic nations, I am anxious to see our country in a position where her moral influence can aid in maintaining the existing autonomy of China, Japan, Corea and Siam.

The Shufeldt convention puts us in that position, a position we should not surrender. And any question of trade between Corea and China, or any reciprocal treaty like the one I inclose, is of minor concern, and can be governed by diplomatic action.

I have said that all these treaties are tentative. I think also that the disposition of the Asiatic nations to enter into treaty relations with each other should be encouraged. We cannot expect from the diplomatists of China and Corea that familiarity with the principles of international law which gives sacredness and prestige to the conventions between the western powers; but the Japanese treaty with Corea last summer, and even this extraordinary treaty, are steps towards western ways and laws, and in that have value. These recent treaties have the Oriental quality of imitation in this, that even the faults of western diplomacy, as so regarded by Oriental statesmen, are faithfully copied when they come to deal with one another. If there is one claim, for instance, which they resent and under which they groan as though it were a heavy burden, it is exterritoriality. We regard it as a security against the application of barbarous procedures to our people. The Orientals feel that it is a principle which, when honestly enforced, must in time affect the existence of the Government which accepts it, and that to extend it is to limit the power of the throne, an apprehension which has a basis in logic if not in experience. Nothing would gratify China and Japan more than for the western nations to abandon this right. Yet when Japan and China, who resent exterritoriality forced upon them by western treaties, come to deal with a sister nation, they compel Corea to grant them the same privilege.

I might add further illustrations in evidence; but the point in the whole discussion which seems essential is, that having opened the door to Corea we should go in and do what good we may.

*　　*　　*　　*　　*　　*　　*　　*　　*

I have, &c.,

JNO. RUSSELL YOUNG.

[Inclosure 1 in No. 85.—Translation.]
Commercial and trade regulations for the subjects of China and Corea.

Corea having been, from ancient times, a tributary state, the canons of her intercourse in all matters with the Government of China are fixed and need not be changed. But inasmuch as other nations have now established commercial relations with Corea, it is manifestly expedient that the interdict against intercourse by sea be at once removed, to the end that the subjects of the two nations may reciprocally enjoy the advantages of commercial intercourse. And it is further expedient that the regulations for trade at the barrier between the territories of the two contracting parties be taken into consideration and slightly modified to meet the requirements of the age.

The commercial and trade regulations hereinafter established are, however, to be regarded as so many concessions on the part of China to her tributary state, and are not within the scope of the "favored nation rule," existing between the several treaty powers and China.

The following regulations are hereby established:

ARTICLE I. Hereafter commercial agents will be appointed by the northern superintendent of foreign trade to reside at the several ports in Corea which are open to foreign commerce, for the superintendence and protection of Chinese subject. Such agents shall correspond with Corean authorities upon terms of equality, and shall be treated with all due consideration.

In case grave matters of business arise, in which the commercial agents deem it inexpedient to assume the responsibility of coming to a decision with the Corean authorities, they will report the facts to the northern superintendent of foreign trade, who will communicate* with the King of Corea, who will direct his council of state to consider and determine the business.

The King of Corea will appoint an envoy to reside at Tien-Tsin, and commercial agents to reside at the other ports in China which are open to foreign trade. The envoy and the commercial agents shall correspond with intendants, prefects, sub-prefects, district magistrates, and other local authorities at the open ports on terms of equality.

In case difficult questions arise, the commercial agents shall be permitted to make suitable representation to the envoy at Tien-Tsin, who may request** either the northern or southern superintendent of foreign trade to take the questions in hand and dispose of them. The necessary expenses of the several agents of the two Governments shall be borne by each Government for itself,

---

* [역주] The Chinese character shows that this communication is to be on terms of equality. [C. H.]
** Not as an equal. [C. H.]

and no extortion or demand for compensation shall be permitted. If any agent of either Government persists in arrogant conduct or manages business in an improper manner, upon communication of such facts either by the northern superintendent of foreign trade or the King of Corea, the agent in question will be at once recalled.

ART. II. Suits at law between Chinese subjects at the open ports in Corea shall be heard and determined by the Chinese authorities. In all civil and criminal cases in Corea, in which Corean subjects are plaintiffs and Chinese subjects defendants, arrests shall be made and the cases heard and determined by the Chinese commercial agents. In cases in which Chinese subjects are plaintiffs and Corean subjects are defendants, it shall be the duty of the proper Corean authorities to arrest and produce the defendants, and, conjointly with the Chinese authorities, hear and determine the case according to law.

All cases at law arising in the ports in China which are open to foreign trade, whether civil or criminal, in which Corean subjects are concerned, either as plaintiffs or defendants, shall be heard and determined by the Chinese local authorities, according to law. The judgment shall be communicated to the Corean agent for record. If the Corean subjects concerned are dissatisfied with the verdict, the high Chinese authorities may be appealed to by the Corean agents to order a new hearing in the interest of justice.

When Corean subjects have occasion to visit the offices of Chinese agents in Corea, or of Chinese local authorities at the open ports in China, in order to lay complaints against Chinese subjects, the constables, clerks, or other servants will not be allowed to extort money or the least compensation from them.

Violations of this rule will be punished with the utmost severity upon proof being laid before the official who is responsible for the guilty party.

If the subjects of either power, whether in their own land or in the ports of the other country which are open to foreign trade, who may be guilty of violation of the laws, take refuge within the territories of the other power upon information communicated by the commercial agents of either power to the local authorities, latter shall take measures to arrest the guilty parties, and shall deliver them into the custody of the nearest commercial agent, to be returned for trial to their native country. Such persons, however, shall not be subjected to any ill-usage in excess of necessary restraint.

ART. III. The merchant vessels of either power shall be permitted, at the option of their owners, to frequent the ports of the other which are open to foreign trade. Export and import duties and all other customs charges shall be paid as provided by the regulations already agreed to between the two Governments.

If the vessels of either power are driven by stress of weather or stranded upon the coasts of the other, their crews shall be permitted to land at the nearest point in order to purchase supplies and to repair their vessels. All expenses shall be borne by the masters of the ships concerned, and all necessary assistance and protection shall be rendered by the local authorities.

If a ship of either power be wrecked upon the coast of the other, the local authorities shall devise measures to preserve life and property. They shall deliver over the passengers and crew to the nearest commercial agent of the Government concerned, who will return such shipwrecked persons to their native land, in order to avoid the expenses involved in the former rules for dealing with such cases.

If the merchant vessels of either country, not being driven thither by stress of weather or to make necessary repairs, clandestinely visit ports of the other country not open to foreign trade, for the purpose of traffic, such vessels and their cargoes shall be subject to seizure and confiscation.

It is, however, agreed that the fishing vessels of either power shall be allowed to frequent the coasts of Ping Au, Huang Hai Tao, in Corea, and of Shantung and Mauchuria, in China, for the purpose of taking fish. The fishermen may land at pleasure to purchase food and water. They shall not be permitted to carry on a clandestine traffic in merchandise, and if found guilty of such conduct the vessel concerned will be subject to seizure and confiscation.

If fishermen are guilty of violation of the laws or regulations of any locality where they land they shall be arrested and handed over to the nearest commercial agent to be dealt with as provided in Article II.

After the expiration of a period of two years from the date of this convention the question of the dues and duties to be levied upon fishing craft shall be taken up and conjointly determined by the two Governments.

[NOTE.—The Shantung fishermen, because the fish are driven over to the Corean coasts, opposite Shantung, by the steamers, go clandestinely in thousands every year to fish among the islands along the Huang Hai Tao, in Corea.]

ART. IV. Subjects of either power proceeding to the ports of the other, which are open to foreign trade, and peaceably attending to their affairs, shall be permitted to lease buildings or land and to construct residences or other buildings thereon. They shall be allowed to traffic in all native produce and other merchandise not declared contraband by law. They shall pay import and export duties and tonnage dues, according to the regulations and tariff mutually fixed by the customs authorities of the two Governments. In addition to such dues and duties, whenever it is desired to transport native produce from one open port to another open port, such produce having paid export duty at the first port shall in addition thereto upon entry at the second port pay half of the export already levied.

Since Corean subjects are permitted by law to trade in Peking, Chinese subjects shall be at liberty to open warehouses at Yang Hua Chin and Han Cheng.* Aside from this privilege the subjects of either power shall not be permitted to transport merchandise into the interior or to open shops there for its sale.

If the subjects of either Government wish to proceed to the interior of the territory of the other in order to purchase native produce, they shall make application through their respective commercial agents to the local authorities, and the two above-named officials will issue a joint permit for the point to which the applicant desires to proceed. He shall be allowed to hire carts, horses, or boats at his option, and will be required to pay all local and *lekin* taxes on the native produce purchased by him.

Subjects of either power desiring to travel in the interior of the territory of the other must make application to the commercial agent concerned, who, with the local authorities, will issue a joint passport allowing them to proceed. If at any point in the interior such persons are guilty of offenses against the laws, they may be arrested by the local authorities and delivered to the nearest commercial agent to be dealt with according to Article II. They shall not, however, be subjected to any ill-usage in excess of necessary restraint.

ART. V. Heretofore trading posts have been established upon the border lines of the two Governments at Icho, Huch Ning, and Ching Yuan, at which points the trade was controlled by officials. Much inconvenience resulted from this system. It is therefore now agreed that trading posts shall be established at Icho and Chamen on either side of the Ya lu Chiang, and at Huci Chun and Kuci Ning on either side of the In Men Chiang, to which the subjects of the two powers shall be freely permitted to proceed for purposes of traffic. At each of

---

* [역주] Two suburbs of Séoul. [C. H.]

these points officials will be stationed by the Government within whose domain it lies to preserve order and collect the revenue.

At the trading posts a uniform *ad valorem* duty of 5 per centum will be levied upon all exports and imports excepting red ginseng. The requisitions heretofore made by the officials at these trading posts for residences, food, &c., are all abolished. Civil or criminal cases at law between the residents on the border shall be dealt with by the respective local authorities according to regulations heretofore made.

The northern superintendent of foreign trade and the King of Corea will respectively detail officers to examine and report minute regulations for the conduct of these trading posts, which will be submitted for the imperial approval.

ART. VI. The subjects of the two powers, whether at the ports open to foreign trade or at the trading posts, are forbidden to traffic in or transport foreign or native opium or munitions of war. Violations of this provision shall be visited with the utmost severity of the laws. Corean subjects are permitted, under existing regulations, to import red ginseng into China upon payment of an *ad valorem* duty of fifteen per centum. If subjects of China clandestinely export red ginseng from Corea without the consent of that Government, the merchandise in question shall be liable to seizure and confiscation.

ART. VII. Heretofore the Government post route between the two countries has been by land *via* Cha Men, and the cost of maintenance has been very great. As the inhibition against intercourse by sea has now been removed, each should be allowed to consult his own convenience and proceed by the sea route. As, however, Corea has neither steam vessels of war or commerce, the northern superintendent of foreign trade will be requested by the King of Corea to appoint for the present one of the vessels of the China Merchants' Steam Navigation Company to make one round trip between china and Corea each month, for which service a certain subsidy shall be paid by the Corean Government. Chinese vessels of war will also cruise along the coast of Corea and visit the various ports for purposes of observation and protection. All contributions by local authorities to such vessels are done away with, and all supplies needed for the vessels will be purchased and paid for by their officers. The officers of such vessels, from the chief of squadron down, will correspond with the local authorities upon terms of equality and shall be treated with all due consideration.

The crews of vessels of war shall be kept under strict control by their officers when they are permitted to land, and not be allowed to molest the inhabitants nor to create disturbances.

ART. VIII. The brief and general regulations as fixed herein shall in the first instance be put into operation in all things stipulated herein, and shall be faithfully observed and kept by the officers and people of the two contracting powers.

Hereafter such additions or alterations as may be necessary will be from time to time discussed by the northern superintendent of foreign trade and the King of Corea, and, when agreed to, will be submitted to His Imperial Majesty for his approval.

Concluded by Chon Fu, customs intendant, &c.; Ma Chien Chung, expectant intendant, superintended by his excellency, Li, &c., &c., on the part of China; and Chao Ning Hsia, senior envoy; Chin Hung Chi, junior envoy; Yü Yun Chung, secretary, on the part of Corea.

———

[Inclosure 2 in No. 85.—Extract.]
Commercial regulations between China and Corea.

(Memorandum.)

PEKING, December 19, 1882.

The Chinese text, from which the foregoing translation was made, was obtained by me indirectly, but was submitted to certain ministers of the foreign office, and pronounced by them to be correct.

As the treaties made by the United States, Great Britain and Germany with Corea are identical in terms, the last two named being merely copies of the first, the comparisons herein made between our treaty with Corea and the Chinese commercial regulations will apply with equal accuracy to the English and German treaties.

If the first sentence in the preamble to these regulations be kept in mind, and the statement that the canons of official intercourse between Corea and China are fixed, be accepted as a fact, as if doubtless is, and it be further borne in mind that the business of negotiating these regulations was carried on in careful conformity to these canons, then much valuable light is thrown upon the question as to the exact relations which exist between the two Governmets concerned. Thus the preamble contains no declaration that the King of Corea acted either in his sovereign right, or even of his own option, in the appointment of envoys to negotiate these regulations. And what is far more important and significant, no provision or stipulation is contained anywhere in them for their ratification or rejection by the King. On the contrary, Article VIII provides that the regulations shall go into effect at once, and that in the future desirable amendments or alterations shall be discussed between the Chinese northern superintendent of foreign trade and the King of Corea, *acting as equals*, and that their conclusions shall be submitted to the Emperor of China, to be approved or rejected by him alone.

The natural inference from this provision, and from the general drift and tenor of the regulations as a whole, would seem to be that His Majesty the Emperor directed his excellency Li and the King of Corea to prepare a series of commercial regulations; that these two high authorities delegated this duty to certain subordinates, and that here the power or authority of the King ended; while, as all the negotiations were conducted at Tien-Tsin, his excellency Li practically superintended and controlled not only the action of his own delegates, but of the Corean delegates as well. There is nothing to show that the King of Corea had either voice or independent control in the business beyond the nominal right to name his substitute.

Articles I, V, VII, and VIII provide that in all negotiations connected with the enforcement of these regulations the Chinese northern superintendent of foreign trade is to correspond upon a footing of equality with the King of Corea. The Chinese text of the articles named shows this beyond the possibility of question. If further proof of this fact were needed, it is found in Article I, in which it is provided that the King of Corea, on his part, shall appoint an envoy and commercial agents to China, and that Chinese commercial agents shall be accredited to the Corean Government, not by the Emperor of China, but by the northern superintendent of foreign trade. Thus, on the part of China, the appointment of commercial agents, or consuls, as we should call them, a prerogative usually reserved to the supreme authority itself, is relegated to a local officer. In other words, these agents are to be appointees of an appointee of the Emperor, and one who, though of high rank, may be removed with or without cause or reason assigned, at the whim of his master.

Article I further provides that the Corean envoy, who is to reside not at

Peking, but at Tien-Tsin, shall rank with an intendant of circuit. And this officer, by the various treaties between China and foreign powers, is made equal in rank with a consul. [See Article X of our treaty of Tien-Tsin, and similar articles in other treaties.]

Article I of these regulations also provides that the Corean envoy may be allowed to address either the northern or southern superintendents of foreign trade only as an inferior addresses his superior. This is incontestably shown by the Chinese text. Thus the Corean envoy to China, or more properly to Tien-Tsin, would appear to rank with a consul, or, at the utmost, with a consul-general.

* * * * * * * * *

Recurring now for a moment to the point already made that these regulations reduce the King of Corea to a level with the Chinese superintendent of foreign trade, it should be added, in order to avoid misapprehension, that this cannot be fairy held to mean an absolute equality of rank or authority. Within certain well-defined limits officials of different rank correspond upon a basis of equality in China. Thus high ministers of state, members of the privy council, correspond upon such a footing with viceroys and even governors of provinces; and what is more to the point, his excellency Li, the northern superintendent of trade, corresponds upon a basis of equality with his imperial highness Prince Kung, who is practically the present head of the Government.

All that is intended to be maintained is that, by these regulations, the head of the Government of Corea is reduces, so far as all official intercourse is concerned, to a level with an appointee of the head of the Government of China. As stated above, these facts throw much valuable light upon the question of the exact relation which exists between China and Corea, and they also raise certain intricate questions which must be determined by our Government in case our treaty with Corea is put into operation, some of which I beg to suggest.

First. If, for purposes of international intercourse, the King of Corea is held as the equal of a Chinese minister of state, what is to be regarded as the status of the President of the United States *vis-à-vis* the King of Korea?

Second. What is to be the basis of official relationship between the diplomatic and consular representatives of the United States in China and the Corean envoy and commercial agents?

Third. What is to be the basis of official relationship between the diplomatic and consular representatives of the United States in Corea, and the Chinese commercial agents to that country appointed by the northern superintendent of trade?

The last clause of the preamble to the commercial regulations, in which it is declared that they are to be regarded as so many concessions on the part of China, "and are not within the scope of the favored nation rule" existing between "the several treaty powers and China," is interesting and might almost be called amusing. As there are absolutely no concessions to Corea found in these regulations which are not already existing in each or all of the treaties between China and the western powers (the recognition of the right of Coreans to trade in Peking excepted), it is quite apparent that this clause was inserted by his excellency Li, under the mistaken idea that it would serve to prevent the application of the "favored nation rule," as found in the recent treaties between the United States, England and Germany on the one hand, and Corea on the other, to the concessions found in these commercial regulations as made by Corea to China, which have not been made by Corea to the three powers named above; and thus to secure to Chinese subjects the exclusive monopoly of certain rights and privileges in Corea. What these rights and privileges are, and their value and importance, will be pointed out in detail further on. It is manifest, without argument, that the clause in question cannot in any sense serve the purpose for which it was intended, and that, so far as the United States are concerned, if can have value only as, and to the extent that, our Government may see fit to recognize it.

Article II of these regulations determines a system of judicial procedure, in all cases in which Chinese in Corea or Coreans in China are concerned. Cases in Corea in which Chinese subjects are alone interested are heard by Chinese authorities; those in which Coreans are plaintiffs and Chinese are defendants are also heard by the Chinese authorities; and those in which Chinese are plaintiffs and Coreans are defendants are heard by the Chinese and Corean authorities sitting as judges, with conjoint and equal powers. Coreans in China are relegated to the exclusive jurisdiction of the local (Chinese) authorities, the Corean commercial agents having only the right to ask a new trial.

Thus China refuses exterritorial jurisdiction to Corea over Corean subjects in China, and assumes it to an extent never claimed by western powers in this Empire, over her own subjects within Corean territories.

The special interest we may feel in this fact centers in the conclusive answer it affords us to any complaints made in future by China as to the injustice of the exterritorial system as maintained by us here. And a more positive and absolute answer would be hard to find.

While it is true that this article gives to Chinese officials a wider range of exterritorial jurisdiction in Corea than is conceded to United States officers in the same country by Article IV of our treaty with Corea, it would not, in my opinion, be advisable for our Government to seek any modification of the stipulations in our treaty upon this point. Our experience for the past forty years in China has plainly shown that the system of joint tribunals unprovided with any common code of laws or judicial procedure, and in which each magistrate must be guided solely by the statues and regulations of his own country, has entirely failed to work to the satisfaction of either Government concerned. The system embodied in Article IV of our treaty with Corea has been found by universal experience in China to produce much more satisfactory results, and is now accepted by all the powers having treaties with this Empire. The provisions of Article III of these commercial regulations relative to vessels in distress and shipwrecks are substantially identical with the stipulations of Article III of our treaty, and need no comment.

It now remains to compare the commercial rights and privileges granted by these regulations to the subjects of either power, with those granted by treaty to subjects or citizens of other nations in either China or Corea; and more particularly to contrast privileges granted to Chinese in Corea with those granted by our treaty to citizens of the United States in the Corean Kingdom.

The commercial concessions to Coreans in China are easily enumerated. The ancient right of Corean merchants to trade in Peking is reaffirmed. But it should be stated that this right is very closely restricted. It does not permit them to establish themselves permanently as merchants here, nor even to open shops or warehouses for a single day. All it amounts to is this: whenever the King of Corea sends an embassy of any sort to the Emperor of China, Corean merchants are allowed to come to Peking in the train of such embassy. They can either sell their wares at wholesale to Chinese dealers, or peddle them in person about the streets. And within three days after the departure of any embassy, on its return to Séoul, all the merchants who came in its train are required to close their business and leave this city. In return for this very meager and questionable advantage, Chinese subjects are permitted by Article IV of these regulations to open warehouses and establish themselves permanently as merchants at

Yang-Hua-Chen and Han Cleng, which are the west and east suburbs of the city of Séoul. Corean subjects are also allowed to frequent two trading posts established in Manchuria near the Corean border, at Chamen and Huci Chun. And as equivalent to this privilege Chinese subjects are permitted to frequent two trading posts established at Icho and Huci Ning in Corea.

As to other trade privileges in China, Corean subjects are placed at a disadvantage by these regulations even as compared with other foreigners in the Empire. Thus, by Article IV, they are forbidden to transport foreign or native produce to the interior under any terms, and can only bring native produce from the interior to a port upon payment of all local taxes and *lekin*. These two privileges are not only granted to all foreign merchants in China, but they can also commute the inland taxes and *lekin* by the use of transit passes. It is true, indeed, that by this same article Chinese merchants cannot take their wares to the interior of Corea, with the exception of course of the two suburbs of Séoul and the trading posts already mentioned. But it must be borne in mind that there are neither inland taxes nor *lekin* in Corea. Hence, while Corean subjects can only bring native produce from the interior of China at a disadvantage, even as compared with foreign merchants, since the use of transit passes is denied them, Chinese can go at pleasure to any point in the interior of Corea and bring native produce therefrom free from any duties or charges whatever save the export duty of five per centum *ad valorem*. Thus, it is manifest that under the terms of these regulations, the lion's share of the benefits of commercial intercourse between China and Corea will fall to the Chinese. And, as though this were not enough, by Article VII, the Corean Government is required to subsidize a Chinese steamship line, by means of the vessels of which this intercourse will be mainly carried on.

To turn now to a particular comparison of the commercial privileges granted by these regulations to Chinese subjects in Corea, with similar privileges granted by our treaty to citizens of the United States in the same country—

First. Citizens of the United States are permitted to establish themselves at such of the ports of Corea as are open to foreign trade, and to pursue their various callings and avocations within the limit thereof. These ports are understood to be, though not specified in the treaty, those open to the Japanese, namely, Fu-San, Ren-Chuan, and Yung Sing. To these is to be added Yang-Hua, which by the convention of August 30, 1882, with Japan, is to be opened within one year to foreign traffic. Chinese subjects are permitted by these regulations to establish themselves and to follow their avocations at all these ports, and, *in addition to this*, to reside at the two suburbs of Séoul, and at two trading posts, already mentioned, in the interior of Corea.

Second. Private citizens of the United States are not permitted to travel in the interior of Corea. Chinese subjects are allowed, by Article V of these regulations, to travel freely throughout the Kingdom under passports, which, upon application, are to be issued by the commercial agents and local authorities acting conjointly. Diplomatic and consular representatives of the United States can travel under passport in the interior by virtue of stipulation of the Japanese convention mentioned above.

Third. Citizens of the United States are forbidden either to transport foreign imports to the interior, or to proceed thither to purchase native produce. Chinese subjects are permitted to transport all merchandise of every class to four points named in the interior, two trading posts, and two suburbs of Séoul, and to proceed to any point of the interior, purchase and bring out native produce, paying no other taxes thereon than the export duty.

Fourth. Citizens of the United States are forbidden to transport native produce from one open port to another open port. Chinese subjects are allowed to transport this class of merchandise from one open port to another, upon payment at the second port of one-half of the export duty; that is to say upon payment of 2½ per cent. *ad valorem*.

Fifth. Citizens of the United States are required to pay an import duty of 10 per centum or 30 per centum *ad valorem* upon all goods imported into Corea, according as such goods fall within one or the other of two general classes. Chinese subjects can import the same articles into Corea, *via* either of four trading posts, upon payment of a uniform duty of 5 per centum *ad valorem*. (See Article V, of the regulations.) As these posts are situated on the banks of two rivers of some size, this discrimination may prove to be of serious importance.

Article IV of the regulations prescribes that the subjects of China shall pay, in Corea, duties and tonnage dues according to regulations and tariff fixed by the customs authorities. As it is not known whether these are or are not the same as those prescribed in our treaty with Corea, it is impossible to say whether there is or is not a discrimination against our people upon this point.

To summarize, the following privileges are denied to our people and granted to Chinese in our treaties with Corea.

A.—To reside and trade at four points in the interior.

B.—To travel in the interior under passport.

C.—To take foreign produce to four points in the interior, and to proceed to the interior and bring out native produce.

D.—To transport native produce from one open port to another; and

E.—A discrimination of ½ in one case and ⅝ in the other to our disadvantage and to the benefit of Chinese importers in the duties on all foreign merchandise imported via certain routes into Corea.

No argument or explanation is needed to show the immense value of the concessions made peculiarly to Chinese merchants and their disastrous effect upon any attempt made by foreigners of other nationalities to build up commercial enterprises in Corea. With the right to establish themselves permanently at four centers of trade in the interior; to take thither all classes of foreign merchandise for sale; to scour the country from end to end, under the protection of passports, in search of new avenues of trade, and in the purchase of native merchandise either for the open ports or for export to foreign countries; to control the coast trade in native produce, which last they readily do, as other foreigners are shut out from this trade, and Coreans have no steamships—with all these exclusive rights it is easy to see that Chinese merchants, with their keen scent for gain, and free from all danger of successful rivalry or competition, will soon fill Corea like a swarm of locusts, and any attempt to build up American trade with that country will be futile.

Making all due allowance for the imaginary or real rights of Chinese as suzerain of Corea is still remains true that these commercial regulations are greatly one-sided.

*　　*　　*　　*　　*　　*　　*　　*　　*

CHESTER HOLCOMBE.

191

閔泳穆(1883. 5/高宗二十年四月) ➜ L. H. Foote

조약비준대표 영접 통보

大朝鮮國督辨交涉通商事務閔 奉書大美國欽差大臣福閣下 頃聞貴大臣啣命 遠涉 已到本國地方 曷任欣喜 本大臣竊以在本國京城換約 實屬親睦 煩請貴 大臣移玉 玆派本衙門協辦洪英植 主事金思轍 前往仁川口岸迎接 卽同貴大 臣到京 惟祈遄臨 順頌勛祺 不一

　　癸未四月初　日　名另肅

高宗(1883. 5. 18/高宗二十年四月十二日) ➡ 閔泳穆

조약비준 전권 위임장

大朝鮮國大君主 督辦交涉通商事務閔泳穆 玆因大美國條約互換 特派卿爲全權大臣 與大美國欽差大臣福妥商辦理 克體委毘之意 欽哉
大朝鮮國開國四百九十二年四月十二日
大君主 安寶

(1883. 5. 19/高宗二十年四月十三日)

조미수호통상조약 비준서

大朝鮮國大君主批曰 這大美國條約予已詳察省覽 各款各節 逐一均可施行
爲此批準 盖用國寶 並親行畵押 用昭憑信
大朝鮮國開國四百九十二年四月十三日
大君主　　御押

| 大朝鮮國 |
| 大君主寶 |

閔泳穆(1883. 5. 19/高宗二十年四月十三日) ➙ L. H. Foote

비준 교환 일자 통보

大朝鮮國統理交涉通商事務衙門督辦閔 爲照會事 照得 本國與貴國上年在仁川口所立條約 玆訂於本日互換 應請貴大臣前臨本署 本大臣不勝欣企之至 相應照會 爲此照會 貴大臣請煩査照施行 須至照會者
　右照會
大美國駐朝鮮欽差大臣　福
癸未四月十三日　　蓋印

閔泳穆(1883. 5. 20/高宗二十年四月十四日) ➜ L. H. Foote

국왕 접견 및 미 대통령 국서 봉정 시각 통보

관련문서 Foote 접견시 의주(儀注)

逕啓者 本大臣將貴大臣進呈國書之由稟明 已奉兪旨 以今日上午十一點鍾訂期先告 煩請貴大臣屆期命駕前詣 順頌勛祺 敬具

癸未四月十四日　督辦交涉通商事務　　　閔泳穆
大美國欽差大臣　　福　閣下

【관련문서】

美使接見儀注

美國國書進呈日 至美欽差公使同參贊官 詣敦化門外下車 奉國書由正門入 公使以下由西門入 參議在門內相候 一同前赴休憩所 督辦協辦承旨先至 設茶少憩 承旨奏請公使進見 上御便殿南面坐 承旨一員史官一員寶劍二員內侍二員侍立 御座前設紅案 督辦協辦參議 引公使同入進見 上起立 公使行三鞠躬禮 上三擧手答之 公使奉國書進呈 上親受轉授承旨 承旨將國書譯漢文讀奏訖 使臣行詞 上擧手溫問 語畢 公使將退 行鞠躬禮 上擧手如初 公使回至休憩所 督辦協辦參議從出 茶罷 由敦化西門出

L. H. Foote(1883. 5. 20/高宗二十年四月十四日)

高宗 알현시 Foote의 답사(答辭)

관련문서 (1) Foote의 전권위임장
(2) 속방조회에 대한 미 대통령의 회답

謄美使廷見時對語

大美國伯理璽天德 特派本大臣 前來貴國京城 將兩國所立條約帶來 因兩國均已批准 昨日業經互換 大美國伯理璽天德 另有函覆呈覽 盖欲兩國政府永相和好 又以本大臣素信于人 是以派來 長駐貴國京城 本國批准條約 將來與朝鮮必能有益 現在尙德之時 非比尙力 朝鮮向未與各國通商 自今以後 定卜永享利益 目下各國 競尙新制 凡製造及土貨等件 自必日有起色 富國富民矣 故大美國伯理璽天德 爲貴國旣已通商 與鄰國和好 不勝欣賀 謹呈國書並函覆 叩見

【관련문서 1】

美國國書譯漢文

大美國伯理璽天德阿禮圖 致書於大朝鮮國大君主 大美國民會 商允務與大朝鮮國通商 玆特派李國聲名素著之員福德 作爲駐貴國二等欽差大臣 該大臣深知合衆國與貴君主及貴政府修好之心 庶與貴國臣鄰彼此往來 永爲和睦 因素悉該大臣公平明愼 料亦貴君主之所欣慰者也 後此辦事自能允治 而兩國政府必加輯睦 換約之後 兩國人民必能長受其益 本國政府信該大臣旣深 亦望貴君主相信之切也 是則願貴君主神明呵護 福德攸隆焉

西紀一千八百八十三年三月初九日
大美國伯理璽天德　　阿禮圖　　畵押

憑　首相　費林輝生
癸未二月初一日

【관련문서 2】

美國答書^{譯漢文}

大美國伯理璽天德阿禮圖　函覆大朝鮮國大君主　今特派欽差大臣福德前往貴國　上年立約之時　曾接奉貴君主來書　玆特修覆　着其代呈　盖朝鮮與中國往來　若無妨碍本國商民之事　此外槪不與聞　亦不詢及朝鮮爲中國屬邦　凡貴國內外等事　已知歸貴君主自爲主持　實深仰慕　而於通商一項　亦猶是自主之國焉　本國民會　旣皆允諾修好　自應批准　除條約內第六款所議數語外　均卽遵行　以此卽作爲自主之國　否則本國槪未與之訂交　故條約內載之言　均極曉暢　兼之立約之時　有中國大官在場　不但不爲阻滯　而反爲助理　益足見和睦之至意焉　遙祝貴君主及臣民同登仁壽矣

西紀一千八百八十三年三月十四日
大美國伯理璽天德　阿禮圖　畫押　　　　　　　　　憑　首相　費林輝生
　　　　　　　　　　　　　　　　　　　　　　　　癸未二月初六日

李鴻章, 張樹聲(1883. 6. 26/光緒九年五月二十二日)

조미조약 제6조의 개정에 관한 상주

爲朝鮮與美國上年議訂條約 現已屆期互換 恭摺仰祈聖鑒事 竊據朝鮮國王咨稱 本年四月初七日 美國全權公使福德航到仁川 該國王特派督辦交涉通商事務閔泳穆爲全權大臣 於四月十三日會同該國公使將上年仁川口所訂條約批准互換 除第六款內一節另行補訂外 按照原約協議施行 咨請轉奏 並將原約第六款補訂一節 及美國國書各棠 錄送前來 伏查上年春間美國與朝鮮結約通好 經臣鴻章遵旨妥籌 代訂約案 奏派候選道馬建忠前往襄助 將議定條約十四款 於光緒八年四月初六日 在朝鮮仁川港由該兩國所派議約大員鈐印畫押 約內聲明仍俟兩國批准 總以一年爲期 在朝鮮仁川府互換 亦經臣樹聲照抄約本奏陳在案 朝美二國之首定是約也 甚非日本所便 上年臣樹聲接出使日本大臣黎庶昌電告 日人喧傳美朝條約美廷批駁不准 意在慫恿改議 今春駐日本英使 亦遣人赴朝鮮煽誘 雖經臣樹聲送飭中書馬建常密告朝鮮君臣 務須堅持原約 拒其所請 然美約未換 簧鼓孔多 常慮朝鮮未嫺交涉 易爲所愚 今美國以一年屆期 特派使臣前赴朝鮮互換條約 實能守敦信修睦之義 查原約第六款內載並不得以土貨由此口販運彼口一節 此次補訂但不禁美國船隻從朝鮮此口至彼口裝出口之土貨 或交卸運來洋貨之意數語 核之原約 於朝鮮自有權利 並無貶損 此外旣稱均卽遵行 自照原約 毫無更改 朝鮮與泰西通好議約 以美國爲權輿 美約換妥 續至各邦均可援據始事 以爲因應 此後遵守勿墜 以維外交 保有權利 以謀內治 是在該國君臣之善其後矣 除照錄朝鮮國王咨文 及補訂原約第六款專條 美國國書 恭呈御覽外 所有朝鮮與美國議訂條約屆期互換緣由 謹合詞恭摺具陳 伏乞皇太后皇上聖鑒訓示 謹奏

198

高宗 ➡ 總署(1883. 6. 27/光緒九年五月二十三日)

조약 비준 통보

관련문서 (1) Foote 신임장
(2) 조미수호통상조약 제6조의 수정

五月二十三日 朝鮮國王文稱 照得本年四月初七日 美國全權公使福德航到仁川 敝邦差員迎入京城 將派督辦交涉通商事務閔泳穆爲全權大臣 於本月十三日會同該國公使將上年仁川口所訂條約批准互換 除第六款一節另行補訂外 按照原約協議施行 該公使仍駐京城辦事 查上年原約悉屬妥善 實由皇上綏靖之恩 亦惟諸王公大人曁北洋大臣經畫遠謨 派大員襄辦 致有今日交際公允 永遠維持 當職謹與一國臣庶 北望攢頌 感戴洪庇 玆將美國原約第六款補訂一節及該國國書二本照錄各案 庸備鑑裁 請煩轉奏天陛 以表小邦無事不達之忱焉 爲此合行移咨 請照驗施行

【관련문서 1】

大美國伯理璽天德阿禮圖致書於大朝鮮國大君主 大美國民會商允務與大朝鮮國通商 玆特派本國聲名素著之員福德 作爲駐貴國二等欽差大臣 該大臣深知合衆國與貴君主及貴政府修好之心 庶與貴國臣鄰彼此往來 永爲和睦 因素悉該大臣公平明愼 料知貴君主之所欣慰者也 後此辦事自能允恰 而兩國政府必加輯睦 換約之後 兩國人民必能長受其益 本國政府信該大臣旣深 亦望貴君主相信之切也 是則願貴君主神明呵護 福壽攸隆焉

西歷一千八百八十三年三月初九日 癸未二月初一日
大美國伯理璽天德阿禮圖畫押 憑首相費林輝生

【관련문서 2】

今將在仁川口壬午年四月初六日 西歷一千八百八十二年五月二十二日 大朝鮮國與大美國所立條約 大朝鮮國大君主大美國伯理璽天德兩國特派全權大臣 於本日互換 先言明以該條約第六條內載幷不得以土貨由此口販運彼口等語 但不禁美國船隻從朝鮮此口至彼口裝出口之土貨 或交卸運來洋貨之意 此約繕寫英漢文字各俱二分存照

大朝鮮國京城 癸未年四月十三日 西歷一千八百八十三年五月十九日立

199

李鴻章 等 ➡ 總署(1883. 6. 27/光緒九年五月二十三日)

청국 연호 미기재(未記載)에 관한 문제

五月二十三日 署北洋大臣李鴻章等函稱 樹聲日前接吳提督長慶函報朝鮮與美國條約業經互換 當卽肅至馳達聰聽 頃接朝鮮國王咨報此事 請爲轉奏 刻卽據咨疏聞 並據附到咨鈞署公文 亦已備牘轉呈 查補訂原約第六款一節 似無大關碍 其餘各款均無更改 尙見美國始終要好 惟原約於朝鮮紀年之下均註明卽中國光緒某年月日 以示春秋遵王之義 此次稱訂專條 未書中國年月 事前馬中書建常曾擧此再三諄告朝鮮 當事逮臨時 該中書未與其事 遂竟不用其言 履霜堅冰 不可不慮 但換約業經竣事 往者已不可諫 幸原約由中國派員苤盟 繫以正朔 炳然可據 現在似祇可於復該國王文內略予語責 俾識天威不違咫尺 以儆其後 是否有當 並祈裁示 專肅 祇頌鈞福

總署(1883. 7. 4/光緒九年六月一日) ➡ 高宗(1883. 7. 19/光緒九年六月十六日)

조약문에 청국 연호 기재를 요구하는 자문

六月初一日 給朝鮮國王文稱 光緒九年五月二十三日 准署北洋大臣張 咨送 貴國王來咨內開 本年四月初七日 美國全權公使福德航到仁川 差員迎入京城 特派督辦交涉通商事務閔泳穆爲全權大臣 於本月十三日 會同該國公使將上 年仁川口所訂條約批准互換 除第六款一節另行補訂外 按照原約協議施行 玆 將美國原約第六款補訂一節及該國國書二本照錄 請轉奏等因 並將抄本移送 前來 查朝鮮國前與美國所訂條約 註明中國光緒某年月日 此次補訂專條 未 經書寫中國某年 與上次辦法不符 嗣後朝鮮國無論與何國辦理交涉文件 仍應 查照上年與美國所訂條約 一律繕寫中國年月日 以符體制 除已由署北洋大臣 將換約情形奏聞外 相應咨復貴國王查照可也

高宗 ➡ 總署(1883.8.16/光緒九年七月十四日)

청국 연호 기재 문제에 관한 자복(咨覆)

七月十四日 朝鮮國王文稱 光緒九年六月二十六日 承准貴衙門咨節 該查朝鮮國前與美國所訂條約 註明中國光緒某年月日 此次補訂專條 未經書寫中國年月 與上次辦法不符 嗣後朝鮮國無論與何國辦理交涉文件 仍應查照上年與美國所訂條約 一律繕寫中國年月日 以符體制等因 謹已閱悉 仍當遵照無違 相應咨覆貴衙門 請煩查照

高宗 ➡ 總署(1883.9.16/光緒九年八月十六日)

보빙사(報聘使) 파견 통보

八月十六日 朝鮮國王文稱 據統理軍國事務衙門狀啓 美國公使福德專來辦事 准約協議 其在修好之誼 合有回禮之擧等因具啓 據此 竊照小邦與美國旣修交好 以禮交聘 今於公使專來之後 理宜有答 玆特派協辦交涉通商事務閔泳翊爲全權大臣 協辦交涉通商事務洪英植爲副大臣 副修撰徐光範爲從事官 已於光緒九年六月十三日裝束發船 除將右項事理謹具咨申 煩乞貴衙門照詳轉奏施行

【關係資料】

1.

(1882. 5. 22/高宗十九年 四月六日)

조미수호통상조약

朝美條約

大朝鮮國與大亞美理駕合衆國 切欲敦崇和好 惠顧彼此人民 是以大朝鮮國君主 特派全權大官申櫶·全權副官金宏集 大美國伯理璽天德 特派全權大臣水師總兵薛斐爾 各將所奉全權字據 互相較閱 俱屬妥善 訂立條款 臚列於左

  第一款
嗣後大朝鮮國君主大美國伯理璽天德 竝其人民 各皆永遠和平友好 若他國有何不公輕藐之事 一經照知 必須相助 從中善爲調處 以示友誼關切

  第二款
此次立約通商和好後 兩國可交派秉權大臣 駐紮彼此都城 竝於彼此通商口岸 設立領事等官 均聽其便 此等官員 與本地官交涉往來 均應用品級相當之禮 兩國秉權大臣與領事等官 享獲種種恩施 與彼此所待最優之國官員無異 惟領事官 必須奉到駐紮之國批準文憑 方可視事 所派領事等官 必須眞正官員 不得以商人兼充 亦不得兼作貿易 倘各口未設領事官 或請別國領事兼代 亦不得以商人兼充 或卽由地方官 照現定條約代辦 若駐紮朝鮮之美國領事等官 辦事不合 須知照美國公使 彼此意見相同 可將批準文憑追回

  第三款
美國船隻在朝鮮左近海面 如遇颶風 或缺糧食煤水 距通商口岸太遠 應許其隨處收泊 以避颶風 購買糧食 修理船隻 所有經費 係由船主自備 地方官民應加憐恤援助 供其所需 如該船在不通商之口 潛往貿易拿獲 船貨入官 如美國船隻在朝鮮海岸破壞 朝鮮地方官 一經聞知 卽應飭令將水手先行救護 供

其糧食等項 一面設法保護船隻貨物 竝行知照領事官 俾將水手送回本國 竝將船貨撈起一切費用 或由船主 或由美國認還

第四款
美國民人在朝鮮居住 安分守法 其性命財產 朝鮮地方官 應當代爲保護 勿許稍有欺凌損毀 如有不法之徒欲將美國房屋業產搶劫燒毀者 地方官一經領事告知 卽應派兵彈壓 竝查拿罪犯 按律重辦 朝鮮民人 如有欺凌美國民人 應歸朝鮮官 按朝鮮律例懲辦 美國民人 無論在商船在岸上 如有欺凌騷擾 損傷朝鮮民人性命財產等事 應歸美國領事官或美國所派官員 按照美國律例 查拏懲辦 其在朝鮮國內 朝鮮美國民人 如有涉訟 應由被告所屬之官員 以本國律例審斷 原告所屬之國 可以派員聽審 審官當以禮相待 聽審官如欲傳訊查訊分訊訂見 亦聽其便 如以審官所斷爲不公 亦許其詳細駁辨 大美國與大朝鮮國彼此明定 如朝鮮日後改定律例及審案辦法 在美國視與本國律例 辦法相符卽將美國官員在朝鮮審案之權 收回以後 朝鮮境內美國人民 卽歸地方官管轄

第五款
朝鮮國商民竝其商船 前往美國貿易 凡納稅船鈔 竝一切各費 應遵照美國海關章程辦理 與征收本國人民及相待最優之國 稅鈔不得額外加增 美國商民竝其商船 前往朝鮮 貿易 進出口貨物 均應納稅 其收稅之權 應由朝鮮自主 所有進出口稅項及海關禁防偸漏諸弊 悉聽朝鮮政府設立規則 先期知會美國官布示商民 遵行現擬 先訂稅則大略 各色進口貨 有關民生日用者 照估價值百抽稅不得過一十 其奢靡玩要等物 如洋酒呂宋煙鍾表之類 照估價值百抽稅不得尚三十 至出口土貨 槪照値百抽稅不得過五 凡進口洋貨 除在口岸完納正稅外 該項貨物 或入內地 或在口岸 永遠不納 別項稅費美國商船進朝鮮口岸 須納船鈔 每噸銀五錢 每船按中 歷一季抽一次

第六款
朝鮮國商民前往美國各處 准其在該處居住 賃房買地起蓋棧房 任其自便 其貿易工作 一切所有土產 以及製造之物 與不違禁之貨 均許買賣 美國商民前往朝鮮已開口岸 准其在該處所定界內居住 賃房租地建屋 任其自便 其貿易工作 一切所有土產 以及製造之物 與不違禁之貨 均許賣買 惟租地時 不得稍有勒逼 該地租價 悉照朝鮮所定等則完納 其出租之地 仍歸朝鮮版圖 除案此

約內 所持明歸美國官員應管商民錢產外 皆仍歸朝鮮地方官管轄 美國商民不得以洋貨運入內地 售買亦不得自入內地 採買土貨 併不得以土貨由此口販運彼口 違者將貨物入官 竝將該商 交領事官懲辦

　　第七款
朝鮮國與美國 彼此商定 朝鮮商民 不准販運洋藥 入美國通商口岸 美國商民亦不准販運洋藥 入朝鮮通商口岸 竝由此口運往彼口 亦不准作一切買賣洋藥之貿易 所有兩國商民 無論僱用本國船別國船 及本國船爲別國商民僱用販運洋藥者 均由各本國自行 永遠禁止 查出從重懲罰

　　第八款
如朝鮮國 因有事故 恐致境內缺食 大朝鮮國君主 暫禁米糧出口 經地方官照知後 由美國官員轉飭在各口 美國商民一體遵辦 惟於已開仁川一港 各色米糧 槪行禁止 運出紅蔘一項 朝鮮舊禁出口 美國人如有潛買出洋者 均查拏入官 仍分別懲罰

　　第九款
凡砲位鎗刀火藥鉛丸一切軍器 應由朝鮮官自行采辦 或美國人奉朝鮮官准買明文 方准進口 如有私販查貨 入官 仍分別懲罰

　　第十款
凡兩國官員商民 在彼此通商地方居住 均可僱請各色人等 勤執分內工藝 唯朝鮮人遇犯本國例禁 或牽涉被控 凡在美國商民寓所行棧及商船隱匿者 由地方官照知領事官 或准差役 自行往拏 或由領事 派人拿交 朝鮮差役 美國官民不得稍有庇縱掯留

　　第十一款
兩國生徒往來學習語言文字律例藝業等事 彼此均宜勸助 以敦睦誼

　　第十二款
玆朝鮮國初次立約所訂條款 姑從簡略 應遵條約 已載者 先行辦理 其未載者 俟五年後 兩國官民 彼此言語稍通 再行議定 至通商詳細章程 須酌照萬國公

法通例 公平商訂 無有輕重大小之別

　　第十三款
此次兩國訂立條約 與夫日後往來公牘 朝鮮專用華文 美國亦用華文 或用英文 必須以華文註明 以免岐誤

　　第十四款
現經兩國議定嗣後 大朝鮮國君主 有何惠政恩典利益 施及他國 或其商民 無論關涉海面行船通商貿易交往等事 爲該國幷其商民 從來未霑 抑爲此條約所無者 亦准美國官民 一體均霑 惟此種優待他國之利益 若立有專條互相酬報者 美國官民 必將互訂酬報之專條 一體遵守 方准同霑優待之利益

其上各款 現經大朝鮮·大美國大臣 同在朝鮮仁川府 議定繕寫華·洋文各三分 句法相同 先行畫押蓋印 以昭憑信 仍俟兩國御筆批准 總以一年爲期 在朝鮮仁川府互換 然後 將此約各款 彼此通諭本國官員商民 俾得咸知遵守

大朝鮮國開國四百九十一年 卽中國光緒八年 四月初六日
全權大官 經理統理機務衙門事 申櫶
全權副官 經理統理機務衙門事 金弘集

大美國 一千八百八十二年五月二十二日
全權大臣 水師總兵 薛斐爾

2.

黃遵憲(1880. 9. 6/高宗十七年 八月 二日)

『조선책략(朝鮮策略)』

朝鮮策略 廣東黃遵憲私擬

地球之上 有莫大之國焉 曰俄羅斯 其幅圓之廣 跨有三洲 陸軍精兵百餘萬 海軍巨艦二百餘艘 顧以立國在北 天寒地瘠 故狡然思啓其封疆 以利社稷 自先世彼得王以來 新拓疆土 旣踰十倍 至於今王 更有囊括四海 幷吞八荒之心 其在中亞細亞回鶻諸部 蠶食殆盡 天下皆知其志之不少 往往合縱而相距 土耳其一國 俄久欲吞之 以英法合力維持 俄卒不得逞其志 方今泰西諸大 若德若英若奧若意若法 皆耽耽虎視 斷不可尺寸之土以與人 俄旣不能西略 乃翻然變計 欲肆其東封 十餘年來 得樺太洲於日本 得黑龍江之東於中國 又屯戍圖們江口 據高屋建瓴之勢 其經之營之 不遺餘力者 欲得志於亞細亞耳 朝鮮一土 實居亞細亞要衝 爲形勝之必爭 朝鮮危 則中東之勢日亟 亞欲略地 必自朝鮮始矣 嗟夫 俄爲虎狼秦 力征經營三百餘年 其始在歐羅巴 繼在中亞細亞 至於今日 更在東亞細亞 而朝鮮適承其弊 然則策 今日之急務 莫急於防俄 防俄之策 如之何 曰親中國 結日本 聯美國 以圖自强而已

何謂親中國 東西北 皆與俄連界者 惟中國 中國地大物博 據亞洲形勝 故天下以爲 能制俄者 莫中國若 而中國所愛之國 又莫朝鮮若 朝鮮爲我藩屬 已歷千年 中國綏之以德 懷之以恩 未嘗有貪其土地人民之心 此天下之所共信者也 況我淸 龍興東土 先定朝鮮 而後代明 二百餘年 字小以涖 事大以禮 當康熙乾隆朝 無事不以上聞 已無異內地郡縣 此非特文字同 政敎同 情誼親睦而已 抑亦形勝昆連 拱衛神京 有如左臂 休戚相關 而患難與共 其與越南之疏遠 緬甸之偏僻 相去固萬萬也 嚮者朝鮮有事 中國 必糜天下之餉 竭天下之力 以爭之 泰西通例 兩國爭戰 局外之國 中立其間 不得偏助 惟屬國 則不在此例 今日朝鮮之事中國 當益加於舊 務使天下之人 曉然於朝鮮與我 誼同一家 大義已明 聲援自壯 俄人 知其勢之不孤 而稍存顧忌 日人 量其力之不敵 而可與

連和 斯外釁潛消 而國本益固矣 故曰親中國

何謂結日本 自中國以外 寂與朝鮮密邇者 日本而已 在昔先王 遣使通聘 載在盟府 世世職守 至於近日 則有北豺虎 同据肩背 日本苟或失地 八道不能自保 朝鮮有一變故 九州四國 亦恐非日本所有 故日本與朝鮮 實有輔車相依之勢 韓趙魏合從 秦不敢東下 吳蜀相結 魏不敢南侵 彼以强隣交迫 欲聯脣齒之交 爲朝鮮者 自當捐小嫌 而圖大計 修舊好 而結外援 苟使他日者 兩國之輪舶鐵船 縱橫於日本海中 外侮自無由而入 故曰結日本

何謂聯美國 自朝鮮之東海而往 有亞美利加者 卽合衆國之所指都也 其土本爲英屬 百年之前 有華盛頓者 不願受歐羅巴人苛政 發奮自雄 獨立一國 自是以來 守先王遺訓 以禮儀立國 不貪人土地 不貪人人民 不強與他人政事 與其中國 立約十餘年來 無纖芥之隙 而與日本往來 誘之以通商 勸之以練兵 助之以改約 尤天下萬國所共知者 蓋其民主之國 共和爲政 故不利人有 而立國之始 由于英政酷虐 發憤而起 故常親於亞細亞 常疏於歐羅巴 而其人實與歐羅巴同種 其國之强盛 常與歐羅巴諸大 馳驟於東西兩洋之間 故常能扶助弱小 維持公議 使歐人不敢肆其惡 其國勢偏近大東洋 其商務獨盛大東洋 故又願東洋 各保其國 安居無事 則使其使節不來爲朝 爲朝鮮者 當遠泛萬里之中洋 而與之結好 況其迭遣使臣 有意以維繫朝鮮乎 引之以爲友邦之國 可以結援 可以紓禍 吾故曰聯美國 夫曰 親中國 朝鮮之所信者也 曰結日本 朝鮮之可將信將疑者也 曰聯美國 則朝鮮之所深疑者也

疑之者曰 日本 自平秀吉 興無名之師 蕩搖我邊疆 凌夷我城郭 茶毒我人民 賴明師攻守而後退 近年日本 變從西出 鷹瞬鶚視 益不可測 江華之役 西鄉隆盛 志在生釁 亦因巖倉大久保諸人 力爭而後已 彼其志 曷嘗須臾忘郢哉 條約之結 本要盟 不得不從耳 及與之曙 是何異閉門而揖盜乎 曰西鄉之議攻朝鮮 二三大臣 獨排衆議 執不可 彼非不欲薦食邊鄙 以厚自封殖 顧度德量力 有所不能 則不如其已耳 朝鮮立國數千來 未嘗無人 未嘗無兵 無論攻之未必勝 卽萬一獲勝 撤兵則復叛 留兵則無力 況日本有事朝鮮 中國勢在必爭 爾時日本 遣其使臣 謁李伯相 伯相告以必爭 又勸以徒傷和氣 毫無利益 故其謀不行 彼知以日本攻朝鮮 旣難操必勝 況加以中國之助 左提右挈 東征西討 而日本必不支 故西鄉之說 卒不得行 旣不敢行 又以朝鮮密邇近隣 存無滋他族 實逼處此之心 故汲汲然講信修睦者 其意欲朝鮮自强 而爲海西屏蔽也 揣時度勢 爲日本計 必不能不出於此 況又今日之日本 外强中乾 朝野乖隔 府帑空虛 自謀之不暇乎 兵家有言 知己知彼 故必知日本所以結朝鮮之故 無所疑 然後 知朝鮮之結日本 亦無可

疑

疑之者又曰 繪圖測地 險旣失 仁川一港 乃我帷闥 容彼往來 藩籬盡撤 非志圖人國 安用測安沿海之暗礁 侵畿輔之要地爲哉 曰古有禁販賣地圖於他國者 殺之無赦者 古有引外國使臣 繞道往來 不使知其我險要者 今非此之謂矣 今天下萬國 互相往來 近而東中 遠而歐美 凡沿海巖礁 皆編爲圖志 布之天下 以便航海 而遠則海濱 近則國都 皆有外使 終年駐箚 此通例也 盖力不足 雖拒之戶外 法取越南之邊鄙 英與緬甸之國政 亦不克自保 力足以自强 雖延之臥榻 英之民 偏居彼得俄都 俄之民 偏居倫敦英京 亦無足爲害也 自强之道 在實力 不在虛飾 況日本 旣不能謀人 則俾熟吾道 乃可以資救援 朝鮮素未知航海 則自識其險 亦可以自守護 從前日本 因兵庫開港 使臣駐京 抵死堅拒 至於一戰再戰而後 蟠然改圖 今行之六十餘年矣 王公守國烏繫乎此哉

疑之者又曰 朝鮮風氣 未與外熟 見彼東人 異言異服 或厚聚觀看 或偶爾詬辱維彼日人 志在恫惕 至於管理之官 亦敢拔刀以殺 苟和好出於眞誠 豈漫無約束 竟肆惡以呈毒哉 或曰 日本性情 好勝而不讓 貪利而寡恥 見小而昧遠 往往如此 特如此事 則兩國細民 猜嫌之未淺 非彼政府之意也 從前草梁一舘 雖曰通商 而朝鮮所以困辱而禁制之者 實無所不備 彼心懷憤怒 非伊朝夕 加以釜山所居 類多對馬窮民 彼輩無賴之徒 祇求自利 安知大體 鬪歐鎖事 固非約束之所則及 觀日本政府 於拔刀一事 撤去山之城 亦可知其志矣 爲朝鮮者 但當恪守條約 於彼之循理者 力加保護 然彼後於彼之無禮者 嚴請究辦 庶情誼相孚耦 俱無猜矣 苟拘拘於薄物細故 不能捐棄 而坐失至計 非知者之所宜出此也

疑之者又曰 日本與我 壤地相接 種類相同 自言結日本 吾固信之矣 若夫歐美諸國 去我數萬里 飲食衣服 不與我同 嗜幣不通 言語不達 彼亟亟然 欲與我結盟者 非鄙利而何 彼利則我害 而子言聯美國 此鄙人之所惑者也 曰美之爲國 分國施政 而合三十七邦 爲合衆國 統而統領 故得土不加廣 隣其南方 有名檀香山國者 意求內附 彼且拒絶 其國尙多曠土 其土多產金銀 其人善於工商 爲天下首富之國 故得土不加富 其不貪人土地 不貪人人民 此天下萬國之所共信者 而顧英法德意諸國 迭來乞盟 此則泰西所謂均勢之說也 今天下萬國 縱橫搏噬 甚於戰國 而列國星羅棊布 欲保無事 必求無甚弱 無甚强 互相維持而可 苟有一國焉 行其并呑則力厚 力厚則勢强 勢强則他國亦不克自安 歐洲一土 群雄角立 彼我之耽耽虎視者 旣無間可乘 故天下知其志必將東向 東向必自朝鮮始 俄苟有朝鮮 則亞細亞全勢 在其掌握 惟意所欲 而狹亞細

亞全局之勢 反而攻歐羅巴 勢殆不可敵 泰西公法 毋得剪滅人國 然苟非條約之國 有事不得與聞 此泰西諸國 所以欲與朝鮮結盟也 欲與朝鮮結盟者 欲取俄國一人欲佔之勢 與天下互均而維持之也 保朝鮮 卽所以自保也 此非獨美爲然 然英法德意 以朝鮮地瘠 必賴戰勝攻取 迭有創傷 以刱盟約 尙非其所願 惟美國 自以爲信義所著 久爲中東兩國所信服 欲以玉帛 不以兵戎 故其來獨先 然則美國之來 非特無害我之心 且有利我之心 彼以利我之心來 反疑爲圖利 疑爲害我 是不達時務之說也

疑之者又曰 朝鮮國小民貧 而與諸大國結盟 誅求無厭 供億無度 藝不將疲於奔命乎 風俗旣殊 禮節亦異 接之非其道 不將疑而滋釁乎 曰古所謂犧牲玉帛 陳於境上 以待强國 以庇吾民者 古人以小事大之禮也 而今則無是 今之小國 若比利時若瑞士若荷蘭國 皆自立 未聞諸大國 督責之 苛求之也 卽使臣聘問 領事駐箚 資粮匪屢 彼自供 初到不過一朝見 終歲不過一宴饗 擧凡郊勞贈賄 皆無有也 安有旣無所供 安有疲應 至於儀文之末 酬應之細 彼亦猶人情 但知我無輕慢鄙夷之心 彼尙有何督過 況朝鮮貧瘠 無所利於通商 彼今者 但欲締盟而已 尙未必遣使臣設領事乎 而又奚疑焉

疑之者又曰 傳敎之士 煽誘小民 干預國政 稍稍以法裁抑 則動啓鬪爭 或激事變 旣與結約 應許傳敎 深患安有窮乎 曰天主敎之橫 天下所共知 顧其敢於橫行者 恃法蘭西左袒之耳 自法敗於普 撤歸護衛敎主之兵 意大利 邊以偏師 取羅馬 逐其敎主 敎主失所依倚 勢遂驟弱 至於近日 法亦屢抑敎士 國勢變而敎門益衰矣 但於立約之始 聲明傳敎之士 須遵國法 若有違犯 與齊民同罪 彼敎士不得肆志 則吾民不知滋事 至於美國所行 乃耶穌敎 與天主敎 根源雖同 黨派各異 猶吾敎之有朱陸也 耶穌宗旨 向不干預政事 其人亦多純良 中國自通商來 戕殺敎士之案 層見疊出 無一耶穌敎者 亦可證其不如患也 彼敎之意 亦在勸人爲善 顧吾中土 周孔之道 勝之何啻萬萬 朝鮮服習吾敎 漸摩旣深 卽有不肖之徒從之 萬不至下喬木而入幽谷 然則令其傳敎 亦復何害 斯又不必疑也

疑之者又曰 誠如子言 天下有疏歐親亞素稱禮儀之美國 聯以爲交 未嘗不可 顧英法德意 從而效尤 接踵而至 則若之何 曰苟欲防俄 正利英法德意諸國之結爲盟約 互相牽制耳 且朝鮮 卽不利諸國之來 能終禁其不來乎 今地球之上 無論大小國 以百數 無一國能閉關絶入者 朝鮮一國 今日鎖港 明日又開 明日鎖港 後日必開 萬不能閉關自守也必矣 萬一不幸 俄師一來 力不能敵 則誠恐國非己有 英法德意 不顧俄人之專有其土 則群起而爭 潰壞決裂 殆不可收拾

前此有波蘭一國 俄德奧取以收分之 去年土耳其之役 俄師未撤 諸國交起 亦割分邊地 與澳與英與德而後已 朝鮮苟爲之續 非吾之所忍言也 卽曰 仗先王先公之靈 群神群祀之福 天祚朝鮮 必無此事 而英法德意迭遣兵船 要刦盟約 不戰則不勝其擾 戰而不勝 則如緬甸之受制於英 安南之受制於法 亦事之所常有 幸不至此 則結一不公不平之條約 百福要求 百端剝削 經歷十數年 兵強國富 不能更改 亦不知何以爲國 正爲防俄之幷呑 憚英法德意之要挾 聯美國 乃不得不亟亟哉 誠使趁美國使者來 而議一公平之條約 則一例泰西之友邦 卽可援萬國之公法 旣不容一人之專噬 又何爲諸國之先導 爲朝鮮造福 卽爲亞細亞造福 此之不爲 尙疑乎哉 群議旣釋 國是一定 於親中國 則稍變舊章 於結日本 則亟守條規 於聯美國 則急締善約 而卽奏請 陪臣常駐北京 又遣使居東京 或遣使駐華盛頓 以通信息 而卽奏請 推廣鳳凰廳貿易 令華商船來釜山元山津仁川港各口通商 以防日本商人之壟斷 又令國民來長崎橫濱 以習懋遷 而卽奏請 海陸諸軍 襲用中國龍旗 爲全國徽幟 又遣學生 往京師同文館 習西語 往直隷淮軍 習兵 往上海製造局 學造器 往福州船政局 學造船 凡日本之船廠炮局軍營 皆可往學 凡西人之天文算法化學鑛學地學 皆可往學 或以釜山等處 開學校 延西人敎習 以廣修武備 誠如是 朝鮮自強之基 基此矣 蓋於無事時 結公平條約 一利也 中東西國 與泰西所締條約 皆非萬國公例 其侵我自主之權 奪我自然之利 虧損過多 此固由來諸外情形 抑亦威逼勢刦 使之然也 今朝鮮趁無事之時 與外人交結 彼自不能多所要挾 卽曰歐亞兩土 風俗不同 法律不同 難遽合利來商人 歸地方管轄 然第與聲明 歸領事館暫管 隨時由我酌改 又立定領事權限 彼無所護符印 不敢多事 而其他 絶毒藥輸入之源 杜敎士蔓延之禍 皆可妥與商量 明示限制 自強之基也 於通商亦有利焉 我亞細亞居天地正帶 物産甚富 中國自唐宋以來 設市舶司 與外人通商 所用金錢 皆從外國輸入 數百年來 不可勝數 至於今日 金錢稍有流出 則以食鴉片烟之故也 日本受通商之害 則以易洋服用洋貨之故也 苟使不食洋藥 不用洋貨 則通商皆有利無害 朝鮮一國 雖曰貧瘠 然其地産金銀 産稻麥 産牛皮 物産固未嘗不饒 吾稽 去歲與日本通商之數 輸入之貨 値六十二萬 輸出之貨 値六十八萬 是歲得七八萬矣 苟使善爲經營 稍稍拓克 於百姓似可得利 而關稅所入 又可稍補國用 此又自強之基也 於富國亦有利焉 英國三島止産煤炭 法國止産葡萄 秘魯止産金銀 皆以富於天下 他若印度之然茶 古巴之糖 日本之綿 皆古無而今有 以人力創興之 竟得大利 朝鮮土尙膏腴 物産亦饒有 其人又多聰明 善工作 彼極南之奧大利亞 極之監察加 皆從古人跡不到之地 尙可開闢蓁莽 化

爲沃壤 況於朝鮮之素居正帶者乎 苟使從事於西學 盡力以務財 盡力於訓農 盡力而惠工 所有者廣植之 所無者移種之 將來亦可爲富國 又況地産金銀 人所共知 若得西人開鑛之法 隨地摧覓 隨時採堀 地不愛寶 民無遊手 利益更無窮也 此又自强之基也 於練兵又有利焉 中國聖人之道 不尙武 不尙巧 誠以自治其國 但求守文守質 以期安靜 不欲以囂凌之習 機械之器 導民以啓爭 然但使他人 不狹其所長 我亦可守舊而不變 今强隣交逼 日要狹我 日侮慢我 同一乘舟 昔以風帆 今以火輪 同一行車 昔以騾馬 今以鐵金道 同一郵遞 昔以驛傳 今以電線 同一兵器 昔以弓矢 今以鎗礮 使兩軍有事 彼有而我無 彼精而我粗 不及交綏 而勝負利鈍之勢 旣判然矣 朝鮮旣喜外交 風氣日開 見聞日廣 旣知甲冑戈矛之不可恃 帆檣槳櫓之無可用 則知講修武備 考求新法 可以固疆圉壯屛藩 此又自强之基也 旣可以圖利 又可以圖强 國無寡小 但使有人有財有兵 卽以自立 彼瑞士比利時 犬牙交錯於諸大之中 尙能爲國 況以朝鮮之素稱名都 獨當一面者乎 朝鮮旣能强 將來歐亞諸大 必將與之合縱以拒俄 苟其不然 坐視俄師之長駈 坐聽他人之爪分瓦解 而害可勝言哉 語有之曰 兩利相衡 則取其重 兩害相衡 則取其輕 況利害相去之甚遠 而可不早決計乎

嗟乎 朝鮮一國 三面海濱 古稱天險 西北壤地 與我相接 數千年來 仰戴聲靈 傾慕德化 惟知有中國 中國爲政之體 極不願疲中以事外 凡在藩服 惟冀其羈縻勿絕 服我王靈 但不敢箕踞向漢 卽不願損一兵 折一矢 以立威 而朝鮮因是之故 朝野上下 皆修文學禮義 中國之衣冠禮樂 屢世恪守 而莫敢失墜 老子所謂 雖有舟輿 無所乘之 雖有甲兵 無所陳之 至老死不相往來 誠天下一樂國矣 譬之 家有慈父 其子飽食安居 無所事 此朝鮮之所大幸也 而不幸至於今日 乃忽有天下莫强之俄羅斯 與之爲隣 而海道四闢 又無險阻之可扼 然猶賴其國僻處海隅 民貧土瘠 故未至如印度之納土與英 如越南之割地與法 如南洋加喇巴小呂宋諸國之幷於荷蘭 幷於西班牙 彼俄羅斯者 又立國偏小 有諸大國與之牽制 未暇東顧 遂得如天之福 世世相承 以至今日 至於今日 防俄之策 其不得不亟亟然 竭朝鮮一國之力 以防俄 小固不可以敵大 寡固不可以敵衆 弱固不可以敵强 以又幸而有中國 可以親 有同受俄患 力不足制朝鮮之日本 可以結 有疏歐親亞 侵人國之美利堅 可以和 斯蓋自先世箕子以來 殆乎今代世宗立國 群后在天之靈 所呵護而庇佑之 乃有此一機也 期所以乘此機者 其正在今矣 前此三十年 中國以焚烟 故議罷互市 而一戰於廣東 再戰於江寧 今此通商者十九處 結約者十四國矣 前此二十年 日本以劫盟 故志於在攘夷 以一戰於馬關 再戰於鹿兒島 今則偏地皆西人 學國學西法矣 當一二十年前 泰

西諸國 船舶猶未堅 槍械猶未精 英法美諸國之要求者 不過通商 故雖戰而敗 敗而成和 雖所締條約 所傷實多 而尙無大實 今則俄人之所大欲 專在關利 其船堅礮土 又遠勝於前俄國 近將樺太洲屯兵 移駐暉春 又於長崎 購煤五十萬銀 運往暉春 又遣大兵船二十餘號 派來太平洋 而朝鮮鎖港之稅仍興 二三年前之中國 日本相類 苟不知變計 恐欲求戰而敗 敗而和 不可復得也 嗟乎嗟乎 時勢之逼 危乎其危 機會之來 微乎其微 過此以往 未之或知 擧五大部 或親或疏之族 咸爲朝鮮危 而朝鮮切膚之災 乃反無聞知 是何異處堂之燕雀 遨遊以嬉乎 惟智慧 能乘時 惟君子 能識微 惟毫傑 能安危 是所望朝鮮之有人 急起而圖之而已 急起而圖之 擧吾策所謂親中國結日本聯美國 力行之 策之上者也 躊躇不決 旣忍需時 親中國 不過守舊典 結日本 不過行新約 聯美國 不過極飄風之船 受印關之書 第求不激變 第求不生釁 策之下者也 第虞我詐 自剪其羽 丸泥封關 深閉固拒 斥爲蠻夷 不屑與伍 迨乎事變之來 乃始卑屈以求全 倉皇之失措 則可謂無策矣 朝鮮立國千數百載 豈謂無人 能悉利害 而顧甘於無策乎 決計 在國主 輔謀 在樞府 講求時務 無立異同 在廷臣 力破積習 開道淺識 在士夫 發奮興起 同心合力 在國民 得其道則強 失其道則亡 一輔移間 而朝鮮之宗社繫焉 亞細亞之大局繫焉 忠言逆耳 利於行 良藥苦口 利於病 豈故爲危悚之言 以聳人聽哉 吾借著而對此策 非吾心所忍 顧以時勢之所逼 不得不出於此 乃不殫強顏以代謀 攖悠以苦諍 若夫吾策旣行 濟之以智勇 持之以忠信 隨時以變通 隨事而因應 下孚其群黎 內修其庶政 斯又環海生靈之慶 非此策之所能盡者矣

3.

R.W. Shufeldt의 개인 서한

(1) R. W. Shufeldt (1880. 4. 28) ➡ M. M. Molly Shufeldt

My dear Moll,

My last letter to you was from Hong Kong, from whence we started for Yokohama, via Luo Choo islands, but fate and adverse winds and seas forced us into this Port, fortunately as [____] say, for on arrival I found it not only much nearer to our objective point, Corea, but the only place in Japan where we could obtain the much needed information about that country. The Japanese have a military settlement at Fusan in Corea and their Consul at that port was here on leave. He readily gave me all the desirable points. He has since returned to his post and I have rec'd from Yokohama a letter from the Japanese Govt. at Yedo, through our Minister, to that official directing him to afford us every possible assistance. In addition to this I have met here the French [____] apoptotic of Japan. Monseigneur [____], who is in correspondence with the French missionaries in Corea and have read their letter in which they say that the Corean Govt. has released all of the Christian captives in the country and is now tolerating the missionaries or at least ceased to persecute them. I have also met the Chinese Consul for their port who informs me that his Govt. has advised Corea to make treaties with foreign powers, as a means to resisting the encroachments of Russia on its northern frontier. Under these circumstances I feel quite encouraged and shall start for Fusan on Monday next. Yesterday I telegraphed this last fact to the Dept. and asked of it how many instructions. I have as yet had no reply. If I only had the squadron now for a few months, to add to the prestige of the flag, I would be almost sure of success, but I shall go anyhow, for here in the East, the opening of Corea, is regarded as one unaccomplished event, of final importance to Western Nations. In the meanwhile the change of climate from the tropics to this sudden cold latitude has had a singular effect upon me personally. A day or two after arrival, I feel an imitation over my body which I must originally attributed to fleas, but on going one night to bed, I discovered myself all covered with welts and red blotches and very soon was so annoyed by the itching that for two nights and days I could not sit, lie or walk, suffered indeed a most cruel inconvenience. The Doctor attributed it to the fever escaping from my system, probably escaping the climate, as the [＿] in the scripture, went out to a herd of swine, and there I hope in my case, as in those into the river [＿] all events I am fine of it now and feel in every way better and brighter.

The months slip around and the time draws near for our start for home. You cannot imagine how impatient I am getting, the routine time of sea life has become almost intolerable to me, besides in my hours of depression, I think cui bono. Why work and worry over matters which after all, are no good to you or yours. If there is no reward here after, there certainly is no reward here for the disinterested labor. The men who idle their time at the dining table or in the salons of Washington, are the men who reap the harvest sown by humbler hands.

Yesterday I went shopping in Old Nagasaki. The town is only a shadow of its former self, European civilization is killing it. I found little if any [＿], no bronzes or lacquer ware, worth the buying, a few plates of Yuan blue and a set of Kaga tea plates and cups, were all I bought and there for their rarity!

If I do not write letters to the boys and to your dear mama, by this mail it is because I am full of wordy dispatches to H.M the King of Corea, which must be concreted here, in order to be translated before sailing and besides my usual work on sea, in waiting up our last port, was prevented by the rough weather, nobody reads these dispatches and everybody would need my letter and yet I write the one and leave the other unwritten, but I do not forget my friends. Soon I hope to greet many, who will receive me with a smile and who with a frown I know of one, who at least will meet me, with that living heart, which is to me the most precious of treasures, the one last link which binds me to life. The bay of Nagasaki, a perfectly landlocked and so quiet as to give one a [＿] of great rest, for the first there almost we lie in a [＿] and this is a great relief after the voyage of 30,000 miles and 40 different ports!

Now my dear, with love to all and until my return from Corea, (when I only go now to send my letter to the King and from there I shall return either here onto Yokohama to give him time to make his reply) I am as ever and forever your loving father.

(2) R. W. Shufeldt (1880. 5. 3) ➡ M. M. Molly Shufeldt

Nagasaki

My dear Moll,

I have just rec'd the mail up to Febry 24. We are underway for the Corea. The telegram from Sidney CB, demanding 1500.90 C5, is a puzzle to me as it was to you. I don't know any such person, didn't know the place, don't owe anybody, I can only suppose it came from a crazy man or a rascal. Your other matters a subject to consideration. I can only say that I do not want the thanks of Congress. I will not join the horde who are seeking for personal advancement. If the Dept. chose to give me the sqdrn well, if not well also, I expect the back from Corea in two weeks, I only go over now to open a correspondence when I return I will with write you more fully.

Adieu my dear daughter don't worry over my advancement- "let us have peace." Your loving father.

(3) R. W. Shufeldt (1880. 5. 22) ➡ M. M. Molly Shufeldt

My dear Moll,

The letter rec'd by last mail were of course matters of great grief to me but I trust that the arrival of Augustus in Washington has dispelled much feeling which you and your mother have entertained in regard to his return home. I leave entirely to him the justification of my action. I am glad to find by a pleasant letter from him dated San Frisco May 4 that he had reached that point in good health and spirits.

Since our arrival here, I have been worried by the slow progress of diplomacy in securing cooperation from the Japanese Govt. for our project in Corea. It was only yesterday that with the very efficient aid of our Minister I succeeded in getting the desired communication to the Corean Govt. My communication to the King of Corea is now on its way, under Japanese cover, to the country. Our Minister says it is an admirable document, "fit for a King," I only hope that it may produce the desired result. The great difficulty has been to get it started beyond the border of the "forbidden land." I was up all last night getting up a history of the present stage of the negotiation for the Govt. at home. My last dispatch from the Navy Dept was dated April 26, in this I was given discretion to remain as long as I deemed admissable. I have now consented to wait 60 days for an answer. This will bring us up to August 1. At that time of [ ], I fervently hope I get a favorable reply. I shall be able to start for home with permission of the Corean Gov to send a U.S. Commissioner to Corea. If snubbed or evaded I shall telegraph Dept for further orders. We sail tomorrow morning for Kobe and there gradually to Nagasaki. I send you slips from the papers here, to show the drift of sentiment among foreigners, on the Corean question, if we can open it, if we finish the cruise very creditably and finish éclat to the Govt. at home. I do not understand the trouble with Dr. Laurie and his parish, I am exceedingly sorry for him and his helpless family whatever the cause may be, I am very tired today my dear daughter and cannot write any more. The slips will give you all the news. With much love to your dear Mother and to all at home, I am an ever lovingly your father.

(4) R. W. Shufeldt (1880. 6. 11) ➡ M. M. Molly Shufeldt

My dear Moll,

    We have just arrived at this port and I am told a steamer leaves here this eve to connect with the mail at Yokohama for San Frisco. We found the Richmond here and during my call upon Admiral Patterson I saw Dr. Gunnell for a moment, he has promised to come and see me this afternoon and says he had a letter from you per last mail.

    So far the Corean project is in good training, my letter to the King having gone forward by special Japanese Courier. I have agreed to wait here for sixty-days if necessary any for the reply. If it should prove favorable we shall probably go to Corea again to commence negotiations, if not it will be for the Govt. to determine its future course. It will be difficult however to retreat now that the movement has been initiated, I have sent to Washington all the data, which will reach about July 4. If then the Dept. chosen to given me this Squadron for the purpose of [ ] the Corea in more force than I now possess, [ ] and good, if not I share probably return to the U.S. on the Ticonderoga and am ordered to advise with the Dept when necessary which I shall do as soon as I hear from Corea. We have just heard of the nomination of Garfield, in my opinion a most excellent choice, I have long since believed that Grant had no chance, ever since it became evident that he and his friends were following [＿] to get it. Your late letters have been so gloomy to say the least, that I have been in bad health, but I hope that your brother has done me the [＿] to see you and his mother. That I not only had nothing to do with his difficulty but that he went home contrary to my advice and wishes. Judging from his letter from San Francisco he must be in better health than when at here. He never looked wise or appeared in full strength while abroad. There seems to be so little that is cheerful in Washington, so small a prospect of a quiet home for you and myself, to say nothing of your dear mother, that I am sometimes sorry that we ever bought the house. Now that Gus is home, perhaps it would be well to shut it up, rent it or sell it and you come at to me either here or wherever I may be. Your mother could no doubt like to be with Gus, wherever he may be situated and I should prefer buying board for Genge rather than keep open house for children who I fear am unappreciative. Perhaps in a few years we might go back, with at least the poor privilege of dying in our own beds. Mason has not written me for six months and Genge has seldom, but in all the time they seem to have lived as if my house was theirs, but I am tired of this selfish, un filial conduct and see no remedy but to shut up the shop and live the life of a wanderer. I feel no responsibility for the support of the boys, only you and myself and yet I am constantly living in short allowance. Why should we continue to do it only my dear sister Martha must have a home whenever she wants it. She and I have grown well together. Whenever her son can share her and we have a roof to shelter us, it must be hers as well as ours. Today I am uneasy and unhappy, as if some evil here impending, perhaps the next mail will clear the sky.

 Today is the first summer day, and I have just been making my calls afloat. The harbor is quiet and the country beautiful, as beautiful only as can be in Japan, I wish my dear daughter you were here to enjoy it, then I should be happy indeed.

 Your loving father,

(5) M. M. Molly Shufeldt (1881. 7. 4) ➡ Mary Howey Shufeldt (mother)

My dear mother,

When I closed my letter at Shanghai, we expected to start that night, or early the next morning for Tientsin, but no steamer sailing, we were delayed until Friday night or rather Saturday morning as it was after midnight when we started. I told you didn't I about the little dinner Mrs. Denning gave for the Spanish and Brazilian ministers. If with it was no loss and a very nice dinner, Madonna Callado the Brazilian Minister's wife, the only lady present except Mrs. Denning and myself, but was particularly lively. Mr. Pindleton called again the night we left. Tell Mary he is looking very well. The Swatara is at Chefoo I fancy by this time and perhaps he may come up here. We came here on the Hae-an, the trip was very pleasant, the weather much brighter than on the other trips, and the ship very clean and comfortable. The captain, a Dane, had his wife on board, a very pleasant and well educated little Germany woman. The Atterburys will not leave till Sunday morning and were detained forty-eight hours by fogs and by mostly high tide at the far Sunday night. While sitting on deck we saw a wonderful bright [___] with an immense luminous tail. We had not seen it before, [___] to the light clouds which covered the entire heavens. Monday morning about 2 A.M. we stopped at Chefoo and remained till after 6 A.M. so that I had a good view of the bay. We took on board a number of passengers all gentleman and foreigners. Mr. Deitring, the Commissioner of Customs being one of them. He was very civil and offered any assistance in his power. Tuesday at 4.A.M. we arrived at the mouth of the Pei-ho river, cruised the bar a little after flood tide, and went on up the river. The most crooked chain you can imagine and besides the [___] sharp bends, very narrow. We were aground once for a few minutes and arrived in Tientsin about 10 o'clock, to find the only two remaining rooms in the Globe Hotel engaged for us by Major Mannix. Mrs. Mannix and the children are well, but dreadfully bitter by sand fleas, or, more likely fleas. This hotel is full of people connected with the new lithograph to be put up from here to Pekin. It is an envious looking place one story high and two rooms deep, built all around like a puzzle, of a white stiff concrete I fancy, and with a wide hall between each block of four rooms. It's not exactly the "Brunsevilo" and does not even remind you much of the

'Higgs' but is much better than I had expected. We had [___] unpacked a little, napped, had dinner and walked a little way along the Bend, or road that close to the river, to the Hae-an then about a block or two into the city and back to the Hotel. Lots of people called on father, none of them very interesting. As the next day began my life in China I might as well give you the singular purpose for each and every day. Most people have coffee &c in bed, but I don't fancy that arrangement, so I have my bath brought in the night before that. I may rise when I choose. After that I put on a dressing gown, a white one, and [___] for coffee, a very small cup, toast without butter, and fruit when it can be had. Then I write or read or sew until Father has bathed and breakfasted when he knocks in for me and will go out into the hall. By that time I have on the [___] you know there I wore at home, which with a blue neck tie.

4.

J. B. Angell (1880. 10. 22) ➜ W. M. Evarts

Duke of Genoa의 조선 방문 report 보고

No. 33
Legation of the United States
Peking
Honorable William M. Evarts
Secretary of State

Sir: -

In my No 21 I expressed the hope that I should soon be able to send you a copy of the official report of the visit of His Royal Highness, the Duke of Genoa to Corea. The report was written by Mr. Wm Donald Spence, of the British Consular service, who accompanied the Duke as Interpreter, and is therefore formally made to the British Minister at Peking. A copy was furnished to Signor de Suca, His Italian Minister. This copy, by the courtesy of Signor de Luca and of Sir Thomas Wade I have been allowed to use with some restrictions. They desire that this communication shall for the present at least not be made public, but be treated as confidential. The Report covers ninety folio pages of manuscript, I should be glad to send the whole, but our clerical force is insufficient to accomplish this in the period during which I feel at liberty to have the manuscript copy.

But I think I can give an accurate idea of it in the full résumé, which I now present, with quotations of several pages. I believe that the information the report contains concerning Corea and the Coreans is of more value than anything I have seen published.

The Duke visited Corea party from curiosity and party to make an attempt to enter into friendly relations with such of the authorities on the coast as he might meet with. An Italian ship had some time ago been wrecked on Quelpart Island, and the only surviving sailor had been kindly treated. The Duke made this the occasion of seeking to open correspondence with the authorities in order to express the thanks of his Government for the kindness shown to the sailor.

The Report states that the books of Oppert and Ross were found to be worthless. Far more valuable proved the Histoire de l'Englise dans la Coreé, and vol. IV of Siebold's Japan.

The first visit was to the harbor of Fusan, or Chosan, which is thus described.

"Its surroundings are fully and accurately described on page 68 of Vol. IV of the China Sea Directory of 1873. It affords a magnificent anchorage for many more ships than are likely to frequent the port, and it is open all the winter. I have little to add to the description given on the publication mentioned. All the sides of the harbor, except the South, are studded with villages, containing a resident population of ten or twelve thousand inhabitants, engaged in fishing. At certain times of the year there is an enormous influx to these fishing towns of people from the interior to catch and cure the ribbon fish which visit the harbor in schools. The Southern shore of the harbor is formed by Deer Island, a densely wooded peak some 1,500 ft. high. It is a Government reservation, where the Government steed of diminutive ponies is turned out to graze. At the time of our visit there were several hundreds of these 'horses' roaming about the lower slopes of Deer Island, and with the exception of their keepers, it is uninhabited. It abounds with hog deer, pheasants, wild pig, and even tigers as I myself can testify.

The country round the harbor is all within the jurisdiction of the prefect [____] of Tung-Tsai-foo [____] or, as it is called by the Coreans and Japanese, Toraifoo. The walled city of Torai is situated a few miles inland, and it is the seat of the local Government. It is with this official, dignified by the name of Governor, that Commodore Shufeldt, on behalf of the United States, and Captain Tournier, on behalf of the French Minister at Peking, tried to enter into official relations. Both these officers availed themselves of the services of the Japanese Consul at Fusan, to carry their letters to the Prefect, but, in both cases, the prefect not only refused to receive or open them, but did so in a rude and offensive manner."

The Japanese Consul stationed here warned the Duke not to land except on Deer Island, lest his party should be attacked, and offered to forward a letter to the local authority at Torai, but gave it as his opinion that the local authority would decline to receive it. The letter was placed in his hands. Two days later the Consul sent a reply, saying that he had forwarded the letter and that the Prefect had declined to receive it because Corean law did not empower him to do so. Mr. Spence was convinced before he left Fusan that the Prefect was there visiting the Japanese Consul on one of the two days intervening between the dispatch of the letter to the Consul and the receipt of the reply. He saw the Prefect in Fusan and was told both by Coreans and Japanese of his presence at the Consuls. He naturally infers that the answers of the Prefect were written by him and the Consul together, and that the Japanese officials are pursuing the policy of throwing obstacles in the way of Europeans, who desire to gain access to the Coreans. It is clear that such access had best be sought at ports not occupied by the Japanese.

"The settlement of Fusan has been inhabited by Japanese ever since the treaty of 1615, between Japan and Corea, with which Fidejoshi concluded his victorious campaigns. It was garrisoned by the Japanese princes of Tsushima for two centuries with three or four hundred soldiers, but, for what purpose, it is hard to say. The garrison was kept under the most severe restrictions by the Corean Government, similar to those imposed by the Japanese themselves on the Dutch at Decima.

From the seat the settlement has the appearance of an ordinary Japanese town, the houses being of wood, and of the usual Japanese type. It is pleasantly situated in a magnificent grove of fir-trees of fabulous age and enormous size. Immediately on the port being opened the Japanese population rose to 700, and it has gone on increasing until there are, today, over 2,300 residents.

Every inducement is held out by the Japanese authorities to encourage settlers to come to Corea. The land on which the settlement is built is leased by the Corean Government to the Japanese for a nominal rent of $50,00 per annum. On application by any Japanese wishing to settle in Fusan, a lot of land is assigned and made over to him by the Consul, free of all charge and expense whatever, whether of initial price, or annual rent. On this lot he is at liberty to build, and he may sell or mortgage his land to any other Japanese subject, provided the consent of the Consul is obtained. The Municipal Government of the settlement is entirely in the hands of the Consul, but in matters where he desires to have the opinion and support of the public he takes no steps until he has consulted the leading merchants. The police, draining, and lighting are all attended to after the manner of European settlements in Japan; there is a Chamber of Commerce, a public hospital with duly qualified surgeons, and I believe, a large Japanese Budhistic temple.

Fusan is, as yet, a free port. There is neither an import nor an export tariff. The Corean authorities have stationed a small custom house at the jetty where goods are landed, but its functions are confined to preventing the importation of articles which are, in Corea, a government monopoly, or articles whose importation has been forbidden by treat. A tariff is at the present time in process of negotiation, and as soon as the amount of duty is agreed upon, it will be put in force.

In the year 1879, the imports were of the value of 560,000 yen. They consisted of English cotton goods, Japanese copper, foreign dye, and Japanese silk goods and notions. I visited nearly all the shops in the settlement, and carefully examined the cotton goods which were exposed for sale. I was surprised to find that they consisted entirely of ordinary English grey and white shirtings of 7 lbs. to 8 lbs. pr. piece. It is notorious in China that Corea is one of the principal markets for American sheetings, and for the heavy and more expensive cotton cloths imported into Shanghai. In the settlement of Fusan however I could not find a single piece of heavy cotton cloth either English or American. All the goods were light weight, had come from Shanghai, and bore the names and marks of BIRLEY, BRAND, REISS, HOLLIDAY, THORNE, and other well-known importing houses. The present consumption of piece-goods is from 5000 to 7000 pieces a month, and is increasing. The exports in 1879 amounted to 670,000 yen. They consist of Rice, Furs, Gold dust, dried fish, seaweed, and medicines. There is no restriction at present to the export of grain.

The volume of the trade of the port is increasing, and for the half year ended June 30th last it amounted to 760,000 yen. It is very surprising that so small a trade can support 2,300 residents. In other ways however than legitimate commerce the Japanese try to make money in Fusan, for I saw more than one large tea house where Japanese girls were entertaining crowds of Coreans with tea, music, singing, etc.

The currency of the port is Corean cash, which are more valuable and better made than Chinese. It is however only suitable for small transactions, and in order to make the smallest purchases a Corean visitor has to have two or three servants to carry the few strings of each he means to spend. The few transactions of any magnitude which take place are done by means of barter, so many pieces of cloth for so many bags of rice. A short time ago the Corean Government interdicted the export of rice, and the consequence was that the Japanese merchants lost heavily through the inability of their Corean customers to complete their contracts, and the whole trade of the port was deranged till the prohibition was removed.

The settlement swarms with Coreans during the day, who come in from the towns and villages in the neighborhood. They are ordered by law to leave every night, but many of them do not do so, and some are engaged by and live permanently with the Japanese as their domestic servants. Every Corean merchant intent on buying is accompanied apparently by half a dozen friends who advise him regarding the transaction he is about to make, and by his servants who carry a load of the international currency. The transactions, as a rule, are trifling in amount, and preceded by an interminable conversation which, in many cases, leads to nothing. Accusations of cheating are freely bandied about on both sides, and it is only after much strong language, and vigorous measurement that a piece of cloth is sold.

There is communication by steamer twice a month with Japan. The trade, besides, gives employment to about a dozen Japanese schooners of foreign type, which ply between Fusan, Simonoseki, Nagasaki, and Osaka.

The Japanese Consul is in official communication with the Prefect of Toraifoo, with whom he corresponds on a footing of equality.

The Japanese in Corea live under their own laws, administered by their Consuls. Attached to the Consulate at Fusan is a Court, a Gaol, a staff of police, and the usual official machinery for the arrest, trial, and punishment of offenders. In deciding mixed cases, as between Coreans and Japanese, in theory a most wise course is procured. When a Corean brings a case against a Japanese, the Consul tries the case by Japanese law; and pari ratione, when a Japanese brings a case against a Corean, the Prefect of Torai trys the case by Corean law. It has taken us many years of experience in China to find out that the only practical and logical solution of mixed cases is for the forum and the lex fori to that of the defendant; but Japan and Corea have blundered upon it at the very outset of their treaty intercourse.

In practice however any supposed offense by a Corean in the settlement is summarily dealt with by the first policeman who catches him, or by any Japanese who cares to assume the task of beating the offender. I regret to say that the Japanese treat the Coreans who come to the settlement merely as visitors, out of curiosity, very badly. The buffet and kick them, as they would beasts, and it seemed marvelous to me how these strong, stalwart men put up with the vile treatment they receive from the Japanese pigmies. I have no doubt that it is for this reason that stones are thrown by the Coreans at foreigners when they try to approach any of the villages which fringe the shore of the harbor of Fusan, and that the timidity and submissiveness which we found elsewhere in Corea were said to be wanting here."

Finding it impracticably to accomplish his purpose at Fusan, the Duke departed and sailed along the Eastern coast of Corea to Yung King Bay. The general aspect of the country is thus described—.

"The physical configuration of the country, in the general outlines resembles Italy. It is traversed from North to South by an avail range of mountains which runs closest and is parallel with the East coast. The Corean rivers which flow into the Pacific are quite small, the main rivers rising to the West of the avail range and flowing Westward to the China Sea. The high east coast line which varies in height from 4000 to 6000 ft with peak rising to 8000 ft, is visible from a long distance at sea. On approaching the coast the country is seen to have a wild but attractive appearance. The mountains which, with their outlying spurs, extend close to the shore, rise in tiers, range behind range and are covered from top to bottom in dense impenetrable jungle and forest. Some of the ranges are harsh and serrated, others again are more soft and rounded; but on all there is the same undergrowth of creepers, roses, dwarf oaks, and stunted conifers on the lower slopes graduating into wild jungle and forest towards the summits. The narrow, deep valleys are cultivated and thickly populated, but the mountains are given over to wild beasts. Tigers abound everywhere and traps to catch them may be seen within a hundred yards of the sea. One is not surprised to learn that they are the plague of the country for the jungle and forests which cover the hills make it a perfect home for them."

The vessel anchored in the northern part of Yung King Bay, called the by the Russians Port Lazareff.

"This is one of the points which the Russians are supposed to have designs upon, as a basis of operations against China. It is one of the finest harbors in the world, perfectly land locked, with waters as unruffled as a lake, and with a practically infinite space of good holding-ground in from eight to nine fathoms of water. Though fringed with ice round the shores the harbor is open in winter. We anchored from five miles from the Northern end of the bay, at which end has rivers run into it. An extraordinary account of the larger of these, from French sources, is given in the China Sea Directory Vol. IV which, however true at the time of the survey, is quite incorrect now. The French Admiral who surveyed it says that he found ten feet of water on the bar; that he sailed five miles up the channel through a smiling and cultivated plain; and that so far as he could judge from the information he procured, and the configuration of the country, the river led to the capital and was navigable a long distance. The trend of the mountain ranges is at right angles to the apparent course of the stream, and to reach the capital the river would have to cross a series of high mountains, and to flow South, instead of North as it does. Of this however when we first arrived we knew nothing, and when we came to anchor we knew no more about the country, the officials, and the people than if we had come to the moon.

The shores of this bay are a series of lovely inlets and coves with the forest and jungle clad hills dropping in a sheet of green, on the border of white sand which masks the seashore. Here and there were meadows and valleys covered with nice fields and villages."

On landing the party was surrounded by crowds of curious people. The medium of communication was Chinese characters traced with the finger or a stick on the seashore. Every person, peasants, fisherman, boys hardly in their teens, classes who in China are uneducated, could read and write Chinese. All who wished were allowed to visit the ship and they thronged it. The next day visitors of a higher class came, including merchants and scholars. They were unwilling to talk about official matters, but were very desirous to get information. They declined to forward a letter to the capital, even when tempted by high remuneration. They said such an act was forbidden by their laws.

An examination of the mouth of the river showed that there were only three feet of water on the bar at high tide.

The following is of interest. "Hempen clothes are universally worn by the laboring classes, and the thread is spun much finer than would be possible with European hemp. I tried to get some specimens of the fibre, but I was unsuccessful. It must be the same I think as the "China flax," which grows in the neighborhood of Newchivang, and as the importation of that fibre into England has long been desired by our flax spinners and is only restricted on account of its high price, attention will probably be called to the Corea hemp whenever the country is open. Unfortunately I did not know the specific Chinese name for the flax of Chihli and Shinking. The better classes wear white cotton clothes, and many of them boast of an overall made of foreign cotton cloth, the gloss and finish of which they much admire, for that they prefer a heavy 'honest' cloth, such as American sheeting. Of silk culture there was none in the country which we saw. They spin however the cocoons of wild ailanthus, and I procured hanks of their silk, which to my inexperienced eye seemed closely to resemble Shantung silk, and several sheets of eggs, for Count Candiani who is much interested in sericulture. Of ornamental artwork, such as porcelain, bronzes, etc. they have none. We saw some worthless pearls, some silver work for feminine trappings and official insignia. The ceramic art is quite rudimentary, and they attach an excessive value to the commonest Japanese ware."

Finally four minor officials appeared saying they had been ordered to visit the ship, and announced that the Prefect also would soon come to visit the vessel. On the day following he came on a junk. He was an old and feeble man. He was seated in a sedan chair which had been lowered into the junk. He brought three secretaries, and a considerable retinue of dirty, ragged fellows, who during the visit ate and drank all that was offered them, thrust the tumblers and empty bottles up their sleeves, as opportunity offered, and stole whatever else they could.

In the conversation with the Prefect he gave his name as Li-chi-chang. He said he was an official of the Board of Transmission and Prefect of Yung Hing foo. In reply to the request to forward the letter to the sovereign, he stated that no official can address the Court directly, no matter how important the matter may be, but that it was his duty to report to the Governor what he should see and hear, and await instructions as to whether he should receive the letter.

A communication to the Prefect, signed by the Duke's aide-de-camp, Candiani, was then placed in his hands. It pointed out the desirableness of having a treaty between Corea and Italy, by which shipwrecked mariners and vessels in want of provisions or assistance should be cared for according to terms agreed upon. It indicated the advantage of treaties with foreign nations, who should be interested then in protecting the independence of Corea, if it should be threatened by some one nation. It asked that the Prefect would bring these things to the notice of his Government so that when after two months the ship should return, the intentions of the Government might be known.

The Prefect promised to report the dispatch and the conversation to the Governor. He respectfully declined a present of cakes and wine, which was tendered to him, saying that is was forbidden by law to take gifts without permission. He appeared to be a man of intelligence and constantly consulted his secretaries as to his answers. In closing the account of this interview, the Report says.

"During the interview and its close the numerous staff which crowded the room regaled themselves with wines, sweetmeats, and cigars. Not one of them showed the respect for Corean laws that was professed by the Prefect, or the same reluctance to take a souvenir of the visit in the shape of an empty bottle or a biscuit-tin. They wrangled for the possession of the most worthless articles, and many of them slipped up their sleeves the tumblers and glasses they had been drinking out of.

The Prefect and his staff at last left the ship. As before he was dragged along the deck by his two youths, and literally bundled down the gangway into his sedan chair in the junk. The noisy and hilarious staff poured in after him laden with the trumpery trophies of their visit with which they had been presented or which they had stolen, all in the highest good spirits. Then came the soldiers and attendants who had spent the time in wandering about the ship. They were similarly laden with gifts of biscuit, etc. by the sailors, who were much amused by their praiseworthy attempts to devour everything given them, even soap. The Prince gave orders for the steam launch to tow the Prefect's two junks to the point where he wished to land. They departed in the midst of much din, for amongst the tatterdemalion followers was a numerous and noisy band of music which blew and banged in the lustiest and the most imposing manner. The spectacle of the two junks crowded with picturesque retainers as they were towed away in a chorus of shouting, laughter, Corean drums and trumpets, and finally, the booming of our big guns, was one of the most diverting and impressive I have ever seen.

The interview lasted nearly four hours, and was in some respects an unpleasant and trying ordeal. The filth of even the official class is extreme, and as an example of what is almost too disgusting to write about, I saw one of the secretaries performing for the hair of his colleague, the same good offices that one monkey may be observed doing for another in the zoological gardens."

A final visit was made on August 15th, to the villages on the shore of the bay. The inhabitants all knew of the visit of the Prefect, and were very cordial. They sold no supplies to the Italians, declaring that if they were found with a foreign coin in their possession, they would be heavily punished and run some risk of losing their heads.

One singular incident is worthy of notice. The natives objected seriously to the gathering of oysters by the Italian sailors, who stripped off their clothes in order to procure the shellfish. On careful inquiry it was found that the objection was not to gathering the oysters, but to the sailors going naked into the water. The nations declared that on account of this indecent conduct their women had been obliged to keep indoors, but if the men would put on some clothing, they might freely take oysters. This modesty is surprising to one familiar with the habits of the Chinese and the Japanese. The poorest classes of the Coreans even while at work in the fields are always decently clad, and the women never show even their faces to strangers.

On the 15th of August the Duke proceeded with his vessel to the lately opened port of Gensan, which is situated on the southern shore of Yung-Hing Bay, about 12 miles distant from the former anchorage. It is the second of the three ports open to the Japanese by treaty. The Report says.

"The third port has not yet been agreed to, as the Japanese wish it to be on the West coast, and in proximity to Seoul. To this the Coreans object. Gensan has only been open four months, and, as yet, there is no trade. The only communication with Japan is one steamer every two months. There are at present 300 settlers, but, of these, nearly one third are soldiers or policemen. The houses in the settlement are being built in the Japanese adaptation of European style which is common in the modern parts of Tokio. The Bay, at this part, is so exposed that the harbor is virtually an open roadstead, and the side of the settlement does not appear to me to be wisely selected, either for an anchorage or as possessed of the best communications with the interior. I understood, however, that the Coreans would not consent to give a site at the Yung Hing end of the bay. A Consul General is stationed at Gensan, and he is in official correspondence with the Prefect of Tê Yïran. He has a large staff of student Interpreters, who are studying the Corean language. Communication between the new port and the capital is bad: a mere footpath over high ranges of hills.

At this port again, I regret to say I have to bear witness to the brutal manner in which the Japanese treat the Coreans. I do not think that the worst class of European rowdies would behave so badly to harmless and inoffensive Asiatics, as one finds the Japanese in Corea behaving to the Coreans. For example I saw one Japanese take a pail of dirty water, and throw it into the face of a grave, dignified, and well dressed Corean, for no other reason than that he was gazing with some interest at the new houses, and probably to make the by standing Japanese laugh, which they did, heartily. I have little doubt that in a year or two it will be as difficult for foreigners to land in the neighborhood of Gensan, as it is reported to be now in the vicinity of Fusan. I told the Consul General what I thought of the conduct of his nationals, but he seemed to think that all Coreans were bad, and that a promiscuous kick could not fail to fall upon a Corean who richly deserved it. He gave the Prince the usual caution about the danger of walking without the settlement limits, unless for a short distance with an escort. The Prince himself had some experience of the Coreans by this time, and had no fear of the unpleasant consequences of country walks. Accompanied by his aides-de-camp and myself, we spent three days very pleasantly shooting, fishing and roaming about the hills and coasts near Gensan. We were molested by nobody. The demeanor of the inhabitants was the same here as we had found it elsewhere. Fine men physically, much finer than the Japanese or Chinese, they have an upright bold manner, and the timidity they exhibit at strange sights and strange sounds is the timidity of ignorance, not of a craven spirit. For the rest, they are exceedingly inquisitive and filthy in their persons."

The visit ended on the 19th of August.

I think you will agree with me that this Report is of great interest and importance. It appears that the trade of Fusan is already more than a million and a half Japanese yen a year or more than a million of our dollars. It appears too that the habits and tastes of the people are such as to promise in due time a considerable market for 'honest' American goods. At Port Lazareff the better classes express a distinct preference for them over the lighter and sized English goods. The peculiar quality of the hemp at the place is also worthy the attention of manufacturers of linen.

It is noteworthy that the mixed Court system, which we are using in China, is in full operation at the Japanese settlements. Doubtless the experience of Western nations here has suggested the adoption of the plan.

Nothing, which is told concerning the inhabitants is more surprising than their modestly and their attainments in reading and writing, unless it be their mildness and kindness to visitors.

The description of the ports, and especially of port Lazareff, on which it is thought the Russians are looking with longing eyes, will attract your attention.

But you will probably consider with special interest the indications that the Japanese authorities are endeavoring to appropriate to themselves whatever advantages are to be gained from intercourse with Corea. I believe there is much other testimony to the same effect. But of course such an effort on the part of Japan must before long prove futile.

I have the honor to be,
Sir,
Your obedient servant,
James B. Angell

5.

申櫶(1882/高宗十九年)
『미국통상실기(美國通商實記)』

美國通商實記

聖上即祚十月九年壬午四月自清國天津北洋大臣肅毅伯李鴻章公亟來到于政府內開云云接準美利堅照會內開聞東洋有高麗國禮儀文物冠於諸國云聞甚欽羨故不容不一次視察次特派大使欲爲通之意文字來着故茲以通知以此準備爲要而美艦不遠間到泊矣自別使派送帶同矣照諒云云自廟堂會議頻繁特定大官時輔國崇祿大夫判中樞府事知三軍府訓鍊院事機務處堂上申櫶德望頗有丙子秋與日本大使黑田靑隆條約江華時有全權大官之例故特差大官兼摠威使從事官三人通譯官二人隨員一人信任若干人擇差待其天津通奇自戶曹自南陽大同船四隻平舖座板左右竹欄干大旗幟華餙靑邊大遮日下設軍幕於中座肅靜口月刀貫耳令翦令旗巡口淸口金皷隨序羅列於船上船頭大吹打雷皷號令於前陪威儀莊嚴也美艦到着于天津北洋大臣迎接欸待命水師提督馬健忠丁汝昌二人與美艦伴到于仁川尾島申大官以交涉次着軍服佩筒介手執摠威司命手旗發船沙工等以巡令手服色手搖櫓以進船體與彼船大有差等故接見時間以辰時約正而船不進行故時近未時受困於海上不勝懣畓之際自淸艦牽導輕如葉片瞬息間當頭于淸艦扶案而登船上揷黃質靑龍紅色如意珠旗先通名啣馬丁兩提督帶歡迎接施禮畢如干敍懷偕徃美艦艦上掛藍質紅橫紋上隅白色米字形多點旗號美使爲人俊秀着鷲絲帽子黑色窄袖短周衣以笑顏握手座定矣大官曰朝鮮原來文恬武嬉都尙文學而已軍艦等尙未設備今日受困於海上時間太過兩國和好之初如是貽笑不勝羞愧也通譯只解淸語故于淸使淸國通譯轉于美使以此交涉極爲不便也四脚高床布呂宋烟紙卷烟草勸吸而言曰大官俄於海上受困必是船隻不利故也請勿爲怪焉本使因前驗深祝朝鮮後日幸福必無窮矣予十八歲初渡印度國港口荒落人物愚昧以年少之致不無鼻笑矣四十六歲時再渡則港口帆牆林立市街鐵道如蛛網家屋道路變作畫裏乾坤然小人物變態心甚驚訝旋用栢悅矣詳聞

內容則爲他人之所點云尚且嗟惜以若浩大地方國民精神未拾故耳今見此地則
山川秀明人物純厚務修自彊之力則不幾年著名於世界矣奚止於軍艦而已哉如
干談話没請邀食堂各色酒肴食料次第而入其慇懃之懷滿于一座讌畢各歸其船
安歇翌朝兩艦名唧來到黑牛假裵柒盋盛白厚洋紙曲書書之清使以梅紅紙書姓
名而探夜安否而去大官扇子紙長唧以架子擔送兩艦午時請邀三使美使則昨日
衣冠携曲頭短杖清使珊瑚鐙子雀羽篩冠黑鍛長袖八褶藍質黑繡鞋頗有鮮明也
食料以上品接待酒則梨薑膏鍍金銀盃三使各七杯全鰒實栢枸杞子菜藥食助岳
正果圓小餠多食矣美使指藥食與助岳而讚曰勿論何地以食料品先驗風土人物
之如何矣今日食料無非珍味果種亦是清新日没將就不言無窮矣何患乎軍艦之
未備耶一場大笑快遊美使曰各國通商本意人種雖曰差異生命保護古今一般故
以和相親培養技術供其有無則民志自然發達國家從此富彊矣豈非幸福耶今日
本使之來別無他意遠聞東洋有朝鮮國禮儀文物冠於諸國公故自議院泒遣本使
一次視察後鞏其和好同享安樂之意而已今見山明水麗人心純古天眞顯於外面
是所心賀然第一言語不通交涉不便請大官與政府諸公會議沒聰俊年少泒遣美
國近日世界形便如何國民之程度詳細視察則語學自然通鮮鐵匣軍艦從此製造
矣豈非今日之急務乎大官大使言論適合於時宜感賀不然會議於政府上稟于大
君主前然後通知于北洋大臣矣丁兩提督亦曰朝鮮禮儀文物自成卓然或有外
變等節相議于中國已成其例且回帆隔日依申大官答言似好也美使唯唯而笑須
臾席散翌日自清艦請邀華榴彫刻交倚華榴四方高床舖黑氈袱回龍香枝水滿玉
鼻連筒白銅水歸臺各色烟草等陳列寒喧畢擧帳請入文房燦爛少傾食料次入來
種種極邑不可勝食以好言一場談話而歸翌朝與美話別爲人偉如言論有序不無
惜別也握手相分沒仍往清艦一場略叙因爲分手前後四日之間其慇懃之懷不能
禁止矣

從事官	朴永世
	姜瑋
	申贊熙
通 譯	李容俊
廳 直	金成俊
	金熙貞
	李汝善
下 人	陳完吉

　　　　　　　　張萬石
　　　　　　　　金聖完
　　　　床 奴　李富成
　　　行首執事　林學基
　　　聽令執事　李浩春
　　　　　　　　梁漢冀
　　　新營監官　張羲恭
　　令翦別武使　許復
　　　　　　　　權有信
　　　　　　　　尹行復
　　　隨廳書吏　金浔鍊
　　　　知彀官　金文恒
　　　　書字的　梁春榮
　　　　　　　　洪翰信
　　　花島別將　金弘信
　　　行首沙工　林榻孫

贐行物種

葛皮　二令

豹皮　二令

鹿皮　三張

竹清紙拾束

扇子紙拾束

各色扇子五拾柄

極細簾　五立

丁學教盡石四幅

紅蔘　拾升

蔘正果　壺缸

大藥果　壺槾

無穴鰒貳拾貼 實栢子武斗

已上美艦巧送

葛皮 各貳令

豹皮各貳令 竹清紙各拾束

別牡紙各拾束

各色扇子各三拾柄

玉果佃席各拾立

細簾各五立

紅蔘各拾升

大藥果各壹樻

蔘正果各壹缸

已上清艦所送

鹿皮各二張

大牡紙各五束

各色扇子各貳拾柄

紅蔘各三升

東醫寶鑑各壹帙

清艦隨貢與通譯處

부록 문서 목록

번호	발신일/수신일*(음력)	문서제목	발신	수신	문서출처	번역문 출처	관련문서 제목	관련문서 출처
(1) 수신사(修信使) 金弘集 파견									
1	1880. 7. 5(高宗 十七年五月 二十八日)	수신사 사폐(辭陛)시 전교	高宗		『일기』高宗 17년 5월 28일			
2	1880. 9. 7/1880. 9. 24(高宗十七年 八月二十日)*	서구 열강과의 수교 권고	井上馨	尹滋承	『동문』4, 「洋情」1, pp. 4175-6; 『왜사』庚辰 8월 21일 啓下; 『수신사』		洪祐昌의 회신	『동문』4, 「洋情」1, p. 4176.
3	1880. 9. 8	서구 열강과의 수교 권고	井上馨	金弘集	『구한국』1(일안 1) pp. 53-4.			
4	1880. 9/1880. 9. 24(高宗十七年 八月二十日)*	부산 세관 설치 재검토 요청	井上馨	尹滋承	『왜사』庚辰 8월 21일 啓下; 『수신사』 「答書契謄本」, p. 159.			
5	1880. 9. 24(高宗 十七年八月 二十日)*	수신사 장계	金弘集	議政府	『왜사』庚辰 8월 21일 啓下			
6	1880. 10. 2(高宗 十七年八月 二十八日)*	수신사 복명서(復命書)	金弘集		『동문』4, 「信行別單」1, pp. 4179-82; 『수신사』「修信使金弘集復命書」, pp. 149-54.		수역(首譯) 李容肅의 문견사건(聞見事件)	『동문』4, 「信行別單」1, pp. 4182-3; 『수신사』, 「修信使金弘集復命書」, pp. 154-5.
7	1880. 10. 2(高宗 十七年八月 二十八日)	수신사 연설(筵說)	金弘集		『일기』高宗 17년 8월 28일; 『수신사』「修信使金弘集入侍筵說」pp. 155-9,			
(2) 『朝鮮策略』의 전래와 신사(辛巳) 위정척사운동									
8	1880. 8. 20(高宗 十七年七月 十五日)	金弘集·黃遵憲 회담(1)	金弘集		『대청』「七月十五日」; 『수신사』「大淸欽使筆談」pp. 171-3; 『何如璋』4, pp. 287-8; 『黃遵憲』上, pp. 808-9.			
9	1880. 8. 21(高宗 十七年七月十六日)	金弘集·何如璋 회담(1)	金弘集		『대청』「七月十六日」; 『수신사』「大淸欽使筆談」pp. 173-7; 『何如璋』4, pp. 288-9; 『黃遵憲』上, pp. 809-10.			
10	1880. 8. 23(高宗 十七年七月 十八日)	金弘集·何如璋 회담(2)	金弘集		『대청』「七月十八日」; 『수신사』「大淸欽使筆談」pp. 175-7; 『何如璋』4, pp. 290-1.			
11	1880. 8. 26(高宗 十七年七月 二十一日)	金弘集·何如璋 회담(3)	金弘集		『대청』「七月二十一日」; 『수신사』「大淸欽使筆談」pp. 177-81; 『何如璋』4, pp. 291-3.			

번호	발신일/수신일*(음력)	문서제목	발신	수신	문서출처	번역문 출처	관련문서 제목	관련문서 출처
12	1880.9.6(高宗 十七年八月二 日)	金弘集·黃遵 憲 회담(2)	金弘集		『대청』「八月二 日」; 『수신사』 「大淸欽使筆談」 pp. 181-7; 『何如 璋』 4, pp. 293-6; 『黃遵憲』上, pp. 811-4.			
13	1880.9.7(高宗 十七年八月三 日)	金弘集·何如 璋 회담(4)	金弘集		『대청』「八月三 日」; 『수신사』「 大淸欽使筆談」 pp. 187-9; 『何如 璋』 4, pp. 296-7.			
14	1880.10.11(高 宗 十七年九月八 日)	『朝鮮策略』에 관한 어전회의	高宗, 李最應		『일기』 高宗 17 년 9월 8일; 『용 호』 4「九月初八 日次對入侍時事 」pp. 445-8; 『실 록』 같은 날; 『日 外』 13, 문서번호 136, 부기 2, pp. 394-6.		제대신헌의 (諸大臣獻 議)	『수신사』 「諸大臣 獻議」pp. 189-91; 『용 호』 4「廟堂 獻議」pp. 448-9; 『中 日韓』 2, 문 서번호 342 의 부건 3, pp. 445-7.
15	1880.10 19(高 宗十七年九月 十六) /1880.12. 30(光緖六年 十一月二十九 日)*	『朝鮮策略』 어 전 진상(進上) 통보	金弘集	何如璋	『中日韓』 2, 문서 번호 345의 부건 1, pp. 452-3; 『何 如璋』 3, p. 235.			
16	1880.11.3(高宗 十七年十月一 日)*	『朝鮮策略』 비 판 상소	劉元植		『나암』「兵曹正郎 劉元植疏(十月初 一日)」 pp. 223-4; 『일기』·『일록』· 『실록』 같은 날			
17	1881.2.26(光緖 七年一月二十 八日)	李裕元-李鴻章 서한(9)	李鴻章	李裕元	『中日韓』 2, 문서 번호 353의 부건 4, pp. 471-2.			
18	1881.3.25(高 宗十八年二月 二十六日)*	영남만인소(嶺 南萬人疏)	李晩孫 等		『나암』「慶尙道儒 生李晩孫等上疏」 pp. 230-6; 『日 外』 14, 문서번호 155, 부속서, pp. 372-5; 『일기』高 宗 18년 2월 26 일; 『일록』·『실 록』같은 날		상소에 대 한 비답	『주연』 34 批 4「嶺南 儒生李晩孫 等論修信使 金弘集罪仍 請斥邪疏 批」; 『일기』 高宗 18년 2월 26일; 『일록』·『실 록』같은 날
19	1881.4.21(高宗 十八年三月 二十三日)*	척사소(斥邪 疏)	洪時中		『나암』「出身洪 時中疏草」 pp. 251-8; 『일기』 高 宗 18년 3월 23 일; 『일록』·『실 록』같은 날			
20	1881.4.21(高 宗十八年三月 二十三日)*	척사소	黃載顯		『나암』「出身黃 載顯疏草」 pp. 250-1; 『일기』 高 宗 18년 3월 23 일; 『일록』·『실 록』같은 날			

번호	발신일/수신일*(음력)	문서제목	발신	수신	문서출처	번역문 출처	관련문서 제목	관련문서 출처
21	1881. 8. 30(高宗 十八年閏七月 六日)*	척사소	洪在鶴 等		『日外』14, 문서번호 156, 부속서, pp. 376-82; 『나암』pp. 259-263, 「江原道幼學洪在鶴疏」; 『실록』18년 윤7월 6일		洪在鶴이 閔台鎬에게 보낸 서한	『나암』「洪在鶴抵閔判書台鎬書」pp. 263-7.
22	1881. 8. 30(高宗 十八年閏七月 六日)*	척사소	申㰌		『실록』18년 윤7월 6일			
23	1881. 9. 1(高宗 十八年閏七月 八日)*	李鴻章 서한 변명소		李裕元	『가오』7 疏箚「申㰌等疏句語對擧疏」; 『일기』高宗 18년 윤7월 8일; 『일록』·『실록』같은 날			
24	1881. 9. 24(高宗 十八年八月二日)*	사직소(辭職疏)	金弘集		『일기』高宗 18년 8월 2일; 『일록』같은 날			
(3) 조약체결 이전 미국의 조선 관련 보고								
25	1874. 3. 30/ 1874. 5. 26*	대원군 실각 보고	S. W. Williams	H. Fish	AADM, pp. 874-5.			
26	1875. 10. 6/ 1875. 11. 9*	雲揚號 사건 보고	J. A. Bingham	H. Fish	AADM, pp. 875-6.			
27	1875. 10. 26	雲揚號 사건 보고	B. P. Avery	H. Fish	ADPP, pp. 42-9.			
28	1875. 12. 28	조선에 대한 일본과 청국의 입장	G. F. Seward	J. L. Cadwalader	ADPP, pp. 50-2.			
29	1876. 1. 5	조선-일본 관계에 대한 청국의 입장	G. F. Seward	H. Fish	ADPP, pp. 53-5.			
30	1876. 3. 9/1876. 4. 3*	조일수호조규 체결 보고	J. A. Bingham	H. Fish	AADM, p. 876.			
31	1876. 3. 21/ 1876. 4. 25*	黑田淸隆로부터 입수한 조선 정보 보고	J. A. Bingham	H. Fish	AADM, pp. 876-7.			
32	1876. 6. 1/ 1876. 7. 5*	수신사 金綺秀 도착 보고	J. A. Bingham	H. Fish	AADM, pp. 877-8.			
33	1878. 4. 8	대조선 수호통상조약 체결 요청 결의안	Sargent		AADM, pp. 880-2.			
34	1878. 10. 29	아프리카, 아시아 미개척 지역 탐사 지시	R. W. Thompson	R. W. Shufeldt	NARA II, M 179, R 523			
35	1878. 11. 9	Shufeldt의 아시아, 아프리카 연안 항행 훈령에 관한 회신	W. M. Evarts	R. W. Thompson	NARA II, M 179, R 523			
36	1879. 1. 24/ 1879. 2. 24*	조일 관세 문제에 관한 보고	S. Stevens	W. M. Evarts	AADM, p. 879.		보고에 대한 회신 (1879. 3. 1)	AADM, p. 879.

번호	발신일/수신일*(음력)	문서제목	발신	수신	문서출처	번역문 출처	관련문서 제목	관련문서 출처
(4) Shufeldt의 서한 전달 시도와 일본의 중재									
37	1880. 2. 13	조선과의 협상 시기에 관한 조언 요청	R. W. Shufeldt	J. A. Bingham	RWS 4			
38	1880. 3. 12	훈령 미도착 통보	J. A. Bingham	R. W. Shufeldt	RWS국편, Vol. 10			
39	1880. 3. 12	Shufeldt를 소개하는 일본 측 서한 요청	J. A. Bingham	井上馨	『日外』 13, 문서번호 169, pp. 435-6.			
40	1880. 4. 1	조선 개항과 관련한 협조 훈령	W. M. Evarts	J. A. Bingham	NARA II, M 77, R 105			
41	1880. 4. 1	Shufeldt 소개 요청 거절	井上馨	J. A. Bingham	RWS 28	[日譯] 『日外』 13, 문서번호 170, pp. 436-7.		
42	1880. 4. 20	부산 주재 영사에게 Shufeldt의 소개장 발송	上野景範	J. A. Bingham	『日外』 13, 문서번호 171, p. 437.			
43	1880. 4. 26	부산에서의 교섭 계획 보고	R. W. Shufeldt	R. W. Thompson	RWS국편, Vol. 10			
44	1880. 4. 26	협상 진전이 없을 경우 복귀 지시	R. W. Thompson	R. W. Shufeldt	RWS 24			
45	1880. 5. 4	高宗에게 올린 Shufeldt 서한	R. W. Shufeldt	沈東臣	RWS 24	[漢譯] 『中日韓』 2, 문서번호 334의 부건 1, pp. 407-11; 『何如璋』 3, pp. 224-5.		
46	1880. 5. 10	서한 전달 실패 보고	R. W. Shufeldt	J. A. Bingham	AADM, p. 895.		近藤眞鋤가 조선 정부에 보낸 소개장의 영역문	AADM, pp. 896-7.
47	1880. 5. 13(高宗 十七年四月五日)*	近藤眞鋤를 통한 Shufeldt의 교섭 보고	沈東臣	議政府	『왜사』 庚辰 4월 5일 啓下; 『일록』 같은 날; 『일록』 高宗 17년 4월 10일; 『실록』 같은 날			
48	1880. 5. 21	Shufeldt 서한 재전달 협조 요청	J. A. Bingham	井上馨	RWS 국편, Vol. 10 ; RWS 24	[日譯] 『日外』 13, 문서번호 172, pp. 438-40.		
49	1880. 5. 24	Shufeldt의 서한 전달 요청에 관한 청훈	井上馨	三條實美	『日外』 13, 문서번호 173, pp. 442-3.			
50	1880. 5. 24	서한 전달 협조 요청 수락	井上馨	J. A. Bingham	『日外』 13, 문서번호 174, p. 443.			
51	1880. 5. 24	Shufeldt 서한의 접수 및 접수 지연 상황에 대한 대처 훈령	井上馨	近藤眞鋤	『日外』 13, 문서번호 175, pp. 443-4.			

번호	발신일/수신일*(음력)	문서제목	발신	수신	문서출처	번역문 출처	관련문서 제목	관련문서 출처
52	1880. 5. 26	서한 전달 협조에 대한 감사	R. W. Shufeldt	J. A. Bingham	AADM, p. 897.			
53	1880. 5. 29	조선 교섭상황 보고 및 무력을 동원한 조약 체결 건의	R. W. Shufeldt	R. W. Thompson	AADM, pp. 890-1; RWS 28			
54	1880. 5/1880. 6. 23(高宗十七年 五月十六日)*	Shufeldt 서한 접수 권고	井上馨	尹滋承	『구한국』1(일안 1) pp. 48-9; 『동문』4, 洋情 1, p. 4175; 『왜사』到付 庚辰 5월 16일	[漢譯] 『동문』4, 洋情 1, p. 4174-5; 『왜사』到付 庚辰 5월 16일	尹滋承의 회신	『동문』4, 洋情 1, p. 4175; 『왜사』到付 庚辰 5월 16일
55	1880. 5. 29/ 1880. 6. 23(高宗十七年 五月十六日)*	Shufeldt 서한 접수 촉구	花房義質	尹滋承	『구한국』1(일안 1) pp. 49-50.	[漢譯] 『동문』4, 洋情 1, p. 4175; 『왜사』到付 庚辰 5월 16일; 『구한국』1(일안 1) p. 50.	尹滋承의 회신	『동문』4, 洋情 1, p. 4175; 『왜사』到付 庚辰 5월 16일
56	1880. 5. 29	일본의 협조에 대한 감사	J. A. Bingham	井上馨	『日外』13, 문서번호 176, pp. 446-7.			
57	1880. 6. 7(光緖六年四月三十日)*	Shufeldt의 서한 전달 시도 보고	何如璋	總署	『中日韓』2, 문서번호 334, pp. 406-7.			
58	1880. 6. 11(光緖六年五月四日)*	Shufeldt의 서한 전달 실패 보고	何如璋	總署	『中日韓』2, 문서번호 335, pp. 411-2.			
59	1880. 7. 31	Shufeldt 서한 관련 예조판서 답신 송부	近藤眞鋤	井上馨	『日外』13, 문서번호 177, pp. 447-8.			
60	1880. 8. 4	Shufeldt 서한의 전달 경과 및 답신 통보	上野景範	J. A. Bingham	『日外』13, 문서번호 178, pp. 448-9.			
61	1880. 8. 6	조선의 서한 접수 거부 사유 통보	J. A. Bingham	R. W. Shufeldt	AADM, p. 901.		조선 예조판서 회신의 영역문	AADM, p. 902.
62	1880. 8. 10	조선의 서한 접수 여부에 따른 대처 계획	R. W. Shufeldt	R. W. Thompson	AADM, pp. 897-8.			
63	1880. 8. 17	조선의 서한 접수 거부 보고	R. W. Shufeldt	R. W. Thompson	AADM, p. 901.			
64	1880. 8. 17	일본 외무당국의 서한 전달상의 실책 비난	R. W. Shufeldt	J. A. Bingham	AADM, pp. 902-3.		Bingham의 회신	AADM, p. 904.
65	1880. 9. 11	일본공사를 통한 Shufeldt 서한의 전달 의뢰	J. A. Bingham	井上馨	『日外』13, 문서번호 182, pp. 451-5.			
66	1880. 9. 18	Shufeldt 서한 전달 의뢰에 대한 회신	井上馨	J. A. Bingham	『日外』13, 문서번호 183, pp. 455-7.			

번호	발신일/수신일*(음력)	문서제목	발신	수신	문서출처	번역문 출처	관련문서 제목	관련문서 출처
67	1880. 10. 13	주선 과정에서 일본의 불성실한 태도 보고	R. W. Shufeldt	R. W. Thompson	AADM, pp. 906-08; ADPP, pp. 106-16.			
		(5) 미국과 청국의 교섭						
68	1880. 5. 4(光緒六年三月二十六日)	Shufeldt의 서한 전달 협조 요청	余瓛	李鴻章	『翰軒』上, pp. 5-7; 『中日戰』2, pp. 347-8.			
69	1880. 6. 14(光緒六年五月七日)	Shufeldt의 중국 해군 자문역 추천	余瓛	李鴻章	『翰軒』上, pp. 8-11; 『中日戰』2, pp. 348-50.			
70	1880. 7. 23/ 1880. 8. 9	天津 회견 요청	李鴻章	R. W. Shufeldt	AADM, pp. 899-900; RWS 국편, Vol. 4			
71	1880. 8. 8	天津 회견 요청 승낙	R. W. Shufeldt	李鴻章	RWS 국편, Vol. 4			
72	1880. 8. 9	天津 초청 서신	余瓛	R. W. Shufeldt	AADM, p. 900.			
73	1880. 8. 9	天津 초청에 대한 회신	R. W. Shufeldt	余瓛	AADM, p. 900.			
74	1880. 8. 13	조선문제 협의를 위한 李鴻章 방문 계획 보고	R. W. Shufeldt	R. W. Thompson	AADM, p. 899.			
75	1880. 8. 16(光緒六年七月十一日)	Shufeldt의 天津 방문 일정 및 자문역 추천	余瓛	李鴻章	『翰軒』上, pp. 21-2; 『中日戰』2, pp. 347-8.			
76	1880. 8. 21(光緒六年七月十六日)/1880. 9. 11(光緒六年八月七日)*	Shufeldt와의 회견 기대	李鴻章	余瓛	『李鴻章』32, 信函 4, G6-07-010, p. 580.			
77	1880. 8. 30	李鴻章과의 회견 보고	R. W. Shufeldt	R. W. Thompson	AADM, pp. 904-5; ADPP, pp. 102-5.			
78	1880. 8. 30	일본의 주선 및 李鴻章과의 회견 보고	R. W. Shufeldt	J. B. Angell	AADM, pp. 905-6.			
79	1880. 9. 13(光緒六年八月九日)	Shufeldt의 중국 해군 개편 의견 찬성	余瓛	李鴻章	『翰軒』上, pp. 23-4; 『中日戰』2, pp. 347-8.			
80	1880. 9. 27	Shufeldt · 李鴻章 회견 및 Prince of Genoa 조선 방문 보고	J. B. Angell	W. M. Evarts	NARA II, M 92 R 56			
81	1881. 3. 3	李鴻章과의 회견 내용 전달	C. L. Fisher	R. W. Shufeldt	RWS 국편, Vol. 7			
82	1881. 6. 20	何如璋의 적극적 협조 보고	J. A. Bingham	J. G. Blaine	ADPP, pp. 121-4.			
83	1881. 7. 1	李鴻章과의 회견 내용 보고	R. W. Shufeldt	J. G. Blaine	AADM, pp. 908-10; ADPP, pp. 125-30; NARA II, M 92, R 58			

번호	발신일/수신일* (음력)	문서제목	발신	수신	문서출처	번역문 출처	관련문서 제목	관련문서 출처
84	1881. 7. 16	조선과의 조약 체결 전망 및 Shufeldt의 해군 고문 고빙 건 보고	J. B. Angell	J. G. Blaine	NARA II, M 92, R 58			
85	1881. 9. 14	井上馨·Bingham 회견 내용 전달	R. W. Shufeldt	J. B. Angell	RWS 국편, Vol. 1			
86	1881. 11. 14	Shufeldt의 임무 통보	J. G. Blaine	C. Holcombe	ADPP, pp. 139-41.			
87	1881. 11. 14/ 1882. 1. 19*	조선 교섭 지침	J. G. Blaine	R. W. Shufeldt	NARA II, DI, China Instruction, Vol. 3; ADPP, pp. 142-8.			
88	1881. 12. 16	李鴻章의 조약 체결 권유에 대한 조선 회자(回咨) 보고	R. W. Shufeldt	C. Holcombe	NARA II, M 92 R 59 ; AADM, pp. 912-3; ADPP, pp. 149-59.			
89	1881. 12. 19	조청(朝淸) 종속(宗屬)관계 보고	C. Holcombe	J. G. Blaine	NARA II, M 92 R 59			
90	1881. 12. 29	조미조약 체결 시 청국관료 파견 제안 보고	C. Holcombe	J. G. Blaine	AADM, pp. 913-4.			
91	1882. 1. 3	李鴻章의 조미조약 초안 일부 전달	C. Holcombe	R. W. Shufeldt	RWS 국편, Vol. 8; RWS 24			
92	1882. 1. 6	조약 체결 관련 지침	F. T. Frelinghuysen	R. W. Shufeldt	NARA II, M-77 R 40; ADPP, pp. 160-2.			
93	1882. 1. 23	전권사절 임명 이후 조선과 청국의 정세 보고	R. W. Shufeldt	F. T. Frelinghuysen	NARA II, M 92, R 59; AADM, pp. 914-5.			
94	1882. 1. 23(光緖七年十二月四日)*	조약체결 전권대사 임명 사실 통보	R. W. Shufeldt	李鴻章	『음청』 pp. 47-8.			
95	1882. 2. 2	조선의 밀사 파견과 회견 방식 통보	李鴻章	R. W. Shufeldt	RWS 국편, Vol. 8; RWS 24			
96	1882. 2. 4	總署 회견 내용 보고	C. Holcombe	F. T. Frelinghuysen	AADM, pp. 915-6.			
97	1882. 2. 6	保定府 회견을 원하는 李鴻章의 의사 전달	周馥	R. W. Shufeldt	RWS 국편, Vol. 8			
98	1882. 2. 8/1882. 2. 13(光緖七年十二月二十五日)*	保定府 회견 요청에 대한 회신	R. W. Shufeldt	李鴻章	NARA II, M 92, R 60	[漢譯]『음청』 pp. 54-5.		
99	1882. 2. 28	Shufeldt의 청국 해군 고빙 건에 관한 보고	C. Holcombe	F. T. Frelinghuysen	AADM, pp. 917-8.			
100	1882. 3. 11	周馥 회견 결과 및 李鴻章 회견 계획 보고	R. W. Shufeldt	F. T. Frelinghuysen	NARA II, M 92, R 60; AADM, pp. 918-19.			

번호	발신일/수신일* (음력)	문서제목	발신	수신	문서출처	번역문 출처	관련문서 제목	관련문서 출처
101	1882.3.25(光緒八年二月七日)	李鴻章·Shufeldt 회견	李鴻章		『李鴻章』33, 信函 5, G8-02-012, pp. 121-2; 『中日韓』2, 문서번호 389의 부건 1, pp. 549-52.			
102	1882.3.27(光緒八年二月九日)/ 1882.3.28(光緒八年二月十日)*	Shufeldt 회견 보고(1)	李鴻章	總署	『李鴻章』33, 信函 5, G8-02-016, pp. 124-5; 『中日韓』2, 문서번호 389, pp. 548-9.			
103	1882.3.31	李鴻章 회견 보고	R. W. Shufeldt	F. T. Frelinghuysen	NARA II, M 92, R 60; AADM, pp. 920-21.			
104	1882.4.5	청국의 조청 종속(宗屬)관계 명문화 요구에 관한 훈령	C. Holcombe	R. W. Shufeldt	RWS 국편, Vol. 8			
105	1882.4.10	조미수호통상조약 초안 보고	R. W. Shufeldt	F. T. Frelinghuysen	NARA II, M 92, R 60	[漢譯] (1) 『李鴻章』33, 信函 5, G8-02-013, pp. 122-3; 『中日韓』2, 문서번호 389의 부건 2, pp. 552-5; (2) 『中日韓』2, 문서번호 393의 부건 2, pp. 561-6.		
106	1882.4.11(光緒八年二月二十四日)/ 1882.4.12(光緒八年二月二十五日)*	Shufeldt 회견 보고(2)	李鴻章	總署	『李鴻章』33, 信函5, G8-02-037 및 G8-02-038, pp. 136-7; 『李文』, 譯署函稿 13, p. 23; 『中日韓』2, 문서번호 392 및 부건 1, pp. 557-8.			
107	1882.4.23	조약체결 중재를 위한 馬建忠 파견 통보	李鴻章	R. W. Shufeldt	RWS 24			
108	1882.4.24	李鴻章 회견 보고	C. Holcombe	F. T. Frelinghuysen	AADM, pp. 927-8.			
109	1882.4.28	조미수호통상조약 최종안 보고	R. W. Shufeldt	F. T. Frelinghuysen	NARA II, M 92, R 60			
110	1882.5.1	Shufeldt의 조약체결 활동에 관한 보고	J. R. Young	F. T. Frelinghuysen	AADM, pp. 929-31.			
			(6) 조선과 청국의 교섭					
111	1879.8.21(光緒五年七月四日)	조선에 조약체결을 권고할 것을 상주		總署	『中日』1, 문서번호 33의 부건 1, pp. 31-2.			

번호	발신일/수신일*(음력)	문서제목	발신	수신	문서출처	번역문출처	관련문서제목	관련문서출처
112	1879. 8. 26(光緒五年七月九日)	李裕元-李鴻章 서한(10)	李鴻章	李裕元	『가오』11, 「答肅毅伯書(2) 附: 原書」; 『용호』4 「直隸總督文閣太學士 李鴻章 抵橘山李相國書」, pp. 433-6; 『실록』16년 7월 9일; 『庸盦外』3, pp. 63-6; 『中日韓』2, 문서번호 309의 부건 2, pp. 366-9; 『淸外』16, pp. 304-6.			
113	1879. 10. 7(高宗十六年八月二十二日)	李裕元-李鴻章 서한(11)	李裕元	李鴻章	『中日韓』2, 문서번호 327의 부건 1, p. 395.			
114	1879. 12. 24(高宗十六年十一月十二日)/1880. 3. 15(光緒六年二月五日)*	李裕元-李鴻章 서한(12)	李裕元	李鴻章	『가오』11, 「答肅毅伯書(2)」; 『실록』16년 7월 9일; 『中日韓』2, 문서번호 329의 부건 1, pp. 398-401.		『龍湖閒錄』수록본	『용호』4 「橘山答書(付 冬至使行便)」
115	1879. 12. 25(光緒五年十一月十三日)/1879. 12. 27(光緒五年十一月十五日)*	李裕元과의 서한 왕복 보고(1)	李鴻章	總署	『李鴻章』32, 信函4, G5-11-002, pp. 502-3; 『李文』, 譯署函稿10, pp. 15-7; 『中日韓』2, 문서번호 327, pp. 394-5.			
116	1880. 3. 17(光緒六年二月七日)/1880. 3. 19(光緒六年二月九日)*	李裕元과의 서한 왕복 보고(2)	李鴻章	總署	『李鴻章』32, 信函4, G6-02-003, pp. 518-9; 『李文』, 譯署函稿10, p. 23; 『中日韓』2, 문서번호 329, p. 397.			
117	1880. 7. 22(光緒六年十月十六日)*	주지조선외교의(主持朝鮮外交議)	何如璋	總署	『中日韓』2, 문서번호 342의 부건 1, pp. 439-42; 『何如璋』3, pp. 229-31.			
118	1880. 8. 14(高宗十七年七月九日)	李裕元-李鴻章 서한(13)	李裕元	李鴻章	『李鴻章』9, 奏議 9, G6-09-005의 부건 1 및 부건 2, p. 173; 『李文』, 奏稿38, pp. 28-9; 『中日韓』2, 문서번호 339의 부건 2, pp. 419-20.			
119	1880. 10. 7(光緒六年九月四日)	조선에 대해 외교 및 자강책 권고 상주	李鴻章		『李鴻章』9, 奏議 9, G6-09-004, pp. 173-4.		근대식 기기 학습을 청원하는 조선 자문	『李鴻章』9, 奏議 9, G6-09-005의 부건 3, pp. 173-4.

번호	발신일/수신일*(음력)	문서제목	발신	수신	문서출처	번역문 출처	관련문서 제목	관련문서 출처
120	1880.10.24(光緒六年九月二十七日)	조선과 서양 각국의 통상 권유 상주	李鴻章		『李鴻章』9, 奏議9, G6-09-031, pp. 190-1; 『李文』, 奏稿38, pp. 46-7; 『中日韓』2, 문서번호 341의 부건 1, pp. 430-1; 『中朝滙』, 문서번호 25, pp. 31-5.			
121	1880.10.25(光緒六年九月二十八日)*	卞元圭와의 회담 보고	李鴻章	總署	『李鴻章』9, 奏議9, G6-09-032, pp. 191-3; 『李文』, 奏稿38, pp. 48-52; 『中日韓』2, 문서번호 341의 부건 2, pp. 432-6; 『中朝滙』, 문서번호 25, pp. 31-5.			
122	1880.12.3(光緒六年十一月二日)*	미국과 조약체결을 위해 밀사 李東仁 파견	何如璋	李鴻章	『李鴻章』21, 電報1, G6-11-002, p. 9; 『李文』, 電稿1, p. 3.		(1) 조미 조약 체결을 위한 淸의 관여 요청 (2) 이동인이 밀교한 조선 내부 의론 (3) 이동인이 밀교한 조선정부회의절략	(1) 『中日韓』2, 문서번호 342, pp. 437-9; 『何如璋』3, pp. 227-9. (2) 『中日韓』2, 문서번호 342의 부건 2, pp. 442-5; 『何如璋』3, pp. 231-3. (3) 『中日韓』2, 문서번호 342의 부건 3, pp. 445-7; 『何如璋』3, pp. 233-4.
123	1880.12.12(高宗十七年十一月十一日)	李裕元-李鴻章 서한(14)	李裕元	李鴻章	『中日韓』2, 문서번호 353의 부건 3, pp. 470-1.			
124	1880.12.22(光緒六年十一月二十一日)*	高宗 밀명 전달	卓挺植	何如璋	『中日韓』2, 문서번호 345의 부건 2, p. 453; 『何如璋』3, pp. 235-6.			
125	1881.2.1(光緒七年正月三日)*	李東仁·卓挺植의 밀보에 관한 보고	何如璋	總署	『中日韓』2, 문서번호 345, pp. 451-2; 『何如璋』3, pp. 234-5.			
126	1881.2.21(光緒七年正月二十三日)*	조약체결시 조청 종속(宗屬) 관계 명문화 건의	何如璋 등	總署	『中日韓』2, 문서번호 349, p. 456; 『何如璋』3, pp. 236-7.			

번호	발신일/수신일*(음력)	문서제목	발신	수신	문서출처	번역문 출처	관련문서 제목	관련문서 출처
127	1881.2.26(光緒七年正月二十八日)	李鴻章·李容肅 회담(1)	李鴻章		『中日韓』2, 문서번호 353의 부건 6, pp. 475-80; 문서번호 355의 부건 1, pp. 484-90; 『李鴻章』9, 奏議 9, G7-02-002, pp. 304-6; 『李文』, 奏稿 40, pp. 13-7; 『清外』1, pp. 497-9.			
128	1881.2.26(光緒七年正月二十八日)	李鴻章·李容肅 회담(2)	李鴻章		『中日韓』2, 문서번호 353의 부건 2, pp. 467-70			
129	1881.3.1(光緒七年二月二日)/1881.3.2(光緒七年二月三日)*	李容肅 회담 보고	李鴻章	總署	『李鴻章』33, 信函 5, G7-02-002, pp. 9-10; 『李文』, 譯署函稿 12, pp. 6-7; 『中日韓』2, 문서번호 353, pp. 461-2.			
130	1881.3.1(光緒七年二月二日)	李容肅 회담 상주	李鴻章		『李鴻章』9, 奏議 9, G7-02-001, pp. 303-4; 『李文』, 奏稿 42, pp. 37-9; 『中日』2, 문서번호 72, p. 32-3; 『中日韓』2, 문서번호 355, pp. 483-4.			
131	1881.3.2(高宗十八年二月二日)/1881.4.30(光緒七年四月三日)*	외교 권고에 대한 회신	金弘集	何如璋	『中日韓』2, 문서번호 361의 부건 1, p. 505; 『何如璋』3, pp. 241-2.			
132	1881.11.17(高宗十八年九月二十六日)	영선사 사폐(辭陛)시 전교		高宗	『일기』高宗 18년 9월 26일; 『음청』pp. 3-4.			
133	1882.1.17(高宗十八年十一月二十八日)	金允植·李鴻章 회담(1)	金允植		『음청』pp. 26-8.			
134	1882.1.17(高宗十八年十一月二十八日)/1882.1.18(光緒七年十一月二十九日)*	대미수교 주선을 청하는 서한	金允植	李鴻章	『운양』11 書牘 上, 「上北洋大臣李鴻章書」; 『동화』1, pp. 1244-6; 『李鴻章』9, 奏議 9, G7-12-002, pp. 540-2; 『李文』, 奏稿 42, pp. 40-3; 『清外』, pp. 496-7.			
135	1882.1.19(高宗十八年十一月三十日)	金允植·李鴻章 회담(2)	金允植		『음청』pp. 29-32.			
136	1882.1.21(光緒七年十二月二日)	조미조약 체결의 필요성 상주	李鴻章		『李鴻章』9, 奏議 9, G7-12-001, pp. 539-40; 『李文』, 奏稿 42, pp. 37-9.			

번호	발신일/수신일*(음력)	문서제목	발신	수신	문서출처	번역문 출처	관련문서 제목	관련문서 출처
137	1882. 1. 23(光緒七年十二月四日)	조미조약 체결 문제를 李鴻章에게 위임하는 상유(上諭)	光緒帝	李鴻章	『李鴻章』9, 奏議 9, G7-12-002의 부건, p. 544; 『中日韓』2, 문서번호 95, p. 45.			
138	1882. 1. 27(光緒七年十二月八日)	黎庶昌·魚允中 회담		魚允中	『中日韓』2, 문서번호 387의 부건 1, pp. 544-7.			
139	1882. 2. 7(高宗十八年十二月十九日)	金允植·李鴻章 회담(3)		金允植	『음청』pp. 44-7.			
140	1882. 2. 14(高宗十八年十二月二十六日)	金允植·李鴻章 회담(4)		金允植	『음청』pp. 52-4.			
141	1882. 2. 15(高宗十八年十二月二十七日)	조청 종속(宗屬)관계 명문화에 관한 상소		金允植	『음청』pp. 55-8.			
142	1882. 2. 27(高宗十九年一月十日)	金允植·周馥 회담(1)		金允植	『음청』pp. 65-6.			
143	1882. 3. 7(高宗十九年一月十八日)	金允植·周馥 회담(2)		金允植	『음청』pp. 72-4.			
144	1882. 4. 4(高宗十九年二月十七日)	金允植·李鴻章 회담(5)		金允植	『음청』pp. 87-9.			
145	1882. 4. 8(高宗十九年二月二十一日)	金允植·周馥 회담(3)		金允植	『음청』pp. 92-4.			
146	1882. 4. 20(光緒八年三月三日)/1882. 4. 21(光緒八年三月四日)*	조미수호통상조약 초안에 관한 의견	李鴻章	總署	『李鴻章』33, 信函 5, G8-03-001, pp. 144-5; 『李文』, 譯署函稿 13, pp. 31-2; 『中日韓』2, 문서번호 393, p. 559.		협상 대리를 청하는 李最應 서한	『李鴻章』33, 信函 5, G8-02-048, pp. 142-3; 『李文』, 譯署函稿 13, pp. 32-3; 『中日韓』2, 문서번호 393의 부건 1, pp. 560-1.
147	1882. 4. 21(高宗十九年三月四日)	金允植·李鴻章 회담(6)		金允植	『음청』pp. 103-6.		(1) 李鴻章의 기록 (2) 조약 초안 조관별 논의	『中日韓』2, 문서번호 394의 부건 3, pp. 571-4.
148	1882. 4. 22(光緒八年三月五日)	馬建忠·丁汝昌의 조선 파견 통보	李鴻章	李最應	『李鴻章』33, 信函 5, G8-03-003, pp. 145-6; 『李文』, 譯署函稿 13, pp. 33-4; 『中日韓』2, 문서번호 394의 부건 2, pp. 569-71; 『나암』pp. 270-1.			

번호	발신일/수신일*(음력)	문서제목	발신	수신	문서출처	번역문 출처	관련문서 제목	관련문서 출처
149	1882. 4. 23(光緒八年三月六日)	조미조약 교섭 전말 상주	李鴻章		『李鴻章』10, 奏議 10, G8-03-017, pp. 55-6; 『李文』, 奏稿43, pp. 34-6; 『中日韓』2, 문서번호 394의 부건 1, pp. 566-9; 『清外』27, pp. 11-3.			
150	1882. 4. 28(光緒八年三月十一日)*	조약초안 관련 高宗에게 보내는 자문	李鴻章	總署	『中日韓』2, 문서번호 397의 부건 1, pp. 575-7.			
151	1882. 5. 5(高宗十九年三月十八日)	조미조약 체결 등에 관한 어전회의	高宗, 洪淳穆, 金炳國 等		『나암』「大臣箚對(三月十八日)」 pp. 271-3.			
(7) 조약 협상 과정								
152	1882. 5. 2(高宗十九年三月十五日)	반접관(伴接官) 임명	統理機務衙門		『일기』高宗 19년 3월 15일; 『일록』·『실록』같은 날			
153	1882. 5. 6	馬建忠과의 회견 통보	R. W. Shufeldt	李鴻章	NARA II, M 92, R 61			
154	1882. 5. 6	조선행 일정 통보	R. W. Shufeldt	C. Holcombe	NARA II, M 92, R 61			
155	1882. 5. 7(光緒八年三月二十四日)	조선 도착 및 조선의 조약 체결 태도 보고	馬建忠	李鴻章	『中日韓』2, 문서번호 420의 부건 10, pp. 619-21.			
156	1882. 5. 8	조선 입국 기록	R. W. Shufeldt		NARA II, M 92, R 61			
157	1882. 5. 8(光緒八年三月二十一日)	李應浚·馬建忠 회담(1)	馬建忠		『中日韓』2, 문서번호 420의 부건 13, pp. 632-3; 『東行初錄』, p. 337.			
158	1882. 5. 11(高宗十九年三月二十四日)	조약 협상단 임명	統理機務衙門		『일기』高宗 19년 3월 24일; 『일록』·『실록』같은 날			
159	1882. 5. 11(光緒八年三月二十四日)*	丁汝昌 파견 보고	李鴻章	總署	『中日韓』2, 문서번호 398, pp. 577-8.			
160	1882. 5. 11(光緒八年三月二十四日)*	조선 입국 경과 보고	李鴻章	總署	『中日韓』2, 문서번호 399, p. 578.			
161	1882. 5. 12	조선 입국 통보	R. W. Shufeldt	花房義質	NARA II, M 92, R 61			
162	1882. 5. 12(光緒八年三月二十五日)	李應浚·馬建忠 회담(2)	馬建忠		『中日韓』2, 문서번호 420의 부건 20, pp. 640-2.			

번호	발신일/수신일*(음력)	문서제목	발신	수신	문서출처	번역문 출처	관련문서 제목	관련문서 출처
163	1882.5.14(高宗 十九年三月 二十七日)	金弘集・馬建忠 회담(1)	金弘集		『미안』1, pp. 1-3.		馬建忠 기록	『中日韓』2, 문서번호 420의 부건 24, p. 643; 『中日韓』2, 문서번호 420의 부건 25, pp. 643-4; 『中日韓』2, 문서번호 420의 부건 26, pp. 644-6.
164	1882.5.16(高宗 十九年三月 二十九日)	金晩植・馬建忠 회담	金晩植		『미안』1, p. 3.		馬建忠 기록	『中日韓』2, 문서번호 420의 부건 27, pp. 646-8.
165	1882.5.17	申櫶・金弘集 소개	花房義質	R. W. Shufeldt	NARA II, M 92, R 61			
166	1882.5.17(高宗 十九年四月一 日)	金弘集・馬建忠 회담(2)	金弘集		『미안』1, pp. 3-5.		(1) 馬建忠의 기록 (2) 조약문 개정 사항 초록	(1)『中日韓』2, 문서번호 420의 부건 28 및 부건 29, pp. 648-51. (2)『미안』1, p. 5.
167	1882.5.17(高宗 十九年四月一 日)	Shufeldt와 미곡수출 교섭결과 통보	丁汝昌	申櫶 金弘集	『미안』1, p. 6.			
168	1882.5.18(高宗 十九年四月二 日)	전권위임장, 조회문 도착 통보	申櫶 金弘集	馬建忠	『미안』1, pp. 6-7.		전권위임장	『미안』1, p. 3.
169	1882.5.19(高宗 十九年四月三 日)	金弘集・馬建忠 회담(3)	金弘集		『미안』1, p. 7.		馬建忠의 기록	『中日韓』2, 문서번호 420의 부건 30, pp. 651-3;『東行初錄』, p. 15.
170	1882.5.20(高宗 十九年四月四 日)	金弘集・馬建忠 회담(4)	金弘集		『미안』1, pp. 7-8.		馬建忠의 기록	『中日韓』2, 문서번호 420의 부건 31, pp. 653-4;『東行初錄』, pp. 15-6.
171	1882.5.20	수호통상 요청 조회문	R. W. Shufeldt	申櫶 金弘集	『미안』1, pp. 8-9.		(1) 전권위임장 (2) 미 대통령 국서	『미안』1, pp. 8-9.
172	1882.5.20 (光緒八年四月 四日)	조선 도착 이후 협상 경과 보고	馬建忠	張樹聲	『中日韓』2, 문서번호 420의 부건 11, pp. 621-3;『東行初錄』, pp. 16-7.		東行日錄	『中日韓』2, 문서번호 420의 부건 12, pp. 623-32;『東行初錄』, pp. 5-16.
173	1882.5.20	조인 일자 통보	R. W. Shufeldt	C. Holcombe	NARA II, M 92, R 61			

번호	발신일/수신일*(음력)	문서제목	발신	수신	문서출처	번역문 출처	관련문서 제목	관련문서 출처
174	1882. 5. 20	대통령의 신임장 제출 및 조인 일자 확정	R. W. Shufeldt(?)		NARA II, M 92, R 61			
175	1882. 5. 21(高宗十九年四月五日)	미 대통령 조회문에 대한 회답 조회	申櫶 金弘集	R. W. Shufeldt	『미안』1, pp. 9-11.		(1) 申櫶, 金弘集 신임장 (2) 종속(宗屬)조회문(屬邦照會文) 초안	『미안』1, pp. 9-11.
176	1882. 5. 21(光緖八年 四月五日)	조약 체결 축하연 초청장	丁汝昌 馬建忠	申櫶 金弘集	『미안』1, p. 11.		축하연 초청에 대한 회신	『미안』1, pp. 11-2.
177	1882. 5. 22(光緖八年四月六日)	조미수호통상조약 조인식 기록	馬建忠		『東行初錄』pp. 355-6.			
178	1882. 5. 22 (光緖八年四月六日)	金弘集·馬建忠 회담(5)	馬建忠		『中日韓』2, 문서번호 420의 부건 33, pp. 655-6.			
179	1882. 5. 29	조약 체결 보고	R. W. Shufeldt	F. T. Frelinghuysen	AADM, p. 931.			
(8) 사후처리 및 비준								
180	1882. 5. 22(高宗十九年四月六日)	金弘集·馬建忠 회담(6)	金弘集		『미안』1, pp. 12-3.		馬建忠 기록	『中日韓』2, 문서번호 420의 부건 32, pp. 654-5.
181	1822. 5. 26(高宗十九年四月十日)	高宗의 馬建忠·丁汝昌 인견(引見) 기록	高宗, 馬建忠, 丁汝昌		『일기』高宗 19년 4월 10일			
182	1882. 5. 27(高宗十九年四月十一日)	金弘集·馬建忠 회담(7)	金弘集		『미안』1, p. 14.			
183	1882. 5. 27(高宗十九年四月十一日)	조미조약 체결 통보	高宗	禮部	『자문』2책 「與美使講定修好通商條規事北京禮部咨」			
184	1882. 5. 27(高宗十九年四月十一日)/1882. 6. 5(光緖八年四月二十日)*	조미조약 체결 통보	高宗	張樹聲	『자문』2 「與美使講定修好通商條規事北洋通商大臣衙門咨」; 『中日韓』2, 문서번호 420, p. 610.			
185	1882. 6. 5(光緖八年四月二十日)*	조영, 조불 조약 체결시 조미조약 원용에 관한 의견	張樹聲	總署	『中日韓』2, 문서번호 413, pp. 585-6.			
186	1882. 6. 8	조미수호통상조약 체결 전말 보고	R. W. Shufeldt	F. T. Frelinghuysen	NARA II, M 92, R 60			
187	1882. 6. 9(光緖八年四月二十四日)	조미수호통상조약 체결 전말 상주	張樹聲		『中日』3, 문서번호 101, pp. 8-10.			
188	1882. 8. 28	조선 무역과 자원 현황	J. A. Bingham	F. T. Frelinghuysen	FRUS1883, Japan, pp. 378-80, No. 203			

번호	발신일/수신일*(음력)	문서제목	발신	수신	문서출처	번역문 출처	관련문서 제목	관련문서 출처
189	1882. 9. 29(高宗十九年八月十八日)	조선의 비준 촉구를 본국 정부에 보고했음을 통보	J. R. Young	趙寧夏 金弘集	『미안』1, p. 15.			
190	1882. 12. 26	조청상민수륙무역장정에 관한 Holcombe의 견해 보고	J. R. Young	F. T. Frelinghuysen	FRUS1884, China, pp. 172-9, No. 72			
191	1883. 5(高宗二十年四月)	조약비준대표 영접 통보	閔泳穆	L. H. Foote	『미안』1, pp. 15-6.			
192	1883. 5. 18(高宗二十年四月十二日)	조약비준 전권위임장	高宗	閔泳穆	『미안』1, p. 16.			
193	1883. 5. 19(高宗二十年四月十三日)	조미수호통상조약 비준서			비준서	『미안』1, p. 16.			
194	1883. 5. 19(高宗二十年四月十三日)	비준 교환 일자 통보	閔泳穆	L. H. Foote	『미안』1, pp. 16-7.			
195	1883. 5. 20(高宗二十年四月十四日)	국왕 접견 및 미 대통령 국서 봉정 시각 통보	閔泳穆	L. H. Foote	『미안』1, p. 17.		Foote 접견 시 의주(儀注)	『미안』1, p. 17.
196	1883. 5. 20(高宗二十年四月十四日)	高宗 알현시 Foote의 답사(答辭)	L. H. Foote	高宗	『미안』1, pp. 17-9.		(1) Foote의 전권위임장 (2) 종속(宗屬)조회에 대한 미 대통령의 회답	(1) 『미안』1, pp. 17-9. (2) 『미안』1, pp. 17-9; 『中日』5, 문서번호 181의 부건 2, p. 7; 『中日韓』3, 문서번호 729의 부건 1, p. 1156. 및 문서번호 732의 부건 3, pp. 1161-2; 『李鴻章』10, 奏議 10, G9-05-006의 부건 2, pp. 189-90.
197	1883. 6. 26(光緒九年五月二十二日)	조미조약 제6조의 개정에 관한 상주	李鴻章 張樹聲		『李鴻章』10, 奏議 10, G9-05-004, p. 188; 『中日韓』3, 문서번호 732, pp. 1159-60; 『中日』5, 문서번호 181, pp. 5-6; 『德宗實錄』163, 甲辰條, p. 17. 『淸外』33, p. 10.			

번호	발신일/수신일*(음력)	문서제목	발신	수신	문서출처	번역문 출처	관련문서 제목	관련문서 출처
198	1883. 6. 27(光緒九年五月十二日)*	조약 비준 통보	高宗	總署	『中日』5, 문서번호 181의 부건 1, pp. 6-7; 『中日韓』3, 문서번호 729, p. 1156. 및 문서번호 732의 부건 1, pp. 1160-1; 『李鴻章』10, 奏議 10, G9-05-005, p. 189.		(1) Foote 신임장 (2) 조미수호통상조약 제6조의 수정	(1) 『中日』5, 문서번호 181의 부건 2, p. 7; 『中日韓』3, 문서번호 729의 부건 2, p. 1157. 문서번호 732의 부건 4, pp. 1162-3; 『李鴻章』10, 奏議 10, G9-05-006의 부건 3, p. 190. (2) 『中日』5, 문서번호 181의 부건 2, p. 7; 『中日韓』3, 문서번호 729의 부건 3, p. 1157. 및 문서번호 732의 부건 2, p. 1161; 『李鴻章』10, 奏議 10, G9-05-006의 부건 1, p. 189.
199	1883. 6. 27(光緒九年五月二十三日)*	청국 연호 미기재(未記載)에 관한 문제	李鴻章 등	總署	『中日韓』3, 문서번호 731, p. 1159.			
200	1883. 7. 4(光緒九年六月一日)/ 1883. 7. 19(光緒九年六月十六日)*	조약문에 청국 연호 기재를 요구하는 자문	總署	高宗	『中日韓』3, 문서번호 735, p. 1165.			
201	1883. 8. 16(光緒九年七月十四日)*	청국 연호 기재 문제에 관한 자복(咨覆)	高宗	總署	『中日韓』3, 문서번호 745, p. 1177.			
202	1883. 9. 16(光緒九年八月十六日)*	보빙사(報聘使) 파견 통보	高宗	總署	『中日韓』3, 문서번호 758, p. 1196.			
관계자료								
1	1882. 5. 22(高宗十九年四月六日)	조미수호통상조약			『朝美條約』(奎 23166); 『실록』19년 4월 6일	[英文] BFSA; 『條約類纂』		

번호	발신일/수신일*(음력)	문서제목	발신	수신	문서출처	번역문 출처	관련문서 제목	관련문서 출처
2	1880. 9. 6(高宗 十七年 八月二日)	『조선책략(朝鮮策略)』	黃遵憲		李瑄根, 1963 「庚辰修信使 金弘集과 黃遵憲 《朝鮮策略》에 對한 再檢討」, 『東亞論叢』 1 수록본; 『수신사』 pp. 160-171, 「朝鮮策略」; 『日外』 13, 문서번호 136, 부기 1, pp. 389-94; 『黃遵憲』 上, pp. 251-8.			
3	1880. 4-6.	R. W. Shufeldt 의 개인 서한	R. W. Shufeldt	M. M. Molly Shufeldt	RWS 16, 17			
4	1880. 10. 22	Duke of Genoa 의 조선 방문 report	J. B. Angell	W. M. Evarts	NARA II, M 92, R 56			
5	1882(高宗十九年)	『미국통상실기(美國通商實記)』	申櫶		『통상실기』			

동북아역사 자료총서 121
近代韓國外交文書 4

2012년 12월 10일 초판 1쇄 인쇄
2014년 11월 24일 초판 2쇄 발행

편   근대한국외교문서편찬위원회
펴낸이   김학준
펴낸곳   동북아역사재단

등록   제312-2004-050호(2004년 10월 18일)
주소   서울시 서대문구 통일로 81(미근동 267) 임광빌딩
전화   02-2012-6065
팩스   02-2012-6189
e-mail   book@nahf.or.kr

ⓒ 동북아역사재단, 2014

ISBN 978-89-6187-287-4 94910
       978-89-6187-444-1 세트

*이 책의 출판권 및 저작권은 동북아역사재단이 가지고 있습니다.
   저작권법에 의해 보호를 받는 저작물이므로 어떤 형태나 어떤 방법으로도
   무단전재와 무단복제를 금합니다.
*책값은 뒤표지에 있습니다. 잘못된 책은 바꾸어 드립니다.